The Production Ecology of Wetlands

Wetlands are unique and fragile environments that provide a transition between aquatic and terrestrial habitats. Focusing on freshwater wetlands with emergent vegetation, this book considers productivity in relation to communities of animals and plants and their environments, mineral cycling, hydrology and management. Emphasis is given to the biological interactions and processes underlying the structure and functioning of wetlands, revealing the need to appreciate the dynamics of the system to establish appropriate management and conservation practices. Based largely on research carried out during the International Biological Programme, this unique synthesis brings together a wealth of information, hitherto widely dispersed in the literature and often difficult to locate. As such, it will be an important resource for all those concerned with the ecology, management and conservation of these sensitive natural habitats.

Derek Westlake is Director of Aquatic Plant Consultancy, following retirement from the UK's Freshwater Biological Association's River Laboratory in Wareham, Dorset.

Jan Květ is in the Hydrobotany Department of the Czech Academy of Sciences' Institute of Botany in Třeboň, Czech Republic and teaches at the Faculty of Biological Sciences, University of South Bohemia in České Budějovice, Czech Republic.

The late Andrzej Szczepański was formerly at the Hydrobiological Station of the Polish Academy of Science's Institute of Ecology in Mikołajki, Poland.

THE PRODUCTION ECOLOGY OF WETLANDS

THE IBP SYNTHESIS

Edited by
D.F. WESTLAKE
Aquatic Plant Consultancy, 100 Wessex Oval,
Wareham, Dorset, BH20 4BS, England.
(Formerly River Laboratory, Freshwater Biological Association,
Wareham, Dorset, UK)

J. KVĚT
Hydrobotany Department, Institute of Botany,
Czech Academy of Sciences, Třeboň, CZ 379 82, Czech Republic

and

THE LATE A. SZCZEPAŃSKI
Formerly Institute of Ecology, Polish Academy of Sciences,
Hydrobiological Station, Mikołajki, Poland

CAMBRIDGE
UNIVERSITY PRESS

PUBLISHED BY THE PRESS SYNDICATE OF THE UNIVERSITY OF CAMBRIDGE
The Pitt Building, Trumpington Street, Cambridge CB2 1RP, United Kingdom

CAMBRIDGE UNIVERSITY PRESS
The Edinburgh Building, Cambridge CB2 2RU, UK http://www.cup.cam.ac.uk
40 West 20th Street, New York, NY 10011-4211, USA http://www.cup.org
10 Stamford Road, Oakleigh, Melbourne 3166, Australia

First published 1998

Printed in the United Kingdom at the University Press, Cambridge

Typeset in Monotype Times 10/13pt, in 3B2™

A catalogue record for this book is available from the British Library

Library of Congress Cataloguing in Publication Data

The production ecology of wetlands: the IBP synthesis/edited by D. F. Westlake, J. Květ,
and A. Szczepański.
      p.   cm.
   Includes bibliographical references and index.
   ISBN 0 521 22822 0 (hb)
   1. Wetland ecology. 2. Biological productivity. I. Westlake, D. F. (Derek Francis)
II. Květ, J. (Jan), 1933– . III. Szczepański, Andrzej. IV. International Biological
Programme.
QH.541.5.M3P76   1998
577.68–dc21   98-15359 CIP

ISBN 0 521 22822 0 hardback

Contents

Contributors

The first address given is the current address for the author. If that is the only address, it was also the address during IBP (apart from political changes). A second address, in italics, was the author's address during IBP.

Day, J.W. Jr
Coastal Ecology Institute, Louisiana State University, Baton Rouge, Louisiana 70803, USA. *Center for Wetland Resources, Louisiana State University, Baton Rouge, Louisiana 70803, USA*

Dvořák, J.
Institute of Botany, Academy of Sciences of the Czech Republic, CZ-252 43, Průhonice, Czech Republic

Dykyjová, D.
Hydrobotany Department, Institute of Botany, Academy of Sciences of the Czech Republic, CZ-379 82, Třeboň, Czech Republic

Hacker, R. (Deceased)
Fish Collection, Museum of Natural History, Burgring 7, PO Box 417, A-1014, Wien, Austria

Haslam, S.M.
Botany School, University of Cambridge, Downing Street, Cambridge CB2 3EA, UK

Hejný, S.
Institute of Botany, Academy of Sciences of the Czech Republic, CZ-252 43, Průhonice, Czech Republic

Holčík, J.
Institute of Zoology, Slovenská Akadémia Vied, Dúbravská cesta 9, SK-842 06, Bratislava, Slovak Republic

Hudec, K.
Institute of Landscape Ecology, Academy of Sciences of the Czech Republic, Květná 8, CZ-603 00, Brno, Czech Republic. *Institute of Vertebrate Zoology, Czechoslovak Academy of Sciences, Květná 8, Brno, Czechoslovakia*

Imhof, G.
Staudgasse 5/4, A-1180 Wien, Austria. *Zoologisches Institut, University of Vienna, A-1010, Wien 1, Austria*

Klötzli, F.
Geobotanisches Forschungs-institut ETH, Stiftungs Rübel, Zürichbergstrasse 38, CH-8044, Zürich, Switzerland

Królikowska, J.
Hydrobiological Station, Institute of Ecology, Polish Academy of Sciences, Leśna 13, PL-11-730, Mikołajki, Poland. *Laboratory of Chemical Ecology, Institute of Ecology, Polish Academy of Sciences, 11-730, Mikołajki, Poland*

Květ, J.
Hydrobotany Department, Institute of Botany, Academy of Sciences of the Czech Republic, Dukelská 145, CZ-379 82, Třeboň, Czech Republic

Marshall, E.J.P.
IACR, Long Ashton Research Station, Department of Agricultural Sciences, University of Bristol, Long Ashton, Bristol BS18 9AF, UK. *River Laboratory, Freshwater Biological Association, Wareham, UK*

Ondok, J.P.
Hydrobotany Department, Institute of Botany, Academy of Sciences of the Czech Republic, Dukelská 145, CZ-379 82, Třeboň, Czech Republic

Opatrný, E.
Palacký University, Faculty of Sciences, Svobody 26, CZ-771 46, Olomouc, Czech Republic. *Silesian Museum, CZ-74601, Opava, Czechoslovakia*

Pelikán, J.
Institute of Landscape Ecology, Academy of Sciences of the Czech Republic, Kvetná 8, CZ-603 00, Brno, Czech Republic. *Institute of Vertebrate Zoology, Czechoslovak Academy of Sciences, Květná 8, Brno, Czechoslovakia*

Pieczyńska, E.
Department of Hydrobiology, University of Warsaw, Banacha 2, PL-02-097, Warszawa, Poland. *Laboratory of Hydrobiology, University of Warsaw, Novy Swiat 67, Warszawa, Poland*

Přibáň, K.
Hydrobotany Department, Institute of Botany, Academy of Sciences of the Czech Republic, Dukelská 145, CZ-379 82, Třeboň, Czech Republic

Raspopov, I.M.
Institute of Limnology, Russian Academy of Sciences, St Petersburg, 97046, Russia

Segal, S.
Prinsensgracht 851 huis, 1017 KB Amsterdam, Netherlands. *Hugo de Vries Laboratory, University of Amsterdam, Amsterdam, Netherlands*

Šmíd, P. (Deceased)
Department of Ecology, Institute of Botany, Czechoslovak Academy of Sciences, Stará 18, Brno, Czechoslovakia

Sukopp, H.
Institute of Ecology, Schmidt-Ott Strasse 1, Technische Universität, 12165 Berlin, Germany. *Institute for Applied Botany, Rothenburgstrasse 12, Berlin 41, Germany*

Szczepański, A. (Deceased)
Laboratory of Chemical Ecology, Leśna Str. 13, Mikołajki, Poland

Úlehlová, B.
Institute of Landscape Ecology, Academy of Sciences of the Czech Republic, Květná 8, CZ-603 00, Brno, Czech Republic. *Department of Ecology, Institute of Botany, Czechoslovak Academy of Sciences, Brno, Czechoslovakia*

Westlake, D.F.
Aquatic Plant Consultancy, 100 Wessex Oval, Wareham, Dorset BH20 4BS, UK. *River Laboratory, Freshwater Biological Association, Wareham, Dorset, UK*

Preface

This book has a long history, which dates back to the early days of the IBP. In 1965–66, when assessment and comparison of biological productivity was recognised as one of the main topics requiring study, plant ecologists proposed that a set of widespread plant species or genera should be selected as test plants. Their production and production processes could be compared, world-wide, in the widest possible range of habitats and experimental sites. *Phragmites australis*, a widely distributed wetland plant, was among those suggested. Many countries, research institutes and individual scientists participating in the IBP, within its PT (Production Terrestrial), PF (Production Freshwater) and PP (Production Processes) sections, took up this idea, and several started research, or modified their current research, on *Phragmites*. However, many other research programmes within the IBP took a different approach, often studying more local species and sites; and it was clear from the start that production by individual species, even if dominant, could only be understood in the context of whole communities and ecosystems. This resulted in a great variety of intensive studies of the littoral zones of water bodies and wetlands in general, particularly as examples of boundary ecosystems (ecotones).

The first opportunity to integrate these results with other research on higher submerged and emergent plants was at the International Conference on Aquatic Macrophytes, convened after an initiative by Romanian and Czechoslovakian specialists, and sponsored jointly by IBP and the UNESCO International Hydrological Decade. This was held in Romania, mainly at Tulcea, in a most appropriate setting at the head of the Danube Delta, in August 1970, and included an excursion into the *Phragmites* wetlands. Most of the papers were published in *Hidrobiologia Bucureşti* vol. 12, 1971. The meeting inspired the formation of an intersectional IBP Working Group on Wetland Ecosystems, which was set up in 1971 with one of the Editors (J.K.) as coordinator. Administrative support was provided by the Praha IBP/PP Secretariat, sponsored by the Czechoslovak Academy of Sciences.

The members met again at the IBP Wetland Symposium, held at the invitation of the Polish Academy of Sciences at Mikołajki in June 1972. A special issue of Polskie Archivum Hydrobiologii (vol. 20, part 1, 1973) published most of the papers. They proposed a summarising book incorporating IBP research on wetlands, which could be one of the series on IBP research being published by Cambridge University Press. Three editors, and nine authors, each responsible for the production of a chapter, were chosen from the members of the IBP Wetlands Working Group.

A working definition of wetland ecology was adopted for this synthesis, covering those research areas and types of ecosystem studied during the IBP which had most to contribute to the understanding of production ecology, and excluding submerged freshwater, brackish, marine and tundra communities which were to be treated by volumes in the IBP series. This 'IBP definition' is relatively narrow in comparison with later definitions and concepts of wetlands, made for other purposes (IUCN, SCOPE, MAB, national surveys and inventories, Project Aqua). However, it could be argued that many of these definitions include much which is totally 'wet' and has no 'land' component. The primary aim of this book, as now presented, is to give a synthetic treatment of the results of the IBP research on such wetlands, in relation to other investigations, and only exceptionally, for the sake of a better understanding, does it take a broader view of wetlands.

The first meeting of the appointed editors and main authors took place at Chlum, near Třeboň, Czechoslovakia, in January, 1974 and was followed by several smaller meetings of the editors, or authors of some of the chapters, especially Chapter 8. Despite the strong initial impetus, subsequent progress was slow. After the termination of the IBP, and with a general change in governmental attitudes to scientific research which reduced funding and emphasised applied research, many of the authors and all three editors were burdened with new duties and had difficulty finding funds and time for intensive work on the book. The main authors of most chapters invited other IBP workers to contribute or co-author sections and subsections, to submit manuscripts or data on specific topics, or to review sections of chapters. This, together with the great range of nationalities co-operating and the consequent range of styles, made the assembly and editing of the text very complex. However, for the completion of Chapter 5, the Austrian Academy of Sciences provided a generous grant which enabled J. Dvořák of Czechoslovakia to spend three months in Austria to work on the chapter together with G. Imhof and other colleagues. Also the Technical University of West Berlin kindly assisted in the completion of Chapter 8, and several institutes helpfully turned a 'blind eye' at critical times. During this period much time and effort was spent on checking, cross-checking and editing to produce a consistent layout, presentation, style and cover throughout the volume, mostly at the River Laboratory of the Freshwater Biological Association in Dorset. In the interests of brevity, many references had to be deleted, but the editors endeavoured to maintain a bibliography which would give thorough access to the topics, and added selected recent references to seminal or comprehensive publications. This all led to a situation where some chapters were virtually complete, while some were at various stages of revision and others had large gaps; which further complicated the scheduling of progress.

The editors and authors became increasingly concerned that publication of the book as a summary of the current status of wetland research would require detailed revision of submitted chapters; and we suffered the premature sad loss of one of the editors, Andrzej Szczepański, in 1983. At a subsequent meeting, initiated by G. Imhof and attended by most of the authors and one of the editors (JK), they agreed (together with the absent editor, DFW) that the book could still meet its original aims and was still worthy of publication as a synthesis of the production biology of wetlands at its climax, which did not otherwise exist. Also, apart from some international activities of ornithologists, the IBP stimulated the first internationally coordinated work on wetlands, which formed a substantial contribution to the results of the IBP as a whole, and which should be recorded to stand alongside the other IBP syntheses. The authors were given the choice of withdrawing their chapters, or letting them stand just with the small corrections especially where there had been significant major developments, and the addition of references to some major contributions and reviews. Only two were withdrawn, neither crucial to the design and balance of the book. The chapter on 'Modelling of Wetland Ecosystems' by J.P. Ondok and J.W. Day Jr dealt with a topic that had undergone rapid change and subsequently has been reviewed elsewhere (e.g. Ondok, 1988; Mitsch *et al.*, 1988; Patten, 1990–91). The proposed chapter on 'Rice – a Wetland Crop' by I. Tanaka and Y. Murata had become particularly outdated and has been superseded by another book (Tsunoda & Takahashi, 1984). However, progress was still very slow.

Despite this long gestation, and the emphasis on IBP sites and on surveying and summarising the achievements of IBP research on wetland ecology, we believe the book has many other valuable features which distinguish it from other recent books on wetlands:

- It accentuates the roles of biological components and processes in the structure and functioning of wetland ecosystems, rather than giving detailed analyses of individual communities and environments, or detailed inventories and surveys of the world's wetland sites.
- It concentrates on the wetlands of lakes, rivers and fens, which are often relatively alkaline or only slightly acid, whereas most other authors have concentrated on peatlands, particularly the acid peats of bogs and moors.
- On the basis of a wealth of both IBP and non-IBP data, it attempts to make a synthetic assessment of the ways in which the productive processes of wetland plants interact with the activities of microbial and animal populations through the creation and fate of detritus, through the creation of micro-habitats in air, water and soil, and through many types of grazing or harvesting activities.
- Special attention is also paid to the structure of wetland vegetation, mineral cycling, micro-climates and water relations.
- There are many references to research in Eastern Europe and the former USSR, which is often not well known in Western Europe and America, and it refers to much research published in theses, government reports and local journals, which are often not to be found in abstracting journals.

A chapter on use and management of wetlands and their biological resources covers the basic range of uses, techniques of management and the scientific basis of wetland conservation. Conservation is desperately needed and is making particular progress in wetlands thanks to the activities of the International Union for Conservation of Nature and the World Wildlife Fund for Nature.

It is hoped that it will be a source of useful data and knowledge; in particular on the invertebrate communities of wetlands, which have not been treated in comparable detail elsewhere.

The long preparation time of this book has meant that some geographical and political names have been outdated by political changes. Generally we have retained the names in use at the time when the original

IBP studies were carried out and we hope that this will not cause any difficulty in locating any sites. Where current names are critical, such as postal addresses of institutes, we have provided this information.

The editors wish to express their appreciation of the organisers and the nations that set up and supported the IBP; their sincere gratitude to all the authors who were patient and co-operative throughout; and their apologies for their major contributions to the delay in publication. In particular, we greatly appreciate the input which our late co-editor Andrzej Szczepański gave to the Polish IBP and to the preparation of this book. We miss the subtle humour and critical assessment that he brought to his editorial tasks. We also owe much to Dr E.B. Worthington, the Scientific Director of the IBP, the late Academician I. Málek, the IBP/PP convener, the late Professor W. Kühnelt, Austrian IBP Committee chairman; and to our friends, the late but unforgettable Dr J. Rzóska, the Scientific Coordinator of IBP/PF, and Miss Gina Douglas, the IBP Scientific Secretary, who stimulated and supported the activities of the IBP Wetlands Working Group. All ceaselessly encouraged the authors' and editors' spirits throughout the many difficulties. Also, the editors thank the many libraries and librarians who went beyond the call of duty when solving reference problems, especially at the Czech Institute of Botany (Třeboň), University College (London), the British Library Science Reference & Information Service, the British Museum (Natural History), the Library of Congress (Washington DC) and the Rossiĭskaya Gosudarstvennaya Biblioteka (Moskva). Likewise, the authors wish to thank the many colleagues and institutes that helped them in their work.

Many of the original contributed manuscripts, data reports, reviews and correspondence are deposited in the library of the Institute of Botany at Třeboň, Czech Republic, where they may be consulted.

Now let us hope that this result of concerted effort by these people, who took an unprecedented interest in wetland ecology, will be used to benefit wetlands. Wetlands well deserve beneficial attention because they are among the most economically valuable ecosystems (Costanza *et al.*, 1997), and yet are the most threatened of all the essential components of the ecology of our beautiful planet.

Derek F. Westlake
Jan Květ
Wareham

Foreword

The editors of this book, Mr Derek Westlake, Dr Jan Květ, and Dr Andrzej Szczepański have made significant contributions to the results of the International Biological Programme (IBP), which ran from 1964 to 1974.

The programme was organised into seven main sections which were inevitably subdivided with a very large number of research projects. By no means all could be brought to conclusion at the end of the programme's decade, so the Cambridge University Press, which had been very helpful throughout, agreed to publish a series of volumes, which record many of the results.

This volume is published in addition to the original IBP Series, and follows on in subject matter from Volume 22: *The Function of Freshwater Ecosystems*, edited by E.D. le Cren and R.H. Lowe-McConnell. As Scientific Director of the IBP with its very wide view of environmental ecology, I have a special interest in its section on inland waters, having spent my early years of research on that subject. I am sure this volume will be welcomed as a valuable contribution.

E. Barton Worthington
Director of the International Biological Programme (IBP)

1
General ecology of wetlands

S. HEJNÝ and S. SEGAL
with a contribution by I.M. RASPOPOV

Introduction

Like all the chapters of this book, this is a co-operative work, written by the two main authors, with a contribution on geographical distribution by I.M. Raspopov, and with the help of comments from colleagues and the three editors.

The term 'wetland' came into use in the 1970s and was soon generally accepted. There is, however, not much agreement about its limits, which are sometimes defined very broadly, and sometimes very narrowly. Generally speaking, wetlands may be defined as habitats where the water table is situated at or near the ground surface, bearing a vegetation adapted to more or less continuous waterlogging (cf. Sjörs, 1948; Ratcliffe, 1964). 'Near' may mean either under or above the ground level.

This definition proves to be vague if we try to fix the limits of wetlands. There is no doubt that littoral habitats and marshes belong to wetlands, but there is less agreement about open water, coastal habitats, mangrove swamps, wet heaths, peat bogs, carrs, and habitats which are waterlogged for only certain periods. One difficulty is that wetlands are very often successional stages. Succession seres often start from open water, under which bottom deposits accumulate gradually causing the community to change over long periods.

Another difficulty arises where the water level changes considerably within brief periods, and the habitat may be waterlogged or flooded only for several short periods per season, or not at all in some years, or as in desert climates, it may be dry for even longer. The behaviour of easily recognised, more or less permanent wetlands along long-lasting water–land boundaries (e.g. in large, stable lakes), is entirely different from temporarily waterlogged habitats such as high-mountain snow fields after thaw, or temporary river-beds and shallow depressions in deserts after heavy rain. Even abruptly arising and brief periods of flooding create specific localised biotic communities.

Wetlands can only be properly understood dynamically. This approach is, of course, necessary for every ecosystem, but is relatively more important in wetlands than, for example, in a stable tropical rain forest. As well as limits in time, we have to consider limits in space, since wetlands very often form part of zonations from aquatic or wet to drier habitats. Sometimes sharp borderlines exist between different communities within such zonations, but very often the communities gradually merge into each other.

To define wetlands, we may start either from the habitat, or from communities, or try to combine these criteria. There is a strong correlation between climatic features, especially precipitation and air humidity, and changes in water level under natural conditions in temporarily water-logged, submerged or flooded areas. These fluctuations in water level vary greatly in different types of wetland and their effects on vegetation are, generally speaking, much greater in dry and warm climates than in temperate and humid climates, where evaporation and mineralisation are slower and peat formation is faster. This makes it very difficult to define wetlands in terms of exact values of water level and we prefer biological definitions.

The biological community point of view is concerned with types of organisms which can be used as indicators. If we look at the biological characteristics of wetlands, we principally use the vegetation. This is not only because the plants are indicators of environmental conditions and primary producers but also because they largely determine the ecosystem structure, including the species composition of all the other biotic communities in the ecosystem. For the **IBP** Wetlands synthesis, the following definition has therefore been adopted:

A wetland is an area dominated by herbaceous macrophytes, which photosynthesise predominantly in the aerial environment and root in a soil which, generally speaking, is entirely saturated with water throughout the greater part of the growing season.

We are aware of imperfections in this, but a brief, precise definition is not possible. We prefer this as a working definition to a more elaborate combination of biological and environmental characteristics. As a consequence of this definition, and some further practical limitations, this synthesis will exclude the following types of habitats, though this does not necessarily imply that they are not wetlands:

1. Freshwater aquatic habitats which are treated in the IBP-PF synthesis (LeCren & Lowe-McConnell, 1980), and, for conservation purposes, in Project AQUA (Luther & Rzóska, 1971).
2. Coastal habitats dominated by seaweeds (although marine and inland littoral saline and brackish habitats colonised by herbaceous vegetation are included). See also Mitsch & Gosselink (1986) for non-seaweed tidal marshes.
3. Saline, inland flood-plain, and wet meadow grasslands used primarily for grazing or hay are excluded as they are included in the IBP-PT 'grasslands' syntheses (Coupland, 1979; Breymer & Van Dyne, 1980).
4. Arctic and high mountain habitats which are treated in the IBP-PT 'tundra' synthesis (Bliss, Heal & Moore, 1981).
5. Ombrogenous peat bogs and *Sphagnum* moors which are treated to some extent in the 'tundra' synthesis, are dealt with extensively in Gore (1983*a,b*), and also by Mitsch & Gosselink (1986). They mainly occur in cold and temperate regions.
6. Shrub and forest vegetation, on waterlogged or flooded ground, not in contact with wetlands dominated by herbaceous vegetation. This belongs to the IBP-PT 'woodlands' group of projects (Reichle, 1981). In particular, this means that carr, flood-plain forests and mangrove swamps are excluded from detailed discussion (see also Mitsch & Gosselink, 1986; Lugo *et al.*, 1990; Patten, 1990).

Wetlands have been defined in a very wide sense by the International Union for the Conservation of Nature and Natural Resources (IUCN, 1972) as:

Areas of marsh, fen, peatland or water, whether natural or artificial, permanent or temporary, with water that is static or flowing, fresh, brackish or salt, including areas of marine water the depth of which at low tide does not exceed 6 m.

However, aquatic habitats containing hydrophytes (submerged plants), fishes and other water animals, planktonic, pleustonic and benthic organisms are not usually treated as wetlands elsewhere.

Typical examples of wetland habitats covered by our definition are littoral belts beside lakes and ponds dominated by *Phragmites*, *Scirpus*, *Typha* or *Cyperus*; river banks dominated by *Echinochloa* spp., *Paspalum repens*, *Prionium serratum* or *Phalaris arundinacea*; swamps dominated by *Cyperus papyrus*, *Zantedeschia*, *Vossia* or *Glyceria*; marshes and fens dominated by *Carex*, *Scolochloa* or *Beckmannia*; coastal marshes and deltas dominated by *Spartina*, *Scirpus maritimus* complex or *Zizania*; and other habitats such as canals, shallow streams with, e.g. *Nasturtium* or *Apium*; periodic pools with, e.g. *Echinochloa* or *Panicum*; and other more or less important periodic water bodies as long as they are colonised by an herbaceous vegetation. Details of habitat types and their dominants are given later in this chapter. Certain important wetland habitats have been selected to show the characteristics of hydroseres in several major phytogeographical regions of the world (in Table 1.3).

Wetlands differ from other biomes studied during the IBP in several respects. Their principal unique feature is a transition, both structural and functional, between the aquatic and terrestrial biomes. Consequently, wetlands have to be regarded as an open 'inter-biome' in all their fundamental ecological characteristics and relationships. The transition from water to land, wet or dry, and back into water, has brought about marked genetically fixed adaptations in many groups of plants and animals. The time scale of the interactions between the aquatic–wetland and terrestrial environments is clearly reflected in the adaptability of various species populations to the varied conditions which they encounter in wetlands. Further, this adaptability is reflected in the various life and growth forms of wetland biota and in the structure and dynamics (spread or retreat as well as stabilisation) of wetland communities. It is therefore understandable that wetlands, being transitional between water and land, are usually species-richer than the water bodies from which they are derived.

The environmental variations, especially the movements of water, both vertical and horizontal, may be regarded as an energy subsidy (E.P. Odum, 1971), which contributes to the high biological productivity of many wetland types such as reedswamps or tidal marshes. Their high primary production is associated with an intense uptake of mineral nutrients by the vegetation and by a great production of dead organic matter. This usually supports a rich and diversified detritus food chain. The grazing food chain, depending on consumption of live-plant biomass, is mostly less important, yet sufficient to support numerous herbivores and predators.

In treating the general ecology of wetlands, we should consider at least the habitat features, biotic structure, dynamics, geographical distribution and types of wetlands. Considerable difficulties arise from a lack of profound knowledge in many respects. In particular, little is known about environmental characteristics and about the ecology of particular species except for some widespread plants like *Echinochloa* spp., *Eichhornia crassipes*, *Salvinia* spp., *Cyperus papyrus*, *Glyceria maxima*, *Oryza sativa, Phragmites australis* (= *communis*), *Typha latifolia, T. angustifolia, Scirpus lacustris, S. maritimus* and *Spartina* spp., which tend to be better known. Usually, we try to summarise generally applicable results and ideas, but we use more restricted studies if these provide insight into general principles or form a basis for discussion or further research. In particular, the study of vegetation structure represents an important starting point for understanding wetland ecosystems.

The early history of wetland studies has been reviewed by Gorham (1953*a*) and Boulé (1994).

Wetland habitats

This section gives only a general picture of wetland habitats, and more detailed information on various habitat components is given in appropriate parts of this book. Some definite complexes of habitat characters mainly influence the structure of communities, others their species composition; some do both. Thus macro-climate is much more important for structure, while species composition is dependent on the flora and fauna of the region, and on the specific requirements of the species with respect to habitat.

Many and voluminous books describe habitat characteristics and human relationships of fresh, brackish and marine wetlands (e.g. Gore, 1983*a,b*; Whigham *et al.*, 1985, 1990; Patten, 1990, 1994; Mitsch & Gosselink, 1986; Gopal *et al.*, 1993; Mitsch, 1994; Hughes & Heathwaite, 1995; Haslam, in press), and give valuable information for local studies of the ecology of wetland organisms and their management. However, their value for understanding worldwide wetland vegetation, animal communities and the functioning of wetlands is generally limited.

Studies of vegetation are the most advanced, but even so, many data from ecological measurements have only a very local significance, or were recorded only occasionally in a changing habitat. In many studies the relation to the functioning of the plants is not clear, for instance, when chemical constituents are measured in water, whereas helophytes are probably much more directly influenced by the chemical characteristics of the substrate. Among the exceptions, although still local, are the thorough studies by Malmer (1962), and several of his pupils, on Swedish vegetation. Some studies exist on the autecology of a few of the helophyte species dominant in wetlands (e.g. Björk, 1967 and Haslam, 1972*b* on *Phragmites australis*). Segal (1965, in Dutch) has given a concise review of habitat requirements of aquatic macrophytes. In view of the limited knowledge, this chapter will only give a brief survey of some habitat characters important for wetland studies. Most ecological factors are interrelated so that any division of the habitat factors is arbitrary.

Geographical and macro-climatic factors

The geographical position (especially latitude and altitude) is as important for wetlands as it is for other ecosystems. The latitude determines the potential input of radiation and its seasonal distribution. Hence it is of great importance for the productivity of wetlands, especially of those in which mineral nutrients or a dry season, do not stand out as factors limiting primary production. The latitude also determines the seasonal distribution of daylength and thus pre-determines, in broad terms, the sets of plant populations that can colonise a wetland. Altitude exercises a further selective influence within a given latitudinal belt, by its correlation with the temperature and rainfall regimes. The relatively higher rainfall, which usually occurs in uplands and mountainous areas, also brings about a relatively faster wash-out of nutrients from the catchment areas into wetlands and possibly from wetlands into running waters and lakes. This factor has become important with the present intense fertilising of agricultural soils now practised in many parts of the world. Otherwise, through the long-term leaching effects of the rainwater, upland and mountain wetlands have become minerally poorer, as a rule, than lowland wetlands. Longitude has certain effects on the occurrence of wetlands as well, especially in continents (e.g. Eurasia) where it is associated with a gradient of continentality, i.e. frequency and distribution of rainfall and temperature range.

Historical factors

Each wetland has its history, although most wetlands are relatively young in geological terms. In boreal regions, their existence dates back to the beginning of the post-glacial period at the earliest. In warmer regions, only some wetlands are of older age such as those situated in rifts which developed in the Tertiary period (e.g. in the Great African Rift), while most tropical and subtropical wetlands are situated in river alluvia and estuaries and hence are of Pleistocene or Holocene origin.

An important factor for the development of any wetland is the ratio between the accumulation and mineralisation of detritus (peat) which determines the rate of its filling with organic deposits, and terrestrialisation. In theory, each wetland represents a transitional stage in a succession from aquatic to terrestrial ecosystems but in practice, this is frequently not the case. Many wetlands are maintained as so-called permanent successional stages by an input of energy from outside (e.g. tidal water movements, flooding, river flow) which prevents further development towards drier types of ecosystems. This energy subsidy may be provided regularly (i.e. tides) or irregularly (e.g. catastrophic floods, storms with strong wave erosion). In the latter case the structure and functioning of a wetland ecosystem oscillate about a certain steady state but, in long-term run, the succession does not proceed further. On the other hand, the terrestrialisation of certain wetlands proceeds quite rapidly and can be slowed down or stopped only through human influence. A classical example are fishponds where sophisticated management is necessary to prevent their filling (see Dykyjová & Květ, 1978). For the process of terrestrialisation of wetlands see pp. 29–53.

The history of human influence is important for understanding the ecology of many a wetland, as is knowledge of its present-day management. Wetlands have been exploited for human needs for a long time (see Chapter 8), and this has not happened without influence on the wetland ecosystems. Frequently, people have also tried to turn wetlands into more accessible or better exploitable ecosystems. Hence drainage, pollution, clearing or regular harvesting of the natural vegetation, hunting, manuring and fertilising, and flooding (accidentally or on purpose) have been practised and have also left their traces in the structure of wetland ecosystems. Of course, people have also strongly influenced wetlands in connection with water-works such as water reservoirs, impoundments, ponds, canals, ditches and drainage or irrigation systems.

Geomorphological factors

These include slope orientation and inclination and other dimensions closely connected with the landscape structure, especially the configuration of the shore.

Wetlands are generally more restricted in space than many other formation types. The surface of a wetland may amount from several square metres or less up to large areas, but often the shape of a wetland is aligned along a water body and the vegetation may be narrow and interrupted. The vegetation stretches out over larger areas only in special cases, for instance, in deltas, flat regions and low-lying basins.

The slope and orientation of shores is important in wetlands attached to larger water bodies, in relation to wind action and dash of waves. Where a distinct wind direction prevails, the wind-exposed shores may be eroded without being colonised by vegetation. The best sites for its establishment are the sheltered shores. The dimensions (surface, form and depth) play an important role in relation to the dash of waves, which is strong in larger lakes. In small water bodies, the surrounding vegetation may reduce wind action. The dimensions may also influence the vegetation structure (see pp. 30–1).

In river beds, quite different morphological characters are of importance (Kopecký, 1965), especially in relation to erosion and accumulation of silt and peat.

Pedological factors

Soil type, silting, peat accumulation, mechanical composition of the substrate and erosion are included here. No complete pedological study on aquatic habitats and wetlands has yet been made. We shall follow the classification of Kubiëna (1953), which is mainly derived from earlier authors.

Main horizons

Wetland soils are generally subaqueous or semi-terrestrial AC-soils. The A horizons are the characteristic humus horizons, showing the highest population densities of organisms and the strongest enrichment with organic matter. The C horizons are composed of unweathered or little-changed parent materials. Profiles of well-developed underwater or ground water soils show grey, grey–blue, grey–green to olive-green-coloured G horizons (gley horizons) instead of the B horizon (see e.g. Fig. 6.4). These are characterised by a lack of oxidation (the colour is due to iron(II) oxide compounds); reduction processes and anaerobic conditions predominate. Gley soils develop where flowing ground water, changing water levels or oxygen from roots and rhizomes cause secondary oxidations, irregular rust-coloured iron horizons and mottling. These are found quite commonly in shallow water habitats which occasionally fall dry, e.g. ditches and cattle holes, and in seepage areas. Strongly contrasting white calcium horizons (Kubiëna, 1953) occur in terrestrial soils and dried-out ground water soils when heavy precipitates of fine calcium carbonate occur. These are also found associated with periodic waters in limestone-rich areas (e.g. in Western Ireland).

Mineral soils, especially clayish soils, in brackish or saline habitats, if flooded intermittently (e.g. by tides) often show a shining black reduction layer at the surface just below a thin äfja (see below) layer which is often composed of *Vaucheria* and blue–green algae. This horizon is not mentioned by Kubiëna and may be called R horizon. Its shine disappears rapidly when cut through oxidation.

Subhorizons

Subhorizons without closer characterisation are the A_1, A_2 and A_3 horizons. The A_0 horizons are mineral-deficient, quite distinct humus layers, lying on the mineral soil, with slight decomposition and humification. *Äfja* is the predominantly green surface layer of underwater soils containing living plants, mostly algae, and scarcely decomposed, almost uncomminuted plant remains. It differs essentially from the (underwater) *förna*, which consists of the remains of higher plants, mainly in shore litter.

Humus

The forms of humus encountered in habitats which are usually covered with water, can be divided into:

R. Raw soil humus without formation of a macroscopically distinguishable humus horizon (in contrast to the next types).

M. Peat if the humus layer is coherent and peaty whereas in the next types it is loose and muddy.

D. Dy if the humus layer is brown and composed entirely of humus flocks. It generally occurs in brown-coloured (dystrophic) waters and consists of amorphous precipitates of humus gels, and is biologically highly inert.

G. Gyttja without or only with a slight smell of putrefaction, rich in animal excreta. Its smell is often slightly inky. Many subtypes are distinguished.

S. Sapropel with strong smell of putrefaction, hydrogen sulphide and other gases of animal excreta.
   Note: The term sapropel is often used in a much wider sense, comprising gyttja in the sense of Kubiëna and decomposed underwater peat, with or without silting or much precipitation of animal excreta and dead animals (mainly M). If no further details are given, it is better to use only the term '(underwater) peat'.

When referring to soils which are not covered with water (or only intermittently), we may distinguish:

A. Anmoor, which is not peaty and is very rich in minerals. When wet, it is muddy, blackish to grey.
L. Low peat moor (drained form), composed predominantly of either reeds or other helophytes, including sedges, or brown moss or carr fragments. Peaty and mineral deficient. This type may be subdivided into reed peat moor (LP), or sedge peat moor (LC), *Hypnum* peat moor (LH), *Sphagnum* peat moor (LS) or carr peat moor (LA) according to the predominant remains.

All these subtypes are macroscopically distinguishable, LP by the size of remains of tall helophytes and stalk nodes, LC by the presence of lustrous dark seeds, LH by remains of plagiotropic bryophytes, LS by *Sphagnum* remains and LA by the leaves, fruits and easily cut woody remains of alders and willows.

In peat anaerobic conditions prevail, which are unfavourable to decomposition of dead plant remains.

Deposition and erosion

Silting is broadly correlated with dash of waves or velocity of water current. In rivers, the measurement of velocity in the midstream may have little relevance to the actual velocities affecting the deposition of silt around a stand of plants, and the degree of silting will be dependent on the degree of turbulence and the supply of silt (Westlake, 1973).

The mechanical characters of the mineral subsoils are related to their texture, those of the peat depend on its composition, decomposition and silting, and in both kinds of soil they depend on the duration of draining and drying out of the soil.

Erosion is highly dependent on the character of the shore (e.g. soil type), hard stony shores and banks being eroded less than those composed of loose or soft materials (sand, clay).

Hydrological factors

By definition, hydrology is of primary importance to the ecology, functioning and conservation of wetlands (examples in Mitsch & Gosselink, 1986; Falconer & Goodwin, 1994; Gilman, 1994; Hughes & Heathwaite, 1995). Aspects of water level, movement and sources are discussed here; evaporation, evapo-transpiration and precipitation are climatic factors affecting the water balance, which arise above and in Chapter 7.

Water level

The influence of changes in the position of the water level has already been mentioned, and examples are given in Chapter 8 (Table 8.4, pp. 432–3). The position of the water level depends strongly on precipitation in the catchment area, but this relation does not always show its effect immediately, especially if percolation takes place through higher-lying soils in the surroundings, e.g. in dune valleys. The effect of precipitation may appear quite regularly several months later, sometimes up to 9 months (Ter Hoeve, 1951), but for soils with smaller porosity than sands, e.g. clay, the time interval is shorter.

The frequency, amplitude and duration of various positions of the water level have different effects depending on the relative elevation or depression of a wetland or aquatic site. The term 'ecophase' has therefore been introduced, which characterises the actual aquatic environment on any site at any given moment. Four principal ecophases are distinguished: hydrophase, littoral, limosal and terrestrial phases (Hejný, 1971; Table 1.1, Fig. 1.2). A certain sequence of ecophases is called an ecoperiod. Ecoperiods *sensu* Hejný (1971) describe, above all, certain trends in the environment and need not necessarily repeat themselves regularly. Three fundamental kinds of ecoperiods may be distinguished, depending on the stabilisation or fall or rise of the water level:

1. ecoperiods with a more or less stabilised water level (hydrophase to littoral phase sequence of ecophases on the deepest sites of a wetland);
2. ecoperiods with a marked fall of water level leading, eventually, to emergence of parts of, or of, the whole bottom (littoral – terrestrial sequence of ecophases);
3. ecoperiods with a marked gradual or sudden rise of water level following an interval of low water level (terrestrial – littoral sequence of ecophases).

The three fundamental types of ecoperiods may combine in reality in various ways so that 'hybrid' ecoperiods may result. In temperate climates, an ecoperiod more or less coincides with the vegetation period, although the winter conditions have to be taken into account as well. In tropical climates, a whole year or only a part of it may be occupied by an

Table 1.1. *Aquatic ecophases (Hejný, 1971)*

Phase	Water level
Hydrophase	Deep water $\gtrsim 1$ m
Littoral	Shallow water ~ 0.1–1 m
Limosal	Waterlogged soil < 0.2 m below soil– < 0.1 m above soil surface
Terrestrial	Dry surface, water within rooting zone, generally > 0.2 m below surface

ecoperiod. The ecoperiods of the types 2 and 3 act selectively on the development of macrophyte communities, each in its own way. If a type 2 ecoperiod is followed by a type 3, this successively creates conditions favourable for the development of all plant life and growth forms that can occur in the wetland – from hydrophilous to hygromesophilous plants. Such a sequence of the two so-called critical ecoperiods marks the termination of one phase of development of the wetland vegetation and the onset of another phase. Combinations of these phases, which repeat themselves over shorter or longer intervals, may be called ecocycles. In the tropics and subtropics, an ecocycle usually takes only 1 year, with a littoral–terrestrial sequence of ecophases during the dry period, and with a terrestrial–littoral–hydrophase sequence during the rainy season.

Practically any wetland site at any given elevation above the deepest bottom level may be regarded as occupying a certain position in a spectrum of more or less widely oscillating ecophases during a certain interval. These oscillations are most conspicuous in climatically dry regions, or in wetlands where the water level is artificially controlled (e.g. in ponds), or controlled by river inflow (e.g. in deltas), and they are least important in wetlands attached to standing waters with a stable water level (e.g. lakes in humid regions with a regular distribution of rainfall). In any case, the concept of ecophases and ecoperiods makes it possible to evaluate various alternative combinations of hydrological conditions in wetlands or water bodies, or in their parts, over longer or shorter time intervals. The effects of these conditions on the wetland habitats and biotic communities can then be predicted if one knows the biology and ecology of the potentially dominant plants and other biota.

If the water level suddenly falls, exposing a soil which remains wet under a water-saturated atmosphere, strong overheating or freezing may occur (see pp. 367–80), both of which may severely affect the plant, animal and microbial life. This harsh micro-climate is one of the reasons why summer annuals often prevail in such habitats. On the other hand, soil aeration is promoted. But this has an unfavourable effect if the soil is rich in sulphide (saline habitats) which is oxidised into sulphate because the result is increased acidity. This happens, e.g. along the Finnish coast, where the ground is rising.

Tides

Tides produce a very extreme ecotope where great differences take place, at short time intervals. These include differences in water content of the substrate and in many correlated features such as salt concentration. In tidal pools, drying out gradually during low tide, this may become far higher than it is in sea water. Only a few species are adapted to such extreme conditions which, however, show a certain regularity.

Water movements

Raspopov *et al.* (1990) have described the influence of water movements on plant communities on the shores of a large lake. In general, a strong dash of waves erodes the shore and diminishes the possibilities for plant settlement. Even on sheltered shores an undercurrent running in the opposite direction to the waves is often responsible for the movement of eroded peat and silt. Where the wave dash has been damped by hydrophytes some wetland species with creeping rhizomes can invade. Once some plants are established, a 'current shadow' allows material to be deposited, and this secondarily influences the possibilities for succession.

Waves and currents have other important secondary effects. The water is usually oxygen saturated and there is also an important relationship between current velocity and kind of substrate (Butcher, 1933; Gessner, 1955). Fast moving water removes coarse sediments (stones), slower currents only finer sediments (gravel, sand) and at still lower velocities only very fine sediments are moved (clay, silt).

Seepage, groundwater

Seepage phenomena and flushes are most apparent at places where water is raised by difference in hydrostatic pressure. This is important not only in mountains and dune valleys but also in polders and elsewhere along dykes and dams. The following phenomena accompany seepage: temperature fluctuations are relatively small, resulting, e.g. in thin and irregular, or no, ice cover, and water which shows a red–brown colour of precipitated iron hydroxides, or hydrocarbonates and a surface cover of an oil-like membrane (consisting particularly of iron bacteria). Seepage and flushes may enrich habitats relatively poor in minerals, e.g. by transport of dissolved calcium carbonate which may give rise to a milky-white or opalescent appearance of the water. However, large quantities of iron may precipitate phosphate ions. Seepage phenomena often occur periodically and locally, depending on precipitation and water level, and on the porosity of the soil in several layers.

Groundwater movements caused by differences in elevation are probably important for understanding pollution and eutrophication of isolated waters (e.g. Verhoeven *et al.*, 1988) together with the air transport of particles and gases.

Ice

The influence of ice cover is manifold. At air temperatures lower than melting point, it has an insulating effect on the water. It reduces light transmission, especially when it supports snow. Another aspect is the mechanical influence of ice, through its pressure and shifting of soil and shore erosion, especially in wetlands situated along windward shores of large lakes.

Physical factors

Physical factors include the radiation and temperature regimes, pressure, wind and fire.

Irradiance

It is clear that the radiation regime is influenced by daylength, sun elevation, cloudiness, sunshine duration, snow and ice cover, and atmospheric pollution, all affecting both irradiance and spectral composition. The influence of these differs with latitude, distance from oceans and with the degree of industrial, agricultural and direct human disturbance in an area.

Radiation is an important factor; most wetland plants are heliophilous, and wetland vegetation is often reduced in the shade of trees. Under water, the irradiance depends on the depth, transparency, turbidity and colour of the water. For further details see Chapter 7, and appropriate passages in Chapter 2 (pp. 116–25). The regime of radiation within wetlands depends on their vegetation cover, whose properties as a radiation-intercepting system have been studied in the IBP (e.g. Straškraba & Pieczyńska, 1970; Ondok, 1977, 1978*a*). Both the transparency and colour of the water depend on the amount of dissolved material, on the planktonic and pleustonic organisms and on the presence of seston. Transparency is usually smaller near the shores than it is in deeper water.

Temperature

The air, water and soil temperatures and their fluctuations, depend strongly on the climate, the topographical position of the wetland and its size, the depth and shape of the adjacent water body, currents, seepage and vegetation, among other factors (cf. Chapter 7). Water is a poor heat conductor which favours the hibernation of plants and animals on or in the bottom. Seepages, flushes and springs extend the effective growing season.

Pressure

Hydrostatic pressure is a physical factor less important in the shallow wetlands than it is in deep lakes, but it may be of importance in particular instances.

Wind and fire

Wind has effects on wetlands through wave action, plant movement and transport of organisms. It is of extreme importance for pollination and propagation by seeds of many wetland plants, among which anemophily and anemochory prevail.

Fire is usually, but not always, of human origin in wetlands. Its effect is mainly a change in chemical composition of the substrate, which becomes enriched in nutrients, e.g. nitrates and potassium. The dead plant remains are good heat insulators. Burning often favours the development of special tall herbs, e.g. *Lysimachia vulgaris*, on some drier places; or *Carex acutiformis* or *Glyceria maxima* in wet habitats in Europe. The effect decreases with the wetness of habitat.

Chemical factors

It is necessary to consider these in water, soil and air, and their interrelations. The hydrochemistry of British wetlands has been reviewed in Hughes & Heathwaite (1995); and Mitsch & Gosselink (1986) and Patten (1990) have chapters on soil and chemistry.

The chemicals in water in wetlands depend on their content in the water which feeds the wetland, but there need not be a direct correlation with the composition of the bottom sediments. Olsen (1950) found great differences in phosphate and nitrate content in the underwater soil both in vertical and horizontal directions, while the chemical composition of the water was nearly constant. For example, Malmer (1962) found in fens in Småland (Sweden) that all elements studied showed much higher concentrations in the soil than in the water. Planter (1973) recorded in Masurian lakes (Poland) that the interstitial water had different properties from littoral water. It possessed mainly a higher conductance, alkalinity and concentrations of different cations. Hence the interstitial water present in the zone of plant roots is likely to be a source of nutrients for macrophytes. The changes in the chemical composition of interstitial water during the vegetation season depend on a complex of co-acting factors: exploitation of the substrate by the plants, mineralisation, carbon dioxide content, redox potential and exchange of water by inflow and outflow in horizontal direction or by vertical movement. Helophytes take part in the exchange by taking up nutrients from the substratum and returning them to the littoral water through mineralisation. Most important are the amounts of exchangeable ions. Conductivity is a measure of total ion concentration. If one strongly dissociated compound occurs in relatively large quantities, e.g. NaCl, conductivity is mainly determined by the amount of this compound. Conductivity, acidity and alkalinity together give a better idea of the hydrochemical properties of a wetland habitat than pH alone. Chapter 6 deals with the chemistry of wetlands in more detail.

Oxygen

As already noted, oxygen is a critical factor in submerged soils. In water, its concentration is, apart from waves and current, highly affected by temperature, and also depends on chloride content, being lower at higher contents of chloride. Oxygen content is positively correlated with redox potential, which is also dependent on pH (so that conversion to a certain pH level is necessary for comparisons). High values of redox potential increase the possibilities of occurrence for free nitrate, sulphate and iron(III) ions; low redox potentials favour the sulphide and iron(II) ions (p. 338).

Phosphorus and nitrogen

According to many authors, phosphate is a limiting factor in many instances. Low phosphate concentrations are often recorded, but little is known about the exchangeability in the inorganic soil–organic soil–surface water systems. Nitrate may often be low as well. Nitrogen fixation may be important in various wetlands (Goldman, 1961; Bristow, 1974), and in some types transitional to shrub and carr vegetation with, e.g. *Myrica gale* and *Alnus glutinosa* (see also Chapter 6).

Trophic status

We shall not deal further with the effects of different ion concentrations here, but some notes have to be made on habitat typification according to hydrochemistry, or the concept of trophy. Although the terms eutrophic and oligotrophic (Naumann, 1919) are generally accepted, great confusion exists concerning their meaning and limitations; even more confusion exists over the term mesotrophic (Segal, 1965). Several authors have proposed more exact definitions based, e.g. on conductivity (Olsen, 1950) or exchangeable calcium (Ratcliffe, 1964), but they are often the result of local observations not suitable for other areas or habitats. Moreover, there exists a difference in the use of the term 'oligotrophy' in botany and limnology. In botany 'oligotrophy' is used in a broader sense including both the 'oligotrophy' and 'dystrophy' of the limnologists. In limnology, some intermediate steps between 'oligotrophy' and 'eutrophy' are distinguished, but their meaning is relative depending, to a large extent, on the attitude of each author. It might be better to avoid these terms when habitat records are available. Some habitats have an unstable chemical composition, e.g. certain disturbed habitats or contact zones between different water types. Leentvaar (1958) and Westhoff (1964) have introduced the term 'metatrophic' where a sudden change in the nutrient economy creates a discontinuity, which finds expression in a sudden shift of the community structure and composition caused by the mixing of different kinds of water (definition in Segal, 1965). Such habitats exhibit an unstable equilibrium. Guanotrophy caused by birds provides an example. The equilibrium in the mineral cycle is disturbed, but the water will have reached a higher trophic level when an equilibrium is re-established. Certain species with a very high production rate are probably favoured in such habitats, e.g. *Typha latifolia*, *Comarum palustre* and *Calla palustris*; this, however, remains to be confirmed.

In some cases, especially in 'Zwischenmoor', when the vegetation becomes isolated from the surface or bottom water (by vertical growth or by a relatively low water level during parts of the succession, or even within a growing season), rainfall may have a great influence during such periods. These 'poikilotrophic' types form, in some sense, transitions to the more ombrotrophic *Sphagnum* peat-bogs. They are, however, rich in species and composition because many micro-habitats exist without a prevailing limiting factor or master factor. This is another argument against using the term mesotrophic, which is often applied to such situations.

Biotic factors

Dissemination

The access of propagules which can develop to a terrain depends on an intricate complex of historical, topographical and geomorphological, as well as physical, chemical and biotic factors. For the migration of any species, its occurrence in the surrounds and the efficiency of its dissemination mechanism are of importance. Sometimes, priority may play a role: that species which becomes established first has a relatively better chance to spread. Since many helophytes show anemochory (wind dispersal) as well as hydrochory (water dispersal), many of them can reach nearly all places over large areas or continents.

Chemical interactions

Observations on the interactions of several plant species have mainly been performed in experiments, e.g. by Borhidi (1970) and Szczepańska & Szczepański (1973). They found that the production of one average seedling of a given species cultivated in monoculture sometimes exceeds the production of an average seedling of the same species growing together with another species.

For example, the production of *Phragmites australis* growing together with *Typha latifolia* or *Scirpus lacustris* amounts, respectively, to only 39 and 63 per cent of the production of *Phragmites* growing in monoculture. On the other hand, *Phragmites* growing together with *Glyceria maxima* is more productive than that growing in monoculture. *Phragmites* growing together with *Carex elata* is more productive than pure *Phragmites* only during the first year of joint cultivation; during the next three years, its production decreases systematically to some 12% of a *Phragmites* monoculture (Szczepański, 1977). *Typha latifolia* cultivated together with other macrophytes also exhibits an analogous differentiation in production. The greatest reduction of *Typha* production, by 46%, results from its joint cultivation with *Eleocharis palustris*, whereas joint cultivation with *Acorus calamus* increases its growth and development to 180% of the production in monoculture.

Polycorms often show concentric growth of their rhizomes, but sometimes the centre of such a polycorm dies so that the polycorm shows a ring form. This has often been observed in *Cladium mariscus* and *Scirpus maritimus* in the Netherlands (and quite often in some species of salt marshes, e.g. *Triglochin maritima* and *Juncus maritimus*, and in *Leersia oryzoides* in newly formed polders). Perhaps self-intoxication may play a role as well as age.

Other aspects of phytogenous factors are peat and litter formation with their influence on temperature, animal life and succession.

Zoogenic and anthropogenic aspects will be described in other parts of this book (Chapters 5 and 8).

All these local biotic and abiotic factors have to be studied in relation to their variations in time and space.

Structure of wetland vegetation

The structural features of the vegetation (synmorphology) include both the *physiognomy* (growth forms) and the *spatial distribution* of the species. In many types of wetlands one species is dominant, consequently its habit determines the physiognomy.

Spatial distribution includes stratification (vertical distribution) and horizontal patterns. Horizontal distribution features combine to form patterns expressed as deviations from a random distribution of the specimens. Patterns can be brought about by differences in the (micro) environment and by relationships between species; they are emphasised by interferences between species. Special attention is focused on homogeneity and boundaries of communities in relation to their zonation.

Adaptability and the life and growth forms of wetland vascular plants

As wetlands have specific habitat types, their vegetation has to be adapted, e.g. to dash of waves or flow, to changing water level and intermittent drainage and flooding of the substrate or to oxygen-poor conditions. Adaptations to common environmental features lead to groups of species which may be taxonomically very different, but resemble each other in morphology, life cycle and behaviour (life forms). However, several criteria have been introduced to distinguish life forms, depending on the emphasis placed on adaptation to particular aspects of the environment. Those of Raunkiaer (1934) based on adaptation to the unfavourable season, are well known. His system, however, is directed mainly to terrestrial plants. Helophytes were defined as plant species with over-wintering buds in water or in the submerged bottom. They are differentiated from hydrophytes in that their vegetative organs are, under normal circumstances, partially raised above water level (Raunkiaer, 1934). That definition includes many wetland plants.

The system of Iversen (1936) is based on different morphological and anatomical adaptations to the water factor. In his system, most wetland plants become either telmatophytes or amphiphytes.

Hejný's (1957, 1960, 1971) system of life forms is associated with the duration of ecophases and ecoperiods and on the character of their sequence. His system, as demonstrated in Fig. 1.1 and Table 1.2, is especially suited for aquatic and wetland plants. This system mainly uses relatively stable vegetative features that determine the ability of aquatic plants to survive two unfavourable seasons, cold or drought; in particular, the types of photosynthetic organs present in both the growth and flowering phases. In Table 1.2 Hejný's definitions have been slightly modified to emphasise this approach, which is consistent with an extension of Raunkiaer's original definition of life forms.

The physiognomic structure of vegetation is more closely related to growth forms, or habit forms. They may show some correspondence with life forms, but are often less stable, so that one species may have different growth forms in different habitats or at different times of the year. Growth forms include categories with different morphological and anatomical characters, and even fruit, seed- or pollen-types may be useful. Not many growth form systems have been elaborated.

Den Hartog & Segal (1964) developed a system for hydrophytes and related wetland forms, which has been modified later by Hogeweg

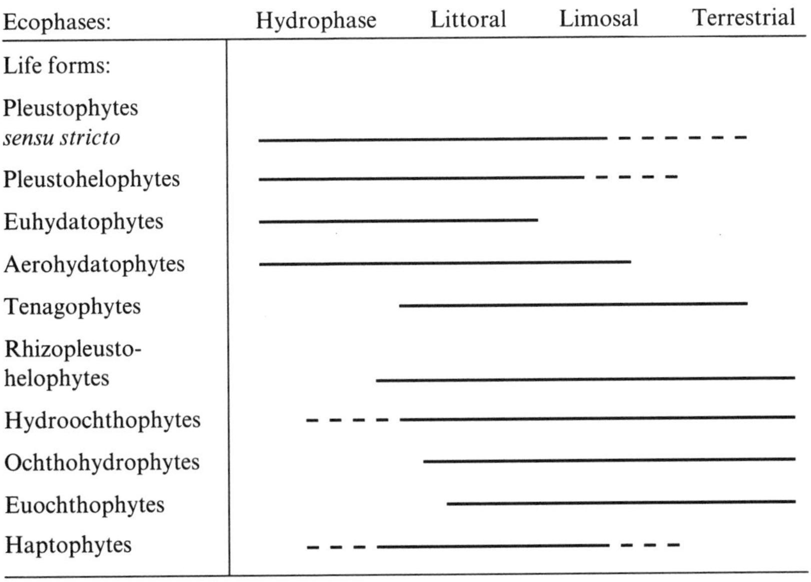

Ecophases:	Hydrophase	Littoral	Limosal	Terrestrial

Life forms:

Pleustophytes
sensu stricto

Pleustohelophytes

Euhydatophytes

Aerohydatophytes

Tenagophytes

Rhizopleusto-
helophytes

Hydroochthophytes

Ochthohydrophytes

Euochthophytes

Haptophytes

Fig. 1.1. Adaptation of the higher plant life forms to individual ecophases (see also Table 1.2).

& Brenkert-Van Riet (1969). These systems are combined here and somewhat further adapted. Although most of these growth forms will only occasionally be found in wetlands, especially the several hydrophyte types, nearly the complete system of macrophytes is given here because all types can be found. The most important characters used are sociability, root system, way of growth of shoots or stems, position of the leaves, anatomy and dimensions. Although adaptation to habitat is only considered secondarily, we will, as far as possible, consider attachment to the substrate (water, soils, stone), site of photosynthetically active tissues (aqueous or aerial), site of reproductive organs, and ecophases, especially for hydrophytes. Riparian zones are not distinguished from littoral zones in the review. The hydrophytes are based on the system of Luther (1949) regarding attachment to the substrate. Haptophytes (attached to solid substrate, e.g. stone) are usually not found in wetlands. Only the pleustophytes and rhizophytes thus remain.

Table 1.2 gives a survey of a combined system of life and growth forms of herbaceous wetland and aquatic vascular plants. This is mainly a

Table 1.2. Survey of life forms and growth forms of wetland and aquatic higher plants (see Notes on p. 26)

Life forms (growth and flowering phase; survival phases)	Growth forms	Examples	Morphology	Habitat
Pleustophytes: *Pleustophytes*	Ceratophyllids	*Ceratophyllum*, many *Utricularia* spp., *Aldrovanda*	(floating plants) fo often dm, ds; rt 0; tu bo; often attached; fo su	su (na) (sh); most Lit, small species Lim
sensu stricto free-na, su or ae; su d often tu	Wolffiellids	*Lemna trisulca, Wolffiella, Riccia* subgen. *Ricciella*	co reduced, en; rt 0 or su; th su (and ae)	su, sometimes ge na, (na) (sh); most Hyd, Lit
	Lemnids	Most *Lemna* spp., *Spirodela, Wolffia, Ricciocarpus, Azolla*	co reduced, en; rt 0 or su; th su and ae	na (sh); most Hyd, Lit
(Transition)	Hydrocharids	*Hydrocharis, Trionea, Limnobium, Phyllanthus fluitans, Salvinia, Ceratopteris* (su rooted; sterile)	fo, dm, en rs or dv; rt su; fo su and ae; sc tu or sc	na (sh); most Hyd, Lit
Pleustohelophytes	Eichhorniids	*Eichhornia; Pistia*	fo en, rs, ar; st; rt su; fo em (and su)	na (sh); most Hyd, Lit
free-na most fo and all fl em; ae d	Callids	*Calla*	fo en, ar; rh; rt su; fo em	na, sh; most Lit, Lim
Rhizophytes: *Euhydatophytes*	Otteliids	*Ottelia, Aponogeton* spp.	(rooted plants) fo en broad, rd; rh ar	su; Hyd, Lit
All fo su; rh, tu, su d	Vallisnerids	*Vallisneria* spp. *Sagittaria lorata*	fo en linear, rd; rh or st ar	su (ae); Hyd, Lit

Magnopotamids	*Potamogeton lucens, P. perfoliatus, Aponogeton crispus*	fo en broad, ca long	su; Hyd, Lit
Parvopotamids	*Potamogeton pectinatus, P. pusillus, Groenlandia, Najas, Zannichellia, Ruppia, Scirpus fluitans, Elodea, Hydrilla, Lagarosiphon, Callitriche autumnalis, Chara*	fo en linear; ca long	su; Hyd, Lit
Aerohydatophytes Some fo ae most su; rh, su d			
Myriophyllids	*Myriophyllum* spp; *Ranunculus circinatus; Hottonia; Hippuris*	fo often dm; ds and en; in whorls; ca long; fo su (and ae)	su (and em); (Hyd), Lit, (Lim)
Batrachiids	Most *Ranunculus* subgen. *Batrachium, Cabomba, Callitriche* sect. *Callitriche, Trapella*	fo dm, en and ds or capillary; ca long; fo su and ae	su and na and sh; Hyd, Lit, (Lim)
Trapids	*Trapa, Jussiaea sedoides*	fo dm, en and ds; ca long; fo su, and su and ae	na and su; Hyd, Lit
Nelumbids	*Nelumbo*	fo dm en broad; su and ae and em	na and em; Hyd, Lit
Nymphaeids	*Nymphaea, Euryale, Victoria, Brasenia; Nuphar; Potamogeton natans, P. gramineus, P. zizii, Luronium; Nymphoides; Polygonum amphibium, Sagittaria guianensis*	fo sometimes dm en broad (su) and ae	na (and su); Hyd, Lit, (Lim)
Marsileids and su st	*Marsilea, Regnellidium*	fo dv small; su, ae, em	na and sh; Lit, Lim
Stratiotids and su st	*Stratiotes*	fo en, rs; ca, su; st long weak; tu bo; fo su and ae or em	na (su and em or su); (Hyd), lit, (Lim)

(continued)

Table 1.2. (cont.)

Life forms (growth and flowering phase; survival phases)	Growth forms	Examples	Morphology	Habitat
Tenagophytes Plants su or em; su d, often ter	Isoetids	Many Isoetes spp.; Littorella, Subularia, Eriocaulon septangulare; Blyxa, Pilularia; Lobelia	fo en linear or needle-like, often stiff; often rd	su (and sh); Hyd, Lit or; (Hyd), Lit, (Lim)
	Subulariids	Subularia, Elatine hexandra, Limosella, Crassula aquatica	fo en small and broad; rh short	(Hyd), Lit, (Lim)
	Peplids	Peplis portula, Ludwigia palustris, Micranthemum, Hypericum elodes, Oxalis natans, O. disticha	fo en, ca leaves and distal rs; fo su and ae or em	na or su; Lit, (Lim)
	Acicularids	Eleocharis acicularis, Juncus bulbosus	fo dm, em awl-like, su soft; ca elong.	sh or su; (Hyd), Lit, optimum in Lim
Rhizopleustohelophytes Fo only ae attached by long stems fl ae; su d or often rh	Decodontids	Decodon, Ludwigia peploides, L. stolonifera, Ipomoea aquatica, Alternanthera aquatica	fo en, rt terrestrial (banks); often ca ar	su and em; Hyd or Lit and Lim or Ter
	Aeschynomenids	Aeschynomene spp., Neptunia oleracea spp.	fo dv; rt terrestrial (banks); ca ar	su and em; Hyd or Lit and Lim or Ter
Hydroochthophytes Some fo su but mainly em, often dm, fl em; usually rts or rh or tu; (or su d)	Sagittariids	Sagittaria most spp., Sparganium emersum, Alisma plantago-aquatica, A. gramineum, Butomus, Peltandra virginica, Monochoria, Glyceria fluitans	fo dm, when su linear ar or with long petioles	em and na and su; Hyd sterile, Lit, Lim (Ter)
	Apiids	Sium latifolium, Oenanthe aquatica, O. fluviatilis	fo dm, when su dv-ds	em and su; Lim; sublit. forms of Lim. species in Hyd sterile

	Cicutids	*Cicuta, Sium erectum, Oenanthe crocata, O. fistulosa*	fo dv or ds, often ar	em (and su) Lit/Lim (Ter)
Ochthohydrophytes Su fo absent or unimportant; rh	Schoenoplectids	*Scirpus* sect. *Schoenoplectus*	fo, dm, su long and weak ae sparse; ca ps rh long	em (and su); (Hyd) Lit (Lim)
	Phragmitids	*Phragmites, Typha, Cyperus, Sparganium erectum, Acorus, Equisetum fluviatile, Glyceria maxima*	fo graminoid, ae; rh long	Lit, Lim (Ter) em (and su)
	Menyanthids	*Menyanthes*	fo en or dv ar; rh	em; (Lit) Lim
Euochthophytes Su fo absent or unimportant; dry phase or winter phase, fibrous rts, or rh (or bulbs or su d)	Pseudacorids	*Carex rostrata, C. acuta, C. acutiformis, C. vesicaria, C. riparia, Iris pseudacorus, Leucojum aestivum*	fo graminoid; rh	em, Lit, Lim
	Paniculatids	*Carex paniculata, C. juncella, C. caespitosa, C. omskiana, C. hudsoni*	fo graminoid; caespitose	em, Lit, Lim (Ter)
	Phalarids	*Phalaris, Calamagrostis canescens, C. neglecta, Scolochloa festucacea*	fo graminoid; st	em; (Lit) Lim (Ter)
	Lysimachids	*Lysimachia vulgaris, Lythrum salicaria, Epilobium hirsutum, Lycopus europaeus, Mentha aquatica Scutellaria galericulata, Rorippa, Nasturtium*	fo not graminoid; rh and/or st, rt	em; (Lit) Lim (Ter)
Haptophytes Attached to su surfaces thalloid; dry phase, flowering and seeds	Podostemids (*sensu lato*)	*Podostemaceae*	fo 0, reduced or present (variable in shape and size); haptera	temporary flowing waters su on bo; Hyd and Lit (Lim)

Abbreviations: ae, aerial (= at surface); ar, aerenchymatous; bo, on bottom; ca, stems (= caules); co, cormus (= plant body based on shoot and root); d, dormancy; dm, dimorphic; ds, dissected; dv, divided; em, emergent; en, entire; fl, floating; fo, leaves (= foliage); ge, generative organs; Hyd, hydrophase; Lim, limosal (ecophase); Lit, littoral (ecophase); na, natant (= surface floating); ps, photosynthetic; rd, radical; rh, rhizomes; rt, roots; rs, rosettes; rts, rootstocks; sc, sporocarps; sh, shores; st, stolons, su, submerged; Sublit, sublittoral (ecophase); tb, tubers; Ter, terrestrial (ecophase); th, thallus; tu, turions; ( ), occasionally.

summary of our knowledge based on observations of the associations between plants and their environment. Further knowledge of the physiological causation of such associations may lead to development and revision. Like most classifications it is imposed on a continuum, and borderline cases will occur throughout. When a species has a range of growth forms, it has been classified under the form showing the greatest achievement of its potential, e.g. *Butomus* is classified as a hydroochthophyte rather than including the form with only submerged leaves under the euhydatophytes.

In limnology the following simpler classification of the forms of vascular water plants is commonly accepted (comprising both growth and life forms).

Amphiphytes – Plants growing at the borderline between water and land, adapted to the life in both environments.

Helophytes – Emergent plants rooted in the bottom with aerial leaves (water depth does not exceed 1.5–2 m).

Nymphaeids – Rooted plants with floating leaves.

Elodeids – Cauline submerged plants, whose whole life cycle can be completed below the water surface or only the flowers are emergent.

Isoetids – Rosette plants growing on the bottom, whose whole life cycle can be completed without contact with the water surface.

Pleuston – Vascular plants without connection with bottom, floating on the water surface or below it.

The frequently used term hydrophytes covers the nymphaeids, elodeids, isoetids, pleuston and partly the amphiphytes, but usually not the helophytes. For details of adaptations of aquatic plants to varying hydrological conditions see, e.g. Sculthorpe (1967).

Stratification of wetland plant communities

Stratification is related to level of organisation. Generally speaking, the more layers that can be distinguished, the higher the organisation. But organisation may be at a still higher level if there is considerable differentiation in plant height without distinct layering. This situation occurs when many species are present. Stratification is also usually reflected in the root systems. It is of importance to study root systems and their underground stratification in order to understand the structure and functioning of the community fully. The vertical structure of plant communities, including wetland ones, has been studied thoroughly with respect to their primary production. Examples of analyses of canopy structure are given in Chapter 2 (pp. 116–21).

Horizontal patterns within wetland plant communities

In discussing the distribution of 'individuals' or 'specimens' in wetland communities it is necessary to consider the definitions of these terms rather carefully. Each stem or shoot above the ground is usually regarded as a specimen, but many of these may be interconnected underground. Many wetland species occur in 'polycorms' which arise from one propagule by extension and branching of rhizomes or stolons, so that each 'individual' extends over a large area. If the original propagule was a seed, the polycorm is a clone; if it was a vegetative structure, the polycorm is merely a separate part of a clone. Sections of the polycorm may become separated by decay or mechanical damage, but the separated parts remain alive, and in their above-ground behaviour may show their common origin (Penzes, 1960).

Specimens of any given species only rarely show a random spatial distribution. A certain degree of overdispersion is the rule, which is partly expressed in the 'sociability' of the species. The sociability, or way of clustering of specimens of the same species, is in many cases a specific characteristic of the species, and may be treated as another kind of 'growth form'. Clearly, sociability will be greatly affected by the growth patterns of the polycorm. If the degree of sociability is low, it may either mean that the specimens are separated or that shoots from the rhizome are not aggregated.

However, in an even environment, the distribution approaches random with increasing quadrat size (Ikusima, 1978). Overdispersion may have several reasons:

1. vegetative spreading by means of short rhizomes or stolons, or caespitose growth;
2. spreading of propagules around a parent within a short distance;
3. small differences in habitat resulting in locally favourable conditions for the development of a certain species, or in unfavourable conditions for other species, e.g. differences in irradiance or micro-relief;

4. interrelations between different species, either direct or indirect, for example, when remains of one species form a favourable micro-habitat for establishment of another species.

Spatial relations between pairs of species can be calculated by means of association (in a mathematical sense), and may be positive, negative or non-existing. Horizontal distributions can be expressed as biomass, frequency, abundance, density or cover. Cover is difficult to measure exactly but it can be readily estimated, the values often being sufficient for the solution of many practical problems.

A vegetation may be more or less homogeneous, mosaic-like or situated in a gradient resulting in zonation. Homogeneity means that nearly all species will be found in representative numbers on any plot equal in size or larger than a certain minimal area selected for the vegetation. In mosaics, several homogeneous communities may alternate.

A vegetation gradient exists if one habitat factor or, usually, more coupled factors change gradually in space. This phenomenon is very common in many wetlands, especially in hydro- and hygroseres[1] showing a gradient of water depth, often accompanied by differences in peat accumulation, as well as in the influence of waves or currents. According to the distance over which it extends, a gradient may be either steep or gradual. Very steep gradients approximate to discontinuous habitat and vegetation boundaries.

At the borderline between water and 'land', either on peaty or on mineral soils, certain environmental conditions change very sharply. This is the explanation why, in the limosal region, there is usually a decrease of structure and species number at the boundary between water and land, where phragmitids often occur, while there is a marked increase in structure and species number of hydrophytes towards the water, and another increase landwards. Strong habitat oscillations may take place at such boundaries.

Zonation, in view of its importance in wetlands, is treated separately in the next section.

---

[1] Successional vegetation in permanent water ('hydro-') and on permanently saturated soils ('hygro-').

Spatial patterns (zones) of wetland communities, their types and classifications

The nomenclature of the zones at the edges of water bodies is not well defined. There are many systems, each influenced by the types of organisms or the dynamics of most interest, and depending on whether the author treats the shore merely as the boundary of open water or as an important region influenced by open water. Figure 1.2 attempts to set the ecophase terminology (see pp. 11–12 & Table 1.1), which refers to the actual conditions occurring at specific times, and has most relevance to wetlands, beside the limnological terminology recommended by Hutchinson (1967) and Wetzel (1975), which is related to the generalised

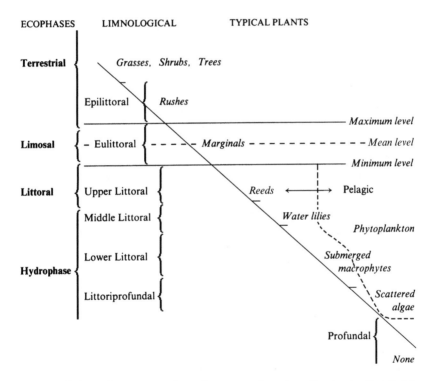

Fig. 1.2. Schematic representation of zones at the edge of water bodies. Bold, Ecophases; Roman, Limnological system; Italic, Typical plants; ⟷, Exchanges. Note that the Limnological System is based on the annual range of water levels and the vegetation; the Ecophase System refers to actual water levels over short periods. Hence, although there is a broad agreement, there are differences in details of levels and in different seasons (cf. Table 1.1).

conditions over the year. Next to the *terrestrial* vegetation, which occupies all land where the water table is well below the surface, comes the *epilittoral zone* where the water table is usually close to but below the soil surface. The *limosal ecophase*, on average, occurs within the *eulittoral zone* which lies between the upper and lower limits of the water level as it fluctuates with season and wave action. The next zone is the *littoral*, but this is limited, in the ecophase classification, to the zone of emergent vegetation and thus often includes the lower eulittoral. In the limnological classification, the *littoral* starts at the highest permanently submerged level and includes all the subsequent zones of macrophytic vegetation. It is subdivided into the *upper littoral* (emergent vegetation, the lower part of the littoral ecophase), the *middle littoral* (floating-leaved vegetation) and the *lower littoral* (submerged macrophytes). The ecophase terminology treats the two latter as the *hydrophase*. Often all zones from epilittoral to lower littoral are loosely referred to as 'the littoral'.

Limnologists also refer to the *littoriprofundal*, with scattered benthic algae and photosynthetic bacteria below the lower littoral, the *profundal* below the photic zone, and the *pelagial*, which is the zone of open water with phytoplankton. The pelagial extends over sward-forming macrophytes of the lower littoral and interacts with wetlands through water exchanges.

In rather narrow strips of wetlands, a simple division into inner and outer littoral zones, may be applied. The water in the former is more or less freely exchanged with the main water body, while the water in the latter is much more isolated (Hejný & Květ, 1978).

The zonation of aquatic macrophytes often exhibits a general sequence from deep water to shore (Table 1.3): submerged rhizophytes (euhydatophytes + tenagophytes) → natant rhizophytes (aerohydatophytes) → helophytes (ochthophytes) → terrestrial vegetation. (True rhizophytes are aquatic plants rooting in the bottom.) In certain situations, especially along shores shelted from wind or waves, where peat accumulation is great, this sequence is extended as follows: submerged rhizophytes → natant rhizophytes → emergent hydrophytes (pleustohydrophytes and pleustohelophytes) → helophytes → terrestrial vegetation.

A unified and synthetic classification of the littoral vegetation zones has not yet been worked out, although numerous attempts have been made. Most of these partial classifications concentrate on reeds as dominants determining the physiognomy of many littorals (e.g. Smirenskiĭ, 1951; Demidovskaya & Isambaev, 1964; Rodewald-Rudescu, 1974). Only a few of the classifications are of a more general character (e.g. Smirenskiĭ, 1950;

Bernatowicz & Zachwieja, 1966; Tadzhitdinov & Butov, 1972; Taubaev, 1970).

The zonation of wetland communities naturally depends on the character of ecocycles prevailing in a given wetland and reflects the local character of land formation through succession of macrophyte-dominated plant communities. The character and frequency of the critical ecoperiods (see pp. 11–12) and the geomorphological character of the shore, e.g. the litho-, psammo- and phytolittoral according to Bernatowicz & Zachwieja (1966), govern the life-forms and the way in which the wetland vegetation contributes to the filling of a water body.

The principles of the spatial patterns of littoral communities are best seen in lakes or other reservoirs with a very long ecocycle, i.e. with a stable water level. Here, the spatial pattern of the vegetation is also quite stable. The opposite situation, short ecocycles and a widely fluctuating water level, is least favourable for the development of regular spatial arrangements of the communities or precludes their existence at all. This problem has been treated thoroughly by Steward and Kantrud (1971) with respect to the classification of ponds, both permanent and temporary or periodic. It is interesting and perhaps also significant that the most detailed classifications of the structure of wetland macrophyte communities have been proposed by authors interested in them from the point of view of game management (Smirenskiĭ, 1950; Stewart & Kantrud, 1971).

General principles of the zonation of aquatic plants have been described, for example, by Segal (1965) and Hogeweg & Brenkert-Van Riet (1969). Littoral vegetation can belong to several types of zonations, all being derived from the general principle that, from deeper water to the shore, we may expect successively: submerged hydrophytes – natant hydrophytes – helophytes – terrestrial vegetation.

The most important habitat factors, at the basis of zonation in waters and wetlands, are water depth, depending on slope or peat accumulation, with associated differences in the radiation climate and dash of waves or current. The most intricate types of zonation can be expected in wetlands associated with a water body which is neither too deep nor shallow, is intermediate in size and in nutrient content, or when no limiting factors, other than those directly related to depth, and no strong fluctuations occur. Other limiting factors may be, e.g. poor irradiance (caused by high turbidity) or exposure to dash of waves or flow. Zonation often shows few zones or only one, e.g. elodeids in some rivers or larger lakes, while more zones exist if the habitat is less extreme.

Tables 1.3(a), (b) and (c) give examples of actual zonations found in

Table 1.3. Examples of wetland zonations of lakes, rivers, swamps and marshes

NOTES

The following principles were observed when compiling the tables:

1. The zonation seres are taken from the literature.
2. The localities were selected so as to provide the basic data needed for possible further comparisons. The geographical location is given by the place, district and state or region. In the absence of exact data in many papers, it has not been possible to give the coordinates and exact altitude.
3. In certain instances, the zonation sere had to be reconstructed from other data given by an author on the vegetation and its zonation and succession.
4. Each zonation sere starts on dry land and leads into a wetland (possibly also into water). In order to give a complete picture, the land end of each sere extends into the adjacent shrub or tree vegetation while the water end extends into floating and submerged aquatic vegetation. Continuation of a sere over more than one line is shown by a + sign.
5. Each stage of a zonation sere is characterised by the respective dominant species with any co-dominant species, linked to the next stage by a + sign.
6. If the literature characterises a stage in a sere by a plant community type (association), not by its dominant species, the name of the community type is presented. It is assumed that this is most important one or two species. This means, for example, that in *Cyperetum papyri*, *Cyperus papyrus* is the dominant species.
7. Zones between ( ) contain few helophytes, pleustohelophytes or tenagophytes and have mainly submerged or floating-leaved vegetation (not wetlands as defined for this book). If not included, they may not have been recorded because of lack of relevance to the research, or problems of sampling; although they may have been absent in a few cases in 1.3(a) and (b) and often in (c).
8. Numbers to the right of zonation seres are water depths. These data are understandably rather scarce in the literature. The water depth recorded on any given day in a tropical wetland, for example, has a much more limited value than a single depth record from say a north European or American wetland adjacent to a lake.
9. The phytogeographical division of the world used in the tables is that made by Good (1953) as modified by Jeník (1972).
10. The original intention to demonstrate zonations in wetlands of different trophy and salinity from each phytogeographical province could not be fulfilled because of lack of the appropriate data from many parts of the world. The absence of a province does not imply that data do not exist. They may have only been beyond the reach of the authors when compiling the tables.

Floristic Province	Locality	Zonation (in order of increasing depth)	Author(s)
(a) Littoral zones of lakes			
Boreal Kingdom			
Arctic and Subarctic	L. Kitenyavr, Kola Peninsula, Russia	*Carex* spp. + *Equisetum fluviatile* + *Sparganium angustifolium* + *Isoëtes lacustris*	Volkova, 1974
	L. Senozero, Kola Peninsula, Russia	*Carex* spp. + *Phragmites australis* + *Polygonum amphibium* + *Isoëtes lacustris*	

	Location	Species composition	Reference
	L. Seĭdozero, Kola Peninsula, Russia	*Carex* spp. + *Equisetum fluviatile* + *Isoëtes lacustris*	Forsh, Drabkova, 1976
	L. Vialozero, Kola Peninsula, Russia	*Carex rostrata* + *Menyanthes trifoliata* + *Nuphar lutea* + *Batrachium dichotomum* + *Isoëtes lacustris*	
Euro-Siberian	Lake Ladoga, Skerries region; Russia	*Carex vesicaria* + *Carex acuta* + *Phragmites australis* + *Potamogeton natans* + *Nuphar lutea* + *Elodea canadensis* + *Potamogeton perfoliatus* *Phalaris arundinacea* + *Carex vesicaria* + *Equisetum fluviatile* + *Potamogeton natans* + *Potamogeton perfoliatus*	
	Lake Ladoga, Southern region; Russia	*Phragmites australis* + *Scirpus lacustris* + *Potamogeton perfoliatus*	Raspopov, 1985
	Lake Onega, Unitzkaya guba, Russia	*Carex acuta* + *Phragmites australis* + *Scirpus lacustris* + *Nuphar lutea* + *Potamogeton perfoliatus*	
	Kontche Ozero, Karelia, Russia	*Carex* spp. + *Alisma plantago-aquatica* + *Eleocharis palustris* + *Sagittaria sagittifolia* *Scirpus lacustris* + *Typha angustifolia* + *Equisetum fluviatile* + *Phragmites australis* + *Scolochloa festucacea* (*Nuphar lutea* + *Nymphaea tetragona* + *Nymphaea candida* + *Potamogeton natans* + *Polygonum amphibium* + *Ranunculus peltatus*) (*Potamogeton gramineus* + *Potamogeton lucens* + *Potamogeton perfoliatus* + *Myriophyllum* spp. + *Ceratophyllum* spp.)	Klyukina, 1974
	English Lake District, Great Britain	*Equisetum fluviatile* + *Carex rostrata* (*Littorella uniflora* + *Juncus bulbosus* var. *fluitans* + *Myriophyllum spicatum* (2–3m) + *Isoetes lacustris* + *Nitella opaca* (–8 m))	Summarised in Hutchinson, 1975

(continued)

Table 1.3. (cont.)

Floristic Province	Locality	Zonation (in order of increasing depth)	Author(s)
Western and Central Asiatic	Asbergenkul L., Group of Sea Lakes (Saline), Delta Amu-Darya, Karakalpak, Uzbekistan	*Tamarix pentandra* + *Aeluropus littoralis* *Bolboschoenus affinis* + *Aeluropus littoralis* *Salicornia herbacea* + *Phragmites australis* *Phragmites australis* (*Najas marina* + *Chara tomentosa* + *Chara intermedia* 0.3–0.5 m) (*Potamogeton pectinatus* + *Najas marina* (0.5–0.7 m) *Ceratophyllum demersum* 1.0–1.5 m)	Tadzhitdinov & Butov, 1972
	Delta Amu-Darya, Karakalpak, Uzbekistan (Altitude 0–50 m)	*Phragmites australis* + *Calamagrostis dubia* *Phragmites australis* + *Typha angustifolia* (0.5–1.0 m) *Phragmites australis* + *Dryopteris thelypteris* (Plaur) (*Potamogeton crispus* + *Ceratophyllum demersum* (1.5 m) *Potamogeton lucens* (2.0 m))	Tadzhitdinov & Butov, 1972
Japanese	Pond Kasumi, Japan Type 1	*Treadenum japonicum* + *Lythrum anceps* *Lobelia chinensis* + *Centipeda minima* *Eleocharis pellucida* (*Myriophyllum ussuriense* + *Nuphar japonicum* *Brasenia schreberi*)	Kamuro, 1957
	Pond Kasumi, Japan Type 2	*Miscanthus sinensis* *Phragmites australis* + *Zizania aquatica* *Eleocharis kuroguwai* (*Brasenia schreberi* + *Trapa japonica*)	Kamuro, 1957

Atlantic North American	North-eastern Wisconsin Lakes, Weber L., USA (Altitude 0–200 m)	*Gratiola lutea* + *Juncus pelocarpus* (0–1 m) *Sparganium angustifolium* + *Elatine minima* (1–2 m) (*Myriophyllum tenellum* + *Isoetes macrospora* (2–3 m)) *Isoetes macrospora* (3–5 m)	Potzger & Engel, 1942
	Weber L.	(*Isoetes macrospora* + *Lobelia dortmanna* (0.5–4 m) *Fontinalis flaccida* + *Drepanocladus fluitans* (10–13 m))	Summarised in Hutchinson, 1975
Pacific North American	Stutsman County, Dakota, USA	(Slightly Brackish) *Salix interior* + *Salix candida* *Calamagrostis inexpansa* *Sparganium eurycarpum* *Typha glauca* (*Ruppia occidentalis*) *Carex aquatilis* + *Cicuta maculata*	Stewart & Kantrud, 1971
		(Moderate Brackish) *Spartina pectinata* *Scolochloa festucacea* *Scirpus acutus* (*Ruppia occidentalis*)	
		(Pond margins) *Carex sartwelli* *Typha latifolia* + *Glyceria striata* + *Phragmites australis* + *Scirpus validus* + *Carex aquatilis* (*Chara* spp. + *Drepanocladus* spp. + *Ceratophyllum demersum*)	
		(Alkaline) *Distichlis stricta* *Puccinellia nuttaliana* *Spergularia rubra* *Scirpus paludosus* (*Ruppia maritima*)	
Palaeotropical Kingdom			
West African	Mohasi L., Ghasal Creekland, Congo Basin, Zaire	*Jussiaea* spp. *Mariscus serratus* + *Leersia hexandra* *Cyperus papyrus* + *Dryopteris stricta* *Mikania scandens* (*Nymphaea hildbraedii* + *Nymphaea magnifica*)	Engler, 1910

(*continued*)

Table 1.3. (cont.)

Floristic Province	Locality	Zonation (in order of increasing depth)	Author(s)
West African (cont.)	Huilla Mountains, Namibia	*Panicum humidicolum* *Saccharum pallidum* + *Cyperus macranthus* (*Potamogeton javanicus* *Ambulia ceratophylloides*)	Engler, 1910
East African	L. Malawi, Malawi/ Mozambique (Altitude 250 m)	*Jussiaetum repentis* *Paspalidietum* *Eragrostidetum hildbraedii* *Aeschynomenetum elaphroxylontis* *Phragmitetum mauritanum*	Gilli, 1975
	L. Naivasha, Kenya (Altitude 1890 m)	*Acacia xanthophloea* *Lanthana camara* *Conyza bonariensis, C. floribunda, C. hypoleuca, C. stricta* *Cyperus papyrus* *Sphaeranthus suaveolens* (*Nymphaea coerulea* *Ceratophyllum demersum*)	Gaudet, 1977a
South African	L. Bangweulu, Zambia	*Cyperus papyrus* *Scirpus articulatus* (*Nymphaea magnifica* + *Eragrostis hildbraedii* + *Ottelia* + *Lagarosiphon*)	Fries, 1914

	L. Kivu, L. Tanganyika, and other lakes in Congo basin (Chefferie Udalishizi), Ruanda Burundi	*Potamogeton pectinatus* + *Cyperus laevigatus* + *Nymphaea lotus* + *Utricularia stellaris* + *U. thonningii* + *Lemna perpusilla* + *Burnatia enneandra* + *Heteranthera kotochyana* + *Oryza barthii* etc. *Phragmites mauritianus* + *Ipomoea fragrans* + *Paspalidium geminatum* + *Panicum meyerianum* + *Polygonum pulchrum* + *Cyperus digitatus* spp. *auricomus* etc. *Cyperus papyrus* + *Dryopteris gongyloides* + *Aframomum sanguineum* + *Melothria cognauxiana* + *M. augustifolia* + *Vigna bukobensis* etc. *Vossia cuspidata* + *Pluchea ovalis* + *Panicum repens* + *Phyla nodiflora* etc.	Germain, 1952
Capensis	Table Mountain, Cape Town, S. Africa	*Scirpus* spp. *Oxalis natans* + *Crassula natans* (*Aponogeton distachyon*)	Walter, 1968
Indian	Dal L., Srinagar, Kashmir	*Typha angustifolia* *Phragmites australis* (*Nymphoides peltatum* (1.5 m) *Myriophyllum spicatum* (2 m))	Kaul & Zutshi, 1967
	Ramgarh L., Gorakhpur, Uttar Pradesh, India (Altitude 95 m)	*Polygonum glabrum* + *Polygonum barbatum* *Ipomoea aquatica* + *Jussiaea repens* *Eichhornia crassipes*	Sahai & Sinha, 1969
	Doodhari L., Raipur, Madhya Pradesh, India (Altitude 280 m)	*Cyperus alopecuroides* + *Echinochloa crus-pavonis* *Oryza rufipogon* + *Eleocharis plantaginea* *Eichhornia crassipes* (*Najas minor*)	Unni, 1971

(continued)

Table 1.3. (*cont.*)

Floristic Province	Locality	Zonation (in order of increasing depth)	Author(s)
Neotropical Kingdom			
Andean	Titicaca Lake, Peru (Altitude 3815 m)	*Scirpus tatora* (*Zannichellia palustris* + *Potamogeton strictus* *Myriophyllum elatinoides* + *Elodea titicacana*)	Tutin, 1940
	East Andes (Cordillera), Bolivia (Altitude 4600 m)	*Distichia muscoides* *Hygrodicranum bolivianum* + *Jamesoniella fragilis* (*Isoetes herzogii* + *Myriophyllum elatinoides* *Nitella* spp.)	Herzog, 1923
	Salina Lakes, Salar de Atacama de Maricuaga, Distr. Atacama, Chile	*Atriplex atacamense* *Ephedra andina* *Tessaria absinthioides* *Distichlis* spp. + *Nitrophila axillaris* + *Triglochin maritima* var. *atacamensis* *Eleocharis melanocephala* + *Calandrinia caespitosa*	Reiche, 1907
Amazon	Varzea Lakes, Amazonia, Brazil	*Leersia hexandra* + *Scirpus cubensis* *Paspalum repens* *Eichhornia crassipes* + *Salvinia* spp. (*Victoria regia*)	Junk, 1933
Antarctic Kingdom			
New Zealand	New Zealand	*Ranunculus limosella* *Glossostigma elatinoides* *Typha angustifolia* (*Pilularia novae-zelandiae* *Potamogeton ochreatus* + *Potamogeton chesemani*)	Cockayne, 1928

Patagonian	Tierra del Fuego, Desolacion, Chile (Altitude 100–150 m)	*Donatia* + *Astelia* spp. *Caltha dioniifolia* + *Caltha apendiculata* (*Isoetes savatieri*)	Reiche, 1907
	West Patagonia, Feuerland, South Rio Grande near Punta Arenas, Chile	*Senecio smithii* + *Marsippospermum grandiflorum* *Gunnera magellanica* + *Caltha sagittata* *Carex darwinii* *Isolepis* spp.	Reiche, 1907

(b) Riparian zones

Boreal Kingdom

Euro-Siberian	R. Zheleznitsa, Nizhnegorodskaya province, Russia	*Carex acuta* (0.5–1 m) *Phragmites australis* + *Typha latifolia* + *Scirpus radicans* + *Scirpus* (*Bolboschoenus*) *maritimus* + *Glyceria fluitans* (*Potamogeton natans* + *Nymphaea candida* *Ceratophyllum demersum* + *Vallisneria spiralis*)	Lukina, 1972
Western and Central Asiatic	R. Amu-Darya (central reaches), Turkmenistan (Altitude ± 160 m)	*Populus pruinosa* + *Populus asiana* *Eleagnus orientalis* *Salix soongorica* *Tamarix* spp. + *Halostachys belangeriana* + *Lycium ruthenicum* + *Halimodendron halodendron* *Calamagrostis dubia* + *Phragmites australis* + *Erianthus ravennae* + *Typha elephantina* *Saccharum spontaneum* + *Calamagrostis dubia* + *Typha minima* + *Tamarix* spp.	Gladyshev, 1975
Japanese	Tamaca R. (middle reaches), Distr. Kanagawa, Japan	*Salicetum integrae* *Setario – Bidentetum pilosae* *Phragmites japonicus* *Phalaris arundinacea* *Polygonum thunbergii* + *Polygonum lapathifolium*	Miyawaki & Okuda, 1972

(continued)

Table 1.3. (*cont.*)

Floristic Province	Locality	Zonation (in order of increasing depth)	Author(s)
Japanese (*cont.*)	Tamaca R. (lower reaches), Japan	*Miscanthus sacchariflorus* *Chenopodium ficifolium* + *Xanthium strumarium* *Oenanthe javanica* *Rumex japonicus* + *Agropyron kamoji* *Beckmannia syzigachne* + *Veronica undulata* *Vandelia angustifolia* *Scirpus triqueter* + *Typha orientalis*	Miyawaki & Okuda, 1972
Pacific North American	Navajo reservoir basin, Colorado and New Mexico, USA	*Tamarix pentandra* *Populus angustifolia* + *Populus fremontii* *Betula pontinalis* + *Salix amygdaloides* *Salix lutea* + *Salix exigua* *Juncus torreyi* *Carex vulpinoidea* *Typha domingensis* (*Cladophora glomerata*)	Seville, 1961
Palaeotropical Kingdom			
North African Highland	Between Saganeiti and Akrur Highland, Ethiopia (Altitude 1900–2200 m)	*Ficus capensis* *Cyperus atronitens* + *Juncus punctorius* + *Juncus fontanesii* *Eleusine floccifolia* *Helosciadium nodiflorum* + *Hydrocotyle natans* *Nasturtium officinale*	Engler, 1910

Region	Location	Species	Reference
East African	Wabbi River, Wabbi Schebel, Somalia (Altitude 200 m)	*Sesbania leptocarpa* / *Typha latifolia* / *Cyperus* spp. + *Scirpus* spp. / *Nymphaea lotus*	Engler, 1910
	Shella Mountains, Mozambique (Altitude 2000 m)	*Salix huillensis* / *Cyperus* spp.	Engler, 1910
Capensis	Southeast Kalahari desert, Bechuanaland	*Salix capensis* + *Rhus viminalis* / *Phragmites australis* + *Riocreuxia torulosa* / (*Polygonum amphibium* + *Hydrocotyle asiatica* / *Nymphaea capensis*)	Engler, 1910
	Table Mountain, Cape Town, S. Africa (Altitude 500 m)	*Prionium serratum* (Palmiet formation)	Walter, 1968
Indian	Islets in Rivers Luni and Sukuri, Distr. Ramasthan, Pakistan	*Tamarix dioica* + *Salvadora oleoides* / *Xanthium strumarium* + *Solanum surattense* + *Tephrosia purpurea*	Saxena, 1972
New Caledonia	Moindam R., New Caledonia	*Pandanus pedunculatus* / *Fimbristylis complanata* / *Pycreus polystachyus* / *Lindernia neocaledonica*	Däniker, 1939

(continued)

Table 1.3. (cont.)

Floristic Province	Locality	Zonation (in order of increasing depth)	Author(s)
Neotropical Kingdom			
Caribbean	Antigua, Guatemala	Saline and brackish stream: *Hippomane mancinella* + *Ruppia spiralis* + *Najas guadelupensis* + *Najas marina* + *Nymphaea ampla* var. *speciosa* + *Echinodorus cordifolius* + *Eleocharis mutata* + *E. geniculata* + *Cyperus articulatus* Freshwater stream: *Echinochloa polystachya* + *Scleria grisebachii*	Loveless, 1960
Andean	Rio Suruth, Distr. Los Andes, Santa Cruz, Bolivia	*Attalea princeps* *Acalypha communis* *Salix marhana* *Gynerium saccharoides*	Herzog, 1923
	Rio Loma, Calama, Chile	*Baccharis juncea* *Tessaria absinthioides* *Distichlis* spp. (*Potamogeton* + *Myriophyllum*)	Reiche, 1907
	Cajon de la Hierba, Loca, Los Andes, Chile (Altitude 3000 m)	*Osychloe andina* (Junc.) + *Colobanthus* (*Myriophyllum proserpinacoides*)	Reiche, 1907
Amazon	Amazon R., Brazil	*Paspalum fasciculatum* *Echinochloa polystachya* *Paspalum repens* *Eichhornia crassipes*	Junk, 1970

Antarctic Kingdom

New Zealand	New Zealand	*Elatine gratioloides* *Limosella aquatica* *Gratiola peruviana* *Arundo conspicua* *Phormium tenax*	Cockayne, 1928
Patagonian	Rio Gallegos, West Patagonia, Chile	*Bolax glebaria* *Caltha sagittata* *Hippuris vulgaris* *Limosella aquatica* *Ranunculus trullifolius* (*Potamogeton juncifolius* + *Potamogeton lingulatus* + *Myriophyllum elatinoides*)	Reiche, 1907

(c) Swamps and marshes

Boreal Kingdom

Western and Central Asiatic	Salt swamp near Khamisa, Oasis Siwa, Saudi Arabia	*Tamarix articulata, T. macrocarpa, T. tetragona* *Nitria* sp. *Alhagi maurorum* + *Zygophyllum coccineum* *Imperata cylindrica* + *Juncus maritimus* var. *arabicus* *Phragmites australis* var. *stenophylla* *Cladium mariscus* *Typha angustifolia*	Rikli, 1929

(continued)

Table 1.3. (cont.)

Floristic Province	Locality	Zonation (in order of increasing depth)	Author(s)
Western and Central Asiatic (cont.)	Hula swamps, Lake Huleh, Israel	Transect W–E: *Prosopidetum farctae* *Rubus sanctus-Lythrum salicaria* ass. *Inulon viscosae* *Cyperetum alopecuroidis* *Polygoneto-Sparganietum neglecti* *Scirpeto-Phragmietum australis* *Cyperus papyrus* – *Polygonum acuminatum* ass. (*Myriophylleto* – *Nupharetum lutei* *Xanthietum strumarii*)	Zohary, 1973
Pacific North American	Grass Lake, Sierra Nevada, California, USA (Altitude 2400 m)	*Kalmio-Pinetum* *Salicetum rigidae* *Poo-Caricetum integrae* *Caricetum nebrascensis* *Caricetum simulo-vesicariae et rostratae* *Mimulo-Caricetum limosae* (*Drepanoclado-Utricularietum vulgaris* *Myriophyllo exalbescentis-Nupharetum polysepali*)	Beguin & Major, 1975
Palaeotropical Kingdom			
West African	Amboland, South West Africa	*Hygrophila affinis* *Cyperus cladium* + *Nephrodium squamulosum* *Limnophytum obtusifolium* *Blyxa radicans* + *Ottelia* spp. *Ambulia baumii* + *Ambulia dasyantha*	Engler, 1910
	Forest swamp, Coquilhatville, Congo basin	*Costus phyllocephalus* + *Aframomum meleguetta* *Clinogyne arillata* + *Sarcophrynium baccatum* *Thalia caerulea*	Engler, 1910

	Forest swamp, Congo River, Congo basin	*Renealmia congolana* + *Aframomum colosseum* + *Trachyphrynium* spp. + *Sacrophrynium* spp. *Thalia geniculata*	Engler, 1910
	Ghasal Creekland, Congo basin	*Costus lucanusianus* + *Aframomum sanguineum* + *Aframomum polyanthum* + *Clinogyne* spp. + *Thalia geniculata*	Engler, 1910
East African	Lake Manyarama, North Tanzania (Altitude 945 m)	*Acacia xanthophloea* + *Phoenix reclinata* *Echinochloa pyramidalis* + *Leersia hexandra* *Cyperus immensus* (Tussocks) *Cyperus articulatus* + *Cyperus longus* + *Fuirena pubescens* + *Pycreus mundtii* *Typha angustifolia* (*Nymphaea caerulea* *Ceratophyllum demersum*)	Greenway & Vesey-Fitzgerald, 1969
South African	Namiro Swamp, Lake Victoria, Uganda	*Dryopteris striata* + *Kotschya africana* + *Aframomum sanguineum* + *Miscanthidium violaceum* + *Loudetia phragmitoides* + *Scleria nyassensis* + *Paspalum commersonii* + *Pycreus lanceus* + *Leersia hexandra* + *Panicum parviflorum* *Fuirena umbellata* + *Eriosema glomerata* + *Digitaria scalarum* *Polygonum pulebrum* + *P. strigosum* + *Cyperus papyrus* + *Impatiens irwingii* + *Hibiscus diversifolius* + *Melastomastrum segregatum* + *Triumfetta macrophylla* + *Limnophyton obtusifolium* (and trees) + *Utricularia* spp. + *Trapa natans* + *Ceratophyllum demersum* + *Nymphaea caerulea*	Lind & Visser, 1962
East African Islands	Îles Comores and Îles Mascarenes, Madagascar	*Typhonodorum lindleyanum*	Engler, 1910

(continued)

Table 1.3. (*cont.*)

Floristic Province	Locality	Zonation (in order of increasing depth)	Author(s)
Capensis	Southwest Cape Province, South Africa	*Wachendorfia thyrsiflora* + *Antholyza aethiopica* *Carex clavata* *Zantedeschia angustifolia* (*Nymphaea capensis*)	Engler, 1910
	Mountain Swamps Table Mount (Altitude 600 m)	*Osmitopsis asteriscoides* *Osteospermum ilicifolium* *Villarsia ovata* *Dovea mucronata*	Engler, 1910
	Table Mount (Altitude 500–700 m)	*Zantedischia aethiopica* *Cladium mariscus* *Typha* spp. (*Potamogeton* + *Nymphaea* + *Nymphoides*)	Walter, 1968
Neotropical Kingdom			
Andean	Coast between Cordillera and Sea, Quinteros, Prov. Valparaiso, Chile	*Drimys winteri* + *Myrceugenia pitra* *Nephrobium spectabile* + *Lomaria chilensis* *Malacochaete riparia*	Reiche, 1907
	Sea Coast between Concepcion and Talcahuano, Chile	*Drimys winteri* + *Myrceugenia apiculata* *Gunnera chilensis* + *Senecio hualtata* *Jussiaea repens* + *Sagittaria chilensis* *Carex* spp. + *Carex riparia* *Malacochaete* *Scirpus* spp.	

Australian Kingdom			
Central Australian	Lake Ipea, New Guinea (Altitude 2500 m)	Transect E–W: *Acorus calamus* *Oenanthe aquatica* *Phragmites dichotomum* (*Gleichenia vulcanica*) *Machaerina rubiginosa* (*Scirpus mucronatus*) *Machaerina rubiginosa*	Walker, 1972
New Zealand	Lowlands *Phormium*-Swamp, New Zealand	*Leptospermum scoparium* + *Hebe salicifolia* + *Coprosma* spp. (Marginal scrub) *Arundo conspicua* *Carex secta* + *Carex virgata* *Phormium tenax* *Azolla rubra* + *Lemna minor* + *Potamogeton* spp. + *Ranunculus macropus*	Cockayne, 1928
	Mountain Swamp, New Zealand	*Carex secta* + *Carex cladium* *Phormium tenax* *Typha angustifolia*	Cockayne, 1928
	Auckland Distr., New Zealand	*Carex virgata* *Cladium articulatum* *Heleocharis sphacelata* *Typha angustifolia* + *Isachne australis* + *Polygonum serrulatum*	Cockayne, 1928

three groups of wetland types representing the world's most important and widespread wetland habitats: littoral belts of lakes and other reservoirs, river banks (riparian zones) and swamps. These tables should facilitate the understanding of the complexity of relationships between individual stages in hydrarch zonations and succession seres. They also demonstrate the variety of plant species populations which act as dominants in these seres. This survey represents just a first attempt and it is clear that all the relevant information cannot be given, even at the level

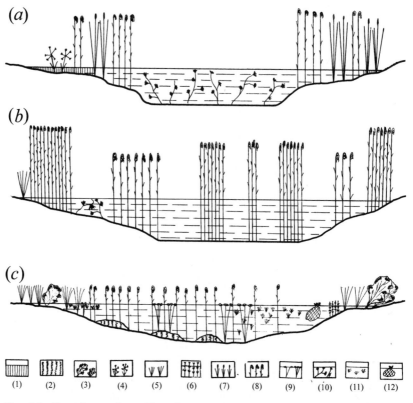

Fig. 1.3. Zonation and profiles of West Siberian shallow pothole lakes (after Smirenskiǐ, 1951, pp. 126, 132 and 142). (*a*) Lake with barrier-like helophyte stands (Lake Sosnovskoe). (*b*) Lake with diffuse helophyte stands (Lake Chany). (*c*) Lake with floating islands (Lake Vikalovo). 1, littoral peat; 2, bottom peat; 3, low shrubs on shore (*Salix* and *Betula* spp.); 4, *Butomus umbellatus*; 5, rhizomatous sedges (*Carex* and *Betula* spp.); 6, *Equisetum heleocharis*; 7, *Typha angustifolia*; 8, *Phragmites australis*; 9, nymphaeids (*Nymphaea* and *Nuphar* spp.); 10, *Potamogeton pectinatus*; 11, *Stratiotes aloides*; 12, floating islands dominated by *Carex gracilis*, *C. rostrata*, *Menyanthes trifoliata* and *Eriophorum polystachyum*.

of the biogeographical provinces according to which the tables are arranged. This, of course, does not fully demonstrate the differences which may distinguish neighbouring regions, for instance, within one province, but the aim of the tables is not to solve biogeographical problems. They only show the variety of seres which exist in wetlands in various parts of the world. Such zonation patterns may vary even within one region, as shown in Fig. 1.3, reconstructed on the basis of Smirenskii's (1957) data.

Dynamics of wetlands

Dynamics has two aspects: periodicity and succession.

Periodicity

Periodicity in wetlands arises from a direct effect of seasonal temperature fluctuations, and often also from seasonal fluctuations of the water level. The latter fluctuations are usually associated with periodic climatic changes (dry and wet season) and often indirectly caused by such changes. Extreme periodicity and tidal effects produce very characteristic vegetation (see below pp. 55–7; 67–71). Periodicity and depth can interact to produce characteristic zones.

Many wetland plant species of temperate regions are late flowering because of the micro-climatic temperature conditions in wetlands (Chapter 7).

In larger lakes during winter, the effect of the dash of waves may become stronger than during summer if they are not covered with ice. The rhizomes loosened from the substrate may either form a narrow belt on the shores or form the basis for floating islets.

Succession

Although numerous schemes of succession in wetlands have been described, particularly by phytosociologists (Tüxen & Preissing, 1942; Neuhäusl, 1965; Mitsch & Gosselink, 1986) our knowledge is still insufficient. Succession is mostly derived from zonation, but this may be dangerous in some cases. Very often the succession starting from one particular situation may go different ways, depending on different vectorial habitat factors (e.g. more or less wind-exposed sites) or on management. Therefore only occasionally can succession be traced as a

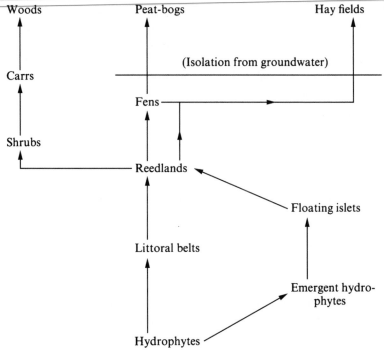

Fig. 1.4. General succession scheme in temperate eutrophic wetlands.

follow-up of vegetation types in a linear sequence. A more intricate scheme of succession in a wetland system is given by Segal (1966). An example, somewhat modified here (Fig. 1.4), shows different series of parallel development in a lowland peat region in the Netherlands. The most intricate seres, with many different stages rich in species, occur in eutrophic habitats, while fewer stages with fewer species are found in habitats either poorer or richer in minerals. The succession is followed vertically from bottom to top. Very poorly developed seres occur in strongly polluted habitats, e.g. where *Glyceria maxima* prevails and no bryophytes are found.

In general, any primary progressive succession (see below), in a similar habitat, is likely to follow the patterns given in Figure 1.4. The scheme also may be used to understand other succession seres, which are generally shorter and may form parts, or are comparable with parts, of the whole scheme. At some sites pronounced zonation develops, which does not indicate any succession, e.g. on relatively steep slopes or in habitats with a fluctuating water level. Succession in very nutrient-poor waters, with isoetid aquatics, may be followed across littoral zones containing small helophytes, to vegetation of the lagg-zone type and finally to peat-bog vegetation which, often very slowly, penetrates into the water.

Dominance of one species or co-dominance of only a few species in wetlands principally means that the habitat is extreme in some way because of some limiting factor(s) or driving factor(s). In such habitats vegetation is structurally underdeveloped. Examples of driving factor complexes are brackish or saline habitats and heavily polluted habitats. In zonation, as well as in succession, several stages may be absent, or the succession stops at a certain stage. Examples are given by Segal (1971). If the plants withdraw mineral nutrients from the substrate, new nutrients are not supplied, and mineralisation is incomplete, a peat bog may arise when the accumulated peat becomes detached from the influence of groundwater. Rainwater then becomes the main source of mineral nutrients.

Wetland successions should lead, theoretically, to the local climax ecosystems, but this happens only rarely. A wetland would abolish itself during such a process. Usually, wetland successions attain long-lasting stages which maintain themselves in a steady state, mostly as wooded wetlands, both in tropical and temperate regions. There may be a widespread rise in general ground level maintaining the water level constant relative to the soil surface within the wetland (Worth, 1972, see p. 56).

Successions may be classified in several ways as follows.

According to substrate

Primary succession The first stage colonises an inorganic substrate with no previous vegetation or only superficial dead fragments of it.

Secondary succession A primary succession sere becomes interrupted and new development takes place in a modified habitat differing from former stages, e.g. after peat has been dug out incompletely, leaving submerged peat layers as a starting point for new development. During the early stages, secondary succession seres often produce communities different from any stage of primary succession. Pleustophytes are a common phenomenon in such cases in standing waters, e.g. *Ceratophyllum* and *Utricularia* species or, in littoral belts, other highly productive helophytes, e.g. *Comarum palustre* and *Typha latifolia*. Disturbances in marshes and fens, for example by fire, may give rise to the establishment of tall herbs as dominants (e.g. *Calamagrostis canescens*, *Eupatorium cannabinum*,

Lysimachia vulgaris or *Epilobium hirsutum*). Several species occur on freshly dredged peaty soils along canals, e.g. *Epilobium hirsutum* and *Sonchus palustris* in Western Europe, or ephemeral nitrophilous vegetation on soft, nutrient-rich soils containing both mineral and organic substances.

According to direction of the changes

Progression Each successive stage becomes more stable, both more persistent and more resilient, showing more differentiation in its species composition and spatial structure. Stability is associated with a higher state of equilibrium in population dynamics.

Temporary replacement of one species by other species May occur after an epidemic or disaster.

Regression Simplification of ecosystem structure is often induced by humans, e.g. by fertilising, eutrophication, pollution, drainage or heavy grazing.

Cyclic changes These may occur where some habitat factor(s) fluctuate(s) periodically, e.g. the water level and intermediate periods are not sufficiently long for normal succession development, e.g. in fishponds.

Progressive succession is the most natural succession type, but it can be interrupted by any disturbance, for example, by a diversion of a river flow or by a heavy flood. Regressive succession usually involves communities poor in structure and composition, e.g. when mixed reedswamp vegetation becomes dominated by tall *Carex* species following eutrophication or by *Glyceria maxima* following a more severe pollution. Cyclic succession may give rise to totally different communities during several periods on the same spot, e.g. semi-terrestrial ephemeral therophyte communities on drained fishpond bottoms where hydrophytes occurred before.

According to the driving force

Autogenic succession The vegetation influences succession in such a way that development of other species becomes possible. The classical example of autogenic succession is peat formation in stagnant waters and the subsequent vegetation development. In this case succession can be reconstructed from the zonation.

Allogenic succession Changes in the vegetation are the result of external changes in the habitat, e.g. by accretion. Allogenic succession is seen in coastal flats where *Spartina* species prevail.

Soil formation in the hydrosere

The deposition of silt and plant materials on the bottom leads to the formation of soils progressively nearer, and ultimately above the mean water level. Plants, restricting water movements and acting as a mechanical filter, enhance this process. Both silting (the deposition of mineral sediments) and the accumulation of plant remains play important roles in the occlusion of water bodies and the transition from wetland to terrestrial communities.

Vigorous stands of giant helophytes such as *Cyperus papyrus* in tropical swamps and *Phragmites australis* in river deltas, act as particularly efficient giant filters clearing suspended materials and nutrients from the water (Thompson 1976; Gaudet, 1976, 1979). In estuaries, stands of *Spartina* and other salt marsh plants fulfil the same role (Blum, 1969).

The relationships between silting and macrophyte vegetation are complex and not all are positive. Waters containing large amounts of suspended materials are less transparent and submerged macrophyte growth is reduced.

In some cases the distribution and stranding of floating islets play an important role in accumulation.

The formation of floating mats and islets

These develop from nuclei of floating plants, by extension of growth from rooted stands out over deep water, or from parts of rooted stands detached from the bottom. The nuclei of islets may be live and dead plant material such as fragments of aerial shoots, rhizomes and roots or larger clusters of partly emergent rhizomes and roots providing conditions favourable for the germination or sprouting of seeds and other propagules and for their subsequent survival (Junk, 1970; Hejný, 1971). Thus the primary vegetation of floating stands comes into being. Once formed they often continue to grow and accumulate live, dead and decaying plant material, various propagules and a loose and sometimes continuous layer of detritus (sapropel, förna or peat).

In boreal temperate regions, the nuclei are formed predominantly of *Sphagnum* and peat, further southwards materials originate from helophytes such as *Phragmites*, *Typha*, *Glyceria* or tussocky tall *Carex* spp.

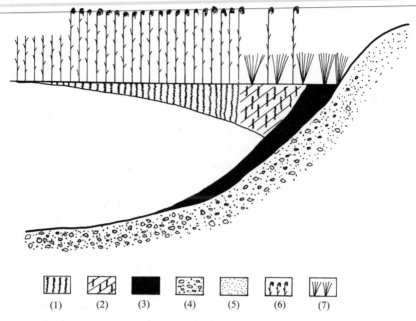

Fig. 1.5. Profile across a *Phragmites australis*-dominated floating mat along a river in Siberia (Upper Irtysh region) (after Smirenskiĭ, 1951). 1, floating mat formed of reed remains; 2, floating mat formed of reed and sedge remains; 3, organic-rich clay; 4, gravel; 5, sand; 6, *Phragmites australis*; 7, *Carex riparia*.

(Fig. 1.5). In temperate regions, floating islets may arise from patches of peat lifted up to the water surface after filling a new reservoir (Balaschov, 1972). Floating mats or islets also arise through the effect of waves, especially in winter or spring, when material is washed away from the littoral belts of larger water bodies, or small pieces of sprouting rhizomes become detached from their polycorms.

In tropical regions, floating mats and islets originate, most frequently, from floating carpets of live plants detached from the bottom during rainy seasons, particularly alongside large rivers and artificial lakes, which then persist for quite long times (Mitchell, 1969; Junk, 1970, 1983; Rzóska, 1974; Thompson, 1976b). Floating islets often travel long distances.

The original vegetation is usually composed of natant plants, both rooted (e.g. *Ludwigia* spp.) and free-floating (e.g. *Eichhornia crassipes* or *Salvinia auriculata*). The floating mats increase in size and become floating islets through increase in size of semiaquatic plants and their colonies, particularly at the periphery of each mat. Large floating islets, however, persist only for 1 to 3 years after which they either fragment or are stranded ashore and dry out during a dry period.

For example, floating mats and islets ('sudd') originate in African artificial lakes by inoculation and propagation of patches of *Salvinia auriculata* around the crowns of drowned trees, which act as 'nurseries' (Lake Kariba, Boughey, 1963). After invasion by other species their coherence is due to the presence of horizontal shoots or stolons of rooting plants such as *Scirpus cubensis*, *Ludwigia stolonifera*, *L. leptocarpa*, *Panicum repens* or *Echinochloa pyramidalis*.

In some important cases, graminoid species are involved in the initiation and development of tropical mats and islets. The genesis and development of communities associated with *Cyperus papyrus* in lakes and swamps of equatorial Africa have been described (Rzóska, 1976; Thompson, 1976*b*). In the middle reaches of the river Amazon, Junk (1970) has made significant observations on the development of annual species in the association *Paspalo-Echinochloetum* on floating mats and islets. As long as the two species occur together *Paspalum repens* is oriented towards the open water surface while *Echinochloa polystachya* is towards the shores. In lakes with a constant water level, however, *P. repens* occurs without *E. polystachya* which cannot exist in such habitats because it needs a dry period for its development. The third grass occurring in floating mats, *Paspalum fasciculatum*, does not develop floating leaves at all and survives flooding in a submerged state. Its leaves are longest of all the three grasses.

Floating islets broken off from floating mats by strong wave action may be stranded ashore when the waves decrease or the level falls. If these enlarge, either before or after stranding, the area of wetland is extended and the accumulation and filling of the water body may be accelerated.

Stability in wetland ecosystems and water level fluctuations

Both regular and irregular water level fluctuations affect the hydrogeological, pedological and ecological characteristics of wetland habitats profoundly. Changes in the habitat characteristics are naturally reflected in changes in the ecosystem structure, especially in its diversity. During periods of a raised water level, terrestrial ecosystems can be flooded and partially 'taken over' by wetland ecosystem species. During periods of low water level, on the other hand, large areas, originally flooded, emerge. This breaks the dormancy of a varied set of dormant terrestrial plant propagules and the rest of the biotic community also becomes more terrestrial. The more regular the water level fluctuations in time, the more balanced ecologically and more adaptable the sets of organisms and communities which are affected by these fluctuations.

In the tropics, in large marshes, swamps and lakes, and along large rivers, the water level fluctuations occur regularly, with approximately the same frequency and amplitude every year, and corresponding regular cyclic changes in species populations and biotic communities take place in many tropical wetlands during a year. In temperate zones, these water level fluctuations take place mainly during the growth season, and they tend to be relatively slow along standing waters while they may be quite rapid along rivers and streams. Hence, it is only the riparian wetland communities that have become adapted to rapid water level changes in the temperate zones.

The accumulation of silt and plant materials, which raises the ground level, is expected to change the depth of water and destabilise the wetland, and indeed this often happens, albeit slowly. However, deposition may take place evenly over a wide area, or sea levels may change, so that the hydrology, relative water levels and distribution of vegetation can remain constant for very long periods despite the change in altitude of the general soil surface. For example, cores at one site in the valley of the R. Frome in Southern England have shown the presence of *Alnus* and *Salix* carr, or, later, *Phragmites*, since soon after the end of the Ice Age, despite the accumulation of 1.5–2.5 m of peat (Worth, 1972). Many valleys, deltas and areas of extensive level wetlands must have had a similar history.

There appear to be three main groups of destabilising factors in wetlands:

(a) In hydrologically stabilised wetland systems, silting and land formation are often the principal destabilising factors. Accumulation of
dead organic matter in a wetland leads towards a change to terrestrial
vegetation, and the mechanism is a biological one. The process is
generally slow, its rate depends on both climatic and biotic factors,
but it is irreversible.

(b) In seemingly hydrologically unstable systems (bi-periodical), with
ecophases shifting from terrestrial to littoral or hydrophase, and
back during a year, the water level fluctuations seem to act as the
principal destabilising factor, with the associated alternating flooding
and emergence of the wetland biotopes. Underwater soils thus
become regularly exposed to aeration and mineralisation of their
organic matter takes place.

The sources of biotic diversity are different in these two instances. In (a) a mosaic pattern with relatively large homogeneous fields prevails, which may be, but need not be, arranged in zones. In (b) the distinct zonation of biotic communities reflects both the frequency and amplitude of the water level fluctuations; and the zones tend to oscillate about their long-term mean positions.

(c) In truly hydrologically unstable systems (polyperiodical) irregular shifts of ecophases destroy an established steady state within a wetland (or terrestrial) ecosystem. The communities, not adapted to these shifts, disintegrate into fragments, and the vegetation changes into a mosaic of more or less isolated populations, leaving open space for invasions of new species (frequently alien) under a changed hydrological regime. The irregular spring drawdown of artificial lakes, leading to the emergence of large littoral areas, provides perhaps the most instructive example of such a situation. Similar phenomena have also been observed in animal communities such as the invasion of a muskrat (*Ondatra zibethica*) population into flooded arable land which was changing rapidly into wetland (Pelikán *et al.*, 1970).

Wetland types – classification

To discuss plant and animal communities, it is convenient to have a classification and a nomenclature, which, at the very least, avoids the need for frequent long descriptions. However, when attempting to distinguish between various types of wetland we meet considerable difficulties arising from the use of different principles, confusion in terminology, the existence of numerous transitional types, and wide geographical differences caused by climatic and geomorphological variation. The terminological confusion is partly due to a lack of precise equivalence of meaning between terms used in different languages and applied in different places to different yet similar communities. We do not attempt to review the whole range of these systems. Many classifications are based on the vegetation, on the assumptions that the vegetation integrates the climate and habitat, and constrains the rest of the community, for which there is considerable justification. Best (1988) discusses the application of classification to wetlands.

Phytosociological classifications after the style of Braun-Blanquet (cf. Poore, 1955; Moore, 1962) or from multivariate analyses (e.g. Rodwell, 1955, UK wetland communities; Holmes, 1983, UK river communities)

Table 1.4. *Major types of CORINE classification of wetlands* (European
Communities Commission, 1991)

More detail given for wetlands as defined for this book.
D – Further divisions; S – Sub-divisions

---

37 Humid grassland and tall herb communities
  37.1   Meadowsweet (*Filipendula ulmaria*)
  37.2   Eutrophic humid grassland; 7D, 11S
  37.3   Oligohumid grassland; 2D, 2S
  37.4   Mediterranean tall humid grasslands
  37.5   Mediterranean short, humid grasslands
  37.6   Eastern supra-Mediterranean humid grasslands; 2D
  37.7   Humid tall herb fringes; 1D, 5S

44 Alluvial and very wet forests and brush
  44.1   Riparian willows (*Salix* spp.); 4D; 14S
  44.2   Grey alder galleries (*Alnus incana*); 2S
  44.3   Medio-European ash-alder wood (*Fraxinus* spp., *Alnus* spp.); 4D, 6S
  44.4   Great river, high flood forest (*Quercus, Ulmus, Fraxinus* spp.); 3D, 2S
  44.5–8   Various local forests, galleries, woods and thickets; 0D, 39S
  44.9   Alder, Willow and Bog Myrtle woods to bogs (*Alnus, Salix* and
              Myrica gale); 3D, 9S
  44.A1–4   Birch (*Betula* spp.) and conifer swamp woods; 0D, 5S

51 Raised bogs
  51.1   Near natural; 6D, 21S
  51.2   Purple Moor Grass Bog (*Molinia caerulea*), managed

52 Blanket bog
  52.1   Lowland, west coastal; 6D
  52.2   Hill; 7D

53 Reed and sedge swamps, water fringes
  53.1   Reedbeds (*Phragmites australis, Scirpus lacustris, Typha* spp.,
              Glyceria maxima, Phalaris arundinacea, tall waterside vegetation);
              6D, 13S
  53.2   Large sedges (*Carex* or *Cyperus* spp.); 2D, 20S
  53.3   Fen Sedge (*Cladium mariscus*); 3D
  53.5   Tall rush swamps (*Juncus* spp.), disturbed
  53.6   Riparian (Mediterranean); 2S

54 Fens, transition mires and springs
  54.2   Rich fens (*Schoenus* spp., *Carex* spp., *Eleocharis quinqueflora,
              Blysmus compressus, Scirpus* spp., herb fens); 18D, 11S
  54.3   Arcto-alpine riverine swamps; 4D
  54.4   Acidic fens; 7D
  54.5   Transition mires; 16D
  54.6   White Beak Sedge (*Rhynchospora alba*)

---

have been widely used, and give some degree of objectivity. However, they rely primarily on the species composition of the vegetation and have no direct relationship to functioning. They can be very dependent on the selection and quality of the samples and on the interpretation of the results, they are rather restricted to their countries of origin, and they often become very formal and elaborate.

Many conservationists and land planners have used the IUCN classification which concentrates more on obvious structural and functional features and less on the vegetation, but lacks coherence. In terminology and species it betrays its North American origins (Shaw & Fredine, 1971), and could be confusing elsewhere. It looks at wetlands from the point-of-view of game and wildfowl, and the common names used are difficult to relate to species or even genus. Subsequently the US Fish and Wildlife Service have used a classification by Cowardine *et al.* (1979), which extends to deep waters.

The recent CORINE classification (European Communities Commission, 1991; Table 1.4) shows a better balance of physical, edaphic, biotic and vegetation features but, similarly, becomes involved in an excess of European detail and it is based on a non-random selection of sites, with an emphasis on rare species.

In this book we propose a system which is probably no more consistent or better than many others, but attempts to provide a 'key' to wetlands which has some functional aspects and has less regional bias. Wetlands are primarily divided into four main classes, according to the type of water body:

1. Related to permanent standing waters;
2. Related to permanent running waters;
3. Related to periodic freshwaters;
4. Related to periodic salt waters.

These are all interconnected by transitional types.

Wetlands related to permanent standing waters

These are inland, mainly along or arising from open waters, both fresh and saline. Peat accumulation may be important. These wetlands accompany lakes, ponds, pools, lagoons, oxbow lakes, peat holes, canals, ditches, etc. All types under consideration are either successional stages or apparently stabilised by certain natural conditions or artificially.

The slope is a very important factor with regard to the ecophases and their duration as well as to the width of the zones in which they occur (see, e.g. Neuhäusl, 1965).

The following types are recognised in wetlands associated with permanent standing water.

Stands of emergent hydrophytes (aerohydatophytes and pleustohelophytes)

Examples are stands of *Stratiotes aloides*, *Pistia stratiotes* and *Eichhornia crassipes*. In smaller water bodies, they may cover the water surface completely as they reproduce rapidly by sprouts and stolons. They are often associated with other aquatic plants, both natant and submerged.

Floating mats and islets

The genesis, stages and phases of floating mat and floating islet development are summarised in the subchapter on dynamics (pp. 53–5). The most characteristic plants are *Cicuta virosa*, *Carex pseudocyperus*, *Calla palustris* and *Thelypteris palustris* in the temperate zone, and *Cyperus papyrus*, *C. cubensis*, *Vossia cuspidata*, *Ludwigia leptospora*, *Paspalum repens*, *Echinochloa stagnina* and *E. polystachya* in the tropics.

Littoral belts alongside lakes and ponds

Such belts are shallow inundation areas with perennial plants adapted to life both in water and air. The soil surface is covered with water or becomes exposed for a short period, but remains waterlogged. Littoral belts are characterised by helophytes *sensu stricto* (ochthohydrophytes) which often grow in polycorms. Attempts at characterising the tropical lake littoral belts and swamps may be found in Thompson (1976*b*) or Gaudet (1977*a*) and the zonation of temperate waters is described above (Table 1.3, pp. 29–49).

Typical temperate species are from *Scirpus* sectio *Schoenoplectus*, *Eleocharis*, *Typha* and *Phragmites*. Tall *Eleocharis* species may replace *Scirpus* species in the tropics, smaller species grow in shallow water bodies. Other tropical species are *Cyperus papyrus* and *Aeschynomene elaphroxylon* in lakes of equatorial Africa. Species like *Scirpus* (*Bolboschoenus*) *maritimus*, *S. paludosus* or *S. acutus* occur in brackish and saline habitats.

Swamps (including some marshes and fens)

These are waterlogged or shallowly flooded habitats which may become dry, e.g. in summer in temperate regions. The terms 'fen' and 'marsh' are often applied to specific situations, for example, in geographical terms like Wicken Fen and Malltraeth Marsh, or for a vegetation dominated by a certain species, for example, sedge fen. In N. America 'swamp' is restricted to wetlands with trees; while a marsh is treeless and dominated by herbaceous, mainly graminoid vegetation in both British and American usage. Our tentative classification of swamps, marshes and fens is based on the life and growth forms of their dominant plants.

In the tropics wooded swamps tend to prevail, but a wide range of types occurs.

Palm swamps These occur in the tropics in depressions filled with clayey soils and in peat-filled backwaters or oxbows. Palms are the dominant plants: *Phoenix reclinata* and *Raphia* in Africa, *Acrostichum* in the West Indies, *Mauritia* in South America. These are accompanied by an equally important and varied cover both of short and tall herbs including the giant *Zingiberales*. Palm swamps occupying old river-beds ('morrichal' in South America) are distinguished by a greatly varied horizontal structure whereby a greater number of dominant and subdominant plants (*Rhynchospora*, *Xyris*, *Heliconia*, *Sauvagesia*, *Cipura paludosa*, *Syngonanthus*) occur in large patches.

Giant-herb swamps These are also found in the tropics. Their species composition and structure vary according to the dominant plants and their groupings.

Zingiberales (Scitamineae) swamps Big herbs belonging to most families of this order act as dominants here: *Heliconia* (*Musaceae*), *Costus*, *Amomum*, *Aframomum* (*Zingiberaceae*), *Phrynium*, *Saicophrynium*, *Thalia* (*Marantaceae*), *Canna* (*Cannaceae*). This type of swamp, usually sheltered by trees, is most picturesque and colourful. Their structure is varied both horizontally and vertically.

Giant Araceae swamps These are more monotonous than the foregoing ones. Tall conspicuous dominants with broad fan-formed leaves prevail here. *Typhonodorum lindleyanum* characterises deeper swamps in Madagascar, *Montrichardia arborescens* characterises swamps accompanying the Amazon river where it occasionally penetrates deeper into the water. *Zantedeschia* sp. is characteristic of African swamps and river banks. The affinity of certain *Araceae* for floating mats is connected with their pleustohelophyte life form and is particularly pronounced in Eurasian boreal swamps and peat bogs (*Calla, Lysichiton*).

Reedswamps and reedlands are more typical of temperate regions but also cover large tropical areas. They have closed vegetation, mostly of tall graminoid helophytes, relatively poor in species, often with two herb layers. In some situations, such as locally in the SE of the USA, broad-leaved herbs may dominate (Penfoud, 1952), producing a similar vegetation, which should not strictly be called 'reedswamp'.

Reedswamps These are shallow areas, flooded for most of the year. Typical dominants include *Phragmites australis*, *Cyperus papyrus*, *Typha* spp., *Glyceria maxima*, tall species of *Scirpus* and of *Carex*. Hydrophytes may be present, especially in small depressions. Mostly, there are few or no bryophytes. In saline habitats, species like *Scirpus* (*Bolboschoenus*) *maritimus* may occur.

Reedlands These are areas without standing water for most of the growing season. Typical dominants are often the same as above, like *Phragmites* and tall species of *Carex* (e.g. *C. acutiformis*) but bryophytes are usually present. A subtropical example is the Florida Everglades, dominated by *Mariscus jamaicensis*. Reedlands may form a transitional stage or a zone between littoral belts or swamps and transitional bog and fens.

Transitional (valley) fens and bogs

Waterlogged habitats usually without standing water for most of the growing season, characterised by medium-sized graminoids, and by the accumulation of more or less mineral-saturated peat. The bryophyte layer, often including *Sphagnum* spp., is frequently well developed. The higher plants usually grow in two or three, sometimes in four, layers: tall herbs, medium herbs, small herbs and a bottom layer with small rosettes, e.g. *Drosera* species or tiny creeping herbs like *Anagalis tenella*. The number of species may be considerable, sometimes more than 70 species of higher plants and bryophytes may be found on an area of a few square metres.

Often several co-dominants occur in different layers. *Carex* species, sometimes rhizomatous *Juncus* species play an important role. In temperate regions the plants usually develop slowly and flower rather late in the season because of the cold air and poor heat conductivity of the substrate. Well-developed examples are becoming rare as they are often dug up, drained, fertilised or eutrophicated.

Tropical examples are characterised by the occurrence of many terrestrial ferns. For example, in Java, they occur in lake bays (e.g. in the system of the lakes Danau di Atas and Singkarak). The principal ferns are here: *Dryopteris gongylodes, Nephrolepis cordifolia, Odontosoria chinensis.* Representatives of the families *Xyridaceae* (*Xyris sumatrana*) and *Eriocaulaceae* (*Eriocaulon blumei, E. trilobum*) are also important. Both families indicate white sands; in the Caribbean and in Guayana, the phytosociological foederatio *Xyrido-Syngonanthion* characterises acid savannah soils, waterlogged for long periods. Along lake shores there are usually floating mats. Thus, the fern species quoted above from Java are joined by others such as *Nephrolepis biserrata, N. radicans, Pleopeltis longissima, Stenochlaena palustris*, as well as *Utricularia bifida* in depressions, fringing the lake Telaga Pangilon in central Java. In northern Sumatra, the large lake basin of the Lake Toba is fringed by vast floating islets in which the succession has reached the stage of floating tussocks with *Vaccinium littoreum, Ilex cymosa* and *Psychotria sarmentosa* and which are rich in insectivorous species of the genus *Nepenthes* (Steenis & Ruttner, 1932).

The following subtypes can be recognised:

1. On peat ridges, transitional to bog.
2. On peat rising or falling with the water level, so the vegetation is rarely inundated, often forming over peat holes between peat ridges. The peat quakes underfoot; 'Quaking fen'.[1]
3. On drying up reedlands or transitional bogs; 'Coarse bog'.[1] The vegetation has tall dicotyledonous dominant, e.g. *Filipendula ulmaria, Lysimachia vulgaris, Epilobium hirsutum.*
4. On heavily grazed or mown transitional bogs; 'Hay bog'.[1] The graminoid vegetation contains many wetland species.

---

[1] Such terms are often derived from Teutonic languages and are not common English usage, e.g. 'transitional bog' = German 'Übergangsmoor' or 'Zwischenmoor'. All these 'folk' terms tend to have a local significance, e.g. 'laagveen' (Dutch) has a slightly different soil and vegetation from 'Niedermoor', and may include 'Zwischenmoor'.

Lagg zones

Lagg zones are situated between mineral-poor waters and higher diluvial soils, e.g. alongside streams, or peat bogs, especially blanket bogs in oceanic regions, or as successional stages of heath pools. They are very sensitive to fertilisation of the higher-situated surrounding areas. The vegetation is mainly small *Cyperaceae* and other Monocotyledonous plants, e.g. *Carex limosa*, *Rhynchospora* spp. and *Scheuchzeria palustris*, mostly with a well-developed bryophyte layer of *Sphagnum* and tiny foliaceous liverworts.

Tropical peat bogs (not treated in 'tundra' synthesis)

In mountains in the tropics, ombrogenous peat bogs are found locally. Their moss layer is formed predominantly by *Sphagnum* species, as in temperate peat bogs, but there are more trees and shrubs. (In this respect, quite a few tropical wetland types differ from corresponding temperate types.) The convex shape and zonation of temperate ombrogenous peat bogs are also seen in the tropical bogs, with a central part which is often nearly devoid of trees and shrubs. Carnivorous plants form an eminent component of these bogs but they need not be the best known ones, i.e. *Drosera* or *Nepenthes*.

Wetlands related to running waters

These are found beside rivers, streams, deltas, estuaries, etc.

Several types listed above are paralleled by comparable types of wetlands alongside running waters, but the latter are often more restricted in width and area and have different species. Thus *zones with emergent hydrophytes* are found in sheltered narrow bends, sometimes as the first stage of oxbow lakes. *Floating islets* occur along shallow shores of slow flowing small rivers, and free-floating in very long rivers such as the Nile or Amazon (Junk, 1983; Rzóska, 1976). *Riparian belts*, similar to *littoral belts*, develop, especially in tidal areas and along river banks and *reed-swamps and reedlands* extend over low-lying land adjacent to rivers. These are sufficiently important to be treated in more detail below. *Transitional valley bogs and fens* usually have little connection with the running water and are similar to the standing water types.

Riparian belts

According to Kopecký (1969; Table 1.5) the riparian belt includes two zones, distinct in geomorphology and hydrology, analogous to the littoral of standing waters (true riparian zones) and to the sublittoral (subriparian zone). The upper subriparian and lower riparian zones provide the most important habitats for wetland vegetation along rivers. The amplitude of the water level fluctuations distinguishes two types of river bank: stenosalentic with the maximum annual fluctuation about 0.6 m and eurysalentic with greater fluctuations, at least 0.8 m, usually about 1–2 m and up to 5 m. The duration of flooding determines ecotopes ranging from submerged (always flooded) to emergent.

According to the intensity of water current, Thienemann (1912) recognised:

1. lentic banks, with the water flowing very slowly or stagnant; and
2. lotic banks, with water steadily or periodically flowing.

When we combine the different bank types and ecotopes with respect to vegetation, we arrive at nine combinations, at least, which are again listed by Kopecký (1969). All of them are represented in both temperate and tropical regions. Peat accumulation varies widely, and is greater in stenosalentic and lentic waters. Terrestrial or pseudoterrestrial vegetation is often developed in emergent ecotopes on layers of peat and silt drying out during succession.

Examples of the vegetation are *Phalaris*, *Zizania* or *Beckmannia* spp. in the Eurasian region; *Paspalum*, *Echinochloa* and *Panicum* in tropical climates; and *Prionium serratum* in the Capensis Kingdom. By contrast to the temperate zones, the riparian banks in the tropics are often vegetated by forest right to the main river flow. A zonation of herbaceous communities is apparent only along the largest rivers in the middle sections of their flow.

Springs, rills and flushes

These are habitats with rapid and localised flow of drainage water near the ground surface which varies greatly in volume and flow rate according to rainfall. The amount of peat accumulation varies widely; true peats occurring only rarely. The water temperature is relatively constant. This wetland type is best represented in hilly regions.

The vegetation usually consists of one layer of small herbs and one layer

Table 1.5. *Vertical divisions of banks of rivers and streams*

Zones		Water levels	Ecotopes	
	Upper riparian	Mean high water	Emersed	
Riparian	Lower riparian	Mean	Semi-immersed	Suprasemi-immersed
		Mean low water		Subsemi-immersed
Subriparian	Upper subriparian	Lowest	Demersed	
	Lower subriparian	Lower limit of macrophytes	Submersed	

Adapted and modified after Kopecký (1969).

of bryophytes or two layers of both. Characteristic are, e.g. *Chrysosplenium*, *Montia* and *Cratoneuron* sp., besides other *Bryales* and *Hepaticae*. In intermittent waters, many hydrophytes are capable of producing land forms when the habitats become dry, e.g. *Ranunculus* subgenus *Batrachium* and *Callitriche* species.

Wetlands in estuaries and deltas including tidal rivers

This type is related to littoral belts and reedswamps and reedlands, but is often poorer in structure and composition. It is often adjacent to swampy woodland on only slightly higher ground. Vegetation may be intermediate between that of freshwater and that of saline or brackish habitats. This is indicated, in Europe, e.g. by the occurrence of *Bolboschoenus maritimus* and *Scirpus tabernaemontani*. Characteristic of tidal rivers, are *Scirpus triqueter* and hybrids of *Scirpus* sectio *Schoenoplectus* species. *Phragmites* and other species often produce luxuriant specimens.

In large deltas such as the Mississippi Delta, a zonation often develops leading from saline to brackish and to freshwater wetlands, their different plant dominants being selected according to their salt tolerance (Penfound, 1952).

Plaurs

Plaurs, i.e. large floating mats, often consist of *Phragmites australis* plants. They are particularly significant in the Danube delta.

Periodic waters

Periodic waters show regular and distinct fluctuations during time intervals of variable length.

Some wetlands associated with periodic running waters have already been mentioned above. Here we deal especially with other types such as intermittent pools, e.g. heath pools, fishponds, coastal marshes and rice fields.

Periodic standing waters with large amplitude fluctuations

All types of standing water wetlands may be regarded as related to more or less periodic waters, especially lakes, ponds, pools, oxbow lakes, lagoons and ditches but the most variable water levels are in heath pools (existing especially in oceanic regions), shallow lakes in dry or arid regions, fishponds and reservoirs. In one geographical region shallow waters with relatively small fluctuations usually support a vegetation of smaller plants than do deeper waters with considerable water level fluctuations during comparable time intervals.

Periodic waters in oceanic regions usually depend on high precipitation during certain periods; those in continental dry regions are more connected with high evaporation at the water surface, and with very low inflow during the dry season. The geomorphological and hydrological structure is particularly important in karst regions. Smaller water bodies in the tropics, especially in the drier areas, show considerable fluctuations of water level for the same reason as those situated in continental regions.

Periodic standing waters with long period fluctuations

Standing waters in which the limosal and terrestrial ecophases occur only occasionally, e.g. during floods (oxbow lakes), during extreme dryness (tree swamps) or during management (e.g. summer-drained fishponds; usually after 6 to 10 or more years). They are inhabited by a characteristic vegetation.

Periodic dry lands (flood-plains)

Periodically flooded large areas of at least several hectares in area, with marsh vegetation. For example, nearly flat areas adjacent to lakes, ponds, reservoirs and rivers, mostly in alluvial plains, are treated as periodic lands. Their colonisation proceeds in various ways:

1. If the substrate is soft and waterlogged and the limosal ecophase lasts for a long time (at least several months), tall aerenchymatous plants occur, e.g. *Oenanthe aquatica*, replaced by *O. fluviatilis* in tidal areas and by *O. crocata* in euatlantic regions of Western Europe. One or two herb layers are present.
2. On soils drained for longer periods, e.g. fishpond bottoms, heath pools and dune valleys, and also in ruts, on wet paths and fields, the vegetation is ephemeral, mainly consisting of annual pelochthophytes, e.g., in Europe, small *Juncus*, *Eleocharis*, *Cyperus* and *Scirpus* subgen. *Isolepis* species and several characteristic bryophytes, e.g. *Pohlia* and *Fossombronia* species. Usually there is one herb layer and often one bryophyte layer.

3. On drained soils rich in minerals, particularly ammonium nitrogen, and often disturbed, e.g. on the bottoms of newly reclaimed polders, in drained ditches and eutrophicated ponds and pools (especially when trodden by cattle or man or polluted); taller therophytes occur in a mostly ephemeral vegetation (e.g. *Bidens* and *Polygonum* species or *Ranunculus sceleratus*).

Rice paddy fields

Rice paddies are shallow standing waters with rice (*Oryza sativa*) as crop. Littoral and limosal ecophases take place during the vegetative season of rice and a terrestrial ecophase is induced before and lasts until after the harvest. Consequently, two types of vegetation develop during one ecoperiod:

1. Helophytic vegetation in competition with rice – *Echinochloa, Ammannia, Rotala, Alisma, Ottelia alismoides, Pontederia* and *Cyperus* – often combined with a synusium of hydrophytes; this is a three-layer vegetation.
2. Pelochthophytic vegetation shortly before and after harvest, not competing with rice – prostrate *Cyperus* and *Juncus* species, *Eleocharis* sp., *Isolepis supina, Lindernia* sp.; this is a one-layer vegetation.

Wetlands of saline habitats

Wetlands of coastal and inland saline habitats dominated by herbs are treated under this heading, including coastal shoals and mud flats. The two latter habitats are often devoid of vegetation.

Coastal marshes

Coastal marshes, if dominated by helophytes, are comparable in structure with littoral belts or saline riparian belts. They support a vegetation poor both in structure and species, often consisting of only one species. *Spartina* species occur on mobile mud flats subject to silt accumulation and erosion, optimally in the eulittoral zone affected by tides. The soil is usually aerated only at the very surface, or not at all. On places in contact with fresh water, stands of *Scirpus* (*Bolboschoenus*) *maritimus* ssp. *compactus* sometimes occur. Coastal marshes show vertical changes which depend on the balance between the frequency and duration of flooding with seawater, the leaching of the ground by rainwater and evaporation. An example is the alternations of the *Spartina alterniflora*, *S. patens* – *Distichlis spicata*, *Juncus roemerianus* and *Salicornia* – *Batis* dominated marshes in the southern USA.

Brackish reedlands

Helophyte stands may occur where conditions are suitable for peat accumulation and there is some contact with fresh water, e.g. with seepage, or in brackish areas of deltas and estuaries. These communities often include *Scirpus* (*Bolboschoenus*) *maritimus* ssp. *compactus*, *Typha* sp. and *Phragmites*. They are poor in structure and species composition.

Shoals

Shoals sheltered from wave action in the upper part of the eulittoral (which may or may not be under tidal influence), often with strongly saline water, generally have therophytes such as *Salicornia*, usually in monospecific stands.

Foreshores

Supralittoral habitats, above the mean high water level and, in maritime regions, extending to the storm tide level. Communities, in contrast to all other wetland types, mainly consist of hemicryptophytes, with some chamaephytes.

1. The lower parts of the foreshore vegetation usually have one layer, e.g. *Puccinellia maritima*, *Limonium vulgare*, *Aster tripolium*, *Halimione* spp.
2. The higher parts of the foreshore vegetation often have a second layer of smaller herbs, including therophytes, e.g. with *Armeria maritima*, *Juncus gerardi*, *Scirpus rufus*.
3. Ephemeral communities including therophytes are found on disturbed nitrogen-rich habitats created by treading, seepage, temporary still water, draining, etc., with marked fluctuations in water and salt content. Usually two layers are present, with, e.g. *Puccinellia* spp., *Spergularia* spp., *Juncus ambiguus* and *Chenopodium chenopodioides*.

Inland salt marshes

Inland salt marshes are usually temporary wetlands, drying out during the hot period, which occur in shallow depressions or in association with shallow water bodies. They are characterised by a high concentration of salts, especially of sulphate or sometimes borate, in the water and/or in the upper soil horizons. This enrichment with salts is due to capillary rise during the periods of high soil surface evaporation. The plants growing in these habitats belong mostly to the same genera as the plants growing in coastal salt marshes but the species or lower taxa may partly be different. Notable is the absence of *Spartina* spp. in the inland salt marshes.

Distribution of wetlands in the world – a survey

This brief survey does not include the types excluded on pp. 2–3, except for some wet forests (as further stages of the succession). The survey is presented continent by continent. More information may be found in Gore (1983*b*) and Whigham *et al.* (1985).

Europe

In northern and central Europe, within the zones of the coniferous and deciduous forest biomes, *Sphagnum* bogs predominate, but other wetlands are present as well. For example, in a small lowland country like Estonia, fens and alluvial wetlands occupy 9.3% of the territory of the republic (Kumari *et al.*, 1974). About two-thirds of them are covered by herbaceous vegetation and one-third by wet forest, dominated mainly by *Alnus glutinosa* (Kats, 1971, 1972).

Both bogs and eutrophic wetlands occupy large areas in the basins of rivers in Poland, Belarus and western Ukraine (Kulczynski, 1949). The eutrophic wetlands are occupied by plant communities with dominant *Equisetum fluviatile*, and *Phragmites*, mixed together or pure, and tall sedges (*Carex* spp.).

In Poland and northern Germany, the river alluvia abound in small patches of wetland dominated by tall sedges, reed and other tall herbs which are rapidly vanishing as a result of drainage (for the north-eastern Germany, see, e.g. Krausch, 1966). Wetlands are also widespread in the south-eastern parts of the Jutland peninsula in Denmark. The woodland vegetation is here dominated by *Alnus* or by *Betula* mixed with *Salix* spp., and the herbaceous vegetation by tall-sedge communities with *Carex rostrata, C. acuta* and *C. vesicaria* as dominants. But in Denmark, similarly also in the Netherlands, large areas of wetlands have been drained and are now used as agricultural land. In the Netherlands, however, notable, although small, areas of various wetland types have still been preserved. For their detailed classification according to vegetation see Westhoff and van den Held (1969).

In the British Isles, bogs are common, but around the lakes and in broad river valleys, mineral-rich wetlands are found especially in East Anglia and Somerset, though mostly relatively small in area. Coastal tidal wetlands occur locally.

The wetlands of the Scandinavian Peninsula are varied, according to their position in relation to substrate and altitude as well as to the gradient of continentality (west to east) and to latitude. Wetlands in the mountains, on crystalline rock, are dystrophic and develop into peat-bogs while mineral-rich wetlands are mostly found in the southern part of Scandinavia (see, e.g. Malmer, 1962; Björk, 1967).

As opposed to the forest biome zone, the forest-steppe zone of Europe is rather poor in wetlands (between 0.25 and 0.7% of the various territories). Among these wetlands, *Phragmites* and *Carex* dominated areas prevail. In river alluvia, besides flood-plain forests dominated by *Salix* and *Populus* spp. or hardwood trees (e.g. *Ulmus*, *Quercus* or *Fraxinus*), small areas are occupied by waterlogged *Alnus* or *Betula* groves. Along the lower Dnieper and other rivers in the Podol and Volyn plateaux (Ukraine & Belarus) *Carex–Hypnum* bogs eventually fill the old river-beds, while *Alnus* groves cover depressions in the parallel river terraces. New large areas of wetlands have arisen in the shallow areas of the newly constructed large artificial lakes forming a cascade of reservoirs along the Dnieper (for further literature see Raspopov *et al.*, 1977). Among them, the Kiev reservoir has been studied intensely in the IBP (Gak *et al.*, 1972). *Phragmites* and other tall graminoids dominate the wetlands in the flood-plains and deltas of the rivers Kubań, Tereka, Volga, Don, Dnieper, Dniester and others (Lavrenko & Zoz, 1931). Floating mats of wetland vegetation occur here as well as in the Danube delta. Here, extensive areas are occupied by *Phragmites* (3.5% of the territory of Romania!). The flood-plain of the Danube is fringed with tall-sedge wetlands. Among the wet-forest types, it is those with dominant *Salix* and *Populus* spp. that prevail, locally also groves of *Alnus* or *Fraxinus* with a *Phragmites* undergrowth (Popp, 1959; Toth, 1960; Rudescu *et al.*, 1965). The wetlands of the rest of the Balkan Peninsula, especially those occurring in the river alluvia, are not very different from those along the Danube.

Around the Mediterranean Sea wetlands are represented in the lowlands of Italy, especially in the flood-plains of the Po and other large rivers, where the plant communities are mainly formed by *Phragmites*, *Arundo*, *Typha latifolia* and *T. angustifolia*, *Scirpus* and other tall graminoids. *Alnus* groves are also present (Kats, 1971; Tyuremnov, 1976). Rice fields occur particularly in the Po lowlands.

The delta of the Rhône, in France, includes the Camargue which is of great importance for migratory birds. There is a very wide range of habitats, from freshwater marshes to salt marshes and extremely saline pans. *Phragmites australis*, *Typha* spp. and *Scirpus maritimus* form extensive stands rich in invertebrates, birds and mammals. Rice fields and various forms of wetland pastures are included. The centre of the delta is now a reserve.

The *Phragmites* reedswamps of the Iberian Peninsula, where wetlands also mainly accompany the lower portions of the large rivers, are famous (e.g. la Doñana on the lower Guadalquivir).

The mountains of Europe have other types of wetlands beside mires, mainly accompanying lakes, particularly in the Alps, and their foothills. In the Caucasus, and its foothills, forest bogs are widespread, e.g. in the Colchis, Kakhetia and in the Alazani river valley (Barsegyan, 1956; Barsegyan & Khursudyan, 1969).

In the south-eastern lowland part of central Europe (Pannonia), large areas of mainly *Phragmites*-dominated wetlands occur in the littorals of lakes, especially of the Neusiedler See, Austria and Hungary (Tóth & Szabo, 1961; Burian, 1973); Lake Balaton, Hungary (Tóth, 1960; Kárpáti & Lantos, 1978) as well as of ponds, e.g. the Nesyt fishpond (Czech Republic, Květ, 1973a). (Most of the examples quoted here were studied in the IBP.) The most important vascular plants colonising these Pannonian wetlands are listed by Hejný (1960).

Shallow lake and fishpond littorals represent important wetlands all over the originally forested part of Central Europe. In the IBP the lake littorals were mainly studied in the Masurian lake district in north-east Poland (Pieczyńska, 1976), while those of the fishponds were studied in South Bohemia and Moravia, Czech Republic (Dykyjová & Květ, 1978; Hejný, Květ & Dykyjová, 1981). For an ecological characterisation of the plant communities of fishponds, see Hejný and Husák (1978). Other studies include those by Hürlimann (1951) on Swiss lakes and Neuhäusl (1965) from the Czech Republic.

Asia

A survey of the Asian wetlands may start from Yakutia (Russia), though only 0.3% of its territory is occupied by wetland: mainly sedge-moss bogs in its central and southern parts. Tall-sedge bogs and wet grassland with shrubs tolerating waterlogging are widespread in the lowlands of the Lena river and its tributaries (Karavaev, 1958).

The Central Siberian uplands and the lowlands along the Angara river are rich in wetlands. The prevailing type is sedge-moss bog, often with shrubs tolerating excessive moisture (Smirnova, 1960; Banyashnikov, 1962; Krasnoborov, 1963). The southern part of western Siberia also abounds in wetlands. In the graminoid and herbaceous vegetation, the prevailing types are those with dominant *Carex* spp., *Equisetum* and *Carex* spp., *Calamagrostis* and *Carex* spp., all with a poor undergrowth of mosses. Sedge-moss bogs are also present.

The steppe zone of western Siberia has wetlands in its western part and in the Basin of Barabinsk which is rich in lakes. Many wetlands are saline here, being therefore devoid of trees and shrubs. Tall grasses (*Phragmites*, *Scolochloa*, *Calamagrostis*) and *Carex* spp. are the principal plant dominants. The steppes and semi-deserts of the Kazakhstan have wetlands in the river deltas (especially of the Amu-Darya and Syr-Darya) and lake littorals (especially of the Aralian Sea). Reedswamps (dominated by *Phragmites*) prevail here (Smirenskiî, 1951; Katanskaya, 1960a; Ganetskaya, 1971). The wetlands of the Volga delta and along the Caspian Sea are similar. An important dominant of the saline wetlands is *Bolboschoenus* (*Scirpus*) *maritimus* ssp. *compactus*.

Reedswamps also prevail among the submontane wetlands occurring along the Altay, Tyan-Shan and Pamir mountains. Higher up, various mires and montane tundra take over (Krylov, 1942; Lavrenko & Sochava, 1956).

The arid regions of Asia, comprising Mongolia, large areas in China, the uplands of Tibet, part of the Indian Penninsula, the plains of Afghanistan and Iran, and the Arabian Penninsula, are occupied by steppe, semi-desert or desert. Wetlands are rather scarce here. Relatively narrow strips of wetlands, mostly dominated by *Phragmites* or *Carex* spp., accompany river beds and lake littorals (Petrov, 1966, 1967). The eastern Mediterranean area is also nearly void of wetlands. An extensive papyrus swamp only fringes the lake Huleh (Forbes, 1940).

Tropical Asia is rich in wetlands, most of them covered with wet forest. They are very rich both in plant and animal species and their most extensive areas are found in river alluvia and deltas (Puri, 1960; Chatterjee, 1964). Rice fields represent cultivated wetlands all over the territory, especially in SE Asia.

Wetlands in the USSR and Malaysia are reviewed in Gore (1983b); in southern Asia by Whigham *et al.* (1985) and in India by Gopal (1992).

North America

Wetlands are numerous but occupy a relatively small area in North America (Hofstetter, 1983). This is due to the dry continental climate predominating in much of the temperate lowlands of this subcontinent and the rocky wind-eroded shores of the Canadian Shield Lakes. Relatively large wetland territories are only found in the alluvia and deltas of large rivers such as the Mississippi and its tributaries and in Georgia and Florida. A good deal of these wetlands have been reclaimed (Penfound, 1952; Thomas, 1956; Kats, 1959). Wetlands are more frequent in the Great Lakes area and further north where, however, *Sphagnum* bogs tend to predominate when advancing in the northern direction. The wetlands of the humid eastern North America, occupied by the deciduous forest biome, are similar to those of temperate Europe. Notable are the coastal marshes along the eastern and south-eastern shores of the USA from Delaware through Carolina to Texas and the inland tree swamps and marshes such as the Okefenokee Swamp (Aumen, 1985) and the Everglades.

Mitsch & Gosselink (1986) review wetlands in the USA.

South America (with Central America)

The tropical part of this subcontinent includes vast wetland territories, occupied either by forest or graminoid vegetation, especially in the Amazon basin, including the upper Madeira basin (Junk, 1983). North and south of this territory, extensive wetlands are found in the Orinoco and Paraná river basins, respectively, both occupied by graminoid and forest vegetation. In Colombia, the river Atrato passes through large wetlands (Braun, 1952; Hueck, 1966). The wetlands of the tropical and subtropical America are highly diverse and may be divided into: (i) permanent graminoid-dominated wetlands; (ii) temporary graminoid-dominated wetlands; (iii) wetlands with pre-dominant shrubs; (iv) those vegetated by forest; (v) palmares – wetlands with prevailing palm trees. Within a certain region, larger or smaller patches of wetlands form a greatly diversified complex of various wetland types (Kats, 1971, 1972).

In temperate South America, both the graminoid- and forest-vegetated wetlands are common, with a species list sharply differing from that of the tropical and subtropical wetlands of this subcontinent. On the mountain plains of the Andes, at an altitude of some 3500 m, particularly in Colombia and Ecuador, the 'frailejones' represent a characteristic wetland type vegetated by tree-form *Espeletia* spp. (family *Compositae*).

In the mountain plains of Peru and Venezuela, these wetlands are replaced by peat bogs with cushion-like *Distichia muscoides* and *Sphagnum* spp. In Chile, *Oxychloe andina* and *Patosia clandestina* (both *Juncaceae*) form the cushions in addition to *Distichia*. These montane wetlands also have grasses and *Carex* spp. and develop around spring and mountain lakes (Troll, 1953; Wilhelmy, 1956).

Africa

This continent includes diverse types of wetlands. They are vegetated either by tall or short graminoids, ferns, shrubs, palm trees and various kinds of forest. Both freshwater and saline wetlands occur in Africa.

Tropical Africa abounds in both permanent and seasonal wetlands whose total area is about $450\,000\,\text{km}^2$ (Thompson & Hamilton, 1983; Denny, 1985; John, 1986; Roggeri, 1995). The most extensive permanent wetlands are found in the inner delta of the Niger river (Hopkins, 1962; Bacalbaşa-Dobrovici, 1971). Large areas of wetland colonised by graminoids, including *Cyperus papyrus*, as well as wet forests occur in the Congo basin both along the lower and middle reaches of the rivers (Lebrun & Gilbert, 1954), and in the basins of other larger rivers flowing into the Atlantic Ocean. Vast permanent swamps (sudd) dominated by *Cyperus papyrus* occupy the upper Nile basin (Rzóska, 1976) as well as the territories adjacent to the Lake Chad, Lake George and other African lakes. *Typha domingensis* dominates around Lake Chilwa. New wetlands will develop along the shores of Africa's artificial lakes such as Kariba, Volta and Aswan.

The eastern part of tropical Africa, despite its dry climate, is relatively rich in wetlands (Beadle, 1974; Gaudet, 1975). For example, they occupy 6% of the territory of Uganda, and the wetlands fringing Lake Victoria are among the largest in the tropics. The wetlands located north of this lake are connected with those occurring in the tectonic depression occupied by a chain of lakes from Lake Alberta to Tanganyika. Here, also, the prevailing dominant plant is *Cyperus papyrus*. The Zambezi and Okowango river basins comprise large areas of graminoid-dominated wetlands, for example the Kafue flats (Ellenbroek, 1987) and the swamp adjacent to Lake Bangweulu, which occupies some $5000\,\text{km}^2$ (Debenham, 1953).

Africa's montane wetlands are both abundant and relatively large in total area. Their biotic communities vary with altitude. At about $2000\,\text{m}$, tall, narrow-leaved herbs predominate but short herbaceous vegetation is also present. At about 3000 m, species of *Sphagnum*, *Lobelia* and *Helichrysum* are common. Higher up, in the subalpine zone, they give way to moss bogs with predominant *Polytrichum* and *Rhacomitrium*. The high mountains of East Africa are rich in wetlands to such an extent that a special wetlands altitudinal zone may be differentiated, e.g. the Sadde plain at some 4000 m, below Mt. Kilimanjaro (Salt, 1954).

Seasonal wetlands vegetated by graminoids occur in river alluvia within the savannah biome (Thomas, 1943). Their number and total area are unknown.

The wetlands of the Isle of Madagascar are diverse (Straka, 1960). Graminoid-dominated wetlands, mainly papyrus swamps, of the northern part of the island occupy some 300 km^2. In its eastern part, these wetlands occupy some 200 km^2, with *Phragmites* and *Typhonodorum* as further plant dominants.

Australasia

Australia is poor in wetlands, which occupy much less than 1% of the territory (Taylor, 1950; Kats, 1971, 1972; Campbell, 1983; McComb & Lake, 1990). Nearly all are located along the sea shore, but a few occur in the mountains in south-eastern Australia. Wetlands colonised by *Eucalyptus* spp. accompany the River Murray and other rivers in the south-east of the continent. In the same region, the coastal marshes are vegetated by graminoids and, to a small extent, by shrubs.

By contrast to the mainland, the climatically humid island of Tasmania is rich in wetlands. Most widespread are graminoid-vegetated swamps with dominant *Gymnoschoenus sphaerocephalus* (Davies, 1964).

New Zealand has numerous littoral wetlands around lakes and a considerable variety of wetlands of impeded drainage (Campbell, 1983; Johnson & Brook, 1989). These include restiad bogs (e.g. *Empodisma minus*), forest swamps (e.g. *Dacrycaspus dacrydioides*, *Agathis australis*) and helophyte swamps (e.g. *Typha orientalis*). There are many alien species.

The tropical island of New Guinea has appreciable flat areas occupied by wetlands, both temporary and permanent, colonised by forest, palm trees or herbaceous vegetation (Taylor, 1959; Reiner & Robbins, 1964).

2

Primary production in wetlands

J. KVĚT and D.F. WESTLAKE
with contributions by D. DYKYJOVÁ, E.J.P. MARSHALL
and J.P. ONDOK

Introduction

The chapter is the result of co-operation between the authors. J. Květ and
D.F. Westlake wrote much of the text, with the help of the contributors.
The contributors researched or wrote the major part of: indirect methods,
and structure and function of the assimilating organs, J.P. Ondok; quality of
net production, genotypic variation and adaptations, Dagmar Dykyjová;
comparisons of standing crop and productivity, E.J.P. Marshall.

Most wetlands are visually dominated by emergent vegetation, often
large reeds or rushes, but the whole community of primary producers
also includes substoreys of floating-leaved submerged macrophytes,
periphyton, filamentous algae and phytoplankton, which may be quite
important in some circumstances. The main emphasis will be on the
behaviour of the dominants, but the other plants will be included where
possible.

It will be assumed that the physiological features common to green
plants are known and the chapter will concentrate on the special features
of photosynthesis and growth by emergent plants. Submerged macrophytes, periphyton and phytoplankton are treated in more detail in the
IBP-PF synthesis volume (Le Cren & Lowe-McConnell, 1980). Bradbury
and Grace (1983) review primary production by *Sphagnum*, along with
other wetland plants. Details on many of the topics discussed here, with
particular reference to *Phragmites australis*, one of the most widespread
dominant plants, will be found in Rodewald-Rudescu (1974).

Methods

Most methods that were used for determining biomass and primary
productivity are described in detail in Handbooks (especially Milner &

Hughes, 1968; Šesták, Čatský & Jarvis, 1971; Evans, 1972; Vollenweider, 1974), and they will be discussed here only briefly to draw attention to particular problems of their application to wetlands and their comparability.

Criteria

Biomass

In most investigations of wetlands, dry weight has been used as the main measure of biomass (B_D), for this is determined easily and accurately and ash contents for most of the dominant species are less variable than for submerged plants (Straškraba, 1968, 20–140 mg g^{-1}). Chlorophyll is a common criterion of biomass (B_C) for algal studies because the problems of sorting algae from non-algal material are avoided. Therefore, it is useful to have chlorophyll data for comparative purposes as well as for its intrinsic importance as the light-absorbing pigment, but determinations have not often been made on wetland plants. There is probably a wide range of 1–20 mg chlorophyll per gram organic weight of aerial shoots, depending on whether the plant consists largely of young green leaves or has a high proportion of stem or older tissues (Bray, 1960; Aruga & Monsi, 1963; Walker & Waygood, 1968; Boyd, 1970a,b; Gaudet, 1973; Rejmánková, 1973b; Szczepański, 1973; and personal (DFW) determinations). To some extent these are complementary, so that plants with much stem or older tissue have a higher biomass than those with mostly young green leaves, and chlorophyll index (cover) (mg chl. *a* m^{-2}) is often relatively constant. Leaf area index (m^2 leaf surface)/(m^2 water or soil surface) is an important parameter for the analysis of growth and of productivity but has no equivalent for algal populations. Chlorophyll index ([mg chl. a] [m water surface]$^{-2}$) is the closest parameter, which may be used to compare algal and macrophyte populations.

Shoot or plant density (*n*, no. m^{-2}), comparable to algal numbers, is a very useful characteristic in populations with well-defined aerial shoots, often revealing otherwise unsuspected aspects of the plant's behaviour.

Production

When considering primary production as an input into an ecosystem, net photosynthesis (*N*) is of more interest than gross because it is only the net production that allows increase in biomass (B) and that can be utilised by heterotrophic consumers. Furthermore, the usual light and dark enclosures used for the measurement of photosynthesis, and respiration (R) cannot give a true value for gross photosynthesis (A_t) because the rate of photorespiration (R_p) is unknown. What is measured is only net photosynthesis plus dark respiration (R_d), which may be called photoassimilation (A) (Marker & Westlake, 1980). However, the different techniques used for macrophytes and microphytes often mean that, while net photosynthesis is available for the former, only photoassimilation is available for the latter, which makes totals and comparisons difficult to obtain.

Further difficulties arise from other differences in techniques. Net production values derived from biomass changes of macrophytes are usually given in terms of dry weights accumulated over long periods, but photosynthetic measurements on microphytes are usually made over short periods in terms of radiocarbon fixation or oxygen output. Dry weights and ash-free dry weights have been interconverted by using published ash contents or the mean content for the same or similar species from Straškraba (1968), Boyd and Scarsbrook (1975b), Dykyjová (1979) or Little (1979).

Energy values would be valuable for discussion of energy flows, but adequate data on energy contents is rarely available. They are usually within 15 to 20 kJ g org.wt^{-1} (3.6 to 5.0 kcal g^{-1}; p. 113; Dykyjová & Přibil, 1975; and papers reviewed therein).

Direct harvesting methods

These are based on sampling the vegetation in quadrats throughout the stand, usually around the time of the maximum biomass, but preferably on a number of occasions during the year (e.g. Westlake, 1966; Burian, 1971; Lack, 1973; Ondok & Dykyjová, 1973; Bernard, 1974; Mason & Bryant, 1975; Schierup, 1978; Westlake et al., 1986). Direct harvesting is particularly difficult in wetlands, partly because of difficulties of access (neither dry land nor deep enough for diving), but also because the populations are prone to have gradients and clumped distributions which (cf. pp. 114–16 and Table 2.8) give high variances. This makes it imperative to consider the size of the quadrats and the sampling pattern very carefully, in conjunction with a statistician (Westlake et al., 1986).

Biomass and production

The increase in biomass observed:

$$\Delta B = B_{t2} - B_{t1} \tag{1}$$

does not necessarily equal the net production (N):

$$\Delta B = N - [L_e + L_b + L_z + L_m] \tag{2}$$

where the losses (L) may be due to excretion (L_e), bacterial and fungal attack (L_b), grazing (and incidental damage) by animals (L_z), or other unspecified mortality (L_m) such as shedding of old leaves and wind damage.

Methods for measuring losses have to be chosen to suit the habitat and species of both plant and consumers. At the simplest, dead material may be collected, but they usually involve frequent sampling of numbers and sizes of shoots, leaves, etc., perhaps even tagging individual shoots, and converting these data to weights by regressions of weight on size (e.g. Westlake, 1975 and in papers quoted in Westlake, 1982), Allen curve techniques may be useful (Mathews & Westlake, 1969).

Biomass changes are rarely a convenient method of measuring algal production because of the very rapid turnover in algal communities, partly due to other losses such as sedimentation and wash-out.

For some ungrazed, mono-specific, fast-growing stands of plants with annual growth or re-growth, like many crop plants, the seasonal maximum biomass $(B_{t\ max})$ can be used as an estimate of the annual production. Even if only the above-ground shoots are measured, small corrections for roots, losses and initial biomass (B_{ti}) may give valid values for the total annual production. However, few natural wetland communities meet these requirements. Often several different species are present, which reach their maxima at different times and which must be accounted for separately (Baradziej, 1974; Whigham *et al.*, 1978). Many wetland species maintain a significant biomass for more than one growing season, or have a rapid turnover of leaves or shoots, or are heavily grazed, and then the production cannot be simply determined. The annual production of the above-ground material of helophytes (ignoring the contribution of translocation, see pp. 82–3, 87–94 and 138–9) has been found to be anything between 0.6 and 3.6 times the maximum standing crop (Westlake, 1982; Table 2.2). Even for a single species the ratios may differ considerably between different habitats or even years, so production should be determined directly.

In most situations many conceptual difficulties can be solved by regarding the annual net production as the sum of all the material that dies in a year:

$$N_y = [L_e + L_b + L_z + L_m]_y \text{ when } \Delta B_y = 0 \qquad (3)$$

At first sight this may seem a surprising definition, but it is valid, particularly for ecosystem studies, and may be an easier quantity to measure if excretion is negligible. It is the total quantity of new organic matter becoming available to secondary consumers in the year, but it could be misleading where studies are concerned with relating production to current environmental conditions, and a year with high insolation and growth, and low mortality, is followed by one with low insolation and growth but high mortality.

Underground biomass

Further serious problems arise because many emergent macrophytes have a large proportion of their biomass underground (Westlake, 1982; Table 2.1), sometimes exceeding 0.9 of the total, and individual organs may persist for many years, although some components are translocated in or out according to season and growth pattern (see pp. 138–9). There are great practical problems in sampling this biomass. To estimate the annual production of the whole plant from biomass data, it is necessary to follow the changes in above- and underground biomass very accurately (e.g. Schierup, 1978; *P. australis*) or to determine the average age of the underground material at the time of the maximum aerial biomass (e.g. Fiala, 1976; *P. australis*), or to determine the annual increment underground directly (e.g. Fiala, 1978b; *T. angustifolia*). The latter technique has been mostly applied to young clones and it is unlikely that the growth of rhizomes and roots will be the same in closed mature stands. When the difficulties of applying it to mature stands have been overcome, it has usually been demonstrated that translocation between old and new rhizome sections causes large errors (e.g. Fiala, 1973; Lack, 1973). Probably most estimates of underground production from biomass changes are subject to large errors from translocation and turnover. The best method at present is to determine underground production as the difference between total net photosynthesis (N_y) and above-ground production (N_A). The latter is determined from changes in standing crop, with corrections for losses and translocation upwards (usually as the initial biomass increment, while the net assimilation rate, as biomass increment per unit leaf area, exceeds $10 \text{ g m}^{-2} \text{ d}^{-1}$). The former has been derived from measurements of leaf photosynthesis, models of above-ground photosynthesis and underground respiration (e.g. Ondok, 1978*b*; Ondok & Gloser, 1978).

If the stand is studied as a whole, translocation should cause no theoretical problems, but once technical problems force the separate study of individual shoots, above- and underground plant parts or parts of different age, it must be allowed for. The standing crop of above-ground shoots of many temperate helophytes partly arises from material produced in the previous year, stored in the rhizomes and translocated upwards in the spring. For example, 0.25 to 0.3 of the above-ground standing crop of *Phragmites australis* is translocated material. It may be convenient to assume that this upward translocation is balanced by downward translocation in the autumn, but then this quantity must not be counted as part of the underground production. When production in tropical stands with constant biomass is being studied by means of the growth of individual shoots and shoot turnover, material translocated from old, dying shoots to new shoots will cause large errors because the product of shoots per square metre per year and the mean maximum weight of shoots can include the same material more than once. This may reach 0.4 of individual shoots in *Cyperus papyrus* (Thompson, 1976; Thompson *et al.*, 1979) and is likely to occur in plants such as *Eichhornia crassipes* for which increase in plant number and mean individual weight is a particularly convenient technique.

Relative growth rate

Some wetland communities (e.g. of *Lemna, Nasturtium, Eichhornia* spp.) often grow by increasing the area covered, keeping their biomass per unit area and their production density relatively constant. It is then necessary to decide if production and biomass are to be expressed in terms of initial area, current area, final area, habitat area, water body area, or some intermediate value; basing this decision on a careful consideration of exactly what question is to be answered or what comparisons made. In such situations it is often more satisfactory to work with relative growth rates (e.g. Rejmánková, 1978).

Relative growth rate, and the other parameters of growth analysis, are also very valuable when discussing the different strategies used by plants to achieve their productivity and to compete (Květ, 1971). Most of the classic studies have dealt with plants with a limited morphological range, few losses and little translocation, and application to wetland communities requires the investigator to carefully define the parameters and to be prepared for unexpected results. Leaf area (S_ℓ) and derived parameters such as leaf area index ($\ell = S_\ell$/ground area S_g), leaf area ratio ($\ell_p = S_\ell$/ dry wt plant B_D) and specific leaf area ($\ell_\ell = S_\ell/B_\ell$) depend on the definition of leaf area as one or both sides of the photosynthetic surfaces. Traditionally, one side has been used. With plants like *Nymphaea* spp. the choice is obviously one side, with plants like *Typha* spp., with nearly erect blade-like monofacial leaves, the choice is very debatable and for *Schoenoplectus lacustris*, with erect conical stems, both 'sides' is the only logical choice (Dykyjová, 1971a).

The observed mean relative growth rate ($\bar{G}$) usually refers to change in biomass,

$$\bar{G} = [\ln B_{t2} - \ln B_{t1}] [t_2 - t_1]^{-1} \tag{4}$$

This has the same dimensions as specific net photosynthesis (N_s; g fixed [g plant]$^{-1}$ h^{-1}) which is obtained from metabolic and algal investigations, but over longer intervals losses or translocation usually mean that $\bar{G}$ does not equal N_s. In theory, for whole plants,

$$N_s = [\ln(B_{t2} + L_{\Delta t}) - \ln(B_{t1})] [\Delta_t]^{-1} \tag{5}$$

where $L_{\Delta t}$ is the total loss of material (by mortality, grazing, excretion etc.) between t_1 and t_2. When $L_{\Delta t}$ is large, or when whole plants are not considered and biomass changes greatly as a result of translocation up or down, very large differences between $\bar{G}$ and N_s are found.

Indirect methods

Application of indirect methods of assessing various biomass and production parameters is advantageous in communities of wetland plants, with their generally large variations in species composition, density, biomass, vertical canopy structure and horizontal distribution patterns. When the growth characteristics of a stand are required, these methods appear to give results with narrower confidence limits than the methods of direct harvesting. They protect the stand from damage by direct harvesting when a large number of replicates is needed due to the high variability, and provide valuable information to aid the interpretation of biomass changes in terms of productivity (see Ondok, 1971a). However, the methods are normally restricted to growth above ground.

Assessment of biomass by means of mean stand density and mean weight of the shoots

The mean shoot density (n) is established by counting shoots in contiguous quadrats of a defined size along a transect laid down through the stand, or by the 'plotless method' on the basis of measurements of distances between individual regularly spaced points (e.g. along a line) and the nearest shoots (for 'nearest distance' method see Clark & Evans, 1954; Cottam & Curtis, 1956). The mean weight of a single shoot (w) is determined by randomly harvesting single shoots along a transect, or by harvesting the shoot nearest to each regularly spaced point on a line. The mean biomass is then obtained as a product of n and w. If statistical parameters of both n and w are known, the confidence interval of the calculated biomass ($n.w$) is obtained by finding the mean and variance of this product. As the product $n.w$ is a function of both n and w, its mean ($\mu_{n.w}$) and variance ($\sigma^2_{n.w}$) may be approximated using linearisation of this function in this way:

$$\mu_{n.w} \simeq \mu_n . \mu_w$$

$$\sigma^2_{n.w} \simeq \mu_n^2 \sigma_w^2 + \mu_w^2 \sigma_n^2 + 2\mu_n\mu_w\sigma_{n.w.} \tag{6}$$

where $\sigma_{n.w}$ is the covariance of n and w. The confidence interval is then constructed by means of these estimates of $\mu_{n.w}$ and $\sigma_{n.w}$ in the ordinary way. If using this method, we suppose that the shoots can be well defined.

Such methods may be applied to find other stand parameters such as leaf area index, mean shoot height, with weight of plant parts, etc. In circumstances where the correlation between shoot density and biomass per unit area is already known, density measurements over a wide area may be converted directly to biomass without further detailed studies of shoots (Ondok, 1971*b*).

Method of standard permanent quadrats

This method can be used with advantage to follow the seasonal growth of a stand. In one or more selected permanent quadrats some non-destructive parameters (e.g. shoot length, number of leaves, leaf area index) are measured for all shoots inside the quadrat at selected time intervals. On each date of measurement, other shoots having the same parameters as the plants measured inside the quadrat are harvested on adjacent plots with approximately the same density as that inside the permanent quadrat. In this way, parallel samples are obtained which approximate very well to the actual biomass inside the quadrat and thus the seasonal growth in the selected plots.

Another variant of this method employs regression equations enabling the biomass to be estimated on the basis of the parameters measured inside the permanent quadrats (e.g. weight/on height). In this variant further samplings are needed to establish the coefficients of the regression equations. These should be made successively during the period of the seasonal measurements inside the permanent quadrat. Details for several littoral stands dominated by *Phragmites australis, Glyceria maxima, Typha angustifolia* and *Scirpus maritimus* are given by Ondok (1971*a*, 1973*a*) and Ondok and Dykyjová (1973). These stands were characterised by gradients of density, shoot height and biomass along transects perpendicular to the shoreline and by irregularities in their horizontal density patterns (produced mainly by gaps within the stand). Simple statistical calculations showed that, using the method of direct harvesting, nearly 100 samples of 1 m^2 size would be needed to reduce the sampling error to 5% limits. Since the indirect method achieved such low errors with much less work, it is clearly preferable in such cases.

It should be mentioned that the variance of a parameter determined using the 'nearest distance' method cannot be calculated in all variants of this method. An indirect way of determining the variance for densities found by the 'nearest distance' method is proposed by Clark and Evans (1954).

Metabolic methods

These primarily involve plants or plant parts in light or dark enclosures and measurements of their carbon dioxide or oxygen exchanges. Since the total production of new organic material potentially available to the ecosystem is the same as net photosynthesis, such measurements can theoretically give information on production as well as on the physiological behaviour of the plants. Probably the greatest difficulties arise because metabolic experiments are best carried out for short periods (minutes), whereas growth and productivity studies are usually concerned with periods longer than a day, up to the whole growing season. Short-term rates fluctuate with environmental conditions so either very numerous measurements or interpolation between fewer measurements are necessary to obtain satisfactory long-term integrations. If integration is attempted by recording the activity of plant stands enclosed for long periods, it is extremely difficult to keep the internal and external conditions similar. Such control is slightly easier with enclosed plant parts, or single shoots, but no part is characteristic of the whole and the behaviour of parts of a plant, when still attached, is affected by the plant structure as a whole (e.g. self-shading, translocation).

In wetlands there are also problems arising from the great horizontal variability of the stands, which makes numerous replicate enclosures desirable. On the other hand, the control of environmental factors may be easier with wetland plants. The adjacent water can often be used to reduce rises in temperature and the combination of high humidity, plants adapted to high humidity and free water around the roots means that water stress limitations are unlikely.

Some valuable studies using measurements of both stand biomass and metabolism have been made, which have shown that the combination is much more informative than either technique separately (Ondok & Gloser, 1978; Burian & Sieghardt, 1979; Sale *et al.*, 1985; Sale & Orr, 1986). Ondok and Gloser made special efforts to overcome the problems of horizontal variability and of the relations between the metabolism of single leaves and the stand over long periods. They developed a model which took account of the structure of the canopy, the incident irradiance, the transmission of light through the canopy, the air temperatures and the field data on photosynthesis and respiration (see pp. 126–32). Determinations of above-ground biomass changes and photosynthesis often show discrepancies arising from translocation and further illuminating studies can be made of the transfer and accumulation of metabolites at different seasons (e.g. Krejci, 1974; Sieghardt, 1977; Fiala, 1978*b*).

When metabolic studies are made of parts or stands of emergent macrophytes, it is usually possible to regard non-plant metabolism as negligible so that photoassimilation, net photosynthesis and dark respiration (see pp. 79–80) may all be determined, and it is often possible to separate most of the epiphytic organisms. When they are used for the metabolism of the submerged periphyton and phytoplankton, it is rarely possible to measure their net photosynthesis directly because of non-plant respiration, and data are normally only available for photoassimilation.

Assumptions about biomass and production

Conversions of above-ground standing crop into total biomass, above-ground production and underground production are often made by assuming standard ratios, such as the P/B ratio (e.g. Vinberg, 1972;

Table 2.1. *Examples of recent values of the ratio of under- to above-ground standing crop for helophytes (at time of maximum above-ground standing crop, as dry wt)*

Species	Notes	B_u/B_a	References
Polygonum hydropiper (dom.)	1 year's growth	0.19	Rejmánek & Velasquez, 1978
Bidens cernua	Annual	0.22	van der Valk & Davis, 1978
Carex rostrata		0.22	Bernard, 1974
Zizania aquatica	Annual	0.41	Whigham, 1978
Carex riparia		0.43	Burian & Sieghardt, 1979
Cyperus papyrus	Tropical	0.45	Thompson et al., 1979
Lepironia articulata	Tropical: burnt or not	0.36–0.60	Ikusima, 1978
Typha latifolia	Different sites	0.4–0.6	Květ & Husák, 1978
Sparganium erectum	Different sites (trop.)	0.44–0.83	Kaul et al., 1978
Typha domingensis	Tropical	0.76–0.90	Howard-Williams, 1973; Kaul et al., 1978
Typha angustifolia	Different sites	0.9–1.2	Květ & Husák, 1978
Eichhornia crassipes	Different sites: subtropical	0.6–5.5[a]	Knipling et al., 1970; Center & Spencer, 1981; Gopal & Sharma, 1981
Acorus calamus	Different sites	0.62–1.9	Lack, 1973; Dykyjová, 1980; Květ & Husák, 1978; Whigham, 1978; Kaul et al., 1978
Spartina alterniflora	Different sites	1–3–(10)	Turner, 1976
Schoenoplectus lacustris	Different sites	2.3–3.9	Květ & Husák, 1978
Phragmites australis		2.3	Schierup, 1978
Phragmites australis	Different sites (temp.)	1.8–9.9	Fiala, 1976
Phragmites australis	Different sites (trop.)	0.62–1.12	Kaul et al., 1978

[a] This range probably shows the inadequacies of the methods of measuring and expressing the productivity of this plant.
Based on Westlake (1982) by permission of the Royal Society of Belgium.

Vinberg *et al.*, 1972). As has been suggested above, and may be clearly seen in Tables 2.1 to 2.3, such ratios vary greatly. For full and accurate investigations it is essential to make direct measurements of underground material and the differences between biomass and production. However, for some more general purposes, in particular to make use of a wide range of existing data for comparative purposes, it is often necessary to make some assumptions. These must be treated very cautiously because the growth patterns of species show great differences which do not fit a standard pattern, and may vary with environmental conditions. In communities with more than one dominant, each may have different growth patterns. Baradziej (1974) has discussed some of the techniques available for such communities, but does not deal with the complications arising from turnover, losses and underground parts. However, provided the obvious pitfalls are avoided, this approach may give useful information.

Proportion of underground material ('Root'/shoot ratio)

The results assembled in Table 2.1 show that the underground parts of helophytes may be from under 0.2 to over nine times the maximum above-ground standing crop, and of course the proportion underground will be higher for most of the year for plants with perennial rhizomes and annual aerial shoots. Even for species of annual plants, there is considerable seasonal variation in the root/shoot ratio (Whigham, 1978). For some, the proportion is high initially and low at or after the maximum standing crop (e.g. *Polygonum sagittatum*), but for others the ratio is highest at some intermediate stage (e.g. *Impatiens capensis, Bidens laevis*). At the time of their seasonal maximum, annuals tend to have a lower root/shoot ratio than perennials, but there is a large overlap in ranges.

For a single species, over a limited range of sites, relatively constant root/shoot ratios have been reported for the seasonal maximum biomass, except at very low biomasses (e.g. Szczepański, 1969; Whigham, 1978). However, as the ranges in Table 2.1 show, there can be large differences between sites.

General conversion factors for all species, or for a single species at different sites, are clearly not advisable. However, for broad comparisons of the biomass of species, using averages over a variety of sites, it may be possible to use a single factor for each species or group of species (e.g. many annual species without rhizomes U/A 0.3, *Typha latifolia* 0.5, *Phragmites australis*, 2.5; Hejný *et al.*, 1981; Westlake, 1982).

Table 2.2. *Some examples of recent estimations of the* **P:B** *ratio for helophytes (annual net production of above-ground parts/ maximum standing crop of above-ground parts: as dry wt)*

Species	Material lost and methods	P/B	References
Typha domingensis	Shoot persistence, leaf loss: age of shoots	> 0.62	Howard-Williams, 1973
Phragmites australis	Leaf and shoot loss: litter collection	1.03	Ondok & Květ, 1978
Phragmites australis	Shoot mortality: wt of dead shoots	1.15	Mason & Bryant, 1975
Typha glauca	Shoot mortality: wt of dead shoots	1.09	van der Valk & Davis, 1978
Schoenoplectus lacustris	Shoot mortality: wt of dead shoots	1.09	Ondok & Květ, 1978
Typha angustifolia	Leaf and shoot loss: wt of dead material	1.06–1.24	Ondok & Květ, 1978
Typha angustifolia	Shoot mortality: wt of dead shoots	1.29	Mason & Bryant, 1975
Glyceria maxima	Shoot and leaf loss: litter collection	1.2–> 1.5	Mathews & Westlake, 1969; Ondok & Květ, 1978
Carex atherodes	Shoot mortality: wt of dead shoots	1.28	van der Valk & Davis, 1978
Lepironia articulata	Shoot mortality: wt of dead shoots	1.3–1.8	Ikusima, 1978
Carex lacustris	Shoot mortality: shoot tags, indirect	1.52	Bernard & Gorham, 1978
Mixed marsh veg.	Numerous spp., leaf loss: spp. max., tags	2.24	Whigham *et al.*, 1978
Spartina alterniflora	Shoot and leaf loss: litter decomp.	1.7–2.6	Kirby & Gosselink, 1978
Cyperus papyrus	Shoot turnover: shoot growth rate	1.8–3.6	Thompson *et al.*, 1979
Nasturtium officinale	Leaf and stem loss: litter decomp.	2.5–3.5	Dawson *et al.*, 1978

Reproduced from Westlake (1982) by permission of the Royal Society of Belgium.

P/B *ratio*

In Table 2.2 various estimates of the annual above-ground net production of helophytes (P_A) are compared with their seasonal maximum standing crop of above-ground parts ($B_{t\ max,A}$). If it can be assumed that the sediment does not release organic material to the water, most of these estimates of production give a practical estimate of the biomass providing a food source to consumers in the water in the current year. They may not give the true total net production (N) of the current year because of translocation up and down (T_U, T_D):

$$P_A = B_{t\,max,A} - B_{t1,A} + [L_e + L_b + L_z + L_m] + T_U = N + T_U - T_D \quad (7)$$

Translocation downwards is allocated to underground structural increments and respiration, as well as to storage for later use to initiate the next season's growth. Hence T_D is greater than T_U and P_A is less than N.

Some of the variations in P/B ratios arise because of the different techniques used, which may not take account of all forms of loss.

Some temperate species have low P/B ratios arising from well-defined growth cycles, stable populations and low grazing (e.g. *Phragmites australis, Schoenoplectus lacustris*). Others have high P/B ratios associated with indefinite growth seasons, rapid turnover and little accumulation of live biomass (e.g. *Nasturtium officinale*). In tropical areas rapid turnover may be associated with a relatively constant, high biomass (e.g. *Lepironia articulata, Cyperus papyrus*). In very stable climates, or in very nutrient-poor habitats persistence of shoots of some species for more than one year leads to P/B ratios much less than one (e.g. *Typha domingensis, Carex rostrata*; and *Arundo donax*, see Ogawa *et al.*, 1961).

The ranges in Table 2.2 cover differences between sites and years. The length of the growing season, particular features of the weather, the fertility of the site and the incidence of grazing or management can all affect shoot emergence, mortality and losses. In a short growing season there may not be time for many shoots to die from senescence before drought or frost kills all the shoots (e.g. *Nasturtium officinale*, Dawson *et al.*, 1978). Mortality is often less in sparse stands than in dense stands, and sparse stands in fertile conditions show high emergence over long periods (e.g. Westlake, 1981). In fertile ponds in the cold winter climate of Czechoslovakia, stands of *Glyceria maxima* and *Typha angustifolia* show high and more stable standing crops, and lower P/B ratios than in poorer conditions in the maritime climate of England (Westlake, 1966; 1981; Mason & Bryant, 1975; Ondok & Květ, 1978).

Table 2.3. *Examples of the ratio of under- to above-ground production for helophytes (as dry wt)*

Species	Methods	P_u/P_a	References
Mixed marsh	Biomass of annual roots	> 0.07	Whigham *et al.*, 1978
Carex lacustris	Biomass change	> 0.10	Bernard & Gorham, 1978
Lepironia articulata	Increments of dead rhizomes	0.12–0.14	Ikusima, 1978
Cyperus papyrus	Biomass and turnover of rhizomes	0.33	Thompson *et al.*, 1979
Typha latifolia	Increments in cultures	0.4	Fiala, 1978b
Glyceria maxima	Root and rhizome dynamics	0.4	Westlake, unpublished data
Acorus calamus	Biomass/age	0.23	Lack, 1973
Acorus calamus	General ratios, cultures, biomass/age	0.5–0.9	Květ & Husák, 1978
Phragmites australis	Modelled net photosynthesis – above ground accumulation	0.34–0.56	Ondok, 1978b
Phragmites australis	General ratios: cultures, biomass/age	0.5–1.0	Květ & Husák, 1978
Phragmites australis	cultures, biomass/age, modelling	0.5–1.0	Burian & Sieghardt, 1979
Phragmites australis	Biomass dynamics	1.4	Schierup, 1978
Schoenoplectus lacustris	General ratios: cultures, biomass/age	1.0–1.2	Květ & Husák, 1978
Typha hybrid	Underground biomass given: divided by est. age by DFW	1.2	Bray *et al.*, 1959
Scirpus maritimus	General ratios: cultures, biomass/age	1.0–1.9	Květ & Husák, 1978

Reproduced from Westlake (1982) by permission of the Royal Society of Belgium.

Total production from standing crop

Attempts to compare the total annual production of different species or communities have often been based only on the seasonal maximum standing crop of above-ground parts. As discussed above, this is rarely valid for wetland plants unless there is enough knowledge of their growth, in their particular environment, to make corrections for accumulation, turnover and translocation. Westlake (1982) has shown that various levels and methods of correction for an example of a pure *Phragmites australis* stand gave estimates of annual total production ranging between 55 and 107% of the best available estimate. Even if the above-ground production can be determined from the seasonal maximum standing crop and corrections for losses and early spring translocation, there remains the problem of underground production. Most comparisons of the relations between above-ground and underground production (P_U/P_A) are subject to errors arising from different method of assessing the annual increments above and below ground and do not take translocation fully into account (Westlake, 1982; Table 2.3).

Many of the differences seen arise from such errors. The highest values of the ratio (0.5 to 2.0) are found in species with large and persistent rhizomes. The annual total production of many such plants is probably about twice the seasonal maximum above-ground standing crop (Westlake, 1982).

Populations, biomass and production

These three criteria of growth, numbers of shoots, weight per unit area and total weight produced in a year, illuminate different aspects of plant behaviour and in comparisons often produce different conclusions. As indicated in the previous section, it is often useful to study the first two in order to understand the third. Otherwise, as always, much depends on the exact reason for the investigation. For example, a study of an animal that consumed growing points would need shoot numbers, a comparison of commercial harvests would need the above-ground biomass and ecosystem research would need annual net production.

Seasonal changes in populations and biomass

Wetland plants show a wide range of types of growth pattern. Relatively stable biomasses and constant rates of production are found particularly in tropical regions where there are no extreme dry or wet seasons, but examples of similar stability, although maintained for shorter periods, may be found in temperate regions. At the other extreme, particularly in extreme climates where only a short period is suitable for growth of wetland vegetation, there are species with rapidly changing biomass and productivity. There are many intermediate growth patterns, even within any one climate, which may arise from one genotype with great adaptability to current circumstances, or from different ecotypes or from different species. Differences in environmental conditions, especially spring temperatures and hydrological factors, may cause year to year differences. Stable biomass often conceals a rapid turnover of individual shoots or thalli. For species that reproduce predominantly from seed, the proportion of the biomass in flowering shoots may be very important. Quite different patterns may be found if the behaviour of young plants growing free from competition is compared with mature stands. The growth patterns seen for the aerial shoots are often a reflection of the behaviour of the underground organs and are more easily interpreted if the whole plant is studied.

The maximum biomass of any plant stand is probably fixed by the balance between photosynthesis and respiration (e.g. Westlake, 1980; and see p. 155). Once the standing crop of aerial shoots is sufficient to absorb most of the incident radiation, photosynthesis of the stand cannot be increased by further leaves, but respiration can. Net growth of new tissues is only possible if older tissue is lost. This often happens by sloughing of the older leaves or by total death of individual shoots or plants (intraspecific competition).

In the following pages growth patterns are presented for several contrasting, widely dispersed species, for which good data are available. Unfortunately, results are rarely available for both above-ground and underground biomass at the same site, so caution must be exercised in comparing the curves given in Fig. 2.1.

Phragmites australis *(*communis*; Common Reed)*

This plant, in the temperate regions, shows a simple, basic growth pattern. The aerial shoots overwinter as buds (Haslam, 1969b) under the soil or water and emerge in spring to grow rapidly (Fig. 2.1(a)). Normally, once the first flush of shoots has emerged in little more than a month, few more emerge and few die (Haslam, 1970b). The density of shoots is then relatively constant, and about 120–140 shoots m^{-2} at good sites, for

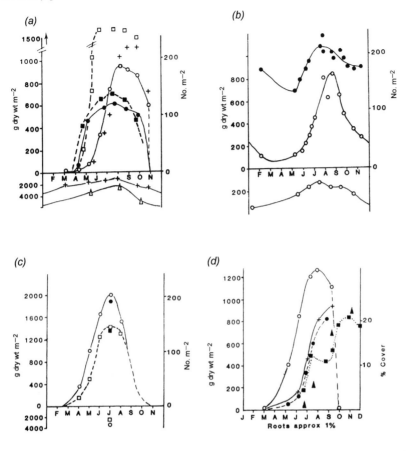

Fig. 2.1. Seasonal changes in standing crop and shoot numbers, or cover, of emergent and floating macrophytes.

(*a*) *Phragmites australis.*
  England, Mason & Bryant (1975); ● Shoot no.; ○ Shoot wt ———;
  Denmark, Schierup (1978); + Shoot wt, and rhizome plus root wt;
  Czechoslovakia $\begin{cases} \text{Dykyjová \& Hradecká (1976); } \triangle \text{ Rhizome plus root wt ———;} \\ \text{Květ } et\ al.\ (1969); \ \blacksquare \text{ Shoot no., } \square \text{ Shoot wt ----.} \end{cases}$

(*b*) *Carex rostrata.* Minnesota, Bernard (1974);
  ● Shoot no.; ○ Shoot wt; and rhizome plus root wt ———.

(*c*) *Phalaris arundinacea.* Czechoslovakia, Kopecký (1967); Spring flooding:
  0 days; ● Flowering shoot no.; ○ Shoot wt ———, and rhizome plus root wt;
  16 days; ■ Flowering shoot no.; □ Shoot wt ----, and rhizome plus root wt.

(*d*) *Nasturtium officinale.* England, Castellano (1977):
  1973; ● % cover ----; ○ Biomass of whole plant per m² plant stand ———;
          + Biomass per m² river ———;
  1972: △ % cover;   1971: ■ % cover ⋯⋯.

(*continued overleaf*)

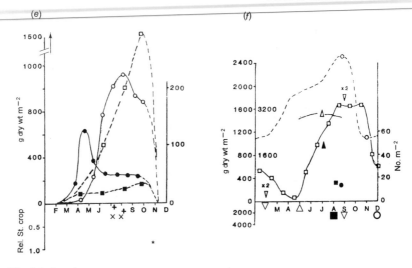

Fig. 2.1. (cont).
(e) Typha spp. (temperate):
England, T. angustifolia, Mason & Bryant (1975); ● Shoot no.; ○ Shoot
wt ——;
Czechoslovakia, T. latifolia, Květ et al. (1969); ■ Shoot no.; □ Shoot wt ---;
Czechoslovakia, young clones, Fiala (1978b); Standing crop underground
relative to late October value (✳); + T. angustifolia; × T. latifolia.
(f) Typha spp. (tropical):
    T. domingensis = angustata. Malawi, 623 m, Howard-Williams (1973); ● Shoot
no.; ○ Shoot wt max. and min. values, --- from text; ○ Rhizome plus roots wt.
Kashmir, 1600 m, Kaul & Vass (1972); ▽ Shoot wt (note half-scale used), and
rhizome plus root wt, both max & min. values. India, Jaipur, 436 m, Sharma &
Gopal (1977); ▲ Shoot no.; △ Shoot wt, and rhizome plus root wt, max. values.
    Typha elephantina. India, Jaipur, 436 m, Sharma & Gopal (1977);
■ Shoot no.; □ Shoot wt ——, and rhizome only wt.

(continued opposite)

about 4 months until their autumnal death. Shoot emergence is controlled
and deaths by intraspecific competition are few. If young shoots are lost
by frost, grazing or physical damage, there may be replacements (Haslam,
1970b). The weight of shoots continues to increase, to give a well-defined
maximum standing crop about the end of July, which is over 1.0 kg dry wt
m^{-2} at good sites. Losses of leaves and a few shoots lead to a slow decline
in weight until shoots start to die rapidly in late autumn. By then, many of
next year's buds are developed underground. Very similar behaviour has
been found at several temperate sites. All shoots that reach full-size flower,
but many shoots, either because their initial buds were small, or because
they emerged late, fail to reach full size (Haslam, 1970b).
    In warmer climates (e.g. Malta) the shoots flower and die later, the buds

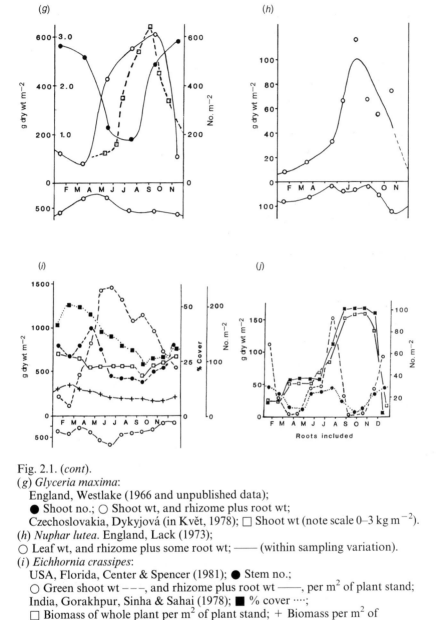

Fig. 2.1. (*cont*).
(*g*) *Glyceria maxima*:
  England, Westlake (1966 and unpublished data);
  ● Shoot no.; ○ Shoot wt, and rhizome plus root wt;
  Czechoslovakia, Dykyjová (in Květ, 1978); □ Shoot wt (note scale 0–3 kg m^{-2}).
(*h*) *Nuphar lutea*. England, Lack (1973);
  ○ Leaf wt, and rhizome plus some root wt; —— (within sampling variation).
(*i*) *Eichhornia crassipes*:
  USA, Florida, Center & Spencer (1981); ● Stem no.;
  ○ Green shoot wt – – –, and rhizome plus root wt ——, per m^2 of plant stand;
  India, Gorakhpur, Sinha & Sahai (1978); ■ % cover ····;
  □ Biomass of whole plant per m^2 of plant stand; + Biomass per m^2 of
  lake; ——.
(*j*) Lemnids. *Lemna minor* and *Spirodela polyrhiza*.

start to develop later and continue, except during the short dormant period, and start to emerge earlier (Haslam, 1969b, 1970b). More undamaged shoots die prematurely, but they are less than 25% of the total (Haslam, 1970b). There are no detailed studies of its growth patterns in more tropical climates; but in Kashmir (34° N, 1600 m) there is a well-defined cycle with a minimum in March which is less than 10% of the August maximum (Kaul, 1971).

The underground biomass is always high, at least twice the above-ground in all cases except some examples from Kashmir (Table 2.2). In the autumn it reaches its maximum of 3–6 kg m^{-2} at good sites, which remains fairly stable over the winter (Fig. 2.1(a)). When aerial shoot buds start growth the underground biomass declines, to reach a minimum in summer. Part of this loss of weight is due to respiration and translocation of reserves, which are replaced in the late summer (see p. 139), but in part is due to death of older parts, which are mostly replaced in the summer and autumn (Haslam, 1969b, 1970b). Individual rhizomes persist for up to 5 years (Westlake, 1968, Ondok & Kvĕt, 1978) but the average life of rhizome material is probably rather less. Many of the shoots for the next year terminate the new rhizomes, but some are tillers from the base of these main shoots and some are tillers or branches from old shoots (Haslam, 1969a).

Carex *spp. (Sedges)*

C. rostrata has a growth pattern which superficially resembles the basic *Phragmites* cycle, with shoot numbers and standing crop varying together (Fig. 2.1(b)), but there is a considerable overwintering biomass and many shoots live up to 2 years. About 70–130 shoots are present for much of the winter, including young (0 + 1) and mature (1 +) shoots (Bernard, 1974; Bernard & Gorham, 1978). Nevertheless, the winter standing crop is only 200–300 g m^{-2}, and both numbers and weight decline further in the early spring. After May both increase rapidly until about July. Then the older shoots, which have all flowered, start to die and are largely replaced by further new shoots and numbers are fairly stable at around 200 m^{-2}. Maximum standing crop (~ 700 g m^{-2}) is reached in August and both numbers and standing crop decline slowly in the autumn. Less than half of the summer population are flowering shoots of the 1 + cohort, and over 80% of the shoots that emerge die before flowering. The number of flowering shoots is therefore equal to the number of surviving shoots.

As in *Phragmites* the underground biomass decreases rapidly during the spring and early summer from about 300 g m $^{-2}$ to less than 100 g m $^{-2}$ and increases throughout the late summer and autumn. Most rhizome growth occurs in July–September and the new rhizomes end in new shoots.

In *C. lacustris*, shoots are also initiated mainly between July and November. However, those emerging in July and August die in the winter, and those emerging later either flower and die in the following summer or remain vegetative and die in the following winter. The number of flowering shoots is very dependent on environmental conditions.

Phalaris arundinacea *(Reed Canary-grass)*

There is a rapid increase from submerged buds in the spring to a well-defined maximum in July–August (Fig. 2.1(*c*)). Kopecký's study (1967) showed the influence of environmental conditions on the growth pattern. The zone that was flooded more in the spring showed later growth, fewer flowering shoots and lower maximum biomass above and below ground.

Nasturtium officinale *(Water-cress)*

This plant has several interesting aspects to its growth pattern, though not all are detectable from data on biomass, percentage cover or shoot number. At the chalk-stream site studied, growth starts from small fragments as soon as they can become entangled in large plants of *Ranunculus calcareus*. In a year when growth of *Ranunculus* is poor and water levels are high (e.g. Fig. 2.1(*d*), 1972), this happens later than in a year when there are low discharges and extensive beds of *Ranunculus* (e.g. 1971 and 1973; Dawson *et al.*, 1978). Floods may check its subsequent extension over the river surface (e.g. 1971) or may stop it altogether early in the autumn (e.g. 1973). If the biomass is expressed in terms of the area of the plant stand, it becomes fairly stable, at about 1.2 kg m $^{-2}$ in summer, but this conceals continued production, both by the continued expansion of area and by the constant death and replacement of leaves and stems that occur during this period. Stem death does not mean death of individual shoots in this case because the stems die progressively from their distal ends. They lose their original roots but continually replace older roots with new adventitious roots. Very similar behaviour was reported by Howard-Williams *et al.* (1982) in a New Zealand stream.

The growth pattern of water-cress as a crop differs in many ways, partly because the cress-beds use a supply of spring water at a constant gentle flow and a constant temperature of 10–12° C, and partly because it is

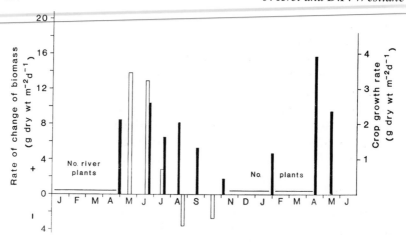

Fig. 2.2. Seasonal growth of *Nasturtium officinale* (water-cress) under cultivation and in a chalk-stream (Stream data from Castellano, 1977; crop data from the detailed original results on which Crisp, 1970 was based, by permission of the author). ■ crop growth rate in cress-bed, dry wt of harvested material/days of growth, per sq. metre of water-cress bed; □ rate of change of biomass in stream, per sq. metre of plant stand. Histograms plotted at mid-point of growth period.

commercially advantageous to manage the beds to produce early salad crops. New beds are established with complete cover using seeds or transplants and a crop is harvested as soon as it is ready. A stubble remains after each harvest and numerous dormant side shoots grow to provide the next harvest.

A bed studied in detail by Crisp (1970) was sown in March and produced a first crop in June. Crops were then taken at intervals of 26–33 days until October, with average crop growth rates of 1.3–3.6 g dry wt $m^{-2} d^{-1}$ (Fig. 2.2). These rates are based on the total cress material removed from the beds at each harvest, about 80% of which is marketable. Material was also removed at other times as part of the management, or to provide transplants, and of course growth of the stems and roots forming the stubble also occurred between harvests. The total net production rate until October was probably between 7 and 14 g $m^{-2} d^{-1}$, very comparable to the rates of change of biomass of 13–14 g $m^{-2} d^{-1}$ observed in the river during June to July (Castellano, 1977), but considerably higher than the rates of 3 to -3 g $m^{-2} d^{-1}$ observed in July to October, when the biomass had stabilised (Fig. 2.2). In the river the dense biomass causes severe self-shading which retards overall growth and the accumulation and death of old material masks the continued production.

Regular harvesting stimulates new growth and removes the older biomass. The crop continued growing during the winter and spring, with harvests in December, March and June (crop growth rates 0.4, 1.2 and 2.4 g m^{-2} d^{-1}, respectively). For much of this period high discharges and low temperatures would prevent growth in the river.

Typha *spp. (Bulrushes, Reedmace or Cat-tails)*

The two temperate species illustrated show growth patterns which differ from each other and from the plants previously discussed (Fig. 2.1(*e*)). Both have overwintering buds which emerge and grow rapidly in the spring. *T. latifolia* stands show further increases in shoot number and standing crop right up until growth ceases in autumn. In stands of *T. angustifolia* numerous young shoots die in May to July and are not replaced. Yet, in both species at the sites studied the final shoot numbers are 35–45 m^{-2} and the standing crops at good sites are over 1.0 kg m^{-2}. The difference in behaviour is less marked in young clones, but *T. angustifolia* then produces fewer shoots than *T. latifolia* during the summer and a greater number of perennating buds in the autumn (Fiala, 1978*a*).

The only appropriate seasonal data on underground parts are for young clones, but these clearly show rapid autumn growth (Fig. 2.1(*e*)). The rhizomes are shorter lived than those of *Phragmites* (~ 18 mo as against 4–5 y; Westlake, 1968) and the ratio of underground to above-ground material in mature stands is correspondingly lower (0.4 to 1.2 as against over 1.8; Westlake, 1982).

The two tropical species show some interesting differences in behaviour, especially at different sites (Fig. 2.1(*f*)). They all show lower standing crops of shoots in unfavourable seasons, but the difference between maximum and minimum shows a very wide range. In Jaipur *T. domingensis* exhibits an almost all the year round growth, in Malawi its minimum is 44% of the maximum, and growth is mainly in December–April and July, while in Kashmir the minimum is 8–22% of the maximum at various sites. The low growth in Malawi around June reflects one of the two minima of insolation, and the cessation of growth in August to October is related to the dry season. For *T. elephantina*, in Jaipur, the minimum is only about 6% of the maxima.

Cyperus papyrus *(Papyrus)*

Nearly all data for emergent vegetation at tropical sites come from high

altitudes or from sites with a marked cold or dry season. *Cyperus*, in more
equable climates, is said to have 'maximum season variations of only 25%
in East African swamps' (Thompson *et al.*, 1979) but there are no
published data for standing crops in different months. There is a constant
death, emergence and regrowth of aerial shoots. At any time there are 6–
23 shoots (culms) m^{-2} and a standing crop of shoots plus young rhizome
and roots of 90–5200 g m^{-2}, depending on site.

Glyceria maxima *(Reed Sweet-grass)*

The growth pattern of this species is very different from all those discussed
above, with the minimum shoot number (~ 40 m^{-2}) occurring close to the
time of the maximum standing crop (Fig. 2.1(g)).

There is a green overwintering standing crop (100–600 g m^{-2}) which
increases rapidly in the spring, while the shoot number decreases. The
detailed development of stands is strongly influenced by soil fertility,
climate and population density. In the mild climate and relatively poor
soil conditions of the English study the maximum stand crop is low (0.6 to
1.1 kg dry wt m^{-2}) and the peak is relatively broad, because old shoots are
dying while new shoots are emerging during July to September. In the
more extreme climate and fertile soils of the Czechoslovakian study the
maximum standing crop is higher (1.2–3.2 kg m^{-2}) and the peak is much
more distinct. The shoot number reaches a maximum in November, when
the shoots are small, and there are many more than for the other species
(about 600 m^{-2} as compared with 40–200).

The behaviour of young clones, without intraspecific competition is
very different (Westlake, 1981). New shoots are produced exponentially
throughout the growing season, while the clone expands. In denser stands
the emergence of some shoots is suppressed and competition leads to the
death of others while still young.

Underground, there is the typical decrease in standing crop while the
young shoots are growing rapidly. In stands new rhizomes start to grow in
early summer which terminate in many of the shoots emerging in July–
September. The rhizomes live for about 18 months so most of those
initiated in one spring are dying while the new ones are growing the
following summer, which reduces the apparent change in underground
biomass. In young clones new rhizomes are produced exponentially
during the growing season.

Nuphar lutea *(Yellow Water-lily)*

Although this is included as an example of a floating-leaved species, the floating leaves were only about 10% of the maximum standing crop in the stand illustrated. There is a very small overwintering standing crop of leaves and a rapid increase to a July maximum at the time of flowering (Fig. 2.1(*h*)). For the rest of the summer, differences are not significant. However, like many other plants, there is probably a slow decline while materials are transferred to the rhizomes, which increase appreciably in the autumn. Van der Velde *et al.* (1979) found similar behaviour by *Nymphoides peltata*.

Eichhornia crassipes *(Water Hyacinth)*

In the subtropical/temperate climate of Florida, *Eichhornia* shows a basic biomass cycle of low biomass in the winter (~ 500 g m^{-2}, one-third aerial) and a high biomass in the summer (~ 1500 g m^{-2}), with most rapid growth in March–June (Fig. 2.1(*i*)). However, there is a long period of intermediate biomass during July–October, possibly because the optimum biomass is then decreased by high temperatures during a period of decreasing insolation. Numbers and biomass both fall in late winter, during cold weather, and rise in the spring. When the standing crop of aerial shoots exceeds 800 g m^{-2}, in April, intraspecific competition causes the number of stems to fall rapidly (from ~ 190 m^{-2}) to a prolonged minimum in June–September (~ 70 m^{-2}). Biomass does not start to decrease to the July–October level until June and decreases rapidly again during October to December. This study was concerned with behaviour within a stand and took no account of expansion in area.

The data for the subtropical Indian population (Fig. 2.1(*i*)) show relatively little seasonal variation, even if changes in cover are taken into account. The maximum total biomass in the lake (area × % cover × stand biomass/100) is only 2.4 times the minimum as compared with 4 in Florida. Also, the highest values occur in the 'winter' period (15–20 °C) when both stand biomass and cover are high. In such relatively stable situations the packing of plants within stands, and the balance between new and dying plants probably have more importance than changes in growth rate. The winter maximum biomass could then be related to the lower temperatures which favour the balance between photosynthesis and respiration, and reduce mortality and grazing, yet give lower initiation and growth rates. These effects, in turn, could lead to an increasing separation of individual plants and the accumulation of a high optimum biomass, despite lower irradiances.

Like *Glyceria maxima*, and probably many other plants, growth free from competition is close to exponential for considerable periods (e.g. Wooten & Dodd, 1976). This, and neglect of the effect of changing areas, have led to considerable overestimates of the natural sustained productivity of *Eichhornia* stands.

Lemnids *(Duckweeds)*

The biomass of these freely floating plants at any point varies very greatly with wind and water movements rather than growth (Duffield & Edwards, 1981). However, data for whole water bodies show distinct seasonal cycles. At temperate sites these are straightforward, with maximum biomass and cover in the summer (Fig. 2.1(j) and Rejmánková, 1973a, 1982). However, the Welsh population reached its maximum in September but in Czechoslovakia most declined after July. Maximum biomasses in the fertile Czechoslovak ponds were much higher (up to 170 g dry wt m^{-2}) and self-shading is known to reduce the relative growth rate.

Growth patterns may be more complex in the tropics. The biomass and cover of a mixed population of *Lemna minor* and *Spirodela polyrhiza* in Gorakhpur showed pronounced minima in March–April and September–October, and maxima in December–January and July (Fig. 2.1(j)). There was a maximum/minimum ratio of over 700 for the total biomass in the lake. Only pH seemed to have any positive correlation with these changes.

For a general review and detailed data see Culley *et al.* (1983).

The quality of net production

Introduction

For the further fate and utilisation of the net primary production in wetland ecosystems, not only the quantity but also the quality of the plant material formed is of importance (Boyd & Goodyear, 1971). Four main components may be considered when evaluating the quality of the plant material:

Water content This is high in most wetland plants; usually between 80 and 94% of fresh weight, see, e.g. Westlake (1965); Boyd (1968a). Differences in water content are rarely of great direct importance to consumers, but may be an important aspect of food quality. For example, Boyd and Scarsbrook (1975*b*) have calculated that, for cattle to obtain their daily energy requirements from *Eichhornia* (94% water), they would need to eat more than twice as much of the fresh material as they are capable of eating each day. Water content and the water relations of wetland plants are discussed further in Chapter 7.

Ash content Some of this is physiologically important to the plant and to its consumers. Often a significant part is of no known immediate nutritional importance to the plant (e.g. stored phosphorus, silica and external carbonate) and none makes a significant contribution to the energy content of the material. Hence, for general purposes it is desirable to use the ash-free organic matter as a criterion of net production. However, it must not be forgotten that the ash may be an important feature of the quality of the material, influencing its utilisation. It is also important when studying the uptake, accumulation and subsequent cycling of mineral nutrients (see Chapter 6).

Organic chemical composition This strongly influences the further fate of the plant matter; which may be consumption by herbivores, decomposition and transformations in the detritus food chain (see Chapter 3) or use by man (see Chapter 8). The organic nitrogen and phosphorus are particularly important.

Energy content Although values for most wetland plants are not very different, the chemical composition of the plant may greatly influence the proportion of the total energy available to a specific consumer. Thus the cellulose and fibre fractions may be little used by many grazing wetland animals.

Ash and elementary content

The ash content of emergent plants tends to be lower than that of submerged plants, often because the latter carry much external calcium carbonate, but also because of some internal differences. Typical values are between 2 and 10% of dry weight for the 'hard' plants (such as reeds and sedges) and between 5 and 20% for the 'soft' plants (such as *Nuphar*, *Eichhornia*, *Sagittaria* and *Lemna*) (Tables 2.4 and 2.6). Apart from oxygen, carbon is the most abundant element by weight (350–480 mg g^{-1}). In most plants the carbon content is influenced mainly

Table 2.4. Elementary composition of aerial shoots of emergent and floating plants (in oven-dry material)

Element	Glyceria maxima	Phragmites australis	Cyperus papyrus	Eichhornia crassipes	Nasturtium officinale	Carex spp.	Schoenoplectus spp. (lacustris and americanus)	Typha latifolia	Sagittaria spp.	Nuphar spp. (lutea and advena)[b]	Lemna spp. L. gibba
Ash (%)	4.6-12	1.8-9.6	5-(20)[a]	5-31	15-23	1-9.1	4.4-13	4.2-12	1.9-15	6.1-9.5	16-19
mg (g dry wt)$^{-1}$											
C	420-450	–	–	350	350-450	–	430-440	–	–	–	–
N	4-30	3-44	7.8-18	10-40	41-74	9.2-25	6-27	4.2-3.5	13-31	38-52	19-53
P	0.5-4.2	0.3-7.9	0.2-1.0	1.0-8.0	1.7-8.5	1.7-5.5	0.3-9.5	0.2-6.6	2.2-8.2	2.4-4.6	6-20
K	3.0-32	2.6-39	15-28	2.0-44	22-60	4.4-18	4.8-37	3.5-50	18-68	14-32	22-57
Ca	1.2-5.7	0.3-7.7	1.4-2.3	0.2-30	16-26	1.0-4.9	1.0-6.4	2.1-25	4.8-9.9	7.5-15	6.2-140
Mg	0.9-3.8	0.2-5.4	0.3-1.1	4.0-11	1.0-19	0.7-8.9	0.6-3.9	1.0-7.7	1.8-4.3	1.7-70	2.4-11
Na	0.2-0.5	0.1-8.7	2.0-4.5	0.1-9.0	7.3-12	0.1-2.9	0.6-2.8	0.7-5.5	0.5-18	0.1-0.7	3.0-19
											L. minor
S	–	0.5-3.7	–	3.3-6.3	–	1.4-7.5	1.1-6.8	1.0-2.0	1.4-3.0	2.0-4.4	3.3-7.8
Si	–	10.1-10.7	20-100	–	–	5.6-9.8	6.0	2.2	7.0-10	0.7-5.6	0.4-5.4
µg (g dry wt)$^{-1}$											
Fe	850-12000	80-1700	80-460	500-14000	98-400	520-5000	300-780	70-200	300-5700	300-9200	250-17000
Mn	7200-25000	50-5000	40-510	87-3900	28-37	190-2400	230-2300	100-3400	100-360	40-7600	100-64000
Zn	–	12-65	–	25-210	48-76	4-43	16-54	17-100	46-200	30-150	110-500
Cu	20-26	4-47	–	7-100	–	–	4-32	3-47	30-68	6-56	5-110

[a] Upper limit: bracteoles only.
[b] Floating leaves only.

(Based on Boyd & Scarsbrook, 1975a,b; Boyd, 1970b; Casey, 1977; Castellano, 1977; Crisp, 1970; Cumbus, Robinson & Clare, 1980; Dykyjová, 1979; Gaudet, 1975; Knipling et al., 1970; Little, 1979; Robinson & Cumbus, 1977; Thompson et al., 1979; Westlake, 1966 and unpublished data). Rounded to two significant figures; a few extreme and unsupported values omitted.

by the ash content, but also by the proportions of carbohydrate, protein and fat. Carbon contents in terms of the ash-free dry weight are less variable.

The other nutrient elements are much more variable, although nitrogen and potassium are normally the next most abundant (generally within 3–50 mg g^{-1}). Phosphorus and calcium contents are generally between 0.2 and 20 mg g^{-1}; magnesium, sodium and sulphur rarely exceed 10 mg g^{-1} (Table 2.4).

The variability of results has been attributed to analytical techniques, seasonal variation, the age of the plant material, specific and genetic differences and the environment (e.g. Dykyjová, 1979). For wetland plants, the concentration factors (internal concentration of an element divided by external) may need to be related to the soil water concentrations, which are often not known, rather than those of open water. However, it should be emphasised that the predominant influence on the contents of major elements is the elemental composition of the normal organic constituents of plants in the proportions needed for growth. Ranges of internal concentrations are always much less than the ranges for external concentrations (Table 2.5) and site, species and age have relatively little influence. Such influence as species and age do have is related to the typical organic composition of the plants and its changes during their life cycle. For example, the mean values for species that are mostly young leaves, such as *Nasturtium officinale* and *Lemna* spp., are higher than for species which have much stem tissue and retain old leaves, such as *Phragmites australis* and *Carex* spp. (Table 2.4).

The influence of external concentrations on internal concentrations of major elements can be seen in suitable circumstances (e.g. Lawrence & Nixon, 1970; Gossett & Norris, 1971; Dykyjová, 1979), but it is often masked by other effects (e.g. Boyd & Hess, 1970; Boyd & Vickers, 1971; Casey & Downing, 1976) and never shows the full environmental range (Table 2.5). Typically, in nutrient-poor environments, the internal concentrations are lower than the critical concentration required for optimum growth (e.g. Gerloff & Fishbeck, 1973; Robinson & Cumbus, 1977; Fig. 2.3), so growth is poor and the nutrient load in the plant (g m^{-2}) is low. In nutrient-rich environments the critical concentration is exceeded (luxury consumption) and growth and nutrient load are high. Usually luxury-consumption tends to a plateau of high internal concentrations (Fig. 2.4), which is less pronounced for phosphorus because specific phosphorus storage compounds exist.

Minor elements show great variability in content (Table 2.4) and their

Table 2.5. *Comparisons of external and internal concentrations of nutrients for wetland plants*

Element	Plant	Nutrient source	Range of external concentrations (max./min.)	Range of internal concentrations (max./min.)	Reference
N	*Eichhornia*	Pond water	–	2.5	1
	crassipes	Pond water		2.0	2
		Culture water	4.7	1.9	3
	Helophytes	Pond soil	37	2.1	4
	Nasturtium officinale	Culture water	1000	1.5	5
P	*E. crassipes*	Pond water	419	5.7	1
		Pond water	–	2.3	2
		Culture water	12	1.8	3
		Culture water	8	2.4	6
	Helophytes	Pond soil	66	2.2	4
	N. officinale	Culture water	1176	4.9	5
K	*E. crassipes*	Pond water	45	4.2	1
		Pond water	–	1.8	2
	Helophytes	Pond soil	16	3.0	4
	N. officinale	Culture water	8.9	2.4	5
Ca	*E. crassipes*	Pond water	53	3.2	1
	Helophytes	Pond soil	9.7	7.5	4

1. Boyd & Vickers, 1971; 2. Lawrence & Mixon, 1970; 3. Boyd & Scarsbrook, 1975*a*; 4. Dykyjová, 1979; 5. Robinson & Cumbus, 1977; 6. Haller & Sutton, 1973.

concentration factors may be very high (often 500; Hutchinson, 1975). This suggests again that uptake is dynamic rather then passive, although uptake of excessive amounts is probably a byproduct of plant activity rather than a necessary feature of their metabolism.

Organic composition

Reviews of organic composition have been made by Straškraba (1968), Boyd & Scarsbrook (1975*b*), Hutchinson (1975) and Little (1979). They show that aquatic macrophytes overall are not greatly different from terrestrial plants, including roughage crops, but they tend to have higher ash, crude protein and fat contents (Table 2.6). The use of means for much of the comparative data in this table conceals wide variations within

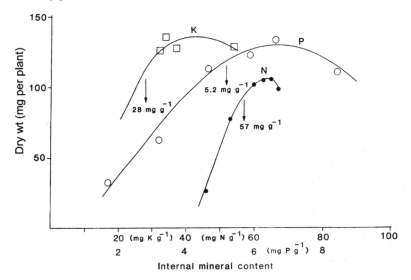

Fig. 2.3. Critical concentrations of nitrogen, phosphorus and potassium for leaves of *Nasturtium officinale* (water-cress) (from Robinson & Cumbus, 1977). Plant growth vs. internal concentrations of: ● nitrogen; ○ phosphorus; □ potassium; → critical internal concentrations for 90% of maximum yield.

species, due to season, age and site, often comparable with that seen in major nutrients in Table 2.4. In general, healthy young shoots, or plant stands of species that have a rapid turnover (e.g. *Lemna* spp., macrophytic algae, *Nasturtium officinale*) have more protein and fat and less fibre than the older shoots of plants with a well-defined growth pattern (e.g. *Zea mais, Phragmites australis*). Boyd (1968*a*) and Tucker and Dubusk (1980) showed that the protein content of the shoots of emergent plants decreased by a factor of 0.5–0.6 between May and August. However, this decrease in protein content may be compensated by the increase in biomass, so that the yield of protein per hectare may remain much the same for several months (Boyd, 1968*a*). The data in de la Cruz and Poe (1975) suggest that the protein content of underground organs is often considerably less than that of the above-ground shoots (0.51–0.99), especially for species with large rhizomes. However, such differences are probably much influenced by season. Fiala (1978*a*) and Burian and Sieghardt (1979) showed that the carbohydrate content of rhizomes was highest in the autumn and winter. The latter authors also report the work of Krejci (1974), showing that the starch was translocated out of the rhizomes in spring and during flowering, and that protein increased when new rhizomes grew after August.

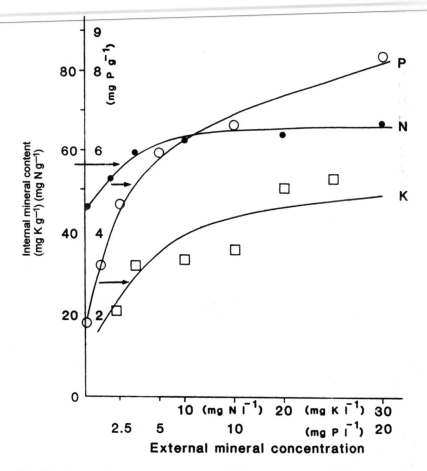

Fig. 2.4. Internal vs. external concentrations of nitrogen, phosphorus and potassium for leaves of *Nasturtium officinale* (water-cress) (from Robinson & Cumbus, 1977). ● nitrogen; ○ phosphorus; □ potassium; → critical internal concentrations for 90% of maximum yield.

More detailed studies of the composition of wetland plants show no great differences from terrestrial plants. Some are relatively rich in vitamins and carotenoids (Little, 1979; Taubaev *et al.*, 1972). The balance of amino acids is quite typical and would give an adequate diet (Table 2.7) although, of the essential amino acids, lysine and methionine are sometimes rather low.

There are a number of widespread and productive wetland species that could be useful as a source of good-quality fodder, but some species have

Table 2.6. *Mean proximate composition of shoots of emergent and floating macrophytes (% oven-dry weight)*

Species	Ash	Crude protein	Crude fat	Cellulose/fibre	Chlorophyll mg (g dry wt)$^{-1}$	Tannin (%)	Energy content (kJ g^{-1})
Eichhornia crassipes	17.0	16.0	3.4	28.1	0.5–3.0[a]	<6	16.0
Jussiaea decurrens	11.7	19.1	3.9	29.5	–	4.1	16.2
Lemna spp.	17.0	18.8	2.9	10.6	10	–	20.8[c]
Nuphar advena	6.5	20.6	6.3	23.9	3.9	6.5	18.0
Glyceria maxima	7.9	13.8[b]	1.2[b]	21.3[b]	6.5[b] (leaves)	–	17.8
Phragmites australis	10	13	3.4	34	0.5–7.5[a] (leaves)	–	17.3
Schoenoplectus lacustris	14	14	1.8	33	1.0[b]	–	16.6
Sagittaria latifolia	10.3	17.1	6.7	27.6	–	2.5	17.2
Typha latifolia	6.9	10.3	3.9	33.2	2.6	2.1	16.7
Mean for 12 submerged angiosperms	18	15	4	28.5	–	–	15.3
Mean for 8 macrophytic algae	18	20	4	22	–	–	(spp.)
Alfalfa hay (*Medicago sativa*)	8.2	14.8	2.0	28.9	–	} <4	18[c]
Corn fodder (*Zea mays*)	5.2	6.8	2.1	21.8	–	}	18[c]
Cow-pea hay (*Vigna sinensis*)	11.3	18.6	2.6	23.3	–	}	17[c]
Mean for 18 roughage crops	8	12	3	29	–	}	18[c]

[a] Range over whole year and a variety of environments; highest value for part of leaf.
[b] Westlake, unpublished data.
[c] Estimated from proximate composition.

(Based primarily on Boyd & Scarsbrook, 1975b and Dykyjová & Přibil, 1975, with additions from Boyd, 1968a; Boyd & Scarsbrook, 1975a; Culley & Epps, 1973; Filben & Hough, 1979; Little, 1979; Rejmánková, 1973b; Sieghardt, 1977; Spector, 1956; Walker & Weygood, 1968.)

Table 2.7. *Amino acid composition of some emergent and floating macrophytes (mg (g dry wt)$^{-1}$)*

Amino acid	Phragmites australis	Schoenoplectus americanus	Sagittaria graminea	19 forages[a]	Eichhornia crassipes	Nuphar advena	Typha latifolia
Aspartic	5.3	16.9	8.8	—	27.3	23.8	13.5
Glutamic	4.7	16.3	8.7	—	24.2	27.4	13.1
Lysine	2.7	4.0	3.2	6.0	12.2	10.6	6.6
Histidine	1.0	2.1	1.3	1.9	4.2	5.4	2.5
Arginine	2.5	3.2	4.5	6.0	1.8	4.0	6.2
Threonine	2.3	4.0	4.3	6.3	9.7	11.7	5.0
Serine	2.4	4.2	4.8	—	9.2	1.7	5.2
Proline	2.2	4.7	4.5	—	9.2	12.1	4.8
Glycine	2.5	3.3	5.4	—	10.6	12.3	6.3
Alanine	3.0	4.3	5.4	—	13.5	12.7	7.5
Valine	2.8	4.9	4.7	5.9	11.6	14.3	nd
Isoleucine	2.7	3.6	3.8	5.0	10.0	11.7	6.2
Leucine	3.7	5.4	7.1	9.5	17.6	22.5	10.5
Half-cystine	t	0.9	nd	Cystine	0.6	0.4	5.7
Methionine	0.9	1.3	1.6	1.9	3.6	3.2	1.6
Tyrosine	1.6	1.9	2.8	5.0	7.6	9.5	3.9
Phenylalanine	2.5	4.0	4.3	6.1	10.6	13.0	6.0
Protein	47	100	100		195	216	105

[a] From Altschul, 1958, assuming a mean protein content of 12% dry wt (see Table 2.6) and that protein is 6.25 N.
Based on Boyd & Scarsbrook, 1975b and de la Cruz & Poe, 1975.

too much mucilage, tannin or ash or an undesirable ionic balance in the ash (Boyd, 1968*b*; Boyd & Goodyear, 1971; Little, 1979; see also Chapter 8). As noted above, a plant with a favourable dry matter composition may not be usable as a food, stored or even cheaply transported until large quantities of water have been removed. Wetland fodder plants are a traditional and important resource in dry regions where the terrestrial vegetation is mostly sparse, sclerophyllous and of low nutritive value (e.g. Taubaev *et al.*, 1972 and Abdullaev, 1972 in Central Asia; author's observations near Lake Skadar, Yugoslavia). Most of such studies has been concentrated on plants like *Eichhornia crassipes* and *Lemna minor* which can be relatively easily harvested and have a high protein content (Culley *et al.*, 1983). The cellulose or fibre content of plants like *Phragmites australis* and *Cyperus papyrus* is sometimes important for the manufacture of paper and boards (see Chapter 8).

Energy content

As in other respects, wetland plants are not greatly different from terrestrial plants and, when expressed in terms of ash-free dry weight, usually contain about 20 kJ (g ash-free dry wt)$^{-1}$. However, as with other components, there are differences between different plant parts, different aged material, species and sites, generally related to the proportions of young growing material and older supporting and storage material. Some examples are given in Table 2.6 and an extensive review has been published by Dykyjová and Přibil (1975), which shows a range of 16.7–21.5 kJ for whole shoots and underground parts (a few very improbable values less than 16 have been omitted). Lipids have a high calorific value (~ 40), cellulose, and other poly-, di- and mono-saccharids have relatively low values (15–18) and materials such as protein and lignin are inter-mediate (~ 25).

It is essential to take account of these differences and to make determinations of the actual components, ash content and energy contents when studying the conversion of solar energy to plant material and the conversion of plant material to secondary production.

Production processes

Production by plants is the end result of a complex system of biophysical and biochemical processes. Clearly, photosynthesis is the most important of these, but net production, chemical composition, growth, seasonal variations, competition and species composition all involve many other interacting processes including aerobic and anaerobic respiration, nutrient uptake, gas transfers, nitrogen fixation and hormone balance. Many of these processes are similar in terrestrial plants where they are well known. This section will concentrate on aspects that are peculiar or particularly relevant to the study of wetland plants. Detailed knowledge of these processes enables models of production and growth to be developed, which relate production to irradiance and other external factors. At present, only irradiance and photosynthesis models can be attempted in detail, but even these give indirect methods of estimating productivity and an insight into the initial stages of the growth of plants.

Structure and function of the above-ground biomass, particularly the assimilating organs

The structure of the stand, i.e. the spatial distribution of the plant organs, affects the spatial distribution of irradiance and thermal energy and thus the interception of irradiance and the temperature regime of the plant. This leads to important causal relationships between stand structure and production. Different patterns in the distribution of plant organs create differing conditions in the stand, which result in differing efficiencies of the production processes. There are, of course, many other aspects of stand structure and functioning which will not be discussed in detail here, as, for example, the effects of translocation of assimilates on the structure, and the interrelations between ageing of a stand and its morphology.

Horizontal structure

This may be expressed in units of biomass (standing crop) or density (number of shoots). The horizontal structure should be determined when precise estimate of stand production over a large area is needed because wetland plant communities show high variation in the horizontal distribution of their density and biomass, even in almost pure monospecific stands. This is caused by distinct clones, by local variations of habitat conditions such as water level, physical properties, changes in bottom substrate, etc. and by growth patterns. In particular zonation may be found in most aquatic communities, especially those of the littoral regions. The zonation refers not only to the species composition of a stand but also to its production. A common feature of littoral stands appears to be gradients of decreasing biomass and production along transects from the

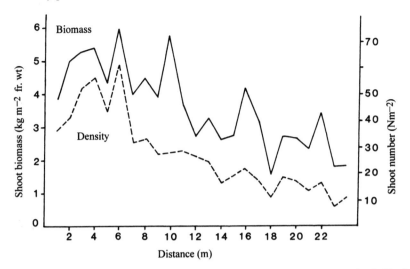

Fig. 2.5. Biomass (aerial shoots) and density gradients in a stand of *Typha angustifolia* along a transect from shore towards open water (Fishpond littoral; Ondok, 1971*b*).

shore toward the open water (see, e.g. Kvĕt & Ondok, 1973). Figure 2.5 illustrates such density and biomass gradients in stands of *Typha angustifolia*.

In stands other than littoral (e.g. in wet meadows, marshes and swamps) the study of horizontal structure is more concerned with patterns of biomass or density in relation to clustering or with the 'gaps' in the stand. Some theoretical considerations, methods and results for several stands of emergent macrophytes are given by Ondok (1971*b*) and Table 2.8 summarises the dimensions of the clusters for several species. Similar clusters were described by Thompson *et al.* (1979) in *Cyperus papyrus* swamps. Ondok found that cluster size does not change if it is defined by biomass rather than by density. More dense stands, with higher productivity, show a more conspicuous clustering. Such clustering arises from the morphogenetic behaviour of the plants in response to competition for space in the air and soil, especially through the distribution and frequency of tillering, and the suppression or promotion of bud emergence and the extension of rhizomes.

Clustering related to habitat factors also occurs, but is much larger in scale and more difficult to study by quadrat techniques. Aerial photography or photographs using fish-eye cameras may be more suitable.

Table 2.8. *The ranges of cluster sizes found in some macrophyte stands* (*Ondok, 1971* b)

Stand	Cluster size (cm × cm)
Acorus calamus	10 × 10 – 80 × 80
Scirpus maritimus	10 × 10 – 40 × 40
Glyceria maxima	10 × 20 – 40 × 80
Phragmites australis	20 × 40 – 40 × 80
Scirpus lacustris	10 × 10 – 80 × 80
Sparganium erectum	80 × 80
Typha angustifolia	10 × 20 – 80 × 80
Typha latifolia	40 × 40 – 160 × 160

Vertical structure

This is usually determined by the stratified clip technique initiated by Monsi and Saeki (1953). The amount of individual plant parts, e.g. weight of living and dead stems, leaves, flowers, etc. is determined for individual layers of defined height, depending on total height of the stand. The vertical structure enables us to follow how the assimilates are distributed above ground during the growing season. Much work has been devoted to establishing the vertical distribution of the assimilatory apparatus (the canopy).

The vertical structure is often summarised in terms of leaf area per unit of ground area, the leaf area index (LAI). Some methodological aspects of the measurement of the LAI of emergent macrophytes are given in Ondok (1968). LAI has been measured for various stands and localities by several authors (some examples are given in Table 2.9).

Generally only the leaf surface area is measured but in some cases surfaces of other plant parts (e.g. stems, sheaths, bracts, flowers) are also involved. The vertical distribution of leaf area is correlated with the vertical attenuation of irradiance penetrating the stand, which may be approximated, according to Monsi and Saeki (1953) by a form of the Lambert–Beer Law:

$$I_z = I_o e^{-KL_z} \tag{8}$$

where I_z is irradiance (W m^{-2}) at horizontal level z(m), L_z is cumulative leaf area index (m^2 m^{-2}) above this level and K is the vertical attenuation coefficient of foliage. The vertical structure of some emergent macrophytes has been studied by Dykyjová (1973*a*) and Dykyjová *et al.* (1970), who compare individual stands from the standpoint of light penetration. Similar results for reedbed stands in fishponds of the South Bohemia region are given in Květ (1971).

Vertical structure influences characteristically the light penetration through stands of the different macrophytes. Some species, mainly those whose stems are growing from the stem base (e.g. *Typha angustifolia, Typha latifolia, Sparganium erectum* and *Acorus calamus*), have most assimilatory surface in low layers. In these species the youngest leaf parts are found in the low layers. Also *Schoenoplectus lacustris* belongs to this type, although the stem surface is the main assimilatory surface. Other species have the majority of their canopy concentrated in higher layers, because their leaves grow in vertical succession on the stem. Examples are *Phragmites australis, Scirpus maritimus* and *Glyceria maxima*. Figure 2.6 illustrates the differences in light penetration for some macrophyte species. The heights within the stand are expressed relative to total stand height to facilitate the comparison. It is evident that the steepest gradients of attenuation are found in *P. australis* and *G. maxima*, which have the majority of their canopy in high layers.

However, the vertical distribution of the canopy is not the only factor determining attenuation in the stand. The term, vertical structure, may be replaced by 'stand architecture' or 'stand geometry' in which leaf inclination and orientation are involved. Theoretical and methodological aspects of the determination of stand architecture have been elaborated by several authors (for review, see Anderson, 1971 and for helophytes, see Ondok, 1977).

The gradient of vertical attenuation in the stand is correlated with the projection of leaf area across the direction of the sun's rays. Leaves arranged horizontally intercept a higher proportion of the insolation, but the higher irradiances experienced by their cells may saturate photosynthesis and lead to low efficiencies, while the leaves also cast more shade on the leaves underneath. For leaves vertically displayed the reverse is true. De Wit (1965) distinguished between planophile (a horizontal arrangement of leaves prevails) and erectophile canopies (a vertical arrangement of leaves prevails). Common-sense suggests that light attenuation is lower for erectophile leaves, which has been confirmed by results of measurements of light interception by different macrophytes. *P. australis* and *G. maxima* stands have higher vertical attenuation than many other macrophyte species because their leaves are, on average, more nearly horizontal. Therefore, the irradiance penetrates more deeply in stands of plants like

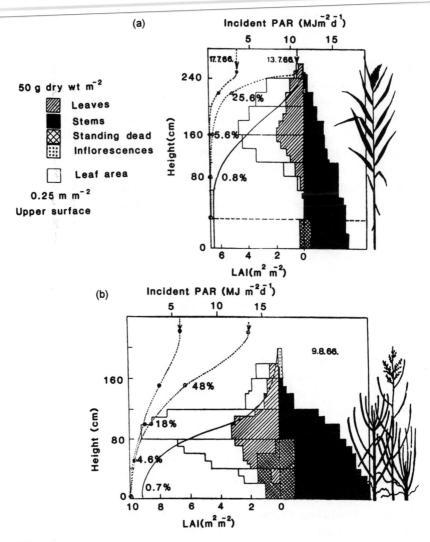

Fig. 2.6. Transmission of irradiance through mature stands of helophytes.
(a) Littoral stand of *Phragmites australis*; partly erectophile foliage high on stem;
(b) Limosal stand of *Glyceria maxima*; erectophile foliage, many leaves and young
shoots near water; (c) Stand of *Schoenoplectus lacustris*: erect stems, no leaves;
(d) Limosal stand of *Typha latifolia*; erectophile foliage, originating from base
(based on Dykyjová, 1971a). Irradiance (PAR); ○ sunny; ● dull; with per cent
incident against sunny curves. – – – water level; —— cumulative leaf area index m²
leaf (m ground area)$^{-2}$. Blocks show size of biomass and leaf area in each stratum.

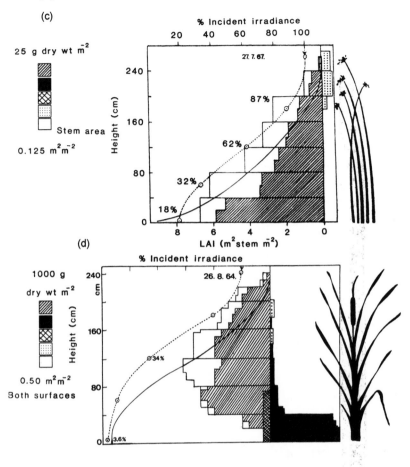

Fig. 2.6. (*cont*).

Typha spp. and *Acorus calamus*, which have nearly vertical leaves. The leaf inclination does not usually remain the same during the growing season. As an example, in *P. australis* the leaves are erectophile at the beginning of the season and then become successively more planophile (see Fig. 2.7).

The measurement of stand architecture is a troublesome and time consuming work and therefore few data on leaf arrangement in macrophyte stands are available. Another difficulty is that the leaves of many species are curved (e.g. in *T. angustifolia* and *latifolia*) so that no

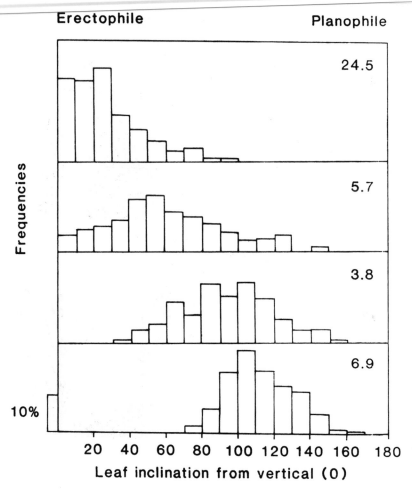

Fig. 2.7. Seasonal change in leaf inclination of *Phragmites australis* (Ondok, 1978*a*).

assessment of inclination is valid for the whole leaf. Ondok (1973*c*) has measured the distribution of both orientation and inclination in stands of *P australis* and Květ *et al.* (1967) have measured leaf inclination in stands of *T. angustifolia* and *latifolia*. The results on stand architecture in *P. australis* show that neither the inclinations nor orientations of the leaves were distributed uniformly. The frequencies had maxima which changed their position during the growing season. For orientation, an anisotrophy has been observed which depends on the prevailing direction of wind.

Table 2.9. *Light interception characteristics of some wetland plants*

Species	Leaf area index ($m^2\,m^{-2}$)	Transmission	Reflection % incident	Attenuation
Acorus calamus	0.9–14.8[a]	2.7	15.1	82.1
Glyceria maxima	6.9–9.3	4.2	12.5	83.3
Eichhornia crassipes	5.8–7.8	–	–	–
Nasturtium officinale	1.8–5.2	–	–	–
Phragmites australis	3–11.5	2.4	10.8	86.6
Schoenoplectus lacustris	7.5–10.2[b]	–	–	–
Sparganium erectum	5.2[a] (– 14.5)	3.3	10.8	85.9
Typha latifolia	5–22.3[a]	2.1	10.3	87.6

[a] Both/all surfaces.
[b] Surface area of stems.
( ) Value not corresponding to further columns.
Květ *et al.*, 1969; Dykyjová & Květ, 1970; Knipling *et al.*, 1970; Dykyjová, 1973*a*; Dykyjová & Ondok, 1973; Ondok, 1975, 1977, 1978*a*; Castellano, 1977.

Interception of irradiance by the canopy

For determining the radiation regime in a stand with given architecture three components of total irradiance must be known: direct sun irradiance, diffuse sky irradiance, and scattered irradiance within the stand. The first two have characteristic daily and seasonal changes and depend mainly on atmospheric conditions. The third depends on the two previous components and on the optical properties of the leaves. The relatively easy problem is to establish the daily and seasonal course of both direct and diffuse sky irradiance for clear days (e.g. Anderson, 1971; Monteith, 1973). The influence of atmospheric conditions is a more sophisticated problem. It may be solved using a stochastic model of the changes in direct and diffuse sky irradiance during their daily and seasonal course (i.e. probable frequencies of a range of conditions). This kind of solution is found in Ondok (1975, 1977). If the components of direct and diffuse sky irradiance have been determined, the third component of scattered irradiance may be evaluated by means of reflection and transmission ratios. Values for *P. australis* leaves are given in Table 2.9, which includes values of transmission, reflection and vertical attenuation of some other macrophyte species. A more direct approach to the evaluation of stand structure has been made possible by using a hemispherical camera (Ondok, 1984).

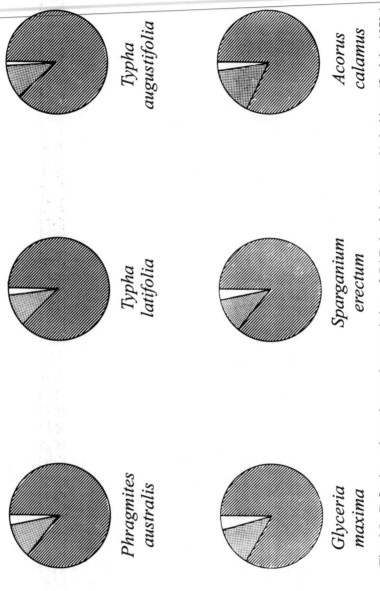

Fig. 2.8. Reflection, absorption and transmission of PAR by helophytes. % incident (Ondok, 1978a). ▨ absorption; ▨ reflection; ▢ transmission.

Table 2.10. *Daily sums of PAR intercepted by foliage* (I_F), *by water* (I_W) *and reflected into the atmosphere* (I_R) *in erectophile and planophile stands (see Table 2.11)*

Date	Planophile (*Phragmites australis*)			Erectophile (*Typha angustifolia*)		
	(% total incident PAR)					
	I_F	I_W	I_R	I_F	I_W	I_R
5.6	76.0	19.8	4.2	51.7	44.4	3.9
22.6	79.4	15.5	5.1	54.5	40.9	4.5
5.7	87.0	8.7	4.3	64.8	31.0	4.1
7.8	92.0	3.9	4.1	50.3	45.1	4.5

Ondok (1977) and unpublished data.

Knowing these three fluxes we may express the radiation regime as three fractions of incoming radiation: (i) radiation intercepted by foliage (or other plant parts), (ii) radiation intercepted by the water, (iii) radiation back-reflected by the stand and water into the atmosphere (albedo). The relative amounts differ in various macrophyte stands (see Fig. 2.8) and have also seasonal courses corresponding with increments of LAI. Table 2.10 compares the proportions of irradiance intercepted by foliage (I_F) by water (I_W) and reflected (I_R) for stands of *Phragmites australis* and *Typha angustifolia*. Both are littoral stands, *Phragmites* having an average density, and *Typha* a low density, typical of shallow fishponds.

The seasonal courses of the radiation regimes within *Phragmites* and *Glyceria maxima* stands are given in Figure 2.9. Very striking seasonal differences may be seen in the amounts of irradiance intercepted by foliage and at water level. Albedo values do not differ substantially and remain at approximately the same level (3–5%) over long periods. Greater differences (2–7%) may be found in the daily time-course, which are produced by the dependence of reflection on the angle of the sun's elevation; the highest values of albedo corresponding with the lowest sun elevation.

Radiation regime and photosynthesis

To use data on radiation regime for the evaluation of stand photosynthesis, three things must be known: the amount of sunlit foliage area

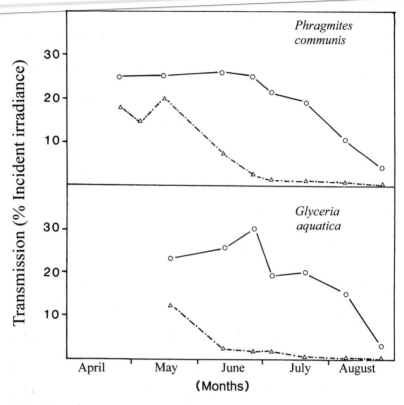

Fig. 2.9. Seasonal changes in irradiance reaching 0.5 m under water surface in open water and plant stands. —○— open water; – –△– – plant stand (Fishpond littoral; Ondok, 1977).

(SLI), the amount of shaded area (SDI) and the distribution of irradiance on the sunlit area of leaf surfaces. These depend on both the stand's architecture and the sun's position. Therefore, they vary within a day and with the changes in stand architecture. The method of determination of SLI, SDI and of irradiance distributions is treated in Ondok (1973*b*) and there applied to a stand of *Phragmites australis*. In addition, the paper determines SLI and SDI separately for the upper and lower sides of the leaf surface, which need not necessarily be involved in a photosynthetic model.

In erectophile foliage SLI is higher than in planophile foliage because the radiation penetrates more deeply into the stand. Uniformly distributed foliage has SLI values between those of erectophile and planophile foliage.

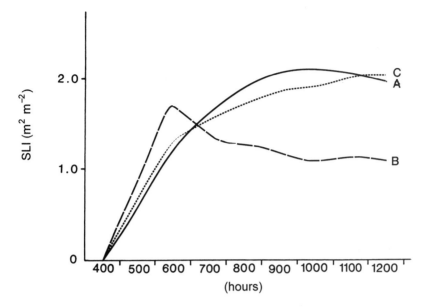

Fig. 2.10. Changes in sunlit foliage area (SLI) with sunlight (hourly changes) and leaf orientation species (characteristics, and seasonal changes). –A– erectophile; – –B– – planophile; ··C·· uniform distribution of leaf orientation (Fishpond littoral; Ondok, 1977).

This is illustrated in Figure 2.10 where the dependence on sun elevation is also given. Modelling the radiation regime gives evidence of the influence of leaf orientation on SLI. A prevailing south orientation of leaves is most favourable for SLI. The distribution of irradiance depends mainly on leaf inclination. In erectophile foliage the distribution of irradiance on sunlit area surface has almost the same shape throughout the whole day. The planophile leaves show a striking shift of maximum frequencies from higher values of irradiance at high sun elevations toward lower values of irradiance at low sun elevations. The erectophile and planophile foliage were defined by measured frequencies of leaf inclinations. This discussion makes it clear that, for the best photosynthetic model, the determination of input data must begin with the determination of leaf geometry. The photosynthesis is then evaluated separately for leaf area of foliage exposed to the direct and diffuse radiation components (SLI) and for foliage exposed only to diffuse radiation component (SDI). However simpler methods may sometimes give adequate answers.

Photosynthesis and respiration

Experimental studies have been made on individual organs in leaf chambers (e.g. Burian, 1973; Gloser, 1976, 1977*b*) and on entire shoots, or groups of shoots in larger chambers (e.g. Walker & Waygood, 1968; Burian, 1969; Gloser, 1977*a*; Sale, 1974; Sale *et al.*, 1985). The large chambers often expose the shoots to unnatural temperatures, humidities and velocity distributions, which are difficult and expensive to control. To obtain whole shoot or stand photosynthesis and respiration from leaf measurements, models taking account of at least vertical differences in metabolic capacity and irradiance must be used (Ondok & Gloser, 1978). Underground respiration is not included.

General morphology and biochemistry

There is no evidence that emergent aquatic plants as a group have any peculiar metabolic features. For a brief summary of the photosynthetic mechanisms in higher plants in general, see Troughton (1975). Morphologically the majority of populations are monocotyledonous, and it is noteworthy that an unusually high proportion of populations do not have leaves as their principal photosynthetic organs, e.g. many Cyperaceae and Juncaceae (stems), *Cyperus papyrus* (stems, bracteoles, rays). Some are C4-plants with the additional C4-dicarboxylic acid cycle (e.g. *Cyperus* spp., *Spartina* spp.; Black, 1971; Jones & Milburn, 1978; Jones, 1988). These C4-plants also have the typical bundle sheath cells, high temperature optima, low carbon dioxide compensation values and low photorespiration. Presumably they also have the low water requirements typical of C4-species, and this may be relevant to their ecology despite the apparent abundance of water (cf. pp. 133–4).

Most species are C3-plants with only the reductive pentose phosphate cycle. Some of these have unusually high rates of net photosynthesis which suggests that they may have some special mechanisms for controlling photorespiration (e.g. *Typha latifolia*, McNaughton & Fullem, 1970; *Eichhornia crassipes*, Patterson & Duke, 1979).

Again, leaf aerobic respiration seems normal (e.g. Gloser, 1976), but many species have particular abilities to carry out anaerobic respiration in roots and rhizomes under the anoxic conditions often encountered by these organs (e.g. Crawford, 1978). However, in practice, this potential is rarely used because the aerenchyma present in wetland plants facilitates

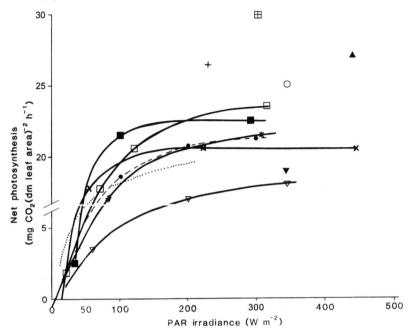

Fig. 2.11. The relationship between irradiance and the net photosynthesis of leaves. (Smoothed curves, generally 20–25 °C, for the most efficient leaves, June–August, assuming PAR 0.48 total sunlight, $\sim$4 W m^{-2} per klux, $\sim$0.2 W m^{-2} per μE m^{-2} s^{-1} and 1.45 dm^2 per g dry wt, where needed.) □ *Glyceria maxima*; $--\bullet--$ *Phalaris arundinacea* (Gloser, 1976); ○ *P. arundinacea* (Chen *et al.*, 1970); × *Phragmites australis* (Burian, 1973); * *P. australis* (Gloser, 1977*b*); + *P. australis* (Pearcey *et al.*, 1974); ▽ *Eichhornia crassipes* (30 °C, Knipling *et al.*, 1970); ▲ *E. crassipes* (31 °C, Patterson & Duke, 1979); ▼ *E. crassipes* (Chen *et al.*, 1970); ⊞ *Typha latifolia*, leaf area of both surfaces used (McNaughton & Fullem, 1970); ■ *Cyperus papyrus* (32 °C, Jones & Milburn, 1978); $\cdots$ *Nuphar japonicum* (Ikusima, 1970).

the supply of oxygen to the roots and rhizomes (Armstrong, 1979 and see pp. 134–7).

Photosynthesis and irradiance

The general characteristics of the responses of the net photosynthesis of individual leaves of emergent plants to irradiance (Fig. 2.11) are a maximum rate of about 20–30 mg CO_2 (dm leaf area)$^{-2}$ h^{-1} at about 20 °C and a light saturation level* around 80–110 W (PAR) m^{-2}

---

* Defined as I_K, the intersection of the initial slope and the final plateau.

(~25 klux), but there is often no clear or complete saturation plateau. Individual results may show considerable differences, for example, the low unit leaf rate of $18\,mg\,CO_2\,dm^{-2}\,h^{-1}$ and the high rate of 22 for *Eichhornia crassipes* in two separate studies (Fig. 2.11). Differences of this sort can arise from pre-treatment of the plants, such as exposure to different irradiance levels (Patterson & Duke, 1979), and probably in many other ways, and should not be given too much emphasis. The basis used for rates of photosynthesis, whether leaf surface area, dry weight, fresh weight, or chlorophyll, can also affect comparisons. Thus *Typha latifolia* appeared to have exceptionally high rates of photosynthesis when expressed in terms of a single leaf surface (McNaughton & Fullem, 1970), but the difference is not so great when the rates are expressed in terms of the area of both leaf surfaces, which is more appropriate for these thick nearly vertical leaves (Dykyjová & Ondok, 1973). Furthermore, in terms of dry weight of leaf (McNaughton, 1973, 1974*b*) *T. latifolia* comes within the range of 3 to $9\,mg\,C\,(g\,dry\,wt)^{-1}\,h^{-1}$ typical of nearly all emergent species. *Eichhornia crassipes* is exceptional on this basis, with a high photosynthetic capacity that reaches $21\,mg\,C\,(g\,dry\,wt)^{-1}\,h^{-1}$, yet is within the normal range of $1\text{–}2.5\,mg\,C\,(mg\,chl.)^{-1}\,h^{-1}$ (Westlake, 1975*a*; Patterson & Duke, 1979) relative to chlorophyll.

Cyperus papyrus is reported to have a rather low unit leaf rate and light saturation point compared with other C4-plants (Fig. 2.11; Jones & Milburn, 1978). It also appears to have a light compensation point over $24\,W\,m^{-2}$, which implies an exceptionally high respiration rate. However, these features may be influenced by the unusual photosynthetic organs, the basis of the comparison (per dm^2) and some uncertainty about the PAR levels used.

Plants with floating leaves tend to have somewhat low rates, between 14 and $25\,mg\,CO_2\,dm^{-2}\,h^{-1}$ (Fig. 2.11; and other results in Ikusima, 1970).

There is little evidence of direct inhibition of photosynthesis by excessive irradiance but high leaf temperatures associated with high irradiance often cause a depression of net photosynthesis around and after noon. This is sometimes attributed to inadequate control of cuvette temperatures or humidities but in other cases it is clearly related to the effect of leaf temperature on light-saturated net photosynthesis (see below) or, in stands, to the high respiration in shaded leaves (Pearcy *et al.*, 1974; Gloser, 1977*a*). Sale *et al.* (1985) found slightly lower rates of photosynthesis by stands of *Salvinia molesta* and *E. crassipes* after noon, even when temperature was well controlled.

Metabolism and temperature

At low irradiances and at high temperatures, net photosynthesis tends to fall with increasing temperature (Fig. 2.12), and much of this effect can initially be attributed to the greater influence of temperature on dark respiration ($Q_{10} \sim 2.1$) than on photosynthesis ($Q_{10} \sim 1.2$), which can be shown by correcting for the dark respiration (Fig. 2.12; cf. McNaughton, 1973). The effect of temperature on photorespiration probably accounts for more.

At higher temperatures inhibition of photosynthesis develops (Fig. 2.14). At light saturation, temperate zone emergent C3-plants have temperature optima for photosynthesis of between 15 and 26 °C (Fig. 2.13). Their compensation points for net photosynthesis rise from about 2 W m^{-2} at 5–10 °C to around 12 W m^{-2} at 30 °C. Ecotypes from different climates show different temperature responses. *Typha latifolia* from a Mediterranean climate has an optimum 3–5 °C higher than plants from a boreal climate (McNaughton, 1973), and *Phragmites australis* from a continental desert climate has a 30 °C optimum (Pearcy *et al.*, 1974). Leaf temperatures in the latter example were up to 8 °C below air

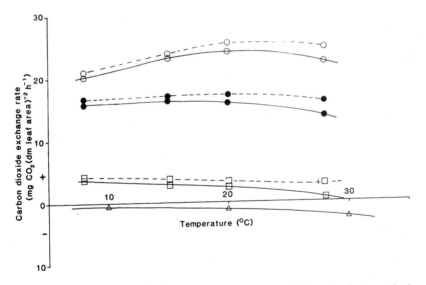

Fig. 2.12. The relationship between temperature, and the net photosynthetic capacity and dark respiration of leaves of *Glyceria maxima* (Gloser, 1976). ——— Light saturated net carbon dioxide exchange rate; – – – corrected for dark respiration ('gross' photosynthesis). ○ 315 W m^{-2}; ● 70 W m^{-2}; □ 10 W m^{-2}; △ 0 W m^{-2} (PAR irradiance).

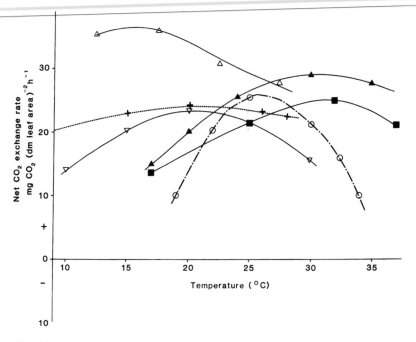

Fig. 2.13. The relationship between temperature and the net photosynthetic capacity of helophyte leaves. Solid symbols, hot climates; open symbols, temperate climates. ·· + ·· *Glyceria maxima*, Czechoslovakia (Gloser, 1976); —▽— *Phragmites australis*, Czechoslovakia (Gloser, 1977*b*); —△— *P. australis*, Austria (Burian, 1973); —▲— *P. australis*, Death Valley, USA (Pearcey *et al.*, 1974); ·—·○·—· *Typha latifolia*, Quebec (McNaughton, 1973); – – –■– – – *Cyperus papyrus*, Uganda (Jones & Milburn, 1978).

temperatures, a greater difference than that found for several other species in the same habitat. *Salvinia molesta, Lemnaceae*, and presumably other species in close contact with the water, often have leaf temperatures above air temperatures (Rejmanková, 1979; Hejný *et al.*, 1981; Sale *et al.*, 1985). The emergent C4-plants have a temperature optimum over 30 °C (e.g. *Cyperus papyrus*, 32 °C, Jones & Milburn, 1978).

Further examples can be found in Burian (1973) and Gloser (1977*a*), and the former gives a series of diagrams of the interactions of irradiance, temperature and photosynthesis (e.g. Fig. 2.14) during the growing season for *P. australis*.

Lethal damage to *P. australis* leaves in Austria is caused beyond about −3 °C and +54 °C, although there are seasonal differences of several degrees in these values. In particular, the lower limit ranges between +2 °C in May–June and −9 °C in November (Zax, 1973).

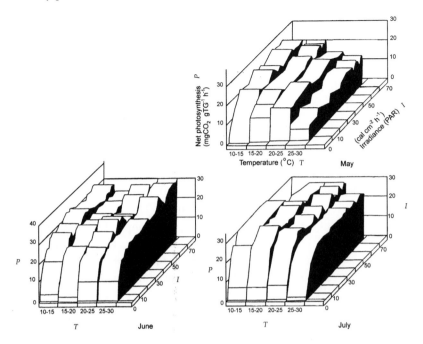

Fig. 2.14. The relationship between irradiance, temperature and net photosynthetic capacity of leaves of *Phragmites australis* during the growing season (Burian, 1973). (This figure is reproduced by permission of Dr K. Burian and the publishers, Springer Verlag.)

Rhizomes can grow even just above 0 °C, but buds do not emerge in Britain until soil temperatures have exceeded about 7 °C for a few weeks (Haslam, 1975). Clones differ in their responses. In December exposed buds can tolerate several days at −9 °C, but in May −2 °C is lethal and even 0 °C may seriously affect further development. Emerged shoots are killed by frost in the autumn. Surprisingly, the leaves of the subtropical species *Eichhornia crassipes* are not much more sensitive, being damaged below +0.5 °C and killed below −3 °C (Penfound & Earle, 1948). However, damage to the leaves leads to the rhizome floating higher and, after 2 days at −5 °C, the entire plant is killed.

Photosynthesis and carbon dioxide

Few species have been studied, but there is the usual distinction between the C3-species, such as *Eichhornia crassipes, Glyceria maxima, Phalaris arundinacea* and *Phragmites australis*, with a carbon dioxide compensation point of 40–60 ppm (Chen *et al.*, 1970; Soekisman, quoted by Gopal & Sharma, 1981; Gloser, 1978); and the C4-species, such as *Cyperus papyrus* (Jones & Milburn, 1978) and *Spartina* spp., with a compensation point of less than 10 ppm CO_2.

Although net photosynthesis is more than doubled by an increase in atmospheric carbon dioxide concentration from 200 to 400 µg l^{-1}, changes within the canopy during the day are about 20 µg l^{-1} (Gloser, 1978), so ecological effects are unlikely. However, some plants, such as *E. crassipes*, may be able to utilise dissolved inorganic carbon sources through their roots (Ultsch & Anthony, 1973) and such sources are likely to show large changes diurnally and seasonally. These sources are likely to be less important for taller plants because of the longer diffusion pathway.

Analysis of carbon dioxide diffusion has shown that the mesophyll resistance is two to three times the stomatal resistance, which in turn is a little higher than the boundary-layer resistance (Gloser, 1978).

Respiration

Specialised aspects, such as photorespiration and anaerobic respiration, are discussed elsewhere. Rates of dark respiration at the optimum temperature for net photosynthesis are usually between 1 and 5 mg CO_2 $dm^{-2} h^{-1}$; 4 to 25% of the optimum net photosynthesis (see references for Fig. 2.11). In terms of dry weight the range is rather less, 3.4–7.3 mg CO_2 $(g\ dry\ wt)^{-1} h^{-1}$. The highest rates are found in the apical, most actively growing leaf, where respiration may be over 20% of net photosynthesis (Fig. 2.15). The lowest rates are found in old leaves but respiration may increase in the oldest leaf (Gloser, 1977*b*).

Over the range of temperatures studied (10–30 °C) the Q_{10} of dark respiration in between 2.0 and 2.2, showing no signs of the inhibition at high or low temperatures that must ultimately occur. The effects of oxygen on dark respiration of emergent plants have not been studied. However, McNaughton (1973) found that net photosynthesis increased in an atmosphere devoid of oxygen, implying that dark and photorespiration were suppressed.

Water relations

The water relations of wetlands are discussed in detail in Chapter 7 and only a few important physiological points need to be stressed here.

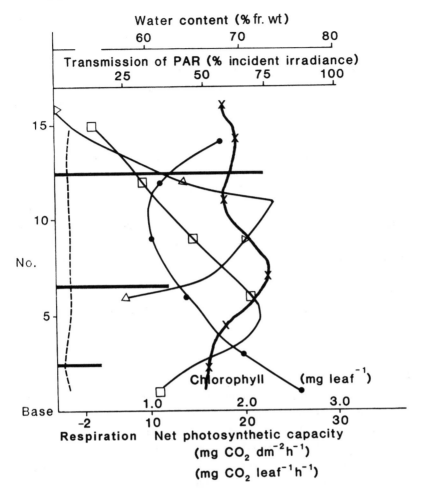

Fig. 2.15. Changes in the physiology of leaves of *Phragmites australis* with age and vertical position (July stands). —●— Water content as percent fresh weight (Rychnovská, 1978); —△— Total chlorophyll content, mg per leaf (Walker & Waygood, 1968); —□— Net photosynthetic capacity per leaf; – –×– – Net photosynthetic capacity per dm² leaf surface; – – – – Dark respiration per dm² leaf surface (Gloser, 1977*b*); ■■■ Percentage transmission of irradiance (PAR) in July (Dykyjová *et al.*, 1970).

Although wetland plants might be assumed never to be short of water, water stress may occur because all the water in the shoots of many species is replaced about three or more times a day (Rychnovská, 1978). The supply of this water may depend on healthy roots; detached shoots of

Phragmites australis, stood in water, soon wilt (Rychnovská, 1973). Appreciable water saturation deficits of between 15 and 22% may be found in *P. australis* shoots during the day and even the leaves may reach 17% (Rychnovská, 1978). However, Pearcy *et al.* (1974) thought the xylem sap pressure of −10 to 17 bar and high leaf conductances (0.5 cm s⁻¹), found in *P. australis* growing at 30–45 °C, were evidence of low stress.

Gloser (1977a) showed that the net photosynthetic capacity of leaves of *Glyceria maxima* and *Phalaris arundinacea* fell to near 50% of its optimum value as soil water potential fell below −5 bar and air humidity decreased to a leaf–air vapour pressure difference of 12 mbar, which are values which occur in wet meadows. The changes in photosynthesis closely parallel changes in diffusion resistance (as shown by porometric values of leaves). Prolonged exposure to dry conditions had no permanent influence on the unit leaf rate under moist conditions, but increased the stomatal resistance and decreased the mesophyll resistance.

Transpiration of *T. latifolia* has been shown to increase linearly with temperature, rising by a factor of over 3 between 20 and 40 °C (McNaughton, 1973).

Aeration

The influence of soil redox potentials and oxygen supply on the species and mobility of nutrients, the concentrations of toxins, the cycling of nutrients in the soil and the root metabolism means that this is an important factor for the growth of wetland plants. Most wetland species have extensive lacunae and aerenchyma throughout their leaves, stems, rhizomes and roots which greatly reduce their resistance to gas transfer (Fig. 2.16). The total gas space may reach 60% of their volume.

There has been much controversy about the significance of these gas spaces, the interactions between plants and sediments and the relative importance of various mechanisms for coping with anoxic conditions, but the main conclusions now seem to be clear in the very comprehensive review by Armstrong (1979) and the recent survey of current research (Armstrong, 1996). In addition to simple diffusion, which is relatively unimportant for large plants, a variety of different physical mechanisms, depending on the plant and its environmental conditions, enable atmospheric or photosynthetic oxygen to be transported from the aerial shoots, through the internal gas space system, to the rhizome and roots, where it can be utilised for respiration or it may diffuse into the soil. There it forms

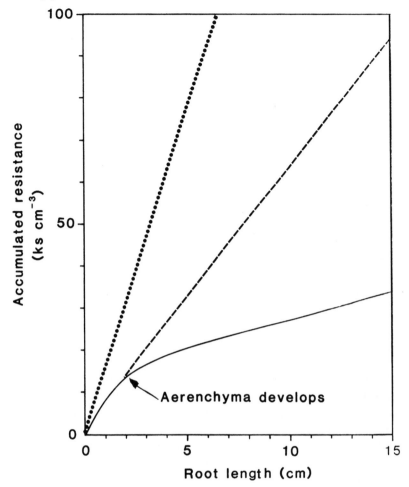

Fig. 2.16. Total gas space resistance (ks = kiloseconds) as a function of root length (from Armstrong, 1979). —— *Oryza sativa* (wetland rice), non-tortuous pores; apical porosity 6.5%; – – – Plants without aerenchyma, straight pores, porosity 6.5%; · · · Plants without aerenchyma, tortuous pores, porosity 6.5%.

an oxidised zone around the roots, which is often easily visible. The extent and location of this zone depend on the gas flow, internal air space resistances and wall permeabilities, and increase with decreasing length and diameter of the roots (Fig. 2.16). As well as facilitating aerobic processes in the soil, this zone protects the plants from anaerobic toxins such as ethylene, sulphide and reduced metals.

For *Phragmites australis*, both humidity- and venturi-induced convections are much more important than diffusion. Humidity generated flows develop from the pressure created within a saturated gas phase separated by a porous partition (such as cells or stomata with intercellular spaces) from the external drier atmosphere. After passing down into the rhizomes, the pressure is vented through broken culms, especially those of previous years. Venturi flows occur when wind blowing across the tops of old culms broken above the water creates a suction pressure which draws gas through the rhizomes from the humidity-generated pressure or from sheltered culms. The vented gas is oxygen depleted and typically carbon dioxide and methane enriched. To some extent in *Phragmites*, and in other helophytes, there can be living inflow and outflow shoots and leaves acting in a similar manner.

In floating-leaved plants, and in some wetland trees, thermally induced pressure differences are more important, though probably not the sole mechanism. In *Nuphar lutea* this thermo-osmosis occurs in young leaves where porous partitions between the palisade parenchyma and the aerenchyma separate warmer air in the aerenchyma from cooler ambient air. During the day the temperature difference arises by absorption of solar radiation, during the night the air cools faster than the water. The gas flows to the rhizomes and is vented through older leaves which are more porous and cannot support thermo-osmosis. Other floating-leaved plants have different circulation systems; for example, *Nelumbo nucifera* has a single leaf to each rhizome node and two specialised return gas channels leading to a central discharge vent in the leaf.

Other processes may have a small role, such as the solubilisation of carbon dioxide into the water surrounding the rhizomes (rather than replacing the respired oxygen in the return flow), simple disturbances caused by wind or wave action, and tidal effects. The primary function of this ventilation is that efficient aerobic respiration in the rhizomes and roots is facilitated, but there are also ecologically important effects on the soil, significant practical effects on the aeration of wetland purification installations, and possibly global effects through the release of methane and other greenhouse gases. Any interference with the gas pathways, such as blocking or perforation by insect or fungal attack, damage by grazing, wind, waves, trampling or boats, or by flooding of broken or cut culms, is likely to affect the health of the plant stands, which may be part of the mechanisms of die-back (cf. pp. 440–2).

The levels at which oxygen concentrations saturate respiration are very low in tissues with a high porosity and are less than 3 kPa (0.03 atm) for the roots of wetland species. This, combined with high diffusivity throughout the plant, and generally low respiratory rates (because of the low proportion of the root volume occupied by cells) ensures the maintenance of aerobic root metabolism.

If the oxygen demand of soil and root exceeds the supply, as for example during long periods of hot sunless weather, or by submergence of the aerial shoots, or over winter, many wetland plants can survive by anaerobic respiration (Crawford, 1978). However, this may produce metabolites which are toxic or, at best, inhibitory, inducing dormancy in the roots and rhizomes. There is little or no evidence that even wetland plants can grow when their roots are starved of oxygen. Root growth usually ceases once respiration is not saturated with oxygen.

When the properties of individual species are compared with each other and their favoured environments, the picture is less clear. For example, *Glyceria maxima*, a species with large air spaces in its rhizomes and a known ability to respire anaerobically, often grows very poorly in dense anaerobic sediments, while *Scirpus lacustris*, which has a relatively solid, almost woody rhizome, is very tolerant of anaerobic conditions.

Nutrient uptake

Little work has been done on the physiology of nutrient uptake by emergent plants. Since few have a significant proportion of their leaves underwater, and most have a well-developed root system, root uptake is likely to be the major route. This applies particularly to pleustohelophytes like *Eichhornia crassipes*, with roots hanging in the water and aerial leaves, but may not be less true of some plants with floating leaves or thalli like the water-lilies or the duckweeds (Bristow, 1975). When most of the roots are in the sediments, sediments are the main source of mineral nutrients but often there are also numerous adventitious, fibrous and functional roots free in the water, especially when the plants are growing in poor soils (e.g. Dykyjová & Hradecká, 1976). General importance of the sediments is supported by several papers on the influence of their nutrient concentrations on growth (Dykyjová, 1978*b*, 1979; Richardson *et al.*, 1978; Barko & Smart, 1979, 1981).

The presence of abundant nutrients in available forms in many organic and anaerobic sediments has been suggested as one reason for the high primary productivity of wetlands (Westlake, 1963), provided the roots can be adequately supplied with oxygen (see above). The ions NH_4^+, Fe^{2+} and PO_4^{3-} are particularly noteworthy and occur in such sediments. Li *et*

al. (1972) have shown that the interstitial phosphorus of lake sediments is
in dynamic equilibrium with phosphorus held by the particulate phase,
and Carignan and Kalff (1979) have shown that this interstitial phosphorus can be the sole source for rooted submerged macrophytes. An
iron-deficient chlorosis occurs in *Nasturtium officinale* (Cumbus *et al.*,
1977), which may be related to high redox potentials in the sediments.
See also pp. 339–42.

Variations in time and space

Most helophytes have a regular pattern of growth in which shoots grow
and bear leaves in sequence. Flowers develop at some stage and ultimately
the shoot dies. Typically, such patterns are seen during the spring and
summer for plants in the temperate zone, during the wet season for plants
in seasonal tropical climates and more or less continuously in other
tropical climates. Different physiological processes dominate at different
times in the cycle and in different parts of the plant. Translocation is most
important during the initial development of the shoot and often also very
important before flowering and again towards the end of its life (see
below). Photosynthesis dominates once a canopy has been established, but
the photosynthesate may be directed towards more leaves or towards
flowers, fruits and seeds. Other changes in activity and physiology occur in
the underground organs in coordination with the shoot activities.

Several authors have found only slight differences in photosynthetic and
respiratory capacity between the youngest and oldest leaves of *Phragmites
australis* when capacity is related to leaf area (e.g. Fig. 2.15). However, the
highest capacities have been reported in the central leaves on a dry weight
basis (Burian, 1973) and in the apical leaves on a wet weight basis (Walker
& Waygood, 1968). In terms of chlorophyll, the latter authors found the
central leaves, with a markedly higher chlorophyll content, were the least
efficient. There is an important vertical gradient in leaf area, with the
largest leaves around 4 to 7 from the base, which means that these leaves
have the greatest potential productivity. However, only about 40% of the
incident irradiance reaches this level, so these leaves will often be light
limited.

Gloser (1976) found rather larger differences between the leaves of
Glyceria maxima and *Phalaris arundinacea*, with the highest capacities in
the second youngest leaf and capacities between 0.55 and 0.8 of the highest
in the oldest leaves. Similarly, McNaughton (1973) found that leaves of *T.
latifolia* 90 days old had capacities about half of leaves 12 days old.

Seasonal changes are presented by Burian (1973) in three-dimensional diagrams of the relations between photosynthetic capacity, temperature and irradiance for *Phragmites australis* (Fig. 2.14). From May to June the light-saturated rate at 10–15 °C rose from about 25 mg CO_2 (g dry wt)$^{-1}$ h^{-1} to just over 30, and then it stayed around 30 in July and August. In May the rate fell sharply at higher temperatures to about 10 mg CO_2 (g dry wt)$^{-1}$ h^{-1} at 25–30 °C, in June there was little difference with temperature and In July–August there was only a small decrease at 25–30 °C.

Translocation and storage

In the winter the underground parts of many temperate zone helophytes have a higher energy content than at other times (18 to 19 kJ (g dry wt)$^{-1}$, Burian & Sieghardt, 1979) due to the accumulation of starch and other reserve materials (Krejci, 1974; Dykyjová & Přibil 1975; Fiala, 1976, 1978b; Fig. 2.17). In spring, when the new shoots grow, these reserves are rapidly depleted and soon reach minimum. Later, they are replenished from the photosynthesate produced by the leaves (July onwards in *Phragmites australis*, September onwards in *Typha* spp.). Krejci detected smaller fluctuations related to the supply of reserves to flowering and the formation of new rhizomes and overwintering buds.

In species with rapid turnover of shoots by initiation and death, translocation between dying and new shoots, connected by rhizomes or stolons, may be less seasonal. This almost certainly occurs in tropical species like *Cyperus papyrus* (Thompson 1976a) and *Eichhornia crassipes*, and probably also in temperate species like *Glyceria maxima* and even *Nasturtium officinale* (cf. pp 99–101). Shoot growth methods may then overestimate annual productivity.

Production in the field

Fluctuations in the environment are integrated through all the above physiological responses into plant growth. Usually, many environmental factors are partially limiting growth. This is partly because growth involves many different processes influenced by different factors; for example, net photosynthesis is the balance between photosynthesis and respiration, both of which are essential to growth. Furthermore, measures of growth are usually averages over long periods and large volumes of stands. For each process different single factors are limiting at certain times of day, in certain seasons and in certain parts of the plant. For

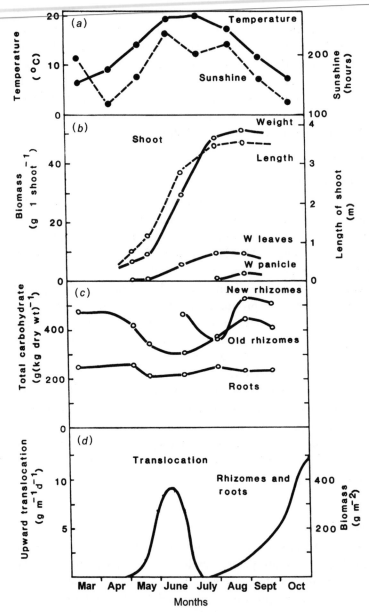

Fig. 2.17. Translocation and storage underground during the growing season of *Phragmites australis*. (*a*) Monthly mean air temperature and totals of hours of sunshine. (*b*) Shoot biomass and length, above-ground. (*c*) Total carbohydrate content of underground organs. (*d*) Rate of upward translocation (calculated from model of photosynthesis) and accumulation of new underground biomass ((*a*)–(*c*) Fiala, 1976; (*d*) Ondok, 1978*b*).

example, low temperatures may inhibit growth early in the year, carbon dioxide may limit photosynthesis of the uppermost leaves in the morning, while light may limit photosynthesis of the lower leaves, and water supply may limit photosynthesis at noon.

Environmental factors

These range from latitude and altitude through water level, and trophic status to micro-climate, which can have particularly dramatic effects (Dykyjová & Hradecká, 1976). The radiation regime is particularly important because water and nutrients are often amply supplied. Therefore, the stand structure and morphology of wetland plants are particularly adapted to use the incident irradiance efficiently, with nearly vertical leaves and shoots which avoid intense heating, reduce the area exposed to irradiances that are far above saturation and minimise self-shading (Dykyjová, 1973a; Ondok, 1977). It follows that, in open stands, enough light reaches the water to support an understorey of floating and submerged macrophytes and planktonic and epiphytic algae (Pieczyńska & Straškraba, 1969; Rejmánková, 1978), even though the leaf area index may exceed $10 \, \text{m}^2 \, \text{m}^{-2}$.

Irradiance and growth

Much of an entire stand is shaded by other parts of the plant. The consequences are that well-developed stands are not light saturated even on clear summer days and that photosynthesis per unit stand weight and the relative growth rate (which are dimensionally identical), or photosynthesis per unit area, change with incident irradiance. This has been shown both by experiments with entire stands and by modelling of entire stands (Fig. 2.18). Also, field growth and standing crop typically follow the seasonal pattern of insolation (e.g. Fig. 2.1) and the maximum standing crop is correlated with latitude, probably because of the influence of latitude on irradiance (see pp. 154–5). However, close correspondence with growth is usually seen only early in the growing season (e.g. Dykyjová & Véber, 1978), and later there is often little correlation (e.g. Fig. 2.17). This is variously due to the increasing influence of plant density, the negative effect of temperature through its influence on respiration, internal factors like flowering and diversion of growth to underground parts, and biotic factors like grazing.

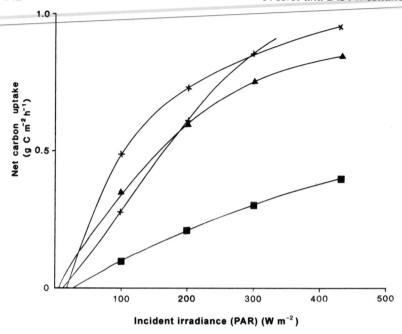

Fig. 2.18. The relationship between irradiance and stand photosynthesis. + *Glyceria maxima* (Gloser, 1977a, by modelling); × *Phragmites australis* (Ondok, 1978b, by modelling); ▲ *Eichhornia crassipes* and ■ *Salvinia molesta* (Sale et al., 1985, by experiment).

Hydrological factors and growth

Flow, water level and changes in water level are uniquely important in wetlands, strongly influencing both species distribution and productivity, which are often expressed in characteristic zonations of vegetation (Gosselink & Turner, 1978; see also Chapter 1). The causal sequences of the responses to hydrological factors are often difficult to prove because hydrology has many direct and indirect effects that are important for growth and survival, such as submergence of shoots, desiccation, frost protection, drag, microclimatic modifications, the nature of the sediments, the redox potential of the sediments and nutrient supply. Effects may derive from responses to average conditions, from the timing of changes, or from the ability to cope with exceptional events.

Rodewald-Rudescu (1974) gives a good example of responses to mean water level during the growing season of *Phragmites australis* (Fig. 2.19), and Korelyakova (1975) gives similar data on the biomasses of *P. australis* and *Typha angustifolia*. Sutcliffe (1974) noted that flood-plain vegetation

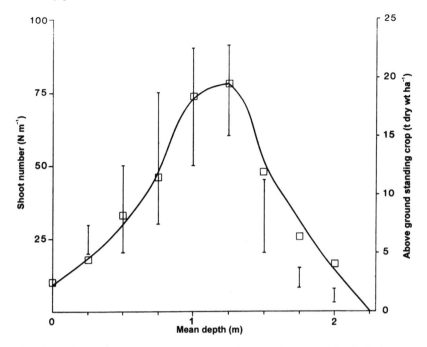

Fig. 2.19. Responses of *Phragmites australis* to mean water level during the growing season in the Danube delta (Rodewald-Rudescu, 1974). I range of shoot numbers per square metre; □ seasonal maximum standing crop.

of the Upper Nile was either 'shallow flooded' (e.g. *Phragmites australis, Oryza barthii,* with deep underground systems) or 'deep flooded' (e.g. *Vossia cuspidata, Cyperus papyrus* with shallow underground systems). For *Cyperus* the range of flood depths may be as important as the maximum depth. Thompson (1974) attributed such differences to the availability of oxygen, although, if water levels fall well below the surface, water supply may also be important. Conner and Day (1976) found that the most productive baldcypress swamps (1.14–$1.92 \, \text{kg m}^{-2} \, \text{y}^{-1}$) were in areas near rivers with seasonal flooding, the least productive (0.19–$0.42 \, \text{kg m}^{-2} \, \text{y}^{-1}$) were slightly higher areas with stagnant water.

Zonation may be seen around the margins of lakes and ponds, across deltas and along flood-plains. Husák and Květ (1973) and Květ and Ondok (1973) have studied changes in species distribution and productivity in Czechoslovak fishponds. The higher summer standing crops were usually in the second littoral zone in from the open water margin; the lowest were in the terrestrial ecophase. In the Opatovický Fishpond the terrestrial zone was populated by *Carex* spp. and grasses and the littoral

zone, where the summer water level was about 70 cm, was dominated by
P. australis; *Glyceria maxima* occurred in the intermediate limosal zone. In
the Nesyt Fishpond *P. australis* was often dominant throughout with little
Carex, and both *P. australis* and *Typha angustifolia* occurred as dominants in the rather shallow littoral zone. Kopecký (1967) analysed the
effects of flooding and sedimentation on *Phalaris arundinacea* growing in a
flood-plain in two years, which differed greatly in hydrological characteristics, although one was close to the long-term average. Floods in the first
3 months of the growing season had the most effect. Production was
generally higher in the average year and the greatest difference was seen in
the wettest zone which was flooded for 91 days in the wetter growing
season instead of 16 days in a normal year. Here, the above-ground
standing crop was never more than 5% of that in the normal years, shoot
numbers were much lower and none flowered. There was less living
material underground and a much higher proportion of dead rhizomes
and roots, which was most marked in the soil with the least air capacity.
The cover by *Phalaris* and *Alopecurus pratensis* decreased and opportu-
nistic species such as *Rorippa* spp. increased.

Responses to floods are particularly noticeable in riparian populations.
After the exceptional summer floods in the Danube delta in 1970, *T.
angustifolia* survived better than *P. australis*, (D. Dykyjová, pers. comm.).
Many populations are adapted to evade and exploit the consequences of
changes in water level. A change in the pattern of flooding would eliminate
such species. The floating meadows of the Amazon (Junk, 1970) survive in
wet patches during the dry season, grow rapidly when water returns and
float on the changing water levels above the turbid water. *Nasturtium
officinale* in English chalk-streams only starts growth when water levels
fall and beds of *Ranunculus calcareus* and silt reach the water surface to
trap small ramets floating downstream. Free from most other competitors, it grows and spreads very rapidly (Dawson *et al.*, 1978) until washed
away by floods, usually in the autumn. However, if the river dries up,
conditions favour *Apium nodiflorum*, which then competes successfully
(Thommen & Westlake, 1981).

Over longer periods occasional droughts may initiate a successional
cycle of development, as seen in prairie glacial marshes by van der Valk
and Davis (1978). During drought years seeds of perennial emergent
plants such as *Typha* spp., *Scirpus* spp., and annual species such as *Bidens
cernua* germinate and form a 'dry marsh' community on the exposed
sediments. When standing water returns, the annual species die and the
emergent plants thrive, with some submerged plants among them ('regen-

erating marsh'). In later years the emergents lose vigour ('degenerating marsh') and are attacked by increasing populations of muskrats until a pond vegetation with few emergents remains (lake stage). The entire cycle may extend over 5 to 20 years. Both the dry marsh and the regenerated marsh show high productivity; during the later stages there is a decrease to low levels (Fig. 2.20).

Hydrological changes are a major factor in successional development from littoral to terrestrial communities (see pp. 29–49).

Nutrient factors

Wetland plants, apart from the floating forms, take mineral nutrients from the sediments by a well developed root system. Plants growing in poor soils often also have numerous adventitious, fibrous roots free in the water (e.g. Dykyjová & Hradecká, 1976), resembling the root system of floating plants. Much of the residual scatter in the relationship between latitude and maximum standing crop can be related to the nutrient status of the habitat (Westlake, 1982; see pp. 151–8 and Fig. 2.21). The mean standing crop of *Phragmites australis* on oligotrophic sites is about one-third of that on eutrophic sites; a highly significant difference. At any latitude the highest productions are found at nutrient-rich sites such as many deltas, fishponds, sewage outfalls and salt marshes. At many such sites organic-rich sediments accumulate but, at others, the sandy sediments are a poor source of nutrients and these are then obtained from the main flow of water.

Early field observations on habitat conditions, leaf nutrient contents, size of shoots and standing crops showed that waters or soils rich in nutrients supported larger shoots of *Phragmites australis*, which had higher nutrient contents in their leaves (e.g. Gorham & Pearsall, 1956; Allen & Pearsall, 1963). Nitrogen appeared to be deficient most frequently, though phosphorus, calcium, magnesium, manganese and potassium deficiencies were also indicated. In the Danube delta the application of either calcium nitrate or superphosphate increased shoot size, shoot number and standing crop (Rudescu, 1965).

Human influences

The management of the catchment as well as of the wetlands themselves have to be considered, as wetlands are particularly sensitive to human activities in both areas.

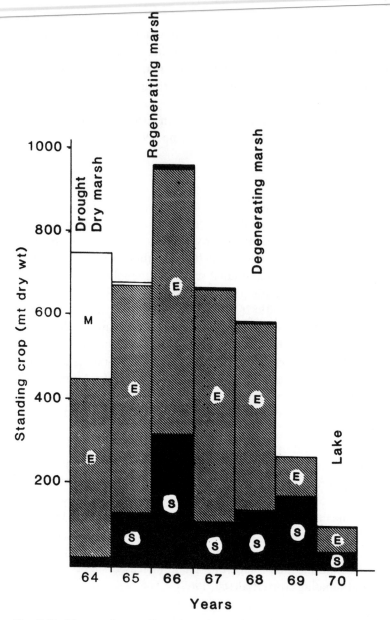

Fig. 2.20. Changes in standing crop of a prairie glacial marsh after a drought. Ⓢ submerged vegetation; ⧆ emergent vegetation; ⊡ mud flat opportunists (From Rush Lake, Van der Valk & Davis, 1978.)

Eutrophication

Wetlands function as large nutrient traps removing excessive nutrients from the run-off from agriculturally or industrially loaded catchments. These nutrients enrich, or change the communities and productivity of the wetlands. However, by natural or artificial mowing, peat cutting and drainage, a significant portion of the organic material produced, and its nutrient content, may subsequently be lost from the wetland.

Changes of wetland areas by enhanced mineral nutrient levels, natural as well as artificial, and the consequences to the succession and productivity of primary communities are described in other chapters. Rudescu (1965) and Rodewald-Rudescu (1974) introduce and discuss many relations between the productivity of reedbed communities; especially of *Phragmites australis*, and the technical management of the Danube Delta, in relation to the rich nutrient inputs from the river water and suspended soil particles, which accumulate in delta areas.

Eutrophication has been included among the factors causing die-back of wetland species (see pp. 440–2) but the evidence is not clear. Neuhaus *et al.* (1993) have suggested that clones growing in low-nutrient habitats may be more sensitive to nutrient increases.

Grazing

Grazing reduces the net primary production and the detritus production of many wetlands. According to Reimold (1972) and Reimold *et al.* (1975*b*), the net production of grazed *Spartina* and *Salicornia* marshes in Georgia was only 40–50% of that of ungrazed areas, but recovery was rapid once grazing was terminated.

Burning

Burning of dry stands at the end of the season also suppresses the helophytes in many wetlands. However, monospecific stands of *Phragmites australis* may be favoured because burning leads to earlier emergence in the spring (Haslam, 1969*b*) and many pests and diseases are eliminated.

Mowing and harvesting

Similarly, winter mowing reduces many noxious insect populations. Husák & Květ (1973) showed that new shoots of *Phragmites australis* growing in stands mowed in the previous year are usually less affected by parasites than those on unmown areas.

Mowing or cutting during the growing season usually significantly lowers the subsequent biomass of helophytes (Haslam, 1969b; Husák, 1973; Mochnacka-Ławacz, 1974b). The reduction depends on the date and frequency of mowing and the species growth pattern (Dykyjová & Husák, 1973). The total of three standing crops mown from reed stands on Mikołajske Lake during the growing season (up to mid-September) was only about one-third of the final standing crop on unmown areas (Mochnaka-Ławacz, 1974b). Repeating cutting at appropriate times can prevent the community regenerating from new shoots and it is completely destroyed.

On the basis of long experience this is the principal method used to control undesirable aquatic weeds in managed fishpond littorals in Central Europe (Hejný, 1971; Dykyjová & Husák, 1973) and in wetlands in other countries (e.g. Haslam, 1969b).

Cutting early in the season, if not repeated, allows regeneration of shoots by buds supplied from the rhizomes, and up to two or three shoots replace each original one, increasing the stand density (Haslam, 1969b; Husák & Květ, 1970; Dykyjová & Husák, 1973). Therefore, in the next year the standing crop often becomes higher in such early mown areas. This response of reedbeds resembles the behaviour of mown meadows.

Mechanical harvesting of reed by heavy harvesters and tractors destroys the rhizomes and buds in soft soils, thus suppressing yields (Isambaev, 1964; L. Rudescu, pers. comm.).

Water level changes

Water level fluctuations or periodic draw-downs, caused indirectly by water abstraction or intentionally, have many effects on aquatic and wetland plants. The effect of periodic, partial or complete summer drainage of Central European fishponds and other shallow water-bodies on the succession and productivity of their littoral communities has been described by Hejný (1971). The productivity of the populations of individual species may be increased, decreased or not changed, which often results in short- or medium-term fluctuations in the species composition of the plant communities along gradients of mean water depth. Species that cannot tolerate the water-level changes may even become absent. Draw-downs at different dates can change the subsequent course of succession (Meeks, 1969; see pp. 165–6).

Efficiency

Very few data are published on the conversion efficiency of insolation. The variation of the energy content in aquatic plants is relatively low, so that the net solar energy conversion efficiency is closely correlated with the total amount of the biomass produced during the season or year. However, as stated by Lieth (1968), the conversion efficiency usually cannot be calculated accurately on the basis of mean values or of constant conversion factors, 'A few measurements selected from the most important part of the yield appear much better'. Thus each individual production measurement for a short period of growth requires individual measurement of biomass energy content, in order to express the results in terms of conversion efficiency.

It may be better in ecological work to calculate the efficiency coefficients of solar energy conversion based on total irradiance, rather than only on the short-wave (photosynthetically active) portion of the total irradiance, as is usual in laboratory photosynthesis experiments (Lieth, 1968). As the production process in the field includes not only photosynthesis, but also respiration, evapo-transpiration and growth, which all are affected by the long-wave radiation, it is often more relevant to express the net efficiency in terms of the conversion of total irradiance. As in many such controversies, much depends on the exact question requiring an answer.

Table 2.11 presents efficiency coefficients of solar energy conversion for wetlands. There is a general increase in net efficiency from April to about July and a decline subsequently (in Northern Hemisphere, temperate climates). Initially, the increasing biomass captures more of the incident irradiance, but later increasing self-shading and higher temperatures increases the plant respiration, and water stress and nutrient deficiencies may decrease photosynthesis. Ultimately, photosynthetic capacity declines with senescence.

Comparisons of standing crop and productivity

Data have been collected for substantially mono-specific stands growing in different climates and habitats at various latitudes. The climates are classified according to Köppen (1923) and, as far as possible, the habitats correspond with Chapter 1.

Table 2.11. *Efficiency of utilisation of solar irradiance in some wetland stands*

$$\% \text{ efficiency } \Phi = \frac{\text{Joules accumulated in biomass m}^{-2} \text{ in growing season} \times 100}{\text{Joules solar irradiance m}^{-2} \text{ in growing season}}$$

Stand		Harvest date	Growth period (d)	Efficiency Φ (%) Total irradiance	PAR[a]
(Above-ground[b] only; Dykyjová & Přibil, 1975)					
Phragmites australis	– erosion zone	12.7.72	82	1.3	2.8
	– accumulation zone	1.7.66	72	3.2	6.6
	– accumulation zone	8.9.66	140	2.7	5.6
Typha angustifolia					
Schoenoplectus lacustris	– erosion zone	26.7.71	86	3.2	6.6
	– accumulation zone	26.7.71	86	4.7	9.7
Glyceria maxima	– erosion zone	12.7.72	87	0.9	1.8
	– accumulation zone	12.7.72	87	3.3	6.9
(Net photosynthesis; Burian & Sieghardt, 1979)					
Phragmites australis		End May	31	1.3	2.7
		End June	30	1.6	3.4
		End Aug.	31	0.8	1.7
		End Oct.	30	0.5	1.1
(Net photosynthesis[c]; Drake & Read, 1981)					
Spartina patens and *Distichlis spicata*		June–Aug.	92	1.7	3.5

[a] Recalculated for PAR 0.48 total irradiance.
[b] Not corrected for underground translocation nor for losses before harvest.
[c] Day-time only; not corrected for night-time respiration.

Climate

Table 2.12 presents a selection of standing crop data grouped according to climate. For each climatic region the first entry is the highest standing crop found for which there is some evidence that it is sustained over a large area. Much higher values may be found for small areas, e.g. up to 20 kg m^{-2} for *Cyperus papyrus* (Thompson, pers. comm.) and over 9 kg m^{-2} for *Phragmites australis* (Korelyakova, 1971). The 10 kg m^{-2} value for *Arundo donax* probably arises because more than 1 year's production accumulates. As far as possible, the other entries are chosen to include several countries, different growth forms, common species or genera and species for which the highest standing crop could be taken from studies at several sites.

There are no obvious correlations between standing crop and climate. High standing crops, around 4 kg m^{-2}, can be found in all of these climates, from tropical Uganda to boreal Czechoslovakia, and the data collected showed that low values, below 0.2 kg m^{-2} are equally widespread. Clearly, standing crop is generally affected by local factors such as species, micro-climate, soil and grazing more than by climate. This is not entirely unexpected. To plants, climates differ primarily in rainfall and in several features which tend to be associated with latitude, including daylength, insolation and temperature. The total area of wetlands in a region is likely to be related to rainfall, but wetlands can occur in arid climates where local topography and river flow allow the accumulation of water. By definition, water shortages are not experienced in any wetlands for much of the year and so rainfall is unlikely to have much influence on wetland productivity. The effects of the other components of climate are rather more complicated, some favouring and others hindering productivity, but detailed analysis does show some relation between standing crop and latitude.

Latitude

Brylinsky (1980) has found a good inverse regression of phytoplankton productivity on latitude. However, there was a lot of scatter and Hammer (1980), using somewhat different criteria and a slightly different data base, found the fit was poor. This difference was probably largely dependent on the range and paucity of acceptable data at low latitudes.

Wetland data include a fairly large set for one species, *Phragmites australis*, which allows us to eliminate variation due to species (Fig. 2.21).

Table 2.12. *Examples of seasonal maximum standing crop of above-ground vegetation of wetlands in different climatic regions*

Climate[a]	Species	Standing crop (kg dry wt m^{-2})	Country	Reference
Tropical rain, no long dry season (rain forest)	*Cyperus papyrus*	4.3	Uganda	Thompson et al., 1979[b]
	Eichhornia crassipes	2.4[c]	Florida, USA	Knipling et al., 1970
	Paspalum repens	1.14	Brazil	Junk, 1970
	Cladium jamaicense	1.13	Florida, USA	Steward & Ornes, 1975
	Pistia stratiotes	0.46[c]	Florida, USA	Davis in Odum, 1957
	Lepironia articulata	0.29	Malaysia	Ikusima, 1978
Tropical rain, long dry season (savanna)	*Arundo donax*	10.0	Thailand	Ogawa et al., 1961
	Typha domingensis	2.54	Malawi	Howard-Williams, 1973
	Salvinia molesta	0.60[c]	Zambia/Zimbabwe	Mitchell & Tur, 1975
Arid (steppe and warm desert)	*Cyperus papyrus*	3.6	Chad	Lévêque et al., 1972[d]
	Phragmites australis	3.6	Ukraine, USSR	Korelyakova, 1971
	Phramites australis	3.2	Chad	Lévêque et al., 1972[d]
	Typha spp.	2.0	Chad	Lévêque et al., 1972[d]
	Phragmites australis	0.6	Uzbekistan, USSR	Abdullaev, 1972
Temperate rain (broad-leaved, evergreen or deciduous forest)	*Typha angustata*	3.86	Kashmir	Kaul et al., 1978
	Phragmites australis	3.00	Austria	Burian, 1971
	Cyperus papyrus	2.9	Kenya	Thompson et al., 1979[b]
	Eichhornia crassipes	2.13[c]	Alabama, USA	Boyd & Scarsbrook, 1975a
	Schoenoplectus lacustris	2.0	Germany	Seidel, 1959
	Nasturtium officinale	1.26	England	Castellano, 1977
	Carex lacustris	1.15	New York, USA	Bernard & Solsky, 1977
	Glyceria maxima	1.00	England	Buttery & Lambert, 1965

Boreal (deciduous or needle-leaved evergreen forest)

Species		Location	Reference
Alternanthera philoxeroides	0.84	Alabama, USA	Boyd, 1969
Trapa natans	0.52[c]	Japan	Koidsumi et al., 1967
Schoenoplectus lacustris	4.2	Czechoslovakia	Dykyjová & Přibil, 1975
Typha latifolia	3.6	Czechoslovakia	Dykyjová & Přibil, 1975
Phragmites australis	3.3	Czechoslovakia	Dykyjová & Přibil, 1975
Phragmites australis	3.0	Austria	Burian, 1971
Glyceria maxima	2.7	Czechoslovakia	Dykyjová & Přibil, 1975
Sparganium erectum	1.9	Czechoslovakia	Dykyjová & Přibil, 1975
Typha glauca	1.5	Iowa, USA	van der Valk & Davis, 1978
Stratiotes aloides	1.2[c]	Belo-Russia	Ekzertsev & Ekzertseva, 1962[e]
Carex rostrata	1.1	Minnesota, USA	Bernard, 1973
Sagittaria sagittifolia	0.47	Belo-Russia	Katanskaya, 1960b

[a] Based on Koppen, 1923.
[b] From biomass of culm-units (including some rhizomes) and aerial parts 88% of culm-units.
[c] Floating plants, roots included.
[d] Converted from fresh weight by assuming dry weights: 20% for *Cyperus*, 25% for *Typha*, 40% for *Phragmites*.
[e] From air-dry weight assuming 8% water.

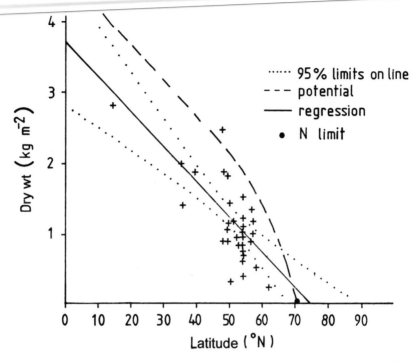

Fig. 2.21. Regression of maximum standing crop of *Phragmites australis* (*B*) on latitude (*L*). Where a paper gave data from more than 1 year, an average has been used. Where a paper gave data from more than one site within a water body, an average value for the more favourable sites has been used. $B = 3.96 - 0.0546L$; $R = -0.712$; $R^2 = 0.507$; t for regression coefficient $= -5.73$; residual mean square $= 0.208$; $N = 34$. This figure is reproduced from Westlake (1982), by permission of the Royal Botanical Society of Belgium.

This shows a highly significant inverse regression of the seasonal maximum standing crop with latitude but, like the phytoplankton data, there are very few data below 40° N or above 60° N, and they are widely scattered. At latitudes around 50° N, where most values have been determined, the highest are four to six times the lowest. Nevertheless, half the variation is accounted for by latitude, leaving half to be explained to local climate, soil and intraspecific differences. Data for *Typha* show a similar picture, but the fit is poor, mainly because of some very high values around 50° N and the wide scatter at low latitudes.

Any site–species combination has a potential maximum biomass which is reached when so much biomass has accumulated that respiration by the underground parts, the stems and the lower, shaded leaves balances the photosynthesis by the upper canopy, and further growth is impossible unless non-productive biomass is lost (cf. the maximum biomass of phytoplankton, e.g. summaries in Tilzer *et al.*, 1980; Steel, 1980). Different species may have different potentials because the ratio between their rates of respiration and photosynthesis (per plant), and their specific light transmission may vary.

This potential is primarily fixed by the irradiance, because the higher the incident irradiance, the more leaves can be adequately illuminated and the higher the photosynthesis of the whole stand. Hence both latitude (sun altitude) and climate (cloudiness) should influence the potential. Other factors such as temperature regime, water conditions, nutrients and toxins may affect the potential through effects on the ratio between photosynthesis and respiration.

In a climate where growth is continuous, and at sites where grazing is slight, this potential is likely to be attained and maintained but in a climate with a no-growth period, the potential can only be achieved if growth is sufficiently rapid for enough biomass to have accumulated by the end of the growing season, when heavy or complete losses of above-ground biomass occur. So, any factors reducing the rate of net photosynthesis or the accumulation of biomass may prevent the potential being reached.

An ideal set of data, if the maximum biomass is limited by irradiance, would be expected to show an upper limit to the biomass, inversely related to latitude, and fixed by the climates with the highest irradiance. Below this line there would be wide scatter corresponding to sites where the irradiance fixes a lower potential or where the potential is not achieved. Although low-latitude, tropical climates are instinctively thought of as hot, moist and bright, and constantly ideal for growth, cloud often reduces the irradiance and heat, without cloud and rain, produces a dry season with low growth and heavy losses. At higher latitudes the irradiance is generally lower and cloudy climates are common. The longer hours of daylight in the growing season at high latitudes probably balance the effect of the longer growing season at low latitudes. Temperature, at sea level, generally increases towards lower latitudes and often acts favourably on growth. Thus the seasonal maximum standing crops of *Carex* spp. and the annual production of *Spartina alterniflora* are positively correlated with temperature over a range of latitudes (Gorham, 1974; Turner, 1976). However, it may have some contrary influence, probably through effects on the dark respiration, particularly where large underground biomasses are present. Thompson *et al.* (1979) found the aerial standing crop of *Cyperus papyrus* decreased with decreasing altitude and increasing temperature. At all latitudes, sites with restricted water supply, poor soils, at high altitudes, or subject to heavy grazing or management are abundant, although perhaps less often selected for study. Thus the reasons for the inverse trend with latitude and the wide scatter are complex.

Habitat

Data were compared for a wide range of habitats, from oligotrophic boreal lakes to fertile tropical ponds, but as might be expected, climatic and specific differences masked most of the habitat differences. A limited comparison of sites dominated by *Phragmites australis* within Austria, Czechoslovakia, Poland and European Russia was rather more revealing (Table 2.13). However, even in a single water body (Opatovický Pond, Czechoslovakia, Dykyjová, 1978a) the maximum biomass varied between 1.03 and 3.25 kg dry wt m^{-2} at different sites and in different years; and objective classification of the water bodies, with the data available, was not easy. In most cases the author's assessment of the trophic status was used, but it seems likely that 'eutrophic', applied to large lakes of the N. Polish plain, refers to less fertile conditions than found in Czechoslovakian fertilised fish ponds or the reservoirs of the lower Dnieper. The 'mesotrophic' group includes a fertilised dystrophic water and two water bodies of uncertain status, which appear to be intermediate from their geographical situation and water chemistry. Most values are averages for all the stands studied, but a few refer to averages for the most productive zone of the reed-swamps. The oligotrophic lakes have significantly lower standing crops then the eutrophic water bodies, and the mesotrophic examples fit neatly between. Björk (1967) found more extreme differences in Sweden, where standing crops were only 10–65 g m^{-2} in oligotrophic waters and reached over 2 kg m^{-2} in eutrophic waters.

In parallel with this range from oligotrophic to eutrophic habitats, Reader (1978) emphasised the low productivity of 'northern bog marshes' (maximum standing crop 0.10–1.01 kg m^{-2}) compared with many other wetlands. These wetlands are transitional fens and bogs as classified in Chapter 1, with low pH, low nutrient input from air and run-off and a peaty soil. Gorham and Pearsall (1956) also emphasised the importance of nutrient input in studies of a range of sites in Northern Britain where the size of the standing crop of *Phragmites australis* increased with the annual mineral accretion. This was particularly noticeable for different sites in single water bodies.

Table 2.13. *Trophic status and average seasonal maximum standing crops of aerial shoots of* Phragmites australis *in NE Europe*

Trophic status		Standing crop (kg dry wt m^{-2})	Reference
Eutrophic	Opatovicky Pond	2.73	Dykyjová & Hradecká, 1976
	Kakhova Reservoir	2.45	Korelyakova, 1971
	Lion Lake	1.86	Fiala, 1976
	Nesyt Pond	1.81	Květ, Svoboda & Fiala, 1969
	Kremenchug Reservoir	1.60	Korelyakova, 1971
	Lake Kotek	1.50	Mochnacka-Ławacz, 1974a
	Šakvický Pond	1.42	Fiala, 1976
	Lake Sniardwy	1.30	Mochnacka-Ławacz, 1974a
	Volgograd Reservoir	1.17	Ekzertsev, 1966
	Smyslov Pond	1.14	Straškraba, 1963
	Lake Warniak	1.02	Bernatowicz & Radziej, 1964
	Skonal Lake	0.95	Mochnacka-Ławacz, 1974a
	Mikołajskie Lake	0.82	Ozimek & Balcerzak, 1976
	Mean and 95% limits	1.17–1.52–1.87	
Mesotrophic	Neusiedlersee	1.86	Sieghardt, 1973
	Taltowisko Lake	1.50	Mochnacka-Ławacz, 1974a
	Ivankovskoe Reservoir	0.98	Ekzertsev & Ekzertseva, 1962
	Rožmberk Pond	0.87	Fiala, 1976
	Dargin Lake	0.83	Bernatowicz & Radziej, 1964
	Uglitch Reservoir	0.51	Ekzertseva, 1961
	Mean	1.09	
Oligotrophic	Üntersee	0.97	Unni, 1977
	Mamry Pólnocne Lake	0.69 ⎫	
	Kasajno Lake	0.57 ⎬	Bernatowicz & Radziej, 1964
	Kirsajty Lake	0.39 ⎭	
	Onega Lake	0.22	Raspopov, 1973
	Mean and 95% limits	0.22–0.53–0.85	

Such comparisons give the best information on the effects of habitat features on productivity. Many papers point out changes in standing crop across the belt of reedswamp on lake shores, from the terrestrial zone, through the limosal zone to the littoral zone (e.g. Husák & Květ, 1973; Ozimek & Balcerzak, 1976; Thompson *et al.*, 1979). The littoral end of this sequence often has the highest standing crop, but this is not always the case. Presumably, at different sites, the relative importance of terrestrial and pelagic nutrient sources and of wave action lead to different distributions of optimum conditions.

Probably the most detailed study of differences between sites is given by

Dykyjová and Hradecká (1976) who investigated two stands of *Phragmites*, one growing in a limosal accumulation zone, the other in a littoral erosion zone. Apart from the major differences in water level and mineral transport, there were other differences in micro-climate and edaphic factors. The aerial standing crop of the accumulation stand was 2.73 kg dry wt m^{-2} as compared with 1.02 in the erosion zone. The explanation of this difference was complex but the greater abundance of nutrients and the milder micro-climate at the accumulation site were most important.

More details of the relations between growth and environmental factors are discussed later (pp. 163–6).

Genotypic variation

The production by natural populations of individual species also depends on the structure and texture and genome of populations composed of the local ecotypes of each species. This is important for comparative assessments of the production of individual species, especially in different regions.

McNaughton (1966) has pointed to the significance of simple uniform communities, characterised physiognomically by one dominant ecotype component, for an analysis of the relationship between an ecotype, its area of distribution, habitat and productivity. Data are given particularly on *Typha* spp., especially on *T. latifolia*.

From Björk (1967), Haslam (1970a) and Raicu *et al.* (1972) onward many authors have focused their attention on the polymorphic wetland dominant, *Phragmites australis*, which is widely variable both in physiological characteristics and productivity. Dykyjová and Hradecká (1973) compared two *Phragmites* stands. D. Hradecká and J. Svoboda (personal communication) assessed differences, some of them significant, between young (several years old) eight clones of *Phragmites* growing in much the same habitat along a stream. The variation, evidently genetical, involved morphological characteristics (including the colour of the inflorescences) as well as such characteristics as the stand biomass, leaf area index and leaf ageing. Hradecká (1973), on the basis of a statistical analysis of flower morphology, has allocated the *Phragmites* populations studied in Czechoslovakia during the IBP, to three freshwater 'forms' (in her terminology, probably ecotypes) and one 'form' growing in saline habitats. Véber (1978) cultivated clones of *Phragmites australis* originating from various parts of Europe (southern Bulgaria, Danube delta, Lake Neusiedlersee, Danube lowlands in southern Slovakia, South Moravia, South Bohemia,

East Bohemia and DDR) in two habitats, mineral soil and peat, in South Bohemia. The differences between the clones pertained to stand biomass, leaf area index, stand density, and leaf ageing as well as to commercial qualities of the reed culms, and they were persistent for three successive growing seasons of the reed cultivation. The differences between the clones originating from relatively warm regions with a longer vegetation period (later flowering and leaf fall) and those from cooler regions, correspond with the differences given by Haslam (1973) for *Phragmites* from the Mediterranean area (Malta) in comparison with that from North-west Europe (Great Britain).

In the Netherlands, van der Toorn (1972) has distinguished and verified experimentally the existence of two principal *Phragmites* ecotypes: (i) a peat ecotype, with short shoots and high shoot density, occurring in peat marshes, and (ii) a riverine ecotype, with long shoots and limited shoot density, occurring mainly in freshwater tidal wetlands. Transitional forms exist between the two ecotypes and the chromosome number, i.e. $2n = 48$, is the same in both (i) and (ii). Results of field experiments (Table 2.14) have shown that as compared with the peat ecotype, the riverine ecotype is distinguished by:

a higher above-ground biomass;
a lower shoot density;
a greater shoot length;
greater tolerance to tidal submergence and salinity and less tolerance to
    ground frosts in spring;
greater susceptibility to infestation by *Arachnara geminipuncta*.

The present distribution of the two ecotypes may be regarded as a result of a selection of genotypes suitable for the habitats given, namely the peaty wetlands, on the one hand, and the eutrophic and/or brackish tidal ones on the other.

Using genomic fingerprinting (Kühl & Neuhaus, 1993) has shown that individual sites may have one to several clones of *Phragmites* while different sites may be populated by different clones or sets of clones. This could mean that different stands would have different responses to environmental changes (Neuhaus *et al.*, 1993).

As to the physiological mechanism responsible for variation in net production, McNaughton (1974*a*) has concluded that this is due to the regulation of the rate of production of leaf tissues rather than to some inherent differences in the assimilation efficiency of the leaves. This is consistent with the same long-proved hypothesis on the leaf area index

Table 2.14. *Ecotypes of* Phragmites australis

	Shoot density (no. m⁻²)	Shoot height (cm)	Above-ground biomass (g dry wt m⁻²)	Tolerance of submersion	Tolerance of frosts	Tolerance of salt	Habitat
					(% 1° shoots killed)		
Netherlands (van der Toorn, 1972)							
'Peak'	220	<250	990	Low	39	Low	Lake margins
'Riverine'	90	>300	2400	High	52	High	Tidal freshwaters
				Underground biomass (g dry wt m⁻²)	Nitrogen biomass load (g N m⁻²)		
Czechoslovakia (Dykyjová & Hradecká, 1973)							
'Littoral'	103	225	1500	5890	28		Fish pond; marginal water
'Limosal'	101	235	2070	3360	47		Fish pond; marginal land

and duration as characteristics determining primarily the net production by crops (Watson, 1952) through the effect on radiation interception by the crop canopies (Anderson, 1975).

Björk (1967) claims that the production characteristics of various *Phragmites* clones do not remain constant when the clones are transplanted into biotopes different from their original ones (mostly into eutrophicated biotopes). Dykyjová (1971b), on the other hand, has found that differences between the morphological and production characteristics of the two *Phragmites* ecotypes mentioned above (see Table 2.14) remained much the same for 7 successive years. It is natural that changed environmental conditions bring about a change in productivity of a certain plant population. It is the relative differences between the populations and their constancy under various conditions that are needed for defining the genotypic variation in various plant characteristics including those pertaining to the primary production. For most wetland plants, except rice, only few data of this kind are available.

The genotypic variation in production efficiency has naturally received most attention in rice. An example is the thorough analysis by Hayashi (1972). The net efficiency of solar energy conversion by the principal Japanese rice varieties was expressed in terms of C_i^ϕ or C_a^ϕ, i.e. as the energy used for the rice dry-matter production related to the energy either intercepted or absorbed by the rice-crop canopy. Positive correlation was found between C_i^ϕ and the product of $L \times K$ (i.e. the leaf area index × the radiation interception coefficient of the canopy), while a negative correlation existed between C_a^ϕ and the product of $L_\ell \times K$ (i.e. the specific leaf area × the extinction coefficient). All three characters concerned, L, L_ℓ and K, possessed a high heritability, mostly over 90%, K being related to the distribution of leaf inclination, which is another character whose seasonal course is largely determined genetically. The increase in C_i^ϕ thus depended primarily on the expansion of a large L in the most advantageous way for radiation interception, i.e. with a small K; the increase in the net assimilation rate of the leaves, $_{s_l}C_B$, was of little importance for either C_i^ϕ or C_a^ϕ. The capacities of the varieties for a high L, small K and large L_ℓ were thus the three principal genetic characteristics positively affecting the production efficiencies of the varieties. It seems that these conclusions could also be tested in other wetland dominants, namely in helophytes of graminoid type, when searching for their highly productive genotypes.

Comparisons with other types of ecosystems

It is difficult to make accurate comparisons when the range of annual production at different sites is so great; and this also applies to most other types of ecosystems. Selecting just the highest value found for each type may be misleading, since this could be in error, or more accurate than the general run of studies, or an especially high value found for one particular type by chance. However, Westlake (1963) found that this approach appeared to give consistent results. Kira (1975) found that, when a large number of sites were studied, a frequency distribution of productivities was obtained which was often slightly skewed, with the longer tail at the high end. Other problems arise because production has been estimated by many different methods, some of which ignore or correct inadequately for losses and underground production.

A large number of values were collected for various types of community, mostly from earlier reviews such as Westlake (1963), Cooper (1975), Lieth and Whittaker (1975) and Le Cren and Lowe-McConnell (1980). Some corrections were made where they were obviously necessary. Where possible, up to 100 values were collected for each type and the ranges of the upper 10% are given in Table 2.15. If only a few values were available, this is noted. This approach reduced the influence of adverse environments and tells us more about the plants. It also probably eliminates stands subject to heavy damage or grazing. Wetlands are much more productive than other freshwater vegetation and more productive than marine vegetation. They are frequently as productive or more productive than most types of terrestrial vegetation, except for intensive agriculture. High productivity is to be expected because of their efficient canopies, their ample water supply and their underground organs which aid long growing seasons, competitive ability and long-term stability. The value of $6.6 \, \mathrm{m.t \, ha}^{-1}$ reported for papyrus after this table was prepared confirms the earlier data (Muthuri *et al.*, 1989). We can also conclude that the genotypic variation of the production of wetland plant populations often seems to be obscured by the effects of environmental factors on the rates of production and growth; and hence the variation can only be assessed in optimum, or near optimum, habitats for the studied species, or by experiments in which the potential limiting factors (usually nutrients or water) are removed.

Table 2.15. *Annual net production of wetlands in comparison with some other ecosystems (based on Westlake, 1982)*

	Probable range of annual production of dry weight at fertile sites (m.t ha^{-1})
Wetlands with helophytes	
Temperate	50–70
Tropical	60–90
Wetlands with pleustohelophytes	
(mostly tropical)	40–60
Cultivated plants	25–85
Forests	20–60
Aquatic	
Submerged macrophytes, temperate, freshwater	5–10
Submerged macrophytes, marine	40–60
Phytoplankton	15–30

Adaptations to the wetland habitat

Wetland plants have many morphological and physiological adaptations to the special conditions of their habitat, many of which have been described above. Mitsch & Gosselink (1986) have a chapter on adaptation of organisms and Brändle *et al.* (1996) contains papers on many aspects of the adaptations of plants.

Here, we emphasise the relationships between adaptation, zonation and succession. The environmental variables controlling wetland plant communities often change along gradients and show marked distributions into micro- or meso-climates. Frost damage provides an example of the latter. The winter buds of helophytes are adapted to the protection afforded by water above the sediments. Exposed to frosts by drainage, they are killed or retarded. Dykyjová and Hradecká (1976) describe two neighbouring *Phragmites* communities growing in the same fishpond littoral which experience such micro-climatic differences, and Šmíd (1973) reports on a similar situation.

Unlike most terrestrial vegetation, which experiences water stress during the growing season, and has no external source of nutrients, wetland vegetation is often well supplied with water-borne nutrients; and then growth is largely controlled by the radiation climate (Willer, 1944; Ondok, 1977). However, water becomes particularly important at the margins. At the upper edge, the wetland plants compete with the terrestrial vegetation more adapted to water stress and, at the lower edge, the depth, temperature and transparency of the water control the extent of the helophytes and the growth of floating and submerged vegetation (Sculthorpe, 1967; Hutchinson, 1975; Spence, 1976).

The typical morphology of helophyte stands, which have perennial plants with extensive rhizomes and near vertical leaves and shoots, facilitates survival at these exposed margins and maximises their exploitation of the irradiance (Jervis, 1969; Dykyjová, 1973a; Ondok, 1973b). The vertical inclination of the assimilatory organs avoids intense heating, exposes a maximum of surface area to light (leaf area indices: *Typha latifolia* 14.6 (Jervis, 1969); *T. angustifolia* (Dykyjová, 1973a)), avoids light saturation, minimises self-shading, and in many stands allows enough light to reach the water to support understorey populations of pleustophytes, hydrophytes, periphytic and planktonic algae (often 15–35% of incident at the water/ground surface, but less than 1% in dense stands, Dykyjová, 1973a; Ondok, 1978a). The rapid development of these photosynthetic organs at the beginning of the growing season, from the large reserves stored in the rhizomes, ensures a long, productive growth period (Fiala, 1978b).

The most characteristic features of wetland vegetation are the pronounced zonations, determined by the hydrological conditions, which often show continuous or cyclic successional changes over long time periods. In the littoral of lakes this zonation is usually parallel to the shore line as the water depth increases, extending from wet meadows or forest (carr) to open water. Not only species but shoot density, height and productivity change across such zonations. Mochnacka-Ławacz (1975) has clearly shown such changes in stands of *Phragmites* and competing species in the littorals of Polish lakes. Fiala and Květ (1971) similarly have described the communities of helophytes along a succession from stands dominated by *Scirpus compactus* and *Typha latifolia* to *Phragmites australis* (Figs. 3 and 4 of their paper). They showed how selective animal grazing (on *T. latifolia* in this case) accelerated the succession to *P. australis* initially, and later led to an unstable mosaic of species in heavily grazed areas. Further examples are given by Květ and Ondok (1973, Fig. 1 and Table 1). Buttery *et al.* (1965) studied the zonation and competition of *Glyceria maxima* and *Phragmites australis*. In this case they showed that neither the nutrients in the soils nor competition for light were important, but the increasingly anaerobic conditions in the mud affected *Glyceria* more than *Phragmites*.

Van der Valk and Bliss (1971) have studied the changes in net primary production with the succession of vegetation in a series of oxbow lakes in Alberta. They showed a typical increase from submerged vegetation, through floating to helophyte communities and to the ultimate decrease in meadow communities. In prairie wetlands Van der Valk and Davis (1978) found a cyclic pattern of communities and productivities in which drought years initiate a 5–10 year sequence, starting from mud flat ephemerals and leading to well-developed emergent stands. Later senescent clones and muskrat activity result in open water with free-floating and submerged plants which last until the next drought.

Auclair *et al.* (1974, 1976) studied an extensive marsh complex in Southern Quebec, covering the species composition, species diversity, biomass, shoot net production and decomposition rates in relation to macro-nutrients and organic matter in the soil, and to the water depth (Fig. 2.22). The dominant species included *Scirpus fluviatilis* and *S. validus*, *Equisetum fluviatile*, *Phragmites australis* and *Eleocharis palustris*. Species diversity was inversely related to net production and biomass, and directly related to perturbations of the system. High levels of soil fertility, efficient nutrient recycling, high biomass and high production apparently promoted stability of the plant communities. A clear succession was seen, going from a community dominated by *Scirpus validus* towards one dominated by *S. fluviatilis*, parallel with an increase in soil fertility.

Gaudet (1977) studied the primary succession on wet mud at the edges of Lake Naivasha, Kenya, and the dynamics and production of *Cyperus papyrus* swamps in relation to the annual draw-down and re-flooding. The succession that started during a fall in lake levels continued after re-flooding and led to a papyrus fringing swamp. Of all the potential dominants present (*Sphaeranthus suaveolens, Cyperus digitatus, C. immensus* and *C. papyrus*), *C. papyrus* was the most adept in competition with hydrophilous annuals.

Meeks (1969) studied the effect of experimental draw-down at different seasonal dates on wetland plant succession for 7 years. The 80-acre experimental area on Lake Erie (Ohio) was separated from the main wetland by dyking, and four units were drained during the next 6 years (March, April, May and June) and re-flooded every September. Plant successions followed the same general trend from semi-aquatic populations to predominantly annual weeds. The early draw-down dates were harmful to breeding muskrats and ducks, but later draining did not have such disadvantages.

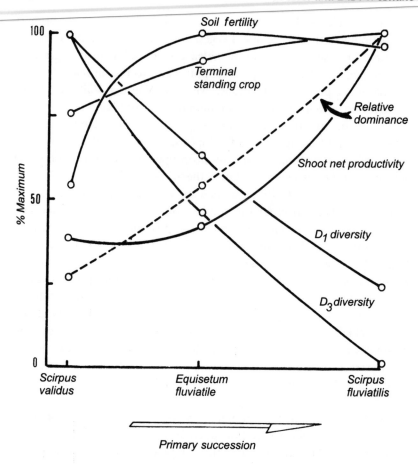

Fig. 2.22. Hypothetical successional gradients in a *Scirpus–Equisetum* wetland (based on Auclair *et al.*, 1974). Based on mean water depth of the three principal emergent communities. All values are species weighted means for gradients of occurrence, expressed as a percentage of the maximum for all species.

Output from primary producers to other trophic levels

In principle, apart from fossilisation, all net primary production is used sooner or later by heterotrophs in the given ecosystem or in other ecosystems. This is also true of wetlands. In most of them, however, the detritus food web predominates over the grazing–predatory food web (see Chapter 3). This leads, in many instances, to a considerable delay in the utilisation of a certain proportion of the organic matter released by the wetland plants. Prior to its consumption by heterotrophs, a greater or smaller proportion of the plant matter dies off and can be recorded as standing dead matter or litter. Various wetland plant communities contain different amounts of standing dead matter or litter and they store them for periods varying, mostly, between a few months and several years. There are big differences along typical temperate littoral wetland transects (Pieczyńska, 1972*a*). At the extreme end, peat is accumulated in some wetlands, whereby the utilisation of a certain part of the primary production is long delayed or practically postponed indefinitely.

Chapter 3 outlines the main pathways of the further utilisation of the net primary production in wetlands, including the various ways of destruction of both live and dead organic matter. Chapters 4 and 5, respectively, deal with the roles of micro-organisms and animals in these processes. At this place, a general statement may be sufficient that it is the quality of the plant matter and the environmental conditions that determine both the way and the rate the plant matter is used and transformed either in the grazing–predatory or the detritus food web. The composition and structure of the heterotroph community is, in fact, determined primarily by these two factors as well. (For the quality of the net primary production, see pp. 104–13.) As a rule, plant materials rich in protein or soluble and/or hydrolysable carbohydrates are both consumed directly and decomposed more readily than materials containing predominantly fibre, which may even be lignified or impregnated with substances whose breakdown is slow. The productive vegetation of eutrophic wetlands is usually richer in the former kind of substances than the less productive vegetation of oligotrophic or dystrophic wetlands. The differences in the output of these substances to the heterotrophs are most clearly seen if they are expressed on a unit ground area basis.

Grazing, although mostly less important than the use of dead plant matter in wetlands, may have a pronounced effect on the structure and productivity of the wetland vegetation (Reimold *et al.*, 1975*b*). This effect may be out of proportion to the small amounts of plant matter generally consumed by the herbivores, and is associated with side effects of their activities such as eutrophication of wetland habitats by bird excrements (see Chapter 3, p. 176), trampling of the vegetation by the bigger birds and mammals, effects on canopy structure leading to changes in competition ability of the plant species affected and, hence, in the plant community structure (e.g. Květ & Hudec, 1971). Another secondary effect of animal activities is changes in assimilate distribution in the affected plants (e.g. Mook, 1971*a* – effects of *Lipara* spp. on *Phragmites*) or the destruction of whole plants or shoots of which only a small proportion is consumed directly (e.g. Pelikán *et al.*, 1970 and Fiala & Květ, 1971 – effects of *Ondatra* grazing on *Typha latifolia* stands). The effects of animal activities on the vegetation are dealt with in more detail in Chapter 5.

Activities of the decomposers, both animals and microbes, also change the wetland biotopes, particularly the chemical properties of the water. The associated release of inorganic nutrients is of importance for the growth and production of the wetland plants (see Chapter 6).

On the whole, the relationship between the primary producers and heterotrophs is not a mere one-way relationship of supplier to consumer but a rather complex one with numerous feedback elements. The feedback relations stand out particularly clearly in highly productive wetlands because of the intense energy flow and passage of mineral elements through such ecosystems.

3

Further fate of organic matter in wetlands

J.W. DAY JR, E. PIECZYŃSKA and B. ÚLEHLOVÁ

Introduction

Organic material produced by primary processes in wetlands, or imported, has various fates: part may be grazed by animals, part may be mechanically destroyed and then decomposed, part may be released into the environment during the life or after the death of primary producers, part may undergo autolysis, part may enter the detritus food chain, part may be sedimented and part may be exported out of the ecosystem. The proportion of organic matter entering these pathways may be very different in various types of wetlands.

The organic matter supports the many different kinds of organisms which feed on it, forming the base of a developed trophic pyramid. In general, it seems to be true that wetlands are typical detritus food chain ecosystems (Odum, 1971). Only relatively few animals consume the plant matter directly. On the other hand, numerous organisms feed on materials pretreated by micro-organisms, on decomposition products, and on micro-organisms carrying out the decomposition. However, qualitative and quantitative data on wetlands about the occurrence of various biota, the trophic pyramids and/or food webs related to the detritus and grazing food chains are still rather scanty. This lack of knowledge is confounded by the extreme diversity and complexity of forms and functions in wetlands.

In order to understand the further fate of the organic matter, it is necessary to know the amounts and quality of different substrates undergoing destruction or decomposition, the processes which take place during these changes, the organisms and their activities participating in such processes and the effects of the ecological conditions.

An attempt to summarise knowledge on the structures and functions of grazing and detritus food chains and to elucidate the further fate of

169

organic matter in wetlands is made in this chapter, which also serves as an introduction to further chapters (4, 5 and 6). Data on closely related terrestrial and aquatic ecosystems are sometimes used to complete the overall picture. Naiman and Decamps (1990) and Hillbricht-Ilkowska and Pieczyńska (1993) have discussed the origins and fate of organic matter in wetlands. Macrophyte decomposition has been reviewed by Polunin (1984) and Webster and Benfield (1986), while Lodge (1991) and Newman (1991) have reviewed herbivory and detritivory in relation to macrophytes.

Origins of organic matter in wetlands

The contents and qualities of organic matter in wetlands vary widely according to their nature and position (e.g. Pieczyńska, 1986). It may be autochthonous (produced within the system) or allochthonous (imported from another ecosystem). The production of autochthonous organic material of plant origin in wetlands was dealt with in detail in Chapter 2. The quantity and quality of autochthonous and allochthonous materials form the nutritional basis for the development of the food web. The details of the paths taken are affected by the prevailing ecological conditions.

Autochthonous material

Several groups of primary producers can be distinguished in any type of wetland, which tend to have different fates: macrophytes, filamentous algae, microphytic algae and autotrophic micro-organisms. These are sources of different kinds of autochthonous organic materials which may undergo consumption, autolysis, breakdown and decomposition at different times and in different ways.

Vascular plants

These form the dominant vegetation in reedswamps, marshes and littorals, especially grasses and sedges, and are relatively highly productive. The seasonal patterns of their growth and biomass change according to the ecological conditions set by the geographical and climatic region, the habitat and the type of vegetation (see Chapter 2). The proportions of living plant parts or whole plants, relative to their standing dead and litter depend on the growth and death rates of the plant species, and the rates of decomposition processes taking place in the standing dead; hence they vary considerably, even at the time of maximum standing crop (Úlehlová, 1976; Table 3.1).

Filamentous algae

These vary in importance depending on the type of wetland and geographical location. Although often associated with the vascular vegetation, the relationship frequently appears to be more one of chance than necessity. They are common constituents of shallow marsh ponds and other areas, regularly, but not necessarily continuously inundated. In contrast to macrophytes, these algae seem to develop and decline quickly and to decompose rapidly.

Microscopic algae

These occur as phytoplankton and as epiphytes, and show pronounced seasonal fluctuations (e.g. Nauwerck, 1980). Their biomass is very low but their turnover rate is high. They are heavily grazed by small aquatic animals and a larger proportion of this material must enter the detritus food chain as herbivore faeces than for macrophytes. However, they are not a large part of the primary production in most developed wetlands, as defined for this book.

Standing dead, litter, and drifting remnants of macrophytes colonised by micro-organisms are the principal forms in which autochthonous production becomes available for decomposition in such wetlands, as the first steps in the detritus food chain from macrophytes. With respect to the standing dead and litter distribution four basic types of plant stands exist in wetlands:
1. standing dead and litter are not accumulated;
2. standing dead is accumulated and litter is decomposed;
3. litter is accumulated; and finally
4. standing dead and litter are proportionally accumulated.

Allochthonous material

Most wetland areas, and especially the marginal areas between land and water bodies (e.g. wetlands connected with lakes, ponds and salt marshes) can be simultaneously supplied with allochthonous matter originating on land and in the water body (organic matter produced in the central parts

Table 3.1. *Percentage distribution of standing dead material and litter as related to total above-ground live biomass in different wetland plant communities at their seasonal maximum biomass.*

Plant community (dominant plants)	Above-ground live biomass (g m^{-2})	Standing dead (% of above-ground live biomass)	Litter (% of above-ground live biomass)	Litter (% of standing dead)
Phragmites australis + *Carex* spp.	432	27	64	236
Carex spp.	468	44	69	164
Carex spp. + mosses	511	52	34	66
Carex spp. + *Phalaris arundinacea*	308	100	111	111
Glyceria maxima	709	51	15	29
Cladium jamaicense	1130	102	–	–

	Above-ground live biomass (g m^{-2})	Standing dead + litter (% of above-ground live biomass)
Carex spp. + mosses + other monocotyledons[a]	224 to 511	190.0 to 285.0
Carex spp. + other monocotyledons[a]	308 to 673	58.5 to 63.3
Carex spp. + dicotyledons[b]	434 to 673	31.0 to 39.0
Glyceria maxima	349 to 964	7.7 to 12.9

[a] Including mostly: *Deschampsia caespitosa*, *Phalaris arundinacea*, *Agrostis alba*, *Molinia coerulea*, *Calamagrostis canescens* and *Juncus* spp.

[b] Including mostly: *Galium palustre*, *Lythrum salicaria* and *Lysimachia vulgaris*. *Carex* spp. including predominantly *C. gracilis* (90% of biomass or more), with *C. vesicaria*, *C. canescens* and *C. acutiformis*.

(Calculated from Westlake, 1966; Květ & Ondok, 1973; Steward & Ornes, 1975.)

of the water bodies which accumulates around the edges). Much less is known about allochthonous matter than about autochthonous production.

The term allochthonous matter is usually applied to organic matter, but in many investigations no distinction is made between organic and inorganic inputs (e.g. total nitrogen or total phosphorus). Under natural conditions, without the visible influence of man, natural organic substances are the main source of allochthonous matter. In the present state of industrialisation and urbanisation, various matter of anthropogenic origin is of great significance, and toxic substances are frequently recorded entering wetlands in large amounts.

Atmospheric precipitation

Precipitation is now taken into account as a significant source of allochthonous material. Earlier, its significance was mentioned only in the case of urbanised and industrial areas.

Schindler (1971) stressed the importance of precipitation as a source of nutrients for Canadian lakes, both as direct input on the lake surface and as run-off. The latter is normally the greater source of material. Quantitative data on the amount of organic substances in atmospheric precipitation in the Voronezh area in Russia are given by Rozinoer, Saprykina and Poroiskaya (1973). They found that carbon amounts to $5.78 \, \text{mg} \, \text{l}^{-1}$ and organic nitrogen to $5 \, \text{mg} \, \text{l}^{-1}$, although these figures are so high as to suggest contamination of some sort. They also point to the relative contributions of particulate and dissolved matter (the latter is of greater significance although the proportion of particulate matter may reach 10%). Kluesner and Lee (1974) found only $0.26 \, \text{mg}$ org. $\text{N} \, \text{l}^{-1}$ in precipitation in central USA, which was calculated to yield about 5% of the annual allochthonous input of organic nitrogen.

Surface erosion

The products of erosion of drainage-basin soils can be of great significance when the drainage areas are large and fertile. The concentration and loading of the matter flowing from the drainage basin varies also according to atmospheric precipitation. Its seasonal character is most marked in areas with alternating wet and dry seasons. The smallest outputs and the lowest concentrations in suspended or dissolved matter are from typically forest drainage areas, whereas the richest are from arable fields, especially those intensively fertilised. Limnological literature shows a simple relationship between the character of the water body and the surrounding area (Schindler, 1971; Vollenweider, 1971; Le Cren & Lowe-McConnell, 1980). These relationships are also true to some extent for wetlands, especially for those connected with water bodies, because the whole allochthonous input reaches the upper littoral zone first and only later on may be transported further to the water body. Products of soil erosion provide mainly mineral particles, for the organic matter content usually does not exceed 10%. However, even this may sometimes be large relative to other sources.

Soil erosion may represent an insignificant contribution to many wetland areas but, in others, erosion may be a very important contributor of allochthonous matter. This is especially true of wetlands situated in deltas and flood plains of the great rivers, such as the Amazon, Danube, Nile and Mississippi. The rivers are the main vectors of allochthonous material in deltaic wetlands and flood plains, and the functioning of these ecosystems depends on them. Not only is there a significant inflow of dissolved and suspended organic material, but also suspended minerals which are deposited and form the bulk of the river sediments. These factors become very apparent when human activities (such as flood protection dykes on the Mississippi and the Aswan High dam on the Nile) disturb the input of sediment. The Mississippi and Nile deltas are now deteriorating because of an insufficient supply of sediments (Chabreck, 1970; Day et al., 1973; Rzóska, 1976; Craig et al., 1979). Rivers may also carry pollution and certain live organisms into wetlands. The role of rivers has also been shown to be similar in estuaries.

Significant amounts of eroded or leached material, especially in solution, may also be transported in less obvious ways such as seepage, underwater springs, drains and direct run-off (e.g. Westlake et al., 1972; Fisher & Likens, 1973; Kluesner & Lee, 1974).

Shore erosion

The erosion of shores by current and wave actions is a source of allochthonous matter only in wetlands connected with water bodies. Its intensity depends on the exposure of the shore to wave action and the susceptibility of the soils to be washed away. For example, shore erosion, calculated for all types of exposure, in Mikołajskie Lake, provides 2 tonnes of dry weight per year, and the maximal measured values are 3–4 kg (m shoreline)$^{-1}$ d^{-1} (Pieczyńska, 1972a).

Shore erosion may also represent a loss of organic matter from wetlands, especially from deltaic wetlands.

Litter fall

This kind of allochthonous matter is the best known and is the easiest to study quantitatively. While other allochthonous inputs have been estimated by insufficiently precise methods, the wind-borne material is usually determined relatively precisely, for example, by using different traps. In several lakes, the autumn inflow of leaf litter has been determined as 100–500 g (m of shoreline)$^{-1}$ (Levanidov, 1949; Szczepański, 1965; Pieczyńska, 1972*a*). These values are rather small and insignificant in whole lake ecosystems but may be important for short periods. In most cases, wind-borne material is less than 1% of the total input of organic matter in lakes. However, analyses of the distribution of leaves outward from the shore and in the bottom sediments have shown that practically all this material accumulates in the littoral wetlands. Close to wooded shores, parts of the inshore zone can be completely covered with leaf litter. The wind-borne material is the dominant source of organic matter here (Pieczyńska *et al.*, 1984).

Even a small amount of wind-borne material can be significant due to its specific components. Smirnov (1964), for example, has pointed to the significance of pollen and spores as sources of vitamins for aquatic animals. Most dust enters wetlands in precipitation (see above).

Allochthonous detritus entering running waters has been intensely studied. It can be the main source of their allochthonous matter and, in some cases, the main source of total organic matter (Mathews & Kowalczewski, 1969; Kaushik & Hynes, 1971; Fisher & Likens, 1973; Dawson, 1976*b*).

Litter fall provides mainly organic particulate matter, but appreciable quantities of nutrients and dissolved organic matter are leached out soon after it falls (see Planter, 1970*b*; Petersen & Cummins, 1974 and p. 184). The organic matter content in fresh tree leaves may be over 90% if they dry before falling. The high structural differentiation of wind-borne material is of great significance for its further fate in the ecosystem. There are all sizes from small particles to large branches. Freshly fallen tree leaves release considerable amounts of dissolved substances and thus can be treated as a source of dissolved matter.

Excreta of birds

In areas where the birds gather in large numbers (e.g. wintering or resting areas) the excreta can become a significant factor, transforming the wetland environment both spatially and trophically.

The birds' excreta cannot always be regarded as allochthonous matter for material produced within the wetland is sometimes processed, but when the feeding place is not the same as the roosting place, birds can fertilise the roosting wetland with a considerable amount of allochthonous matter. Dobrowolski (1973a) in his studies on Mazurian lakes found that coot (*Fulica atra*) produce 3.75 t y^{-1} of excreta in Lake Łuknajno, 5.5 t in Lake Śniardwy, 156 kg y^{-1} in Mikołajskie Lake and 100 kg y^{-1} in Lake Warniak. Swans (*Cygnus olor*) produce 1.7 t y^{-1} of excreta in Lake Łuknajno (the lake is a swan reserve) during the growth season. A considerable part of the excreta accumulates on the shore and changes the environment completely. Leah *et al.* (1978) found that the phosphorus budget of a lake in East Anglia (England) could be balanced by the large input ($\sim$70% of total phosphorus loading) from roosting blackheaded gulls (*Larus ridibundus*) which fed elsewhere. They also provided a large nitrogen input. Geese have been shown to play a similar role in the USA (Manny *et al.*, 1975).

Domestic and industrial sewage, manure

Wetlands are often exposed to sewage which contains both mineral and organic matter. Such input at a low level fertilises the ecosystem and can be mineralised there, but an excess causes a degradation of the system. Average municipal sewage contains about 50% of organic matter, of which over 50% is dissolved. The literature provides some data on the transformation of different littoral communities (mainly of macrophytes) by sewage (Suominen, 1968; Adams *et al.*, 1971; Bernatowicz *et al.*, 1974; Pieczyńska & Ozimek, 1976; Ozimek, 1978; de Nie, 1987; Pieczyńska *et al.*, 1988). In all cases analysed, a marked effect of sewage was observed, but it is rarely clear if the effects are caused by increases in inorganic nutrients, the input of organic matter or other constituents.

In many ponds in Central Europe, that are used for the industrial culture of carp (*Cyprinus carpio*) and other fish, the application of organic farm manure provides considerable inputs of allochthonous material which drastically change their biological structures and functioning.

From the water body associated with the wetland

The accumulation of detritus and aquatic organisms on shores of water bodies, mainly lakes and reservoirs has been observed in numerous instances. This is due to wave action and to currents. The accumulation of planktonic organisms on the shore has been described as the 'shore effect', regarded in the limnological literature as an important process (Welch, 1952; Szczepańska, 1967; Braginski *et al.*, 1968; Pieczyńska, 1972*a*). Detritus and macrophyte debris also accumulate there. Sebestyen (1950) observed the intensive accumulation of detritus due to wave action on the shores of Lake Balaton. Data given by Björk (1967), Hejný (1971) and Pieczyńska (1972*a*) show great accumulation of macrophyte fragments on the shores. The drifting material is frequently over 90% aquatic in origin, by dry weight, including both algae and aquatic macrophytes.

This accumulated material supplies the shore zones with considerable amounts of organic matter and is an important element modifying the spatial structure of the littoral biotope. For example, the material accumulating isolates fragments of the littoral by forming small lakeside pools with different environmental conditions (Pieczyńska, 1972*a*).

Differentiation of allochthonous materials

The various kinds of allochthonous material usually differ qualitatively in proportion of dissolved compounds, size of particles, physical structure and chemical composition, as well as in quantity. Furthermore, there are great differences in input dynamics, in space and time. For example, the role of litter fall differs according to the adjacent plant cover, being significant in afforested areas and often of no significance in grassland areas. The spatial differentiation of shore erosion is also great. Over time, the surface inflow depends on the distribution, nature and intensity of precipitation and litter fall. The latter is much influenced by wind and the phenological cycle of plants. Pieczyńska (1972*a*) has shown that over 70% of the annual leaf-fall occurs in 3 months in Lake Mikołajskie in Northern Poland. All these variations affect the significance of the allochthonous matter in the ecosystem and the ways in which it is transformed.

The proportions of autochthonous and allochthonous organic matter in various wetlands

The majority of aquatic and terrestrial environments show a definite prevalence of a particular source of organic matter, and the proportions of various autochthonous and allochthonous sources therefore vary in different wetland areas. Most data on the relative proportions of autochthonous and allochthonous organic material deal with whole water bodies and show the allochthonous component may be from less than 10% to more than 80% of the total input (Saunders *et al.*, 1980). However, similar variability occurs between and within wetlands. Large areas, for example, may be only poorly supplied with allochthonous organic matter, except along their boundaries, while narrow strips of wetland can be much more affected by allochthonous organic matter. In eulittoral wetland sites related to lakes, there may be several sources or organic matter in addition to local photosynthesis, such as considerable contributions of matter of drainage-basin origin (due to the vicinity of arable land) and simultaneous accumulation (due to wave action) of matter produced in other parts of the lake. For example, sites in the eulittoral of Mikołajskie Lake (Northern Poland) are supplied with $8800 \, \text{kJ} \, \text{m}^{-2} \, \text{y}^{-1}$ of organic matter produced on-site (predominantly by algal photosynthesis), $20\,300 \, \text{kJ} \, \text{m}^{-2} \, \text{y}^{-1}$ of material produced elsewhere in the lake and transported by wind and wave action (mostly reeds), and $8100 \, \text{kJ} \, \text{m}^{-2} \, \text{y}^{-1}$ of terrestrial material (mainly from soil erosion and leaf litter) (Pieczyńska, 1972a).

In Mikołajskie Lake, used here as an example, and in other lakes, the role of various allochthonous and autochthonous inputs of organic materials differs in various littoral environments. For example, in several lakes, parts of the littoral, several hundreds of metres long, are shaded by trees, with a meagre primary production. This environment is affected noticeably by large inputs of organic matter of terrestrial origin. Frequently, parts of the eulittoral are particularly exposed to wave action and have broad inshore shallows where organic matter of lake origin is constantly being accumulated. Primary production is usually of greatest significance in sheltered areas occupied by helophytes or unshaded, quiet bays separated from the lake by a broad belt of helophytes. In many lakes, considerable parts of the eulittoral are affected noticeably by sewage.

In the saline marshlands of South Louisiana (USA), the net production of the dominant emergent macrophyte (*Spartina alterniflora*) was estimated as $25\,100 \, \text{kJ} \, \text{m}^{-2} \, \text{y}^{-1}$ and algal net production (in the shallow fringing lakes) was estimated as $21\,600\,\mathrm{kJ\,m^{-2}\,y^{-1}}$ (Day *et al.*, 1973). Here terrestrial input was very low because of the size of the marsh.

Losses of biomass

The incoming organic matter, both allochthonous and autochthonous, depending on the kind of material and environmental conditions, undergoes various transformations in wetlands. These processes can be illustrated by the example of the fate of macrophytes which are the dominant producers and the most significant 'environment-forming' factor in wetlands.

The literature on the fate of macrophyte production is rather poor. Most often the losses of macrophyte material prior to the time of the maximum biomass are studied as an essential part of the determination of the annual production from maximum biomass (see Chapter 2, pp. 80–2). The majority of these estimates pertain to an overall biomass loss without mentioning the causes, and only a few quantitative studies distinguish between the effects of particular factors on the losses of macrophyte production.

Living vascular plants, or their parts, may enter the food chains throughout the whole year because of animal grazing, fungal and bacterial attack, viral diseases, mechanical destruction by wind, waves and animals, human management and natural aging death. The turnover of living submerged macrophyte vegetation is often a continuous process, but less rapid than in algal populations (Williams, 1966; Westlake, 1982).

Losses of macrophyte material by animal grazing

Macrophytes can be used as food by many herbivores: fish, birds, mammals and aquatic and terrestrial invertebrates. Gaevskaya (1966/69) has compiled numerous references to their activities and there is further discussion in Chapter 5. Nevertheless, there is great diversity of opinions in the literature on the quantitative significance of grazing and the utilisation of macrophytes under natural conditions. Some macrophytes are grazed more than others, particularly if selective grazers are present (e.g. Perkins & Maddox, 1976). Again, there is considerable diversity of opinion as to whether emergent plants are more or less likely to be heavily grazed than submerged plants. It is probably not sensible to generalise, for much will depend on local circumstances and the type and abundance of particular grazers.

Even where grazing is unimportant as a fate of macrophyte production, it may nevertheless be important to maintain particular populations of species which are obligate herbivores, especially if they are selective.

Most grazing losses are based on observations of damage attributed to grazing, on qualitative observations of gut contents or on laboratory experiments. It is not clear to what extent macrophyte tissues found in the guts are assimilated, or to what extent they reach the gut quite incidentally with detritus, algae or animal food and are subsequently defaecated to be used in the detritus food chain. However, Hansen *et al.* (1971) have shown the consumption of *Eichhornia* unequivocally, using radioactive tracers.

In some circumstances a high grazing pressure can lead to relatively great damage (e.g. Pelikán *et al.*, 1970; Sheldon, 1987), but more often the total amount of macrophyte directly consumed is quite a small proportion of the net primary production. Imhof and Burian (1972) in their study on the reedbelt of the Neusiedlersee (Austria) and Ondok and Květ (1978), on the basis of investigations of wetlands connected with fishponds in Czechoslovakia, show that only a small percentage of the energy bound in reeds is ingested by herbivores. Similar data have been obtained in other quite varied wetland environments (see Chapter 5).

On the basis of considerable literature data, it is justified to conclude that macrophyte grazing is of relatively little importance on salt marshes and that the majority of consumers inhabiting these types of wetlands, especially at the lower trophic levels, are at least partially detritivores (Golley *et al.*, 1962; Teal, 1962; Heald, 1971; W.E. Odum, 1971; Pomeroy & Wiegert, 1981; Polunin, 1984; Day *et al.*, 1989).

Invertebrate grazing

Soszka, G.J. (1975) examined the feeding of invertebrates on four species of submerged macrophytes, and the losses of macrophyte material due to grazing in the shallow littoral of Mikołajskie Lake. Feeding on *Potamogeton* species was particularly intensive. In June over 60% of the leaves of *P. lucens*, and almost 80% of the leaves of *P. perfoliatus* had holes, most probably as a result of grazing. The leaf biomass losses increased during the vegetation season; by autumn, they amounted to an average 60% for *P. perfoliatus* and 40% for *P. lucens*. At many sites over 90% had been lost. *Elodea canadensis* and *Myriophyllum spicatum* were eaten to a much lesser extent. The percentage of their leaves showing damage gradually increases during the season, but even by autumn it does not exceed 20% for *Elodea* and 40% for *M. spicatum*. The maximum losses of biomass do not exceed 7% for either species. Similar preferences were found by Kořínková (1971*b*). Kashkin (1961) estimated the monthly losses of submerged plants due to total invertebrate grazing in a reservoir as 0.1– 0.01% of plant biomass but, in contrast, Wesenberg-Lund (1943), in Danish ponds, reported that, by autumn, the Trichoptera larvae destroy the leaves of *Potamogeton natans* almost completely.

Mining species are often important (Urban, 1975), again particularly in *Potamogeton* species. Unlike the grazing fauna living on macrophytes, which uses mainly leaves, the mining organisms often penetrate the stems. McGaha (1952, 1954) working in various lake and river environments, has found so many canals in macrophyte leaves due to mining of Diptera larvae that the leaves would break even without any wave action, and the leaves of *Nuphar* were sometimes completely destroyed by young Lepidoptera larvae. According to Gaevskaya (1966/69) some larvae of Diptera move on to new leaves after damaging several leaves so that eventually all leaves are perforated. These observations indicate that mining may weaken plant tissues and thus accelerate detritus formation (cf. Soszka, H., 1974). One of the authors of this chapter (E.P.) has observed that, by autumn, such invertebrates sometimes destroy almost the whole mass of vegetation they colonise. These are, of course, exceptional situations, and similarly there are situations where mining does not occur at all.

Smirnov (1961*b*) has analysed the feeding of ten species of invertebrates on plants with floating leaves in Lake Poletskoye and has found that the daily losses of leaf biomass may reach 7% at some sites. Imhof (1973) has estimated the energy intake by all phytophagous insects feeding on the emergent *Phragmites australis* as about 170–250 kJ m^{-2} y^{-1}, which is less than 1% of the net primary production.

Smirnov (1961*b*) considered that emergent plants are consumed in the living state, whereas submerged plants are consumed dead, along with their aufwuchs, and Soszka, G.J. (1975) found that, given a choice, *Asellus aquaticus* preferred dead leaves and periphyton. However Marcus *et al.* (1978) have shown that *Asellus* consumes, and grows fast on, live *Elodea canadensis* in the laboratory, and in most of the examples above live submerged tissue are being consumed.

Vertebrates

Birds are an important group of grazers on macrophytes in wetlands. Many species found in wetlands use them both as living and feeding sites and as resting areas (migratory waterfowl). The concentrations of birds may be high (see in Smart, 1976 and the series of Bulletins of the International Waterfowl Research Bureau). Although their grazing effect is rarely estimated quantitatively, it is undoubtedly quite considerable (see pp. 299–300 and 315–16).

Other vertebrates can also act as considerable consumers of wetland macrophytes. The muskrats (*Ondatra*) can be mentioned here (see Errington, 1963; Pelikán *et al.*, 1970; Pelikán, 1975). Fish can also be of great significance, such as the grass carp (*Ctenopharyngodon idella*) acting as specialised macrophyte grazers (e.g. van Zon, 1977).

Chapter 5 gives more details of the consumption and use of macrophytes by animals.

Mechanical destruction of macrophytes

The detachment of entire plants from the substratum or fragmentation, is normally due to wind and wave action, animal activity, or action or side effects of the human exploitation of wetlands. In several cases the faunal activity is undoubtedly a considerable element of destruction of live wetland plants, such as by large muskrat or coypu populations (e.g. Pelikán *et al.*, 1970; Mason & Bryant, 1975). Also, a considerable length of leaf mines is probably made for animal movement rather than for consumption (Soszka, H., 1974).

Partly damaged macrophytes, detached from the substrate, often survive for some time, being utilised in the grazing food chain and excreting dissolved organic matter. Depending on the type of damage, a whole plant or shoot can be detached or only a small fragment. In the first case, a submerged plant can survive for a long time, floating free in the water.

By wave action macrophyte material is accumulated on the shore. In Mikołajskie Lake, Pieczyńska (1972a) has shown that about 80% of the annual *Phragmites* production accumulates on the shore by early in the year following its death and breakdown. A distinct periodicity was observed in the accumulation of leaves, panicles and stalks of reeds. About 80% of the annual accumulation of stems was observed in spring (April, May) after the ice cover had broken up material from the previous year. The leaves accumulated mainly in late autumn (leaves of the current year's plants), and in spring (leaves of the previous year's plants). During summer the accumulation of emergent plant material was at a minimum, which has been found elsewhere by Úlehlová (1976).

All submerged species found in Mikołajskie Lake have been observed stranded ashore (Pieczyńska, 1972*a*). Plants colonising the shallow parts of the littoral accumulated most intensely, such as species of *Potamogeton*. The most dense accumulation of macrophytes has been observed in large lakes with a considerable wave action, where the configuration of littoral allows the waves to reach the shore. In small and completely overgrown lakes or ponds, such accumulation is less, as the waves are weaker and do not reach the shore.

Death of plants

In this context 'dying' is limited to mortality unrelated to grazing or damage. Such death may arise from the natural growth and ageing cycle of the plant, unfavourable environmental conditions, inter- and intra-specific competition and, in practice, from diseases (though this is energetically a form of grazing and grazing damage). Most interest attaches to mortalities during the growing season (before the maximum biomass in communities with seasonal growth patterns) because these affect the population dynamics and are less easily measured than mass mortalities such as occur at the end of growing seasons, or after epidemics.

Some examples of differences in mortality patterns may be seen in Chapter 2, where the population dynamics of several species are described. In relatively stable species and undisturbed environments (e.g. many *Phragmites australis* reedswamps) losses of green parts are usually between 1 and 15% of the seasonal maximum above-ground biomass (Borutskiĭ, 1949; Květ, 1971; Hejný, Květ & Dykyjová, 1981). However, some temperate species (e.g. *Glyceria maxima*, *Nasturtium officinale*), and many tropical and subtropical communities in equable climatic and hydrological environments (e.g. *Cladium jamaicense*, *Typha domingensis*, *Cyperus papyrus*) have leaves and shoots continually dying along with initiation and growth (Westlake, 1966; Mathews & Westlake, 1969; Howard-Williams, 1973; Steward & Ornes, 1975; Dawson *et al.*, 1978; Thompson *et al.*, 1979). Further examples and the effects on the P/B ratio are discussed in Westlake (1982). This means that, at the end of growth seasons, there is often a considerable weight of dead plants in temperate freshwater, tidal and salt marsh and swamp ecosystems, where grazing is slight and most of the organic production dies. The proportion of standing live and dead vegetation varies seasonally and according to the species and environment (see Table 3.1).

The excretion and leaching of dissolved organic matter

Excretion of organic material during growth, and the role of this process, in freshwater and marine ecosystems have been investigated by several authors. Allen (1971) and Wetzel and Allen (1972) studied lake macrophytes and showed that excretion of dissolved organic matter by plants represented a significant portion of their gross photosynthesis. In their opinion the dissolved organic matter (DOM) released by macrophytes is likely to be utilised to some extent by epiphytic algal and bacterial populations living on macrophyte plants, before the organics reach the aquatic environment. The problem of release of DOM by living plants arises only for submerged plants and the submerged root and rhizome systems of emergent plants. Otherwise losses of dissolved organic matter from emergent plants are connected mainly with processes occurring in dead plant material.

As plant cells die and their plasmalemmas lose integrity, autolysis and leaching of soluble organic compounds occur once the tissues fall into the water or are washed by rain. This is a rapid process which occurs in a time scale of days and is also important with fresh allochthonous material. In field studies, this has been difficult to document because the sampling interval used has not been short enough. However, Boysen-Jensen, as early as 1914, reported a decrease in the protein content of the submerged aquatic plant, *Zostera*, from 14% in live leaves to 9% in dead yellow leaves. More recently Kirby (1971) reported a decrease in energy contents of dead standing *Spartina alterniflora* compared with live plant tissue from $17.2 \, \text{kJ g}^{-1}$ to $16.3 \, \text{kJ g}^{-1}$ dry weight. In a controlled laboratory test, Burkholder (1957) showed an extremely rapid initial growth of bacteria when incubated with *S. alterniflora*, and attributed this to leaching of soluble compounds. If microbiological inhibitors are used, 50 to 80% of the weight lost in the first 2 to 3 weeks can be attributed to leaching (Hobbie *et al.*, 1980; Polunin, 1982*a*).

It can be concluded that the release of DOM is an inevitable, although little known fate of part of macrophyte production. The released organic compounds are taken into the cycling of matter mainly by micro-organisms.

The fate of algal biomass

Less is known about the fate of algal biomass in wetlands. Algae are known to be heavily grazed by many small invertebrates and it may be assumed that grazing is often more important than for macrophytes. Soszka, H. (1974), for example, found that periphyton was the main component of gut contents, even in insects mining in angiosperm leaves. Large sessile and floating filamentous algae also provide an excellent substrate for diatoms that are grazed (Smalley, 1958; Kirby & Gosselink, 1976). Pieczyńska (1986) reports that algae are broken down in the littoral several times faster than macrophytes.

The fate of animal biomass

The processes that utilise animal biomass have been less studied than those affecting plant materials, except perhaps for predation. Animals are autolysed and decomposed much faster than plant materials, and are more difficult to study. The diversity of the animal materials is much greater, related to the levels of animal organisation and behaviour.

The fate of allochthonous material

The other sources of organic matter in wetlands undergo similar transformations. Although several authors point to the possibility of allochthonous detritus as direct food of invertebrates (Gaevskaya, 1966/69; Minshall, 1967; Kaushik & Hynes, 1971; and others), it seems that the main decomposition of this matter is due to bacteria or fungi (Sorokin, 1967; Mathews & Kowalczewski, 1969; Kaushik & Hynes, 1971; Pieczyńska, 1972a; and others). Many components are not readily usable by animals.

The leaching of dissolved compounds from particulate allochthonous matter is a very rapid process over a short period; up to 30% of dry weight per day, depending on the kind of matter and environmental conditions, especially temperature (Kaushik & Hynes, 1971).

The change to detritus

A large part of the organic input, both autochthonous and allochthonous, enters the detritus food chain directly or indirectly and is utilised by detritus feeders or undergoes decomposition by micro-organisms (e.g. Pieczyńska, 1986). The rates of the processes involved depend on abiotic factors such as temperature, oxygen concentration water chemistry and water movements (Godshalk & Wetzel, 1977), as well as on the properties of particular species (size, chemical composition and morphology, e.g.

Mason & Bryant, 1975; Úlehlová, 1976) and, especially in the case of plants, on the differing properties and initial location of their specialised parts (leaves, roots, rhizomes, tubers, etc.).

Detritus formation and transformation

As the material breaks down, it is changed in size, and in chemical composition and a considerable proportion becomes dissolved (Godshalk & Wetzel, 1977). Mechanical fragmentation and chemical modification of the detrital materials are not easily separable processes, since one influences the other. Breakdown is usually thought to involve colonisation by micro-organisms which, through enzyme activity, attach the detrital materials. These then become easily fragmented by currents and wave action (W.E. Odum *et al.*, 1973). The bacteria, protozoa, fungi and other micro-organisms enrich the detritus in protein and make it an attractive food for a number of detritivores (e.g. Hargrave, 1976). The latter, in turn, appear to skim or digest off the micro-organisms, returning faeces to the detrital pool for recolonisation (Fenchel, 1970).

The grinding and tearing action of the detrital feeders may be an important process in itself. Furthermore, digestive enzymes secreted into the material as it passes through the intestine contribute to chemical degradation. Finally, repackaging of very fine fragments occurs in the faecal pellets, making these fragments more available for further exploitation (Hargrave, 1976). These faecal pellets and other excrements are important sources of organic matter. Mason and Bryant (1975) showed that the oxygen consumption of faeces and of fragmented material was often higher than that of the initial litter. Thus the microbial action and the feeding activity of detritivores reinforce each other.

Pieczyńska (1972a) and Godlewska-Lipowa (pers. comm.) stress that, in the border zone between land and the littoral of lakes, where there is a great amount of organic detritus, the number of micro-organisms is considerably larger than either in the terrestrial or aquatic parts of the lake basin. The decomposition rate is also highest there. Hargrave (1970) showed that bacterial production was stimulated by grazing of the deposit-feeding amphipod *Hyalella azteca*. Fenchel (1970) showed a much increased breakdown rate when *Thallassia* leaves were exposed to amphipods. Mason and Bryant (1975) found no significant difference in the rates of breakdown of *Typha* and *Phragmites* in the presence and absence of animals, but complete breakdown took longer when animals were absent.

The way in which micro-organisms operate in this system has often been queried. There seem to be doubts that microbial action on surfaces is an important aspect of breakdown. The initial microbial colonisation of the surface of the detrital material has been inferred largely from chemical analyses which showed increasing protein content with decreasing detritus particle size (Odum & de la Cruz, 1967; Heald, 1971; Kirby, 1971; E.P. Odum, 1971). However, Paerl (1973) showed, through scanning electron microscopy, that heterotrophic activity and colonisation of detritus in Lake Tahoe, USA were correlated directly and Hargrave (1976) showed an apparently simple relationship between surface area, organic matter content, and the size and metabolism of communities of organisms associated with diverse aquatic sediment and detritus particles. On the other hand, surface microbial density is always low; usually only about 1% of the surface area of the colonised particle is occupied. It is possible that significant microbial activity occurs through organisms not directly attached to detrital particles, but utilising organic substrates leached or excreted from the detrital complex.

The meiobenthos is particularly important in breakdown (nematodes, amphipods, harpacticoid copepods and other small crustaceans, annelids and insect larvae). The nature of the faeces will vary greatly with the digestive efficiency of the organisms and their specific metabolic features, but very little is known quantitatively (Fenchel, 1970).

Composition of detritus

During weathering and decomposition, the nature and chemical composition of the original materials change because of elution processes, enrichment with mineral elements, microbial colonisation, mineralisation, humification, grinding, disintegration, etc. All sorts of material are initially depleted in nutrients by leaching but in later stages of decomposition nitrogen, phosphorus and some minerals (but not sodium and potassium) increase in concentration in the residual material (e.g. Mason & Bryant, 1975). Chemically, the live wetland vegetation is usually rich in cellulose and relatively poor in nitrogen. Initially, after death, the soluble materials are leached out and both the energy and protein contents decline. As fragmentation occurs, the protein and energy contents of the detritus plus microbiota increase at the expense of carbohydrates, crude fibre (cellulose and lignin), and lipids. This has been shown in *Phragmites* wetlands by Úlehlová (1976), in red mangrove by W.E. Odum (1971) and Heald (1971) and in *Spartina* marshes by Odum and de la Cruz (1967).

Gosselink and Kirby (1974) reported a fivefold increase in the content of particulate nitrogen in microbial cultures which used ground *Spartina alterniflora* as their organic substrate. The increase probably came from microbial incorporation of inorganic nitrates and ammonia from the incubation medium.

Younger plant materials may be decomposed faster than older, due to their more favourable histological and chemical composition, especially the higher nitrogen content, of their biomass. The old vegetation is characteristically poor in organic nitrogen and rich in lignified tissues.

The greatest differences in chemical composition of organic matter, as can be expected, are to be found between materials of plant and animal origin. A high C/N ratio and carbohydrates, mostly cellulose, starch and similar polysacharides, with lignins, prevail in plant materials, while the material of animal origin is characterised by a low C/N ratio and high protein content. While the proteins and nitrogen-rich compounds are easily decomposable, carbonaceous substances are resistant and are decomposed in several stages. Úlehlová (1976) gives examples of chemical composition of some materials.

Partly decomposed plant material supports a nitrogen- and phosphorus-rich diverse and productive micro-community on a relatively inert cellulose–lignin substrate. Its value as food seems to depend on the attached community rather than on the cellulose substrate, which is often passed relatively unchanged through the gut of animals. The microorganisms are therefore an important component of detritus. No data are available on the actual chemical composition of microbial cells existing under the natural conditions of wetland ecosystems. Cultured bacterial cells contain higher amounts of nitrogen, phosphorus and magnesium than macrophytes and algae, and less potassium and calcium. Excretion of organic matter and autolysis of microbial cells are common and are of great importance for the overall rates of decomposition.

The small biomass, short generation times and high turnover rates of micro-organisms result in looser bonds to the habitat than is the case with higher plant vegetation. Micro-organisms, because of their small size, their manifold enzymatic activities, their rapid adaptability to the new environment, and their ability to survive long periods under bad conditions, may grow rapidly anywhere and at any time under favourable conditions.

Sedimentation

The particulate organic matter formed during the breakdown of dead material settles, according to size and density, towards the bottom. Not all is respired and mineralised in the food chain and some accumulates as sapropel (cf. humus in terrestrial soils). This is mainly composed of complex relatively inert, materials such as humic acids, but varies in nature with the original materials and the dominant pathways of decomposition. Although resistant, they may be slowly used as an energy source and have important roles in modifying the physico-chemical environment (e.g. as antibiotics, or chelating agents). Little is known quantitatively about the rates of accumulation or the origins from allochthonous or autochthonous sources. Godshalk and Wetzel (1977) have suggested that rapid accumulation in sediments only occurs in very productive lakes where large amounts of resistant macrophyte material settle in anaerobic conditions.

Export

Yet another fate of organic material may be export out of the ecosystem. Since macrophytes are the main producers in developed wetlands, most interest attaches to their export. Macrophytes exported from a wetland can have several fates. They may be removed artificially either for industry or weed control (see Chapter 8). The terrestrial animals (birds, mammals, insects, reptiles) which feed on wetland macrophytes cause the indirect export of macrophyte material. They use and export to the neighbouring areas live plants, dead plants or the detritus from decomposing plant material.

Wetland areas are also penetrated by aquatic organisms, e.g. fish, which graze and carry part of the material beyond the given system. Prejs (1973) and Pieczyńska (1973) have shown that the eulittoral of Lake Warniak is regularly penetrated by fish and used as a feeding place. In the gut contents of carp, tench and crucian carp *Cylindritomidae*, *Liriopeidae*, *Tabanidae* and *Stratiomyidae* occur, which are typical of the boundary zone and are not found in other than the eulittoral lake zones. The magnitude of this kind of export is unknown.

In many wetland environments water flow is of considerable significance in the export of material beyond the system. Tidal water movements in coastal areas and heavy rains in inland marshes provide the mechanisms for loss of organic materials from marsh surfaces. This export, accompanying flushing, is probably the most important route for organic material leaving wetlands, either in the form of dissolved or particulate matter.

Reimold (1972) estimated the loss of inorganic phosphates from *Spartina alterniflora* plants and found that flooding water leaches significant quantities of phosphates. Few estimates exist of dissolved organic matter leached from whole plant stands. Turner (1978) reported that loss of DOM from salt marsh stands in Georgia during submergence was nearly equal to the net respiration of the planktonic community. Some of this soluble organic matter is undoubtedly refixed by the marsh epiphytes, but it is usually assumed that most of this dissolved material is exported.

Particulate organic loss seems to be the most important type of export in tidal wetlands but this may not be the case in wetlands that are flushed less frequently, or more gently. Flood waters are important in the mechanical degradation of detrital particles. This process must be size dependent, but no reports have been discovered which would describe the size dependence of the process. Odum and de la Cruz (1967) measured the flux of total particulate material out of a small tidal creek in the salt marshes of Georgia. They estimated a net export of 140 kg and 25 kg of organic matter for spring and neap tides, respectively, from a 10–25 ha marsh area in one tidal cycle. It has been estimated that from 30% to 50% of net production of coastal swamps and marshes is exported into adjacent water bodies (Golley *et al.*, 1962; Teal, 1962; Heald, 1971; Day *et al.*, 1973). Happ *et al.* (1977) showed a clear gradient of organic carbon concentration in a Louisiana estuary. Highest levels were in water bodies fringing the wetlands, and lowest were found in the Gulf of Mexico, indicating export from the marshes to the Gulf of Mexico. Nixon (1980) has reviewed studies on organic export from salt marshes and concluded that export did not always take place, but was site specific.

Material leaving wetlands around lakes will be decomposed in the lake or transported to wetlands on other shores.

General conclusions

Irrespective of the initial pathways entered by organic material the final fate of the material supplied by autochthonous and allochthonous inputs may be:

1. respiration and mineralisation (utilisation);
2. export;   ⎱ both may lead to humification and long-term
3. sedimentation. ⎰ accumulation in sediments

The IBP studies in the Nesyt fishpond marginal wetlands may be used as an example summarising the breakdown and losses of organic materials (Květ, 1973a; Úlehlová, Husák & Dvořák, 1973; Úlehlová, 1978). The main input is from *Phragmites* which produces about $1.5 \, \text{kg m}^{-2} \, \text{y}^{-1}$ above ground. Not more than 5 to 10% of this can be consumed by animals during the year but 40 to 50% may be exported by human beings if the stands are harvested. Some 5% becomes available for decomposition in the course of the growing season. Most of the remainder, about 70% of unharvested above-ground production, enters the detritus food chain from autumn onwards. Leaves, flowers and some stems become litter during autumn, winter and early spring, but some stems remain as standing dead until the next autumn.

The data discussed in this chapter stress that the classic trophic chain of producer–herbivore–carnivore does not fit most wetlands because of the low level of direct grazing and, in some cases, the high allochthonous input. A better, more representative model is producer (+ import)→ micro-organisms→herbivore→detritivore→carnivore which recognises the importance of micro-organisms in forming detritus and suggests the microbial complex as a distinct trophic compartment. This has been implied or shown in many ecosystem treatments of wetlands (e.g. E.P. Odum, 1971; Imhof, 1973; Pieczyńska, 1976; Úlehlová, 1976; Dykyjová & Květ, 1978; Good *et al.*, 1978; Pomeroy & Wiegert, 1981; Gore, 1983a,b; Howard-Williams & Gaudet, 1985; Day *et al.*, 1989).

4

The role of decomposers in wetlands

B. ÚLEHLOVÁ

Introduction

The organic matter produced by primary producers is subject to two basic decomposition processes.

Mineralisation This accompanies the assimilation of organic matter by different organisms, varying according to the level of organisation. Some of the substances are used for building their own biomass (secondary production), but the rest is released as mineral or simple organic compounds (e.g. K^+, Na^+, CO_2, CH_4, H_2O, NH_4^+, NO_3^-, SO_4^{2-}, $CO(NH_2)_2$, H_2S, PO_4^{3-}).

Humification This is a relatively long series of various fermentative and other biochemical processes, wherein different organic metabolites become gradually transformed into complex organic heteropolycondensates with bonds of different strength, called humus. The formation, as well as the decomposition and stability, of humic substances are affected to a considerable extent by bonding with some of the mineral constituents of the medium such as ions and clay minerals.

Different ecosystems can vary in their mineralisation/humification ratio, depending on the environmental conditions and the diversity of the organisms present. Individual structures of the wetland ecosystems, i.e. standing dead, litter, bottom sediments, soil and subsoils, vegetation zones, etc., are subjected to changing conditions of water level, thermal stratification, moisture content and air humidity in the course of the growing season. The feeding materials, sources of energy for microbial populations, vary as well, and change through the trophic levels. Some organisms modify the original substrates, for example, by fixation of atmospheric nitrogen, or release of metabolically active and important compounds. In this way the trophic potential of modified substrates may become suitable for other microbial groups. Specialised organisms can remove particular components selectively from the media (nitrifiers, denitrifiers).

The changing physical and trophic conditions of the micro-habitats contribute to the seasonal dynamics and successions of microbial populations with diverse metabolic activities and requirements, and to food webs of varying complexity.

In wetlands, the detritus food chain dominates, in which micro-organisms inhabit and transform the primary material. A number of animals feed on micro-organisms responsible for decomposition, on decomposition metabolites, byproducts and end products accumulating in the medium, and on materials pre-treated by micro-organisms. The microbial decomposition of more resistant materials is often preceded by mechanical disintegration and partial digestion during the feeding processes of animals.

Spatial distribution of decomposers and decomposition processes

The spatial distribution of local micro-habitats provides diverse conditions. The decomposition processes may take place:

1. in the air;
2. in the water;
3. in the soil;
4. at the interfaces of the three above-mentioned environments; or
5. in the digestive tracts of animals.

The decomposition taking place under fully aerobic conditions on the surface of standing dead plant material, above the water or soil will often be limited by drying of decomposing material, and will therefore be dependent on air humidity. The total amount of material decomposed here will be rather small. A fungal flora predominates.

In the water, different freshly dead and semi-decomposed plant materials as well as particulate and dissolved organic compounds, support the growth of various groups of micro-organisms with different enzymatic activities, belonging to different parts of the complicated food web and forming the base of the heterotrophic pyramid. Local gradients of oxygen, organic and mineral substances can be important by producing a variety of changing conditions, and establishing successions of microbial populations.

In the soil, dead rhizomes or roots are destroyed by the activities of quite different types of organisms from those in water or air. Here, also, local gradients can play an important role.

The soil surface in predominantly terrestrial areas comprises numerous micro-habitats in which organic material, accumulated as litter and enriched with mineral salts from interspersed soil particles, is decomposed. The nature of the organic material, the nutritional character of the soil, and the moisture and temperature conditions co-determine the rate of the decomposition process.

The surfaces both of living, dead and inorganic materials periodically wetted support a prolific 'aufwuchs'. These mixed communities of bacteria, algae and invertebrates display commensalism to mutualism. The bacteria make use of organic substances from dead plant material, simultaneously diminishing its mechanical strength. Both ample water supply and good aeration are the important factors.

Dead intricate organic material, at more or less advanced stages of decomposition, accumulates by sedimentation, at the surface of submerged soils. According to the rates of water movement and of accumulation and quality of organic matter, further decomposition may proceed under either anaerobic, or semi-aerobic to aerobic conditions.

The digestive tracts of animals contain diverse associations of intestinal micro-flora which carry out specific short-term decomposing cycles.

A complete description of sites of decomposition would be impossible because wetlands are composed of a multitude of micro-environments, each representing a separate biological–chemical–physical unit supporting a specific microbial community.

Redox conditions

The local redox status is the most important influence on the rate of decomposition processes and determines whether decomposition follows the aerobic or anaerobic path. The oxygen storage capacity of freshwater at 100% saturation is between 7.04 (at 35 °C) and 14.16 (at 0 °C) mg O_2 l^{-1} at 1 bar pressure. Swift-flowing streams and rivers, or rough waters of lakes or ponds, tend to be saturated with oxygen. During the summer thermal stratification occurs in lakes and the store of oxygen, especially in deeper water layers, is depleted. There are spatial (horizontal, vertical) and temporal (diel, seasonal) variations in oxygen content. The oxygen regime of the littoral zone of a water body has particularly marked diel and seasonal patterns. In general, photosynthesis generates large amounts of oxygen and can cause supersaturation, while decomposition needs oxygen and can cause oxygen deficits.

Waterlogged leaves or twigs at the mud–water interface often decompose under aerobic conditions because the topmost few millimetres of mud have a higher diffusion rate when there is a stirring action of overlying turbulent water and invertebrate activity. The thickness of the oxidised surface layer depends on the supply of oxygen at the surface and on the oxygen consumption rate in the substrate. Patrick and Delaune (1972) state that waterlogging changes the properties of soils. Redox potentials of aerated soils are in the range of 400 to 600 mV, moderately reduced soils are -100 to $+100$ mV, and highly reduced are -300 to -100 mV. Some redox systems become unstable under reducing conditions. Reduced iron and manganese become soluble in the surface mud layers and diffuse out into the water, while phosphorus ceases to be absorbed by these cations, comes into solution and is available for biota. Thus anaerobiosis leads to a chain of chemical changes (Willoughby, 1974).

Microbial processes taking place in the oxidised zone of waterlogged soil are similar to, or identical with, those in moist but well-aerated soils (Brady, 1990), while the processes taking place in the underlying reducing zone are due to the activities of facultative and true anaerobes. When oxidation of organic material takes place under aerobic conditions, about 50% of original carbon is used for respiration and released as carbon dioxide and the other 50% is incorporated into the biomass of the microbial population. The end products of aerobic decomposition are carbon dioxide, sulphate and nitrate, and the resistant residues.

During anaerobic decomposition a number of intermediary products arise, but much less microbial biomass and carbon dioxide are produced. The rate of decomposition is also slower. The intermediary products can be further metabolised by new populations of micro-organisms or when oxygen becomes available. The end products of anaerobic decomposition include methane, hydrogen, ammonia, amines, mercaptans, and sulphides (Tenney & Waksman, 1930; Sircar et al., 1940). The ratio of carbon dioxide to methane indicates the degree of anaerobiosis (Úlehlová, 1970; Wetzel, 1975). Wiebe et al. (1981) examined the major anaerobic pathways in the salt marshes in Georgia, i.e. fermentation, dissimilatory nitrogenous oxide reduction, dissimilatory sulphate reduction and methanogenesis. The emission of methane, a 'greenhouse gas', from wetlands has become recognised as an important component of the global heat balance (Mathews & Fung, 1987; Adams et al., 1996).

Materials undergoing decomposition

Organic materials utilised by heterotrophic micro-organisms in wetlands in the course of decomposition vary widely according to their origin. They may be autochthonous or allochthonous; of plant, animal or microbial origin; living, moribund, dead, or decomposing. They may be in the form of structured matter, or of different liquid or gaseous products of plant, animal or microbial metabolisms, such as different exudates, excreta, etc.

The greatest differences, as can be expected, exist between materials of plant origin, with high C/N ratio and high carbohydrates, and of animal origin, with a low C/N ratio and high protein (see pp. 187–8). Some developmental stages of insects contain considerable amounts of chitin, which is resistant to decomposition. Nitrogen and lignin contents in decomposing material are important factors determining the rate of decomposition.

Each decomposing material comprises substances which are easily decomposable, slowly decomposable and refractory. The substances that are metabolised slowly, or in more steps, such as lignin, hemicellulose and cellulose, support long and complicated trophic chains. After the first stages of microbial colonisation, plant litter often may become more palatable to animals consuming it. Live plant parts as well as plant remains are mechanically disintegrated by feeding animals, the increased surfaces being colonised by new populations of micro-organisms, and enriched by enzymes and organisms of their alimentary tracts. During the decomposition process the plant material thus passes several times to and fro between the grazing and decomposition food chains, involving plants, micro-organisms and animals in manifold, complex and successional interactions.

Specific differences are more important for animal materials because the fauna is represented by hundreds of species even in the structurally poorest habitats, contrasting with the tens of species in the higher flora of the most structurally rich ecotopes (Dvořák, 1971 and Chapter 5). The major part of energy assimilated by animals is lost in respiration, while another part passes in the form of excreta, urine, organic remnants and dead bodies into the decomposition food chain. Thus, the decomposition food chain is entered not only by the overwhelming part of the primary production but also by the whole secondary production, comprising metabolites, dead biomass and litter of animals and micro-organisms.

Micro-organisms have a carbon content around 47% of dry weight. The organic matter of bacteria can be separated into the acid soluble and insoluble fractions. The first one contains inorganic substances, sugars, organic acids, amino acids, nucleotides, vitamins, etc.; the second one lipids, lipoproteins, nucleic acids and proteins. Cell walls of micro-organisms are refractory. The chemical composition of cell walls is characteristic of different taxonomic groups of micro-organisms.

The metabolites of plants, animals and micro-organisms are mostly easily decomposable. Microbial exudates or metabolites may account for up to 50% of net microbial biomass production, so both these products and microbial biomass are important food sources for the microbial and micro-planktonic communities. The dissolved organic matter in waters includes low equilibrium concentrations of these, which may vary spatially and seasonally.

Micro-organisms

The heterotrophic micro-organisms participating in decomposition processes are relatively small (the diameter of a bacterial cell varies about 1 μm) and complicated mutual relationships usually develop among different taxonomic units. Individual taxa and coenoses possess differences in their metabolic activities. Taxonomically, they can be divided into bacteria, actinomycetes, lower fungi, algae and protozoa. For any ecotope it is important to know the taxonomic composition of microbial populations and their productive characteristics such as biomass, growth rate and generation time. However, knowledge of these characteristics is deficient. The occurrence of individual species of these groups in different parts of a wetland ecosystem may vary according to local conditions of the individual micro-habitats or micro-environments.

Although the population densities may not correspond necessarily with specific enzymatic activities of the respective physiological groups or species, the rate of growth is the important criterion of the participation of the organisms in different stages of the decomposition process. The micro-organisms may be present either in dormant or in active state, and the rates of growth of the active forms are under the control of a number of internal and external factors.

Dickinson and Pugh (1974) summarise the knowledge of the biology of plant litter decomposition in different environments. Jones (1974) reviews the taxonomy, ecology, physiology and biochemistry of aquatic fungi.

Table 4.1. *Bacteria of different wetland environments*

Environment	Bacteria	References
Water	*Myxobacteria* sp., *Cytophaga* sp., *Pseudomonas* sp., *Vibrio, Flavobacterium, Achromobacter, Escherichia, Micrococcus* sp., *Serratia marcescens, Bacillus megatherium, B. cereus, B. c.* var. *mycoides, B. pumilus, B. alvei, B. subtilis, Alcaligenes* sp., *Azotobacter chroococcum*	Oláh, 1969 Kocur *et al.*, 1961 Romanenko & Kuznetsov, 1974
Sediments	*Bacillus, Achromobacter, Vibrio, Chromobacterium, Pseudomonas, Nocardia, Micromonospora, Bacillus firmus, Mycobacterium*	Hood, 1970 Oláh, 1972
Freshwater sludge	*Spirillum, Spirocheta plicatilis, Sphaerotilus natans, Beggiatoa* sp., *Thiopedia rosea*	Marvan & Sládeček, 1973
Paddy soils	*Escherichia freundii, Klebsiella aerogenes, Erwinia* sp., *B. licheniformis, B. cereus, B. pumilus, B. circulans, B. polymyxa, Clostridium putrefaciens, Cl. lentoputrescens, Cl. cadaveris, Cl. indolgenes, Cl. bifermentans, Cl. capitovale*	Takeda & Furusaka, 1970 Kobayashi, 1971

Qualitative composition

Data on taxonomical distribution of different microbial groups in wetlands are very scarce. Complete lists of microbial taxa in different wetland environments are, and for a long time will be, impossible to prepare. Table 4.1 lists some species of bacteria isolated from different types and environments of wetlands and Table 4.2. lists fungi on some dominant wetland plants.

The association of fungi and particular macrophytes has been described by several authors (Pugh & Dickinson, 1965a,b; Pugh & Williams, 1968; Taligoola, 1969; Pugh & Mulder, 1971). They isolated fungal species from living generative organs, seedlings, leaves, stems and roots, and from dying and decaying plant parts, both in the aerial and soil environment. Each of the plant species seems to possess a specific colonisation pattern during the life period as well as decomposition. Several stages of succession were observed: hyaline-spored fungi were common on buried stems, leaves and roots, whereas the dark-spored fungi predominated on the standing dead material. The first colonisers of young *Typha latifolia* leaves

Table 4.2. *Fungi on some plants*

Salsola kali L.	*Typha latifolia* L.	*Spartina alterniflora* L.
(Pugh & Wiliams, 1968)		(Pugh, 1962)
Cephalosporium sp.	*Aureobasidium pullulans*	*Alternaria maritima*
Fusarium sp.	*Cephalosporium* sp.	*Cladosporium herbarum*
Acremoniella atra	*Cladosporium herbarum*	*Phoma* sp.
Alternaria tenuis acut.	*Mortierella hygrophila*	*Haligena spartinae*
Botrytis cinerea	Sterile mycelium	*Leptosphaeria albopunctata*
Camarosporium obiones	*Alternaria tenuis*	*L. discors*
Cladosporium herbarum	*Epicoccum nigrum*	*L. marina*
Epicoccum nigrum	*Phoma typharium*	*L. pelagica*
Stemphylium sp.	*Sporobolomyces* sp.	*L. typharum*
Chaetomium sp.	*Leptosphaeria typharum*	*Lulworthia medusa*
Other fungi	*Dactylaria candida*	*Lignincola laevis*
	Heliocorhoion sp.	*Pleospora herbarum*
	Leptosphaeria licatensis	
	Ophiobolus herpotrichus	
	Pleospora typhicola	
	Stagnospora typhoideaum	
	Isaria sp.	

emerging from water were the first four species listed in Table 4.2. Bacteria were also relatively common in young plant parts and declined with increasing age of plant organs. The nematophagous fungi *Arthrobotrys arnoides*, *Dactylaria candida* and *Dactylella leptospora* colonised the litter of the previous year mostly in the summer months when it was in an advanced state of decay. Thus the micro-flora of wetlands is greatly influenced by the type of vegetation that is predominant.

The micro-flora of submerged sediments differ from that of overlying water, although many species are common to both environments. Micro-organisms within finer bottom deposits are facultative anaerobes, which can grow either with or without oxygen. There are usually many more spore formers in sediments than in water and they exhibit a greater physiological versatility, in general, than those isolated from water. Kobayashi (1971) has stressed the role of photosynthetic bacteria in paddy soils.

Yeast and fungal populations have been reported from salt marshes in Barataria Bay, Louisiana, by Meyers (1971). The most abundant yeasts were of the genera *Pichia* and *Kluyveromyces*. Actinomycetes are well known in lake water and sediments (Willoughby, 1974) and have been reported in various wetland habitats. Among the most common protozoa of wetland communities are ciliates and foraminifera. Fenchel (1969) reported that the dominant ciliates were *Euplotes* spp. Most ciliates feed on bacteria, diatoms or small protozoas.

Quantitative distribution in space and time

Spatial or seasonal variations in counts of micro-organisms may be estimated by cultivation from materials on different nutritive agar media, by direct microscopic observation of materials, or by counting organisms on membrane filters. From the amount of organisms enumerated, microbial biomass can be calculated. The adenosine triphosphate (ATP) method measures microbial biomass on the basis of uniformly distributed cellular constituents (Sorokin & Kadota, 1972; Rosswall, 1973; Romanenko & Kuznetsov, 1974). The 'fumigation' (Jenkinson & Powlson, 1976) and 'respiration with an excess of substrate added' (Anderson & Domsch, 1978) methods have often been used for microbial biomass estimation, especially in terrestrial soils.

Generally, in spite of great seasonal variations and specific characteristics of water bodies, bacterial numbers and biomass increase from oligotrophic ($50 \times 10^3 - 340 \times 10^3$ organisms ml^{-1}) to eutrophic lakes ($2200 \times 10^3 - 12\,300 \times 10^3$ organisms ml^{-1}). Numbers of micro-organisms decrease markedly in acidic dystrophic lakes (Wetzel, 1975). Production of bacteria estimated over a short time period increases with increasing productivity of lakes and the average generation time decreases with increasing trophic level of the lake (Wetzel, 1975).

Vertical and horizontal distributions of heterotrophic micro-organisms can change very rapidly. The energetic sources actually available for microbial populations are the main controlling factors for their growth and development (Saunders, 1971; Úlehlová, 1976). Table 4.3 gives annual averages in counts of micro-organisms, cultivated on meat-peptone agar, of plant materials, soil and water, collected in three different littoral zones of the Nesyt fishpond, Czechoslovakia. Standing dead of *Typha angustifolia* is more densely colonised than that of *Phragmites australis*. Both kinds of dead material collected in aquatic habitats yield higher counts of micro-flora than those from terrestrial ones. Seasonal ranges of microbial counts in different materials studied are given in Table 4.4.

Coveney *et al.* (1977) estimated standing crops of bacteria from their total number determined by epifluorescence microscopy, and the growth rate constants in water of the eutrophic Bysjön, Sweden, over a 2-month

Table 4.3. *Annual average counts of micro-organisms of different plant,*
water and soil materials in three littoral zones of the Nesyt fishpond
(counts per g dwt of material or per ml of water estimated on meat-peptone agar; original data)

Material analysed \ Zone	Terrestrial	Littoral	Aquatic
Standing dead:			
Phragmites australis	0.7×10^7	0.4×10^7	
Typha angustifolia	4.9×10^7	35.7×10^7	
Litter:			
Phragmites australis	15×10^7	31×10^7	
Typha angustifolia,			
floating, semi-decomposed			36×10^8
Sapropel, soil	0.1×10^7	1.0×10^7	1.2×10^7
Water	5.1×10^3	9.9×10^3	5.0×10^3

Table 4.4. *Seasonal ranges of microbial counts in different*
materials in littoral of the Nesyt fishpond
(counts per dwt of material or per ml of water; estimated on meat peptone agar;
original data)

Material	Min.–Max.	
Standing dead	0.4–35.7	$\times 10^7$
Litter:		
Terrestrial	15.1–17.0	$\times 10^7$
Aquatic	31.1–36.0	$\times 10^7$
Aquatic, decomposed	0.3–30.0	$\times 10^8$
Sapropel, soil	0.1–1.2	$\times 10^7$
Water	4.8–9.9	$\times 10^3$

period during spring circulation. Mean number of bacteria varied from
2.7×10^6 to 13×10^6 cells ml^{-1} of water and mean calculated bacterial
biomass ranged from 0.4 to 2.2 mg fresh weight 1^{-1} of water. Mean
bacterial biomass was from 0.10–0.21 g C m^{-3} of water and the bacterial
production was at least 0.0–0.023 g C m^{-3} d^{-1}. Part of the bacterial
production is grazed by animals.

Christian *et al.* (1981) calculated spatial and temporal distributions of
organisms from ATP concentrations in the salt marsh soils and estuarine
waters at Sapelo Island, Georgia, USA. In all salt marsh soils studied,

ATP concentrations decreased with depth, but the ATP concentrations in the 'tall *Spartina* marsh' decreased less with increasing depth than those in the 'short *Spartina* marsh'. The highest concentrations of ATP in the top 10 cm occurred during July.

Hanson and Snyder (1979) reported that particulate organic carbon (POC) concentrations and viable bacterial densities in water decreased with distance from the *Spartina* marsh in several locations in freshwater, but ATP concentrations were similar at all locations. Soil concentrations of ATP were three orders of magnitude greater than concentrations in the tidal water. Of the biomass of the microbial community 79% was associated with the soil in the marsh. Microbial carbon in salt marsh soils lies in the range of $0.052–0.011$ mg C cm^{-3} in tall *Spartina* marsh and of $0.096–0.008$ mg C cm^{-3} in short *Spartina* marsh (using the conversion factor carbon: ATP = 100:1).

Microbial activity

Microbial biomass and production data give no information on the metabolic capabilities or activities of the microbial populations of the ecosystem. These are responsible for the actual decomposition and transformation of materials formed by the primary and secondary producers; for the release and reintroduction of mineral constituents from and into the individual structures (as plants, animals, micro-organisms, soil, water, air), i.e. for mineral cycling and for the maintenance of material equilibria. A number of authors have attempted to characterise and measure the microbial activities, using different methods, often rather sophisticated. Most of the methods may be described as non-specific, i.e. they measure the extent of transformations performed by the whole microbial population without distinguishing the role played by any individual component of that population.

Growth rates

Meyer-Reil (1977) has followed the growth rates of bacteria from Kiel Bight and Kiel Fjord on membrane filters in a flow system culture apparatus by using fluorescence microscopy. Hossell and Baker (1979) have followed the increase in bacterial numbers on fronds of *Lemna minor*, growing in a river, by direct counting, and have corrected these results for bacteria settling or being washed off. Another approach is to directly measure the change in bacterial numbers in natural water, filtering to remove zooplankton (using membrane filtration before and after exposure). Counts may be converted into biomass and differences into production by measurement of all sizes (e.g. Straškrabová & Sorokin, 1972).

These studies have shown a wide range of generation times, from 2.5 to 1000 h. They are often very long because natural water is a very dilute solution of resistant substrates, and the shortest times are usually found on surfaces in the early spring and late autumn when organic material may be a little more abundant and more labile. Very few of these studies have adequately considered other causes of change in bacterial numbers such as imports, sedimentation, or grazing, and the effects of the experimental treatments.

Paired plots

One of the frequently applied methods for measuring the extent and rate of decomposition under natural conditions is the 'paired plots method' described by Wiegert and Evans (1964). The instantaneous relative rate of disappearance of dead material from these plots can be calculated as:

$$L_b = \ln (W_0/W_1) (t_1 - t_0)$$

where L_b = disappearance rate in $g\,g^{-1}d^{-1}$, W_0 = weight of dead material at time t_0, W_1 = weight of dead material at time t_1, $(t_1 - t_0)$ is time interval in days.

This method was used by Ketner (1973) in the plant communities of *Junco-Caricetum extensae* and *Plantagini-Limonietum* on the Fresian island, Terschelling. The amounts of plant material decomposed, measured in monthly intervals, ranged from 0 to 145 g dry wt m^{-2} in the *Junco-Caricetum* and from 0 to 105 g m^{-2} in the *Plantagini-Limonietum*. The seasonal pattern of decomposition was similar in both plant communities; maxima of decomposition occurring both in spring and autumn. The summer minimum in the *Junco-Caricetum extensae* recurred regularly in July, while that in *Plantagini-Limonietum* plant community was seen in August. The relative rate of decomposition calculated, according to the formula of Wiegert and Evans varied in the course of the year from 0 to 40 mg g^{-1} d^{-1} in the *Junco-Caricetum* and from 0 to 20 mg g^{-1} d^{-1} in the *Plantagini-Limonietum*. The lowest decomposition rates were usually observed during the summer months of June and July, the highest ones were in the autumn (September, October). The extent and rate of decomposition varied from year to year.

Table 4.5. *Comparison of litter decomposition rates in different communities estimated by two different methods: 'paired plots' and 'litter bags'*

Reference	Area	Plant stand	Method used	Average relative decomposition rate (mg g^{-1} dry weight d^{-1})	
Ketner, 1973	Netherlands Terschelling	*Junco–Caricetum extensae*	Paired plots	Range	0–40
				Annual mean	14 (Loc. 1)
					18 (Loc. 2)
			Litter bags	Range	1–14
				Anual mean	5.5 (Loc. 1)
					6.0 (Loc. 2)
Úlehlová (original data)	Czechoslovakia Lanžhot	*Glycerietum maximae*	Paired plots	Range	7.3–15.4
			Litter bags	Range	3.8–8.0

Litter bags

Decomposition in ecosystems is often studied using the litter bag method, which consists of enclosing plant material of known mass and chemical composition in plastic mesh bags. A large number of bags is placed in the field and at several subsequent sampling dates a randomly chosen set of bags is retrieved and analysed for loss of mass and changes in the chemical composition. Wieder and Lang (1982) critically evaluated this method and recommended single and double exponential models for evaluation and description of mass losses over time using data obtained from litter bags.

The litter bag method underestimates actual decomposition in comparison with 'paired plots' as can be seen from data in Table 4.5. Nevertheless, it seems that data from litter bag studies reflect trends in decomposition of naturally occurring litter and allow comparisons of decomposition among species, sites and experimental treatments.

This method has often been used for the evaluation of decomposition of organic matter in different types of wetlands. Brinson *et al.* (1981) have summarised data on decomposition rates from a large diversity of wetlands. Several studies reported loss rates as percent remaining after one year. The decomposition rate coefficient, k, is calculated from the exponential decay formula:

$$k = \ln (x/x_0) /t$$

where x_0 is the dry weight of litter initially present and x is the dry weight of litter remaining at the end of the period of measurement, t is the duration of the experiment. Decomposition rate may be measured on different time scales (weeks, months, seasons, years). According to Brinson *et al.* (1981), the mean annual decomposition coefficient for northern peatlands (0.3) differs significantly from that (0.9) for other wetlands. A latitudinal gradient in loss rates exists, for they are faster at lower than at higher latitudes. Loss rates are species specific.

Chemically better defined material, such as pure cellulose, may be used in litter bags instead of litter. Cotton wool or filter paper serve as test materials. Hundt and Unger (1968), Tesařová and Úlehlová (1968) studied the rates of cellulose decomposition in several wetland plant communities in Central Europe. Úlehlová (1973) measured the cellulose decomposition rates in different pond littoral plant communities in Czechoslovakia, and Brinson (1977) in an alluvial swamp forest in North Carolina.

Table 4.6 summarises the data on decomposition rates in wetlands

Table 4.6. *Some decomposition rates in wetlands*

(a) Mean relative annual rate of decomposition

Wetland type	Location	Litter type		Rate of decomposition k (y^{-1})	Reference
Northern Peatlands	Michigan	*Carex* sp.		0.45	Brinson *et al.*, 1981
	Manitoba	*Carex rostrata*		0.25	
	Norway	*Carex nigra*		0.53	
	Canada	*Carex* sp.		0.24	
	Michigan	*Salix* sp. leaves		0.46	
	Manitoba	*Salix babbiana*		0.34	
	Norway	*Salix* sp.		0.33	
	England	*Eriophorum vag.* + *ang.*	leaves	0.20–0.27	
	Canada	Herbs and shrubs	leaves	0.07–0.49	
	Europe	Herbs and shrubs	leaves	0.16–0.60	
	Canada & Europe	Herbs and shrubs	stems	0.08–0.15	
	England	*Phragmites australis*		1.09–1.26	
		Typha angustifolia		0.64–0.69	
Cypress stand	Florida	Site mixed litter		0.39–1.39	
Freshwater marsh	USA, Canada	Different species		0.21–1.29	
	South Carolina	Floating leaves		4.0	

(b) Percentage of annual production remaining after 1 year

Wetland type	Location	Litter type		Annual residue (%)	Reference
Spartina marsh	Mississippi	*Juncus roemerianus*			Hackney & De la Cruz, 1980
		leaves		52.3	
		roots 5 cm		82.5	
		rhizomes 15 cm		92.1	
		Spartina cynosuroides			
		leaves		73.9	White *et al.*, 1978
		roots 5 cm		70.5	
		rhizomes 15 cm		93.0	
	Lousiana	*Spartina alterniflora*		0	
		Spartina patens		38	
		Juncus roemerianus		20	
Alluvial forest	North Carolina	*Nyssa aquatica*	leaves	28	Brinson, 1977
			twigs	82	

(c) Mean relative daily rate of decomposition

Wetland type	Location	Litter type		Rate of decomposition ($mg\ g^{-1}\ d^{-1}$)	Reference
Emergent eulittoral	Poland	Litter of macrophytes		0.5–10.3	Pieczyńska, 1972a
Borderline of land and swamp				22.8–79.6	
Swampy shore area				44.3–135.0	
Littoral				1.5–37.2	
Stream	England	*Nasturtium officinale*	leaves	358	Castellano, 1977
			stems	24	
Nesyt Fishpond	Czechoslovakia	Cellulose		5.0–37.4	Úlehlová, 1973
Open water				2.0–28.0	
Littoral					

measured by various methods and published by several authors. The examples, and the data collected, demonstrate that the microbial activities in different types of wetlands differ under the influence of temperature, soil type, moisture conditions and nutrient level, but also with the decomposability of the respective organic materials.

Metabolism

Another way of estimating micro-heterotrophic activity is based on the measurement of carbon dioxide production, oxygen consumption, or the uptake of glucose or other organic compounds (Hobbie & Wright, 1965). A number of authors (MacFadyen, 1963; Teal & Kanwisher, 1961; Houghton & Woodwell, 1980) have used the measurement of the released carbon dioxide as a means of obtaining integral, holistic information on the particular ecosystems. Schiemer and Farahat (1966) measured oxygen consumption in soils from four diverse reed zones of the Neusiedler See and on small saline lakes 'Zicklacken' in the Small Hungarian Lowland. Gallagher and Pfeiffer (1977) studied oxygen consumption of standing dead *Spartina alterniflora* and *Juncus roemerianus* in a salt marsh. Respiratory rates had similar seasonal pattern: they were lower in winter, increased in the spring, decreased in late June and July and increased in late summer and early autumn. Respiratory rates of *Juncus* material were lower than those of *Spartina*.

Hanson and Snyder (1980) estimated glucose concentration and flux in the Duplin River, Sapelo Island, Georgia, at low and high tide. They used also maximum uptake velocity, V_{max}, as an index of potential heterotrophic activity. Increases in potential activity in the creek were attributed to the higher number of bacteria. Bacterial counts were correlated positively with glucose uptake. According to Christian *et al.* (1981), in Sapelo Island studies, micro-heterotrophs in the Duplin River and marsh creeks, were the major consumers of labile DOC, and utilised glucose, glycolic and lactic acids more readily than aspartic acid and alanine. Glucose V_{max} values ranged from 0.04 to 25 mg C m^{-3} h^{-1} in waters of 'Sapelo estuary', whereas in estuarine waters of North Carolina the range was 0.06–9.6 mg C m^{-3} h^{-1} (Crawford *et al.*, 1974).

Cavari (1977) measured the nitrification potential (NP) of the water and sediments of Lake Kinneret, Israel. The process of nitrification includes a lag period of variable duration, which is dependent on the number of nitrifying bacteria initially present in the sample. The author calibrated the NP measurement in terms of number of nitrifying bacteria and supposed that the mixing of the upper layer of the sediments causes the distribution of the bacterial inoculum throughout the lake water.

Quantitative variation

Factors controlling rates and patterns of decomposition are manifold. Mesh size influences the rate of decomposition, for slower rates are reported in bags with smaller meshes. Soil water content is often a limiting factor for decomposition in terrestrial ecosystems but is less relevant in wetlands. From published data, it appears that flooding, its duration, water flow, turbulence and water stagnation may influence the rate of decomposition in wetlands. Alternating wetting and drying results in higher respiration, mineralisation and litter disappearance. Most rapid decomposition rates occur with aerobic conditions under some optimum regime of wetting and drying. Alternations between aerobic and anaerobic conditions result in somewhat lower rates of decomposition and continuously anaerobic conditions in the lowest ones (Brinson *et al.*, 1989).

Temperature is the chief controlling factor of decomposition rates in habitats well supplied with moisture and oxygen.

Heal and French (1974), studying decomposition of tundra plant materials, showed that the order of decreasing decomposition rates was soft leaves > hard leaves and shrub shoots > mosses > lichens and wood.

Mineral cycling

Micro-organisms are responsible directly or indirectly for recycling of nutrients (see also Chapter 6). During this mineralisation of organic materials, simpler organic and inorganic compounds are released, which enter new pathways and new cycles in the same or other habitats. Many papers (Odum & De la Cruz, 1967; Úlehlová & Dobrovolná-Vašulková, 1977; Brinson, 1977; Sharma & Gopal, 1982; Kulshreshtha & Gopal, 1982; Polunin, 1982b; Killingbeck et al., 1982) have described chemical changes during decomposition of different wetland plant litter. The data indicated that the first phase of the process involves passive leaching of nutrients and decomposition of water soluble organic substances which may account for 6–30% dry weight loss, according to the character of plant material, within about a 14-day period. Important trends in the decomposing substrates were an increase of both nitrogen and lignin levels while most inorganic elements decreased steadily, although calcium and magnesium tended to increase. With time the material becomes less easily decayed. It seems that, while in early stages of decay nutrients, such as nitrogen and phosphorus, may be limiting to decomposition, later on the availability of labile and decomposable organic matter may become limiting in microbial activity. Substrate-related factors and their changes in time probably play a key role in regulating the nature and rate of decay processes (Polunin, 1982*b*).

Cycling and fluxes of phosphorus and nitrogen within the wetland ecosystems are often reported. For example, Pomeroy (1970) estimated that the short-term cycling of phosphorus in coastal waters is independent of inputs, both from the marshes and from ocean. Kistritz (1978) discussed the role of aquatic macrophytes, blue-green algae and mud surface in terms of recycling of nitrogen and phosphorus. Valiela and Teal (1979) gave a nitrogen budget for Great Sippewissett marsh, Massachusetts. The main inputs of nitrogen into the marsh were by groundwater, rain and biological nitrogen fixation. Losses occurred through tidal export, denitrification and volatilisation. Gaudet (1982) considered the effect of papyrus swamps on nitrogen and phosphorus budgets of two African lakes. The decomposing plants fragment and much of their nitrogen and phosphorus enter the sediments, though Gaudet found about 35% was recycled. The ultimate balance between accumulation in the whole sediment–plant system and losses is dependent on many physical, chemical and biological processes. Phosphorus accumulation appears to be 20–25% of the annual input in the papyrus swamps, although some relatively unavailable organic phosphorus may be released. Nitrogen is lost as mineral and organic compounds, but particularly as gaseous nitrogen from denitrification. On the other hand, nitrogen fixation probably exceeds denitrification in the papyrus swamps.

5

The role of animals and animal communities in wetlands

J. DVOŘÁK and G. IMHOF
with contributions by J.W. DAY JR, R. HACKER,
J. HOLČÍK, K. HUDEC, J. PELIKÁN and
E. OPATRNÝ

Introduction

This chapter is primarily a summary of results of studies on selected animal groups and communities inhabiting various types of wetlands in Europe, Asia, Africa and America. Many of the data were obtained during the International Biological Programme.

The rules governing the formation and development of wetland animal communities and their productivity are still insufficiently understood. First of all, a synthetic approach to their study is largely lacking for several reasons, mainly the recent recognition of many of the problems involved. Wetlands have been studied intensely only during the last 40 years or so and a relatively small number of zoologists specialise in the study of wetland animal communities and their productivity. Another reason is the great ecological variety of wetland ecosystems (see Chapter 1), leading to generally fragmentary and inconsistent knowledge about them and about their animal components in particular.

For these reasons, the present chapter has been conceived more as a review rather than as a true synthesis. The authors have also confined their attention to the most-studied and best-known animal groups and communities living in wetlands, without attempting to provide a complete and exhaustive picture of all animal life and its role in these ecosystems.

Some manuscripts, data, reviews and correspondence used in writing the chapters are deposited in the library of the Institute of Botany at Třeboň, Czech Republic, where they may be consulted.

The chapter is a collective work. Gerhard Imhof collected the basic materials, wrote several parts and later commented on drafts. With the assistance of further collaborators, Jan Dvořák completed and edited the chapter. These collaborators were: John W. Day Jr – general remarks and conclusions; Rainer Hacker – fish; Juraj Holčík – fish; Karel Hudec –

birds; Evžen Opatrný – amphibians and reptiles; Jaroslav Pelikán – mammals. The chapter also makes use of unpublished manuscripts which were contributed on request on the following topics: fish communities and production by Tadeusz Backiel (Inland Fisheries Institute, Zabieniec, Poland); ecology and productivity of animal communities of North American coastal marshes by John W. Day Jr and James Gosselink (both from Louisiana State University, USA); the ecology of paddy fields by Syun'iti Iwao (Kyoto University, Japan); and animal communities associated with *Cyperus papyrus* swamps by Tomislav Petr (FAO, Rome, Italy).

The authors are indebted to the following colleagues for valuable comments and suggestions on the text of the chapter during the final phase of its elaboration: A.F. Alimov (Zoological Institute, Leningrad, USSR; now St Petersburg, Russia); M. Skuhravá (Encyclopedic Institute, Praha), V. Skuhravý (Institute of Entomology, Praha), M. Straškraba (Hydrobiological Laboratory, České Budějovice) which institutes were formerly of the ČSAV but are now of the Academy of Science of the Czech Republic; and J. Vijverberg (Tjeukemeer Field Station, Limnological Institute, Oosterzee, the Netherlands) and the three editors of the book.

Following a suggestion from Professor W. Kühnelt (University of Vienna, Department of Zoology), the former chairman of the Austrian Committee for the IBP, the Austrian Academy of Sciences provided a special three months' grant to J. Dvořák in early 1977, enabling him to visit several Austrian scientific institutions and to collaborate closely with the Austrian co-authors of this chapter, which could thus be completed. This grant is acknowledged particularly gratefully. Thanks are also due to H. Pruscha for his hospitality to J. Dvořák during his stay in the Department of Zoology, University of Vienna.

I COMPOSITION AND STRUCTURE OF ANIMAL COMMUNITIES

Macro-invertebrates associated with emergent shoots of plants

Introduction

The invertebrate animals encountered among emergent wetland vegetation can be distinguished into three ecological groups according to their relations to the plants:

(i)   herbivorous animals feeding on emergent plant organs during a
      major part of their active life cycle;

(ii) adult insects emerging from the water or soil, the major part of their life cycle taking place under water (the emergent vegetation mainly provides shelter and/or facilities for mating and spawning, although some feeding may occur, e.g. flies sucking plant secretions);

(iii) parasites and predators feeding on the first two groups.

The relative diversity and abundance of these ecological groups differ in different types of wetlands. This is particularly evident in emerging insects which are governed by their submerged environment. Generally, this ecological group is richer in freshwater than in marine wetlands.

Relatively little attention had been paid to the structure and dynamics of these animal communities. Some insight has been gained from investigations in coastal *Spartina* marshes of Georgia (Smalley, 1959) where classical energy flow studies were performed (Teal, 1962) and of North Carolina (Davis & Grey, 1966) and California (Cameron, 1972). Also, IBP work in littoral reedbelts of shallow lakes and ponds in Central Europe added knowledge (Imhof & Burian, 1972; Pelikán *et al.*, 1973). A study on the faunal succession in umbels of *Cyperus papyrus* growing by the Upper White Nile was published by Thornton (1957).

Herbivorous insects

Systematic composition and ecological peculiarities

Most papers on aerial wetland invertebrates deal with the life history and distribution of herbivorous species and with the trophic relationships with their food plants. The fauna of rice (*Oryza sativa*) and common reed (*Phragmites australis*) has been particularly studied because of the economic importance of these plants. A large number of observations have been collected by Gaevskaya (1966/69) in her extensive review on trophic relationships between animals and higher aquatic plants. Her data reflect the unequal attention given to different consumers of emergent macrophytes. Most phytophagous insect species have become known in the course of investigations on the control of pests of rice. Walker's preliminary list (1962) includes more than 1400 species of insects (both aerial and aquatic) as pests of rice throughout the world. Pathak (1968) reviewed the distribution and ecology of 33 common insect pests of rice all over the world (excluding the Soviet Union), and found that about 20 species are of major significance. Generally less than ten are important in any single locality (Kiritani, 1972; Table 5.1).

Aerial invertebrates feeding directly on live helophytes are found

Table 5.1. *Regional differences in pest status of rice-inhabiting insects in Japan (Kiritani, 1972)*

Species	Order/Family	From south to north							
		Kyushu	Shikoku	Chugoku	Tokai-Kinki	Kanto	Hokuriko	Tohoku	Hokkaido
Tryporyza incertulas	Lepidoptera, Pyralidae	+	+	−	−	−	−	−	−
Chilo suppressalis	,,	++	++	+	+	++	++	+	+
Nephotettix cincticeps	Homoptera, Jassidae	++	++	+	+	++	++	+	−
Laodelphax striatellus	Homoptera, Delphacidae	+	+	+	+	+	−	−	−
Sogatella furcifera	,,	++	++	++	++	++	++	−	−
Nilaparvata lugens	,,	++	++	++	++	++	++	−	−
Scotinophara lurida	Heteroptera, Pentatomidae	+	+	+	+	++	+	−	−
Nezara viridula	,,	+	+	−	−	−	−	−	−
Chlorops oryzae	Diptera, Chloropidae	(+)	(+)	(+)	(+)	(+)	+	+	+
Agromyza oryzae	Diptera, Agromyzidae	−	−	−	−	−	+	+	+
Hydrellia griseola	Diptera, Ephydridae	−	−	−	−	−	+	+	+
Oulema oryzae	Coleoptera, Chrysomelidae	−	−	−	−	−	+	+	+

++ vectors of virus diseases, + injurious pests, − absent or potential pests.

mainly in the insect orders Orthoptera, Thysanoptera, Heteroptera, Homoptera, Coleoptera, Lepidoptera and Diptera. The families with the most numerous species are listed in Table 5.2. Although these insects belong to orders primarily evolved in terrestrial environments, breathing air by spiracles, nearly all representatives living in wetlands are more or less adapted to the aquatic environment. Most species can move on the water surface, and most are able to survive below water for up to several hours. Several species, belonging to different systematic groups, spend part, or even most of their life cycle under water, such as larvae, and sometimes adults, of Curculionidae and Chrysomelidae (subfamily Donacinae), as well as the lepidopteran larvae of *Cataclysta* and *Nymphula* during certain stages.

Insects have several different ways of consuming plant production: (i) ingesting plant tissues by means of chewing mouth-parts; (ii) sucking plant sap through piercing mouth-parts; (iii) absorbing plant secretions through sponging mouth-parts. They may also damage plants by burrowing in the tissues or using shoots in case building without actually eating them. Examples of all these types in the fauna of salt marshes are shown in Table 5.3.

It is a peculiarity of the herbivorous insect fauna of wetlands that substantial grazing rarely occurs on external plant tissues. It seems that the kind of feeding depends mainly on the mechanical properties of the food plants. Internal populations are more important and three types can be recognised: (i) mining in leaf and stem tissues; (ii) living free in, and feeding on, the internodes of the stems; (iii) forming galls. No sharp boundaries can be drawn, however, between these types.

External grazers

External feeders are specialised for plants with relatively soft organs (for some examples see Tables 5.3 and 5.13). Larvae and imagines of numerous species in the Chrysomelidae feed externally on such plants, many being restricted to only a few plant species. Members of the subfamily Galerucinae also attack Nymphaeceae. The most important is the polyphagous, holarctic species *Galerucella nymphaeae*, which feeds on at least 14 floating-leafed plants and seven semi-submerged plants (Gaevskaya, 1966/69) and all stages live on the leaves of their food plants.

Emergent vegetation with tough epidermal tissues is less suitable as food for small biting and gnawing animals. Only in some *Spartina* marshes are grasshoppers (family Tettigoniidae) important external consumers. In

Table 5.2. Numbers of insect species feeding on aquatic and semi-aquatic macrophytes (Gaevskaya, 1966/69)

Order/Family	Feeding exclusively on plant groups				Feeding on plants of all groups
	Semi-submerged	With floating leaves	Completely submerged	
Coleoptera					
Chrysomelidae	46	9	2		8
Curculionidae	31	11	3		2
Others	1	1	2		1
Diptera					
Agromyzidae	26	0	0		0
Itonididae	7	0	0		0
Chironomidae	26	12	15		18
Ephydridae	3	5	3		11
Others	16	4	0		2
Lepidoptera					
Pyralidae	13	3	0		8
Noctuidae	34	1	0		0
Others	16	0	0		0

Table 5.3. *Characteristic insects connected with* Spartina alterniflora *in North America (Davis & Grey, 1966)*

Food (feeding type)	Species	Order/Family	Habitat confinement	Recorded in: 1	2
Plant tissue (chewing mouth-parts)	*Orchelimum fidicinium*	Orthoptera, Tettigoniidae	*Spartina alt.* specific	+	+
	Conocephalus spp.	"	Marsh general	+	
	Mordellistena spp.	Coleoptera, Mordellidae	*Spartina alt.* specific	+	+
Plant sap (piercing and sucking mouth-parts)	*Prokelesia marginata*	Homoptera, Delphaceae	*Spartina alt.* specific	+	+
	Sanctanus aestuarium	Homoptera, Cicadellidae	"	+	
	Draeculacephala portola	"	"	+	
	Ischnodemus badius	Hemiptera, Lygaeidae	"	+	+
	Trigonotylus uhleri	Hemiptera, Myridae	*Spartina* spp.	+	
Plant secretions (sponging mouth-parts)	*Chaetopsis apicalis*	Diptera, Otiidae	Low marsh	+	+
	Ch. fulvifrons	"	"	+	
	Conioscinella infesta	Diptera, Chloropidae	Marsh general	+	
Omnivorous, nesting in stalks	*Crematogaster clara*	Hymenoptera, Formicidae	"	+	+

1 – Carteret County coast, North Carolina (Davis & Grey, 1966).
2 – Sapelo Island, Georgia (Teal, 1962).

the North American Atlantic coast marshes, *Orchelimum fidicinium* is reported as a dominant species (Smalley, 1959; Davis & Grey, 1966). Smalley (1960) calculated a mean density of adults of $3.5\,\mathrm{m}^{-2}$ during the summer in the Sapelo Island marshes. Rudescu (1965) reports that *Locusta migratoria*, which has a spreading centre near the coast of the Black Sea, in dry years occasionally invades the western areas of the Danube Delta and oviposits at the bases of *Phragmites* stems. When an inundation occurs, the population is lost and needs about 7 years for recovery.

Hygrophilous grasshoppers, such as members of the widely distributed genus *Conocephalus*, occur in different types of wetland vegetation, such as *Phragmites, Spartina anglica* (Payne, 1972), and *Oryza*, but they are omnivorous and do not play an important role as grazers. They inhibit mainly the floral parts, like the migratory locusts in *Cyperus papyrus* stands, which are known to feed directly on the umbels (Weber, 1942). Similar restrictions to inflorescences are also known for other external feeders. Cole (1931) found that four species of lepidopterous larvae were specialised to feed on flowers and seeds of *Typha latifolia*.

Plant-sap suckers

The majority of herbivorous insects in wetlands are types which pierce and suck plant saps, or miners and inhabitants of hollow plant organs, which feed on the soft inner tissues. The sap-suckers on emergent wetland plants are represented by three groups of Homoptera; plant-hoppers, coccids and aphids and several Heteroptera. Coccids and aphids, together with thrips form a characteristic community on *Cyperus papyrus* stems (Rzoska, 1974; Howard-Williams & Gaudet, 1985). Among the plant-hoppers, members of the family Delphacidae appear as characteristic inhabitants of marshes and reedbeds. Being mostly small species, they can occur in large numbers, such as the North American species *Prokelesia marginata* which is the most abundant plant-hopper in *Spartina* marshes (Smalley, 1959; Davis & Grey, 1966) or *Euidella speciosa* in reedswamps of Central Europe (Schubert, 1961).

Surprisingly little is known of the biology of wetland coccids, although they seem to be common on most emergent plants. They are generally steno- or monophagous and settle on distinct parts of their food plants, e.g. *Chaetococcus phragmitidis* within the leaf sheaths of *Phragmites*. Coccids, particularly of the family Pseudococcidae, are bound to a single host plant during the whole life cycle.

In contrast, aphids tend to change host regularly. Hydrophytes and helophytes of the temperate zones are inhabited only during summer, when aphids perform their asexual cyclophase, but most species are relatively selective with regard to their summer hosts. A remarkable exception is the worldwide species *Rhopalosiphum nymphaeae*, which has been identified on 27 host species (Gaevskaya, 1966/69), mainly of the genera *Nymphaea, Nuphar* and *Lemna*, which they invade in spring from fruit trees. Another relatively well-known species is *Hyalopterus pruni* (mealy plum aphid), which also has a worldwide distribution and changes its host between *Prunus* in winter and emergent water plants in summer. *Phragmites australis* is the primary host, but later on it forms parthenogenetic colonies on the leaves of *Typha* and *Scirpus* spp. Pintera (1973) studied the population dynamics of *H. pruni* during its stay in *Phragmites* stands of South Bohemia, which lasted from June to the end of August. The extent of the colonies developing then depends mainly on the initial attack of winged females. The number of gynoparae arising in late summer, which form the winter stock, does not depend on the total population density on the reed, but is apparently connected with the nutritive conditions in the host plant.

In European reed stands a pest mite, *Steneotarsonemus phragmitidis*, may also occur in masses on *Phragmites* (Durska, 1970; Skuhravý *et al.*, 1975).

Several species of Jassidae and Delphacidae are important pest insects in rice fields. The green leaf-hopper of rice, *Nephotettix cincticeps* has an annual cycle of three generations during which it changes its host from wild grasses such as *Alopecurus aequalis* to rice in paddy fields (Hokyo, 1972). The density of adults at the peak (third) generation is very stable every year in spite of considerable density variations of the invading (first) generation (Kuno, 1968; Kuno & Hokyo, 1970). The equilibrium density of *c*. 22 adults per hill* in the peak generation (corresponding to $370 \, \text{m}^{-2}$) is much lower than the carrying capacity of the rice plant. More than 400 adults (i.e. $> 6700 \, \text{m}^{-2}$) could be reared under caged conditions. Mechanisms of population regulation, discussed by the above authors, as well as by Kiritani *et al.* (1971) and Sasaba and Kiritani (1972) are: reduction in adult fecundity in the preceding generation by density-dependent emigration; density-dependent egg and larval parasitism; and predation. They conclude that different mechanisms operate at different

* 'Hill' means a group of rice plants transplanted together which forms a unit similar to an individual tillering plant. In Japan these are usually 15 to $20 \, \text{m}^{-2}$.

density levels, and that escape of the population from one mechanism automatically brings another density-dependent mechanism into action.

In contrast to *N. cincticeps*, which maintains a stable population cycle within the local grassy and paddy ecosystem complex, the injurious plant-hoppers *Nilaparvata lugens* and *Sogatella furcifera* are migratory species, possibly immigrating annually from overseas (Kisimoto, 1971). Their densities fluctuate violently in both time and space. The population development of *N. lugens* is characterised by initial concentrations in round areas covering several hundred or more hills, with densities of individuals up to 500 per hill ($8000 \, \text{m}^{-2}$), which result in the entire loss of crop in these places. The dense colonies are built up of the rather immobile brachypterous progeny of the immigrating macropterous generation. In the third generation, migratory macropterous adults start to increase again, according to the degree of crowding during the larval development (Kisimoto, 1965).

Whereas leaf-hoppers and plant-hoppers injure leaves and basal organs of the rice plant, there are several heteropterous bugs that suck the sap of developing rice grains. They appear not to be strictly bound to rice, because they usually also live on grasses in the vicinity, where they feed and reproduce during the growth phase of rice. Subsequently they migrate to flowering rice fields, to which they are strongly attracted. Most important representatives of this ecological type are the rice bugs *Leptocorisa* spp. in tropical and subtropical Asia, the rice stink bugs *Oebalus* spp. in the United States and the Caribbeans, and the southern green stink bug, *Nezara viridula* in East Asia and Australia. The latter attained particular significance in southern Japan after the introduction of early paddy, which, in conjunction with middle-season and late-planted rice, provides extraordinarily suitable conditions for population propagation (Kiritani, 1964, 1971; Kiritani & Hokyo, 1970).

Miners and stem borers

True leaf miners are mainly in the microlepidopteran families, Yponomeutidae, Elachistidae and Momphidae. Also, the larvae of the dipteran family Agromyzidae occur as specialised feeders in numerous wetland plants, but little special work has been done on their biology. Among the rice pest insects of tropical Asia there is also a coleopteran, *Hispa armigera*, which has larvae which mine in leaf blades.

Larvae of Noctuidae and Pyralidae (Lepidoptera) feed by boring in stems and appear to be common in all types of tall wetland vegetation.

The existence of stem borers is recorded from *Spartina* salt marsh as well as from tropical swamps with *Cyperus papyrus*, but detailed knowledge is sparse. Most attention has been paid to stem borers of rice, because of their economic importance, and to a lesser degree to those in the freshwater littoral belts of Europe, mainly in *Phragmites* (Grünberg, 1909; Schütze, 1931; Cole, 1931; Pruscha, 1973; Skuhravý *et al.*, 1981). Gaevskaya (1966/69) listed 11 species known in *Phragmites* nine of them exclusive and eight species in *Typha latifolia*, five of them exclusive; but only six species boring in *Phragmites* have been objects of more recent field investigations (see Table 5.4). Several species live mainly in the above-water part of the stem and cause considerable damage by destroying the growth tip. Others, particularly the pyralids, tend to penetrate the underwater parts down to the rhizomes, or are even restricted to the submerged internodes, like the only reed-inhabiting species of Cossidae (*Phragmataecia castaneae*) or to rhizomes, as is the noctuid *Rhizedra lutosa*. Stem borers which are specialised for the same host species respond differently to environmental conditions. Our knowledge is insufficient to explain their distribution and habitat selection and more intensive investigations would be desirable, especially with regard to the management of reed areas.

Ecological investigations have also been made on rice-inhabiting stem borers, particularly on the impact of pesticides used for their control on the invertebrate communities of rice (see. pp. 310–11). IBP activities included a symposium on rice stem borers (Rothschild & Waterhouse, 1972), and a special IBP handbook (Nishida & Torii, 1972) on field and laboratory methods dedicated to these insects.

Of the 12 common species (ten of Pyralidae and two of Noctuidae), the rice stem borer *Chilo suppressalis* is dominant in the temperate zone, and the yellow-striped rice borer *Tryporyza incertulas* predominates in tropical and sub-tropical regions. Their life cycles vary according to local climate and cropping system (one or more crops). In temperate areas there may be one or two distinct generations; in tropical regions, however, there is continuous breeding throughout the year, and as many as ten or more generations may be produced annually.

The best-known species, *Chilo suppressalis*, brings forth two generations a year in most parts of Japan, and hibernates as full-grown larvae in a diapause state. Eggs are laid in masses (50–80 eggs per mass) on rice plants, and hatching larvae tend to live in aggregations in a single stem during their early instars and then disperse to adjacent stems of the same or other plant hills (for detailed biology see Kiritani & Iwao, 1967). The

Table 5.4. *Stem borers* (*Lepidoptera*) *in* Phragmites australis, *on which recent biological investigations have been conducted*

Species	Geographical distribution	Remarks on life history and damage	Author
Cossidae			
Phragmataecia castaneae	Palaearctic (possibly cosmopol.)	In submerged parts of stem; biennial life cycle; no damage	Pruscha (1973)
Noctuidae			
Archanara geminipuncta	Europe	In stem up to the growth tip, which is destroyed; changes the host stem; annual lie cycle, over-wintering as egg or larva	Mook (1971a,c) Wyninger (1963) Skuhravý (1976) Skuhravý et al. (1981)
Archanara dissoluta	Europe, Soviet Central Asia	Like *A. geminipuncta*	Durska (1970)
Rhizedra lutosa	Palaearctic	In rhizomes of dry stands; 1 generation/year; overwintering as egg	Mook & van der Toorn (1974)
Crambidae			
Schoenobius gigantellus	Europe, Soviet Central Asia	In submerged parts of stems and rhizomes, destroying several young shoots	Pruscha (1973)
Chilo phragmitellus	Palaearctic	In all parts of older stems; probably biennial life cycle	Pruscha (1973)

most important mortality factors, such as the parasitic wasps *Tricho-gramma japonicum* and *Telonomus dignus*, operate in the egg stage. Rothschild (1971) demonstrated in Sarawak that *Chilo* eggs were heavily attacked by orthopterous predators such as *Conocephalus, Oxia* and *Anaxipha*, and inferred that about 90% of the total mortality of the eggs and young larvae would be due to the combined action of predators and parasites. In late larval and pupal stages, there are many species of parasitic wasps and a fungus disease *Isaria farinosa* (Yasumatsu & Torii, 1968).

The patterns, both of seasonal and annual population fluctuations, have been analysed mainly on the basis of long-term data on light-trap catches of the moths. These data have been accumulated in various parts of Japan in order to predict the population trends. According to the number, timing and relative height of the peaks in the collections, Ishikura (1955) classified seven types of seasonal prevalence of moths, from a one-brood type in cool regions, through varieties of two-brood types, to three-brood types in the southern regions. The pattern is determined not only by climatic conditions but also by cultural practice and genotypic characters of the populations (Fukaya, 1948; Kiritani & Iwao, 1967).

Annual fluctuations appeared to be irregular, but moderate; the peak density rarely exceeds six times the long-term average density, but crop damage becomes quite severe when the density increases three to five times over the average. Rapid population growth which continues over two or three generations, may be initiated by unusually low temperatures in early summer, which delay the emergence of the moths of the overwintered generation. Most egg masses are then laid in transplanted rice fields, which increases the proportion of effective eggs. Utida (1958) suggested that a relatively low reduction of egg fecundity by egg parasitism, which was observed for the generation preceding explosive increase, is another cause of initiation of an outbreak. On the other hand, the percentage of parasited eggs becomes high at, and after, the peak generation. Egg parasitism is therefore considered to act as a density-dependent mechanism of population regulation. There are also some indications of a regulatory effect of crowding: the percentage of unfertilised eggs in an egg mass increases in the generation following an outbreak (Miyashita, 1963). The mean population level is, of course, strongly affected by the intensity of artificial control and the system of cultivation used (see p. 310).

The general level of abundance of *Tryporyza incertulas*, for which the population dynamics are much less clear, is also closely related to cropping management (see p. 311). Peak densities can be 50 to 100 times the long-term average.

Gall-formers

Stem-inhabiting and gall-forming species on *Phragmites* occur in the families Cecidomyiidae, Chloropidae and Dolichopodidae. Waitzbauer *et al.* (1973), who surveyed the endophagous Diptera in the littoral reed belt of the Neusiedlersee, recorded 13 species (Table 5.5), the majority of them being concentrated at the landward edge of the reedbelt. In this zone, with relatively poor reed growth, inundated only during winter and early spring, 50% of all stems were infested. The mean number of individuals per m^2 of all species together (which are generally univoltine) was calculated from a winter sample as 275. The respective figures for the permanently flooded zone were 5% and $42 \, m^{-2}$. The rather large number of species occurring in one stand can be explained by differences in habits and biology which lead to spatial separation within the stems (Waitzbauer *et al.*, 1973).

The best-known endophagous insect of *Phragmites* is the gall-forming species *Lipara lucens* (Ruppolt, 1957; Mook, 1967, 1971*b*; Waitzbauer, 1969; Durska, 1970; Pokorný, 1971; Chvála *et al.*, 1974; Skuhravý *et al.*, 1981). The settlement of the larva in the apical region of the young stem provokes a conspicuous cigar-like gall including several shortened internodes, and causes stunting of further growth by destroying the growth tip. The species is distributed in Western, Central and Southern Europe and recently appeared in North America (Connecticut). The unequal local distribution, even in homogeneous environments, was analysed by Mook (1967, 1971*b,c*), who showed that the fly has only a small colonisation capacity because of restricted flying mobility. The growth conditions of the reed act as a decisive environmental factor influencing the local distribution. For oviposition the females prefer stems of medium thickness, while the survival of young larvae, before reaching the growth tip, is greatest in stems of the thinnest diameter. Thus the highest gall densities occur in stands in which the basal stem diameter ranges between 2.5 and 4.5 mm. Such stands grow under suboptimal conditions in places without, or with only a brief period of, inundation.

The galls of *Lipara lucens* provide a habitat for a number of inquilines, living mainly as saprophages or omnivores (Waitzbauer, 1969). These inquilines, their parasites, the parasites of *Lipara* itself (8 Hymenoptera known), and arthropods periodically inhabiting or hibernating in the galls form a striking community dependent on the occurrence of *L. lucens*.

The larvae of several gall-midges, in the genera *Lasioptera, Giraudiella* and *Microlasioptera* (Table 5.5) develop inside reed stems causing fragility and breaking, often late in the year.

In Bohemia *Giraudiella inclusa* has one or two generations a year, but only causes appreciable losses in heavily infested stems. The first generation develops in the lower internodes of the reed stems and the second generation in the upper internodes, or on lateral shoots. Most galls are between the second and sixth internodes. They are grain-like, but their shape depends on the structure of the stem tissues (Skuhravá & Skuhravý, 1977).

Larvae of *L. arundinis* develop in lateral shoots growing out when the vegetative top of the reed has been destroyed by the fly *Platycephala planifrons*, the moth *Archanara geminipuncta*, the mite *Steneotarsonemus phragmitidis*, or rarely by species of the genus *Lipara*. *L. arundinis* itself is never the primary agent influencing the development of lateral shoots on the reed stems. Larvae hatched from eggs move along a narrow strip in the direction of the apex of the lateral shoots, disseminating a fungus of the genus *Sporothrix* and entering the lateral shoots. Beginning in September, larvae of the third instar move into tiny enclosures within the galls, where they persist until pupation by the end of May the next year (Skuhravý, 1975; Skuhravá & Skuhravý, 1981).

Larvae of *Lasioptera hungarica* develop within internodes of the main stem, along with growths of the same fungus sheathing the walls inside, which harbour the larvae (Skuhravá & Skuhravý, 1981).

A fourth species, *Microlasioptera flexuosa* is very rare, but very interesting. It has been reported from a limited area of the Pannonian plain and its northern extension, where very low-growing reed occurs in halophytic grassland communities. The infested state of the reed appears to be undamaged, although about 30–50 larvae live inside the terminal part of the stems, with undeveloped inflorescences. No fungal hyphae are present in the infested internodes. The adults are released from the stem only after it has been broken by either biotic or abiotic factors (Skuhravá & Skuhravý, 1981).

There is also a gall-forming dipteran, *Pachydiplosis oryzae* which is a pest of rice. In contrast with the gall-forming dipterans of *Phragmites*, it changes its host within five to eight overlapping generations per season. The flies become active at the onset of the monsoon, when it completes one or two generations on other grasses before the rice is planted, and then

Table 5.5. *Endophagous Diptera in* Phragmites australis, *on which biological investigations have been conducted (inquilines of galls and parasites excluded)*

Species	Geographical distribution	Remarks on life history and damage	Author
Chloropidae			
Platycephala planifrons		One larva damages the growth tip; One generation/year	Waitzbauer et al. (1973) Skuhravý & Skuhravá (1978)
Lipara lucens	Europe (immigr. in N. America)	One larva in the stem, forming a large top gall and preventing further growth; prefers suboptimal stands	Waitzbauer (1969) Doskočil & Chvála (1971) Chvála et al. (1974) Mook (1967, 1971a,b) Skuhravý et al. (1981)
Lipara similis	Europe	Similar to *L. lucens*, but galls are more slender	Doskočil & Chvála (1971) Chvála et al. (1974) Skuhravý et al. (1981)
Lipara pullitarsis	Europe	Similar galls; prefers dispersed reed stands between trees and bushes	Doskočil & Chvála (1971) Chvála et al. (1974) Skuhravý et al. (1981)
Lipara rufitarsis	Europe	Similar galls; prefers dry stands	Doskočil & Chvála (1971) Chvála et al. (1974) Skuhravý et al. (1981)
Dolichopodidae			
Thrypticus smaragdinus	?	Mining in the stem wall; one generation/year	Waitzbauer et al. (1973)
Thrypticus bellus	?	As above	Waitzbauer et al. (1973)

Cecidomyiidae			
Giraudiella inclusa (syn. *G. incurvans*)	Central and NE Europe	Grainlike galls inside the lower or upper internodes of the stem; one or two generations/year; prefers thick stems	Mook (1971*a*,*b*,*c*) Waitzbauer *et al.* (1973)
		In main stem and also in lateral shoots; two generations/year	Skuhravá & Skuhravý (1977, 1981)
Lasioptera arundinis	Central, West Europe	Numerous larvae in deformed lateral shoots inside black mass of hyphae of the genus *Sporothrix*	Waitzbauer *et al.* (1973) Skuhravý (1975) Skuhravá & Skuhravý (1981)
Lasioptera hungarica (syn. *Thomasiella massa*), *Lasioptera erdösi*	Central, West (South) Europe	Up to 250 larvae inside the stem in black mass of the hyphae of the genus *Sporothrix*; one generation/year; causes breaking of the stems, prevents flowering	Waitzbauer *et al.* (1973) Skuhravá & Skuhravý (1981)
Microlasioptera flexuosa	Small areas in Central Europe	Numerous larvae inside the stem; one generation/year; no damage	Waitzbauer *et al.* (1973) Skuhravá & Skuhravý (1981)

finally migrates to the rice fields. Newly hatched larvae creep down the leaf sheath to the growing point of tillers, where its feeding stimulates the development of a tubular gall resembling an onion leaf. Knowledge of the bionomics and ecology of this species was not sufficient to develop a satisfactory control method.

Other stem inhabitants

Other animals inhabit stems beside those using the tissues as a food source or in galls. Although they are not all herbivores, it is convenient to consider them here. The interior of stems may serve as a shelter for nesting and hibernation. In *Spartina* stems, the ant *Crematogaster clara* is very common and can be found there throughout the year (Davis & Grey, 1966; Teal, 1962). As it breeds in the stems, this species is not limited by tidal inundation. The same habit enables several species of ants to reside in papyrus stands (Thornton, 1957), sometimes older channels of stem borers are inhabited by ants expanding them into large galleries which may then serve them as a habitat or become a refuge for other small insects. In flooded reed stands of the temperate zone, no stem-inhabiting ants are known. Old broken or cut stems of *Phragmites* are, however, commonly used as winter refuges by the permanent arthropod fauna, mainly predatory beetles and spiders.

Predators and parasites of animals living on plants

Predators

Data on carnivorous invertebrates in emergent vegetation exist mostly as brief notes scattered in faunistic surveys.

Intrinsic food chains are known for some groups of herbivorous insects, e.g. aphids which form the feeding basis for coccinellid and syrphid larvae. The dominant and most characteristic predators among the invertebrate community are spiders, preying mainly in winged insets, using the populations emerging from the water, populations trophically connected with emergent vegetation and casuals visiting in search of food and water. The importance of spiders is seen in all major types of tall wetland vegetation. In a tidal marsh of *Spartina alterniflora* in North Carolina, which is regularly flooded, the spider community of 22 species (see Table 5.6) is confined completely to the upper parts of the vegetation; no ground forms were recorded (Barnes, 1953). On the contrary, a characteristic

Table 5.6. *Characteristic spiders connected with* Spartina alterniflora *(Barnes, 1953)*

Species	Family	Habitat confinement	Recorded in 1	2
Grammonota trivittata	Micryphantidae	*Spartina* specific	+	+
Dictyna savanna	Dictynidae	Low marsh	+	+
Eustala anastera	Araneidae	Low and intermediate marsh	+	+
Hyctia pikei	Salticidae	Marsh generally	+	+

1 – Carteret County coast, North Carolina (Barnes, 1953).
2 – Sapelo Island, Georgia (Teal, 1962).

community of 'ground' spiders is known in reeds even during inundation; some species of the families Pisauridae and Lycosidae being well adapted to activity upon the water surface. However, most spiders in reeds are in the upper layers of vegetation. Pühringer (1975) recorded about 25 species of this type in the permanently flooded zones of the littoral reedbelt of the Neusiedlersee, eight of them breeding in the panicles of *Phragmites* (see Table 5.16). In the late spring, at the time of egg-laying, the initial population density of the five largest of the species that inhabit panicles was $1.5\,m^{-2}$. Although numbers of individuals increase later on, the maximal biomass occurred at that time. Other population densities are, for example, $20\,m^{-2}$ in Californian *Spartina* marsh (Cameron, 1972), $40\,m^{-2}$ in a rice field in Sendai, north-eastern Japan (Kobayashi & Shibata, 1973), and $150\,m^{-2}$ in Kochi, a warmer part of Japan (Kawahara *et al.*, 1969)*, all figures referring to all species together during summer, when a maximum is reached.

Parasites

The endophagous insect larvae appear to be used by a considerable variety of parasitic Hymenoptera but knowledge is rather fragmentary. Eight parasitic species are known for *Lipara lucens* (Waitzbauer, 1969) and for another gall-forming species *Perrisia inclusa* (Erdös, 1957). Erdös also reported five species parasitic on the stem borer *Archanara*

* Dominant spider species in rice fields of Japan are: *Gnathonarium dentatum, Oedothorax insecticeps, Lycosa pseudoannulata, Pirata clorcki* and *Pirata piratica.*

geminipunctata. The parasite communities must be considered as an important regulating factor for the endophagous insect populations.

Structure and dynamics of aerial invertebrate communities

Species structure: spatial and temporal variation

As mentioned above, only a few authors have discussed problems of structure and dynamics of the aerial invertebrate community in wetlands as a whole. Davis and Grey (1966) analysed the zonal and seasonal distribution of the insect communities in the herbaceous layer of salt marshes in Carteret County, North Carolina. Based on frequencies, densities, and special observations they recognised distinct associations of characteristic species for each marsh type (for low *Spartina alterniflora* marsh see Table 5.3), most of these species being generally restricted to maritime and submaritime conditions. Differences in the size of the insect communities on sites with different types of vegetation and different exposure to tides were, however, more influenced by the morphology and structure of the vegetation and by food supply than directly by the tides. During summer, when the whole community is richest, different insect types show different degrees of constancy of abundance.

Most of the homopterans had a definite peak period, but the most abundant species, *Prokelesia marginata*, varied considerably in the time of maximum abundance from year to year and in maximum densities in different stands. Similar inconstancies have been shown for rice plant-hopper populations as well as for the dominant cicadellid *Euscelis obsoletus* in a *Spartina anglica* marsh in Britain (Payne, 1972), and for the inconstancy of the time course of population development which was described by Pintera (1973) for the reed aphid *Hyalopterus pruni.*

Most species of salt marsh insects pass the winter in the egg stage, which contrasts somewhat with the reed communities, which are dominated by endophagous insects hibernating mostly in the larval or pupal stage.

An interesting aspect has been mentioned by Thornton (1957). As *Cyperus papyrus* stems have a relatively short life cycle, during which umbels sprout, grow, mature, and die throughout the year, a faunal succession was observed, which was season independent, but strongly correlated with the stage of umbel development. This was particularly striking for the plant-suckers, like Thysanoptera, and it suggests that as the umbel ages the condition and availability of its sap changes. The early animal populations on the young umbels are isolated until the length of the ray is such that the umbels begin to contact one another in the canopy, so that even apterous species can migrate to another umbel which provides a suitable developmental stage. The richness and succession of the fauna indicate that the papyrus umbel is the site of an intricate food web, the pattern of which changes as the umbel grows, matures and dies.

Species diversity and trophic structure

Cameron (1972), studying the adult insect assemblage in a small intertidal marsh of *Spartina foliosa* in California throughout a year, made an attempt to relate the trophic structure and seasonal dynamics to the species diversity. He came to the conclusion that seasonal fluctuations in species diversity corresponded with fluctuations of food resources. Positive correlations were found: (i) between herbivore diversity and plant standing crop; (ii) between detritivore diversity and litter accumulation; and (iii) between predator diversity and prey diversity. The diversity changes of herbivores and detritivores were attributed to changes in species numbers, not by abundance. These, in the case of herbivores, were caused by the temporary occurrence of species which are present only during the growing season. Indirect evidence supported the hypothesis that both persistent and temporary herbivores are specialists in relation to their food, which enabled the maximum number of species to co-exist in the habitat, and the optimal use of nutritional resources.

A remarkable species diversity has also been seen in artificial wetlands, such as rice fields. M. Kobayashi (pers. comm.) commented that the community structure is not simple, and that polyphagous predators are more abundant in paddy fields than in other kinds of habitats. Many insect species use the paddy field only as a temporary habitat during a part of their life cycle. Thus the interchange of populations between the paddy field and adjacent habitats of other kind, is an important factor determining the community structure in this type of wetland.

Macro-invertebrates associated with submerged parts of plants

Introduction

In contrast with the communities associated with emergent parts of plants, the invertebrate macro-fauna under the water is much more diverse, including representatives of many taxa (Cnidaria-Hydrozoa, Bryozoa, Turbellaria, Oligochaeta, Hirudinea, Gastropoda, Lamellibranchiata,

Acarina, Araneae, Isopoda, Amphipoda, Ephemeroptera, Odonata, Heteroptera, Coleoptera, Megaloptera, Trichoptera, Lepidoptera and Diptera).

The structure of the water macro-fauna is less obvious and more complicated than in aerial invertebrate communities. Considerable heterogeneity in vegetation structure, frequency and length of hydroperiod, food resources and other ecological conditions such as temperature, oxygen or hydrogen sulphide content, result in the high spatial and temporal variety of animal communities inhabiting various types of wetlands. In contrast to open water bodies, no sharp distinction can be made between benthic and epiphytic communities, particularly if both living and dead plant material are present with other debris in a shallow water layer. There are also considerable difficulties in establishing trophic categories. Only a minority are true phytophages feeding on fresh plant tissues of macrophytes or on algae exclusively. Most species have an intermediate or unspecialised trophic position somewhere between fresh plant tissues and well-decayed organic substances. Bacteria and unicellular algae also play an important role in the nutrition of detritophagous animals. Even many carnivorous animals are not solely restricted to living prey. Cummins (1973) studied the trophic relations in aquatic insects and concluded that most of them are polyphagous, their food selection being determined mainly by the particle size and mechanical properties of the organic matter present. Similar conclusions hold also for some deposit- and filter-feeders (Taghon *et al.*, 1978; Doyle, 1979).

In spite of the heterogeneity of the published research, we attempt to review the relatively rich information on the biology and structure of the macrofauna of submerged plants in various kinds of wetlands.

Herbivorous invertebrates

Gaevskaya's review (1966/69), on the trophic relationships between animals and higher aquatic plants, shows a correlation between the terrestrial or aquatic origin of aquatic animals and their trophic relations to living plant tissue. Pure phytophages feeding on macrophytes are almost exclusively insect larvae, which are, in terms of evolution, secondary inhabitants of the aquatic environment. The only primary aquatic invertebrates, reported to feed predominantly on living tissues of macrophytes, are some species of crayfish of the genera *Astacus*, *Cambarus* and *Cambaroides*, which are well adapted to consuming rhizomes and other storage organs of emergent macrophytes.

External grazers

Specialised consumers of fresh macrophytes are found within the coleopteran families Chrysomelidae and Curculionidae. Although belonging primarily to the aerial community (see pp. 213–15; Table 5.2), larvae of several species also graze on underground parts of water plants. As they obtain their respiratory oxygen from the aerenchyma of their food plant, most species occur on large helophytes and Nymphaeaceae. They tend to spend their whole life cycle on a single individual plant. Some of the most effective external grazers on water macrophytes in European wetlands are caterpillars of several species of the family Pyralidae (*Cataclysta lemnata, Elophila nymphaeata, Paraponyx stratiotata* and *Acentropus niveus*) which are adapted to aquatic respiration, and larvae of caddis-flies *Phryganea, Limnephilus* and *Leptocerus*.

The Lepidoptera feed particularly intensively on macrophyte tissues (see Table 5.2). In contrast with terrestrial caterpillars and semi-aquatic stemborers, the water-dwelling lepidopteran larvae are mostly non-selective with regard to their food plants, but prefer soft parts of submerged and floating macrophytes (Kashkin, 1959).

Like the aquatic Lepidoptera, caddis-fly larvae are also mostly polyphagous and avoid tough helophytes. *Phryganea grandis* and species of the genus *Limnephilus* are among the most effective grazers. For example, *L. stigma* is one of the very important pests of rice fields in Soviet Far East (Mischenko, 1940).

Many of both the lepidopteran and caddis-fly larvae make cases using plant material, and break up more than they consume (e.g. Dawson, 1976*a*).

Gastropoda, Isopoda, Amphipoda and larvae of Chironomidae, which are dominant major groups in overgrown, shallow waters, feed on fresh plant tissue to a smaller extent, or only occasionally (Glowacka *et al.*, 1976; Kobuszewska, 1973; Marcus *et al.*, 1978). The basic foods of *Radix ovata* and *Bithynia tentaculata* living upon plants were periphytic algae and detritus of periphytic origin (G.J. Soszka, 1975).

Miners

The mining larvae of the dipteran families Ephydridae and Chironomidae are a special type of macrophyte feeder. The former comprises the genera *Notiphila* and *Hydrellia* the members of which are characteristic elements of the marsh fauna; rather little is, however, known of their biology. A good deal of information has been gathered on mining chironomid larvae by Berg (1950), Gripekoven (1921), Kalugina (1959, 1961), Thienemann (1954) and others. Berg (1950) and Thienemann (1954) have listed mining chironomid species belonging to the following genera: *Cricotopus, Polypedilum, Pentapedilum, Lenzia, Glyptotendipes* and *Endochironomus.* However, only a few groups of mining species play a significant role in transformation of the fresh plant matter, e.g. some representatives of the family Orthocladiinae and the genera *Glyptotendipes* and *Endochironomus.* Berg (1950) distinguished between 'true miners', which feed only on the mesophyll between two epidermal layers, and 'semi-miners' which make open galleries and leave only one epidermal layer untouched. The mines also serve as residental tubes for the mining larvae; the miner's respiratory movements lead to water exchange in the mines. The water streaming through brings in fine detritus and algae also serving as food. Consumption of fresh plant tissues combined with detritophagy seem to prevail for the big larvae of some species of the subgenus *Phytotendipes* and the *Endochironomus.* Many mining species are not restricted to living tissues, but also consume the plant tissues in various stages of decay.

Glowacka *et al.* (1976) examined the composition of the food of larvae of *Glyptotendipes gripekoveni* and *Endochironomus tendens,* which both live on the surface of plants in residental tubes built of fine particles, and in mines as true miners. For larvae living on the surface of plants, plant tissues were 2.5% of the whole food in *G. gripekoveni* and 2% in *E. tendens.* In the mining larvae the percentage reached a maximum of 17 for *G. gripekoveni,* and five for *E. tendens.* Periphytic algae and detritus formed the major part of the food of both groups of larvae in both species.

The trophic specialisation of chironomid mining larvae ranges from monophagy (e.g. *Cricotopus brevipalpis* in *Potamogeton natans*) to polyphagy. The different species of helophytes are not equally suitable as host plants for mining chironomid larvae. Some phytophilous chironomid species posses a certain degree of specifity, selecting certain species or groups of species of host plants within a single locality. This phenomenon is apparently caused by the diverse morphological and biological properties of the plants (Dvořák, 1970*b*) and by synchrony between the life cycles of the host plant and the miners.

Detritus feeders, periphyton scrapers and scavengers

Wetlands are predominantly detrital systems in which the products of photosynthesis die and are microbially enriched before use by higher trophic levels (see Chapter 3). However, in areas with a sufficiently deep light penetration, autochthonous autotrophic periphyton and phytoplankton also develop well. Much food in littorals is brought in to the littoral by the water motions as phytoplankton of pelagic origin. Dead bodies of consumers are a food source before they are completely decomposed. Detritus, micro-flora of different origin, as well as protein-rich dead matter serve as the main food support for the most substantial part of the invertebrate macro-fauna, that is detritus feeders, scrapers of periphyton, and scavangers. However, no sharp lines can be drawn between these categories because of the tendency to omnivory in many of the invertebrate macro-fauna.

Many detrivorous animals are collectors or filtrators of detritus. The former group includes some Oligochaeta, for example, the roving *Stylaria lacustris* (Rehbronn, 1937), and the burrowing species of the genera *Tubifex, Limnodrilus* and *Lumbriculus*. Other collectors are developmental stages and adults of insects, e.g. some ephemeropteran nymphs (Baetidae, Caenidae and Siphlonuridae), many Trichoptera, beetles of the family Hydrophilidae and larvae of flies of the families Culicidae and Chironomidae. Of the latter family, some species of the genera *Microtendipes, Chironomus* and *Endochironomus* are among the most efficient collectors.

Some bivalves of the genera *Pisidium, Sphaerium, Musculium*, and *Dreissena* are true filtrators. They play a substantial role in the ultilisation of tripton (Alimov, 1967; Zhadin, 1962, 1965). One adult specimen of *Sphaerium corneum* is able to filter about 60 ml h^{-1} of water, and *Dreissena polymorpha* filters some 40 to 50 ml h^{-1}. Another type of detritus-filtering invertebrate is represented by the oligochaete *Ripistes parasita*, its filtering apparatus is formed by groups of long bristles on the anterior segments. Larvae of several mosquito species are also filtrators. *Anopheles* takes its food from the surface layer of the water and larvae of some species of the genera *Aëdes* and *Culex* feed on tripton of planktonic origin.

The food of scrapers consists mainly of periphytic algae with associated detritus and dead plant tissues. The scrapers include many species of snails possessing a special cutting plate in the mouth (the radula), the nymphs of *Caenis* and chironomid larvae with a specially adapted labial plate (e.g. *Endochironomus* and *Phytotendipes*). Some species of mosquitos in *Theobaldia* and *Aëdes* also belong to this group.

It is generally known that organic material of plant origin is likely to pass through more than one animal gut successively during its breakdown.

Table 5.7. *Groups of carnivorous invertebrates in underwater communities in European wetlands*

Mostly microphagous	Mostly macrophagous	Ectoparasites

Coelenterata
  Hydra spp.
Turbellaria
  Dendrocoelum spp.
  Microstomum spp. (often eats *Hydra*)
  Macrostomum spp.
Oligochaeta
  Chaetogaster diaphanus
Odonata nymphs
  Zygoptera (*Agrion, Erythomma,* and *Lestes* spp., also eats periphytic algae)
  Anisoptera (*Sympetrum* spp. and some other Libellulidae and Cordulidae)
Trichoptera larvae
  Cyrnus spp.
  Holocentropus spp.
  Molana angustata
  Psychomyidae
  Leptoceridae (some spp.)
Coleoptera larvae and adults
  Dytiscidae (minute species)
  Gyrinidae
Diptera larvae
  Chaoboridae (*Chaoborus* spp.)
  Tanypodinae
	Turbellaria
	  Polycelis some spp.
	Hirudinae
	  Herpobdella spp.
	  Haemopis sanguisuga
	Hemiptera adults
	  Nepa cinerea
	  Notonecta spp.
	  Naucoris cimnicoides
	Megaloptera larvae
	  Sialis spp.
	Odonata nymphs
	  Anisoptera (*Anax* spp. *Aeschna* spp., some Libellulidae and Cordulidae)
	  Dytiscidae larvae and adults (large species of subfam. Dytiscinae)
	Arachnida
	  Argyroneta aquatica
		Oligochaeta
		  Chaetogaster limnaei (on gastropods)
		Hirudinae
		  Glossiphonia spp. ⎫ (on gastropods and
		  Helobdella stagnalis ⎬ chironomid larvae)
		  Piscicola geometra (on fish)
		  Protoclepsis tessulata ⎫ (on birds and
		  Hirudo medicinalis ⎬ mammals)
		  Batracobdella paludosa (on amphibians)
		  Haementeria costata (on tortoise *Emis orbicularis*)
		Neuroptera
		  Sisyra sp. (on sponges)
		Diptera (Chironomidae)
		  Parachironomus varus (on *Physa*)
		  Xenochironomus sp. ⎫ (on sponges and
		  Demeijera sp. ⎬ bryozoans)

Dölling (1962) made experimental studies on the food ranges and food preferences of several common aquatic animals from a stagnant pool which was supplied with plenty of litter. Several non-selective species (*Gammarus pulex, Dero limosa* and benthic Chironomidae) were found to feed on dead plant material as well as on faeces of other phytophagous animals; in this sense they are both primary and secondary decomposers. Most freshwater snails, the larvae of the caddis-fly *Limnephilus flavicornis*, and *Asellus aquaticus* were regarded as primary decomposers. The secondary decomposers, which feed mostly on faeces and on the associated bacteria are mainly Nematoda, Copepoda, Ostracoda and several Oligochaeta.

Scavengers are defined as animals feeding on not yet fully decomposed corpses, arising from animals (carrion) either dwelling or falling in the water. In the aquatic invertebrate fauna this feeding type is mainly represented by largely omnivorous species of various systematic status: Lymnaeidae, Planorbidae, Viviparidae, *Asellus aquaticus*, Limnephilidae, big Hydrophilidae and occasionally *Chironomus*. Also, a few species of Turbellaria and Hirudinea belong to this group.

As stressed earlier, the majority of the primary decomposers take in a more or less wide range of food often depending on the most available source. However, many observations lead to the conclusion that most detritivores have distinct food requirements, or at least preferences, related to the physical and chemical properties of the food materials. The apparent sensitivity to such changes in food material arising during the natural ageing and deterioration process of plants may be some reason for the confusions and apparent contradictions found in investigations of the food of animals in these groups.

Predators and ectoparasites on animals

These are a relatively numerous group of invertebrates. The predominance of predators over parasites in the aquatic communities of wetlands is in some contrast to the emergent communities where parasites play the more important role (pp. 228–30). In overgrown littorals the variety of carnivorous invertebrates is much greater than in open water bodies. This is due to the more diverse environment on the one hand, and by the different evolutionary origin of the predatory animals, on the other. The carnivores can roughly be divided into three groups (Table 5.7).

The micro- and macro-phagous carnivores

The micro-phagous species prey on zooplankton, animals of aufwuchs communities and young developmental stages of various invertebrates. The macro-phagous carnivores mostly prey on invertebrates belonging to the macro-fauna and, occasionally, on small vertebrates, e.g. fry of fish and amphibian larvae. Most of the invertebrate carnivores masticate or swallow the bodies of their prey. However, the larvae of Dytiscidae, the water spider *Argyroneta aquatica*, and the aquatic Hemiptera suck up the body fluids after the prey has been infused with digestive secretions.

The ectoparasites

These include invertebrates feeding on surface mucus, blood and tissue fluids of different groups of animals, and are associated with both poikilotherm and homeiotherm hosts. The larvae of *Xenochironomus* and *Demeijera* possess a special mode of feeding, eating living water sponge and bryozoan colonies (Thienemann, 1954).

Structure and dynamics of aquatic macro-invertebrate communities in wetlands

The macro-fauna of wetlands is formed both by primary and secondary inhabitants of the aquatic environment. Therefore, from the evolutionary point of view, the macro-fauna appears as a rather heterogeneous and very plastic group of populations. The species found in water range from those which must live totally submerged all their life (the permanent fauna), through those that live only part of their life cycle underwater (temporary fauna) or are restricted to the water surface, to those that occasionally enter the water (see Berczik, 1973*a*).

   Substantial spatial and seasonal changes in the species structure of macro-fauna have also been observed. This results in difficulties if attempts are made to determine the characteristic species structure of the macro-fauna for a particular wetland habitat. On the other hand, the macro-fauna provides good indicators of community responses to environmental changes.

Species structure: spatial variation

Analyses of the species structure and diversity of the macro-fauna inhabiting the stands of inshore and wetland vegetation are based mostly on studies of littoral regions of European lakes, ponds and broads.

The lake eulittoral is a typical ecotone, in which terrestrial and aquatic organisms are found, as well as specifically littoral organisms. In the eulittoral zone of several Mazurian lakes in Poland, an edge effect has been observed (Pieczyńska, 1972a), which results in the occurrence of a greater number of species, and greater density of some populations in the ecotone than in the adjacent terrestrial and aquatic habitats.

Mason and Bryant (1974) used abundance/frequency analyses to study species structure in a *Phragmites* dominated reedswamp in Alderfen Broad (Norfolk, UK). In their opinion, a large degree of subjectivity must necessarily enter into any attempt to delimit communities and describe their structural components. The most important animals in the community structure were considered to be those which were both abundant and frequent. However, there were a number of groups where animals may have been abundant but occurred in few samples only, or were widely distributed yet scarce. This latter group probably contained a number of vagrants to the community. Three rather different communities were recognised in the reedswamp, corresponding to three types of biotope: outer marginal fringes exposed to the open water ('littoral ecophase'), central part with puddles of water amid mosses ('littoral-limosal ecophase') and inshore fringes near the upper limit of the reeds ('limosal ecophase'). The species diversities and equitabilities of the macro-fauna of the outer fringe and centre were very similar but they were smaller in the inner fringe. This was also less structured because it was less stable, drying out during summer and flooding during winter, thus making colonisation by primarily aquatic or terrestrial species difficult.

Dvořák and Lišková (1970) and Dvořák (1970a) studied macro-faunal structure in the stands of emergent vegetation in fishpond littorals in South Bohemia, especially in stands of *Glyceria maxima*, and tried to define certain species as characteristic of a certain biotope. They selected the species encountered most frequently in each biotope, which were able to stand the fluctuations of life condtions and formed a substantial constituent of the respective macro-faunas.

A very specific environment for a macro-fauna is found in stands of *Stratiotes aloides*, which often form an important stage in the water to land succession. In the growing season it grows in both emergent forms (mostly adult plants) and submerged forms. The well-developed emergent plants, growing in the central and marginal belts bordering on the pelagic zone, form an ecotone within the larger ecotone of the swamp zonation and succession (Higler, 1975). Here, the highest number of animal species was found (cf. Pieczyńska, 1972*a*). Another distinct group of animal species occurred on the submerged plants. Higler (1977) also considered the possibility that different sites in the *Stratiotes* vegetation could be characterised by means of functional units of macro-fauna based on their food relations. He found that the differences in community structure along a transect from the shore to the open water of the broad were mainly due to different physico-chemical characteristics of the sites (especially fluctuation in oxygen content, occurrence of ammonia and hydrogen sulphide). Differences in the depth of water, thickness of the sapropel layer and density of the vegetation also played a substantial role. The *Stratiotes* plants acted as substrate and habitat modifiers.

The water-facing fringe of *Cyperus papyrus* swamps has also been found to be the biologically richest habitat in the whole swamp system; the stand–water interface is also by far the most complex habitat in the swamp (Rzóska, 1974; Thompson, 1974). Monakov (1969) estimated the biomass of *Entomostraca* and found the fringe to be 10 to 100 times richer than the open water of the 'sudd'. According to Rzóska (1974) insects are the most productive group in the papyrus fringe of the Sudanese sudd, and this was also confirmed for the papyrus swamp fringe in the lakes Victoria and George in Uganda (T. Petr, pers. comm.). The standing crop of the invertebrates in papyrus fringes in Uganda is often dominated by the ephemeropteran nymph *Povilla adusta* (Petr, 1973).

The distribution of invertebrate fauna in the stands of *Leersia hexandra* was studied in the Amazonian region (Fittkau *et al.*, 1975). These data also confirm the importance of the marginal fringes for the secondary production of whole wetland biotopes. A conspicuous decrease in total abundance occurred, depending on worsening oxygen conditions from the fringe towards the centre of the stand, where the ephemeropterans, trichopterans and conchostracans disappeared completely.

Most studies of tidal salt marshes have also indicated the richness of the grass stands along tidal creeks as compared with those growing further away (Teal, 1962; Smalley, 1958). Unlike wetlands attached to standing and tidal waters, in some running water biotopes the water current does not allow the fauna to inhabit the stand–water interface in larger numbers. Junk (1970, 1973), investigating the ecology of wetlands along the middle Amazon, found an increasing density of organisms with increasing distance from the margins (total biomass of $0.3 \, \text{g}$ dry wt m^{-2} to $4.2 \, \text{g}$ m^{-2}).

Table 5.8. *Relations between the density of* Elodea canadensis *and the quantity of invertebrates in a carp pond (Kořínková, 1971a,b)*

Positive	Negative	None apparent
Young *Lymnaea peregra*	*Gyraulus albus*	*Helobdella stagnalis*
Young *Physa fontinalis*	*Cloën dipterum*	*Glossiphonia* sp.
Plea atomaria	*Caenis* spp.	*Cymatia* sp.
	Mystacides spp.	*Corixa* spp.
	Triaenodes spp.	*Erythromma najas*
	Chaoborus sp.	*Ischnura elegans*
	Endochironomus sp.	*Elophila nymphaeata*
	Eucricotopus sp.	and others
	Psectrocladius sp.	

Another approach to the assay of phytophilous community structure is that chosen by Zimbalevskaya (1981). She studied invertebrates in various water bodies on the River Dnieper. When the invertebrate species were ranked by magnitude by their respiratory metabolism, associations were found, not only with different body size but also with different habits of nutrition. This may be considered as a manifestation of the degree of community structure. An inverse relationship between the invertebrate densities and their individual biomasses revealed successive changes in the community structure and in the proportions of different components of the energy-flow through the community.

The distribution of macro-fauna on Lemnaceae, both floating (*Spirodela polyrhiza* dominated) and submerged (*Lemna trisulca*) was studied by Kobuzsewka (1973). Despite the environmental differences between those two groups, there were not many species of animals exclusively characteristic of either the floating or submerged Lemnaceae. The few differences observed concerned Anisoptera and Neuroptera, and were probably due to the different spatial structure of the vegetation.

In submerged macrophyte vegetation the species structure of animal communities is mostly influenced by the morphological and biological properties of the host plants and by the environmental factors dependent on the vegetation (e.g. light distribution, temperature, oxygen content and pH). Kořínková, (1971*a,b*), analysed the quantitative relations between submerged macrophytes and invertebrate populations in a carp pond in South Bohemia, and distinguished three groups of animals whose population densities showed different correlations with the density of *Elodea canadensis*; positive, negative and no apparent correlation (Table 5.8).

Specific interrelationships between some phytophilous larvae and certain submerged plant species are mostly caused by the feeding and other ecological requirements of the larvae, on the one hand, and biological properties of the plants, on the other. Müller-Liebenau (1956) found such relations between *Cyrnus flavidus* larvae, and *Potamogeton lucens* and *P. pectinatus*; between *Acentropus niveus* and *P. perfoliatus* and *P. pectinatus*; between *Paraponyx stratiotata* and *Potamogeton lucens*; and between *Hydrellia* larvae and *P. lucens, perfoliatus* and *crispus*. Similar relationships were also observed for emergent or floating-leaved plants (Dvořák & Best, 1982), between *Tinodes waeneri* and *Lype phaeopta*, and *Phragmites australis, Typha angustifolia* and *Polygonum amphibium*; between *Nonagria* and *P. australis*; between *Bezzia* spp. and *Palpomyia lineata*, and *P. australis, T. angustifolia* and *P. amphibium*. Particularly close associations are generally found between miners and their host plants.

On the basis of this information, some generalisations can be made. The littoral vegetation, even that with a single helophyte dominant, does not provide a homogeneous environment. The governing influences exerted by the sheltering effect of plants and alternations of ecophases on the species structure of the macro-fauna is apparent. Gradients of most of the ecological factors are found, especially in food supply (both qualitative and quantitative differences), in the volume of aquatic living space, temperature, oxygen content or in the occurrence of hydrogen sulphide and other toxic matters dissolved in the water. The most conspicuous gradients have been found during summer from the outer edges of the helophyte stands towards the land. These environmental gradients are reflected in a conspicuous spatial distribution of macro-faunal components. The communities inhabiting the zone along the water–stand interface mostly contain actively swimming aquatic animals, with higher oxygen requirements, and air-breathing species as well as true benthic elements, for instance leeches, may-flies, some damsel-flies, water bugs, large dytiscids and especially chironomids. Conversely, near the terrestrial edge of the stands the macro-fauna consists of a large number of semi-terrestrial or terrestrial components, e.g. the larvae of *Pericoma, Ptychoptera, Kempia, Limnophyes* and *Cyphon* as well as of Oligochaeta, Zonitidae, and carabid, staphilinid and hydrophilid beetles. The air-breathing species often form a preponderant part of the invertebrate assemblages. Inside the stands the various characteristic species structures of the macro-fauna are formed by the combined influences of mechanical, trophic, and biological properties of

Table 5.9. *Trophic structure of invertebrate populations of the vegetation of a lake margin (Dvořák & Best, 1982)*

	Percentage of total invertebrate biomass	
Guild	Range	Mean
Grazers	0–16	2
Miners	0.15–22	6
Detritivores, periphyton scrapers and omnivores	22–69	44
Filter-feeders	4–65	36
Carnivores	4–22	12

the stand, fluctuations of the water level and seasonal life cycles of the animal species.

When the central region of the stands is in the littoral ecophase, the substantial part of the invertebrate communities is often formed by species ecologically closely attached to the plants (macro-epibionts) while the proportion of true benthic elements, which are rich at the stand–open water interface, is reduced (Rudescu & Popescu-Marinescu, 1970).

Trophic structure

Wetlands are predominantly detrital systems and the utilisation of fresh plant material is usually much lower than might be expected. Dvořák and Best (1982) have shown how this is expressed in the invertebrate communities (Table 5.9) of seven species of vascular water plants, including emergent, floating-leaved and submerged types, in a small lake. However, the differences between different species of plant were large, and there were strong seasonal changes which were affected by the population dynamics of the detrital feeders and omnivores (molluscs, chironomids and other insect larvae), on the one hand, and the carnivores (dragonfly nymphs, carnivorous caddis-fly larvae, etc.) on the other.

The differences in species structure within wetlands, as along the gradient from the outer edges of helophyte stands towards the land described above, are, as a rule, paralleled by changes in a diverse trophic structure. While the food in the outer fringes is mainly supplied by easily utilised, penetrating and sedimenting phytoplankton and fine detritus of pelagic origin, the central region contains predominantly coarse detritus of autochthonous origin from the helophytes, and the inshore margins receive much resistant allochthonous detritus from trees and shrubs.

The favourable oxygen and feeding conditions along the outer margins result in mass development of populations of invertebrates collecting or filtering detritus, namely oligochaetes, ephemeropteran nymphs and especially chironomid larvae (*Microtendipes, Chironomus,* and some species of *Glyptotendipes* and *Endochironomus*). A higher proportion of predators is found in the total macro-fauna of the margins than inside the stands. Dvořák and Lišková (1970) found that carnivores were 26% of the whole macro-faunal biomass of the margins, but only 6–15% inside the stands. An extreme situation was observed in the margins of a pure stand of *Glyceria maxima* (Dvořák, 1970*a*), where the large carnivores formed as much as 80% of the biomass of all free-living macro-fauna. The contrasting conspicuous prevalence of detritivores and scrapers of periphyton inside the stand was partly a consequence of the seasonal mass development of new generations of oligochaetes, snails and mosquitoes, and chironomid and *Cyphon* larvae, and partly of the absence of large predators (Dytiscidae, *Ilyocoris*, etc.).

Kořínková (1971*a*) calculated the ratio between the predators and their prey in stands of three submerged plant species. In *Elodea canadensis* predators formed, on average, 21% of the animal biomass, in *Ranunculus aquatilis* 23% and in *Potamogeton lucens* as high as 32%. Higler (1975), when constructing the trophic web in *Stratiotes* vegetation, also found a large number of top predators (leeches, dragonflies, caddis-flies) but almost no fish. The phenomenon could be explained by the substantial food for predators provided by zooplankton of both pelagic and local origin. These data on the high share of carnivores in the macro-faunal biomass point to the fact that the macro-fauna cannot be looked at as a distinct community, but only as an assemblage of populations of large animals forming an integral part of more complex animal communities.

Seasonal dynamics

The species structure of macro-fauna and its quantitative development are subject to substantial seasonal changes. Unfortunately, only a little is known on the winter patterns of macro-faunal communities.

In *Stratiotes* mats in the Dutch broads, Higler (1975) found almost no mortality of fauna beneath the ice as long as the oxygen content was sufficient. In the winter beneath the ice, and in spring, the same combination of species was found on the sunken and decaying plants of *Stratiotes aloides* as was on the living ones in summer and autumn. In littoral stands of *Glyceria maxima* and various *Carex* species in South Bohemian ponds, most macro-faunal components move to hibernate in the outer waterward margins of the helophyte vegetation where oxygen conditions are more favourable; particularly the leeches, snails of the family Lymnaeidae, mayflies, caddis-flies, chironomids and other dipteran species. Another part of the macro-fauna (Enchytraeidae, several species of Planorbidae and *Aplexa hypnorum*, as well as some hydrophilid beetles and heleid larvae) tend to hibernate along the upper terrestrial edge of the stands (J. Dvořák, unpublished data).

Most information on the dynamics of macro-fauna comes from the warmer period of the year, namely from the period April–October in the northern temperate zone. The combined effects of several factors operate, namely alternation of ecophases, life cycles of the most important species, feeding activity of fish consuming the macro-fauna and physico-chemical conditions. A generally accepted pattern of seasonal development of the macro-fauna cannot be given because of the highly variable combinations of ecological factors in various biotopes.

The alternation of ecophases is the main determinant of the seasonal dynamics. For each ecophase certain leading organisms can be found, the life cycles of which determine the pattern of the whole macro-faunal dynamics, e.g. in the hydrophase and littoral ecophase of the European wetlands, leeches, Tubificidae, Naididae, Physidae, Lymnaeidae and chironomid larvae; in the littoral ecophase, Lymnaeidae, Planorbidae, Hydrobiidae, gammarids, *Asellus*, mosquitoes and helodid larvae; in the limosal ecophase, Enchytraeidae, *Eiseniella tetraedra, Lymnaea (Stagnicola) palustris*, beetles of the subfamily Sphaeridiinae and some dipteran larvae (Forcipomyinae, some Orthocladiinae, Tabanidae, Syrphidae). Even when anoxia occurs in some parts of a wetland, there are some airbreathing animals which can colonise these parts and develop there in great masses, e.g. larvae of the dipteran families Psychodidae, Ptychopteridae and Syrphidae (*Eristalis*) and beetles of the genus *Cyphon*.

Best known are the seasonal dynamics of macro-fauna living in hydrophase and littoral ecophase. In stands of emergent water vegetation of the Northern temperate zone, usually two or three peaks, both of abundance and biomass occur during the warm period of the year (Mordukhai-Boltovskoi *et al.*, 1958; Mordukhai-Boltovskoi, 1974; Shcherbakov, 1961; Sokolova, 1963; Dvořák & Lišková, 1970; and others). If a spring peak occurs, it is usually the consequence of immigration and growth of animals that hibernate in the sublittoral as well as of the development of new spring generations (especially may-flies, caddis-flies and non-biting midges). The main maxima mostly arise in the summer (June–August), sometimes in early autumn (September–beginning of October). These main maxima result from mass appearance and development of summer generations of most of the macro-faunal components (especially Mollusca, Oligochaeta, Crustacea and insects, mostly Chironomidae). The late autumnal peaks are due to hatching of the individuals of the winter generations before their migration to the places of hibernation.

Kobuszewska (1973) found two factors simultaneously affecting both the biomass of Lemnaceae and the fauna inhabiting them. On the one hand, the fluctuations are due to direct fish grazing on the plants and consumption of the associated fauna; on the other hand, the Lemnaceae expand into new habitats; which may result in irregular growth of the plants and also in irregular changes in the quantity of associated fauna.

The seasonal dynamics of the phytophilous fauna of submergent macrophytes is mostly correlated with the growth patterns of the host plants.

Rice fields exhibit a clear-cut succession of ecophases which results in very substantial changes in animal populations. Washino and Hokama (1967) outlined the seasonal changes in Californian rice fields, from flooding and seedling stages to harvest. Aquatic Coleoptera and Hemiptera mostly reached a single seasonal peak in early summer. Some Hemiptera had a second peak later in summer and may-flies appeared in late summer. Among Diptera the peak abundances were in late May to mid-June for chironomids, in June for the mosquito, *Culex tarsalis*, and in late summer for another mosquito, *Anopheles freeborni*. Detailed data on periodic changes of animal communities inhabiting rice fields also come from Hungary. Berczik (1971, 1973*b*) reports the succession of benthic and phytophilous (mining) animals during the developmental period of the rice fields and ditches, with two peaks (March–April and end of September). The chironomid larvae played a leading part, both in qualitative composition and in peak development of the whole fauna.

Planktonic and epiphytic micro-fauna

Zooplankton

Zooplankton is an important constituent of animal communities in water bodies. Most information is for populations of the pelagic zone and only little attention has been paid to flooded areas with emergent macrophytes. Some quantitative studies on zooplankton have been made in littorals of backwaters and fishponds (Straškraba, 1963, 1965b, 1967; Poštolková, 1967; Losos & Heteša, 1971; Amoros, 1973). These mainly focus on aspects of fish culture (e.g. influence of fish populations on zooplankton communities; changes in plankton composition caused by pond management), but give insight into the structure and dynamics of zooplankton in some emergent macrophyte communities. Some detailed information on zooplankton within littoral communities of several helophytes, in Russian reservoirs and lakes, is given by Mordukhai-Boltovskoi *et al.* (1958), Shcherbakov (1961) and Sokolova (1963).

The most important components of zooplankton within the macrophyte stands are Cladocera and Copepoda, which numerically exceed the Rotatoria during the vegetation period when zooplankton is abundant. Straškraba (1965b) reports a ratio Crustacea : Rotatoria of between 2 and 5 : 1 in moderately dense emergent vegetation, and between 5 and 15 : 1 in dense submerged vegetation. A similar result was obtained earlier by Reinisch (1925). Rotatoria dominate only during winter.

The zooplankton of the littoral zone is not as clearly defined as in the pelagic zone because the crustacean and rotatorian species present are associated with the substrata to varying extents. Straškraba (1967) distinguishes four ecological groups in this respect (Table 5.10):

Littoral species These, although capable of swimming, mostly creep on vegetation, scraping periphyton or preying on organisms attached to or moving on plants; larger forms prevail.

Tycholimnetic species They are usually swimming free amongst vegetation, but also occur in open water regions; they are mostly filter-feeders dependent on phytoplankton and are generally smaller species.

Pelagic species They inhabit mainly the pelagic region of water bodies, but may be common in the littoral region, particularly in sparse stands of emergent macrophytes, when phytoplankton is abundant.

Benthic species They are associated with the bottom surface and sediments.

However, no sharp boundaries can be drawn between these groups, as

Table 5.10. *The most abundant representatives of different ecological groups of littoral zooplankton in Eastern and Central Europe and British Isles (Gliwicz & J.I. Rybak, 1976; Shcherbakov, 1961; Smyly, 1957; Straškraba, 1967)*

Littoral species
Cladocera: *Simocephalus vetulus, S. exspinosus, Scapholeberis mucronata, Sida crystallina, Ceriodaphnia megops, C. reticulata, Alona affinis, A. guttata, A. costata, A. quadrangularis, Eurycercus lamellatus, Acroperus harpae, Graptoleberis testudinaria, Alonella exigua, A. nana, Pleuroxus aduncus, P. trigonellus, Chydorus sphaericus*
Copepoda: *Macrocyclops albidus, M. fuscus, Eucyclops macruroides, E. macrurus, E. serrulatus, Acanthocyclops vernalis, A. viridis, Microcyclops bicolor, Canthocamptus staphylinus*
Rotatoria: *Platyias patulus, P. quadricornis, Notholca squamula, N. acuminata, Euchlanis deflexa, E. dilatata, Mytilina ventralis, Lecane luna, Cephalodella* sp., *Testudinella patina, T. parva, Trichocerca capucina, T. tigris, Chromogaster testudo, Colurella obtusa*

Tycholimnetic species
Cladocera: *Diaphanosoma brachyurum, Scapholeberis mucronata, Sida crystallina, Ceriodaphnia pulchella, C. quadrangula, C. affinis, Bosmina longirostris, Chydorus sphaericus*
Copepoda: *Mesocyclops leuckarti*

Pelagic or pure planktonic species
Cladocera: *Daphnia pulex, D. longispina, D. cucullata, Bosmina longirostris*
Copepoda: *Eudiaptomus gracilis, E. graciloides, Cyclops vicinus kikuchii, Mesocyclops leuckarti, M. (Thermocyclops) oithonoides, M. (T.) crassus*
Rotatoria: *Brachionus angularis, B. calyciflorus, B. quadridentatus, B. urceus, Keratella cochlearis, K. quadrata, Kellicottia longispina, Asplanchna priodonta, Synchaeta* sp., *Polyarthra dolichoptera, P. remata, Filinia longiseta, F. terminalis, Conochilus unicornis*

Benthic species
Cladocera: *Iliocryptus sordidus, Macrothrix laticornis, Chydorus globosus*

has been shown by species which occupy different categories in different water bodies; many species are in such intermediate positions.

According to such differences in biology and trophic relations, a remarkable species diversity may occur in littorals. Straškraba (1967) reports 77 species of 'zooplankton' in a small backwater of the Labe river in Bohemia, of which 34 species were Cladocera. Numbers of Cladocera species in comparable littorals range from 13 in an English moorland pond (Smyly, 1952) to 59 in a eutrophic pond in Silesia (Langhans, 1911).

In narrow littoral belts with sparse vegetation, the species composition resembles that of the open water, but in denser and extensive stands, with little exchange with the open water, littoral species become dominant. They seem to replace the tycholimnetic species. This is also expressed through different seasonal cycles; whereas tycholimnetic species have their maximum in summer, littoral species show bimodal cycles with a well defined maximum in spring and a less defined one in autumn (Straškraba, 1965*b*). In the extensive, uniform reedbed of Neusiedlersee, a distinct zonation of zooplankton composition has been found from the land margin to the waterside stands over a distance of more than 1 km (Löffler, 1979*b*). This zonation cannot be attributed, so far, to differences in environmental conditions. However, Thomas (1961) found a correlation between the amount of light falling on the water in a papyrus swamp, and the number of Cladocera present there. Far more Cladocera were found in the part of the swamp where papyrus had been cut than where it was growing densely; he thought that the amount of light, by regulating the primary production and hence the dissolved oxygen concentration in water was determining the density of cladocerans. In a sunlit swamp pool in Uganda he found five species in one litre of water, totalling (in two samples) 110 and 320 individuals, respectively, which compares favourably with other water bodies. In the weed beds of Lake Chad, in Central Africa, Dejoux and Saint-Jean (1972) report that the crustacean fauna inhabiting dense stands of *Ceratophyllum* and *Potamogeton* are very different from the benthic and pelagial fauna of open places, even those within the plant stands.

Apart from the presence of higher plants, other abiotic and biotic factors can strongly influence the composition and seasonal dynamics of zooplankton species. In unstable waters like drained fishponds, the ability to form developmental stages resistant to desiccation (ephippia, resting eggs of Cladocera, ovarial sacs of Copepoda or even certain copepodite stages) at any time when drainage may occur, is an important selective factor. This ensures rapid re-population when the pond is refilled. Amoros (1973) stressed the importance of this phenomenon for fish culture. Those species which resist drainage, excavation and cultivation of the pond, belong to larger size classes preferred by carp as food, whereas in ponds not drained for several years, small species become dominant. Fish themselves influence the species composition by selective feeding as has been shown by fencing experiments (Straškraba, 1965*b*; Poštolková, 1967) or total removal of the fish fauna (Vladimirova, 1963; Straškraba, 1967).

In the Amazonian flood-plains, where Junk (1973) made an intensive investigation of the fauna of the floating meadows, the populations of Cladocera and Copepoda, inhabiting the interstitial spaces within the tight root entanglement of the floating mats, respond quickly to changes in water quality. After the dry period, rising water loaded with tripton, and phytoplankton development, lead to a rapid increase in zooplankton, which sharply decreases when the current speeds up and whitewater, loaded with inorganic suspended material, penetrates the flood-plains. After the end of whitewater flushing, the zooplankton increases again until the mat becomes dry. This somewhat simplified scheme is modified on different types of sites according to the local water regime. In such unstable conditions, zooplankton plays an important role; after the rapid increase, the zooplankton biomass can be as much as half the biomass of the macro-fauna and crustacean micro-fauna together.

Several authors have estimated zooplankton abundance and biomass in littorals of lakes, ponds and reservoirs. Besides the problem of species associated with plants, spatial variations such as swarming complicate the estimates. Dense swarms of pelagic zooplankton may appear near the shoreline, particularly in the narrow littoral zones of small water bodies. Sládeček (1973) reports a density of some $4000\ 1^{-1}$ for Crustacea in a swarm in the Nesyt fishpond littoral (South Moravia), whereas at the same time only $73\ 1^{-1}$ were found on a comparable site. In the Poltruba backwater in Bohemia a density as high as $27\,000\ 1^{-1}$ was found, as against the normal 2000 during maximum abundance (Straškraba, 1967).

Abundance and biomass figures mostly refer to concentrations. By this scale, zooplankton abundance and standing crop are commonly up to tenfold higher in littorals than in the respective pelagials (Lipin & Lipina, 1951; Mordukhai-Boltovskoi et al., 1958; Rudescu et al., 1965; Straškraba, 1965b, 1967). Related to unit area, however, the biomass in littorals is equal to, or less than in, pelagials. Biomass figures per square metre of surface, which are more suitable for comparisons between different wetland types, are rather rare. As an example for littorals of a large basin in the temperate region, Zimbalevskaya (1972) reports a mean zooplankton energy of biomass during the vegetation period of about $33.6\ \mathrm{kJ\ m^{-2}}$ from macrophyte stands in the Kiev reservoir in the Ukraine. Similar values were found by Junk (1973) in the rhizosphere of floating mat meadows in the Amazonian region, with peaks up to about $84\ \mathrm{kJ}$ $\mathrm{m^{-2}}$, and by Straškraba (1965a) in the Labíčko backwater (North

Bohemia), where the crustacean zooplankton in a *Typha* stand, with additional submerged vegetation, reached a mean value of 105 kJ m^{-2} during the season of maximum abundance.

The 'aufwuchs' community

The 'aufwuchs' community which settles on the surfaces of submerged parts of macrophytes, and other objects, includes a larger variety of microfaunal elements than is represented in the zooplankton. In temperate freshwaters the animal constituents of the aufwuchs is represented by Ciliata, Porifera, Hydrozoa, Rotatoria, Nematoda, Oligochaeta, Bryozoa, Ostracoda, Copepoda, Cladocera, and larvae of different insect groups, mainly chironomids. The species composition and ecology of this community has been studied for a long time (e.g. Duplakov, 1933; Meuche, 1939). Qualitative composition and population density is dependent on several ecological conditions, of which the duration of flooding and the lifespan of macrophytes serving as substratum are of basic importance.

The population density on different submerged macrophytes (*Potamogeton, Myriophyllum, Elodea*) analysed by Bownik (1970) showed a maximum in autumn on plant species decaying during the winter (*Potamogeton*) and in autumn and spring on overwintering macrophytes (*Myriophyllum, Elodea*). The main animals colonising submerged macrophytes are Nematoda, Oligochaeta and Chironomidae. Sessile forms such as Spongillidae and Bryozoa are restricted to stems of emergent plants which persist for several years.

In many papers dealing with colonisation the problem is discussed whether it is the chemical or the mechanical properties of the substratum that most influence the composition of the aufwuchs. Pieczyńska and Spodniewska (1963) experimented with different natural and artificial substrates, which resulted in no significant differences in the composition and dominance structure of at least the aufwuchs fauna (Nematoda, Oligochaeta, Chironomidae). This supports the use of glass plates in investigations of aufwuchs animal production. Great differences have been found, however, on substrates of the same kinds in different lakes and even at different sites of the same lake. This was also shown by investigations of aufwuchs on helophytes in several Mazurian lakes (Pieczyńska, 1960*a,b*).

Trophic conditions seem to be the dominant controlling factor for the spatial distribution and seasonal variation of aufwuchs, which may be considerable. Pieczyńska (1970*a*) distinguishes three trophic types of aufwuchs:

1. autotrophic type with less than 10% animal biomass;
2. autotrophic–heterotrophic type with an animal community with similar biomass to algae, at least partly dependent on detritus;
3. heterotrophic type with more than 90% of animals, often consisting of monospecific masses of Spongillidae or Bryozoa.

These types can substitute for one another on different sites and during different time periods, the heterotrophic type, however, prevailing during autumn and winter. Also, the abundance peaks during this season, found by Bownik (1970) on submerged plants, are partly attributed to the supply of decaying plant material colonised by bacteria–detrital complexes which seem to provide the main nutrition for the aufwuchs microfauna.

Data on the abundance and biomass of aufwuchs animals involve the same problems of comparability as for those on phytophilous macrofauna. As the surface of solid substrata is the relevant dimension for spatial limitations of aufwuchs, figures related to surface area are more suitable for comparisons than those related to weight or volume units. However, with submerged macrophytes the surface is usually difficult to measure, and with helophytes the aerial leaf area is usually determined, which is not relevant to aquatic populations.

Invertebrates of the root region of macrophytes

Introduction

The root region of plants comprises the rhizosphere, the roots and rhizomes, etc. and their surfaces (Parkinson, 1967). The fauna of the root region is not well known; most attention has been paid to Nematoda which form a substantial part of the meio-fauna of roots and rhizomes (Prejs, 1973). For the macro-fauna, there is a lack of information on the more complex relations between the specific animal communities and the root region of various species of aquatic macrophytes. The bottom macro-fauna in stands of macrophytes has been usually studied as a whole without special regard to the part closely related to the roots ecologically.

Species structure

Meio-fauna

Nematodes are the most numerous meio-fauna inhabiting the root region of macrophytes, frequently more than 90% of the total. The rest are mostly oligochaetes and chironomid larvae (Prejs & Wiktorzak, 1976). The nematodes live both freely in sediments and penetrating into tissues of roots and rhizomes. The root region and bottom sediments along the plants usually have higher numbers of Nematodes than the bottom sediments of non-overgrown zones of littorals.

Prejs and Wiktorzak (1976) analysing the meiofauna of the stands of *Potamogeton lucens* and *P. perfoliatus* in littoral of Mikołajskie Lake (Poland), found 45 species of Nematoda representing 16 families. In the root region of these plants, species of *Dorylaimus* and *Mesodorylaimus* were most common. Representatives of the genera *Tobrilus, Ironus* and *Chromadorita* were also abundant. Bottom sediments among the plants were mostly inhabited by species of *Chromadorita* and *Tobrilus*; the non-overgrown zones were dominated by *Tobrilus, Monhystera* and *Chromadorita*. Almost all species of Nematoda noted in bottom sediments around the underground parts of plants were also found penetrating into roots and rhizomes, but their dominance structure was different. Prejs (1973, 1977) and Prejs and Wiktorzak (1976) comment on the existence of specific groupings of nematodes living in the root region and penetrating into the tissues of roots of pond weeds.

Invertebrate macro-fauna

Oligochaetes (especially Tubificidae) and Chironomid larvae usually form the most numerous macro-invertebrates of the root region. They mostly live in bottom sediments among the roots and rhizomes of plants. Some Mermithidae, larvae of *Donacia* and some Curculionidae, as well as the larvae of several species of dipteran families, Chironomidae, Tipulidae and Ephydridae are directly related to the underground organs of water plants, which provide them with favourable feeding and living conditions. As a rule, the macro-fauna of the root region has greater taxonomic variety than that living in non-overgrown areas of littorals because of the presence of phytophilous species. These qualitative differences are usually paralleled by quantitative ones; for example, in *Nuphar lutea* stands the macro-fauna of the root region was 26 to 195 times more abundant than in non-overgrown places, while in *Potamogeton perfoliatus* the macro-fauna of the root region was 10 to 26 times higher (Prejs & Wiktorzak, 1976).

Relation between invertebrates and the underground parts of plants

Nematodes

According to their feeding characteristics Prejs and Wiktorzak (1976) distinguished three groups of Nematoda associated with underground parts of water macrophytes.

Those feeding on live plants (e.g. *Hirschmanniella, Dorylaimoides, Mesodorylaimus* and *Chrysonemoides*) possess spears for puncturing the plant tissue. Representatives of the superfamily Dorylaimoidea faculta-tively utilise plant saps; they can be called semi-parasites. *Hirschmanniella oryzae* and *Heterodera oryzae* are important pests of rice and may be regarded as parasites.

Many feed on dead plant tissues and bacteria (e.g. *Chronogaster, Plectus, Panagrolaimus* and *Cryptonochus*). Both parasites and detriti-vores penetrate plant tissues and may make the underground organs accessible to secondary infections by various pathogenic micro-organisms thus causing more harm than the nematodes.

Nematodes of other trophic groups (predators, omnivores and certain stadia of parasites of invertebrates, for example, Mermithidae) use the intercellular spaces of roots and rhizomes as a habitat and shelter.

External grazers and miners

Macro-invertebrates trophically bound to the underground organs of water macrophytes are represented mainly by external grazers and miners. Larvae of *Donacia* species graze on rhizomes of various water macrophytes; their presence is evident from grazed and withered frag-ments of roots. Analyses of gut contents of *Donacia* larvae show the presence of plant tissue. They also puncture the tissues to obtain air from intercellular gas spaces. Larvae of some water weevils are known to damage the roots of rice, e.g. *Lissorhoptrus oryzophilus* which has been reported as a common and destructive pest of rice in the USA (Pathak, 1968). Mining chironomid and tipulid larvae damage the roots of water plants; they are also serious rice pests (Gaevskaya, 1966/69).

Vertebrates in wetlands

Fish

The shallow littoral belts and wetlands bordering standing waters, as well as paddy fields and flood-plains of rivers, are frequently utilised by fish populations as spawning and feeding grounds. Indeed, the data analysis by Fernando and Holčík (1982, 1984, 1991) revealed that most freshwater fish in standing waters are limited to the littoral. This is due to the riverine origin of fish communities which are not adapted to lacustrine habitats and with increasing offshore distance and depth, the number of species and density of fish decrease markedly. The few exceptions from this rule are only ancient lakes such as Lake Baikal or lakes in the Rift Valley in Africa for instance, which also harbour endemic lacustrine species living in both the pelagial and at depth.

Relations between the reed standing crop, size of the littoral zone and the fish in Polish lakes were studied by Szajnowski (1970). The author divided the fish species into two groups: the first group consisted of fish species strongly related to the littoral (*Tinca, Esox* and *Rutilus*); the second one consists of species having a lesser or negative relation to the littoral (*Alburnus, Perca, Abramis* and *Anguilla*). The author explains these results by a positive or negative correspondence between the biological properties of the fish species with the trophic and spawning conditions provided for them in the littoral. The biomass of pike, *Esox lucius*, in several Dutch waters appeared directly related to the percentage of the lake area covered with vegetation (Grimm, 1989).

It has been repeatedly suggested that papyrus swamps, and particularly the papyrus–open water interface, serve the fish as a breeding and feeding habitat and provide them with a shelter, but serious research has yet to be done in this respect. In the Sudan's sudd 17 species of fish belonging to 11 families were found (Sandon, 1950). Greenwood (1966), Sandon (1951) and Sandon and El Tayib (1953) list fish species which commonly visit or inhabit the swamp fringe for food, shelter or breeding. Elder *et al.* (1971) refer to considerable fish movement from and towards the swamp fringe. Similar observations were made in Lake Victoria and Lake George in Uganda (Gwahaba, 1975; T. Petr, pers. comm.).

The summaries by Welcomme (1979, 1985) for large tropical rivers show that the flood-plains, and shallow areas around man-made lakes, are of vital importance for reproduction and feeding of fish which undergo regular lateral migrations on and off flood-plains.

Spawning

In the northern temperate zone, early in the spring, many fish species migrate to inundated areas or shallow waters sheltered by reedbelts from the wave action to lay their eggs (e.g. *Esox lucius*, northern pike). Other species follow and the deposition of eggs may last until August, depending on the local climate. These species were classified by Kryzhanovskiĭ (1949) and Balon (1975), as phytophils, that is fish which require submerged, live or dead aquatic or recently flooded terrestrial plants for deposition of eggs. *Cyprinus carpio*, the common carp, is a phytophil. Fish culturists in Central Europe, knowing this requirement, have constructed special spawning ponds for centuries which amount to artificial wetlands.

Another group of fish which is more or less dependent on wetlands is the 'indifferents' (Holčík & Hruška, 1966) or, according to the latest classification, phyto-lithophils (Balon, 1975, 1981). They deposit eggs in relatively clear water habitats on submerged plants, if available, or on submerged objects such as logs, gravel and rocks (e.g. *Abramis brama, Alburnus alburnus, Perca fluviatilis*).

Wilkońska and Żuromska (1967) observed the spawning sites of *Esox lucius* (pike) and *Rutilus rutilus* (roach) in a 120 km^2 complex of Polish lakes for 8 years. They estimated that the spawning grounds in the entire lake complex occupied 6.6% of the total lake area (8.8% of the total length of the shoreline) for pike, and 0.4% of the area (22.0% of the length) for roach. These proportions vary from lake to lake being greater in small than in large lakes.

From many studies on lakes and reservoirs with controlled water levels (Frazer, 1972) one can infer that denudation of these littoral sites during spring causes heavy losses in fish production.

Fish spawning may also be an important contribution to the food web in littoral zones. Ingenious sampling of fish eggs and just hatched fry carried out on selected spawning grounds by Żuromska (1967*a,b*) illustrates this point. She worked in the Polish lake area already mentioned. Her sampling procedure showed that the number of roach eggs laid varied from 35×10^3 m^{-2} to 1.25×10^6 m^{-2}. Żuromska also estimated the numbers of fry which were only from 0.12 to 6.34% of the number of eggs estimated 8 to 19 days before the fry sampling. The average loss of individuals during that short period was about 99%. This high mortality rate of eggs and just hatched fry is usually caused by several physiological and biological factors (Schäperclaus, 1961) but the predation activity of many water invertebrates (e.g. nymphs of dragonflies, beetles of the family Dytiscidae, water bugs and carnivorous larvae of caddis-flies) must be of great importance. The juveniles of roach were also preyed upon by juvenile pike, but mortality due to parasites (*Dactylogyrus* sp., *Trichodina* sp., metacercaria of *Sphaerostomum globiposum*) was of minor significance.

The example concerns just one species of fish, but there are many others which deposit eggs on similar, or even the same, places. Thus, the wetland sites frequented by fish for spawning supply a substantial amount of food suitable for secondary consumers.

Feeding

As already stressed, wetlands provide favourable feeding conditions for fish populations. Studies of the diet and behaviour of feeding fish have shown great variety of and adaptability to food sources.

Direct consumption of macrophytes is well known for several species of fish. According to Gaevskaya (1966/69) the obligate phyto-stenophages, feeding exclusively or predominantly on vascular or lower water plants are mostly representatives of the family Cyprinidae (*Ctenopharyngodon idella, Acanthorhodeus asmussii, Megalobrama terminalis, Parabramis pekinensis, Scardinius erythrophthalmus, Schizopygopsis stoliczkai* and *Schizothorax argentatus*). The grass carp or white amur (*Ctenopharyngodon idella*) is the best known. This species originates from the Far East, being distributed from the northern part of the Indonesian peninsula northwards over the whole of China to the river Amur and its tributaries. It has been introduced into many other countries as a biological weed control agent and a human food source (Krupauer, 1967, 1968; Fischer, 1968, 1973; Chapman & Coffey, 1971). Its feeding habits have been reviewed by Gaevskaya, (1966/69). In the youngest developmental stages *C. idella* feeds mainly on zooplankton, changing from zoophagy to pure phyto-phagy during maturation. Young and mature fish show selectivity of the species consumed (e.g. Duthu & Kilgen, 1975; Fowler & Robson, 1978 and pp. 298 and 458). In Europe, the most herbivorous native species is rudd (*Scardinius erythrophthalmus*) which inhabits vegetated lake littorals and slow-flowing rivers; although fish up to 4 cm long feed on zooplankton. Adult bitterling (*Rhodeus sericeus*) and quite often adult roach (*Rutilus rutilus*) and chub (*Leuciscus cephalus*) also exhibit herbivory (e.g. Leszcynski, 1963; Prejs, 1973).

Wetlands also provide suitable food for other fish species having wider diets but which include vascular plants both living and in various stages of decay; for example, the Indian species *Labeo rohita, Cirrhinus mrigala* and

Catla catla. Among African species, *Sarotherodon* (*Tilapia*) *mossambicus* is the best-known herbivorous species. The Far East species, *Aristichthys noblis* and *Hypophthalmichthys molitrix* are sometimes included into this group, but the former feeds on zooplankton and the latter is specialised for phytoplankton.

All these species have been introduced into fish culture in many countries of Asia, Europe and America, where some are successfully cultured and applied also to water weed control. Several investigations indicate that the grass carp (*Ctenopharyngodon idella*), if properly used, can be a very effective tool for the control of submerged vegetation (e.g. van Zon, 1977; see also pp. 457–9), and may even affect emergent plants.

A greater number of fish species predominantly feed on periphytic, planktonic or benthic algal and animal communities inhabiting various wetlands. However, the feeding demands differ from species to species and in different age categories of fish. To appreciate the feeding conditions provided by wetlands for fish, the whole complex of ecological peculiarities of those biotopes should be considered, especially their trophic status, oxygen conditions, water temperatures and water level fluctuations.

In shallow water bodies that have become eutrophic, mass development of blue-green algae regularly occurs, both in natural waters and in basins used for fish culture. The consumption of blue-green algae by *Sarotherodon* (*Tilapia*) *niloticus* (Nile perch) and *Haplochromis nigripennis* in tropical waters was studied by Moriarty and Moriarty (1973) and Moriarty (1973). The role of these species in the Lake George ecosystem is described by Moriarty *et al.* (1973).

The littorals of lakes and ponds of the Northern temperate zone provides favourable but complicated feeding conditions for many fish species. The summer diet of *Abramis bjoerkna* (*Blicca bjoerkna*) was studied in the littoral reedbelts of the Neusiedlersee in Austria (Hacker, 1974; Meisriemler, 1974). The composition of their food appeared to be variable regionally as well as seasonally. Benthic algae (epipelic diatoms) were the main food components of *A. bjoerkna* in the fringes (interface between reed and open water). In general, their importance decreased with increasing distance from the reed stands towards the centre of the lake whilst the animal components (zooplankton) increased.

Dvořák and Lišková (1970) also proved the value of narrow littoral belts of helophytes as a source of natural food for fish in fishponds. The phytophilous planktonic and epiphytic fauna plays a highly important role in the summer diet of common carp fry.

In the Polish Lake Warniak, Zawisza and Ciepielewski (1973) showed

Table 5.11. *Average numbers of food items per fish in the alimentary tract of three species of fish in a Californian rice field (Washino & Hokama, 1967; Washino, 1968)*

Food items	Cyprinus carpio	Gambusia affinis	Lavinia exilicauda
Cladocera	5.2	6.3	28.9
Podocopa	1.3	0.7	1.7
Eucopepoda	0.3	0.9	0.6
Chironomidae	47.5	4.2	7.7
Others	2.0	3.2	1.2

that shallow littoral areas were frequented by young specimens of tench (*Tinca tinca*), crucian carp (*Carassius carassius*), perch (*Perca fluviatilis*) and roach from spring till late autumn, except for very warm days in summer; whereas adult fish occurred there mainly in autumn. Prejs (1973) studied feeding habits of fish in the same lake and found that certain Diptera larvae occurring only in the eulittoral were eaten by the common carp, tench, crucian carp and roach, only in spring and autumn. On the contrary, the analysis of food composition of 2- and 3-year-old common carp (*Cyprinus carpio*) from south Bohemian ponds showed an increased proportion of phytophilous chironomid larvae (especially *Glyptotendipes*) in the total amount of food in the summer (R. Faina, pers. comm.). These larvae were, at that time, a very typical component of fauna of the margins of the helophyte stands, while the benthos of the ponds was rather poor at that time (as a consequence of metamorphosis of many of the benthic chironomid species as well as of feeding activity of the fish).

In paddy fields, common carp, common bluegill (*Lepomis macrochirus*), and hitch (*Lavinia exilicauda*) move from irrigation canals after flooding and live in paddy field water throughout the growing season. *Gambusia affinis* is often stocked artificially for biological control of mosquitoes. These fish are carnivorous, and examination of their digestive tracts has indicated that they feed predominantly on Cladocera and Chironomidae. *G. affinis* has a tendency to surface feeding, and so it also feeds on terrestrial insects (e.g. aphids and adult Diptera) as well as aquatic animals, while carp tends to feed on benthic organisms. In spite of such differences, both these fish tend to eat any currently abundant species of water invertebrate (Table 5.11). The examples mentioned here represent only a fraction of the work done in this field, but they have been chosen to illustrate some particular aspects of the subject.

Adaptations to life in wetlands

Physiological adaptations of fish to certain ecological peculiarities of wetland biotopes, especially the lack of oxygen and dry periods, are of great interest. In papyrus swamps which dry out periodically, the lungfish (*Protopterus* spp.) is common, and its aestivation period has been well described (e.g. Nikolskiĭ, 1971). Also *Polypterus* spp., *Clarias* spp., *Mastacembelus* and *Ctenopoma* spp. have various respiratory adaptations which enable them to utilise atmospheric oxygen, and thus they are able to inhabit water with low concentrations of dissolved oxygen.

In swamps and temporarily inundated lands of South-eastern Asia there are several fish species adapted to the peculiar conditions, by having some accessory respiratory organs. Several species of the families Anabantidae, Channidae and Clariidae also can live in water practically devoid of oxygen. In European waters *Misgurnus fossilis* can take air into its alimentary tract and respire via an especially developed part of the intestine. Another interesting fish is *Umbra krameri*, living in the floodplains, swampy channels and shallow overgrown lakes of the Danube and Dniester river basins. Its air bladder is coated by a dense network of capillaries and serves as an accessory breathing organ. Crucian carp (*Carassius carassius*) can also be regarded as a wetland-dwelling species, although it occurs also in lakes and slow-flowing rivers. It is able to live for a considerably long time in completely anaerobic conditions, even in water bodies with some hydrogen sulphide, because it is able to produce oxygen by means of glycogen splitting, (Blažka, 1958).

Amphibians

Amphibians rank among the most typical vertebrates of freshwater wetland biotopes. The existence of the overwhelming majority of amphibians at a larval stage requires a water environment, and many species continue to live in water as adults. But, individual amphibian species differ in the type of biotope preferred and the time they remain in the water in the course of a year.

General biology and life cycles

The ecological role of amphibians in wetlands has been so far assessed only in qualitative terms. Very little is known of their role in the energy flow through the wetland ecosystems – even in regions where they occur in large numbers. The brief survey given here therefore presents only a few examples of the importance of wetlands and shallow waters for the life of amphibians, drawing mainly on knowledge from Europe.

Smaller standing waters are inhabited mostly by newts (*Triturus*) that move there early in spring to deposit eggs. During summer they leave and return to a terrestrial, noctural way of life. Lowlands of Central Europe are rich in the smooth newt (*Triturus vulgaris*) and the warty newt (*T. cristatus*). Towards Western Europe the palmate newt, (*Triturus helveticus*) and the marbled newt (*Triturus marmoratus*) increase. Salamanders behave similarly. For example, only the larval development of the fire salamander (*Salamandra salamandra*) takes place in forest streams, and the adults live in forests, out of the water. The alpine salamander (*Salamandra atra*) is less dependent on water because it is viviparous.

In the Salientia the fire-bellied toad (*Bombina bombina*) is one of the species dependent most continuously upon lowland wetlands; occupying small areas of shallow standing waters. Sometimes, it is even found in rather polluted pools. The adult midwife toad (*Alytes obstetricans*) of Western Europe occurs in wetlands only for a short time, when the male carrying fertilised eggs on his hind limbs brings them to the water to get them moistened. The tadpoles continue living in the water. Another species, the spade-foot toad (*Pelobates fuscus*), finds small standing waters just at the time of egg deposition and its big conspicuous tadpoles live in the water.

Toads (*Bufo*) are common inhabitants of pools and ponds in spring. Early in March the common European toad (*Bufo bufo*) and the natterjack toad (*Bufo calamita*) begin egg deposition, and the green toad (*Bufo viridis*) starts about a month later. After leaving the water, the adults live mostly on land. Shallow, overgrown waters and wetlands are sought by the European tree frog (*Hyla arborea*) at the time of reproduction.

Some species of the genus *Rana* are the most characteristic inhabitants of lake and pond shores and slow-flowing channels. Over most of Europe the well-known edible frog, *Rana esculenta*, abounds. In warmer regions the marsh frog (*Rana ridibunda*), one of its bigger relatives, occurs. These frogs do not leave water during the whole year, being buried in mud in winter. Other species of *Rana*, the common frog (*Rana temporaria*), the field frog (*R. arvalis*) and the agile frog (*R. dalmatina*), look for water at the time of copulation. In *R. dalmatina* the males hibernate in water while the females hibernate mostly on land (Opatrný, 1968).

Feeding

The food of amphibians usually consists of some small invertebrates. Larvae of various water insects form a substantial part of the newt's food. Bellied toads are important predators on larvae of several species of blood-sucking flies (Lác, 1958). These species capture their prey by grasping directly with their jaws, which enables them to catch even in water. On the other hand, frogs and toads which capture using an everted tongue can only catch on land, or on the water surface (Schneider, 1954). The major component of the food of *Bufo bufo* is ants and other insects, *B. viridis* feeds mainly on ground beetles, spiders and so forth. Even water frogs feed mainly on animals caught ashore. Under certain circumstances, e.g. in shallow waters, they may sometimes even catch a small fish. *Rana esculenta* and *R. ridibunda* are among the most predatory species. Cannibalism is common among them and the stomachs of some big individuals have been found to contain mice, lizards and small birds. During the time of reproduction some frogs, e.g. *Rana temporaria*, do not take in food for many days.

In contrast with adult amphibians, tadpoles feed on vegetable food, especially on algae and withered parts of aquatic plants, and dead animal bodies (occasional scavengers).

Both tadpoles and adult amphibians are consumed by other animals such as some predatory fishes, water birds (ducks, herons, storks, etc.), water turtles and snakes, mink, hedgehogs and polecats. In some countries, the big frogs' thighs are eaten by humans, and frog breeding for human consumption has started. Many frogs and toads are also used as experimental laboratory animals.

Reptiles

Reptiles, unlike amphibians, are not intrinsically dependent upon a water environment. Even the species living in water and searching for food there, usually reproduce on land, with their eggs being deposited on solid ground.

As for amphibians, very few quantitative data are available on the role which reptiles play in the functioning of wetland ecosystems. Their feeding habits, however, place most of them among the predators or even top predators (especially crocodiles). Apart from crocodiles, the examples of life of various kinds of reptiles in wetlands come from Europe.

In warmer regions of Europe the European pond tortoise (*Emys orbicularis*) inhabits mainly sunny shallow standing or slowly running waters, rather loosely overgrown by macrophytes. It climbs ashore to bask in the sun and to deposit eggs. It catches its food (small fish, amphibians, water insects, molluscs, etc.) only in water. It hibernates buried in mud (Wermuth, 1952).

The ringed or grass snake (*Natrix natrix*) is spread over the whole of Europe. From Central Europe to the South and South-East there is also the tessellated water snake (*Natrix tessellata*). Ringed snakes sometimes live in small pools and sometimes move quite far from water, searching for food both in water and on land, feeding mainly on amphibians, small fish and invertebrates. The tessellated water snake prefers the margins of fast-running streams, not moving very far from water and mainly catching small fish. The food of other water snakes is similar.

In addition, European wetlands contain the viviparous lizard (*Lacerta vivipara*) whose existence is not inevitably linked with wetlands and which, in Central Europe, lives mainly in mountains. In mountain peat-bogs, it looks for places of concealment from a potential danger in shallow waters. In lowlands, it is relatively rare, but is usually found in wetlands or in alluvial forests (Opatrný, 1973).

Birds

Birds are characteristic and functionally important components of all wetland ecosystems and they are the most conspicuous animals. They have always attracted human attention to wetlands and are indicators of change taking place in these ecosystems (Turček, 1972). Bird species inhabiting wetlands are mostly closely adapted to life on water, on mud flats and in littoral stands of emergent macrophytes. By their spatial diversity, these ecosystems offer the birds numerous ecological niches. These are created, for example, by different depths of water and types of bottom and submerged vegetation, and, above all, by both the vertical and horizontal distribution of the littoral emergent vegetation. Although the latter frequently consists of only a few dominants (e.g. *Phragmites, Typha, Carex, Cyperus*), the stands are stratified and their height, density, and plant species composition, and the extent of water lagoons within them vary depending on the depth of water. All that, together with trophic specialisation, encourage a rich diversity of avian species both within the helophyte vegetation and on the adjacent open water (Palmgren, 1936; Beecher, 1942; Festetics & Leisler, 1968; Dobrowolski, 1969, 1973a,b; Day et al., 1973; Bezzel & Reichholf, 1974; Böck, 1974). Peat-bogs show a much simpler vegetation structure, and, hence, a lower species diversity (Kumari *et al.*, 1974).

Communities

Bird communities have been studied in wetlands in various parts of the world. For example, Day *et al.* (1973) analysed the communities inhabiting North American salt marshes, establishing the main ecological groups of birds and describing their seasonal abundance, food habits, biomass and respiration. A little information is available on the birds inhabiting *Cyperus* swamps. Thornton (1957) reports *Ardeola ralloides, Balaeniceps rex, Anhinga rufa* and *Actophilornis africanus*. Of the passerine birds, *Ploceus capitalis, P. jacksoni* and *Centropus superciliosus* have obviously the same relationship to the papyrus swamps as the starlings to *Phragmites* stands in Europe. Also, the information on rice cultures is scanty. Granivorous passerines of the family Estrildidae, particularly the mannikins of the genus *Lonchura* are major consumers of rice. Large flocks of them visit the paddy fields and roost in swamps. The above family also includes the Java sparrow (*Padda oryzivora*) a notorious pest of rice cultures.

The species diversity of birds inhabiting wetlands varies both in space and time. Naturally, the principal avian life forms are taxonomically most closely related within individual zoogeographic regions. Thus the wetlands of Europe and North America are inhabited by birds mostly belonging to the same genera but different species (literature cited above, also Blackard *et al.*, 1972). Similarly, tropical wetlands include the same life forms (see e.g. La Bastille, 1974) but some different genera and systematically more distant forms (e.g. *Balaenicipitinae* in the papyrus wetlands). To a limited extent, ecologically different life forms develop, occupying specific niches (e.g. Jacanae running over floating leaves of Nymphaeaceae).

The time variation in avian communities inhabiting wetlands is of two kinds. The species diversity of the community changes, in the temperate zone, in the course of the year with the departure of the breeding species; in the tropics, on the contrary, with the arrival of the wintering species. Long-term changes are also known, such as the increasing range of occurrence of *Aythya ferina* and *A. fuligula* in Central Europe within the past 100 years (Nowak, 1971).

In the remainder of this section the use of wetlands for shelter, roosting, breeding and food supply is mainly illustrated by the birds of Central

European littoral reedbelts. Similar behaviour is seen in other temperate wetlands.

Migratory birds

During migration time, the open water surface is the main resting place for all species of geese, ducks, swans and the other waterfowl. Many of these species also forage in the terrestrial surroundings and are of indirect importance for the wetland ecosystems by importing various substances to water in the form of faeces (Kalbe, 1981). Mud flats, either temporary or permanent, are the principal feeding places for migrating waders. Feeding on various invertebrates, they export considerable amounts of animal biomass, which may be of functional importance for the wetlands.

Migratory top carnivores in Europe include non-wintering *Pandion haliaetus* (osprey) and wintering *Haliaetus albicilla* (white-tailed eagle).

Birds roosting or breeding in wetlands, often feeding outside

Reedbelts serve as roosting places for certain passerine birds, especially in late summer and autumn. In Central Europe, large flocks of swallows, sand martins and starlings, besides some other passerines, roost in reed-swamps. Of these, the swallow (*Hirundo rustica*) and similarly the swift (*Apus apus*) also feed by reedswamps, catching insects close over the stand as well as over the water surface. North American wetlands serve as gathering places for numerous flocks of grackles (*Quisculus quiscula*) and redwing blackbirds (*Agelaius phoenicus*).

Many species breeding in wetlands are only dependent partly on them for food. The ducks, *Aythya ferina, Anas platyrhynchos* and to a smaller extent, *Netta rufina, Aythya nyroca* and *A. fuligula* are one such group. They are mainly satisfied by the presence of lagoons inside the stands. The grebes (*Podiceps*), which usually breed at the edge of the reedbelts near water, are trophically dependent on the open water rather than the littoral reedbelt (Böck, 1974). Breeding colonies of gulls (mainly *Larus ridibundus*) are often an important ecological factor in reedswamps and littoral belts. The gulls may physically damage the stands and import material or faeces. Of minor importance are herons (*Ardea, Casmerodius*), ibises (*Plegadis*) and spoonbills (*Platalea*).

In winter, when ice covers the water surface, the reedswamps and littoral belts of Central Europe become a refuge of *Phasianus colchicus* (pheasant). The insectivorous warblers are then replaced by tits (mainly

Parus caeruleus), while *Panurus biarmicus* consumes hibernating insects and seeds of *Phragmites*.

All these birds enrich the wetlands by foraging in the environs and importing this material in the form of faeces and birds dying in the wetland. When the flocks are large, the amounts of faeces may significantly alter the wetland (e.g. Leah *et al.*, 1978). In addition, roosting birds damage the aerial plant parts, thus increasing the amount of detritus and accelerating decomposition.

Birds breeding and feeding in wetlands

Such bird species in wetlands of Central Europe belong to several trophic groups. Only a small number of species are herbivorous or partly herbivorous, despite the high primary productivity of wetlands. This group includes *Panurus biarmicus* and *Emberiza schoeniclus* of the passerine birds and *Fulica atra, Anser anser* and *Cygnus olor* from the remaining birds. The overwhelming majority of avian species occurring in wetlands are carnivorous. They are differentiated with regard to numerous trophic niches, and often form the terminal links of the grazing–predatory food chains. Passerine carnivores include insectivorous warblers (*Acrocephalus, Locustella*), gathering their food mainly from the upper strata of the reed stands. The lower strata, including the submerged parts, are the main foraging places of crakes (*Porzana*) and rails (*Rallus*).

Circus aeruginosas (marsh harrier) is a top carnivore feeding in wetlands during the breeding season.

Mammals

Mammals living in wetlands have been mainly studied in Europe and North America. The species diversity of the mammal communities inhabiting wetlands in Central Europe is higher than generally believed. In particular, the wide littoral reedbelts, comprising a zonation of ecophases from hydrophase to the terrestrial ecophase, harbour terrestrial mammals recruited from the surrounding habitats, in addition to the expressly aquatic and amphibious species. In the area of the Neusiedlersee, Bauer (1960) recorded 19 mammal species frequenting the reedbelt; either permanently or temporarily (Böck, 1974). Additionally four to six species of bats hunt near waters (Bauer, 1960). In the fishpond reedswamps in Southern Moravia (Czechoslovakia), Pelikán (1973, 1975) recorded 21 mammal species; in addition to these there are about four species of bats (J. Gaisler, pers. comm.).

Central European wetlands

Qualitative, and some quantitative, data on the mammals occurring in Central European littoral belts are presented in Table 5.12, where the species are arranged according to their trophic behaviour and ecological importance in the reed ecosystem. Bats are excluded from the table as well as from subsequent considerations in view of the complete lack of quantitative data.

The species diversity has been compiled from Bauer (1960), Spitzenberger (1966), Pelikán (1973) and Böck (1974). On the basis of these data, the occurrence of the species in the various zones (limosal, littoral and terrestrial ecophases) is expressed semi-quantitatively.

The composition of the food consumed by rodents in these wetlands was studied by Holišová (1970, 1972, 1975). Table 5.12 contains annual averages ascertained in the littoral reedbelt of the Nesyt fishpond in Southern Moravia. The values for *Apodemus agrarius* (field mouse) originate from Holišová (1967) in Northern Moravia; the composition of food of *Microtus oeconomus* (field vole) was studied by Kratochvíl and Rosický (1955). For all the remaining species, the food composition is indicated semi-quantitatively by crosses.

The population densities of rodents and insectivores, given in Table 5.12, were obtained in the reedbelts of the Nesyt fishpond in 1971 to 1973 (Pelikán, 1975). Only the data on *Ondatra zibethicus* (muskrat) and *Arvicola terrestris* (water vole) come from another southern Moravian locality (Pelikán *et al.*, 1970; Pelikán, 1974). These numbers per hectare give an idea of the relative proportions of the species involved.

Of the herbivores, the muskrat (*Ondatra zibethicus*) is undoubtedly the greatest destroyer of emergent macrophytes. Of substantially less importance is *Arvicola terrestris* whose density is highest on step-like stream banks. Along water bodies with flat shores, the density was two to ten times lower (Pelikán, 1974). Competition with the muskrat affects the water vole population negatively (Bauer, 1960; Abaschkin *et al.*, 1972; Boulenge, 1972). The typical wetland mammals also include *Micromys minutus* (harvest mouse), *Microtus oeconomus* and *Apodemus agrarius* (Bauer, 1960; Kratochvíl & Rosický, 1955; Zejda, 1967; Holišová, 1967) but no quantitative data on their densities and influence on the littoral vegetation are available.

Table 5.12. *Species diversity and some semi-quantitative data on mammals in Central European littoral reedbelts (for references see text)*

Species	Occurrence in ecophases[a]			Food composition (% of volume)		Population density (N ha^{-1})	
	lit.	lim.	terr.	plants	animals	averages	maximum
Herbivorus							
Ondatra zibethicus	++	++	+	100.0		4.0–40.0	55.0
Arvicola terrestris	+	++		100.0		6.1–8.1	15.1
Micromys minutus	++	++	++	64.2	35.8	–	–
Microtus oeconomus		+	++	100.0		–	–
Microtus arvalis		+	++	100.0		3.0–212.9	447.6
Clethrionomys glareolus		+	++	88.1	11.9	9.4–42.2	49.8
Rattus norvegicus		++	+	+	+		
Mus musculus			+	74.6	25.4	0.6–2.8	11.1
Apodemus agrarius		+	++	72.5	27.5	–	–
Apodemus sylvaticus			+	74.9	25.1	0.8–7.9	15.9
Apodemus flavicollis			+	37.2	62.8	0.3–1.4	3.2
Apodemus microps			+	100.0		0.1–1.3	6.6
Lepus europaeus			+	+		–	–
Capreolus capreolus		+	+	+		–	–
Cervus elaphus			+	+		–	–
Sus scrofa			+	+	+	–	–

Insectivorous					
Sorex araneus	+ +	+ +	+	0.9–31.6	70.0
Sorex minutus	+ +	+ +	+	0.9–32.9	70.6
Neomys anomalus	(+)	(+)	(+)	–	–
Neomys fodiens	+ +	+ +	+	–	–
Crocidura suaveolens		(+)	+	–	–
Erinaceus europaeus		+	+	–	–
Talpa europaea		(+)	+	–	–
Carnivorous					
Mustela nivalis	+	+	+	–	–
Mustela erminea	+	+	+	–	–
Putorius putorius	+	+	+	–	–
Vulpes vulpes	+	+	+	–	–

Scale of occurrence: + + frequently present, + present, (+) accidental occurrence, – no data.
[a] Abbreviations for ecophases: lit. – littoral, lim. – limosal, terr. – terrestrial.

Of the ten remaining rodent species occurring in the limosal and terrestrial ecophases of Central European reedswamps, only a few attain high numbers in peak years. Only then can they play an important part in the grazing–predatory food chain. They include *Microtus arvalis* (common vole), immigrating from the surrounding fields, and *Clethrionomys glareolus* (bank vole), originating from the forest. The density of the former may attain $450\,ha^{-1}$, that of the latter is about ten times lower. The importance of the remaining rodent species is negligible: *Rattus norvegicus* (brown rat) and *Mus musculus* (house mouse), occur only in the vicinity of human settlements. Larger herbivores (*Lepus, Capreolus, Cervus, Sus*) seek wetlands for shelter rather than food and are of no practical importance for the energy flow.

The ecological importance of insectivorous shrews lies in their high density (particularly the two *Sorex* spp., see Table 5.12), high amount of food consumed and high metabolic rate. The density of *Neomys fodiens* (water shrew) is five to ten times lower, the remaining species are rare.

Of the carnivores, *Mustela nivalis* (weasel) attains the highest density in reed swamps, but the fox (*Vulpes vulpes*) is of greater trophic importance; preying on rodents and, above all, pheasant (*Phasianus colchicus*).

N. America

Day *et al.* (1973) studied the mammals of Louisiana salt marshes with regard to the energy flow through their populations. Again, the muskrat (*Ondatra zibethicus*) is the most important herbivore in ecological respect. In *Spartina* marshes, the density of the muskrat population attains only $0.3\,ha^{-1}$ on the average. The coypu (*Myocastor coypus*), an introduced species, attains five times lower densities. Even the racoon (*Procyon lotor*) is partly herbivorous, attaining a density of only $0.06\,ha^{-1}$. The top carnivores of these marshes are the mink (*Mustela vison*) and the otter (*Lutra canadensis*), showing about equal densities. Further data are required on the remaining mammal species living in the *Spartina* marshes, particularly the small ones.

Tropical wetlands

No data are available on the mammal species inhabiting African swamps, dominated by the emergent macrophyte, *Cyperus papyrus*. Only Thornton (1957) reports the hippopotamus (*Hippopotamus amphibius*) and the swamp-buck, or sitatunga (*Tragelaphus spekei*) as the main herbivores, and the African otter (*Aonyx capensis*) and the marsh mongoose (*Atilax paludosus*) as the main carnivores. No information seems to be available on the mammals inhabiting rice fields in South or East Asia.

II SECONDARY PRODUCTION AND THE ROLE OF ANIMALS IN FOOD CHAINS

Macro-invertebrates

Invertebrates associated with aerial parts of emergent and floating vegetation

The invertebrate communities of wetland vegetation show rather great diversity of feeding habits and ecological relationships to the plant substratum. The mechanical properties of plants, especially their toughness or softness, play an important role in this respect. The toxicity of some plants does not prevent them being eaten, but limits the number of consumer species. For many invertebrate species the emergent vegetation serves as shelter only (adults of Chironomidae, Culicidae, Ephemeroptera, Trichoptera, etc.). However, several groups of organism are important in the overall ecosystem energy budget, especially external grazers and some special feeding types (see pp. 215–24).

External grazers

Gaevskaya (1966/69), using Smirnov's data, summarises information on the extent of consumption of emergent parts of vascular plants by insects, predominantly beetles. The adult populations of two coleopteran species, *Donacia denata* and *Hydronomus alismatis*, together consume not less than 6% of leaf biomass per day from *Sagittaria sagittifolia*, when most abundant. Both *D. dentata*, and *D. crassipes* grazing on *Nymphaea candida*, have been found to consume 2.6% per day (see Table 5.13). Another criterion of grazing activity is the daily consumption of plant biomass expressed as a percentage of the consumer biomass. Results in Table 5.13 suggest that emergent vascular plants with tough tissues (e.g. *Typha*) were consumed less than softer and less sclerotised floating plants (e.g. *Spirodela* and *Nymphaea*). Glowacka *et al.* (1976) gives data on consumption by caterpillars for several genera (*Paraponyx*, *Acentropus* and *Nymphula*). Average populations of about 7–10 m^2 can consume about 0.5 g fr.wt d^{-1} of water plant, which is roughly equal to one small

Table 5.13. *Examples of daily consumption of emergent and floating vegetation by insects*

Insect species (developmental stage)	Species of food plant	Daily consumption of leaves (in 24 h)		Reference
		(% plant biomass)	(% consumer biomass)	
Donacia dentata (imago)	*Sagittaria sagittifolia*	2.6		
Hydronomus alismatis (imago)	*Sagittaria sagittifolia*	3.5		
Galerucella nymphaeae (larval)	*Nymphaea candida*	0.4	106–295	Smirnov (1959, 1960, 1961a)
Galerucella nymphaeae (imago)	*Nymphaea candida*		224	
	Nuphar lutea		130	
Donacia crassipes (imago)	*Nymphaea candida*	2.6	54	
Donacia vulgaris (imago)	*Typha latifolia*		29	
Elophila nymphaeata (larval)	*Typha* sp.		24–103	Kashkin (1958)
Elophila nymphaeata (larval)	*Nymphaea candida*		36–168	
Cataclysta lemnata (larval)	*Typha* sp.		18	
Cataclysta lemnata (larval)	*Spirodela polyrhiza*		163	

plant of *Potamogeton perfoliatus*. However, their feeding intensity depends both on their age and on the species grazed. The older the larvae, the lower is the mean daily consumption in proportion to body weight. In some species (e.g. *P. stratiotata*) this daily food ration is halved during larval development. Therefore, such rates of daily consumption indicate only an intensity at which the biomass of plants is eaten by animal populations during the main feeding season, but give no indication of the annual food consumption. The size of this is determined by a whole complex of factors (e.g. seasonal dynamics of consumers, changes in properties of the plant parts eaten, temperature). Smirnov (1961*b*) estimated the consumption of *Alisma plantago-aquatica* and *Oenanthe aquatica* by *Donacia dentata* at 3 and 6.1%, respectively, of their annual production. For *Sium latifolium* consumption has been estimated as 6.3% (Straškraba, 1968), and grazing on *Glyceria maxima* by *Succinea putris* has been estimated as less than 0.5% of the annual production (D.F. Westlake, pers. comm.).

Internal grazers

Comprehensive data on productivity of such invertebrates, trophically directly dependent on *Phragmites australis*, come from studies which were carried out in extensive stands of *Phragmites* in the Neusiedlersee (Austria). Waitzbauer *et al.* (1973) estimated the total autumnal biomass and its energy equivalent of the dominant endophagous dipteran species (Table 5.14). For the gall-forming dipteran species *Lipara lucens* Waitzbauer (1969) has estimated the production of the undisturbed larval population during the feeding period, and the total amount of food consumed (Table 5.15). For the stem boring larvae of *Phragmataecia castaneae* the production was 12.5 kJ m^{-2} stand area during the 2-year development from August of the first year to November of the second year, and consumption of the plant tissues was 57.4 kJ m^{-2}.

Total grazing fauna

Imhof (1973) attempted to assess the total significance of phytophages in the food chain in the reed ecosystem in the Neusiedlersee. The production and food consumption were known for only a few species of the main feeding types, so approximate estimates were made for the remaining species, using their known biomass and knowledge of the energetic regimes of ecologically closely related species. The total energy intake by

Table 5.14. *Autumnal biomass and energy content for larvae of endo-phagous Diptera* (Giraudiella, *Lasioptera,* Lipara *and* Platycephala) *from the* Phragmites *stand in the Neusiedlersee, Austria (Waitzbauer* et al., *1973)*

Biomass (mg dry wt m^{-2})	Energy content (J (mg ash-free dry wt)$^{-1}$)	Total autumnal energy of biomass (J m^{-2})
138.6	23.4	3240

Table 5.15. *Production and total consumption by the larval population of* Lipara lucens *in the* Phragmites *stands of the Neusiedlersee during the feeding period (Waitzbauer, 1969)*

	June to mid-September (J (m stand area)$^{-2}$)		
	Production *P*	Consumption *C*	*P/C*
Inland terrestrial strip of *Phragmites* amidst the stands of *Carex acutiformis* and *Juncus* sp.	480	710	0.68
Extensive terrestrial stand of *Phragmites*	160	240	0.67

all phytophagous insects in the *Phragmites* stand was estimated at 170 to 250 kJ m^{-2} y^{-1}. The net production of *Phragmites* at the locality was estimated as 63 MJ m^{-2} y^{-1}, and the energy intake by all phytophagous insects is thus only 0.3 to 0.4% of this value. This, however, does not fully reflect the complex effect of invertebrate consumers on the stand. Imhof (1973) gives an example: the stem borer *Phragmataecia castaneae* takes 6.3 kJ per stem of *Phragmites* per year (Pruscha, 1973) but does not visibly affect the plant's growth, whereas the gall-forming *Lipara lucens*, using only 0.25 kJ (Waitzbauer, 1969) inhibits stem growth markedly and prevents flowering.

Predators

In the invertebrate community associated with the emergent parts of *Phragmites* the main predators are dragonflies and spiders of different habits. Imhof and Burian (1972) give the energy budget of the population of the web-spider *Araneus cornutus*, which preys mainly upon *Chironomidae* and *Culicidae*. This species showed a very high production efficiency (Production/consumption = 0.66), and a high ratio of production to average biomass ($P/\bar{B}$ = 5.2). Further data, gathered by Pühringer, on the panicle-inhabiting spider community from *Phragmites* in the Neusiedlersee are in Table 5.16. These confirm the high production efficiency (P/C = 0.61) of *A. cornutus* but other reed dwelling spiders have lower efficiencies ranging from 0.42 for *Clubiona juvenis* to 0.51 in *Singa phragmiteti* and *Arundognatha striata*.

Zooplankton in aquatic vegetation

Some quantitative data on zooplankton populations inhabiting stands of water macrophytes of different types of water bodies are given in Table 5.17. To illustrate the relationships between littoral zooplankton and some other links of the food chain in littoral, two examples were chosen for this section.

Data gained during the studies of trophic levels in the Kiev reservoir (Gak *et al.*, 1972) enable the littoral zooplankton to be compared with the pelagic zooplankton and phytophilous macro-invertebrates (Table 5.18). There was no substantial difference in mean zooplankton biomass between the macrophyte stands and the pelagic zone, but a difference was found in the productivity of filtrators which, in the stands, was 1.44 times that estimated for the pelagial. The prevalence of herbivorous zooplankton production over the production of non-predatory macro-fauna (23-fold) was striking.

Straškraba (1963) tried to estimate the contribution of the littoral regions overgrown with helophytes to the productivity of South Bohemian carp ponds. The estimates were based on a comparison between the production of herbivorous zooplankton and the total consumable primary production (periphyton and phytoplankton net production plus 10% of macrophyte production to represent the decayed material available to the zooplankton; see Table 5.19). Assuming that 10% of the food consumed would be utilised for growth and reproduction of the zooplankton, the primary production did not seem able to fully supply the energy needed by the zooplankton, especially since this calculation made no allowance for consumption by herbivorous macro-fauna. The littoral secondary producers therefore, have to draw energy from sources outside

Table 5.16. *Quantity and metabolism of the spiders (adults and subadults) inhabiting panicles of* Phragmites australis *(Neusiedlersee, Austria; littoral ecophase) (Pühringer, 1975)*

Species	Maximal abundance (N m^{-2})	Mean biomass $\overline{B}$	Production P	Respiration R	Consumption C	P/C	$P/\overline{B}$
			($J\,m^{-2}\,y^{-1}$)				
Araneus cornutus	0.18	105	531	314	878	0.61	5.1
Singa phragmiteti	0.35	84	301	255	586	0.51	3.6
Clubiona phragmitidis	0.18	38	134	168	314	0.43	3.5
Clubiona juvenis	0.54	34	113	147	272	0.42	3.3
Arundognatha striata	0.15	92	406	364	795	0.51	4.4
Totals or averages	Σ 1.40	353	1485	1248	2845	Σ/n 0.50	4.0

the stands, most probably as pelagial phytoplankton and detritus with bacteria.

This could explain the negative correlations found between the production of herbivorous zooplankton and the autochthonous primary production of littoral helophyte belts, and between the width of the littoral belt and the size of the littoral zooplankton concentration relative to the pelagian zooplankton (Table 5.19). Odum *et al.* (1959) suggest a similar phenomenon within marine littoral stands of macro-algae. Such edge effects are very characteristic of narrow littoral belts and marginal fringes with aquatic vegetation.

Invertebrate macro-fauna associated with the submerged parts of the vegetation

Results in this field are inconsistent: most authors have used their own sampling method, with sieves of different mesh size; bottom fauna has been involved in most studies of emergent plant stands, while zooplankton has not; submerged plants have been mostly sampled without the bottom fauna, but in some instances, with the zooplankton. For most studies, these are no quantitative measures of the plant (biomass, surface area, etc.) although these are essential for valid comparisons (Dvořák & Best, 1982). Most authors have limited their attention to the biomass of the fauna, and consumption and production estimates are rare. Comparisons of such variable data enable only limited generalisations.

Biomass

Table 5.20 contains data on biomass found in different types of vegetation from diverse waters of the northern temperate, and tropical zones (items 1 to 17), calculated per unit bottom area. When comparing the data gained from plants only (not including the bottom fauna), the highest biomasses of macro-fauna (3.2–10 g dry wt m^{-2}) were found on *Lemna trisulca* (item 6), *Potamogeton crispus* (item 10), *Schoenoplectus lacustris* (item 8) and on *Ranunculus aquatilis* and *Elodea canadensis* (item 5). Other plant species studied supported 0.2 to 1.9 g m^{-2}. There are often no apparent differences found between the colonisation of submerged and emergent plants (items 2 and 10).

In helophyte stands the relatively small water depth together with many plant remains at various stage of decay make it impossible to distinguish the macro-invertebrates specifically associated with plants from the

Table 5.17. *Quantity of littoral zooplankton in various water bodies in Europe*

Water body		Dominant plant species	Abundance ($N\,l^{-1}$)	Biomass ($J\,l^{-1}$)	Reference and notes
Vel. Pálenec fishpond, (South Bohemia)	loc. C	*Glyceria maxima*	260 (20–1274)	110 (5–445)	Straškraba (1963)[a] Crustacea; Season, April–October, mean values and (min.–max.)
	loc. F	Mixed stands of *Glyceria maxima* and *Schoenoplectus lacustris*	321 (40–1227)	140 (6–370)	
Smyslov fishpond, (South Bohemia)	loc. A	*Phragmites australis*	181 (33–468)	90 (20–220)	Data on production in Table 5.19
Labičko backwater, (Central Bohemia)	loc. B	*Glyceria maxima*	1400	250	Straškraba (1965a)[a] Crustacea; Summer maxima
	loc. C	Mixed stands of *Typha latifolia*, *Myriophyllum* sp., *Hydrocharis morsus-ranae* and *Lemna* spp.	1400	250	
	loc. D	Mixed stands of *Nuphar lutea*, *Hydrocharis morsus-ranae*, *Myriophyllum* sp. and *Ceratophyllum* sp.	5500	375	
Poltruba backwater (Central Bohemia) and removal of fish	before	Mixed stands of *Phragmites australis*, *Nuphar lutea*, *Ceratophyllum* sp. and *Hydrocharis morsus-ranae*	500	125	Straškraba (1967)[a] Crustacea; Summer maxima
	after		1370	500	

Rybinsk reservoir (basin of river Volga, USSR)	Glyceria sp., Carex spp. and various swamp Gramineae	Polyphemus sp. 125 Ceriodaphnia spp. 415 Copepoda 400	40 (0.6–110)	Mordukhai-Boltovskoi et al. (1958)[b]. Season, April–November. Abundance, maximal values per season; biomass, mean values per season and (min.–max.)
Uchinskoe reservoir (Moscow district, USSR)	Typha latifolia Schoenoplectus lacustris Phragmites australis Potamogeton pectinatus	136.8 105.2 201.3 838.0 (73–2948)	60 85 95 345 (6–1280)	Sokolova (1963)[b]. Season, June–September. Whole zooplankton community (Rotatoria, Crustacea and Ostracoda). Mean values per season and (min.–max.)

[a] Energy contents from 1 μg N ≡ 0.25J.
[b] Energy contents from 1 mg fr. wt ≡ 2.0J.

Table 5.18. *Production of littoral zooplankton and non-predatory macro-fauna in Kiev Reservoir (Gak et al., 1972)*

Faunal component	Mean biomass May–October $(kJ\ m^{-2})$	
	Within macrophytes	In pelagic zone
Zooplankton – filtrators	32.3	31.0
Zooplankton – predators	0.2	0.65
	Seasonal production May–October	
Zooplankton – filtrators	1047	729
Non-predatory phytophilous macro-fauna	45.2	–

benthic fauna (vertical migrations must also be considered). However, Sokolova (1963) has shown that the aquatic macro-fauna of plant stands of *Typha latifolia* and *Phragmites australis* is, on average, 42% of the abundance and 67% of the biomass of the macro-benthos. In most of the studies dealing with the macro-fauna in helophyte stands, both faunal components are summed (items 3, 4, 8, 9, 13 and 15). The highest values of macro-fauna biomass (13–40 g dry wt m^{-2}) have been found in a stream on *Nasturtium officinale* (item 13), and in standing waters in *Sparganium erectum* (item 3) and *Typha latifolia* (item 8). The lowest data (0.05–2.0 g m^{-2}) come again from *Typha* and from *Phragmites* (item 4).

The biomass of the macro-fauna inhabiting the vegetation of tropical water bodies (items 14, 15 and partly 16) does not differ substantially from that found in waters of the Northern temperate zone. However, the annual production is not determined only by the biomass, but also by the duration of the productive season and the turnover rates of faunal components. Unfortunately, the available material is insufficient for more detailed analysis of differences in production between tropical and temperate waters.

Controlling factors

The invertebrate biomass or productivity cannot simple be related to the standing crop or production of the host plants (Kořínková, 1971a,b;

Table 5.19. *Some properties and production of littoral belts in two South Bohemian fishponds (Straškraba, 1963)*

Pond (locality)	V. Pálenec (F)	V. Pálenec (C)	Smyslov (A)
Dominant plant species	*Glyceria maxima* and *Schoenoplectus lacustris* with sections of *Typha*	Mostly monospecific stand of *Glyceria maxima*	Monospecific stand of *Phragmites australis*
Average width of belts (m)	3.4	5.1	6.0
Consumable primary production (kJ m^{-2} season^{-1})	2746	2530	3083
Production of herbivorous zooplankton (kJ m^{-2} season^{-1})	454	353	303
Ratio of production of herbivorous zooplankton/consumable primary production	1/6.0	1/7.2	1/10.2
Ratio of standing crop of zooplankton in pelagial/standing crop of zooplankton in littoral (per unit volume)	1/5.2	1/4.2	1/1.5

Table 5.20. *Biomass of phytophilous macro-fauna in various types of wetlands and shallow waters*

Item	Type of habitat and plants studied	Reference, region	Sampling season	The data represent:	Energy of Biomass (g dry wt m^{-2})	biomass (kJ m^{-2})
A						
I	North temperate zone (items 1–6) Fishponds (items 1–13)					
1	*Glyceria spectabilis* *Sparganium erectum* *Phragmites australis* *Acorus calamus*	Arenkova (1965) Fishponds of western Ukraine	One-time sampling during the summer	Macro-fauna of plants, individual values	1.6 1.7 0.6 0.9	33.5 35.6 12.6 18.9
2	Helophytes: *Typha* spp., *Sparganium erectum*, *Phragmites australis*, *Glyceria* sp., *Schoenoplectus lacustris*	Arenkova (1970) Fishponds of western Ukraine	Warm period of the year	Macro-fauna of plants, data originally expressed as biomass of fauna per 1 kg of plants; seasonal mean values	0.3–2.1	6.3–44.0
	Hydrophytes: *Potamogeton lucens* and *P. pectinatus*				0.3–1.3	6.3–27.2
	Pleustophytes: *Trapa natans* and *Polygonum amphibium*				0.5–1.9	10.5–39.8
3	*Glyceria maxima* with *Carex elata* (central area inside the stand)	Dvořák & Lišková (1970) Carp ponds in South Bohemia	April–September	Macro-fauna of plants and bottom; seasonal mean values	8.4	176.0
	Sparganium erectum (stand–open-water interface)				13.2	276.5

	Reference / Location	Sampling period	Notes		
4 *Typha* sp. *Phragmites* sp. *Scirpus* spp. *Potamogeton* spp.	Slepukhina (1969) Steppe ponds of Caucasia	Sampling during the growing season (summer?)	In *Typha*, *Phragmites* and *Scirpus* macro-fauna of plants and bottom, in *Potamogeton* spp. bottom fauna only; individual values	0.05 0.05–2.0 2.1 5.3	1.0 1.0–42.0 44.0 69.1
5 *Ranunculus aquatilis* *Elodea canadensis* *Potamogeton lucens*	Kořínková (1971a,b) Carp ponds, South Bohemia	Sampling during the growing season	Macro-fauna of plants, benthos not included; seasonal mean values	3.2 3.2 1.9	67.0 67.0 39.8
6 *Lemna trisulca*	Lipin & Lipina (1951) Fish ponds of USSR	Summer sampling	Phytophilous macro-fauna; summer mean values	10.0	210.0
II Littorals of lakes and reservoirs (items 7–12)					
7 *Equisetum heleocharis* *Phragmites australis*	Shcherbakov (1961) Lake Glubokoe, USSR	May–October	Macro-fauna of plants only; seasonal mean values	0.8 0.2	16.8 4.2
8 *Typha latifolia* *Schoenoplectus lacustris* *Phragmites australis*	Sokolova (1963) Uchinskoe reservoir, Moscow district, USSR	June–October	*Typha* and *Phragmites*, plant and benthic fauna, respectively; *S. lacustris*, macro-fauna of plants only; seasonal mean values	16.9 6.4 3.1	354.1 134.1 65.0
9 *Phragmites australis* and *Typha latifolia*	Beattie *et al.* (1972) Polder lake, Tjeukemeer, Netherlands	April–November	Macro-fauna of plants and bottom; seasonal means	5.1	107.0

(continued)

Table 5.20. (cont.)

Item	Type of habitat and plants studied	Reference, region	Sampling season	The data represent:	Biomass (g dry wt m^{-2})	Energy of biomass (kJ m^{-2})
10	*Phragmites australis* *Equisetum heleocharis* *Schoenoplectus lacustris* *Potamogeton crispus*	Lipin & Lipina (1951) Lake Udomlia, USSR	Not given	Macro-fauna of whole community; *Potamogeton crispus* – plant fauna only; seasonal means	3.5 5.3 1.9 8.2	73.3 111.0 39.8 171.8
11	*Myriophyllum spicatum* *Utricularia vulgaris* with *Potamogeton pectinatus* and *Najas maritima*	Andrikovics (1975*b*) Little lake, Hungary	One-time sampling in August	Macro-fauna of plants only; individual values	1.2 1.1	25.1 23.0
12	*Ceratophyllum submersum*	Andrikovics (1975*a*) Gravel-pit lakes, Hungary	One-time sampling in August	Macro-fauna of plants only; individual values	0.02	0.4
III	Streams (item 13)					
13	*Ranunculus penicillatus* var. *calcareus* *Nasturtium officinale*	Westlake *et al.* (1972) Chalk-stream, Dorset, England	Summer sampling (July)	Macro-invertebrates of whole community; individual values	6.0 40.0	126.0 838.0
B IV	Tropical habitats (items 14–17)					
14	*Azolla* sp. *Trapa* sp. *Eleocharis* sp.	Ambasht (1971) Tropical ponds in India	Method not mentioned	Phytophilous fauna only, bottom fauna not included	0.2 3.0 3.8	4.2 62.8 79.6

15 *Utricularia* sp., sand and detritus *Sagittaria* sp.	Reiss (1973) Freshwater lagoons of North Brazil	December; one-time sampling	Macro-fauna of plants and bottom; individual values	1.6 0.5	33.5 10.5
16 *Paspalum repens* (narrow belt) *Leersia hexandra* (central zone of the meadow, anoxic)	Junk (1973) Floating meadows, várzea lakes of Amazonian region	November samples	Crustaceans and insects ('perizoon'); individual values	4.9–10.2 0.16–0.20	102.7–213.7 3.4–4.2
17 *Pistia stratiotes*	Petr (1968) Artificial lake	Vegetation season during their filling	Invertebrate fauna of the roots; individual values	1.2–7.0	25.1–146.6

(If fresh wt is given in original papers, the dry wt and energy are calculated by means of conversion factors of 0.2 to dry wt and 1 g dry wt ≡ 210 kJ).

Table 5.21. *Examples of daily consumption of submerged vegetation by insects*

Insect species (developmental stage)	Food plant species	Daily consumption (in 24 h) (% consumer biomass)	Reference
Acentropus niveus (larval)	*Potamogeton perfoliatus*, *P. lucens* and *Elodea canadensis*	100	Glowacka, Soszka & Soszka (1976)
Elophila nymphaeata (larval)	*Potamogeton perfoliatus*, *P. lucens* and *E. canadensis*	74	
Elophila nymphaeata (larval)	*Potamogeton lucens*	22–68	
	Potamogeton lucens	21–97	
Phryganea grandis (larval)	*Ceratophyllum* sp.	52	Kashkin (1958, 1959)
	Elodea sp.	4	
Paraponyx stratiotata (larval)	*Potamogeton lucens*	8–350	
	Potamogeton perfoliatus, *P. lucens* and *E. canadensis*	48	Glowacka, Soszka & Soszka (1976)
Cricotopus brevipalpis (mining larvae)	*Potamogeton natans*	(Volume ratio: length of the gallery to the length of larvae 400 to 600:1)	Lipina (1928), Müller-Liebenau (1956)
Hydrellia albiceps (mining larvae)	*Potamogeton natans*		
Hydrellia obscura (mining larvae)	*Potamogeton natans*		

Dvořák & Lišková, 1970). The life form, size of colonisable plant surface and physiological state of the host plants must be taken into account.

When invertebrate biomass is expressed per unit of the bottom area, no consistent differences are found between various species or life forms of plants (Table 5.20). In this respect the species composition of the vegetation appears not to be a controlling factor for development of the biomass of the macro-fauna. Differences do appear when the quantity of invertebrates is related to the specific surface area of plants (surface area per unit of the plant biomass; Dvořák & Best, 1982). Submerged vegetation with dissected or densely packed leaves offers more surface area for colonisation than massive, simply built (and often sclerenchymatous) emergent macrophytes. Floating-leaved plants like *Polygonum amphibium* have an intermediate position. These differences reflect positively in differences of the total invertebrate biomass when the data are expressed per unit biomass of these life forms of plants. This holds only for live plants or fresh plant material; dead and decaying plants behave quite differently (e.g. invertebrate biomass is higher on last year's stems of *Typha angustifolia* than on live stems of the current year).

It may generally be assumed that the amounts of detritus and periphyton are the prime trophic factors governing the productivity of these invertebrate communities. Although they are often called phytophilous, they mostly consist of detritivores and consumers of aufwuchs, for which the living plants provide suitable environmental conditions, namely shelter and the basis for detritus sedimentation and development of the aufwuchs. Some invertebrate species directly consume the living tissues of submerged plants (see Table 5.21), but these species are generally a rather low and highly variable proportion of the total community. Their feeding period is also restricted to certain, often relatively short, seasons. On the contrary, the soft, decaying and bacterially enriched plant tissues are consumed, for longer periods, in much greater measure than the fresh ones.

The input of food of allochthonous origin, as detritus, seems to play a particularly important role (cf. Structure, pp. 243–4).

Invertebrate production and budgetary studies

Most studies of the phytophilous macro-invertebrates deal only with consumption or production in individual species or particular components of the ecosystem; few enable their role in the total budget to be quantified. Food consumption rates in some phytophagous insects and predatory

Table 5.22. *Production of various types of invertebrates in Lake Krivoe* (*Alimov* et al., *1972*)

	$(kJ\ m^{-2}\ (season)^{-1})$				
	Mean biomass $(\bar{B})$	Production (P)	Consumption[a]	$P/\bar{B}$	K_2' [b]
Chironomidae	0.38	1.13	6.2	3.0	0.3
Sphaerium suecicum	0.46	0.71	3.6	1.5	0.3
Gammarus lacustris	1.89	1.38	15.1	0.7	0.15
Ephemera vulgata	0.96	1.77	19.2	1.2	0.1
Sialis flavilatera	0.25	0.38	4.6	1.5	0.1

[a] Amount of food consumed = 'ration'.
[b] Efficiency of use of assimilated food: $K_2' = P/(R + P)$ where R is respiration.

spiders have been discussed previously (see pp. 271–5). Information on the efficiency of utilisation of assimilated food for production of some macro-invertebrates is given by Alimov *et al.* (1972; Table 5.22) from Lake Krivoe, expressed as K_2' which may be considered as net production efficiency of the population. K_2' values decreased from Chironomidae (0.3) to the lowest value in *Ephemera vulgata* and *Sialis flavilatera* (0.1). On the basis of experiments on the growth and metabolism of the larvae, the lowest K_2' values can be explained by high metabolic rates, coupled with low growth rate for these animals. The $P/\bar{B}$ ratio, indicating the production turnover rates of populations, was highest in Chironomidae (3.0), while it was very low in *Gammarus lacustris* (0.7). Similarly Kajak *et al.* (1972) found the highest $P/\bar{B}$ values in phytophilous Chironomidae (12.1) and rather low values in Hirudinea (0.8) (see Table 5.23).

Production and turnover rates were also estimated in populations of aquatic pulmonate snails in the reedbeds of the Neusiedlersee (Imhof & Burian, 1972). For four species the $P/\bar{B}$ ratio decreased roughly with decreasing length of life and body size of the species (Table 5.24). Data on population productivity of three carnivorous water bugs come from the same locality (Waitzbauer, 1976; Table 5.25). The relatively low values of turnover rates $(P/\bar{B})$ in all species studied are due to the high biomass which the populations sustain for a long time, and to the low rate of production. The species have one generation a year (with one hibernation as imagos). The highest values of efficiency (K_2') occurred in all species in summer, being high in adult *Naucoris* and in the last nymphal stages of *Notonecta* and *Ranatra*.

Table 5.23. *Biomass and production of some macro-faunal components of litttoral zoobenthos in Mikołajskie Lake (Kajak et al., DR 104)*[a]

| Faunal component | (kJ m^{-2} (season)$^{-1}$) | | |
	Mean biomass ($\bar{B}$)	Production (P)	$P/\bar{B}$
Chironomidae[b]	41.5	503.2	12.1
Ephemeroptera	5.3	24.0	4.5
Trichoptera	5.3	24.0	4.5
Hirudinea	10.6	8.4	0.8

[a] IBP PF Data Reports are held for inspection by the Freshwater Biological Association, Ferry House, Ambleside, England.
[b] *Glyptotendipes gripekoveni, Microtendipes chloris, Limnochironomus tritomus* and others.

Table 5.24. *Production of aquatic pulmonate snails in the reedbelts of the Neusiedlersee, Austria (Imhof & Burian, 1972)*

| Species | Life cycle | (kJ m^{-2} y^{-1}) | | |
		Mean annual biomass ($\bar{B}$)	Annual production (P)	$P/\bar{B}$
Lymnaea ovata	Annual	4.6	20.1	4.4
Planorbis planorbis	Biennial with annual reproductive periods	8.4	32.7	3.9
Lymnaea stagnalis	Biennial with annual reproductive periods	11.3	25.1	2.2
Planorbarius corneus	Biennial with annual reproductive periods	13.0	27.6	2.1

The contribution of the littoral stands to the total production of the benthic invertebrate communities in reservoirs and lakes may be relatively high, ranging from 8.4% (Gak *et al.*, 1972) to 50% (Chambers, 1971*a,b*; Beattie *et al.*, 1972). The lowest value comes from Kiev Reservoir built on the River Dniepr (Ukraine). The highest concentration of the fauna (*Gammarus lacustris*, Hirudinea, Trichoptera, Chironomidae and Ephemeroptera) was observed in clumps of *Stratiotes and Potamogeton* (12 to 29 g kg^{-1} of host plants, both in wet weight), while lower values were

Table 5.25. *Population productivity of three carnivorous species of water bugs in the littoral reedbelt of Neusiedlersee, Austria (Waitzbauer, 1976)*

Species	Production (P) during the nymphal period (from first to fifth stage) (kJ m^{-2} nymph. period^{-1})	Production reached at the climax of the adult population (summer–autumn) (kJ m^{-2} climax period^{-1})	Production (P) estimated at the end of life of the population (spring of the next year) (kJ m^{-2} life span^{-1})	Mean energy of biomass $\overline{B}$ (kJ m^{-2})	$P/\overline{B}$	K_2' [a]
Naucoris cimicoides	5.60	9.93	9.62	3.52	2.8	0.76
Notonecta glauca	1.37	3.10	2.77	1.22	2.5	0.62
Ranatra linearis	0.29	0.67	0.65	0.24	2.8	0.62

[a] $K_2' = P/(R + P)$ where R is respiration.

found in *Typha* and *Phragmites* (4 to 6 g kg^{-1}). Data on the biomass and production of phytophilous macro-fauna for the whole vegetation season are given in Table 5.26.

Production estimates by Chambers come from the polder reservoir Tjeukemeer in the Netherlands, where the fauna of inshore stands of *Typha latifolia* and *Phragmites australis* was dominated by three species, *Gammarus tigrinus, Asellus aquaticus* and *A. meridianus*. Most of the total production by the littoral fauna was by *Gammarus* and chironomids. *Gammarus tigrinus* was chosen for detailed production studies (Table 5.27; cf. data from Lake Krivoe, Table 5.22). The littoral fauna of Tjeukemeer contributes significantly to the production of the benthic fauna as a whole. The stands of *Typha* and *Phragmites* are only 1% of the whole lake area, but they contribute 30 to 50% of the total benthic production of the lake. Examination of fish stomachs shows that *Gammarus* forms an important part of the diet of *Anguilla anguilla* and *Gymnocephalus (Acerina) cernus*.

Fish

Natural wetlands around lakes and in river flood-plains are important for the biology of fish in many water bodies and as sources of fish for human populations. Artificial systems such as fishponds are influenced by their wetland components, and rice fields are also artificial wetland systems producing fish (see also Chapter 8).

Lake wetlands

Attention has usually been concentrated on pelagic lake fisheries. Holčík (1970) has studied two shallow inland lagoons, with abundant emergent and submerged vegetation, in Cuba. He found 177 822 and 8584 fish per hectare, and the corresponding biomasses were 32.1 and 32.6 g fr.wt m^{-2}. The 'available' productions (i.e. that part which survived and was present at the time of sampling) were 21.6 and 27.7 g m^{-2} y^{-1}, respectively. The same author also investigated a backwater forming a part of an extensive marsh on the southern coast of Cuba, situated about 200 m from the sea. He found 148 611 fish per hectare (5.7 g m^2). While the fish population of this backwater was composed of six indigenous species, the fish fauna of the two lagoons was composed of seven and five species respectively; with 91 and 93% of the total density, and 90 and 96% of the total biomass consisting of two North American centrarchids (*Lepomis macrochirus* and *Macropterus salmoides*) introduced to Cuba in 1927.

Table 5.26. *Production of macro-fauna living on macrophytes in the Kiev Reservoir (Gak et al., 1972)*

Macro-fauna	Mean biomass $\bar{B}$	Production P	$P/\bar{B}$	K_2' [a]	($kJ\ m^{-2}$ growing season^{-1}) Respiration R	$R/\bar{B}$	Assimilation A	Consumption C
Non-predatory	15.1	45.2	3.0	0.3	101.4	6.7	145.0	185.2
Predatory	4.2	12.2	2.9	0.3	28.1	6.7	40.2	50.3
Total Mean	19.3	57.4	3.0	0.3	129.5	6.7	185.2	235.5

[a] $K_2' = P/(P + R)$.

Table 5.27. *Biomass and production of* Gammarus tigrinus *in littoral stands in Tjeukemeer, the Netherlands (Chambers, 1976)*

Year and period of investigation	Dominant plant species	Mean biomass ($\bar{B}$)	Annual production P	$P/\bar{B}$
		(kJ m^{-2})		
1969 13 June–17 Nov.	*Typha latifolia* and *Phragmites australis*	58	365	6.3
1970 15 June–16 Nov.	*Typha latifolia* and *Phragmites australis*	81	604	7.43
1969 13 June–17 Nov.	*Potamogeton* sp.	–	4.2	–

Flood-plains

Flood-plains are defined as the low-lying areas bordering rivers, which are seasonally inundated by overspill from the main river channel (Welcomme, 1975). In some cases the main river-bed is branched to form many anastomosing arms ('braided').

There are strong correlations between the depth of flooding of wetlands and their subsequent productivity, which can be applied to the modelling of catches (Welcomme, 1985; and see p. 418).

Kapetsky (1974), Holčík *et al.* (1981) and Holčík (1996) give total annual productions ($P = G\bar{B}$) of 103.9 g fr.wt m^{-2}, and 34.9–327.2 g fr.wt m^{-2} in the Kafue and Danube flood-plains, respectively. For the Danube arm of the investigated flood-plain it was found that only about 20% of production came from autochthonous food, and the remaining 80% probably came from the main channel by immigration of fish (Holčík, 1996). It was also found that, in a year after a high water year, both the growth rate and the production were increased.

In accordance with the higher fish population densities in flood-plains, the catch of fish is higher than that from the main river channel (Table 5.28). According to Antipa (1912) the mean annual catch from two lower Danube flood-plains at Crapina and Braila, in 1901–1908 was 6131 metric tonnes, i.e. about 7.7 g fr.wt m^{-2}. Analysing the catch of fish from the Czechoslovak section of the Danube, Holčík *et al.* (1981) found the mean

Table 5.28. Fish biomass ($kg\ fr.\ wt\ ha^{-1}$) in the main river channel and flood-plain of the Danube river and some African rivers (selected from Holčík & Bastl, 1976, 1981 and Welcomme, 1975) (± standard error)

River		Main river channel	Flood-plain		
			Overgrown	Open	Grass marsh
Kafue (Zambia)	in flood	337	2682	337	64
	low water	348 ± 60	879 ± 268	575 ± 123	
Chari (W. Africa)		870–2170		370–5260	
			Sand–mud	Sand	Mud
Sokoto (Sudan)			1029 ± 536	475 ± 148	144 ± 83
			Permanent channels		Intermittent pools
Danube (Europe middle stretch)	high water	35	327 ± 77		265 ± 60
	low water		257 ± 94		

annual catch from the main stream in years 1962–1972 was 0.44 g fr.wt
m^{-2}, while the catch from flood-plain arms was 13.5 g fr.wt m^{-2}. The
mean annual catch of the Czechoslovak–Hungarian section of the Danube
for those years was 4.1 g fr.wt m^{-2}, while that taken from the adjacent
lower-lying Hungarian section, where the flood-plain practically does not
exist, was only 2.2 g fr.wt m^{-2}, i.e. about half.

Available data on tropical and subtropical waters also show the
cardinal importance of flood-plains for fisheries. The mean annual catch
of 12 African flood-plains listed by Welcomme (1975) is 3.8 ± (S.E.) 2.3 g
m^{-2} ha^{-1}, but as the author indicates, this figure is low because some of
the flood-plains studied are considerably underfished; the potential catch
from these flood-plains is 834 000 metric tonnes annually. The total
freshwater fish harvest in all Mekong-related waters, which are considered
to be among the most productive, has been estimated to be greater than
200 000 metric tonnes annually (Bardach, 1972). Of similar importance is
the fishery of flooded areas in the central plain of Thailand, covering about
2 million hectares and yielding between 6 and 18 g m^{-2} of fish annually
(Yamamoto & Backiel, 1968). The upper Nile in the Sudan flows, in part,
across an extended plain flooded every year. Rough estimates showed
that, in 1950–1960, some 700 000 people inhabited the flood-plains and
caught at least 3000 metric tonnes of fish annually (Hickling, 1961).

The main principles of fish population dynamics in flood-plains seem to
be the same regardless of their geographical position (see Chevey &
Lepoulain, 1940; Bardach, 1972), and there are only minor specific
differences. In rapid flowing rivers, such as the middle reaches of the
River Danube, the main river channel does not offer optimal conditions
for the reproduction, feeding and growth of fish, and most fish stay in the
waters of the flood-plain. The spawning period in the Danube basin
coincides with periods of high water and inundated flood-plains offer
important and vast spawning areas. During the floods fish migrate into the
flood-plain from the adjacent section of river and are washed down from
the upper part of the river. Accumulation of nutrients brought by floods,
together with rising temperature, support a rapid growth of zooplankton
and other forms of aquatic life, thus forming the food basis for all age
groups of fish. The higher the spate in one year, the higher is the fish
biomass in the following year.

In tropical flood-plains the fish also find ideal conditions for
reproduction, feeding and growth during the outburst of productivity
that follows the migration of the fish from the river channels into the
flood-plain at the beginning of the flood period (Welcomme, 1975).

Similarly, the creation of large artificial lakes, particularly in tropical areas, often extends over several years, leading to yearly shallow flooding of new areas covered by terrestrial vegetation which decays. As soon as the oxygen conditions become favourable, the great majority of the fish stock of associated riverine systems enters these shallows for spawning and feeding. The permanency of inundation in such water bodies prolongs the spawning period and provides them with an abundant food supply, while the predatory pressure in these areas is greatly reduced (Jackson, 1961). The initial rises in fish biomass and commerical fish catches that follow, lasting several years, gradually decline as the submerged terrestrial vegetation decays, nutrients decrease and predation pressures increase (Mikheev & Prokhorova, 1952; Henderson *et al.*, 1973; Holčík, 1977).

There is found to be no significant difference between the production values for fish of temperate and tropical flood-plains (Welcomme, 1985; Holčík, 1996). It has to be noted, however, that the sources supporting fish production in the temperate and tropical regions are different. The fish production of the tropical flood-plains may be considered to be natural, due to the high input of flood-plain nutrients in the form of accumulations of dung, rotting vegetation and ash from fires which sweep through them towards the end of the dry period. In the temperate flood-plains the current production seems to be supported mostly by increasing eutrophication due to the constant and increasing influx of nutrients from the human activities in their basins.

Deltas and coastal waters

The regular rhythms of water level fluctuation in rivers are of great benefit also for fisheries of deltas and even on seas, as is well known from the Nile, and damming the rivers can cause irreparable damage. As shown by George (1972), after the building of the Aswan High Dam on the upper Nile in 1965, Egypt suffered a great decline in the eastern Mediterranean fisheries. In 1962, the total fish catch was 30 600 metric tonnes but after the impoundment of the rich floodwaters it declined to 12 000 metric tonnes 10 years later. Due to reclamation of land, the area of brackish lakes on the Nile Delta decreased substantially and, as can be seen from the figures given by Libosvárský *et al.* (1972), the mean catch of only one lake (Borullus) declined from 15 253 metric tonnes in 1966 to about 10 000 metric tonnes in 1970. This, and the eastern Mediterranean decline, has caused a destabilisation of the Egyptian fishery and an Atlantic trawler fleet has had to be established to compensate for this loss (George, 1972).

Cultivated wetlands

Cultivated wetlands that provide fish for human consumption include rice paddy fields, fishponds with floating emergents such as *Eichhornia crassipes*, and the marginal areas of fishponds. Some details are given in Chapter 8, pp. 418–19.

Productivity and food supply

Growth rates and production of fish populations based on natural food sources can be more or less positively correlated with the productivity of the biotope. This has been demonstrated by field experiments carried out by R. Hacker (1974) and P. Meisriemler (1974) and personal communications on *Gymnocephalus cernuus* (*Acerina cernua*) and *Abramis* (*Blicca*) *bjoerkna* in the littoral stands of the Neusiedlersee (Austria). Both fish species were rather common in shallow regions of the lake. *G. cernuus* fed on chironomid larvae living in the surface layer of the mud (epipelic species, mainly *Tanypus* and *Procladius*) and almost omitted the phytophilous species. The diet of *A. bjoerkna* consisted mainly of benthic algae and planktonic invertebrates (see p. 258). Therefore, the growth rates of the two species could reflect the productivity of epipelic and planktonic communities as well as living conditions for fish in the littoral stands.

Growth rates of both fish species were measured after exposure in cages placed at three different sites within plant stands, for the period from mid-July to end of September. The first site was situated in an open pool in the marginal fringe of the stand of *Phragmites australis*, the second was amidst *Myriophyllum*, close to the boundary line between *Phragmites* and *Myriophyllum* stands, and the third was in dense *Myriophyllum* about 450 m waterwards from this boundary line. Cages were stocked with ten individuals per 1 m^2 of either one or the other species, the initial weight of individuals was about 5 g for both species. Positive increments were found only in the cage placed in the pool in the marginal fringe of *Phragmites* (for *Gymnocephalus cernuus* + 47%, for *Abramis bjoerkna* + 7%) while smaller or even negative changes were found in the other two cages (+ 5% for *G. cernuus* and − 4% for *A. bjoerkna* in the second cage, and + 13% for *G. cernuus* and − 8% for *A. bjoerkna* in the third one).

The results are in accordance with the anticipated high trophic value of marginal helophyte stands, in which overgrown areas alternate with open pools and channels. In such places fish concentrate to graze on rich invertebrate populations. Similarly, in Danubian reedbeds disturbed by

Table 5.29. *Daily food consumption of plant biomass by*
Ctenopharyngodon idella *(modified from Gaevskaya, 1966/69)*

Plant species	Daily food consumption (24 h) (Fresh wt, % of body weight)
Potamogeton crispus and *Pot. filiformis*	up to 200 or even more
Hydrocharis morsus-ranae	145
Ceratophyllum spp.	114
Elodea spp.	109
Lemna spp.	102
Myriophyllum spp.	36
Typha spp.	31
Carex spp.	14–31
Phragmites australis (old leaves) and *Scirpus* spp.	17

harvesting of the reed, the fish production was found to be two to three times higher than in undisturbed stands (Rudescu & Popescu-Marinescu, 1970).

In these examples the production of fish was based mainly on grazing on invertebrate populations. For herbivores, such as *Ctenopharyngodon idella* (grass carp), the efficiency of assimilation changes greatly with the food supply. Quantitative data on the daily ration (food consumption per unit body weight in terms of fresh weight) have been summarised by Gaevskaya (1966/69, see Table 5.29). She found the approximate mean food coefficient ($C/\Delta B$) to be 30, but values varied from 14–21 in good trophic conditions, up to 54 when insufficient food was offered. The coefficient was much influenced by the species of plant eaten. In terms of dry weight the food coefficient is lower, varying from 1.7 to 2.0 (Rottman, 1977). This author emphases that, contrary to popular opinion, grass carp convert aquatic vegetation to fish flesh efficiently and can be compared favourably with other intensively cultured fish. However, when the food is composed of emergent or terrestrial vegetation with more indigestible cellulose and fibre, their efficiency is less (Rottman, 1977).

Birds

In the area of Port Royal Sound (South Carolina, USA), Blackard *et al.* (1972) determined the numbers of breeding pairs of certain bird species associated with wetlands. On an area of $1.6 \, \text{km}^2$, including various habitats, 0.32 nests of six species of herons and egrets occurred per hectare and the egg production was 0.99 eggs ha^{-1}. For *Rallus longirostris* (a rail), up to 5 nests ha^{-1} occurred (mostly 0.25 to 0.75 nests ha^{-1}) and for *Pandion haliaetus* (osprey) only 0.003 nests ha^{-1} were found.

Day *et al.* (1973) present a detailed analysis of communities inhabiting *Spartina* salt marshes in Barataria Bay (Louisiana, USA). The mean annual biomass of the birds was 0.131 g fr.wt m^{-2} (0.044 dry) and total net production was about half that (0.022 g dry wt m^{-2}). The total metabolic rates were (in g dry wt m^{-2} h^{-1}): consumption 7.33, respiration 5.11 and urine and faeces 2.20. Since the majority of bird species inhabiting marshes are zoophagous, the majority of the food intake will be animal.

Hudec (1975) investigated the production of birds in reedswamps in Southern Moravia (Czechoslovakia). On average, 20 pairs of birds bred per hectare of the reed stand on Nesyt fishpond (about 13 passerines, 3 grebes, 1.7 ralliformes, 1 greylag goose, 0.5 ducks and 0.04 marsh harrier). In addition, a breeding colony of *Larus ridibundus* (black-headed gull) contributed 83 breeding pairs ha^{-1} (averaged over the whole area of the reed stands). The highest densities were twice the average. The mean biomass of breeding birds (in fresh weight) was 4.44 g m^{-2} for gulls and 1.12 g m^{-2} for the remaining birds. The annual production of all eggs laid was 246 eggs ha^{-1} for gulls, and 171 eggs for the remaining species on average (i.e. 0.815 and 0.226 g fresh wt m^{-2}, respectively). The mean net production (in g fresh wt m^{-2} y^{-1}) of fledged young was 2.01 for the gulls and 1.36 for the remaining species. The respective losses of young from nests were 1.23 and 0.41. Hence, the resulting total annual production of young birds was about 3.25 g m^{-2} for gulls, and 1.77 for the remaining species on average (or 1.09 and 0.60 g dry wt m^{-2} y^{-1}). Hence the total mean production of eggs plus young was about 4.06 g fresh wt m^{-2} y^{-1} for the gulls, and 20.0 g m^{-2} y^{-1} for the remaining birds. Throughout, the maximum values were about twice the average.

Dobrowolski (1973*a*) gives some rough estimates of the consumption and energy flow through animal populations in central European reed-swamps. He considers that *Fulica atra* (coot) and *Gallinula chloropus* (moorhen) consume about 22 kg fresh weight of plant biomass per bird per growing season, ducks about 16–19 kg, geese and swans about 240 kg or more (i.e. in some situations 9.5 kg (m plant stand)$^{-2}$ season^{-1}). The total consumption by herbivorous birds was estimated as 2% of the annual primary production of the macrophytes, but it may be much more in very dense populations (Uspienski, 1967).

Hammack and Brown (1974) discuss several models for describing population changes of mallard (*Anas platyrhynchos*). Important variables were the area of wetland suitable for mallard, hunting pressure and some feature of spring weather. No particular model behaved well under all conditions studied. Increases in wetland area were much more rewarding than increases in the density of breeding birds in a constant wetland area. Hence, under natural conditions cyclic variations in ponds (e.g. pp. 144–5) may be a major influence on waterfowl populations.

Mammals

Day *et al.* (1973) also evaluated the production and energy flow in the mammal populations in *Spartina* marshes. For *Ondatra zibethicus* (muskrat) there was an annual average of 0.31 animals ha^{-1} (90 g dry wt ha^{-1}) which consumed 12 kg ha^{-1} y^{-1} of dry plant. They therefore produced 324 g dry wt ha^{-1} y^{-1} assuming production/consumption was 2.7%. The population density of *Myocastor coypus* (coypu) was about one-fifth of the muskrat density, consuming 2.4 kg ha^{-1} y^{-1}, and producing about 65 g ha^{-1} y^{-1}.

Very detailed data provided by Errington (1963) show that in reedbelts in Iowa (USA) dominated by *Typha* and *Phragmites* normal high population densities of muskrat were 4 ha^{-1} in the spring and about 12 ha^{-1} in the autumn. In 3 peak years, 1944–1946 the autumn muskrat density of 50–63 ha^{-1} was the maximum recorded so far.

These values match the peak densities of 6–8 ha^{-1} in spring and 48–55 ha^{-1} in autumn, found in the South Moravian Kobylské Jezero marsh (Czechoslovakia) by Pelikán *et al.* (1970). Here, the annual mean density was about 17–23 ha^{-1} and the production was 23–31 kg fr.wt ha^{-1} y^{-1} (assuming 30% dry weight found by Day *et al.*, 1973, this would be 6.9–9.3 kg dry wt ha^{-1} y^{-1}). Assuming a *P/C* efficiency of 2.7% (as used by Day above and the same as found for *Arvicola terrestris* by Pelikán, 1974), this corresponds to a consumption of 255–344 kg dry plant ha^{-1} y^{-1}, i.e. about 1.5–2.0% of the net above-ground production of the *Typha* stand.

Since damage by muskrats may be two to three times as high as consumption (Lavrov, 1957) the amount of vegetation destroyed by dense muskrat population is about 4.4–8.7% of the annual net above-ground primary production (Pelikán *et al.*, 1970). On the Havel River near Berlin, with a lower population density, Sukopp (1968) estimated the destruction of *Typha* stands by muskrats at 3%. The usual levels of destruction caused by normal populations are expected to be lower still.

Of the remaining herbivores, production by *Arvicola terrestris* (water vole) was found to amount to 1.97–2.60 kg fr.wt ha^{-1} y^{-1}; the amount of consumed and destroyed biomass was 75–140 kg dry wt ha^{-1} y^{-1} (Pelikán, 1974). Rough estimates for *Microtus arvalis* (field vole) in the reedbelt of the Nesyt fishpond (Pelikán, 1975) are: production, 0.6–5.8 kg fr.wt ha^{-1} y^{-1} (the latter value relating to a peak year), consumption of aerial plant about 8–77 kg dry wt ha^{-1} y^{-1}. For *Clethrionomys glareolus* (bank vole) the production was 1.0–2.4 kg fr.wt ha^{-1} y^{-1}, and the consumption was 10.6–24.3 kg dry wt ha^{-1} y^{-1} of plant and 1.1–2.6 kg dry wt ha^{-1} y^{-1} of animal food. The production and consumption by the remaining rodent species amounted to about 50% of the *Clethrionomys* values. The amount of mechanically damaged plant biomass was about two to three times the biomass consumed.

The secondary production of all rodent species, except the muskrat, amounted to about 4.1–12.0 kg fr wt ha^{-1} y^{-1} and the total destruction of plant by these species to about 150–600 kg dry wt ha^{-1} y^{-1}, i.e. about 0.8 to 3.4% of the annual net above-ground primary production. The upper limit is probably the maximum.

Only Day *et al.* (1973) give any data on the secondary production of insectivores and carnivores in wetlands. They estimate the production of *Procyon loctor* (the racoon) in *Spartina* salt marshes at about 80 g dry wt ha^{-1} y^{-1}, with an overall consumption of animal food of 11 kg dry wt ha^{-1} y^{-1} ($C/P = 138$).

III IMPACT OF ANIMALS ON VEGETATION

Introduction

This subchapter deals with the activities of animals that are significantly detrimental to the growth, populations and reproduction of wetland vegetation. This may arise from general mechanical damage to the whole stand of vegetation caused by grazing, trampling and nesting, typically by birds, mammals and some fish; or by more specific effects, typically by invertebrates, which often attack only certain host plants. The term 'pest' is usually applied to animals that have adverse, economically harmful effects on plants that are managed or grown as crops, but it is convenient here to use it also for any invertebrate seriously damaging any wetland vegetation.

It is difficult to present this topic without involving the general biology and production biology of the animals, which have already been discussed in the preceding subchapters, and some repetition cannot be avoided. In

Table 5.30. *Influence of invertebrates on the production of* Phragmites australis *in Czechoslovakia* (*Skuhravý et al., 1981*)

Species	Decrease of dry matter production by attacked stems (% of undamaged stem weight)	Average number of damaged stems (% total)	Total decrease of dry matter production in Czechoslovakia (% normal)	Damage	Scale of importance of insect pests (see p. 303)
Archanara geminipuncta	52	3.0	1.56	Destroy the growing point	4
Giraudiella inclusa	36	3	1.08	Drooping of stems	5
Hyalopterus pruni	minimum	0 to 100	–	Damage to leaves	10
Lasioptera arundinis	–	1	–	Galls on lateral shoots	11
L. hungarica	50	1.5	0.75	Drooping of stems	8
Lipara lucens	60	1.5	0.9	Gall on growing point	7
L. pullitarsis	45	7.0	3.15	Gall on growing point	1
L. rufitarsis	47	4.5	2.12	Gall on growing point	3
L. similis	47	2.0	0.94	Gall on growing point	6
Platycephala planifrons	46	0.03	0.01	Destroy the growing point	9
Steneotarsonemus phragmitidis	48	6.5	3.1	Gall on growing point	2
All stem species (weighted mean)		30	14		

the invertebrate section, we start from the main species and groups that are host plants, rather than from the functional types of invertebrate. Then we concentrate on specific information on rates of infestation, damage caused and, in the case of crops, control measures.

Invertebrates

Pests of Phragmites australis

Many invertebrates are specialised for *Phragmites australis* as a host plant. For some species the common reed serves mainly as a shelter. However, there is a group of invertebrates closely bound to this plant trophically. Various developmental stages of these species feed on the sap or on living tissues of the reed, often causing malformations of its organs, or withering and breaking of the shoots, or suppression of flowering. The data presented in this section originate from Central and Western Europe and Great Britain. In Central Europe, most invertebrates attack the reed from mid-May to mid-June, reducing the mature height of stems by 35 to 60%. The pests infesting stems in July are of much less importance because the reed has already reached over 80% of its full height. Infestation of the stands of reed by individual pests at individual localities greatly varies, from 1 to 90% of the shoots. However, there is no conspicuous fluctuation in the occurrence of individual pests in successive years at the same locality; except for *Hyalopterus pruni* their abundance remains unchanged (Skuhravý *et al.*, 1981).

Infestation often results in losses of reed crop. As the reed is used as a source of cellulose or for roofing in some countries, these pests thus become important economically. For example, in Czechoslovakia, about one-third of the reed stems were injured or damaged by insect pests, causing a reduction of annual above-ground net production by 13 to 14% (Skuhravý *et al.*, 1981; see Table 5.30). The decrease of the crop is mainly caused by the pests damaging stems; the pests of leaves are almost of no importance in this respect.

Skuhravý *et al.* (1981) arranged the invertebrate reed pests in Czechoslovakia in the following order of importance: 1 *Lipara pullitarsis*, 2 *Steneotarsonemus phragmitidis*, 3 *Lipara rufitarsis*, 4 *Archanara geminipuncta*, 5 *Giraudiella inclusa*, 6 *Lipara similis*, 7 *Lipara lucens*, 8 *Lasioptera hungarica*, 9 *Platycephala planifrons*, 10 *Hyalopterus pruni* and 11 *Lasioptera arudinis*. Waitzbauer (1972) divided these pests into three groups, namely visible gall-formers, stem-miners and shoot- or leaf-suckers. A modified division is proposed by Skuhravý et al. (1981):

1. Species damaging the growing point of the reed and checking the growth of stems; leading to suppression of flowering and lateral branching of the shoots.
   (a) Species destroying the growing point without causing the formation of galls;
   (b) Species causing gall formation on the growth tip.
2. Species developing inside the stems and causing them to break.
3. Species causing secondary damage by attacking lateral shoots.
4. Species living on reed leaves.

Species injuring the growing point of reed stems without causing the formation of galls

These are mainly represented by *Archanara geminipuncta*, *A. dissoluta*, and *Platycephala planifrons* (see also Tables 5.4 and 5.5). The caterpillars of *A. geminipuncta* develop earliest, and infested stems have only four to seven normally developed internodes. The shoot apex becomes dry outside and foul inside. The damage becomes conspicuous at the beginning of June and the infested apical part of the shoot falls off completely after mid-July. Having damaged several internodes as well as the stem apex, the larva leaves the infested stem and attacks another one; one larva can damage up to seven stems. Infested stems form one to seven lateral shoots mostly from the third to seventh internodes (Skuhravý, 1976).

Pruscha (1973) took quantitative samples along a transect through the extensive littoral reedbeds of the Neusiedlersee (Austria), and recorded six species of stem borers, infesting between 15 and 20% of the reed stems; on average, 12%. The different species showed population maxima in different zones. Erdös (1957) estimated that 20% of stems were infested by *Archanara geminipuncta* in the reedbeds of Lake Balaton (Hungary), and Wyninger (1963) recorded infestation figures lying between 10 and 20% in six, and higher than 20% (up to 48%) in two out of 22 reed stands investigated in south-west Germany.

Information on *A. dissoluta* is given by Durska (1970) from Poland. Like the previous species, it damages the upper parts of stems and the plants never bloom. The species is one of the most common pests of reed in Poland causing great damage by making shoots unsuitable for industrial purposes. Infested stems are up to 47% shorter than healthy ones.

Table 5.31. *Influence of gall formation by* Lipara *species on the length of* Phragmites *stems at Bohemian localities (Pokorný, 1971)*

Species	Length of infested stems/ length of healthy stems
Lipara lucens	0.43
L. pullitarsis	0.56
L. rufitarsis	0.58
L. similis	0.73

External damage of common reed caused by *Platycephala planifrons* is similar to that caused by *Archanara* species. The infestation results in desiccation of the apical leaves and in destruction of the inner parts of the stem. Infested stems form only four to six normal internodes and develop lateral shoots similar to those attacked by *Archanara geminipuncta* but, in contrast to that species, one larva of *P. planifrons* destroys only one stem (Skuhravý & Skuhravá, 1978).

The caterpillars of *Arenostola* spp. also belong to this group. With an 80% infestation of the stems, the larva can completely destroy patches of reed stands in Great Britain (Haslam, 1973a,b,c). Young shoots die if attacked. If half-grown shoots are infested, the mature base (*ca.* 30 to 60 cm) is left, the immature tip is lost, and narrow lateral shoots grow up from below. Full-grown shoots are hardly affected.

Species transforming the growing points of the reed into galls

The most serious such pests of reed stands are the larvae of four species of fly, of the genus *Lipara*, namely *L. lucens*, *L. similis*, *L. rufitaris* and *L. pullitarsis*. The galls initiated by their action are formed by bundling of the leaves which grow from the stunted internodes (giving a cigar-like shape). The galls of *L. similis* are rather inconspicuous and slender, often indistinguishable from normal non-flowering shoots (Pokorný in Skuhravý *et al.*, 1981). Pokorný (1971) reports, that in Bohemia and Moravia nearly all reed stands are infested by two, three or even all four *Lipara* species (Table 5.31). *L. pullitarsis* occurs in the largest numbers (Pokorný in Skuhravý *et al.*, 1981). In reed stands of the South Moravian Nesyt fishpond, the infestation of *Phragmites* stems by all four *Lipara* species varied between 8 and 10%, resulting in a decrease of shoot biomasses by 36.8% and in shortening of the stems by 36.1%

Table 5.32. *Changes in dimensions of internodes of* Phragmites australis *caused by* Lipara spp. *infestation (percentage of the dimensions of unaffected stems; internodes numbered from top) (Durska, 1970)*

Internodes	Length of internodes			Diameter of internodes			Strength of internodes			Total stem
	First	Fourth	Ninth	First	Fourth	Ninth	First	Fourth	Ninth	
Lipara lucens	111	88	–	76	72	–	42	33	–	57
L. rufitarsis	103	102	80	95	94	96	86	68	50	74

(Rychnovský, 1973). Waitzbauer (1969) found that reed stems infected by
L. lucens in Austria were 40% shorter than healthy ones; the same effect
was found for *L. pullitarsis* in Czechoslovakia (Rychnovský in Skuhravý
et al., 1981). Durska (1970) evaluated the changes in reed condition caused
by infestation by two *Lipara* species in the Mazurian and Pomeranian lake
districts in Poland (Table 5.32). An estimation of the total effect of *Lipara*
spp. on the production of common reed can also be made on the basis of
data gained by Rychnovský (1973) and Husák and Květ (1973) at the
Nesyt fishpond where infestation by *Lipara* spp. accounted for approximately 3 to 4% of the losses of annual above-ground net production (see
also Table 5.30).

Recorded gall densities of *L. lucens* are: Neusiedlersee (Austria; Waitzbauer *et al.*, 1973), $3 \, m^{-2} = 5\%$ of all stems; Nesyt Fishpond (South
Moravia; Rychnovský, 1973), 8–10% of all stems; Flevoland Polder
(Netherlands; Mook, 1967), $10–20 \, m^{-2} =$ up to 20%. Including all four
species of *Lipara*, Pokorný (1971) reported between 5 and 40% of stems
infested in different localities of Bohemia and Moravia.

Another gall-former is the mite *Steneotarsonemus phragmitidis* which
causes warts in the inflorescence, and curled leaves surrounding the
panicles. The galls are 29 to 129 cm long and 0.5 to 3 cm in diameter. In
Poland, Durska (1970) estimated losses in the most heavily infested
stands, where diseased stems attained only 67.6% of the height of the
healthy ones and only 41.6% of the diameter at the level of the ninth
internodes. The infestation prevents flowering, and attacked stems form
lateral shoots (Skuhravý *et al.*, 1975).

Species mining the stems

These occur in warmer regions of Europe. Data on infestation rates of
Phragmites by mining larvae of *Phragmataecia castaneae* and their effect
on the host plants are given by Pruscha (1973) for the Neusiedlersee
(Austria; see Table 5.4). The caterpillars of *P. castaneae* feed on submerged, less lignified parts, of the stems. No substantial external changes
were observed in infested plants as compared with healthy ones except for
earlier fading and shedding of leaves in autumn. The infested stems did
not break until the following year, when they were dead anyway. This
species thus causes no serious production losses. The pattern of infestation
of *Phragmites* stems by *P. castaneae* and some other butterfly caterpillars
in the Neusiedlersee is given in Table 5.33.

Also in this group are some butterfly species of the family Crambidae;

Table 5.33. *Infestation of* Phragmites australis *by butterfly caterpillars and some characteristics of the affected stand at Neusiedlersee (Pruscha, 1973)*

| | | Mostly pure *Phragmites* | |
	Short mixed *Phragmites* mostly in terrestrial ecophase	Flooded with terrestrial ecophase during the summer	Permanently flooded
Mean stem length (cm)	166	218	215
Number (stems m^{-2})	65	75	–
Water depth (cm)	0–25	25–50	50–110
Infested stems (% total)			
by *Phragmataecia*	8.2	12.2	10.1
by *Pyralidae*	7.8	1.0	2.7
by other miners	0.8	0.5	0.8

namely *Schoenobius gigantellus* and *Chilo phragmitellus* (see Table 5.4), which, despite their low population densities, cause much greater losses in production. Larvae attack young shoots which are emerging approximately 30 to 40 cm from the water surface. They gnaw a deep, ring-shaped furrow into the inner tissue of the shoot close to the water surface, so that the growth tip dies off, the shoot breaks easily and perishes completely. One larva of *S. gigantellus* attacks and damages several young stems during its 2-year development. This species infested up to 5% of young shoots in the Neusiedlersee (Pruscha, 1973).

Injury of reed stems is also caused by caterpillars of *Rhizedra lutosa* (Netherlands; Mook & van der Toorn, 1974). They attack young stems first, which die off, and then they bore down to the rhizomes, which are also heavily damaged. Studying the development of an experimental, dry, reed field in Ijsselmeer Polder (Zuid Flevoland), a few years after the onset of reed growth, they found infestation rates of *Rhizedra*, together with *Archanara geminipuncta*, were sometimes over 70%.

Larvae of gall-midges (see also Table 5.5), develop inside the reed stems, causing fragility and breaking. *Lasioptera arundis* larvae enter lateral shoots and cause a thickening of the internal tissues. These lateral shoots become strongly swollen, with shortened internodes containing 20 to 60 larvae living in a black mass of symbiotic fungi (Skuhravý, 1975). Internodes of the infested lateral shoots are only 1 to 3 cm long, while the length of healthy internodes is 3.8 to 4.8 cm. The dry weight of infested lateral shoots, including the galls, is two to three times the weight of healthy shoots, even though the latter are longer (Skuhravá & Skuhravý, 1981).

L. hungarica can have up to 250 larvae inside the stems, with black masses of fungal growths. Such galls prevent flowering and may cause breaking, but groups of 20 to 30 larvae may not cause obvious damage. Birds of the genus *Parus* open infested stems from the beginning of September, preying on the larvae, and the stems then become more prone to breaking (Skuhravá & Skuhravý, 1981).

Giraudiella inclusa also forms galls in reed stems but losses are appreciable only with heavy infestation. Infested stems are easily distinguished by the exit holes, which are usually numerous and small, in contrast to the larger and isolated holes drilled by caterpillars of butterflies. The affected stems sometimes thicken where galls have developed, and they tend to break off there during the winter. In Bohemia, the infestation of reed stems by this midge varied from 0 to 50% (Skuhravá & Skuhravý, 1981).

The leaf- and shoot-suckers

Hyalopterus pruni (aphid) and *Chaetococcus phragmitidis* (coccid), and others (see pp. 218–20) cause no substantial losses. The aphids of *H. pruni* stay on the reed for 60 to 70 days (late June to early September), when the infestation can be easily recognised by the curled leaves. Pintera (1971) showed, in field experiments in South Bohemia, that there is normally no significant difference in stem length, stem weight and leaf area between infested and uninfested stems at the end of the season. The shoots tend to be lighter, to grow slower and to be slightly less fertile only in heavily infested plants.

Pintera (1973) observed that inundated reed stands are much more attacked by this aphid (up to 95% of all stems) than terrestrial stands, which was also reported for the Neusiedlersee (Austria) and for the Ijsselmeer polders (Netherlands) (Mook, 1971*b*).

Pests of **Oryza sativa**

As in *Phragmites*, these rice pests can be divided into several groups, including stem borers and miners of various parts of the plant, leaf- and plant-hoppers, gall-formers and grain-suckers (Pathak, 1968; Gaevskaya, 1966/69; see also Table 5.1 and pp. 219–25).

Stem borers

Stem borers cause great damage, especially Lepidoptera (Pyralidae and Noctuidae). A phenomenon known as a 'dead heart' appears in attacked stems and these plants form no panicle. If the plants are attacked after panicle initiation, 'white heads' appear, the panicles become dry and do not produce grain. Infestation after partial grain formation leads to shrivelled grains. The plants can compensate for a low percentage of early dead hearts, but for every 1% of white heads a 1 to 3% loss in yields may be expected (Pathak, 1968). The dominant species are often *Chilo suppressalis* in temperate, and *Tryporyza incertulas* in tropical regions. Particular attention was paid to stem borers during the IBP (Rothschild & Waterhouse, 1972; Nishida & Torii, 1972).

The percentage of stems infested by *C. suppressalis* in one field varies widely from zero to almost 100. In unsprayed fields the mean density of late-stage larvae often exceeds $80 \, \mathrm{m}^{-2}$ in Japan and the Phillipines, but appears to be much less in Sarawak. Much research has been on the impact of insecticides on their population dynamics, particularly in Japan (Ishikura, 1955; Miyashita, 1955, 1963; Utida, 1958). Population levels became very low in many Japanese localities, attributed by Miyashita (1971) to the heavy use of powerful insecticides, particularly granular types. Other possible reasons lay in the increasingly widespread practice of extraordinarily early planting of the rice, which may disturb the seasonal synchronisation of the life cycle with the host plant; and in the treatment of straw after harvest, which reduces the hibernating population.

Much work has been done on the relationship between injury level and the reduction in grain yield. Generally, injury of rice by the first (summer) generation larvae does not reduce the yield seriously because of the compensatory tillering of the rice plants after infestation. Takagi *et al.* (1958), using records of yield and infestation of 5000 hill* samples from 100 different fields with 11 different rice varieties, calculated the pooled regression of yield (Y, in percentage of maximum yield) on the percentage of infested stems per hill for the second generation (X) as: ($Y = 100 - 0.097(X - 10) - 0.0059(X - 10)^2$) (for $X \geqslant 10$), under the assumption that yield loss due to less than 10% infestation is negligible. According to Ishikura (1952, 1967), the maximum loss of yield caused by the combined infestation of the first and second generations is about 50%.

---

* See p. 219 for explanation of 'hill'.

Less is known about the population dynamics of *Tryporyza incertulas*, which occurs in tropical regions and the warm, southern area of Japan. Like *Chilo suppressalis*, the cropping system has been used as a method of control. Delayed planting of rice, once practised to escape injury by this insect in Japan, reduced the population drastically through asynchronisation of its life cycle with the host. The same effect is seen when rice is planted very early. However, after the 1950s, when this species caused considerable damage, only drastic insecticidal control decreased the population of this monophagous species to a very low level (Miyashita, 1963). This was facilitated by the strict host selection shown by this species. Multicropping is associated with high mean densities.

The miners

The miners, *Tipula conjugata*, *T. longicauda*, *T. parva*, *Hydrellia griseola* and some *Chironomus* spp. can also severely damage rice plantations (Gaevskaya, 1966/69), by attacking the roots. Serious damage on rice fields in Hungary was reported by Berczik (1970). In June 1969, the young rice fields were suddenly infested by mining chironomid larvae of species *Cricotopus sylvestris* and *Cricotopus bicinctus*. The damage attained nearly 100% in 48 hours in the severely afflicted areas, about 15% in lesser infested areas.

According to Mischenko (1940) the trichopteran *Limnephilus stigma* (an external grazer), and the ephydrid *Hydrellia griseola* can destroy up to 75% of the rice crop in the Soviet Far East, if they appear in masses.

The most important leaf-hopper and plant-hopper species

These are *Nilaparvata lugens*, *Nephotettix* spp., *Sogatella furcifera*, and *Sogatodes oryzicola*. These insects damage the plants by sucking the sap and by the mechanical influence of their feeding activity, which exposes the plants to fungal and bacterial infection. Light infestation during the early stages of plant growth only impairs the condition of the plants, but after panicle initiation a similar infestation greatly increases the percentage of unfilled grains (Pathak, 1968).

After the early 1950s, *Nephotettix cincticeps* became an important pest in Japan, following the extensive use of BHC and DDT for controlling the stem borer *Chilo suppressalis*. The insecticides destroyed its natural enemies; spiders particularly were found to be much more susceptible than the leaf-hoppers (Kobayashi, 1961; Sasaba *et al.* 1973).

The gall-forming midge

Pachydiplosis oryzae damages the rice plants by transforming normal tillers into tubular ones, which dry without bearing panicles, and is a serious pest in tropical Asia (Reddy, 1967). It can only infest the crop in the tillering phase, so late planted fields are more exposed to attack by the greatly increased midge population than fields planted earlier. It seldom infests the second crop and has not been observed in the third. The attacked tillers usually have only one larva, but die off without bearing panicles.

Grain-sucking species

These include the rice bugs of the genus Leptocorisa (subtropical and tropical rice cultures) and the rice stink bug (Oebalus pugnax, an important pest in the southern United States). Both nymphs and adults feed on grains at the milky stage, the grains remaining empty or only partially filled thus causing serious losses. The rice stink bug can also feed on developed and ripening grains. Also the southern green stink bug Nezara viridula, is an occasional rice pest in Japan.

Other rice pests

The larvae of the rice water weevil, Lissorhopturus oryzophilus, feed on and within the roots, reducing the rice yield in the USA. Rice roots are also attacked by nematodes Hirschmanniella oryzae and Heterodera oryzae (see p. 254). Rice hispa, Hispa armigera, damages the leaves in South-east Asia. This insect is a perpetual problem in Bangladesh, infesting about 600 to 800 km^2 every year and causing losses of about 20% in yield (Pathak, 1968).

Pests of other emergent plants

Two major problem weeds, Eichhornia crassipes and Salvinia molesta, have many invertebrate pests. More than 90 species attacking Eichhornia are reviewed in Gopal and Sharma (1981), ranging over a great many families which graze, suck and tunnel the leaves, petioles and roots. Although some are specific, and some can cause considerable damage in suitable situations, their use for biological control is not as successful as the biological control of Salvinia. This is also attacked by a variety of species, but a beetle, Cytobagous salviniae, which burrows in the rhizomes and growing points, is particularly successful in practical applications in Australia, Papua New Guinea and Namibia (Thomas & Room, 1986).

Damage caused to *Typha* spp. and *Schoenoplectus lacustris* is well known. The parts most affected are roots and rhizomes, and young shoots or leaves. Attacked young shoots often perish, and damage to the roots results in decreased vigour, so both kinds of attack reduce the primary production considerably.

Severe damage to *Typha latifolia* is caused by larvae and adults of the beetle *Calandra pectinax* (Claassen, 1921), and by *Donacia vulgaris* (Smirnov, 1961*b*). Also *Glyptotentipes paripes*, feeding on the roots, can affect its production considerably (Gaevskaya, 1966/69). *Nonagria typhae* is a well-known lepidopteran borer in *Typha*. The American river crayfish *Cambarus clarkii* consumes leaves and rhizomes of *Typha* sp., and has been used successfully for controlling *Typha* in fishponds (Viosca, 1937).

Information on the effects of invertebrate pests on *Scirpus* in Michigan is given by Frohne (1938, 1939*a,b*). Larvae of *Chilo forbesellus* and *Occidentalia comptulatalis* form galleries in *Scirpus* stems, and often kill the plants. In Europe, larvae of *Phytochironomus latifrons* mine stems of *Schoenoplectus lacustris* and cause losses in production when abundant (Goetghebuer, 1928; Thieneman, 1954).

In England the watercress crop (*Nasturtium officinale*) is attacked by *Phaedon cochleariae* (mustard beetle), *Phyllotreta undulata* (flea beetle), *Limnephilus lunatus* (caddis-fly) and *Aphis nasturtii*. The caddis-fly larvae mostly cause damage by case making. The presence of chironomid larvae and *Gammarus* reduces the value of the crop but these do not graze directly on the leaves (Stevens, 1983).

Pests of plants with floating leaves

In plants with floating leaves, such as Nymphaeaceae, *Polygonum amphibium* and *Potamogeton natans*, and in part, *Sagittaria*, infestation of leaves by invertebrate external grazers causes mechanical injury as a first step of damage. This exposes the leaves to microbial infection and mechanical damage by wind and wave action. The leaves begin to die and the primary production and vigour of plants is reduced. Examples are populations of *Galerucella nymphaeae*, consuming leaf tissues of *Nymphaea candida*, *N. stellata* and *Nuphar advena* (Weiss & West, 1920; Scott, 1924; Smirnov, 1960). *Donacia* species and *Hydronomus alismatis* may consume appreciable proportions of the biomass (see Table 5.13).

The species *Donacia crassipes*, *D. pubescens*, *D. proxima* and *D. piscatris* are closely bound to Nymphaeaceae. As the adults feed on the leaves and the larvae on the roots and rhizomes, they are particularly damaging to the host plants. According to Wilson (1928), larvae of trichopterans *Limnephilus marmoratus, L. rhombicus* and *Halesus radiatus* are the most serious pests of cultivated *Nymphaea*, feeding on their buds and leaves.

Of the sap-suckers, the aphid *Rhopalosiphum nymphaeae*, is well known as a serious pest of both the wild and cultivated Nymphaeaceae. This species infests floating leaves in masses, causing extensive damage to the plants (Wilson, 1928; McGaha, 1952).

Lemnaceae are attacked by selective coleopterans *Tanysphyrus lemnae* and *Scirtes* spp., and several dipteran larvae (*Lemnaphila scotlandae, Hydrellia albilabris* and *H. williamsi*), all causing substantial changes in *Lemna* populations. *Cataclysta lemnata* can eliminate a large part of a *Lemna* cover by feeding and case building (Wesenberg-Lund, 1943). Equally drastic effects can be produced by the feeding of pulmonate gastropods, e.g. *Lymnaea stagnalis, L. palustris* and *Radix ovata* (Alsterberg, 1930; Frömming, 1952, 1956).

Pests of submerged plants

Submerged plants are also frequently severely damaged by invertebrate populations. Müller-Liebenau (1956) states that when there is heavy insect infestation of *Potamogeton* stands, the lifespan, both of individual plants and whole beds, can be very much reduced, especially when various insect pests infest different parts of the same plant simultaneously. For example, some mining Chironomidae (*Endochironomus tendens, Phytochironomus severini, Glyptotendipes paripes*) damage the plants from inside, and simultaneously several external grazers consume the leaves and stalks (some butterfly and caddis-fly larvae such as *Acentropus niveus* and *Phryganea grandis*). The damaged plant tissues rapidly decay and the whole plant dies. Other *Potamogeton* pests are mollusc (*Lymnaea stagnalis*) and the chironomids (*Cricotopus trifasciatus* and *C. brevipalpis*). The Brazilian snail, *Marisa cornuarietis*, capable of consuming considerable quantities of *Ceratophyllum*, has been used to control this plant (Chapman & Coffey, 1971).

Vertebrates

Herbivorous fish

Obvious effects on the higher aquatic vegetation are produced by the feeding activities of phytostenophagous fish, especially several representatives of the *Cyprinidae*. Among the best known is the grass carp, *Ctenopharyngodon idella*, which has also proved to be one of the most powerful means of biological control of water weeds in China, India, USSR, Japan and Taiwan. Adult grass carp feed both on submerged and emergent macrophytes, as well as on accessible terrestrial plants in some cases, substantially affecting their development and production (see also pp. 456–9 and Table 5.29). Chapman and Coffey (1971) found that the young specimens of grass carp consume some water weeds much more rapidly than they grow. In comparative experiments (using two young fish and 500 g of weed during 14-day trial periods) it was found that the rate of consumption of *Lagarosiphon* exceeded the net primary production seven times. This factor was 14 times for *Egeria* and 8 times for *Ceratophyllum*.

The effects of selective feeding by grass carp on tank populations of mixed macrophytes were studied by Fowler and Robson (1978). They found the favoured species were greatly reduced and were replaced by less palatable species, which were only attacked by dense, starving populations.

Birds

The number of bird species consuming emergent vegetation is surprisingly small. Where numerous, the greylag goose (*Anser anser*) is the most important consumer throughout the period of its presence (Hudec, 1973*b*), with plant material forming 90% of its diet (Dobrowolski, 1973*a*). It consumes mainly green parts of plants, from young sprouts that are still submerged, to the tips of stems which it bends down actively. *Anser* mostly pinches off plants at about 25 cm above the water surface. Their grazing results in the presence of permanently short stands along the edges of open water surfaces. Their grazing also affects the growth of the plants as well as the presence of various helophytes. In Central Europe *Anser* prefers plants in the following order: *Phalaris arundinacea, Glyceria maxima, Phragmites australis, Bolboschoenus maritimus, Scirpus lacustris, Typha angustifolia* (Květ & Hudec, 1971). Outside the growing season, the greylags also feed on underground plant parts, especially of *Bolboschoenus* *maritimus* (Hudec & Rooth, 1970; Hudec, 1973*a*). These, too, are their main food when in wintering grounds (for instance, in the Marismas in the Guadalquivir Delta, Valverde; in Bernis, 1964) when they even invade rice fields (cf. Delacour & Jabouillet, 1931; Hudec & Rooth, 1970).

Fulica atra (coot) and other species of that genus, numerous in most wetlands all over the world, consume mainly fresh green matter, and a few seeds. However, plants make up only part of the diet of these omnivorous species (Glutz *et al.*, 1973; 85%, Dobrowolski, 1973*a*).

All the remaining waterfowl species consume helophytes to a negligible extent or not at all. Some species consume submerged plants, especially anseriform species, both swans and geese as well as certain species of ducks. As a rule, with about 50% of their diet being plant material (Dobrowolski, 1973*a*), these species do not forage inside the helophyte stands but from open water surfaces. For the selection of plant species consumed, see Gaevskaya (1966/69).

Jupp and Spence (1977) showed that changes in submerged macrophytes were correlated with the consumption of shoots and tubers by changing populations of *Cygnus olor* (mute swan), *Fulica atra* and *Aythya ferina* (pochard). Plant growth was improved where birds were excluded.

Mechanical damage and transport of plants and their parts by birds accelerate the decomposition process. Dense populations of greylag geese create, inside the stands, a system of canals some 0.5 m in width, which they enlarge by pinching off the reed stems. Here they become a 'landscape forming' element (Koenig, 1952; Leisler, 1969; Hudec & Rooth, 1970). The effect of swans (*Cygnus* spp.) is similar.

Helophyte stands are also utilised as material for nest building (*Fulica, Gallinula, Aythya, Netta*, etc.) or for building a roof over the nest (mainly Ralliformes). Most nests, however, are built of dead plant material; this is particularly true of nests built early in spring (geese, swans, Ardeiformes). The material is mostly collected or broken off in the surrounds of the nest. Larger species create bare areas round their nests in this way, 1 to 5 m in diameter (geese, swans). Smaller birds transport broken stems to their nest from greater distances. Lariformes (gulls, terns) also collect and transport material from areas outside reed swamps. In general, however, the destruction of plants by nest building is negligible (KoŽená-Toušková, 1973).

Mechanical damage of plants is also caused by birds congregating in reeds to roost. This is particularly evident with larger birds (*Sturnus* etc.).

Bird excreta can often drastically change the trophic status of small water bodies (see p. 176).

Mammals

Data are reviewed on the impact of mammals on the vegetation only for the European and North American wetlands. There, the muskrat (*Ondatra zibethicus*) is the principal consumer damaging the emergent vegetation. Although the composition of the food of this species is varied (Hoffmann, 1958; Artimo, 1960; Krasovskiĭ, 1962; Errington, 1963; Gaevskaya, 1966/69; Akkermann, 1974), the species mainly consumes *Typha latifolia*, *T. angustifolia* and, particularly in spring, shoots of *Phragmites*. *Ondatra* also utilises parts of these plants to build its houses.

Pelikán *et al.* (1970) found that, around an average muskrat family house, the stand of *Typha* was damaged up to a distance of 14 m from the centre of the house, i.e. over an area of 615 m^2, where 20% of the above-ground production of *Typha* was destroyed. In Kobylské Jezero (Southern Moravia), there were 16 muskrat houses of varying size per hectare. With the spring population density of two to four pairs per hectare, the total destruction of the *Typha latifolia* stand amounted to 800–1600 kg of dry weight by the autum, i.e. 5 to 10% of the annual primary production. The amount of plant material per muskrat house (dry weight) varied from about 7 to 166 kg; the average amount of utilised material was thus 690 kg ha^{-1}. Removal of shoots and rhizomes from runs also damages the stand (Akkermann, 1974). This has not been evaluated.

The number of muskrat houses is generally used as a measure of the muskrat population density: five muskrats per large house is a reasonable number for estimates (Dozier, 1948). In spring, however, only about one-quarter to one-third of all houses are occupied by breeding pairs (Pelikán *et al.*, 1970; see also Akkermann, 1974). The densities of muskrat houses are usually small. In eutrophic lakes in Finland, Artimo (1960) found only 0.2 to 2.3 houses per hectare (average 0.7 houses ha^{-1}). The average density of 16 houses ha^{-1}, with the maximum number of 31 houses, reported by Pelikán *et al.* (1970), is quite exceptional but corresponds with the densities found by Errington (1963) in central Iowa, or Abashkin *et al.* (1972) on the Ob River, in years of peak densities.

The destruction of helophyte vegetation by the remaining mammalian herbivores is substantially less than that due to the muskrat. With medium densities of *Arvicola terrestris* (water shrew), the next most important mammalian herbivore in European wetlands, the amount of plant biomass consumed annually was 25 to 35 kg dry wt ha^{-1} (Pelikán, 1974). The plants remaining were about two to three times as high and, hence, the total loss of plant biomass was about 75 to 140 kg ha^{-1} y^{-1}. With a net primary production of 18 to 20 t ha^{-1} this would be about 0.4 to 0.7%.

IV GENERAL CONCLUSIONS

Wetlands of various types often form transitional zones between terrestrial and aquatic habitats. Such transitional zones or ecotones are usually more productive than any of the bordering ecosystems and the water movements in wetlands bring nutrients and organic material. Day *et al.* (1973) showed that productivity and biomass of *Spartina alterniflora* were highest next to the marsh–water interface. Biomass of invertebrate animals and some vertebrates (especially birds) was higher in the near-shore marsh than in marsh further from the interface. Aquatic meiofauna was also highest in the submerged sediments nearest to the shore. Evidence of the high primary productivity of marginal fringes of eulittorals and wetlands in various parts of the world has been discussed in Chapter 2.

Wetland ecosystems have a high degree of 'connectivity' *sensu* Gallopin (1972). This means that, rather than simple straight food chains, there is a very complex food web. Gallopin states that, 'biologically, the most important vertices (species or compartments) in a food web are those with the greatest number of incident wedges' (the greatest number of connections). It has been stated earlier (Chapter 3, pp. 191–2) that wetlands are predominantly detrital systems. Gallopin uses Darnell's (1961) description of detritus in Lake Pontchartrain, Louisiana, USA as an example of an important component (or vertex) of estuarine systems. Judged in this manner (i.e. number of connections) detritus is one of the most important 'species' of the wetland ecosystem, because it is directly connected to almost every species or compartment. Problems of delimitation of the term detritus were dealt with by Wetzel (1975), who gives the most synthetic definition of it. The higher carnivores may also be considered important in that they are connected to virtually all macroscopic creatures in the wetlands. Thus there are only very few specialists in the wetlands; most species are generalists. McArthur (1955) suggested that stability of a community increases as the number of links in its food web increases. A highly connected wetland ecosystem should therefore be stable. It has achieved this stability through a diversity of connections rather than through a diversity of species.

6

Mineral economy and cycling of minerals in wetlands

D. DYKYJOVÁ and B. ÚLEHLOVÁ

General characteristics of wetland habitats

Generally speaking, wetland plant communities are so dependent on the chemical processes in their submerged or waterlogged soils (or sediments) that they indicate the chemical properties of their biotopes.

The content of nutrients and other minerals in the aquatic environment depends on the chemistry of the parent rock, subsoil and soil and on the chemistry of the inflowing, running or spring waters. In wetland eco-systems that are managed or interfered with, such as fishponds and farm ponds or aquacultures, or polluted areas in river deltas and estuaries, the degree of either eutrophication or saprobity is decisive.

Wetland biotopes may be classified according to the limnological categories based on the relationship between mineral nutrient contents, and productivity (Thienemann, 1925; Naumann, 1932) as dystrophic, oligotrophic, eutrophic, auxotrophic (Björk, 1967) polluted and saprobic, etc. For the organisms in wetlands the physico-chemical environment, as a whole, is as important as the total nutrient concentration in the aquatic environment; and the ionic interactions (antagonism or reinforcement) are particularly important. A number of wetlands are distinguished by high concentrations of dissolved and suspended organic substances, which act as intense polyionic (macromolecular) buffer systems, functioning on a large scale, especially in the interstitial water of the bottom sediments. The limits of mineral nutrition are therefore not determined by the total nutrient concentrations, but by the absorption capacity of the relevant buffer system for each ion.

Wetlands combine many structural and functional attributes of both terrestrial and aquatic ecosystems. These are usually characterised by a highly developed detritus food chain (see Chapter 3). Processes controlling the cycling of minerals may occur in the soil, water or aerial environment and all three are linked (see Fig. 6.1).

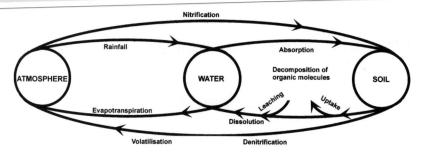

Fig. 6.1. General scheme of mineral cycling in a wetland ecosystem.

Differences in the availability of oxygen, ranging from full aeration to anoxia, control the equilibria between different forms of many mineral constituents in wetland ecosystems, e.g.

$$SO_4^2 \rightleftharpoons HS^-, NO_3^- \rightleftharpoons NH_4^+, Fe^{3+} \rightleftharpoons Fe^{2+}$$

Their availability is different to different organisms. The uptake and release of mineral nutrients by organisms particularly by micro-organisms, benthic animals, higher plants and higher animals, together determine the rates and paths of cycling of the elements.

These biogeochemical cycles may be followed at different levels and employing different time scales: from the global (e.g. Holdgate, 1977) with turnover times of up to 10^6 years for nitrogen, to the ecosystem or subsystem level (see, e.g. Reimold & Daiber, 1970; Úlehlová *et al.*, 1973) with turnover times of the order of years or days or even less. The extent of external exchanges and internal cycling for each ecosystem depends greatly on the complexity of its structure (Hillbricht-Ilkovska & Pieczyńska, 1993). Different types of wetlands vary greatly in these respects (see Chapter 1 and Whigham *et al.*, 1994). Mineral cycles would operate on the Earth even without participation of living organisms (Morowitz, 1974) but many biological processes form links in mineral cycles taking place partly or entirely in the biosphere. Studies initially based on Liebig's 'theory of the minimum', i.e. that the mineral nutrient which is least accessible to a crop acts as the limiting factor, have revealed that several nutrients together may be limiting, depending on the interactions between various elements and the chemical bonding they enter, as well as on physiological and ecological interactions. The directions and rates of flows of elements between individual ecosystem compartments indicate the relative importance of the elements in each ecosystem.

The acceleration of the global flow of some mineral nutrients, caused by human beings during the last century, results in changes in the normal pattern of biogeochemical cycles. While nutrient export prevails in terrestrial ecosystems thus disturbed, nutrients accumulate in most aquatic biotopes and wetlands (E.P. Odum, 1971).

Gore (1983*a*), Mitsch and Gosselink (1986) and Patten (1990) include chapters on soil chemistry and mineral recycling, often with special emphasis on peats. Ross (1995) gives an excellent discussion of the hydrochemistry of wetlands, from their water sources, through soil processes and recycling to practical applications; with many recent references.

Sources of nutrients

The immediate sources of nutrients in wetlands, which govern the rates of supply, are numerous, including the atmosphere, the incoming water, the soil, detritus, plant and animal materials and activities in adjacent ecosystems. These sources are now discussed in detail.

Atmosphere

This is the main source of oxygen, carbon and nitrogen. All aerobic organisms, i.e. emergent and floating higher plants, many micro-organisms and all animals need oxygen. Ultimately, the atmospheric pressure and temperature control the oxygen concentration in the water, but at times a large proportion of the oxygen originates from photosynthesis. For further information see Hutchinson (1957, pp. 575–652).

The carbon dioxide in the atmosphere (300–600 $mg\,l^{-1}$) forms a permanent pool for the carbon cycle through the photosynthesis of emergent and floating macro- and microphytes. The submerged autotrophic organisms are dependent on the carbon dioxide and bicarbonate dissolved in the water (Raven, 1970, 1981). In calcium- (or magnesium)-rich waters, bicarbonate may be used by many submerged plants as their carbon dioxide source for photosynthesis, incidentally giving rise to different incrustations and to the biolithogenesis of calcareous rocks (e.g. travertines) (Gessner, 1959, pp. 197–213, 287–306, 481–485). The carbon dioxide output from the respiration of all categories of wetland organisms plays an important part in the maintenance of the carbon dioxide equilibrium.

The atmosphere is the largest reservoir of nitrogen, which is continually entering wetland ecosystems via nitrogen-fixing micro-organisms as well as through effects of atmospheric electricity, pollution and rainfall. In the littoral or coastal areas of lakes and seas in paddy soils, the nitrogen-fixing blue-green algae and aerobic bacteria are of great importance (Stewart, 1975). In peat-bogs, the blue-green *Chroococcus turgidus* is adapted to pH values of about 4. Many species of blue-green fixers, such as *Anabaena, Aphanizomenon, Nostoc,* or *Cylindrospermum*, occur abundantly in polluted habitats. Some species of purple bacteria also fix molecular nitrogen (for details, see Fogg *et al.*, 1973). Nitrogen-fixing bacteria living in the rhizosphere of higher wetland plants make a significant contribution to their total nitrogen uptake, e.g. for the marine angiosperms *Thalassia testudinum* and *Zostera marina* (Patriquin & Knowles, 1972), for *Carex paleacea, Spartina alterniflora* and other salt marsh species (Patriquin & Keddy, 1978), for *Glyceria borealis* and *Typha* sp. (Bristow, 1974), and for *Alnus* sp. (Stewart, 1975).

This non-symbiotic nitrogen fixation was calculated to be 100–1700 kg N ha^{-1} y^{-1} for *Thalassia*, 60 kg N ha^{-1} y^{-1} for *Glyceria* and 115 kg N ha^{-1} y^{-1} in a rice field (Yoshida & Ancajas, 1971). The fixation of atmospheric nitrogen by blue-green algae, *Azobacter* and other soil microorganisms in rice fields has been investigated by many authors (see Stewart, 1975).

Water

Water is often the main source of all minerals estimated as ash in the dry matter of wetland organisms. The content of minerals dissolved in water fluctuates within a wide range, from very soft rainwater to 40–50 g l^{-1} in saline waters. The qualitative and quantitative characteristics of the mineral composition of different types of fresh, brackish or sea waters are described in various textbooks (Hutchinson, 1957; Gessner, 1959; Golterman & Kouwe, 1980).

Nitrogen or phosphorus often seem to be limiting in natural freshwater ecosystems (E.P. Odum, 1971; LeCren & Lowe-McConnell, 1980) as well as in estuarine habitats (Day *et al.*, 1973). However, with the combined water pollution by fertilisers and sewage wastes, their contents rise progressively in many ecosystems (Stewart, 1968; National Academy of Sciences, 1969; Edmondson, 1970; Royal Society, 1983). The concentrations of many other elements show the same increasing tendency. Furthermore, the rainfall derives nutrients and other minerals from polluted atmospheres.

Rainfall

Some wetlands, in raised bogs, depend mainly on the nutrients from atmospheric precipitation. The amounts of nutrients contained in atmospheric water can be significant (Hutchinson, 1957).

Rainwater differs only little from very soft waters. Polisini *et al.* (1970) calculated the total annual input of nutrients in rainfall for a small oligotrophic pond. Although rainfall was the main source of elements, the concentrations of cations (Ca, Mg, K and Na) in the pond water were greater than in the rainwater, whereas the concentrations of anionic elements (N, P and S) were lower. Although concentrations are low, the annual input from rainfall is considerable, for example, between 6 and 20 kg ha^{-1} y^{-1} (Úlehlová, 1976). Today, human activities affect the quality of rainwater. Atmospheric nitrogen oxides alter ombrogenic mires and acid rain adversely affects wetlands low in bases.

Freshwater from lakes, rivers and groundwaters

Many wetlands represent, in fact, subsystems of larger lake or river ecosystems. Lake waters are dependent mainly on the chemical nature of influent waters, which depend on the type of soils through which the water has percolated. The run-off from surrounding land surfaces is also important. The mean ionic concentration of many rivers was calculated by Livingstone (1963) as 120 mg l^{-1}. These data may, however, need revision because of the subsequent drastic eutrophication and pollution of natural waters. The mean chemical composition of the large rivers of the world, has been compiled by Maybeck (1976). Data on the nutrient content of rivers, lakes and springs in the United States have been published by Sanders (1972).

Hutchinson (1957) reviewed the general tendency towards an overall uniform composition as freshwaters pass through rivers and lakes, despite differences in the parent rocks of the drainage basins. This alteration of the initial composition of the headstreams may be due to base exchange reactions with clay minerals in soils and freshwater sediments. Individual lakes, however, show differences in the contents of alkalis and alkaline earths, as well as in their whole salinity, and Golterman and Kouwe (1980) considered the differences to be far more important than a trend to uniformity. These differences extend to the chemistry of wetlands in the lake littorals.

The mean salinity of soft drainage waters, from acid igneous rocks and especially in the mountains, fed by precipitation or melting snow, is less than 50 mg l^{-1} (Hutchinson, 1957; Gessner, 1959). In hard waters, derived from the drainage of calcareous sediments, Ca^{2+}, Mg^{2+}, CO_3^{2-} and SO_4^{2-} increase the salinity to about 200 mg l^{-1}. Some inland lakes in closed basins with arid climate and high evaporation contain high amounts of carbonate, sulphate, borate or chloride, and their salinity is extremely high (Hutchinson, 1957, pp. 564–571).

Groundwater has many of the characteristics of river water, but its variability in time and space due to local conditions, such as agricultural practices, water table management and local permeability, has important effects on the distribution of vegetation in wetlands (e.g. Niemann, 1973; Verhoeven *et al.*, 1988).

Sea water

The salinity of sea water fluctuates between 32 and 38 g l^{-1}, but the relative amounts of different minerals remain constant, with sodium chloride prevailing. The brackish water in river deltas and estuaries differs in salinity in accordance with the inflowing freshwater and tidal activity. Brackish waters are classified following the international Venice system (Gessner, 1959, p. 355) into three main categories (with four subcategories):

hyperhaline	*euhaline*	*mixohaline*	*freshwater*
>40 g l^{-1}	~40 to ~3 g l^{-1}	~3 to ~0.5 g l^{-1}	<0.5 g l^{-1}

Increasing salinity, producing increasing osmotic values, is a determining factor in the differentiation of plant and animal communities in brackish and salt water wetland biotopes.

Submerged soils and bottom sediments

Soil types

Many attempts have been made at classifying aquatic soils and vegetation according to the nutrient status, e.g. Veatch (1932), Lundh and Almerstrand (1951*a*, *b*), Spence (1967). Any comparisons must, however, consider the specific environmental conditions. The chemistry of submerged soils may play a significant role in the differentiation of species and ecotypes of wetland plants (e.g. Wooten, 1973, for populations of *Sagittaria graminea, S. platyphylla* and *S. cristata*).

Ponnamperuma (1972) has classified submerged soils into four categories:

Gley soils These are intermittently water saturated so that a mottled gley (G) horizon, arising from alternate oxidation and reduction, occupies most of the profile. They occur in almost all climatic zones.

Marsh soils These are almost permanently water saturated or submerged and are characterised by a high accumulation of detritus in the surface horizon, coupled with a permanently reduced G horizon. In freshwater habitats, this horizon is blue or green, in brackish wetlands it is green or dark grey. Upland freshwater marsh soils are mainly fed with rainwater, consequently they are poor in bases, with a pH of 3.5 to 4.5. Lowland marsh soils tend to be base saturated and their pH is about 5.0 to 6.0. Transitional types occur. These soils have been investigated in detail in the English Lake District and other similar biotopes (Pearsall, 1938; Misra, 1938). Pearsall and Mortimer (1993), and others have investigated the oxidation–reduction state of these soils in relation to the distribution of natural plant communities. Gorham (1953b) has described the nutrient status of the plants in relation to the soil chemistry.

Salt marsh soils, when submerged and in anaerobic conditions, have a neutral reaction. The presence of iron(II) sulphate is characteristic. If the water recedes and oxidation occurs, the pyrites in the soil are oxidised into iron(III) sulphate and sulphuric acid, often producing an acid sulphate soil.

Paddy soils These are managed for the wet cultivation of rice in soil flooded with standing water for 4–5 months.

Subaquatic soils These are sediments deposited in rivers, lakes and seas. Their uppermost layer is usually loose, and consists of soil components in which typical soil-forming processes proceed. These soils contain high amounts of organic matter and living micro-organisms; their metabolism is similar to that of submerged marsh soils.

Soil exchanges

Most nutrients accumulated from the atmosphere and water pass to wetland plants, and indirectly to benthic organisms, through the submerged soils or bottom sediments, which act as a nutrient pool and a site of ionic interchange between overflowing water, interstitial water and colloid particles.

The chief difference between submerged and drained terrestrial soils is the reduced state of submerged soils arising because gas exchange is curtailed between soil and atmosphere. Unless aided by the activities of burrowing animals, or by the presence of lacunae in plants, oxygen can enter only by molecular diffusion through the interstitial water. This process is about 100 times slower than the diffusion in gas-filled pores of drained soils (Ponamperumma, 1972) and only the surface layer of the submerged soil can then be oxidised by contact with oxygenated water. This surface layer is very thin, but ecologically most important because of its high metabolic activity, affecting profoundly the nitrogen and phosphate economy of the ecotope (Patrick & Khalid, 1974). These processes have been investigated, especially in paddy soils (see, e.g. Ponamperumma, 1972) and by experimental tracer studies (Tusneem & Patrick, 1971).

Higher plants rooted in submerged soils absorb nutrients arising in an oxygen-free medium. The plant tissue may receive oxygen from the aerial parts through gas spaces connecting all organs (Armstrong, 1979). Some of this oxygen may diffuse into the rhizosphere and modify soil chemistry (e.g. Wium-Andersen & Andersen, 1972; Tessenow & Baynes, 1975; see also pp. 132–7).

Soil chemistry

Stangenberg (1949, 1967) studied the interrelations between mineral components and organic matter in the bottom sediments of Polish lakes and fishponds. In his early studies he found correlations between phosphorus and iron, and between organic matter and calcium concentrations in deep lacustrine sediments. The bottom sediments of shallow fishponds (Stangenberg, 1949, 1967), or of shallow lake littorals (Szczepański, 1965; Pieczyńska, 1972a) contain far more organic carbon and nitrogen than deep lake sediments (see also Stangenberg & Zemoytel, 1952; Rybak, 1969). The close correlations between organic matter and nitrogen, sulphur and cation exchange capacity found by Boyd (1970c), in new ponds on clay soils with little organic matter (0.37 to 6.42%) probably do not apply to the older and deeper organic sediments in lakes.

Peaty bottoms are rich in organic matter ($<80\%$) and carbon ($>40\%$) and organic N ($>2.8\%$). Clay or clay-calcareous sediments contain little organic matter (5 to 8%) as well as organic nitrogen. But the C/N ratio is as high or higher in these inorganic sediments than in the peaty sediments. The Polish data (Stangenberg, 1949, 1967) correspond with those of Misra (1938) and Mortimer (1941) on the lake muds of the English Lake District. Gorham (1953*b*) extended these observations into bogs and fens. The nitrogen content of the soils rose with increasing organic matter content, but nitrogen as a proportion of the organic matter declined, being least in raised bog peats (< 2% of dry organic mass).

The cation exchange capacity depended on the humus content, rising from a few mmol per 100 g in the least organic underwater soils to between 52 and 163 mmol in the highly organic peats and in some black lake muds. Marsh soils of similar organic content, but with recognisable organic detritus, showed much lower exchange capacities. The content of total exchangeable bases was relatively high in underwater soils in close contact with moving water. In the raised bogs, on the other hand, the content of exchangeable bases was low: 3 to 35 mequiv. per 100 g dry weight.

The inorganic marsh soils were generally more acid and less base saturated than the underwater soils. Their pH values remained at 4.5 to 7.0, but in the raised-bog peats the pH values fell below 4, as low as 2.9. The plants from underwater sites were richest and those from raised bogs were poorest both in minerals and nitrogen, reflecting the differences in soil base status quite clearly.

The concentrations of some ions in littoral waters are often correlated positively with their concentrations in the bottom sediments, but the relationships are not always clear. Planter (1970*a*, 1973) studied the physico-chemical properties of the water in reedbelts of the Mazurian lakes and characterised the littoral (using the classification of Bernatowicz & Zachwieja, 1966) as a separate lake zone, the chemistry of which depends on several factors such as the shore configuration, wave motion, chemical and mechanical composition of the bottom sediments, the abundance of mineral salts and of overgrowing vegetation. The water of isolated reed zones is richer in mineral salts than that of open reedbelts, owing to intense decomposition and mineralisation of organic matter. Much the same phenomenon has been described by Pieczyńska (1972*a*).

Similar differences have been found in the interstitial waters of different littoral sediments (Planter, 1973). A gradient along the transect across an isolated reedbelt to an open reedbed is shown in Figure 6.2. Comparisons of the nutrient content in littoral and interstitial water suggest that the latter is a rich source of plant mineral nutrients (see Fig. 6.5(*b*) and (*c*)). Haslam (1978) found that dissolved nutrient

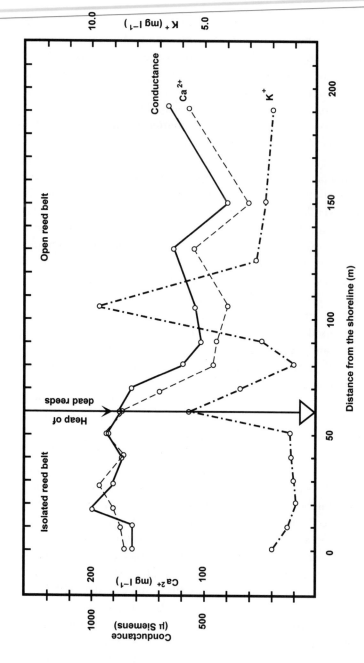

Fig. 6.2. Changes with distance from shoreline in the composition of interstitial water in the reedbelt of Lake Śniardwy, July 4, 1968 (Planter, 1973).

concentrations in sediments (per kg wet soil/per kg water) were 6–20 times higher than in open water.

The helophyte stands take part in the exchange of nutrients between the littoral sediments and the littoral water, by taking up nutrients from the substrate and returning them to the lake water by excretion or in the mineralisation process. Such a 'helophyte nutrient pump' has been suggested by Björk (1967, p. 235) and other authors (e.g. Schröder, 1973; Dykyjová & Hradecká, 1976; Prentki *et al.*, 1978). In this way, helophyte communities overgrowing large littoral areas may contribute substantially to the eutrophication of whole water body, as was proved in the Bodensee by Schröder (1973). Dykyjová (1973*a*) has calculated that the decomposing above-ground biomass of helophytes in a highly fertilised fishpond (mainly *Phragmites*, *Typha* and *Glyceria*) returns some 112 kg N, 139 kg K, 18 kg P, 25 kg Ca and 11 kg Mg per hectare

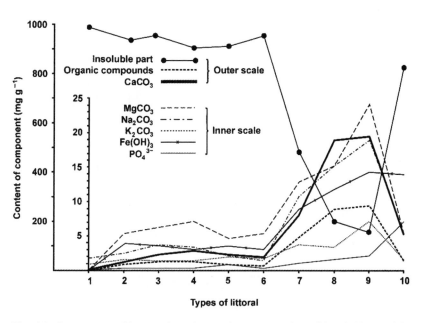

Fig. 6.3. Occurrence of inorganic and organic compounds and insoluble particles in bottom deposits in various types of lake littorals (Bernatowicz & Zachwieja, 1966; analyses according to method of Stangenberg & Zemoytel, 1952). Types of littoral: 1. litholittoral; 2. psammolittoral; 3. psammolittoral with large-lake helophytes; 4. large-lake phytolittoral; 5. phytolittoral of medium-sized lakes; 6. small-lake phytolittoral; 7. pond-type phytolittoral; 8. marsh phytolittoral; 9. degenerating phytolittoral; 10. artificially changed phytolittoral.

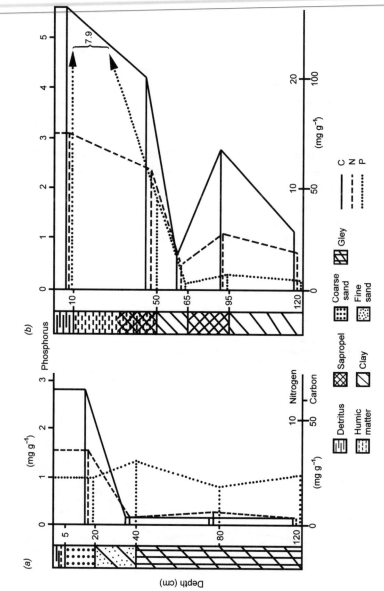

Fig. 6.4. The contents of Kjeldahl-N, organic C and P (extracted with 20% HCl) in the soil profiles below *Phragmites australis* growing (*a*) in an erosion biotope, and (*b*) in an accumulation biotope at the Opatovický fishpond (Dykyjová & Hradecká, 1976).

of helophyte-colonised area to the water each year. Similar exchanges have also been observed in salt water by McRoy *et al.* (1972, for *Zostera marina*) and Reimold (1972, for *Spartina alternifolia*).

Bernatowicz (1960) distinguished different types of lake littoral, correlated with types of plant succession (Bernatowicz & Zachwieja, 1966), and with increasing amounts of organic matter and both soluble and insoluble chemical substances in the bottom deposits (see Fig. 6.3). Calcium, for example, is deposited mainly in the zone of submerged plants. Similar increases may be seen in the amounts of magnesium, potassium and phosphorus, the latter usually accompanied by larger quantities of iron (see also Fig. 6.4). In all these soils there are large changes in concentration down the profile (Fig. 6.4).

Detritus

The rate of mineralisation of organic material of plant or animal origin depends on the susceptibility of different organic components to decay, on the functioning of the necessary relevant micro-organisms and on the ecological conditions under which the decomposition takes place (see Chapters 3 and 4).

The amounts mineralised can be quite large and of great economic interest. In Central European fishpond management the surplus of aquatic and littoral 'weeds' has encouraged analyses and experiments with their composting (e.g. Solski, 1962; Vavruška, 1966). Similar experiments have been made in other temperate and tropical regions (for review see Little, 1979). The explosive growth of certain aquatic plants and the fate of their biomass, after killing or removal from the water, has raised a serious question. What can be done with the decomposing plant material which releases nutrients back into the water body and primes the biotope for a new plant explosion? These problems are discussed in more detail by Little (1979) and Boyd (1970*a*, 1971*b*).

The decomposition of organic matter is of foremost importance for the functioning of any wetland ecosystem (see Chapters 3 and 4). Nichols and Keeney (1973) have analysed the release of nitrogen and phosphorus from decaying *Myriophyllum verticillatum*. Planter (1970*b*) has followed the elution of mineral components out of dead reed in laboratory experiments. Boyd (1970*b*) has found that the mineralisation of initially dry tissues decaying in water is much faster than in aerial conditions above the water surface. Boyd (1974) has also found that the growth of *Scenedesmus dimorphus* increased in proportion to the contents of nitrogen in decaying

Table 6.1. *Mineral elements in dead and decomposing materials in different vegetation zones in the Nesyt fishpond (Úlehlová, 1976)*

	Ash	N	P	K	Ca	Organic matter (% dry wt)	C (% org. wt)	C/N
			(mg (g dry wt)$^{-1}$)					
Locality 1: *Phragmites australis, Typha angustifolia, Carex riparia* (swamp)								
Phragmites stems standing dead	60.0	2.6	0.3	1.2	3.8	94.0	47	180
Typha leaves standing dead	62.5	3.5	0.4	2.7	25.2	93.75	47	134
Mixed surface litter 0–5 cm layer	92.7	10.6	0.8	2.5	12.6	90.73	45	42
Decomposing litter 5–10 cm layer	293.3	14.9	1.4	3.5	28.9	70.67	35	23
Locality 2: *Phragmites australis* (littoral hydrophase)								
Phragmites stems standing dead	62.5	3.7	0.3	1.2	3.5	93.75	46.8	126
Litter bottom surface 0–5 cm layer	201.6	8.9	1.3	1.8	14.2	79.84	37.4	42
Decomposing litter bottom 5–10 cm	156.3	20.9	1.6	2.7	32.8	84.37	42.2	20
Drift – algae, *Lemna* spp.; August	199.5	26.6	5.0	18.0	60.0	80.05	40	15
Drift – algae, *Potamogeton pectinatus, Hippuris vulgaris*; September	276.5	28.0	4.7	10.4	37.7	72.35	36	12.9

Table 6.2. *Comparison of mineral elements in the dead material from three stands of marsh plants in the cool and in the warm season in Georgia salt marshes (Reimold et al., 1975a)*

Element	Tall form *Spartina alterniflora* March	Tall form *Spartina alterniflora* August	Short form *Spartina alterniflora* March	Short form *Spartina alterniflora* August	*Juncus roemerianus* March	*Juncus roemerianus* August
(mg (g dry wt)$^{-1}$)						
N	10.0	8.0	5.0	8.0	6.0	6.0
P	1.1	10.0	1.2	1.1	0.8	0.8
K	4.3	3.2	3.2	4.2	2.2	2.5
Ca	0.8	1.3	1.3	3.2	1.4	2.2
Mg	2.3	4.1	3.1	10.9	2.7	5.3
(μg (g dry wt)$^{-1}$)						
Mn	107	109	166	102	242	288
B	25	37	33	50	35	45
Cu	8	7	9	8	6	6
Zn	17	18	14	13	10	9
Mo	12	14	14	16	4	5
Sr	14	27	20	58	22	35

plants in cultures, where these were the only source of nitrogen. Decaying algae were a better source of nitrogen than higher plants such as *Typha* or *Eichhornia*. However, Boyd (1973) did not consider the possible effects on the growth rates of some inhibitory or growth substance leaching from the decaying plant material. Mineralisation and excretion processes taking place in lakes have been described by Wetzel and his co-workers (see Wetzel, 1964; Wetzel & Manny, 1972; Wetzel *et al.*, 1972), and those taking place in reedbelt biotopes in fishponds have been discussed by Úlehlová (1976; see also Chapters 3 and 4).

Composition of plant detritus

Some differences in the quality of deposited plant materials, affecting the rate of mineralisation, are illustrated by Úlehlová (1971) and Reimold *et al.* (1975a); see Tables 6.1 and 6.2. The composition varies between species with time of decomposition and with season.

Algae and other micro-organisms have a much smaller C/N ratio than the cellulose-rich higher aquatics, and this ratio can be traced in

Table 6.3. *Mineral elements in filamentous algae at two different stages of algal mat development in a fertilised fishpond (Nesyt fishpond; Lhotský & Marvan, 1975)*

Date	Dry biomass (kg ha^{-1})	(t per fishpond)	Site[a]	Nutrients in biomass (mg (g dry biomass)$^{-1}$)				Nutrients in the algal biomass of the whole fishpond area (kg ha^{-1})			
				N	P	K	Ca	N	P	K	Ca
May 25 1972	480	144	A	18.2	5.1	11.8	18.0	8.6	2.3	6.0	23.7
			B	17.8	4.6	13.6	50.7				
June 13 1972	800	239	C	12.3	3.8	5.8	42.1				
			D	12.3	8.2	25.2	48.0	8.7	5.1	14.5	35.1
			E	8.0	7.2	23.2	41.5				

[a] The species composition on the sites A and B: *Oedogonium* 46%, *Spirogyra* 38%, *Cladophora fracta* 17%. The community on the site C was dominated by *Oedogonium*, on the sites D and E by *Cladophora fracta*.

lacustrine sediments (Stangenberg, 1949). According to Vinberg (1971) the ash content in phytoplankton varies from 40 to 100 mg (g dry wt)$^{-1}$ (green or blue-green algae), to 0.5 to 0.7 g g^{-1} in many diatoms, and the nitrogen content is about 80 mg g^{-1}. Many filamentous algae and *Characeae* are encrusted with carbonate (e.g. Boyd & Lawrence, 1967). According to Szczepańska (1970), the percentage of calcium in periphytic algae of the Mazurian lakes fluctuates within the limits of 0.11 to 0.20 g g^{-1}.

There is little information on the elemental composition of algae in wetlands, but as a general rule algae are richer in mineral elements than rooted plants (cf. Tables 6.1, 6.2 and 6.3). The ash, nitrogen and phosphorus determinations by Gerloff and Skoog (1954, 1957) were mostly made on planktonic blue-green algae. However, Boyd and Lawrence (1967) analysed for many elements, finding the levels of most varied considerably, both within and between genera. Sirenko (1972) made similar comparisons (for C, N, P and K) and Lhotský and Marvan (1975) analysed filamentous algae (Table 6.3). Selective accumulation of one or more elements above the usual levels has been observed in several genera. Almost all genera contained relatively high levels of copper, iron, manganese and zinc.

The biomass of algal blooms containing significant quantities of mineral nutrients is a substantial component of the mineral nutrient turnover in aquatic ecosystems, and often also in adjacent wetlands. The rapid turnover and decomposition of algae, as well as the difficulties in separating the analysed material from zooplankton and various impurities, render adequate calculations impossible. Pieczyńska (1972*b*) estimated that total mineralisation of *Cladophora glomerata* took 5 days, and of *Gleotrichia echinulata* took 3 days. Below heaps of reed in the eulittoral the process took 3 days more. Lhotský and Marvan (1975) give information on the productivity of filamentous algae and on the nutrients they found in a highly fertilised fishpond (Table 6.3). The specific and temporal differences in the nutrient contents in the biomass of algae complicated the calculations of the total nutrient content in the whole fishpond. The mineral contents of some of the phytoplanktonic algae, at the time of 'blooming', fluctuated by a factor of 2 or 3. Therefore dense blooms might contain 0.4–6 g N m^{-3}, 0.1 to 0.9 g P and 0.09 to 0.46 g K depending on their current nutrient content and their biomass (see Priimachenko & Litvinova, 1961).

Composition of animal detritus

Only some very general statements can be made on the mineral content of
animal detritus (Vinberg, 1971). The soft tissues decompose as rapidly as
the planktonic algae. The ash content in zooplankton is about 100 mg (g
dry wt)$^{-1}$, in mollusc bodies it is low (30 mg g^{-1}) in the soft parts but high
when referred to the total weight with the shell included. The same
probably applies to all aquatic animals with encrusted parts of their
body. The nitrogen content in ash-free dry weight of zooplankton and
fishes is about 100–120 mg g^{-1}, in bacterial cells it is about 100 mg g^{-1}.

**Total inflow of mineral nutrients from surrounding terrestrial and aquatic
ecosystems**

Within the area draining to a wetland, dissolved mineral and organic
materials, together with particles of the same compounds, enter water
bodies as direct surface run-off from the surrounding landscape and as
percolated water through the deep soil and rocks. In a landscape with
rooted perennial vegetation cover (meadows, woods) the direct run-off is
reduced but more time is available for water percolation and the solution
of substances increases (Hynes, 1972). For agricultural drainage, see e.g.
Ohle (1965), Biggar and Corey (1969), Cooke (1976) and Royal Society
(1983). Armstrong and Rohlich (1969) found that agricultural land
contributed 42% of the phosphorus in USA water supplies. For forest
drainage and nutrient output, see Cooper (1969), Tamm *et al.* (1974) and
Likens *et al.* (1977). Sawyer (1947) has found that, in Wisconsin, the run-
off contributed about 7.7 kg NO_3^--N ha^{-1} y^{-1} and 0.38 kg of phosphorus. The steeper the slope of the surrounding area, the greater was the
contribution.

Appreciable amounts of dissolved and particulate organic substances,
containing minerals, are present in surface waters, and are essential in the
food chains of micro-organisms and zooplankton. Even the primary
producers absorb and secrete some nutrients, such as nitrogen and
phosphorus, in organic form (Wetzel, 1968; Wetzel & Allen, 1972; Wetzel
et al., 1972).

The nutrients carried in rivers, streams and drains, whether inorganic or
organic, dissolved or suspended, accumulate in areas of sediment deposit,
which often develop into wetlands. Papyrus swamps filter much of the
detritus and minerals from water flowing through them into lakes and
rivers (Thompson, 1976*b*).

On a miniature scale, this accumulation process has been studied where the mouth of a stream enters a shallow fishpond (Dykyjová & Hradecká, 1976; cf. Fig. 6.4(*b*)). The luxuriant helophyte vegetation of *Glyceria aquatica* and *Carex gracilis* does not utilise all the nutrient reserves present in the sediments. The detritus accumulated in the surface layer adds new nutrient sources to the humus-rich A horizon.

In streams overgrown with aquatic vegetation, the concentrations of dissolved nutrients may fall slightly during the season of active plant growth because the plants act as traps for nutrients. Anchored vegetation, however, does not utilise all nutrients contained in water or the sediment layers (Rodewald-Rudescu, 1974; Casey & Westlake, 1974).

Waste waters and pollution

Human beings have always used waters to dispose of all kinds of impurities and wastes. All settlements pour their sewage, waste and industrial effluents into natural or artificial rivers, lakes, estuaries and seas, as well as into wetlands. McLusky (1971) estimated that the crude sewage from 280 000 people was added daily to the estuary of the River Tees, England; in addition, effluents from coke treatment plants then contributed daily 2 t of tar acid and 0.8 t of cyanide. The Rhine is heavily polluted by 40 million people and by the largest industrial centre in Europe. An equivalent of 400 t of concentrated sulphuric acid was released daily at the head of the estuarine Chesapeake Bay. The inhabitants of Washington DC daily added 10 t of phosphorus and 30 t of nitrogen into the Potomac estuary in the form of sewage (McLusky, 1971, p. 107). Such pollution often accumulates in wetlands; indeed, wetlands are often used to purify polluted water (see Chapter 8, pp. 420–2).

Atmospheric sources of pollution must also be considered. Initially radioactive fall-out from nuclear bomb tests and reactor accidents had most attention, but more recently the fall-out of mineral acids (mostly sulphuric and nitric), derived from the combustion of coal, petrol and plastic wastes, causing acidification of water bodies, is the main concern. Most literature deals with forests, bogs and lakes, especially where soils and waters are initially neutral or acid (e.g. Rimes, 1992), and low in calcium (Patrick *et al.*, 1995). Most wetlands, as here defined, are relatively high in calcium and well buffered. However, the nitrogen acids may be a significant source of extra nitrogen, capable of changing the vegetation (Verhoeven *et al.*, 1988).

The recent drastic increase of eutrophication has changed and disturbed aquatic and wetland habitats. All future investigations of mineral cycling in wetland biotopes must be, therefore, either an abstraction of natural processes or realistic measurements of artificial changes.

Soil processes

The major inorganic reactions in wetland soils (Ponnamperuma, 1972; Ross, 1995), and the broad outlines of organic decomposition (Polunin, 1984; see Chapters 3 and 4), are well known. Both are carried out by micro-organisms and are very dependent on the aeration or redox potential of the soil.

Redox reactions

There is a suite of reactions spanning four stages (Patrick, 1978).

Stage 1 Oxygen not completely absent, phosphorus absorbed on ferric and manganic oxides, nitrate begins to be reduced to nitrite and then to ammonium, Mn^{4+} reduced to Mn^{2+}, Eh_7* 820 to 200 mV;

Stage 2 No oxygen or nitrate, iron(III) (Fe^{3+}) reduced to iron(II) (Fe^{2+}), phosphate can be precipitated by iron(II) ions; both stages 1 and 2 involve facultative anaerobes and the reactions are readily reversible if oxygen increases, Eh_7 0 to -150 mV;

Stage 3 Sulphate (SO_4^{2-}) reduced to sulphide (S^{2-}, usually as iron(II) or hydrogen sulphide), usually reversible, Eh_7 -150 to -230 mV;

Stage 4 Carbon dioxide reduced to methane, Stages 3 and 4 involve true anaerobes, normally irreversible, $Eh_7 < -230$ mV.

The reversal of Stage 3 may lead to strongly acid waters containing sulphuric acid or heavy precipitates of iron(III) hydroxide (ochre), both of which are serious pollutants.

Denitrification converts nitrate, via ammonia, to nitrogen gas (or in acid conditions to nitrous oxide, N_2O), usually by chemoheterotrophs. This requires a supply of nitrate, but low oxygen levels. Highest field rates are found at redox potentials of about 200 to 400 mV, and optimal

---

*Eh_7 is related to pH 7, being the measured redox potential referred to the value it would have at pH 7.

conditions arise in heterogeneous organic soils where aerobic and anaerobic conditions occur close together (Patrick & Reddy, 1976; Baker & Maltby, 1995; Maltby *et al.*, 1995).

Nitrogen-fixing heterotrophic or autotrophic bacteria or algae can reverse denitrification by taking up nitrogen gas and converting it to ammonia and thus to protein. These organisms can be free-living, but many are symbionts in plant roots such as legumes and, in wetlands, rice and *Alnus* spp. which contain blue-green algae. Optimal conditions for non-symbiotic fixation are near neutrality, available carbon and low pH (Ross, 1995).

Cations and anions

These may involve chemical solution or precipitation, or absorption or desorption with organic materials, especially peat, minerals, especially clays, and iron oxides (Brady, 1990). Apart from the cation exchange capacity of the clays, the exchanges are influenced by the pH of the soil. The complexity arising means that it has been difficult to quantify the interactions and effects on the accumulation and release of nutrients.

Uptake of mineral elements by plants and animals

Mechanisms of mineral nutrient uptake by wetland plants

In a symposium on ion transport in plants (Anderson, 1973), about 35% of the contributions dealt with higher aquatic plants and filamentous algae. The rest referred to theoretical models or to barley roots.

The old controversy over the role of leaves and roots as sites of nutrient uptake by submerged macrophytes has been concluded by experimental studies (see the literature reviewed by Hutchinson (1975), Bristow (1975) and Denny (1980)). Nutrients are taken up from both water and soil, the proportions depending on the plant's morphology and on the relative availability of the nutrient.

On the other hand, helophytes such as *Phragmites*, *Typha*, *Scirpus* and *Carex* have less absorptive shoot tissues submerged and take up mineral nutrients not only via their 'edaphic' roots, penetrating into the bottom mud or subsoil, but also via their accessory aquatic roots. These play an important role in the mineral nutrition of the plants (Roman *et al.*, 1971; Rodewald-Rudescu, 1974; Dykyjová & Hradecká, 1976; Cumbus & Robinson, 1977).

Nutrient absorption takes place through contact cation exchange between roots and soil or mud colloids, between roots and the aqueous phase of bottom sediments or by foliar absorption from the water.

Submerged plant parts such as leaves or stems not only absorb electrolytes, but they also readily release substantial amounts of nutrients back into the water (McRoy *et al.*, 1972 – *Zostera*; De Marte & Hartman, 1974 – *Myriophyllum*). The experiments with ^{32}P absorption in *Zostera marina* made by McRoy and Barsdate (1972) are particularly instructive.

The higher solubility of iron, manganese and aluminium phosphates at the low redox potential in anaerobic mud enables the rooted plants to take up more nutrients than they would from the water alone (Shapiro, 1958; Ponnamperuma, 1972). Thus the rooted plants do not have to compete with non-rooted macrophytes or phytoplankton. Only non-rooted macrophytes and those without any absorptive roots compete with

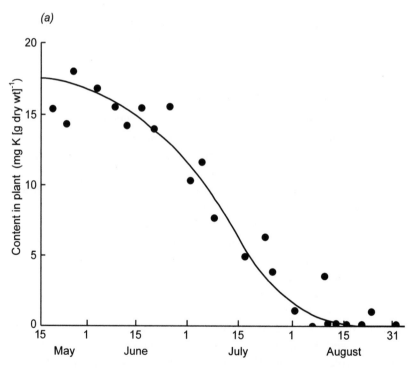

Fig. 6.5. Seasonal variation of potassium content (*a*) in the biomass of *Phragmites australis*, (*b*) in the soil, and (*c*) in the water in its habitat, a littoral stand (Bayly & O'Neil, 1972*a*).

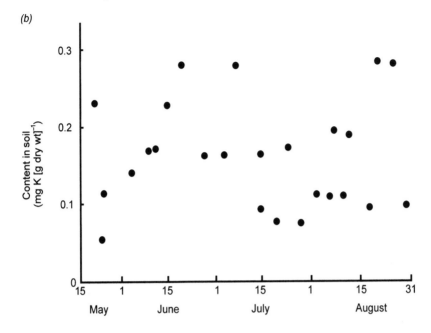

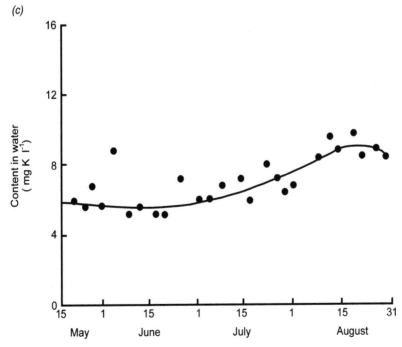

Fig. 6.5. (*cont.*)

Table 6.4. *The content of mineral components in emergent macrophytes of Lake Warniak at maximum biomass in comparison with the mineral content of water (Bernatowicz, 1969)*

(a) *Minerals in the plants*

	Ash	N	P	K	Ca
Species		(mg (g dry wt)$^{-1}$)			
Nymphaea alba	101	28	4.2	11	1
Stratiotes aloides	167	21	3.9	64	6
Acorus calamus	64	18	0.3	7	6
Scirpus lacustris	78	17	0.3	5	2
Menyanthes trifoliata	70	17	3.5	13	4
Hydrocharis morsus-ranae	158	17	0.5	23	12
Calla palustris	97	16	0.8	20	8
Equisetum limosum	132	14	3.3	10	2
Phragmites australis	59	12	0.1	4	1
Typha latifolia	51	12	0.2	3	4
Cicuta virosa	143	–	0.4	41	23

(b) *Minerals in the water*

	Inorganic N	PO$_4$P	K	Ca
Date 1966		(mg l^{-1})		
April 18	0.27	0.016	1.3	32
May 19	0.24	0.029	0.9	32
August 29	0.02	0.000	0.7	19

phytoplankton for nutrients dissolved in the water (Boyd, 1971*b*; Mulligan & Baranowski, 1969). Generally, the internal concentrations of elements are much greater than the environmental concentrations for both major and minor constituents (e.g. Table 6.4 and Fig. 6.5; see also Tables 6.5, 6.8 and 6.12).

Problems and errors arising from methods of sampling and analysis

Any comparisons of the uptake, metabolic pathways and contents of minerals in organisms have to assume that the chemical analyses of the organisms and their environmental sources of minerals are reproducible and comparable with other methods. Numerous methodological problems have to be taken into consideration which are discussed by Straškraba (1968) and Boyd (1968c). The conclusions of these authors on the role of macrophytes in the ecology of freshwaters sometimes differ because Straškraba was interested in their effects on pelagic waters, while Boyd tackled those of the littoral. Most of their conclusions are, however, similar.

1. Analyses of aquatic plants reported earlier are rarely comparable because they did not respect intraspecific variation due to age, phenophase and type of plant organs analysed (see Tables 6.7 and 6.11; Figs 6.5(a), 6.6 and 6.7; Boyd & Scarsbrook, 1975b; Dykyjová, 1979).
2. The mineral concentrations in the water and soils may influence the production and mineral content of some species to a high degree (see Tables 6.6, 6.8, 6.9, 6.10 and 6.11 and Fig. 6.8; see also Boyd & Scarsbrook, 1975b; Dykyjová, 1979; Little, 1979).
3. The three different groups of vascular wetland plants, emergent, floating and submerged differ in ash and mineral contents. Submerged plants have a higher water and ash content then the emergent vegetation, while floating species are in between these two groups (Westlake, 1965; Straškraba, 1968 and Table 6.4). Compare also data in Mayer and Gorham (1951), Gorham (1953b), Hutchinson (1975) and Dykyjová & Květ (1982).
4. Besides the natural sources of variability in the chemical composition of aquatic plants, many discrepancies exist in the analytical techniques used. Even the data on water content are often not comparable; drying may be at 60, 70, 80 or 105°C in ovens, or only air drying. Similar problems apply to comparisons of the ash content (see also Westlake, 1965, pp. 234–235) if different temperatures have been used without considering possible losses of volatile or unstable components. Many submerged plants are heavily encrusted with external calcium carbonate, which obscures not only the values of the internal ash content, but also the proportions of other minerals or nutrients in the dry matter. According to Wetzel (1960) the marl encrustations in the biomass of several submerged plants may exceed 50%.
5. Further discrepancies occur when attempts are made to correlate the mineral nutrient content in the plants with the chemistry of either water or soil. In most comparisons between different biotopes, as reported in the papers cited in this chapter, different soil extracting procedures have been used, and many authors only refer to handbooks written for other habitats.

The opinions of Boyd and Lawrence (1967) and Boyd (1968c) are applicable to wetland ecosystems:

Analyses of bottom soils, water and biota, in conjunction with equilibrium rates between various phases of the system, will be necessary to establish the level of availability of a particular element. In large deep oligotrophic reservoirs water analyses are probably indicative of the nutrient supply. In shallow eutrophic reservoirs, the store of soil minerals is probably of greater significance, and in addition a large quantity of nutrients are bound in biomass. Water analyses therefore, are of limited value in estimating anything other than the concentration of solutes at the instant of sampling. Soil samples are usually analysed for the total amount of a particular nutrient, or extracted for analysis with solvents used in agricultural soil testing. Agricultural procedures ideally extract a fraction of nutrients, which is correlated with plant response. Nutrients extracted from muds by these procedures have no particular relation to aquatic plant growth. Just as in terrestrial species, aquatic plant growth is related to available nutrients and not to the total supply. Only when the proportion of aquatic soil nutrients available to plant growth is ascertained, and extraction procedures are calibrated against nutrient availability and plant response, can valid interpretations of bottom soil chemical analyses be made.

Therefore, only broadly conceived comparison can be made between the fertilities of different wetland habitats and the behaviour of different species, unless the comparisons are limited to particular techniques.

Bioassays

A better picture of the mineral nutrient supply in the habitat is often provided by tissue analyses of active plant organs at the stage of maximum vegetative growth, particularly if these can be related to the concentrations found in plants shown experimentally to be growing at their optimum rate (the critical concentrations; see below). Such techniques have been used for the elaboration of many methods for testing nutrient supplies and deficiencies in crop plants. Lundegårdh's (1951) leaf tissue analysis is based on the mineral element concentrations in metabolically active plant tissues, reflecting the availability of mineral nutrients in the environment. Such leaf analyses reveal the status of available nutrients in the habitat more precisely than soil or water analyses. They have also been applied to aquatic macrophytes (Gerloff & Skoog, 1954; Allen & Pearsall, 1963; Björk, 1967; Robinson & Cumbus, 1977). Many of the methodological and technical problems are discussed by Gerloff and Fishbeck (1973), and further investigations are necessary before this useful bioassay can be extended widely. Difficulties in elaborating appropriate bioassay techniques for several aquatic plants arise mainly from their specialised physiological features (see, e.g. Wilson, 1972; Caines, 1965; Goulder & Boatman, 1971), but also from difficulties in achieving rapid and repeatable growth in culture.

One particular feature, which restricts the general application of bioassay techniques for nutrient availability, but provides opportunities for detecting low concentrations of minerals, is the well-known selective absorption capacity of several species for particular ions (Hoágland, 1948; Hutchinson, 1975). The concentration factors for individual nutrients, calculated from the ratio of the level of an element in the plant tissue to the level of that element in the water, are sometimes extremely high. In algae, the concentration factors for most elements range from 3000 to 12000; for manganese they are as high as 100000 to 250000 (Boyd & Lawrence, 1967). Higher aquatic plants are also marked accumulators of particular elements. Boyd (1969) reports concentration factors (on a dry weight basis) for several elements in *Justicia americana*, sampled in lakes with different water hardness in Alabama and Florida (Table 6.5; see also Tables 6.4, 6.8 and 6.12 and Fig. 6.5).

Varenko and Lubyanov (1973) reported on the accumulation of some trace elements in submerged, floating and emergent macrophytes in the bays of two Dnieper reservoirs. The accumulation coefficients for copper were higher in half-submerged plants than in submerged ones. The greatest amounts of zinc and cobalt were found in floating plants.

Caines (1965), analysing seven submerged species growing in Scottish lakes before and after fertilisation with calcium superphosphate, showed that only *Myriophyllum alternifolium* and *M. spicatum* had significantly increased their uptake of phosphorus following the addition of fertiliser.

Gramineae, Cyperaceae and Juncaceae usually have a high potassium to calcium ratio (Duvigneaud & Denayer-De Smet, 1962; Denayer-De Smet, 1964), said to result from a low capacity for calcium uptake (Iljin, 1936), a relatively slow water turnover rate (Rychnovská *et al.*, 1972) and the accompanying slow passive transport of cations (Stocker, 1967). These high ratios have been confirmed for aquatic species by Dykyjová (1979; see Table 6.6).

Table 6.5. *Water analysis and concentration factors for littoral stands of* Justicia americana *(Boyd, 1969)*

(*a*) *Analysis of different water bodies*

Analysis	Lake Seminole	Cahaba River	Halawakee Creek	Chewalca Creek
pH	7.3	7.4	7.2	7.6
Total alkalinity $(mg\,l^{-1}\,CaCO_3)$	25.0	89.5	20.5	105.8
Elements in solution $(mg\,l^{-1})$				
P	0.03	0.05	0.03	0.04
Ca	4.4	19.5	3.0	23.5
Mg	1.2	3.7	1.6	4.3
K	2.2	1.5	1.2	1.0
Fe	0.18	0.06	0.12	0.04
Mn	0.030	0.004	0.020	0.006
Zn	0.16	0.02	0.04	0.01
Cu	0.021	0.004	0.011	0.006

(*b*) *Concentration factors in different water bodies*
(concentration of element in dried plant/concentration of element in water; for convenience the tabulated values have been divided by 10^3, and rounded)

Analysis	Lake Seminole	Cahaba River	Halawakee Creek	Chewalca Creek
P	43	42	47	47
Ca	2	1	5	1
Mg	3	2	3	1
K	28	21	36	37
Fe	4	7	3	17
Mn	6	29	14	31
Zn	1	14	3	17
Cu	2	10	2	7

Accumulation of mineral nutrients by plants in relation to species, organs, seasons and type of habitat

Species differences

Though samples of each species show a range of nutrient contents, even when the sites, times of sampling and plant parts are standardised, distinct differences between species still occur (Table 6.6; see also Table 6.4).

Table 6.6. *Ranges of mineral contents of wetland species at sites of different nutrient status*

(a) *Above-ground parts at maximum stand development, July–August. From Opatovický fishpond (Dykyjová, 1973b)*

	N	P	K	Ca	Mg	Na	S	K/Ca
				(mg (g dry wt)$^{-1}$)				
Phragmites australis	17.7–21.3	1.9–2.8	10.8–17.4	0.3–2.9	0.8–1.7	0.3–0.5	—	4.2–9.0
Typha angustifolia	11.5	1.6	11.6–16.5	1.8–7.3	1.3–1.8	2.5	—	2.3–6.4
Sparganium erectum	14.2–25.5	3.2–4.8	36.0–41.0	1.8–12.3	1.9–2.9	3.9–4.4	—	5.8–5.9
Acorus calamus	12.6–19.2	2.0–13.5	18.5–36.7	3.4–8.5	1.4–2.1	0.9–2.4	—	5.8–11.0
Scirpus lacustris	10.3–17.7	2.3–3.4	13.6–16.9	0.7–2.5	0.9–1.5	3.4–4.0	—	6.0–6.7
Glyceria maxima	12.9–18.2	1.8–3.1	17.0–23.0	1.2–1.9	1.0–1.3	—	—	9.5–18.0
Scirpus maritimus ssp. *maritimus*	13.6–17.9	2.8–3.5	14.0–26.9	0.8–6.3	1.0–1.7	1.6–6.6	—	4.3–18.0

(b) *From Balaton Lake (Kovács et al., 1978)*

	N	P	K	Ca	Mg	Na	S
				(mg (g dry wt)$^{-1}$)			
Mean, culms and leaves *Phragmites australis*	19.8	1.0	10.1	—	2.3	0.35	—

(c) *From 17 habitats of different nutrient status USA*

	N	P	K	Ca	Mg	Na	S
				(mg (g dry wt)$^{-1}$)			
Whole plants (Boyd & Vickers, 1971) *Eichhornia crassipes*	13.3–33.3	1.4–8.0	6.0–67.0	6.6–21.0	2.0–8.8	1.7–7.5	3.7–6.3
Above-ground parts (Boyd, 1971a) *Juncus effusus*	8.7–13.3	0.5–2.0	10.3–20.6	1.0–3.0	0.4–1.2	0.2–3.7	1.2–3.0

Difference between plant organs

The accumulation of minerals in individual organs differs according to their metabolic activity. The highest content of nutrients is generally in the stems and leaves but some nutrients, such as sodium, may be higher in stems and phosphorus and magnesium may accumulate in flowers and fruits (Fig. 6.6; see also Table 6.11). The mineral content of underground storage organs such as bulbs and rhizomes is usually lower than leaves because of 'dilution' by organic reserves, but it may be higher when young buds are present in great numbers.

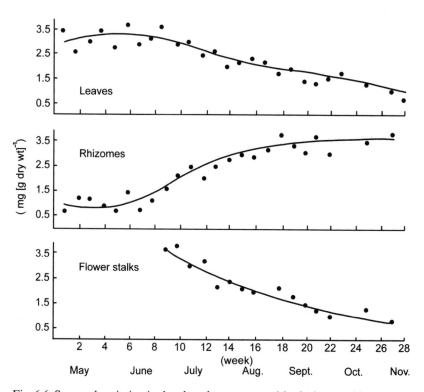

Fig. 6.6. Seasonal variation in the phosphorus content* in the leaves, rhizomes and flower stalks of *Typha glauca* in a marsh (Bayly & O'Neil, 1972b). *The absolute values given in the original appear improbably high. The scales here have been divided by ten.

Table 6.7. *Seasonal changes in the ash and mineral contents of aerial shoots of* Typha latifolia *in a littoral stand (Boyd, 1970b)*

Constituent (mg (g dry wt)$^{-1}$)	Date					
	April 16	May 1	May 16	May 29	June 18	July 17
Ash	101.3	95.0	73.3	58.0	49.1	42.1
N	24.0	19.6	10.1	8.7	5.1	5.1
P	3.1	2.4	1.7	1.2	1.1	0.9
S	1.8	1.9	1.8	0.9	0.9	0.8
Ca	7.7	9.2	9.3	8.9	5.6	5.3
Mg	1.8	2.1	1.9	1.8	1.1	1.0
K	34.6	19.3	20.5	19.1	20.7	16.0
Na	1.8	2.1	2.8	2.4	2.4	1.9

Seasonal differences

The seasonal changes in the accumulation of nutrients in the macrophyte biomass play an important role in the mineral cycles of wetland ecosystems. In the aerial parts, concentrations of most nutrients, except calcium and possibly sodium, tend to decrease during the growing season (Table 6.7; see also Figs 6.5, 6.6 and 6.7). Seasonal, and even daily fluctuations in nutrient uptake are related to gradients in metabolic activity during the growth, development and ageing of the plant. In the initial growth processes, the uptake of essential metabolic nutrients occurs more rapidly than the net production rate of organic matter, later it declines (Boyd, 1970*b*; Dykyjová, 1979; see Table 6.7 and Fig. 6.7). Therefore, the percentage contents of metabolic elements decrease during the seasonal plant development.

Those aerial or submerged organs, which decompose each season, release their nutrients into the environment. The large underground storage organs, such as the rhizomes, roots or tubers of perennial macrophytes, retain a substantial part of the accumulated nutrients for two or several seasons and enrich the bottom or subsoil with nutrients only after decomposition.

Differences between habitats

The mineral nutrient status in the bottom and water may influence the distribution and production of wetland plant populations. The

Table 6.8. *Contents of elements in the rhizosphere and vegetation of two wetlands (from Dykyjová & Květ, 1982)*

	Content of rhizosphere		Content of vegetation[a]	
	Bog 0–200 mm	Wet meadow 0–250 mm	Bog (Whole plant; at maximum biomass)	Wet meadow
	$(mg\,(kg\,dry\,wt)^{-1})$		$(mg\,(g\,dry\,wt)^{-1})$	
N	–	–	8.7–24.1	17.6–24.6
P	36	115	1.3–2.6	1.5–3.2
K	83	259	4.4–9.8	3.8–19.0
Na	227	202	0.4–1.3	0.4–0.8
Ca	242	2710	1.3–6.9	1.6–2.4
Mg	102	37	0.5–2.0	0.7–1.1
			$(\mu g\,(g\,dry\,wt)^{-1})$	
Fe	284.0	2.0	180–3600	–
Mn	27.2	159.7	49–457	–
Zn	66.6	203.9	37–74	–
Co	1.86	22.3	0.7–1.8	–
Cu	6.10	69.2	5.5–20	–
Cd	0.60	1.92	0.2–1.1	–

[a] Vegetation: Bog – *Sphagnum* spp., *Eriophorum vaginatum, Vaccinium* spp., *Ledum palustre, Pinus* × *rotundata*; Meadow – *Calamagrostis canescens, Carex gracilis.*

relationships between the mineral constitution of submerged soils and water and the mineral composition of plant biomass have often been discussed. Many authors have related the nutrient content in the plants to the trophic conditions of their hydrosoils and waters (Gorham, 1953*b*; Rodewald-Rudescu, 1974; Allen & Pearsall, 1963; Björk, 1967; Wallentinus, 1975; Dykyjová, 1979). Usually plant populations growing in hard waters and nutrient-rich habitats accumulate more mineral ions than those growing in poor habitats. This can be seen between extreme situation such as acid bogs and fertilised fishponds, and even between accumulation and erosion sites in a single water body at certain times (Table 6.8 and Fig. 6.7; see also Tables 6.6 and 6.12). Very wide ranges may be shown by trace elements (Table 6.9). Differences in biomass and biomass load of nutrients (g in biomass per square metre) often correspond with differences in nutrient content in soil (see Fig. 6.8).

In very fertile habitats however, there may be little or no relationship between internal and external concentrations (e.g. Casey and Downing, 1976) and in plants from mesohaline waters internal concentrations are

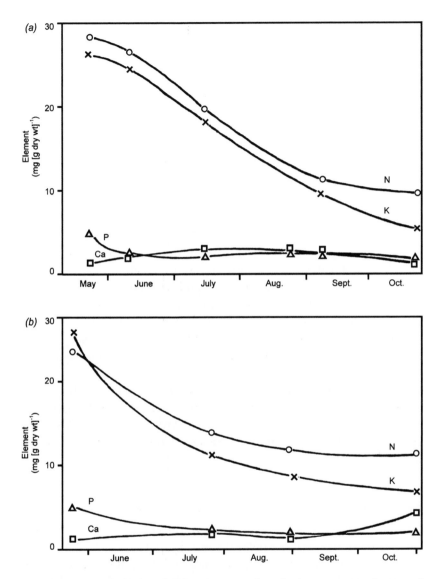

Fig. 6.7. Seasonal changes in the contents of total nitrogen, potassium, total phosphorus and calcium in (*a*) stands of *Phragmites australis* and (*b*) *Scirpus lacustris* in fishponds (Dykyjová, 1973*b*).

Table 6.9. *Ranges of trace element contents in* Eichhornia crassipes *from 17 different habitats (Boyd & Vickers, 1971)*

	Minimum	Mean	Maximum
Element	\$(\mu g\ (g\ dry\ wt)^{-1})\$		
Fe	522	3 420	14 440
Mn	87	270	400
Zn	25	67	209
Cu	7	15	100
B	15	20	25
Mo	2	12	40

within the range found in plants from freshwaters (see Table 6.6). Dykyjová and Véber (1978) cultivated reedbelt helophytes in outdoor hydroponics with sandy substrates in solutions with increasing concentrations of all nutrients. Biomass analyses of 1- and 2-year-old cultures showed an increase in the mineral nutrient contents of the plants up to an optimum concentration of the nutrient solution; at higher concentrations the nutrient amounts in the biomass declined and the net production was also lower (Table 6.10).

The high stand density and net production achieved by forced mineral nutrition (4–12 kg dry m^{-2} tank area after 2–3 years) were accompanied by increased mineral content (Dykyjová, 1978b). This calls attention to the possibilities of enhancing the production of many wetland plants.

Uptake and accumulation of mineral elements by animals

Data on the uptake and accumulation of mineral elements by wetland animals are very sparse, except for the enrichment factors of radionuclides in animals along food chains (e.g. Nelson *et al.*, 1972). Bootle and Knauer (1972) reported on the accumulation of heavy metals, through detritus-feeding crabs of *Spartina* salt marshes. The faecal material contained concentrations of As, Co, Cu, Fe, Mn, Cl and Zn 2.3 to 14 times higher than originally present in their diet of brown algae. Chapman and Coffey (1971) gave results of experiments with herbivorous fish controlling macrophytes such as *Lagarosiphon*, *Elodea canadensis* and *Egeria densa*. These alien water weeds grow in lakes of New Zealand fed by thermal

Table 6.10. *Content and load of mineral elements in second-year shoots of* **Phragmites australis** *cultivated in hydroponic sand cultures at increasing concentrations of the nutrient solution (Veber, 1973)*

Concentration of nutrient solution (relative to basic)		0.1	0.25	0.5	1.0	1.5	2.0		Composition of the basic (1.0) nutrient solution	
								Element	($mg\,l^{-1}$)
Shoot ($g\ dry\ wt\ m^{-2}$)		809	832	1353	1430	1250	857		Amine-N	280
Panicles ($g\ dry\ wt\ m^{-2}$)		17	49	33	10	0.9	1.5		Nitrate-N	110
Total N	Content	19.20	26.60	29.70	32.50	28.70	30.40		Ammonium-N	
	Load	15.57	22.13	40.25	46.80	35.87	26.09		Phosphate-P	155
Total P	Content	3.15	3.15	3.29	3.08	3.50	2.80		K	195
	Load	2.55	2.62	4.45	3.43	4.37	2.40		Mg	193
K	Content	9.82	18.00	24.50	24.50	21.20	20.90		Ca	136
	Load	7.94	15.02	33.15	35.28	26.54	17.95		(With sulphate, trace elements and EDTA)	
Ca	Content	1.12	2.04	2.53	2.46	2.28	2.36			
	Load	0.91	1.69	3.42	3.44	2.85	2.02			
Mg	Content	0.58	0.90	0.92	0.85	0.56	0.79			
	Load	0.47	0.75	1.25	1.20	0.70	0.67			

Nutrient content in above-ground biomass ($mg\ (g\ dry\ wt)^{-1}$) and load ($g\ m^{-2}$)

springs containing considerable amounts of soluble arsenic. The accumulations of arsenic in the plants and even more in the fishes are considerable; over 80 mg kg^{-1} in the muscle and bone.

Mineral cycling in examples of different wetland types

Bogs, fens and transitional types

In inland areas of impeded drainage of cold and temperate zones some characteristic waterlogged habitats occur. Some of these provide the poorest conditions for plant life from the point of view of nutrient supply. Large areas of the circumpolar and boreal zones are covered by poor plant communities, accumulating peat in the upper soil horizons, and have characteristic populations of higher plants. These have been classified into many categories from the point of view of hydromorphology or vegetation structure (see Gore, 1983*a*).

Major types

Raised bogs Raised bogs are the extreme ombrogenous dystrophic or highly oligotrophic peatlands (mires), independent of the groundwater and receiving water and dilute nutrients mainly from rainfall. In general, they are not treated in this book, but their mineral nutrient regime is included here for the sake of comparison. The pH values are low and the decomposition of organic matter (mainly *Sphagnum*) is extremely slow. The interstitial water and plant biomass are poor in nitrogen, phosphorus and other dissolved nutrients. Large areas of natural intact raised bogs occur at present only in boreal regions in cold and humid or oceanic climatic conditions. In more continental climates, as in Central Europe, only small relics are found in highlands.

Fens Fens are topogenous minerotrophic (meso- to eutrophic) peatlands (mires) with a neutral reaction (pH 6 to 7), related to groundwater eluting mineral sediments or rocks in the subsoil and consequently mineral saturated, with a more rapid decomposition of dead plant material, usually reeds or *Carex* sp.

Transitional Transitional types between raised bogs and fens are common. They receive water and nutrients from rainfall as well as from the running or standing waters in the surrounding raised terrain, or from subterranean springs.

Such differences in the nutrient contents between raised bogs and fens in relatively unpolluted regions are described by Gorham (1953*b*), Walter (1968) and Gore (1983*a*).

Minerals in bogs

The low nutrient content in peat-bogs, especially in raised bogs, makes this environment extremely difficult for the life of plants, small animals and micro-organisms. It is possible only by highly specialised adaptations. The organic deposits decompose very slowly because of the lack of essential nutrients, and because microbial life is inhibited by the high acidity of the surrounding water and by inhibiting substances formed during the decay of the sphagnoid mosses. Another source of poisonous material may be provided by the high acidity of peat-bogs allowing aluminium, manganese, iron and nickel to reach toxic concentrations. Concerning the aluminium toxicity see, e.g. Clymo (1962). The physiological adaptations of bog plants, aimed at avoiding toxic accumulation of manganese and aluminium by selective exclusion by the roots during absorption, are described by Small (1972*a*).

In ombrotrophic mires there is a poor nitrogen supply from rainfall, increasing with atmospheric pollution. However, Granhall and Solander (1973), working in the Swedish IBP Tundra Biome Project, on a subarctic ombrotrophic mire situated near Abisko in Lappland, recorded some biological fixation of atmospheric nitrogen, mainly by species of *Azotobacter*, adapted to high acidity in elevated areas. In wet depressions and pools, fixation by epiphytic or intracellular blue-green algae, associated with *Sphagnum* and *Drepanocladus*, often occurred in appreciable quantities. These inputs of nitrogen are several times higher than that from precipitation.

Small (1972*b*), comparing the deciduous plants of bogs with non-bog deciduous species, has found that the bog plants are potentially capable of producing about 60% more photosynthate per unit of nitrogen acquired, before losing it by leaf fall. In turn, evergreen bog species, which retain their leaves for several seasons, can potentially produce about 2.4 times more photosynthate per unit of nitrogen acquired than can deciduous bog species. This efficient internal nitrogen recycling is an ecological adaptation of evergreens to nutrient deficiency in the peat substrate.

The supply of phosphorus is also limited in peat-bogs, as its concentration is very low in rainwater (Gorham, 1955, 1957). In addition, its availability falls substantially in acid soils with a high organic content because complexes are formed with organic compounds, iron and aluminium (Patrick & Mikkelsen, 1971).

The cations K^+, Na^+, Ca^{2+}, Mg^{2+}, occurring in the peat water and in sphagnoid mosses are also very scanty, especially in the very acid hummocks of *Sphagnum* sp. The concentration of organic acid anions in the water surrounding the *Sphagnum* plants is far from stoicheometrical equivalence with the H^+ and other cations. It was recognised very early (for review see Gessner, 1959, pp. 260–262) that the high acidity in the raised bogs is caused by *Sphagnum* plants, live or dead, acting as cation exchange materials with the surrounding water containing dilute cations, and that the equivalent organic acid anions are retained in complex structural components in the plants. These cation exchange processes enable both *Sphagnum* and the higher plants of bogs to use all mineral ions, with maximum efficiency in their competition with other plants in a nutrient-poor environment.

Higher plants living successfully in acid peat are adapted to nutrient deficiency, having developed economical nutrient cycles (Small, 1972*a,b*). However, phosphorus and nitrogen remain as limiting factors for many trees growing in bogs such as black spruce (*Picea mariana*) in Northern Minnesota (Watt & Heinselam, 1965) and red maple (*Acer rubrum*) in Massachusetts upland bogs (Moizuk & Livingston, 1966). Numerous measurements of nutrient uptake have been made with *Eriophorum vaginatum*. Goodman and Perkins (1959), in their study of efficient mineral cycling during the year, found that *Eriophorum* accumulated potassium and phosphorus in its living leaves and that these elements were translocated away prior to the death of the leaves.

According to Tamm (1954), *Eriophorum vaginatum* responds only to the addition of phosphorus, but the same species was limited by potassium and phosphorus in a British bog (Goodman & Perkins, 1968). The availability of both elements was increased by adding limestone (pure powdered $CaCO_3$) to an acid bog (Goodman, 1962).

Minerals in fens

In areas of less precipitation, and where the hydrology or the accumulation of plant remains enables water to be retained for long periods over impermeable strata, fens develop. The soils are flooded for much of the year and the water level never sinks below the plant roots. In such biotopes, the mineral nutrition of the vegetation is independent of local precipitation, and the status of available nutrients depends on the nature of the parent rock or sediment. On calcareous rocks, the calcium content in the water is higher and produces a neutral to alkaline reaction. On granite, sandstone, or many other crystalline rocks, the water reaction remains rather acid. In a humid climate, in oceanic or some boreal regions, a leaching process takes place to produce podzolic soils. In such regions, the plant cover accumulates acid raw humus or peat as in typical raised bogs. On the other hand, in more continental regions with temporarily dry summer periods, the less soluble cations, especially calcium, accumulate, shifting the soil and water reaction to neutral or alkaline and transitional mires or fens prevail. The acidophilous plants disappear and are replaced by alkalitrophic communities.

The typical fen plants possess various adaptations to the higher nutrient status and lower water level during the dry periods. The osmotic potential in the mesophyll cells reaches about 1.5 to 2.8 MPa in tall sedges, *Phalaris* and *Phragmites* (Walter, 1968, p. 667). Some xeromorphic features of the assimilatory and transpiratory apparatus are present even in the helophytes. The nutrient content in the plant tissues is also higher, especially in populations growing in nutrient-rich habitats.

Gorham and Pearsall (1956) and Allen and Pearsall (1963) studied the relations between shoot size, production and mineral supply for the common reed (*Phragmites australis*). Allen and Pearsall proved the importance of the principal nutrients for shoot production of *Phragmites* in a calcareous fen using the method of leaf analysis. On some sites the concentration of leaf calcium appeared to limit shoot growth, on others shoot production was correlated with the amount of nitrogen per leaf.

Symbiotic nitrogen-fixation is carried out by micro-organisms associated with lichens and *Alnus* in transient minerotrophic mires and in fens (Stewart, 1975; Gordon *et al.*, 1979).

Littoral swamps and marshes

Many of the principal freshwater wetland ecosystems are found in the undrained and periodically flooded regions beside lakes, backwaters or artificial ponds. These habitats may be classified roughly into four principal groups according to water chemistry (Walter, 1968):

Oligotrophic With calcium on calcareous parent rocks in highlands, or without calcium on acidic subsoils, mainly in oceanic climates.

Eutrophic Rich in nitrogen and phosphorus, mainly on silty soils in agricultural landscapes (artificial ponds for fish farming also belong to this group).

Dystrophic Acid, with coloured water percolating from peat-bogs or other raw humus layers.

Halotrophic In closed basins in arid areas, with chloride, sulphate or carbonate waters, saturated with these anions in various ratios.

The change from oligotrophic to eutrophic Intense studies on mineral cycles have been undertaken in littoral wetlands, related to the eutrophication of oligotrophic lakes and ponds. Björk (1967) has studied the reaction of *Phragmites* populations to the eutrophication of lakes by sewage in central South Sweden, an area of originally oligotrophic lakes, in comparison with eutrophic lakes in Sweden and Denmark. His results give numerous comparable data on the water and bottom soil chemistry and structure and on their influence on the mineral contents in the sap, the production, and the size of *Phragmites* plants. Despite the great variability and dissimilarity in the development of genotypically different *Phragmites* clones, quantitat-ive increases in response to eutrophication by sewage were clearly demonstrated.

Managed fishponds

The IBP investigations on the fishpond littoral wetlands in Czechoslovakia during the years 1965 to 1973 produced numerous comparative analyses of the contents of mineral ions in the communities of emergent and floating macrophytes in relation to the chemistry of bottom soils and water, and to fishpond fertilisation. Two regions were compared differing both climatically and in the mineral status of the waters and soils. The first area was Southern Bohemia, with a cooler suboceanic climate where the fishponds are situated on peat or sandy clay in an originally swampy region (dystrophic to eutrophic wetland ecosystems, according to Walter, 1968). The other area was Southern Moravia in the Pannonian Lowlands, with a warmer subcontinental climate and with shallow fishponds and

Table 6.11. *Ranges of mineral contents and surface loadings in the shoots of littoral invasion stands of* Phragmites australis *at the peak of the growing season (late July to mid-August 1968) in 14 fishponds in South Bohemia and South Moravia (Květ, 1973c)*

Element	Content (mg (g dry wt)$^{-1}$)		Load (g m^{-2})
	Leaves	Stems[a]	Whole shoots
N	33.50–51.0	11.20–23.40	18.81–34.67
P	1.52–2.40	0.84–1.85	1.06–2.67
K	12.10–20.70	5.5–13.90	8.29–21.30
Ca	2.45–6.51	0.62–1.29	1.42–3.98
Mg	1.20–2.09	0.30–0.60	0.61–1.32
Na	0.35–0.80	0.45–1.30	0.46–1.35
Biomass (dry weight, 4–5 samples from 1 m^2)			824–1511

[a] Including leaf sheaths and panicles.

marshes showing a tendency towards salinity (eutrophic to halotrophic wetland ecosystems).

The absorption of mineral nutrients, and mineral cycles taking place in the shallow fishpond littorals, were compared throughout several seasons (Úlehlová *et al.*, 1973; Dykyjová, 1978*b*, 1979). The highest and lowest mineral contents and surface loading of minerals for reed stands harvested at the peak of the growing season in 14 fishponds from both areas investigated are shown in Table 6.11. Dykyjová (1973*a*) has presented similar spatial differences in the nutrient content of different species, sampled in one highly fertilised fishpond in Southern Bohemia, distinguishing accumulation and erosion sites (see Table 6.6 and Fig. 6.8).

The differences in the chemistry of the water, sediments and underlying bottom soils between representative fishponds from both the eutrophic and halotrophic habitats, are described by Úlehlová and Přibil (1978). The higher contents of alkalis and alkaline earths in the water and soil of the halotrophic habitat (Nesyt fishpond) are, however, little reflected in the chemical composition of the plant tissues, with the exception of the underground organs (Květ, 1973*c*). Fertilising and manuring of the fishponds in Czechoslovakia distort the original differences in water and hydrosoil chemistry and also cause wide seasonal and spatial fluctuations in the analytical data.

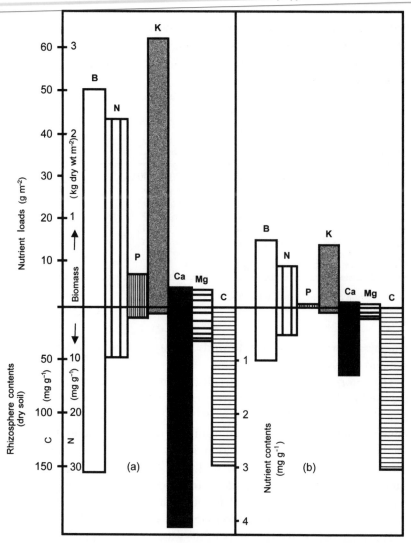

Fig. 6.8. Plant biomass (B), nutrient loads in the biomass, and the nutrient content and organic carbon content (c) of the rhizosphere of (a) an accumulation-type biotope and (b) an erosion-type biotope of *Glyceria maxima* in the littoral of Opatovický fishpond (Dykyjová, 1978b). (Minerals extracted with 2% citric acid; N and C are totals.)

Meso-haline lake littorals

In continental temperate wetland habitats, which sometimes dry up temporarily, the water becomes more saturated with less soluble minerals, especially in regions with calcareous rocks. Nutrient-rich to alkalitrophic fens then tend to prevail. In some cases more or less saline lakes occur, such as the lakes Neusiedler (Löffler, 1979*a*) and Velencei in the Pannonian basin (Austria and Hungary).

The water chemistry has been analysed at several sites in the reedbelt of the Neusiedlersee (Schiemer & Farahat, 1966). Total and suspended phosphorus are lower within the reedbelt than in the lake, while hydrolysable phosphorus is higher; orthophosphate is not consistently different. Such differences probably occur in most lakes. The average salinity is given as 1.5 g l^{-1} but at low water level the salt content can increase to 13.5 g l^{-1} (Burian, 1971). Tóth and Szabó (1958) also give similar analyses from the Pannonian Balaton Lake. They analysed ripe *Phragmites* culms and green leaf blades (September–October) with respect to the technological quality of the reed stems at various erosion and accumulation habitats in the lake littoral. The nitrogen content increased slightly between plants taken from a strong erosion zone and plants from a limosal accumulation zone. Ash, calcium and silica showed irregular differences not related to this sequence. None of the element contents differed greatly from freshwater values (Table 6.6; Kovács *et al.*, 1978).

Freshwater river alluvia and deltas

Some river alluvia and deltas in the temperate zone may be considered as freshwater wetland biotopes with highly eutrophic waters and submerged soils. Rodewald-Rudescu (1974), in his monograph on *Phragmites*, described two main types of reedbelt soil in the Danube delta:

1. Alluvial alkaline sandy soils rich in carbonate (up to 10%) and poor in humic matter ($<5\%$), annually enriched with nutrients owing to regular flooding.
2. Floating mat or island soils (plaur), peaty and acidic (pH = 5.8 to 6.8), poor in carbonate (1%) with more than 40% of organic matter.

The soils are periodically flooded with water from the river rich in silt and nutrients. Rodewald-Rudescu (1974) gives several examples of the chemical composition of flood waters and of both flooded and drained (aerated) soils. Drained soils have higher concentrations of soluble nutrients. The

Table 6.12. *Mineral elements (min.–max. values) in shoots of three Phragmites australis populations from different biotopes in comparison with the soil analyses (0–25 cm) (van der Toorn, 1972)*

Area and Transect no.	Shoot biomass (g dry wt m^{-2})	Elements: in soil (mg (l wet soil)$^{-1}$) in shoots (mg (g dry wt)$^{-1}$) August					
		K	Na	Ca	Mg	P	N
Kalenberg (peat ecotype)	(soil)	12–45	9–22	214–710	26–57	2.10–4.20	2.00–2.90
I	288–1496	7.22–7.96	0.87–1.28	1.75–2.54	0.90–1.13	0.71–1.26	11.10–13.70
II	75–993	3.73–6.44	0.79–1.88	2.24–2.59	1.00–1.52	0.74–1.19	12.10–17.50
Biesbosch (riverine ecotype, Rhine–Maas estuary)	(soil)	57–81	9–30	1940–3200	116–156	444–1106	6.80–95.60
III	416–1734	10.26–16.53	0.57–1.26	1.28–1.98	0.58–0.74	1.31–1.94	12.10–19.60
IV	1165–1550	10.38–12.91	0.56–1.06	1.82–2.98	0.64–0.87	1.33–1.46	13.80–17.80
Zuidland (brackish tidal populations, Rhine–Maas estuary)	(soil)	249–329	573–685	1362–1888	564–694	406–535	1.20–3.50
V	600–828	10.44–11.74	1.67–2.19	1.44–1.78	0.79–1.05	1.30–1.53	12.60–13.30
VI	772–1073	11.78–16.19	1.92–2.70	1.29–1.92	0.75–1.39	1.66–1.85	15.60–18.90
VII	569–1141	10.56–12.87	1.26–2.04	1.45–2.05	0.82–1.05	1.20–1.48	12.60–13.40

mineralisation of nitrogen and phosphorus compounds in the sediments brought in by floods in the Danube delta is described by Neagu-Godeanu *et al.* (1968).

Van der Toorn (1972) gives comparisons of the nutrient contents in three types of *Phragmites* populations in three different habitats in the Netherlands: peaty, nutrient-rich and brackish. The selective absorption capacity of the reed plants, especially for potassium, calcium and magnesium is very striking (see Table 6.12). Gaudet (1975, 1976, 1977b, 1982) has described the behaviour of nutrients in papyrus swamps. Where they grow on inflow deltas, they act as nutrient filters.

Estuaries

Salt marshes develop along sheltered sea coasts on loamy soils. Salt water marshes cover $0.2 \times 10^6 \, km^2$ of flat land supporting salt-tolerant marsh plants and some specialised animal populations (Ponnamperuma, 1972, p. 32). They occur chiefly in the large river deltas in temperate zones. In the tropical zones, mangrove swamps occur in similar habitats. For the literature, see Chapman (1977) and Ketchum (1983).

Many papers deal with the problems of different adaptive reactions of freshwater aquatic and swamp plants to high salinity in the water and soil, and vice versa. Seidel (1955) reports on the plants of *Scirpus lacustris* ssp. *lacustris* transplanted from the littoral of freshwater lakes to the shores of the North and Baltic seas, with a salinity of 1 to $7 \, g \, l^{-1}$ sodium chloride. New shoots sprouting from the transplanted plants were similar to the more halotrophic *S. lacustris* ssp. *tabernaemontani*. On the other hand, *S.* ssp. *tabernaemontani*, transplanted from Dutch coastal biotopes to German freshwater lakes, tended towards *S.* ssp. lacustris after 4 years of cultivation. The ash analyses of both species from both biotopes, however, did not show any significant differences in the chemical composition of the plant tissues. Similar results were reported by Waisel and Rechav (1971) on glycophytic and halophytic populations of *Phragmites*. These authors presume that the similar rates of uptake of sodium and chloride ions and a similar distribution of these ions in both types of plants are due to an adaptive mechanism which ensures that salts are kept at the same low level.

Specialised halophytes such as *Salicornia*, *Spartina*, *Salsola* or *Limonium*, absorb and accumulate chloride ions in the cell sap of their transpiring organs to high osmotic values (2 to 4 MPa), surpassing those of the soil solution in the rhizosphere. The selective absorption capacity of halophytic plants, high for chloride ions, and less marked for sulphate ions, enables the plants to maintain internal ratios different from those in the soil. The succulent character of halophytes is caused by a specifically high hydration of their protoplasm by chloride ions. The cations Na^+, Ca^{2+}, K^+, Mg^{2+} are rather indifferent, the sulphate anion produces a xeromorphic effect. Carbonate soils with calcium sulphate often show enhanced alkalinity caused by ionic interchange between calcium and sodium cations giving rise to highly alkaline ('natron' or 'solonchak') soils containing $NaCl + Na_2CO_3 + Na_2SO_4$. These soils are common in many arid areas such as Egypt, India, California, Central Asia and also in the estuary of the Rhône (La Camargue).

For other adaptations and the chemistry of plants and soils occurring in the extreme saline marshes or in inland sulphate, carbonate and chloride lakes, see Gessner (1959), Walter (1968), Epstein (1969), Pigott (1969) and Reimold and Queen (1974).

According to Williams (1972), in most estuaries, bays and other coastal areas, available nitrogen limits the production of phytoplankton for most of the time; in contrast to freshwaters, where phosphorus is most commonly the limiting nutrient. Williams gives several examples of both polluted and unpolluted estuaries on the North American Atlantic coast. Rooted plants, especially *Spartina alterniflora* and *Zostera marina* may often outproduce the phytoplankton. Research described by Pomeroy and Wiegert (1981) and McRoy *et al.* (1972) indicates that two main processes combine to produce levels of phosphorus adequate for the growth of phytoplankton. Firstly, a large amount of phosphate is adsorbed on the sediments in the estuaries, which, through purely physical adsorption–desorption processes, tends to maintain a suitable concentration in the water. Secondly, *Spartina* or *Zostera* plants take up phosphorus from the deeper sediments and by excretion, consumption and decomposition of their detritus provide another source for the water. Williams (1972) states that the marsh sediments contain enough phosphorus to last for millenia, within reach of the *Spartina* roots. The mathematical model of the flux of phosphorus in a Georgia estuary described in Pomeroy and Wiegert (1981) shows that a thousandfold reduction of the amount of phosphorus initially present in the ecosystem would have slight effects on its living components. They concluded that the high stability of estuaries, in terms of population density and species composition, metabolic rates from year to year, and nutrient concentrations, is largely the result of the presence of a nutrient reserve in the sediments and of a mechanism for mobilising this reserve.

Nitrogen, on the other hand, is often highly deficient in shallow estuaries and coastal areas, in contrast to open oceans (Williams, 1972; Daiber, 1974; Day *et al.*, 1973; cf. soil nitrogen and phosphorus in fresh and brackish water soils in Table 6.12). Nitrogen transformations lead to a relative accumulation of phosphorus even in waters which initially have an N:P ratio of 15:1 (an average for surface oceanic water). Day *et al.* (1973) considered that one of the most important sources of new nitrogen for the estuary was probably nitrogen fixation by bacteria and blue-green algae.

Williams and Murdoch (1969) studied the potential importance of *Spartina alterniflora* in conveying radionuclides of zinc, manganese, and iron into estuarine food chains. The elemental composition indicated the maximum amount which might be available to animals from the grass, and can be converted to concentration factors assuming a normal sea water. These concentrations factors range from 370 (Zn, mature shoots) to 164 000 (Fe, dead material). Concentrations were slightly higher in young material than in mature shoots and were much higher in the dead material. The high iron content of dead *Spartina* may raise the iron content of organisms feeding on it. The analyses of faecal material produced by detritus-feeding crabs (Bootle & Knauer, 1972), and the values mentioned by Ho and Barrett (1975), also show the importance of increasing concentrations in the food chains.

Springs, streams and rivers

The ecology of such wetland sites may be regarded as intermediate between the flood-plain and deltaic areas, with a constant input of nutrients, and lake littorals, with prolonged or permanent inundation. Emergent vegetation is normally present only as a narrow marginal zone, unless the stream is very slow and shallow.

In many rivers the supply of nutrients far exceeds the demand of the plants, and physical and biotic factors are more important (Casey & Newton, 1973; Westlake, 1975b). The growth of plants then makes little difference to the ionic concentrations in the water, which are governed by inputs, exchanges with the sediments and microbiological activities. In nutrient-poor waters, or very small, densely populated streams, nutrients may be more important and plants can influence their concentrations during rapid growth (Casey & Westlake, 1974; Haslam, 1978).

Adams *et al.* (1973) have investigated the mineral content of 15 species of emergent rooted macrophytes (and 30 species of submerged and floating plants), collected from 52 locations in the Delaware, Susquehanna and Allegheny catchments in Pennsylvania. The collection sites were characterised according to different categories of land use: forestry, recreation, mining, optimalised agriculture, urban and industrial. The results show a wide range of interspecific as well as intraspecific variations, and of differences between sites, presumably related to the status of the elements in the environment.

7

Micro-climatic conditions and water economy of wetlands vegetation

J. KRÓLIKOWSKA, K. PŘIBÁŇ and P. ŠMÍD

Basic features of the micro-climate

Shallow waters

The production processes in all ecosystems are dependent on the physical properties of the environment. Radiation, temperature and water supply are among the basic factors influencing photosynthesis, respiration, growth and other physiological processes in autotrophic plants. Other ecosystem processes, such as the decomposition of dead organic matter, and the activity, food uptake, respiration and reproduction rate of animals, are also influenced by temperature, humidity and radiation.

The macro-climate of a given area is determined by its geographical position and large-scale air circulation. The plant cover, perhaps more than any other active surface, alters the climatic conditions in its surroundings. Studies on the micro-climate within the plant cover and an evaluation of the feedback effects of the plant biomass, both live and dead, on the micro-climate are indispensable for an understanding of ecosystem functioning. The immediate result of the mutual relationship between vegetation and micro-climate is the water economy of the vegetation. For general information on these subjects, the reader is referred to Geiger (1961); Monteith (1973, 1975–76), Slavík (1974) and Kreeb (1974).

Wetlands are more complicated than either purely aquatic or purely terrestrial ecosystems because three phases are present: air, water and soil. Moreover, the relative importance of these varies considerably in both space and time. Despite the frequent large-scale uniformity of wetland plant stands, they show a considerable diversity of micro-environments in space and time, caused in the first place by variations of water level, plant density and management.

The physical processes taking place in the boundary between an active surface and the lower layers of the atmosphere may be expressed in units of energy flux (J m^{-2} s^{-1} for instantaneous values and MJ m^{-2} for the hourly or daily totals). The principle that energy can neither be created nor destroyed allows the energy inputs and outputs to be written in the form of the energy balance equation:

$$R_n = G + C + \lambda E + D \qquad (1)$$

where R_n is the net radiation flux to ($+$, usually during the daytime), or from the surface ($-$, at night), G is the heat flux from the surface into the deeper layers of ground ($+$, in opposite direction $-$), and C is the flux of sensible heat into ($+$) or from ($-$) the atmosphere, caused mostly by mixing of the air masses, which are in turbulent motion. λE is a similar flux of latent heat, i.e. used for evaporation ($+$), or gained from condensation ($-$); λ being the latent heat of vaporisation, and E the evaporation or condensation rate. The last term D is the rate of energy input ($-$) or output ($+$) horizontally, by advection. It may be of sensible, as well as of latent, heat and depends on the wind speed and on the horizontal gradients of temperature and water vapour content of the air, in the direction of the wind. These gradients are usually negligible for large homogeneous areas (with the upwind 'fetch' from an observation site of the order of 100 m), but for smaller water bodies, wetlands, or irrigated fields they may be considerable, and an advective energy income causes an increase of the latent heat flux up to several hundred J m^{-2} s^{-1}.

For plant communities, two other terms may be needed, i.e. J and A_Λ, which are the net fluxes of energy into physical and biochemical storage in the column enclosing unit horizontal area of vegetation, respectively. But, the term J (rate of change of the sensible or latent heat content of the vegetation and of the air within the column) is negligible except in the case of forest, and A_Λ (for energy stored by carbon dioxide assimilation, the specific energy fixation for CO_2 is about 1.15×10^4 J g^{-1}) does not exceed 16 J m^{-2} s^{-1}.

Typical values of the energy budget over vegetation (upwind fetch at least 100 to 200 m) for mid-day without clouds are: $R_n = +500$, $D = \pm 25$, $G = +25$, $J = +2$, $A_\Lambda = +12$, and $(C + \lambda E) = +461$ J m^{-2} s^{-1}. For a more detailed description, the reader is referred to Monteith (1975–6, pp. 93–100).

Net radiation may also be defined as the sum of all the radiative inputs to and outputs from a given surface:

$$R_n = I_d - I_u + L_d - L_u \qquad (2)$$

where the subscripts d and u indicate downward and upward fluxes respectively; I_d is the incident short-wave radiation (direct from the sun and diffuse from the sky), and I_u is the short-wave radiation reflected by the surface. Their relation:

$$= I_u I_d^{-1}$$

is named reflectivity of the surface (or less accurately 'albedo'). L_u is the long-wave radiation of the surface, which is a function of the emissivity and temperature of the surface and the Stephan–Boltzmann constant. The long-wave radiation of the sky reaching the earth (L_d) depends mainly on the content of water vapour and on the temperature of the air, and may vary from $100 \, \text{J m}^{-2} \text{s}^{-1}$ in a very cold, dry atmosphere to $500 \, \text{J m}^{-2} \text{s}^{-1}$ on a cloudy day.

The value of the net radiation flux for water is determined primarily by the usually small reflection of short-wave radiation (albedo), which depends, more than that of other surfaces, on sun elevation, but it is only about 10% even at a sun elevation of 40°. The albedo of the dark rough intercepting surface of a coniferous forest is comparably small (Geiger, 1961).

Contrary to most other natural surfaces, in water the radiation is not totally absorbed or reflected by the uppermost thin layer, but some wavelengths penetrate to considerable depths. The other physical peculiarities of water, significant from the viewpoint of energy balance, are its large heat capacity, $4.184 \, \text{J cm}^{-3} \, \text{K}^{-1} = (1.0 \, \text{cal cm}^{-3} \, \text{K}^{-1})$ and its considerable thermal conductivity, 5.4 to $6.3 \, \text{W cm}^{-1} \, \text{K}^{-1}$ (1.3 to 1.5 cal $\text{cm}^{-1} \, \text{s}^{-1} \, \text{K}^{-1}$). Owing to the large heat capacity, the ground heat flux component in the energy balance equation is larger for water than at a soil surface. The heat accumulated in water is released as either sensible or latent heat for heating the air and/or for evaporation. According to their area and depth, water bodies tend to reduce the amplitude between day and night or winter and summer temperatures.

For the life in cold and temperate waters, the thermal anomaly of water is highly important as the density of water is greatest at 4°C. Hence, deeper layers of water maintain this temperature and remain fluid even if the water surface is frozen and the water shallow, except in extreme conditions. Hibernating plant organs, animals and micro-organisms survive in water near the bottom without damage.

In shallow waters, rapid increases of temperature (in mornings and in spring) and mean water temperatures (in the afternoon and in summer) higher than that of the free air (about 2 to 3°C or more) are usually observed (Szumiec, 1973, 1986; Figs. 7.1 and 7.2). A possible explanation

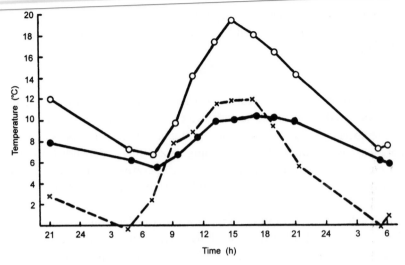

Fig. 7.1. Daily course of air temperature at 2 m height (×—×) and of water temperature at 10 cm depth in a cut (O—O) and uncut (●—●) reed stand. (Holhovecký fishpond, Czechoslovakia, 14–16.4.71; Šmíd, 1973).

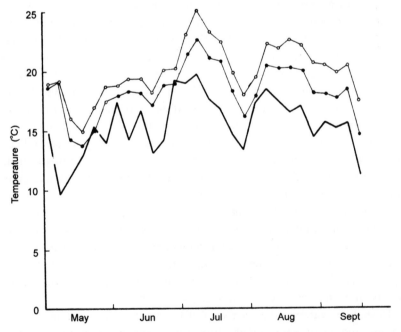

Fig. 7.2. Annual course of temperature of the air (——) and water in a fishpond (O—O) and in a narrow strip of reed (●—●), both at 20 cm depth (Opatovický fishpond, Czechoslovakia; K. Přibáň, original data).

Table 7.1. *Temperature fluctuations (°C) at various depths of water in an English lowland pond on a sunny day (10 June 1968, sunshine duration 11.1 h) (after Martin, 1972)*

	Air temperature	Water temperature at depth (cm)		
		0–2	10–12	58–60 (bottom)
Minimum	4.4	10.6	13.9	17.0
Maximum	23.6	28.3	19.8	17.9
Amplitude	19.2	17.7	5.9	0.9

is that the net radiative input to the water is greater (owing to its smaller reflectivity) than to the solid surface. Also the long-wave radiative loss during night is probably decreased by a considerable amount of vapour in the air above water. The heat accumulated in the water in these ways causes the relatively rapid rise in temperature despite the water's large heat capacity. This enables algae and macrophytes to grow very fast during this period.

In such shallow waters, which are the usual habitats of hydro- and helophytes, stratification into epi-, meta- and hypo-limnion does not occur. If the water area is large and/or exposed to wind, the water is stirred and mixed by waves. The temperature and chemistry are almost uniform at different depths. On the other hand, in small water bodies, where the mixing effect of turbulence is less efficient, a conspicuous thermal stratification often develops which is less permanent than in deep waters. Martin (1972) measured the water temperature in small lowland ponds (10 to 50 m in diameter, in England). He found significantly different temperatures as well as amplitudes at different depths. The thin water layer near the surface was warmer than the surrounding air, especially at the time of the night minimum temperature of the surface water (see Table 7.1).

In spring, when night frosts occur, Šmíd (1973) has observed that the air temperature near the water level remained above freezing point and that rime did not occur on the leaves or stems of helophytes growing in the water, while an adjacent meadow was fully covered with rime. The heat absorbed by the water during the day heats up the lowest air layer during the night or is used for evaporation. Under usual summer conditions, even though the absolute humidity of this air layer is high, its relative humidity remains low and condensation does not take place during the night

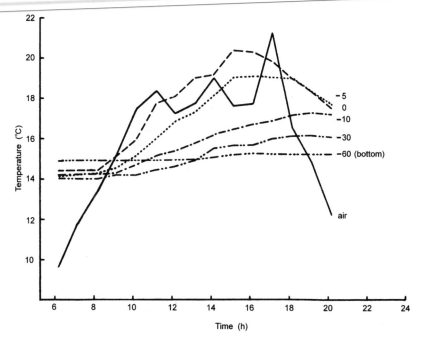

Fig. 7.3. Daily course of temperature in and above a dense, submerged stand of *Ceratophyllum demersum* and *Stratiotes aloides* on a sunny day. Depths in cm (20.8.67, Overijssel, the Netherlands; Úlehlová, 1970).

(Willer, 1949*a*; Šmíd, 1973). Along a transect across the whole wetland zonation, from open water to a sedge marsh and alder (*Alnus glutinosa*) carr, the most extreme summer temperature conditions (amplitude between the daytime maximum and early morning minimum) occurred in the short sedge (*Carex* spp.) marsh with a *Sphagnum* undergrowth (Květ, 1984).

In submerged or floating aquatic vegetation

A dense vegetation of submerged plants greatly reduces mixing of the water by waves and a large part of the incoming radiation is intercepted by the plants present in the upper water layers. A steep temperature gradient usually develops below the very warm surface water. For example, the temperature conditions in submerged stands of *Stratiotes aloides* were measured in north-west Overijssel, Netherlands, by Úlehlová (1970). She found a significant thermal stratification (see Fig. 7.3). Similar temperature conditions were found by Martin (1972) in water thickly covered by filamentous algae.

The effect of floating plants is very similar to that of submerged plants. The floating leaves not only absorb much of the incoming radiation but they reflect more than an open water surface. The albedo of horizontally situated leaves is about 20% or more (compare with the water albedo given above). Gessner (1955) measured the penetration of radiation in stands of several plant species with floating leaves and found only 3 to 7% was transmitted. Owing to the smaller energy income, the water remains colder below the floating leaves, but a thin surface layer with the leaves is overheated. Gessner (1955) found the difference between the daily temperature maxima of the surface water and that below a thick layer of *Najas guadalupensis* to be 10 °C in tropical marshes of South America; in open water the difference was only 0.2 °C. Similar conditions have been found by Martin (1972, pp. 461–4):

A thick surface layer of algae or other surface plants reduced the amplitude and rate of fluctuation in the water temperature.... The water temperature near the surface did not fall to the same minimum [i.e. as in open water] when surface algae and plants were present and was never inversely stratified.

Few, if any, data are available on the heat budget of waters with submerged or floating vegetation. The temperature conditions in water covered by *Lemna* have been illustrated by E. Rejmánková's results (in Přibáň *et al.*, 1977; Fig. 7.4). They indicate that the net radiation income of the water below *Lemna* over 24 hours is reduced, probably because of the increased reflectivity. The ground heat flux is also reduced but the overheated vegetation cover increases both the sensible and latent heat fluxes. The water vapour pressure gradient above a *Lemna* cover is steeper than above open water, which indicates that evapo-transpiration from water with duckweeds will be higher than the evaporation from open water (see Dale & Gillespie, 1976 and below, p. 384). Přibáň *et al.* (1986) found the same for cover by *Nuphar lutea*.

In vegetation of emergent macrophytes (helophytes)

Emergent macrophytes usually do not grow in water deeper than 2 m, but very often they form stands on sites situated above the normal water level in zones which are flooded only temporarily and/or are waterlogged. According to the position of the water level, littoral, limosal and terrestrial ecophases may be distinguished (Hejný, 1960, 1971). The water depth

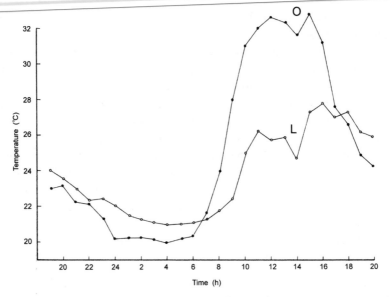

Fig. 7.4. Daily course of temperatures in the near-surface water layer in open water
(O, O—O) and in a thick cover of duckweeds (*Lemna gibba*) (L, ●—●) (Lednice
fishponds, Czechoslovakia, on two bright and hot summer days 28–29.7.71; data
by E. Rejmánková in Přibáň *et al.*, 1977).

considerably influences the species composition, micro-climatic conditions and the production processes in wetland ecosystems. Temperate
dense reed (*Phragmites australis*) stands may be taken as an example of
helophyte communities (Figs. 7.1, 7.2, 7.5–7.9). From the micro-climatological viewpoint, the most effective factor is the considerable amount of
organic matter present in the helophyte communities, which may be living
or dead, and the latter often persists for a long time (e.g. the resistant dead
stems of *Phragmites*). Such standing dead material may be removed by
wind and waves from more exposed sites, or by human intervention
(cutting), making marked differences between sites (compare the temperatures in cut and uncut stands in Fig. 7.1). A thick layer of litter
accumulating at the base of the stands influences the micro-climate, and
plant growth and survival, particularly by its heat-insulating effect (Přibáň
et al., 1997).

Thus the temperature and humidity conditions in wetlands change as
the amount and proportions of biomass and dead plant material vary in
both space and time.

As the helophyte stands develop a typical vertical structure (see Chapter 2) up to the height of several metres, a porous medium is created, which strongly reduces air movement near the water or ground surface. Willer (1949*a*) has measured wind speeds at the edge of a dead *Phragmites* stand fringing an ice-covered lake in winter at 15 m from the edge; the wind velocity was reduced to some 10% of that in the open. Rudescu *et al.* (1965) and Bernatowicz *et al.* (1976) present similar results.

During perennation the dry stem surfaces absorb the incoming radiation, and most of its energy is transformed into heat which increases their temperature. The turbulent sensible heat flux into the atmosphere is reduced because of the small wind speed inside the stand. Consequently, the evaporation from the *water surface* is also low in littoral stands, and it is even less in limosal and terrestrial stands. In winter or early spring the differences between the air temperature inside and 2 m above the stand may attain 3 °C or even more. The highest temperatures occur deeper in the stands at mid-day than in the evening, in dependence on sun elevation (Fig. 7.5). The higher temperatures and little air movement make the reed stands a suitable refuge for a number of animals during the cold seasons. There is little difference in water vapour pressure within the stands.

The freezing depth of the water and soil in the reedbelt seems to depend on total water depth and on the amount of the dead plant material present. Figure 7.6 shows the freezing depth in different zones of a fishpond littoral during a winter with a high water level. The ice was thicker nearer to the open water; in terrestrial reed stands the soil froze only superficially. The difference is probably due to the much greater heat conductivity of water as compared with the soil rich in organic matter and insulated by reed litter. The thick mats of dead material from sedges (*Carex*) and grasses have a similar insulating effect. In early spring, the ice persists below a dense undergrowth of *Carex* within limosal *Phragmites* stands longer than anywhere else in the reedbelt. This phenomenon contrasts with the frequently occurring high air temperature observed immediately above the dead sedge leaves on sunny days in the spring. Higher temperatures are found in the soil in terrestrial stands than in the limosal stands; evidently, the smaller amount of standing dead plant material intercepts less radiation and the drier soil warms up rapidly. However, the most favourable early spring conditions occur in littoral reed stands; here, the average water temperature is often higher than that of the air (Fig. 7.7).

Removal of dead reeds from littoral stands (e.g. by harvesting) further

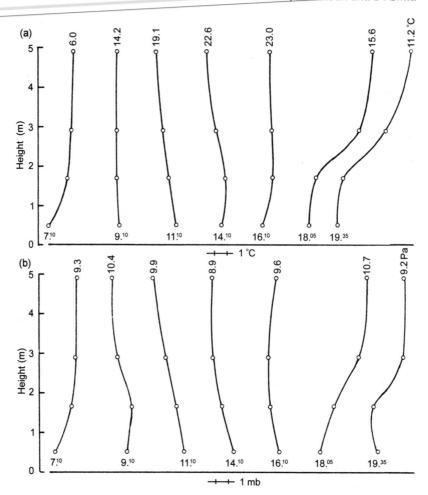

Fig. 7.5. Vertical profiles of temperature (a, °C) and water vapour pressure (b, mb or 100 Pa) in a terrestrial reed stand. Each profile shows temperature or vapour pressure at the top and time (h) at the bottom (Nesyt fishpond, Czechoslovakia, 21.3.74; P. Šmíd, original data).

improves the temperature conditions, and the relatively high water and bottom temperatures promote a fast and even growth of the young reeds as well as the development of a rich plant and animal life in the water. On the other hand, in terrestrial reed stands, winter harvesting exposes the unsheltered young reeds to late night frosts. The regenerated shoots are usually smaller and thinner. The sprouting of reeds in limosal stands with a sedge undergrowth starts much later than elsewhere and is

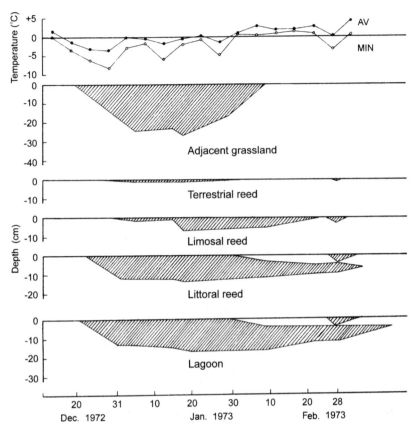

Fig. 7.6. Mean (AV ●—●) and minimum (MIN ○—○) air temperatures, and depth of ice (shaded areas) in various zones of the reed belt (Nesyt fishpond in the winter of 1972–73, when the fishpond was filled with water; P. Šmíd, original data).

uneven, probably because of the variable thickness of the litter layer. Haslam (1969*b*,*c*) has discussed the effects of frost on reed growth in the spring.

With the growth of the reed (or other helophytes), the micro-climatic conditions change. The biomass increases and can be about 2 kg dry wt m^{-2}, or more, at the peak of the growing season. The leaf area also increases and the leaf area index (LAI) usually attains values between 4.5 and 7.0 so the developing canopy intercepts more and more incoming radiation. The reflectivity is quite high, about 18% (see p. 000). Gessner (1955) measured the light penetration into a reed stand at the water level and arrived at values of 3 to 60% of the incoming radiation, the mean

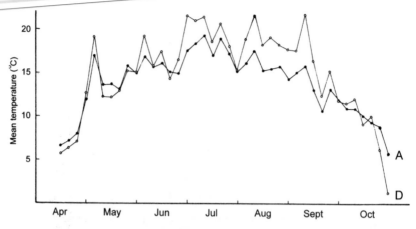

Fig. 7.7. Seasonal course of temperatures, averaged over 5 days, of water in a large stand of reed at 10 cm depth (D ●—●) and of the air at 5 m above water level (A ○—○) (Nesyt fishpond, 1973; P. Šmíd, original data).

value being about 16%. Data on reed stands of different density are given by Straškraba and Pieczyńska (1970). The light interception in helophyte stands has been thoroughly examined by Dykyjová (1971a) and Ondok (1977) (see Chapter 2).

The considerable amount of leaves, usually well saturated with water (see Rychnovská, 1967, 1973), evaporates large amounts of water. In mature reed stands, the leaf temperature is much the same as that of the surrounding air (Tuschl, 1970; J. Gloser, pers. comm.).

As a result of the development of helophyte stands, the temperature gradients in the air near to the vegetation surface become only small and the humidity gradients become steeper (Šmíd, 1973). Below a dense extensive canopy, the air remains colder throughout the whole day.

Similar temperature profiles (characterised by maxima in the middle canopy layer) have been found in rice fields, where the sensible heat flux was upwards above a level at about 40% of the stand height and downwards below this. The heat transferred downwards is mainly used in evaporation from the water surface (Uchijima, 1976).

Water and bottom temperatures in littoral reed stands are lower than the average temperatures of the free air and open water during most of the vegetation season, because of the decreased energy income (e.g. the free air and reed stand water temperatures in Fig. 7.7). Uchijima (1961) found the average temperatures (over 10 days) of the water in paddy fields to be 2–3 °C higher than the free air temperatures in the early growing season

(May, first half of June) but about 1 °C lower in summer (July and August) when the stand was fully developed. The winter temperature regime was comparable to a winter-cut reed stand.

In the reedbelts in contact with the warmer open water, the water as well as air temperatures depend on the degree of mixing of the cool reed stand water and air with those from the open water area (Fig. 7.2; Přibáň, 1973), and the air inside may be warmer than the free air overnight (Bernatowicz *et al.*, 1976; Květ, 1984).

The presence of a stable source of water vapour and the reduced air movement increase the air humidity in the littoral reed stands. An example for a bright summer day (sunshine duration 12 h), with a maximum wind speed of about 5 m s^{-1} in the afternoon, is given in Fig. 7.8. Further data on air humidity in reed stands are given by Rudescu *et al.* (1965), Šmíd (1973), Bernatowicz *et al.* (1976) and Přibáň *et al.* (1977, 1986). Willer (1949*a*) recorded higher relative air humidity inside a littoral reed stand than above the open water surface during a whole summer day. According to Willer, the summer micro-climate in reed stands is comparable with that in the tropical rain forest. This environment is very suitable for a great many animal populations, especially insects.

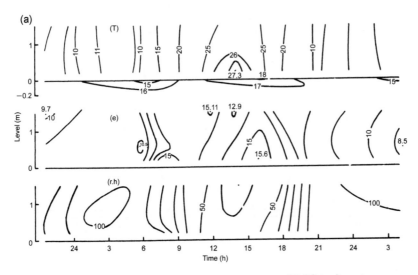

Fig. 7.8. Isolines of air and soil and water temperatures (T, °C top), water vapour pressure (e, Pa, middle) and relative humidity (r.h., %, bottom) over 24 h in a terrestrial (*a*) and a littoral uncut (*b*) reed stands, 18.8.71 (Šmíd, 1973).

(*continued*)

Evapo-transpiration from wetland vegetation

Theory

The typical micro-climatic conditions evidently influence the energy balance in wetlands. Data on the radiation balance in wetland vegetation are very scarce. Measurements taken at the Nesyt fishpond, Czechoslovakia, indicate that the reflectivity of a fully developed dense *Phragmites* stand is about 18%. This is less than the reflectivity of grass (about 20 to 25%) and more than that of forests (about 10 to 13%). As the temperature of the leaves does not differ much from the ambient air temperature, the long-wave emission may be assumed to be smaller in the reed stands than in most other plant communities. Since the ground heat flux mostly depends on the radiation income to the water or soil below the canopy, which is very small in fully developed stands, the ground heat flux rarely exceeds 10%.

The other components of the heat balance, the sensible and latent heat fluxes, are usually treated as their ratio, known as the Bowen ratio (β). This is defined as:

$$\beta = H / LE \tag{3}$$

usually calculated according to the formula:

$$\beta = 0.66 \times \Delta T / \Delta e$$

where ΔT and Δe are, respectively, the differences in temperature (°C or K) and water vapour pressure (mb or cPa) between two levels of measurement. In rice fields with a fully developed canopy ($LAI = 4$), a Bowen ratio of 0.18 was found on a bright August day. Corresponding values found in a maize field and above shallow water were 0.55 and 0.08, respectively, on days with similar weather. The mean Bowen ratio in rice fields was 0.27 for the period July to September, with a considerable increase during the ripening of the rice crop (Uchijima, 1976). In accordance with the seasonal changes of the temperature gradient as described above, positive values of the Bowen ratio were recorded in the reed stands at Nesyt in spring and autumn when both H and LE were negative, but they were about zero or sometimes negative in summer, with LE negative and H positive, when *Phragmites* was fully developed (Fig. 7.9). When the Bowen ratio becomes negative, the heat needed for evapo-transpiration is usually obtained from the air as well as from the radiation income. A negative Bowen ratio may also result from heat advection

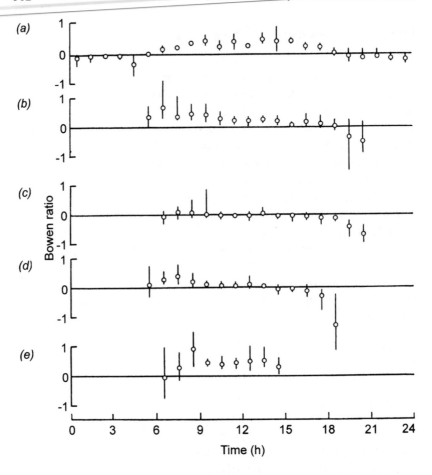

Fig. 7.9. Bowen ratio (H/LE) for a littoral reed stand at the Nesyt fishpond; ranges (vertical bars) and means values (○) for groups of cloudless days: (a) 10, 12 and 13 May; (b) 18, 21, 22, 28, 29, 31 May and 1 June; (c) 17, 18 June and 2, 3, 4 and 17 July; (d) 6, 7, 8, 10, 11 and 12 August; (e) 16 September and 3, 5, 6 October (Šmíd, 1975).

('oasis effect'), and then it depends on wind speed, dryness of the surrounding area and, indirectly, on the distance from the boundary with warmer areas (fetch). Such increased evaporation has been observed and examined, for example, in irrigated rice fields in the semi-arid region of Australia (Evans, 1971; Lang, Evans & Ho, 1974).

In temperate regions, where the daily sum of net solar radiation can reach 23 MJ m^{-2}, the total daily evapo-transpiration from a large reed stand, increased by heat advection may be up to 10 mm (of water column, 10 kg m^{-2}). Such values are reached only by well-developed reed stands at the peak of the growing season, see the discussions by Šmíd (1975) and Rychnovská *et al.* (1980). The average seasonal values for temperate wetlands are 2 to 4 mm d^{-1}, with daily maxima of up to 7 mm d^{-1} (Přibáň & Ondok, 1985, 1986).

Evapo-transpiration from wetlands in comparison with evaporation from open water

Many authors have attempted to solve this question, which is of great importance for water management, but the results have been contradictory. The first shortcoming of many such comparisons is that the evapo-transpiration from a plant community is compared with that from a body of open water which is usually deeper than the water in the wetland; the depth affects the energy balance components significantly, especially by increasing the ground heat flux and decreasing the water temperature and hence the evaporation. The evaporation from a lake, especially in arid regions, also depends on the dryness of the surroundings. According to Linacre (1976, p. 342):

When the country was dry, the swamp evaporation over four day-time hours was only a third of the lake, whereas, after heavy rain had wetted the entire region, lake evaporation was reduced to about that of the swamp. This change emphasises the importance of the oasis effect on the relatively small lake, and differences between the lake and swamp vegetation are trivial in comparison.

In general, it is extremely difficult to set up experimental conditions to measure water loss accurately, which represent conditions in real water bodies, particularly with regard to area of surface, wind velocity, and fetch, but also to other aspects of the micro-climate. Small isolated groups of helophytes often have a higher leaf area index than large stands and they evaporate rather as three-dimensional bodies (Królikowska, 1987). Although experiments may not give absolute values, they serve to elucidate the action of some of the important factors (Mitchell, 1974), and the results may provide useful information for an evaluation of evaporative water loss from sites such as narrow channels and ditches overgrown by helophytes. Both experimental and field studies have rarely adequately characterised the biomass and vitality of the vegetation which influence the evapo-transpiration.

The total evapo-transpiration from a stand is the sum of evaporation from the exposed water surface (E_w) and transpiration from the plant (E_c). Occupation of the surface by the plant and the formation of a relatively still, humid micro-climate greatly reduce evaporation from the water (e.g. Kuznetsov, 1954, annual rate 0.35 of open water rate (E_o); Burian, 1971, growing season, 0.57; Bernatowicz et al., 1976, 3 years, 0.47). Uchijima (1976) found the daily evaporation (E_w) in a paddy field to be about 3 to 5 mm in spring, but less than 1 mm (about 20% of the total stand evaporation) when the stand was fully developed.

Experiments comparing the water losses from containers with floating plants, such as _Salvinia molesta, Lemna_ sp. and _Eichhornia crassipes_, with containers containing water only, showed that evapo-transpiration was increased relative to evaporation (E_o) by increase in temperature, increase in wind speed, decrease in humidity and by greater size and vigour of plants (Little, 1967; Gavenčiak, 1972). The ratios of evapo-transpiration to evaporation varied from 0.45 : 1 to 6.6 : 1 with environmental conditions, species and time of year.

Piasecki (1967), who examined the behaviour of stands of _Lemna_ and other freely floating plants, states that:

The hydrophytes, floating on or below the water surface, increase the evaporation in the first half of the vegetation season, but they reduce it from September to November, as compared with open water. During the whole vegetation season the evaporative water loss from the water surface covered with plants floating on and below the water surface was 103 and 110 per cent of open water evaporation, respectively.

The results of Gavenčiak's examinations (1972) of _Lemna_ evaporation were not very different. In his experiments, the evaporation from a tank with duckweed was about 1.2 times that from a tank without vegetation during the hottest month. The yearly total was also 12 times greater at one of the experimental stations, but a little smaller (about 0.98) at another station.

According to Timmer and Weldon (1967), pools covered with _Eichhornia crassipes_ lost 3.7 times more than open water. The high ratios found for this plant, often over 3 and up to 6.6, suggest that it may be a greater danger to water stored in tropical reservoirs if it behaves similarly in entire stands. Similar experiments have been set up with helophytes, including _Phragmites australis_ and _Typha_ spp. Evapo-transpiration rates found by Rudescu et al. (1965) and Bernatowicz et al. (1976) were quite high (900–1600 mm y^{-1}). The latter study showed that the losses from the containers with plants were three to five times the loss from adjacent containers of

Table 7.2. *Correlations between: I evaporation and evapo-transpiration, II maximum daily temperature and evapo-transpiration, and III wind velocity and evapo-transpiration for different aquatic and wetland species (compiled from Brezny* et al., *1973)*

	Correlation coefficient		
Plant species	I	II	III
Cyperus rotundus	0.78	0.73	0.63
Typha angustifolia	0.88	0.72	0.74
Ipomea aquatica	0.84	0.64	0.57
Eichhornia crassipes	0.98	0.76	0.81
Trapa natans	0.89	0.50 ns	0.38 ns
Pistia stratiotes	0.15 ns	0.48 ns	0.31 ns

ns, not significant.

open water, and that the rates of loss from isolated containers on land were much higher than from containers placed within the reed belt. The values obtained by Gavenčiak (1972) were particularly high, for example, the maximum values of daily evapo-transpiration of *P. australis* were 17.9 and 17.8 mm d^{-1} on two distinct sites in southern Slovakia. The influence of advection of dry air was probably considerable in these experiments.

Several authors have used earlier data to calculate values for their own situations. Brezny *et al.* (1973) calculated, on the basis of reliable data obtained by Otis (1914) from measurements on stands in tanks placed in natural situations, that the evapo-transpiration of *Typha latifolia*, *Acorus calamus*, *Scirpus validus* and *Nymphaea odorata* would be, respectively, 3.1, 2.5, 2.0 and 1.0 to 1.2 times greater than the open-water evaporation. According to Otis, the reasons for differences between the species are in their different anatomical and morphological structure and stand structure. The uneven horizontal stand biomass distribution, vertical canopy structure and micro-climatic conditions are probably important as well.

On the basis of experiments measuring the daily fall in water level in tanks of plants, probably stood in a garden, Brezny *et al.* (1973) examined the correlation between evapo-transpiration of several species and individual meteorological factors. Significant correlations were found with the evaporation from an evaporimeter, maximum daily temperature, and daily mean wind velocity for four out of six species (Table 7.2). They also found that the evapo-transpiration of their dense experimental stands of

Eichhornia crassipes, Typha angustifolia and *Cyperus rotundus* was, respectively, about 0.3 to 0.4, 0.6 to 0.7 and 1.3 to 1.5 times that of open water in equivalent conditions. Kuznetsov (1954) and Kovařík (1958) suggested ratios of 1 to 3 for various species of helophyte.

Many of the errors inherent in experimental studies are overcome by placing the containers of plants or water within an extensive stand of plants. Tuschl (1970) and Bernatowicz *et al.* (1976) thus obtained similar results for the Neusiedlersee (Austria) and the Mazurian Lakes (Poland). Evapo-transpiration rates in dense stands were 500–1400 mm y^{-1}, while evaporation rates from the open water were 430–700 mm y^{-1}. The latter authors showed that the ratio could vary from lake to lake (0.92 to 1.27) according to the specific composition and weight of the vegetation and the relative area covered. It can be deduced that an extensive, relatively sparse stand, that is sufficient to reduce wind speed and evaporation from the water surface within the stand, will produce a low ratio, especially if the dead stems persist throughout the winter (e.g. *Phragmites*). Migahid (quoted by Penman, 1963) found that the yearly mean evapo-transpiration of a swamp of *Cyperus papyrus* in Africa was 2190 mm y^{-1}, much the same value as in an open lagoon (2230 mm y^{-1}).

Another technique determines evapo-transpiration from micro-climatological methods as part of a heat budget. Rijks (1969) used this approach to estimate the evapo-transpiration from a large area of a *Cyperus papyrus* stand, and Penman's (1948) formula for the evaporation from the water surface. The mean value of *C. papyrus* stand evapo-transpiration obtained over 15 days was only about 0.6 that of open water. A probable explanation of the discrepancy between these results and Migahid's is that he used recently transplanted papyrus in tanks. The dead foliage of the mature stand probably impeded evaporation considerably.

Linacre *et al.* (1970) using three micro-meteorological methods, obtained results which were very similar to those of Rijks. The evapo-transpiration from a swamp overgrown by patches of cattail (principally *Typha orientalis*) in Australia was found to be about two-thirds that from an open lake (instantaneous values on several hot days at mid-day). They claim that: '...perhaps the best general summing up would be that, in dry climates, they may enhance it'. (Linacre *et al.* p. 385). This effect may be due to a partial or full closure of stomata, resulting from a water saturation deficit in the helophyte leaves.

Idso and Anderson (1988) very clearly demonstrated the importance of the surface area of plants exposed at the periphery of tanks. The true influence of extensive stands of vegetation can be shown by extrapolation to the point where the peripheral area becomes insignificant. This showed that evapo-transpiration of *Eichhornia* and *Typha* was about 0.8 of open water evaporation, and that this value would be affected by the height of the plants and their stomatal conductance.

Transpiration rates by helophytes

It is clear that water loss from helophyte stands mostly depends on the transpiration of the plants, and has to be studied in connection with all the physiological factors participating in water uptake, transport and loss. The transpiration rate may be expressed:

per unit of transpiring area of biomass,
per unit ground area in plant stands,
or as a fraction of water content in a given plant.

Most transpiration data have been obtained by gravimetric methods, i.e. weight losses from cut-off parts or whole shoots are measured over short periods. There is some evidence that this overestimates the real transpiration. Weight losses from entire plants are more reliable (e.g. Slavik, 1974). Rychnovská *et al.* (1980) have compared measurements of the transpiration of reed plants and stands (*Phragmites australis*) by means of the gravimetric method, Bowen ratio method and the thermoelectric method of measuring the xylem water flow. The estimated daily water outputs of the stand were: 5.3, 6.0 and 4.0 mm d^{-1}, respectively.

The values of the observed rates of transpiration by helophytes are highly variable, caused by both internal and external factors. For example Přibáň and Ondok (1978, 1980) have calculated the evapo-transpiration from wetland communities in southern Bohemia. For two communities the components of the heat balance were calculated from micro-meteorological data recorded on eight selected sunny days during the growing season and the evapo-transpiration was estimated from values of the Bowen ratio. The evapo-transpiration from the wetter community, dominated by *Carex gracilis*, varied between 0.2 mm d^{-1} in April and 4.6 mm d^{-1} in June. In the drier community, dominated by *Molinia coerulea*, the corresponding variation was between 0.1 and 4.0 mm d^{-1}. Elsewhere, they attempted to calculate the seasonal energy budgets for a South Bohemian sedge-grass marsh dominated by *Carex gracilis* and *Calamagrostis canescens*, which exhibited the highest evapo-transpiration in May to July (Přibáň & Ondok, 1980). The average energy conversion into latent heat of evaporation (including transpiration) during the whole

Table 7.3. *Maximum transpiration rates (mg cm^{-2} h^{-1}) of hydrophytes and mesophytes under optimum conditions for evaporation (compiled from Gessner, 1959)*

Hydrophytes		Mesophytes	
Potamogeton natans	64.8	*Syringa vulgaris*	12.8
Eichhornia crassipes	37.8	*Viola tricolor*	15.0
Alisma plantago-aquatica	27.0	*Taraxacum officinale*	15.5
Nymphaea alba	17.6	*Artemisia monogyna*	24.6
Sagittaria sagittifolia	13.8	*Rhus mollis*	6.3

growing season (May to October) was 75% of the energy of total incident global radiation; 20% of this energy was transmitted to the atmosphere as sensible heat while the ground heat flux accounted for as little as 5%. The highest daily sums of evapo-transpiration were 6.5 mm d^{-1} and seasonal average daily evapo-transpiration was 2.6 mm d^{-1}.

Under conditions favourable for transpiration, the transpiration of hydrophytes exceeds that of mesophytes, but such species as *Sagittaria sagittifolia* or *Nymphaea alba* transpire at about the same rate as mesophytes (Table 7.3; Gessner, 1959).

Differences in the transpiration rate of stands of emergent macrophytes may be correlated not only with different rates of transpiration per unit transpiring surface area of the plants but also with differences in the ratio between this area and leaf or shoot biomass. This may be illustrated by a comparison between *Phragmites australis* and *Schoenoplectus lacustris* (Antipov, 1961). The transpiration rate per unit surface area is smaller in *Phragmites* than in *Schoenoplectus*, but the former species has a larger transpiring surface area per unit fresh weight (leaf area ratios of 70.1 and 31.7 cm^2 g^{-1}, respectively).

The transpiration per unit ground area is smaller in helophytes such as *Schoenoplectus*, which have practically no leaves when emergent. In reservoirs covered by helophyte stands of medium density the respective mean hourly values of transpiration per sq. m ground area were 1.019 mm, 0.768 mm and 1.695 mm in the stands of *Schoenoplectus lacustris*, *Equisetum limosum* and *Glyceria maxima*. These values were reported to increase to 1.903 mm, 3.468 mm and 5.026 mm per hour, respectively, at the time of maximum transpiration rate in July and early August (Lisitsina & Ekzertsev, 1971). These values are quite high and various factors may have resulted in overestimates of the transpiration rates.

Table 7.4. *Transpiration of* Phragmites australis *in different stands*

Transpiration rate		
Mean per unit leaf area and hour $(mg\,cm^{-2}\,h^{-1})$	Maximum per unit ground area and day $(mm\,m^{-2}\,d^{-1}$ or $kg\,m^{-2}\,d^{-1})$	References
–	12.4	Kiendl (1953)
–	9.5	Forsh (1957)
22.00	15.6	Rudescu (1960)
10.00–15.00	–	Antipov (1961)
16.86	10.2	Tuschl (1970)
17.60	–	Khashes & Bobro (1971)
18.48	11.7	Królikowska (1971)
18.00–21.00	7.9	Květ (1973b)
–	4.7	Burian (1973)
16.76	6.9	Rychnovská & Šmíd (1973), Rychnovská et al. (1980)

Phragmites australis, the most cosmopolitan species among helophytes, exhibits different transpiration rates according to habitat. The mean values of its transpiration per unit leaf area in freshwater littoral stands seem to be much the same throughout the wide range of its geographical distribution; but the maximum values per unit ground area are highly variable (Table 7.4), because of the differences in biomass.

The ratio between stand transpiration (E_c) and evaporation from a free water surface (E_o), both of the same ground area, is called relative transpiration (E_c/E_o). Gessner (1956) states, that the relative transpiration of aquatic and marsh plants is usually less than 1, but for some species, e.g. *Phragmites*, it may be greater than 1. Rudescu (1960), studying large stands of *Phragmites* in the Danube delta, discovered a considerable variation in relative transpiration rates, usually greater than 1 (Table 7.5). The highest value (3.42) was obtained at the seasonal maximum of biomass.

The water turnover rate (WTR) is the weight of water transpired per unit weight of water content per unit time $(g(g\,H_2O)^{-1}\,d^{-1}$; 'day' being the period during which the plants transpire). It shows how many times the water content of an organ or whole shoot is exchanged during a certain period of time (Rychnovská et al., 1972). Differences in transpiration rates are reflected in different water turnover rates (WTRs) as shown in Table 7.6.

Table 7.5. *Relative transpiration (transpiration/evaporation from open water) by reed in the Danube delta (after Rudescu, 1969)*

Period	Evaporation (E_o) (mm)	Transpiration (E_c) (mm)	E_c/E_o
1959			
1 June–23 June	164	534	3.25
24 June–22 July	60	120	2.00
23 July–22 Aug.	208	417	2.10
23 Aug.–19 Sept.	142	485	3.42
1960			
14 Apr.–12 May	68	74	1.15
1 June–30 June	62	60	0.98

Table 7.6. *Daily transpiration and water turnover rate for* Glyceria maxima *investigated on 6 June 1968, 5 to 20 h (after Rychnovská et al., 1972)*

Plant organ	Transpiration $(g\,(g\,d\,wt)^{-1}\,d^{-1})$	Water turnover rate Water loss $(g\,(g\,water\,content)^{-1}\,d^{-1})$
First leaf	34.1	15.0
Second leaf	36.8	14.2
Fourth leaf	24.7	9.0
Flowering shoot	12.4	3.7
Non-flowering shoot	12.2	3.5

Květ (1973*b*), examining the water economy of *Phragmites* growing in littoral and dry terrestrial habitats, found water turnover rates to vary according to environmental conditions, and between the apical and basal parts of the green shoots. The WTR values were 7.5 (apical parts), 4.8 (medial parts), 3.2 (basal parts) and 4.5 (whole shoots) in the littoral stand and, respectively, 6.2, 6.2, 3.0 and 5.2 $g(g\,H_2O)^{-1}\,d^{-1}$ in a dry terrestrial stand. Rychnovská and Šmíd (1973) determined the water turnover rates for terrestrial *Phragmites* and *Glyceria* as 7.9 and 4.3 $g(g\,H_2O)^{-1}\,d^{-1}$, respectively.

Under the usual favourable conditions of water supply, transpiration of helophyte stands is proportional to their above-ground biomass which is expressed in the transpiration coefficient, transpiration (E_c) over biomass (B). In a terrestrial and a littoral stand of *Phragmites* studied by Rychnovská and Šmíd (1973) the daily canopy transpiration coefficients were nearly the same (9.4 and 8.8; E_c in kg m^{-2} d^{-1}, B in kg dry wt m^{-2}). For *Glyceria* they found $E_c/B = 11.9$. However Bernatowicz *et al.* (1976) found considerable differences in growing season transpiration coefficients ($E_{c,g}$ in kg m^{-2} (120 d)$^{-1}$, B_{max} in kg m^{-2}) between plants in isolation on land and those within the reedbelt; and between species ($E_{c,g}/B_{max} = 391$ to 691 on land, 320 to 593 in reedbelt).

The rate at which hydrophyte stands transpire is related to the amount of their emergent live plant material (Eisenlohr, 1966) and/or to the surface area exposed to the aerial environment (floating leaves).

Internal factors regulating transpiration rate

Stomata and conductive elements

Plants lose water to the atmosphere through their stomata and cuticle. The cuticular transpiration is relatively unimportant in most plants, but it may be of relatively higher importance for plants with floating leaves than for helophytes. Stomata enable the plants to regulate their transpiration. The greater the number of stomata per unit area of plant surface, the better the effect of this regulatory mechanism.

The anatomical structure of all macrophytes, including helophytes, is appreciably affected by habitat. The number of stomata as well as the length of conductive elements (vessels) per unit of epidermal surface area have been proved to vary with changes in the environment. This has been demonstrated in *Phragmites australis*. Demidovskaja and Kirichenko (1964) found that the leaf epidermis of *Phragmites* growing in a wet meadow had about 30 more stomata mm^{-2} than *Phragmites* growing in water. In plants growing on peat the number of stomata depended on the depth of the groundwater level (450 and 333 stomata mm^{-2} with water level at 1.5 m and 0.5 m depth, respectively). On saline soils as many as 670 stomata mm^{-2} occurred.

The relative length of vessels is affected in a similar way. In the saline habitat there were 38 cm (cm leaf surface)$^{-2}$ and in littoral stands 116 cm cm^{-2}. In general, both this length and the stomatal density are smaller in helophytes than in mesophytes. Within one plant, the length of the vessels may vary with the leaf position in relation to water level, e.g. from 91 to 104 and from 68 to 71 cm cm^{-2} in aerial and floating leaves of *Nelumbo*,

Table 7.7. *Stomatal density (per 1 mm² leaf surface area) for some
common helophytes and hydrophytes*

	Stomatal density		
Species	Upper side	Lower side	References
Phragmites australis	757.9	935.0	
Typha latifolia	501.6	485.7	
Butomus umbellatus	48.9	43.7	
Sparganium simplex	106.2	84.8	Antipov (1961)
Alisma plantago-aquatica	40.1	29.9	
Sagittaria sagittifolia	43.1	47.3	
Stratiotes aloides	39.7	38.7	
Schoenoplectus lacustris	225.0	–	
Glyceria maxima	170.0	85.0	Lisitsina & Ekzertsev (1961)
Equisetum fluviatile	85.0	–	

respectively (Gessner, 1956). A typical feature of the leaves in contact with water is a decreased number of anastomoses between vessels.

The anatomical characters are also influenced by the leaf position on the stem. In *Phragmites*, more stomata are found on the upper leaves than in the lower ones (Demidovskaja & Kirichenko, 1964).

Pazourek (1973) and Björk (1967) describe the dependence of stomatal density on plant age, developmental stage, and ecotype in *Phragmites*. The differences in stomatal density may be regarded as adaptations to environmental conditions.

Representative data on the stomatal density of common helophytes are given in Table 7.7.

Osmotic pressure of the cell sap

Osmotic pressure of plant cells varies significantly in different ecological groups of plants. Freshwater helophytes, regardless of their systematic position, are characterised by relatively low osmotic values. Like the number of stomata, the osmotic pressure varies according to the position of the leaf; in general, the osmotic pressure of the upper leaves is higher (Rychnovská, 1967, 1973). In macrophytes growing in water and forming both submerged and emergent leaves, the latter have a higher sugar content in the cell sap and hence a higher osmotic pressure.

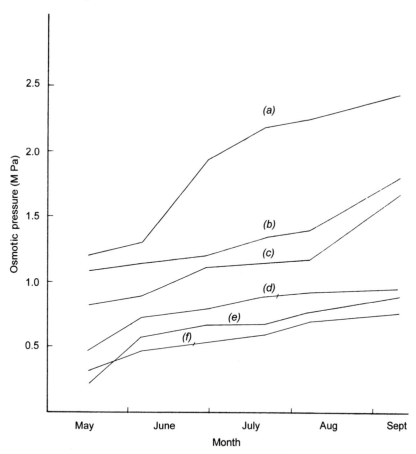

Fig. 7.10. Seasonal course of osmotic pressure in some helophytes: (*a*) *Phragmites australis*, (*b*) *Carex stricta*, (*c*) *Scirpus lacustris*, (*d*) *Trapa natans*, (*e*) *Polygonum amphibium* and (*f*) *Nuphar luteum* (Müller-Stoll, 1938).

Typical daily and seasonal courses of osmotic pressure can be observed. Diurnally, lower values are found at night and the maximum is at mid-day, related to the accumulation of photosynthesates in the leaves during intense transpiration (Gessner, 1959). The seasonal course of osmotic pressure in several macrophytes is shown in Fig. 7.10.

The osmotic pressure in cells of hydrophytes with submerged or floating leaves is usually only about half of that in helophytes such as *Phragmites* (Gessner, 1959).

Suction tension (diffusion pressure deficit or water potential)

The suction tension is of great importance for the water economy of plants because it determines the uptake of water by plant cells. Transpiration is the immediate reason for the suction tension in the leaf cells. Like the osmotic pressure the suction tension is highest at mid-day and lowest at night, when the cells are fully saturated with water and dissolved assimilates have been transported away from the leaves (Gessner, 1959). The suction tension exhibits pronounced gradients within one shoot as well as within a single leaf lamina (Rychnovská, 1967).

Uptake and conduction of water

The rate of uptake of water may differ between ecologically different plant groupings. The submerged macrophytes absorb and conduct water with the aid of osmotic pressure (Gessner, 1959), but in macrophytes with floating leaves this process is connected with transpiration. Their poor capacity for water uptake is usually compensated by a thick cuticle and a relatively small number of stomata, which are placed only on the upper leaf surface. Special cells, called hydropots, which have no cuticle and are located on the lower leaf surface, are able to absorb water (Gessner, 1959).

The emergent macrophytes take up water from the soil and water with their roots. In this case, the water potential in the leaves, increased by their transpiration, is of primary importance for the uptake and conduction of water. The rate of water conduction in helophytes, as in other plants, varies during the day, being higher at mid-day and falling to zero during night. The uptake is correlated with both the daily course of transpiration rate and internal properties of the plant tissues, particularly by their anatomical structure. Such helophytes as *Schoenoplectus*, *Typha* and *Phragmites* have a partly xeromorphic anatomical structure and a well-developed aerenchyma as well as water-conducting elements. Their water content is relatively small.

Water content and water saturation deficit

The water content in aquatic and littoral macrophytes varies according to both species and individual organs. Emergent helophytes contain less water in their leaves than in the underground organs. But, such plants as *Alisma* or *Sagittaria* contain large amounts of water not only in their

Table 7.8. *Water content in leaves of several helophytes and hydrophytes (percentage of fresh weight) (compiled from Antipov, 1961, 1964)*

	Month			
Plant	June	July	Aug.	Sept.
Phragmites communis	68	58	50	50
Schoenoplectus lacustris (stems)	74	69	61	62
Typha latifolia	76	75	72	65
Butomus umbellatus	85	83	80	80
Sparganium simplex	85	80	80	80
Alisma plantago-aquatica	85	84	81	81
Sagittaria sagittifolia	86	84	81	80
Stratiotes aloides	89	89	87	85
Nymphaea candida	87	80	87	85

underground parts but also in their shoots and petioles even when they grow in a terrestrial ecophase (Antipov, 1973). The colloids of these macrophytes are less hydrophilous than those of emergent helophytes such as *Phragmites*, *Typha* and *Schoenoplectus*, and even less than those of *Nymphaea*. According to Antipov (1973) the more hydrophilous are the colloids, the better the plant can endure relatively drier periods and higher temperatures.

The water content in the leaves of macrophytes fluctuates during the day. It also depends on the developmental phase of a plant and on its habitat. The leaves of emergent helophytes contain less water at the time of intense transpiration at mid-day than they do in the morning and evening (Fig. 7.11; Królikowska, 1974). The water content of the leaves of a single plant depends on their position on the stem, like the number of stomata and osmotic potential. The lower leaves contain more water than the upper ones (Królikowska, 1974; Rychnovská, 1978) in *Phragmites* (Fig. 7.12).

Seasonal fluctuations of the water content in macrophytes have been recorded, e.g. by Antipov (1961, 1964; Table 7.8).

Different plant organs contain different amounts of water. The tabulated values (Table 7.9) have been recorded for organs of four common European species of helophytes. Antipov (1973) has found correlations between the water contents in the leaves and flowers of aquatic and littoral plants. *Phragmites australis* and *Glyceria maxima* contain less water in their flowers and inflorescence stalks than in leaves, whereas species like

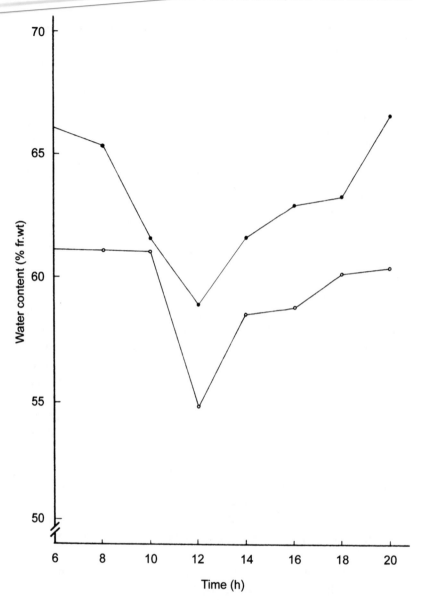

Fig. 7.11. Diurnal changes of the water content in the leaves of *Phragmites australis*; ●—● July, ○—○ August (Królikowska, 1974).

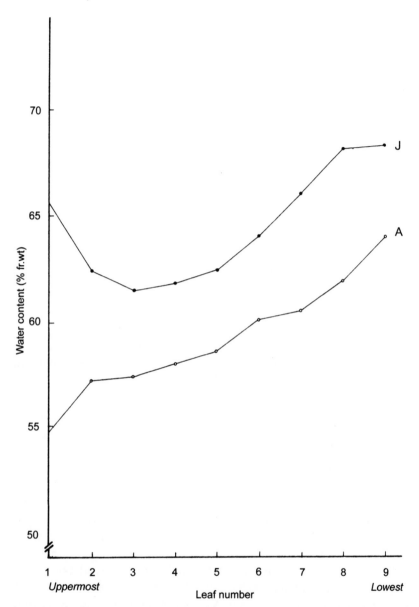

Fig. 7.12. Water content successively from the upper to the lower leaves of
Phragmites australis: J, ●—● July, A, ○—○ August (Królikowska, 1974).

Table 7.9. *Average water content in different parts of helophytes (percentage of fresh weight) (original data; J. Królikowska, unpublished)*

Species	Phragmites australis	Glyceria maxima	Typha latifolia	Typha angustifolia
Panicle	66	53	83	74
Stem	55	67	81	74
Leaf sheaths or bases (in *Typha*)	63	72	87	83
Leaves	56	69	70	68
Underground parts	78	84	86	84
Young shoots in water	89	93	93	92

Stratiotes aloides, *Sagittaria sagittifolia* and *Sparganium simplex*, contain more water in their flowers than in leaves.

These data show that the water content is closely related to the anatomical structure, environmental conditions and transpiration of the plants.

The ability of plants to survive periods of water stress depends on their ability to endure a decreased water content. The sublethal water deficit is defined as the maximum water loss which may occur without killing the plant, expressed as a percentage either of dry weight or of 'normal' water content at full turgidity. For hygro- and hydrophytes the values of the sublethal water deficit are about 20% of the normal water content (Gessner, 1959). For *Phragmites* growing in water, the sublethal water deficit was 21%, but for that growing in a meadow it was 32% of the normal water content. Small, harmless deficits are often observed; in the upper leaves 7.8% and in the lower leaves 3–4% (Rychnovská, 1978).

Rychnovská *et al.* (1972) estimated the water saturation deficit (Vassiljev, 1931) as the difference between the morning (maximum) and current values of water content in *Glyceria maxima*. There was a considerable variability in the peak (afternoon) values of the water saturation deficit in individual leaves and between the developmental stages of any given plant (Table 7.10). Rychnovská (1973), studying the *Phragmites* stands at the sites of Květ's (1973b) transpiration measurements, found that the maximum saturation deficit did not exceed 6% and 3% in the dry terrestrial and littoral *Phragmites*, respectively. Only shoots detached from their root systems suffered severely from water stress. The root system seems to be highly important for the water supply to the intensely transpiring shoots. Like other characteristics of water relations

Table 7.10. *Daily maximum and minimum water content (at certain times of day) and water saturation deficit in* Glyceria maxima *(on 6.6.1968) (after Rychnovská et al., 1972)*

Organ	Water content in % of dry weight				WSD (%)
	max.	at h	min.	at h	
First leaf	259	6	218	12	16
Second leaf	281	6	252	12	10
Fourth leaf	335	7	314	12	6
Flowering shoot	373	6	331	14	11
Non-flowering shoot	438	7	378	13	14

in *Phragmites* plants, the water saturation deficit varies markedly with the level of leaf insertion and the position of the leaf tissue in a lamina (Rychnovská, 1973, 1978).

External factors affecting the transpiration rate

Meteorological factors

The transpiration rate depends on the same factors as evaporation; especially on air humidity and temperature, incoming radiation, and wind speed. The external control of transpiration is particularly evident in the open and patchy vegetation of shallow water and mudflats or growing along the shoreline in partially filled lakes or ponds (Květ, 1975). The daily courses of these factors are reflected in the daily course of transpiration rate (Fig. 7.13). Curves showing the daily course of transpiration usually have a single peak at mid-day. Depressions due to water deficit and stomata closure may occur only when helophytes are grown under extreme conditions (open terrestrial stands, saline soils, etc.).

The night transpiration is usually very small. For example, Tuschl (1970) gives a value of about 0.78 mg (cm leaf)$^{-2}$ h^{-1} for *Phragmites* during nights with no dew formation. In most instances, the leaves are cooler than the surrounding air, dew is formed and no transpiration can be detected (Królikowska, 1971).

The influence of meteorological conditions is also reflected in the seasonal course of helophyte transpiration in the northern temperate zone, where the highest values are usually recorded in summer (Table

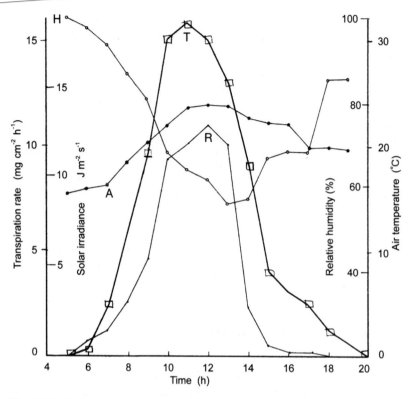

Fig. 7.13. Daily course of transpiration by *Phragmites australis* as compared with main meteorological factors: T, □—□ transpiration, A, ●—● air temperature, R, •—• global radiation and H, ○—○ relative air humidity (Królikowska, 1971).

7.11). Another reason for intense summer transpiration is the large surface area of transpiring leaves. The seasonal changes of leaf area index in the important helophyte communities are discussed in Chapter 2.

The transpiration of leaves, belonging to a single shoot, varies according to leaf position. The upper leaves, exposed to more radiation and wind, transpire much more than the lower leaves (Fig. 7.14) but this is also partly due to the age differences between the leaves. Forsh (1967) found the following differences in hourly transpiration of *Phragmites* leaves, according to their position on the stem: the upper leaves, 0.976 g (g fresh wt)$^{-1}$ h^{-1} the middle leaves, 0.653 and the lower 0.399. The transpiration of the leaves in the middle part of the stem amounted to about 97% of that of all foliage, which was due to the long lifespan of the middle leaves.

Table 7.11. *Monthly totals of transpiration (mm) for two helophyte communities in Central Europe (Kiendl, 1953)*

Month	Glycerietum 1951	Phragmitetum 1950
January	0.0	0.0
February	0.0	0.0
March	0.3	0.0
April	20.0	19.1
May	144.1	86.1
June	362.3	188.1
July	333.6	255.9
August	320.7	384.1
September	218.0	240.1
October	120.0	119.5
November	42.5	12.0
December	26.6	0.0
Annual total	1588.1	1304.9

Water and humidity conditions

In monospecific helophyte stands the transpiration will vary according to the position of the water level. Plants of *Phragmites* transpired more when growing in water (littoral ecophase) than in a terrestrial stand (Królikowska, 1971). Beydeman (1960) found a very low transpiration rate (only about half the normal value) for *Phragmites* growing in saline soil with a ground water level at about −5 to −6 m. The anatomical structure of these *Phragmites* leaves also changed (see p. 391) so this behaviour must be regarded as the result of an interaction between external and internal factors.

According to Antipov (1973) the transpiration (per unit of transpiring area) is less in helophytes than in hydrophytes with floating leaves or aerial leaves near the water surface (Table 7.12). These plants, however, never form such dense canopies as *Phragmites*, *Typha* and other helophytes of that type.

Biotic factors

The transpiration rate may be affected considerably by infestation by pests and parasites. The transpiration of *Phragmites* leaves heavily

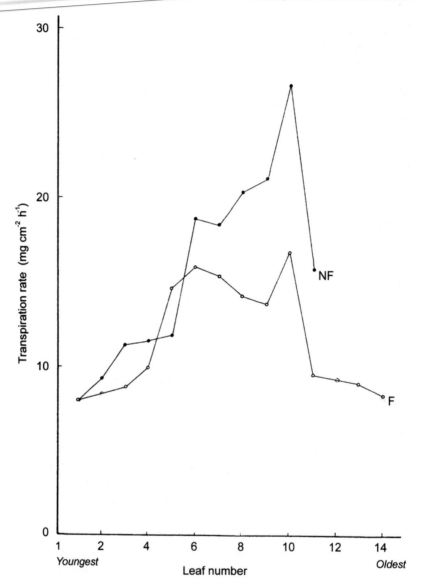

Fig. 7.14. Transpiration by successive leaves on a shoot of *Phragmites australis* (from the youngest to the oldest leaf): NF, ●—● shoot without panicle; F, ○—○ flowering shoot (Królikowska, 1971).

Table 7.12. *Hourly transpiration (in g (g fresh wt)$^{-1}$ h^{-1}) by several wetland plants under comparable conditions (calculated from Antipov, 1973)*

Plant species	Transpiration
Phragmites australis	0.735
Glyceria maxima	0.864
Stratiotes aloides	1.160
Plantago amphibium	1.254
Sparganium simplex	1.424
Sagittaria sagittifolia	1.500

attacked by *Ustilago grandis* was found to be only one-half of that of the healthy leaves. According to Durska (1972), external factors normally enhancing transpiration were much less effective on infested plants. *Deightoniella arundinacea* reduced *Phragmites* transpiration by about 54% and in one case by as much as 85%. This decrease was more pronounced in a terrestrial than in a littoral reed stand (by 65% and 49%, respectively).

Young *Phragmites* leaves infested by *Puccinia phragmitis* transpired less than healthy leaves of the same age, but the old leaves transpired more. On average, this rust decreased transpiration by 13% (Durska, 1972). Aphids, which cover the leaves with a thin layer of sugar exudates, may have a similar effect on transpiration as the parasitic rusts and blight fungi.

Where suitable conditions (increased air humidity) result in a regular and abundant occurrence of pest organisms in wetlands, the decrease in transpiration rate may be important.

Chemicals used in agriculture

With the increased use of chemical pesticides, more and more chemical substances are washed off into aquatic ecosystems. The pollution of water in wetland habitats results in disturbances in their plant life. The effects on plant–water relations may be significant, as has been shown for *Typha latifolia*. Experiments have proved that the decrease of transpiration rate was proportional to the concentration of the herbicides applied (2, 4-D and MCPA) to the pots with *Typha*, as well as to the duration of their application (Królikowska, 1972). The standard triazine herbicides increase the transpiration of *Typha* during the first days following application and later reduced it to 50% of that of the control plants (Królikowska, 1976).

8

The management of wetlands

S.M. HASLAM, F. KLÖTZLI, H. SUKOPP and
A. SZCZEPAŃSKI

Introduction

The main authors were assisted by several collaborators who provided information on specific topics: wetland fisheries by T. Backiel (Inland Fisheries Institute, Poland), lake restoration by S. Björk (Institute of Limnology, Sweden); changes in wetlands by R.J. de Boer and V. Westhoff (Netherlands). Some of these manuscripts and data are deposited in the library of the Institute of Botany at Třeboň, Czech Republic, where they may be consulted.

It used to be said that most wetlands were commercially useless, but they have long been used, and their varied uses and importance have slowly become recognised (National Academy of Sciences, 1976; Szczepański, 1983). The first uses were for fishing and hunting (fowl and mammals), and, in times of stress, as refuges for the local populations. Shelters could be built, and roofs covered, by wetland materials. Some species could be used for fodder. Early specialisations included more-developed hunting and fishing, and the cultivation of rice. Most of these are still practised, even in affluent and industrial countries, and in some countries wetlands are used on an industrial scale. Large-scale 'uses' involving habitat destruction, such as conversion to arable land through drainage, etc. are not discussed here.

In sparsely populated non-industrial countries, especially in the tropics, large flood-plains (e.g. of the Upper Nile, Niger, Central African Republic) are very important for grazing and fishing. In the advanced industrial countries, in contrast, large wetlands are more often under complete human control, and are rarely as important for living space.

Wetlands, merely by their existence, regulate water regimes, acting as storage reservoirs. They are also biological filters, changing the quality of percolating water by adsorbing or releasing nutrients, decreasing suspended matter, and retaining many pollutants. They provide materials for handcrafts as well as for industrial use. Their peat is used in horticulture and for fuel. Fowl and mammals are sought for food and sport, and marshes and waters are becoming used increasingly for other forms of recreation. Much food for domestic animals can also be obtained from them.

Wetlands have relatively fast rates of succession, and have been relatively undisturbed. They are therefore, especially suitable for the study of plant succession. Their importance is increased by frequent presence of the remains, in peat, etc., of earlier stages of the successions. Palaeobotanists, palaeolimnologists and phytosociologists can fruitfully investigate wetlands as models of natural ecosystems. Both undisturbed and managed wetlands act as refuges for plants and animals, often having a unique flora and fauna. The gene pools and structure of wetlands should therefore, be protected against alteration or destruction, and when new reserves are acquired, wetlands should be given priority.

Thus the users of wetlands may consume their production, utilise their physical and chemical properties, enjoy their recreational potentialities or conserve their life and environment.

Wetlands are living entities, taking many years to form. They are often slowly changing, or undergoing cyclic changes. Forms of exploitation not based on sound ecological theory tend to upset the pattern of development and lead to rapid destruction of the ecosystem. Regeneration may be impossible, very costly, or very slow. Many wetlands are thus seriously endangered by change of any sort.

Large areas of wetland are often drained in order to increase arable land. Wetlands are also imperilled by channelling and deepening rivers, by water abstraction, and by the consequent lowering of the groundwater table. Examples are the proposal for diverting the White Nile (Jonglei Investigation Team, 1954; Howell *et al.*, 1988) which would completely alter present papyrus swamps; and drainage operations in Florida and Louisiana which are damaging the Everglades and coastal swamps (Stone *et al.*, 1977).

They are exceptionally susceptible to mechanical damage to the underground parts of the plant populations because these long-lived organs are required for the maintenance and propagation of the community. Consequently, damage by harvesting, heavy vehicles or other management practices must be prevented.

Management, properly based on ecological principles, maintains the wetland habitat and permits the exploitation of wetland species, without prejudicing their survival. In order to ensure economic returns over long periods of time therefore, management is linked with conservation. Awareness of this ecological principle is especially necessary when industrial exploitation is involved, since heavy vehicles are used for harvesting and transport.

When growing vigorously, helophytes may interfere with management plans, and so control is sometimes necessary. Pests, chiefly insects, may become too numerous in wetlands, and these, also, may need to be controlled.

Many chapters in Patten (1990 and 1994), describe relationships between wetland ecology and management, and Naiman and Decamps (1993) present wetland management in terms of ecotones.

Uses of wetland production

Industrial use of plants

Industrial uses fall into two classes: the non-destructive uses such as materials for the building and chemical industries, and the destructive large-scale removal of peat. The latter eliminates the habitat, and so will not be discussed here.

The common reed (*Phragmites australis*) is the species principally used for industrial production. The basic differences between reedswamp or reedland and other agricultural habitats mean that using dry land practices in the wetland normally leads to its destruction. Reedswamps and reedlands are relatively simple ecosystems in an early stage of succession, with production exceeding respiration. Part of the organic matter produced accumulates as peat. Deposition of organic and inorganic sediments accelerates the succession, which may proceed towards swamp forest (eutrophic habitats) or acid bog (dystrophic habitats). Commercial exploitation may prolong the reedland seral stage, and delay succession, keeping the community juvenile, or it may, by preventing the deposition of organic matter, change the community altogether. Correct exploitation removes organic matter and may delay, but does not change the natural processes of the ecosystem.

In reedswamps and reedlands, the underground stems are an essential part of the community, as next year's shoots develop from them. Their destruction during harvesting leads to the destruction of the whole plant community. These communities, unlike those of arable land, are not re-created each year, and for continuous production, management must take this into account.

Harvesting is the main difficulty. Manual harvesting is a skilled craft, but is slow, often unpleasant, and frequently badly paid. Recruitment of staff may be difficult or impossible. Small harvesters, with their operators on foot, are satisfactory for small areas and on soft soil. They are much quicker than scything, but still slow when large areas are concerned. Tractor-type harvesters vary in size but even the smallest can be bogged down in soft soil. On firm soil, larger harvesters can be used, but the heavier ones cause damage to the soil and below-ground parts, which, in turn, leads to the deterioration or destruction of the bed (e.g. in Romania, Rudescu *et al.*, 1965; USSR, Krotkevich, 1960). Specialised amphibious vehicles with buoyancy tyres are often useful. Heavy machines can be safely used only when thick ice is present during harvesting.

The problems with papyrus (*Cyperus papyrus*) are particularly intractable (Steenberg, 1968). The German factory in the Sudan, the 'Tybro' plant in Uganda, and the South African pulp factory all closed because of harvesting difficulties (K. Thompson, pers. comm.).

For commercial use, stands must be continuously monodominant, and vigorous, with high production. Management techniques, on a large scale, are the timing and height of the cutting, the regulation of the water supply, and burning. Different species have different requirements. *Phragmites*, for example, is harvested in late winter in Europe, when the aerial shoots are dead and dry. It is favoured by a regular water regime, and spring burning (e.g. Haslam, 1972*b*). Efforts to increase production by water regulation, and by conversion to polders have proved unsuccessful in Romania except on an experimental scale (L. Rudescu, pers. comm.).

Management regimes favourable for the appropriate species can be continued for long periods, but plant diversity in such wetlands is necessarily low. If large areas are cut in each season, this can be disadvantageous for some birds and mammals.

Cellulose and paper

Historically, papyrus was used widely. *Phragmites* has been used for cellulose production in China, Korea, Romania and USSR for it contains over 50% cellulose. Good-quality writing paper, however, must have no more than 20% fibre, although wrapping and corrugated papers may contain up to 60%. In Romania, once the leading country in this field, the production in the Danube Delta reached about 8×10^5 t annually, of which 80% was processed (Rudescu *et al.*, 1965). In USSR the annual reed production for cellulose was 7×10^7 t (Krotkevich, 1970).

Building materials

Reedboard (thatchboard) is a building board. It is made of parallel reeds (less commonly, other wetland species) without inflorescences but sometimes with leaves, the stems being compressed and linked (e.g. by galvanised steel wires), or first reduced to fibre, possibly with added wood fibre for strengthening. It can be made either by hand, or in a special type of press. The boards are commonly *ca.* 1.5 × 2.4 m in size, and *ca.* 2–7.5 cm thick.

Reedboard is widely used for ceilings, floors, light buildings, etc. in, e.g. Austria, Czechoslovakia, Hungary, India, Iraq, Poland, Romania and USSR. In USSR over 20×10^6 m^2 of reed slabs were produced in 1965 (Zezin, 1968). Prefabricated elements used in house buildings are also manufactured in Poland.

Houses of reedboard should be well insulated, with damp courses, good foundations and plaster for protection against atmospheric and ground moisture. In the climate of Central Europe properly built houses last for about 50 years. In the tropics the incidence of damage from termites may be the controlling factor. In wattle-and-daub buildings, reed mats can form the supporting wattle under the plaster.

Reeds can also be used to reinforce lime mortar (e.g. Iraq; Anon., 1972).

The decay of reeds and reedboard can be slowed by impregnation with preservatives (Rozmej, 1952), but these are not often used on a commercial scale.

Thatching

Thatched roofs are covered with dried plant material, usually reed-like. In general, terrestrial plants are used (straw, palm leaves, etc.). Near wetlands, however, thatching is naturally done with marsh species and their use is becoming more widespread as agricultural practices produce less suitable straw. Impoverished communities often use thatch as it is free. Affluent ones may use it from tradition or for novelty. Good thatch is as effective and long lasting as tiles (and has better insulation), but poor thatch is not.

Phragmites spp. are the most commonly used, and *P. australis* is the chief component of good thatch. *Arundo donax, Cladium* spp., *Cyperus* spp., *Festuca macrophylla, Oryza sativa, Saccharum* spp., *Scirpus* spp. and *Typha* spp. are the main other species (Beetle, 1950; Miyawaki, 1956;

Perdue, 1958; Anon., 1972). *Typha* spp., being hygroscopic, are used in arid regions only.

The plants may be spread as a general covering, may be woven into mats in the softer species, or may be bundled and laid with the ends facing downwards and outwards, as in good thatch. Mud plaster sealing of the underside can greatly reduce fire risk (Anon., 1972), like the ceilings of more affluent areas. If harvesting is frequent, the cutting regime must permit the continued dominance of the desired species.

Commercial thatching reed (*Phragmites australis*) comes mainly from W. Europe, where large *Phragmites* stands occur, with small and thin reeds which are all dead and leafless during the cold winter. Access for harvesting in later winter (unflooded beds or thick ice), and for removing the crop (by boat, tractor, etc.) is also needed.

Quality is somewhat improved by management, but some biotypes are genotypically better than others. Good thatching reed is short (e.g. 1.26–2 m), straight, hard, even, durable and dense. Spring burning, autumn drying and regular cutting increase quality. Very soft reed may have little sclerification, but good quality reed varies. Some biotypes can be cut for thatching in the third winter, others are soft enough for reed to fall after one winter. The best reed comes from regular water regimes, with at least periodic flooding, and not very stagnant conditions. Spring burning and summer flooding decrease competitors and hence improve reed. Severe pollution is damaging or disastrous.

Annual harvesting is usually accompanied by increases in burning and other interferences and so, usually, the density increases. Biennial harvesting is advantageous in nutrient-low beds, and for wildlife, in that only half the bed is cut each year. Harvesting normally increases primary production, although it somewhat decreases shoot length. Harvested reed is bundled, and stacked to dry.

Many reedbeds have been developed by, and for, reed harvesting. Beds subsequently treated differently may deteriorate.

For detailed discussions of many of these points, see Rudescu *et al.* (1965); Hübl (1967); Fiala and Květ (1971); Cooper (1972); Haslam (1972*a,b*); van der Toorn (1972); Klötzli (1974).

Phragmites is too stiff to bend over the roof ridge, where litter (see below) or *Cladium mariscus* may be used. *Cladium* occurs in mesotrophic fens, on summer flooded (or, with management, summer dry) places. It is harvested in summer, usually every 3–4 years, a treatment which also depresses the accompanying *Phragmites*. More frequent cutting produces litter instead.

Protein

Wetland plants are a potential source of leaf protein on a commercial scale. Nitrogen or crude protein values vary greatly between species, but many species contain similar percentages to plants with other growth habits (see Table 2.6; Boyd & Scarsbrook, 1975*b*; Little, 1979). Morphological forms found in emergent plants are similar to those represented by forage species, so protein extraction procedures for crop plants should be directly applicable. Protein from these natural crops could supplement traditional protein supplies in many localities (Boyd, 1971*c*).

Among the species tested, fairly good protein extractability (25 to 54% of the total nitrogen) was obtained for *Justicia americana, Alternanthera philoxeroides, Sagittaria latifolia* and *Orontium aquaticum*, and poor, for *Typha latifolia, Scirpus* sp. and *Polygonum* sp. (Boyd, 1971*c*). Floating species such as *Eichhornia crassipes, Pistia stratiotes, Lemna* spp. and *Spirodela* spp. are also possibilities which would be easier to harvest (Pirie, 1970; National Academy of Sciences, 1976; Culley *et al.*, 1983).

At present, too little is known to justify a large-scale policy of extracting protein from wetlands. The problems are easily defined, however, and the necessary research would not be expensive (Pirie, 1970).

Non-industrial uses of plants

Rice

Rice, a wetland plant, is the world's most important cereal crop. It is unique in the extent and variety of its uses, and its adaptability to a wide range of climate, soil and cultural conditions. While most is grown in shallow flood (wet paddy), some is grown as an upland cereal, and some, in deep floods. Its biology is reviewed in Tsunoda and Takahaski (1984).

Rice benefits from standing water, but its water requirement is little different from other field crops. Rice is mostly found below 40° latitude; grown in Asia, from the Middle East to Japan (91%), in Africa (2.2%), in South and North America (3.9%), and to a limited extent in Europe.

There are many thousands of cultivars, traditional and recently developed. The 'Green Revolution' in higher-yield rice started with the IR8-type in the late 1960s, and continues by breeding and genetic manipulation for many features of the plant. New varieties tend to take 120–125 days from seed to harvest, compared with 150(–200) for older varieties, an obvious advantage. With present technology, 100-day growth may be the

Table 8.1. *Some wetland foods (including cooked foods, excluding medicines)*

Aerial shoot or whole plant	Fruit or seed	Underground parts	Pollen
Azolla spp.	*Glyceria fluitans*	*Acorus calamus*	*Typha* spp.
Ceratopteris thalictroides	*Nelumbo nucifera*	*Aponogeton* spp.	
Eichhornia crassipes	*Nymphaea* spp.	*Butomus umbellatus*	
Ipomoea aquatica	*Oryza sativa* (rice)	*Calla palustris*	
Nasturtium officinale agg. (water cress)	*Trapa* spp.	*Colocasia esculenta*	
Neptunia oleracea	*Zizania aquatica*	*Cyntospermia edule*	
Ottelia alismoides		*Cyperus esculentus*	
Typha spp. (young bases of leaves)		*Eleocharis dulcis*	
		Lotus nelumbo	
		Phragmites australis	
		Sagittaria spp.	
		Typha spp.	

shortest without greatly lessening the grain yield. In paddies with controlled water level, modern technology has its greatest effect. Short high-yield rice is of little use in regular floods of 5 m. Hardy low-yield local strains are best for those depending on unpredictable monsoon rains for watering.

In the late 1980s, rice covered *ca.* 145 million hectares and produced nearly 470 million tonnes of grain. Rice is the staple food of over half the world (millions of Asians eat little but rice). The fastest growing populations are in rice-eating areas.

Rice may be sown on the fields or paddies, or be transplanted after 11–70 days. Transplanting is the commonest in Asia. Crop management varies greatly: weeds are more of a problem in upland than in deep-flooded rice, for instance, but attention is needed to choice of variety, water regime, nutrient regime, pests, diseases and competitors. Most harvesting is by hand (sickle or knife), although where both capital investment and habitat are suitable, mechanical harvesters are used (these need large areas with sufficiently firm soil and shallow water, and grain ripening at the same size).

Rice paddies are so far removed from even much-managed fens or bogs (as wheat fields are from oak forests) that the details of rice production are not described here (see Mikkelson & Datta, 1991).

Other foods for man and fodder for domestic animals

Apart from rice, wetlands produce little food for human beings and have only minor or local importance (Table 8.1; see also Sculthorpe, 1967). The most widespread and general use of wetlands, however, is for feeding domestic animals by grazing on wetland pasture, or by eating marsh hay cut from wet meadows and flood meadows of various types (Table 8.2). Until the decline of horse transport, this use of wetlands was even more important in countries with good communications.

Fodder comes from many wetlands, dry or shallow in summer, and from those which can be drained to this extent. For grazing, land must be dry in summer, but tall grasses such as *Glyceria maxima* and *Phalaris arundinacea* can be cropped from flooded marshes, although for the latter, the marsh must dry by mid-summer. Both species can be cropped up to five times a year. Such grazing was once of considerable agricultural importance (e.g. Wein, 1942; Klapp, 1965). With decreasing use, tall dicotyledonous herbs and coarser grasses invade, and rough marsh, reed-swamp and carr have increased (e.g. Weber, 1928; Haslam, 1965). Silage

Table 8.2. *Some fodders from wetland*

Vegetation	Management	Water regime	Nutrient regime
Agrostis stolonifera, Arrhenatherum elatius, *Poa* spp. and tall dicots	Rough grazed	Usually not inundated	High or medium
Echinochloa coarctata	Mown	Flooded in spring	High
Echinochloa crus-galli	Mown	Flooded in spring	High
Eichhornia crassipes (also as silage)	Gathered	Still	Generally high
Glyceria maxima, Phalaris arundinacea and (*Phragmites australis*)	Mown	Usually flooded	High
Glyceria spp., *Alopecurus geniculatus* and small dicots	Mown or grazed	Flooded in winter	High or medium
Lemna spp.	Gathered	Still	Variable
Phragmites australis	Mown	Usually flooded	Variable, not low
Pistia stratiotes	Gathered	Still	High
Salvinia spp.	Gathered	Still	High
Spartina townsendii	Grazed (or mown)	Tidal	High
Stratiotes aloides	Gathered	Still	Medium

can also be produced (e.g. Hubbard & Ranwell, 1966). In arid regions wetlands may support the only productive vegetation and the dried plants are important as fodder (e.g. Lake Skadar, Yugoslavia; J. Květ, pers. comm.).

Animal bedding; insulating material

Litter is dried (soft) vegetation used for covering plants etc. and for animal bedding. Litter develops in summer-dry habitats harvested during summer and autumn annually or biennially. It is usually dominated by grasses (e.g. *Calamagrostis* spp., *Glyceria* spp., *Molinia* spp., *Phalaris arundinacea, Phragmites australis*) or rushes (*Juncus* spp.), with a high proportion of dicotyledonous herbs. Meadows underused for litter production, or made more nutrient rich, develop more of the latter (e.g. *Eupatorium cannabinum, Filipendula ulmaria, Hypericum* spp., *Mentha* spp.). The parts of *Phragmites* shoots left over by the industry can be used as litter, too.

Crafts

Crafts may be for free staple items for impoverished dwellers near wetlands, or for sale to the more affluent. As only small quantities of plant are used, management is seldom needed (but see Hashimoto, 1958, Japan; Täckholm & Tackholm 1941, 1950, Egypt). The long, durable leaves or shoots of, e.g. *Arundo*, Cyperaceae, *Juncus, Phormium, Phragmites, Scirpus, Typha*, etc. are, or have been, used wherever they occur.

Specialist crafts See Watt (1983); Anon. (1947, 1956); Beetle (1950); Täckholm and Drar (1950); Bittmann (1953); Golovanov (1955); Seidel (1955); Perdue (1958); Walker and Willans (1961); Bohr with Guest (1968); Khan *et al.* (1969); C. Burrows, E. Lund, M. Rix, J.M. Shay, K. Thompson & C.J. Ward, pers. comms.

Baskets are made from most genera. Rush-bottomed chairs, ropes, string and plaited work, and containers (cartons, sacks, etc.) are made mainly from *Cyperus, Phormium, Phragmites, Scirpus* and *Typha*. 'Reeds' for woodwind instruments are made from *Arundo donax*, mainly from coastal S. France, although cane of apparently equal quality comes from Mexico and Texas.

Boats – hull, spars and nails – are made from *Scirpus tatora* in S. America. Simpler rafts, sometimes with rims, are made from bunched *Cyperus papyrus* or *Phragmites* in Africa and *Phormium tenax* in New

Zealand. *Lepiromia* is used for junk sails, and *Typha* in houseboats in India.

Lesser crafts include fishing equipment (mainly *Arundo, Cyperus* and *Phragmites*), walking sticks (*Arundo*), writing pens, sieves (*Festuca* spp., often *F. macrophylla, Phragmites* and *Typha*), clothes (*Phormium*), and bird traps (*Phragmites, Typha* and *Festuca* spp.). Stuffing for cushions, mattresses etc. comes from fruits (e.g. *Phragmites, Typha*) or leaves (e.g. *Cyperus*). *Arundo* and *Phragmites* were formerly used for arrows.

Ornamental (also see below) Purely ornamental skilled craftwork is infrequent (but occurs, e.g. in the decorative panels of *Phormium tenax* in New Zealand, C. Burrows, pers. comm.). Useful articles are frequently ornamental.

With increased prosperity, skilled craftwork often declines and easily made articles may increase, e.g. dried inflorescences (in bouquets), craft pictures, reed-thatched bird tables, reed and sedge dolls.

Outdoor unspecialised uses See Täckholm & Täckholm (1941; 1950); Perdue (1958); Bohr with Guest (1968); E. Lund and C.J. Ward (pers. comms.).

Arundo and *Phragmites* are used for windbreaks and greenhouse shades (e.g. in market gardens) and for ornamental or cheap fencing. *Arundo* stems are used for trellises, lattices for drying fruit, etc., and for propping up plants. Simple huts of *Arundo, Phragmites* or *Typha* are used as dwellings, or as hides for shooting, bird watching, etc. Houses can also be made with a framework of arched pillars of bunched *Phragmites*, the walls and roofs being filled in with matting (see also industrial use, above). Stems, bunched, matted or woven can be used for lining watercourses, and *Arundo donax* (living or dead) can be used to break the force of water in intermittently flowing streams.

Other crafts Acorus and *Cyperus* are used for scenting, *Cyperus* and *Typha* are used for clearing muddy water, and *Phragmites* can be a substitute for cork. Seed or chaff (*Phragmites, Typha*) can be used for binding mortar and adobe brick (Täckholm & Täckholm, 1950; Bohr with Guest, 1968), and 'fibre' from both larger and smaller marsh monocotyledons is used to bind mud for walls (e.g. Danube Delta, Africa).

Herbal medicines Herbal medicines are still used in various ways in many cultures, but are now often replaced by cheap, easily obtainable and effective commercial drugs. Species currently or recently used for medicines are listed in pharmacopœia but most medicinal species are not so listed (though some appear in floras). *Acorus, Hypericum, Mentha, Menyanthes* and *Valeriana* are useful in Europe, and may be used direct from the wetlands, or be cultivated in gardens first. *Acorus calamus* was first introduced to Europe as a medicinal plant, but is now an integral part of several European wetland plant communities.

Miscellaneous minor uses

Wetland plants are used only seldom as fertiliser or mulch, as decomposition is often slow. Submerged plants, including coastal algae and weeds from eutrophic lakes are more beneficial. In remote places, plants can be burnt for salt (e.g. Africa, *Cyperus papyrus*; E. Lund, pers. comm.). Powdered *Equisetum* can be used as an abrasive and polishing agent; *E. hyemale* in Japan being of particularly high quality (Townsend & Guest, 1966). Grass turf for lawns can be sold, in affluent and populous areas, from summer dry wetlands. After harvest, new grass is sown and managed for *ca.* 4 years.

Shoots or rhizomes are locally used for fuel (e.g. Africa and Asia; Täckholm & Täckholm, 1941; Beetle, 1950; Perdue, 1958; Bohr with Guest, 1968).

Uses of mammals, birds and fish

Several categories are harvested or otherwise used:

1. Domestic animals pastured on the wetland (see above).
2. Waterfowl, fish and to a lesser extent, deer and other mammals, caught for recreation (see below).
3. Waterfowl, fish, etc. harvested for human food. This is usually of minor importance in wetlands without extensive open water.
4. Fur-bearers, etc. These are important in N. America, and form a minor crop in some other countries.

Fur and feathers

The species used for fur include: *Castor fiber* (beaver), *Lutra lutra* (otter), *Mustela vison* (mink), *Myocastor coypus* (coypu) and *Ondatra zibethicus* (muskrat).

These animals are usually trapped. Land management for fur bearers is little and recent, as it has been needed only with the decrease in undeveloped land. Management is applied to the proportions of open water, marsh and woodland, the changes in water regime, and the distribution of the mammals and their trapping points. It has proved successful (e.g. Bourn & Cottam, 1950; Steenis *et al.*, 1954). A few species, e.g. *Mustela vison* and *Myocastor coypus*, are also farmed for fur.

Feathers and down of birds may be collected.

Fish

Wetlands besides lakes are important feeding grounds for fish, subsequently harvested from the lake. Seasonal floods on river plains can be very productive, indeed, in tropical regions the most important inland fisheries are on such plains (see also pp. 293–6). These include the Cambodian part of the Mekong River and Grand Lac, and central Thailand (Hickling, 1961; Yamamoto & Backiel, 1968).

From the fishery point of view, such wetlands can be regarded as gigantic natural systems of hatcheries and breeding, nursing and wintering ponds, and in times of heavy spates they also operate as holding tanks (Holčík & Bastl, 1976; Holčík *et al.*, 1981).

Antipa (1912) was probably the first to point out the importance of floodplains for fisheries, emphasising that the floods in the flood-plain region of the lower Danube have a positive influence on the catch of fish. Later on, it was shown that there are statistically positive correlations, not only between the water levels and catch of fish in the current year (Ivanov, 1959; Stankovič & Jankovič, 1971) but also between the water levels of the preceding year and the catch in the current one, and that these correlations can be used to predict the future fish catch (Holčík & Bastl, 1977). The same principles are also valid for other rivers throughout the world (Welcomme, 1985). He stressed that any alterations in the intensity or duration of the floods can lead to changes in the fish populations in the following year. Welcomme & Hagborg (1977) developed a model of the relationships between African river fisheries and flood regime. They showed that both biomass and catch are dependent on the extent of flooding during high water and the amount of water remaining in the system during the dry season.

Wherever rice has been cultivated, fish have been harvested from the rice fields. Yields vary from a few kg to *ca.* 1800 kg ha^{-1} y^{-1}. Coche (1968) has reviewed this subject from the point of view of human food supply, and described various practices of combined fish-and-rice culture, or just simple capture of fish in the paddy fields.

In China there are specialised farms for breeding the fish in the paddy fields (Tapiador *et al.*, 1977). In addition to 4 t ha^{-1} of rice from the first rice crop and 5.3 t ha^{-1} from the second one, almost 1 t ha^{-1} of fish was also harvested each year, especially in the Kwantung province. Here, mainly carp and *Sarotherodon* spp. (probably *S. mossambicus*) were bred; in many other areas where rice has been cultivated further fish species have been used.

However, with the growing application of pesticides on wet rice fields, this kind of fish culture is losing its significance in agriculturally developed regions. For example, combined rice and tench culture was practically abandoned in Italy in the 1940s. Coche (1968) also discussed several attempts to control weeds, snails and mosquitoes in the paddy fields by means of fish. The problem has a health aspect, for snails are vectors of bilharzia, and mosquitoes are vectors of malaria. He reported some success in Shaba (Zaire), Indonesia and Malaysia, but the idea seems to have been abandoned, again mostly because of chemical control of these vectors and diseases.

Uses of sediments

Fen peat can be used for animal bedding. In affluent areas, however, it is sold for garden use. Peat cutting lowers the ground level (which effectively raises the water level) but can seriously deplete the available supply and damage or destroy the fen. Substitutes are being urgently sought. (The large-scale commercial use of peat for fuel, particularly to produce electricity, is not described, as acid bog peat is usually used and its use largely destroys the habitat.)

When new wetlands are made (e.g. for duck) in affluent and populous areas, the sale of the excavated soil can nearly cover the excavating costs (Anon., 1969).

Uses of physical and chemical properties of wetlands

Wetland ecosystems act on the flow of energy, water and materials passing through them, often producing changes beneficial to humans; although they sometimes act disadvantageously.

Purification of waters

As an extension of the natural tendency of wetlands to accumulate and metabolise sediments and nutrients (Louckes & Watson, 1977) they can filter, clarify and purify polluted water passing through them. The application of macrophyte stands for the purification of polluted waters was developed initially by Dr K. Seidel (1955, 1966, 1971; Bittmann & Seidel, 1967), and in the years after the IBP became widely used, e.g. Krotkevich, 1976, in Russia; Cooper & Green, 1995, in the UK and Moshiri, 1994, Kadlec & Knight, 1995, in the USA. For further examples see Klötzli (1967); Culley & Epps (1973); Toth (1972); National Academy of Sciences (1976) (review); Pieterse (1978) (review); Little, (1979) (review); Blake & Dubois (1982) (review); Haslam (1994) (report) and Ross (1995) (review).

Plants stands may purify because:

their presence creates heterogeneity and surfaces in the soil and water, which provide suitable conditions for a variety of chemical and biological interactions;

their rhizosphere and aufwuchs organisms absorb many pollutants and break down organic matter and toxins;

root exudates can eliminate pathogenic bacteria and promote mineralisation;

the macrophytes can transport oxygen into the soil. The macrophytes themselves can take up, accumulate and metabolize pollutants; but

their efficiency may decrease in winter, or as minerals, toxins and silt accumulate, and the community changes.

They are particularly suitable for cleaning up dirty effluents, stripping treated effluents of minerals, cleaning domestic water supplies and (when planted as barrier zones or buffer strips) for preventing the nutrients in diffuse run-off reaching water bodies. They are especially suited to cheap installations at remote sites where tourists cause severe seasonal pollution (Sloey *et al.*, 1978) and in the tropics, where year-round treatment is assured. They require only a low expenditure of capital and energy; although they do have a high requirement for land area.

Wetland types and species differ greatly in their ability to treat effluents and this can vary seasonally, even fluctuating between storage and release. Generally, they are efficient filters for suspended solids and organic matter and transformers of nitrogen, but vary more in their metabolism, absorption, precipitation and long-term storage of toxins and stable minerals

Table 8.3. *Efficiencies of removal of pollutants by wetlands*
(Pollutant removed/Pollutant input × 100)
(Sources of variation include species, retention time, over- or through-soil)

Natural		Schmitz *et al.*, 1982	
C.O.D.	>98%	Metals	10–98%
NO$_3^-$ N	99%	Bacteria	96–99%
Constructed		from Blake & Dubois, 1982 Maeseneer *et al.*, 1982 Haslam, 1994	
Nitrogen	25–99%	Toluene, benzene	99%
Phosphorus	14–95%	Pathogens	86–99%
Iron	82–99%	C.O.D.	71–90%
Manganese	9–98%	B.O.D.	55–90%
Heavy metals	'Substantial'	Suspended solids	55–90%
Sulphur compounds	'Substantial'	Chloroform	32%

such as phosphorus and metals (e.g. Blake & Dubois, 1982; Table 8.3). Individual species (and their micro-flora) may be particularly efficient at removing specific pollutants (e.g. Kickuth & Tittizer, 1974, *Iris pseudacorus*, toluene; Ozimek & Klekot, 1979, *Glyceria maxima* better than *Schoenoplectus lacustris* at accumulating nitrogen, phosphorus and some metals).

In temperate regions in Europe *Phragmites australis* is the species used most often in constructed purification wetlands. It is ecologically and physically tough, grows well in a wide range of habitats, and has good root and rhizosphere structure with good oxygen transfer. *Typha latifolia* is used more in North America (where it is commoner than *Phragmites*) and in warmer climates floating species like *Eichhornia crassipes* and *Lemna* spp. are favoured. It is even becoming possible to control the micro-flora, either by using pre-packaged selected organisms (Kostecki & Calabrese, 1991) or by acclimation to a specific pollutant.

There are various types of purifying wetlands, varying from the simple, such as buffer strips, or natural ponds or marsh with control over throughflow, to the complex, with specified gravel types, aeration, etc. (see Hammer, 1990; Kadlec & Knight, 1995). The most important features, of both design and management, ensure that the polluted water flows through the upper soil (roots of floating plants), and not over the top. Similarly, buffer strips need to be carefully sited with respect to the natural direction and depth of water movements in the soil. Some efficiencies achieved are summarised in Table 8.3, but more information is needed on how long these can be maintained before the artificial wetland needs reconstruction.

The mechanisms of removal vary with the pollutant but are basically similar to processes occurring in natural wetlands (cf. Chapters 1, 3, 4 and 6). The important oxygen may be supplied by the incoming water, by diffusion from the atmosphere or, particularly, by the transfer of atmospheric or photosynthetic oxygen from the leaves to the roots and soil by means of diffusion and wind-forced ventilation through the internal air spaces (see pp. 134–7). Organic materials, suspended and dissolved, are filtered out and decomposed, either aerobically to carbon dioxide or anaerobically to methane. Nitrogenous materials are broken down to ammonia or nitrates, and then taken up by plants. The plant nitrogen, unless harvested, is recycled, but ultimately much of the total nitrogen is lost as nitrogen gas by denitrification. Organic toxins accumulate in soils, micro-organisms and plants and often decompose at varying rates, while metals just accumulate, unless the plants are harvested or the soils changed. Phosphorus also accumulates in soils and plants, and for long-term treatment harvesting or soil changing is needed when saturation is attained (Richardson, 1985). Most of these processes are much slower in winter, which may restrict the application of constructed wetlands in temperate climates.

Storing excess water

Low-lying ground near main watercourses may be embanked to receive flood water. Extra water may be useful to drying wetlands, provided it is not more eutrophic or toxic than the natural water.

Shore protection

Reedswamp plants can be used to protect shores from erosion by waves or current. Their shoots decrease the water movement at ground level, and the underground parts consolidate the soil (Bittmann, 1957). Techniques of creating this biological barrier are described by Bittmann (1953, 1973).

This use declined after 1945 with the spread of cheap building materials, but interest has recently revived. Protection by plants is part of the ecological management of the shore, and is the most aesthetically pleasing technique.

Biological drainage of polders

Phragmites australis has been used in new polders in the Netherlands. When salinity is low enough, fruit is sown (by air). *Phragmites* increases water loss and prevents the establishment of species less easy to eradicate. Ploughing and arable crops follow in a few years (D. Bakker, pers. comm.). Similar water losses from reservoirs are disadvantageous (see Chapter 7).

Recreational uses of wetlands

These are discussed by Fritz (1977) and Odzuck (1978). Recreation usually comprises:

In the wetland	*Beside the wetland*
Viewing the scene	The activities done in the wetland,
Rambling	and:
Picknicking, camping, etc.	Boating (manually, sail and power
Photography, recording, etc.	propelled)
Nature study (including bird	Swimming
watching)	Fishing
Shooting (hunting)	

The demand for recreation rises with the prosperity of the visiting population, and the amenity value and ease of access of the wetland.

Mutually compatible activities

These usually involve few people. They include nature study, fishing, viewing, rambling, picnicking, photography, etc., provided visitors are few. There are three main types of wetland likely to be used.

1. Neglected or untouched wetlands in inaccessible areas, or small ones with a potentially somewhat higher visitor density. Small wetlands are aesthetically pleasing, but most visitors remain on the dry land alongside. Invasion by trees should be prevented, because of the loss of habitat diversity, the fundamental change in physiognomy, and the development of acid peat under conifers, but no other management is required unless changes are impending, in habitat or visitors.
2. Wetlands with traditional management for economic use. Limited recreation is satisfactory, though extra facilities may be desirable (see below).

3. Nature Reserves, which may also be (1) or (2) above. Their primary purpose is the conservation of all or part of the ecosystem, ideally all.

However, a wetland managed for plants may permit destructive shooting, or eutrophication and flooding may be allowed to alter the natural vegetation of one managed for waterfowl, etc. Visitor density varies with the aim of a Reserve, e.g. a reedbed managed for *Phragmites* and moths tolerates more visitors than the same bed regarded as a bird sanctuary. Wardens and car parks are needed if visitors are frequent.

Management should provide the maximum educational and aesthetic benefit with the minimum damage. Nature trails suit both purposes and can provide essential instruction on the importance of wetlands. Specialist leaflets are recommended (e.g. elementary and advanced, botanical and entomological, worksheets for schools). Escorted tours provide more information and protection, and may be organised for general viewing (more glamorous by boat) or study. Unescorted visitors should be directed by ditches, wet soil, *Urtica dioica*, etc., rather than by 'No Entry' signs. A summer dry path with little use needs mowing perhaps twice a year. With increased use, it must be widened or protected by boards, gravel, etc. In wetter places paths may be raised on rubble, etc., or constructed on stilts. Unescorted boats should be prohibited in reed-swamps, because of mechanical damage (e.g. Sukopp, 1971*a*). Escorted boat tours are advantageous in areas where substantial damage is possible.

Bird watching is often the main form of recreation. Birds and larger mammals tolerate less disturbance, and so need more protection, than other organisms. If visitors are numerous, it is advisable to have, e.g. hides (blinds, which also aid viewing), screened paths, and visitors limited to certain seasons or days. Occasional major disturbances are preferable to continual minor ones (Atkinson-Willes, 1969). Angling should be restricted to specified sites and seasons, e.g. through club membership. High densities of visitors restrict birds to tame species such as ducks.

Wetland fishing is mainly for recreation, as reedswamp and shallow water are unsuitable for large nets. It may, however, have the best fishing, as the fish, their eggs and their food supply are protected (see below). If the reedswamp surrounds a much-fished lake, it may be stocked. Access, and prevention of boat damage to reedswamp, must also be arranged. In more remote areas, wetland fishing may provide animal protein for the people living near.

Shooting

This is incompatible with other activities at any one time. Larger mammals (e.g. deer, fur-bearers) may be shot for sport or limitation, but large-scale harvesting is mainly trapping of fur-bearers. Management of populations, and of the proportion of open water, etc., improves both conservation and crop (e.g. Smirenskiĭ, 1950; Steenis *et al.*, 1954). Hides, screens and access are needed in more populous areas.

The shooting of duck, geese, etc. is mainly for recreation (although it sometimes forms an important source of animal protein). In some countries any birds may be shot (e.g. Malta). Where conservation laws are enforced, in remote parts and sanctuaries, shooting is negligible. The third extreme is when a small specified number of named species may be shot at specified times by licensed, brightly coloured hunters (e.g. parts of N. America, see Shaw & Fredine, 1971). Intermediates, of course, occur.

Pheasants, whether or not specially reared for sport, may depend on wetlands for shelter in winter and cover for nesting. Grazing or other removal of standing dead vegetation decreases nesting. Wetland drainage may decrease the crop of pheasants (e.g. Gates, 1970).

Waterfowl live, not only on wetlands, but also on adjacent open water and dry land. Many are migrants, and are thus targets for wildfowlers in many different places. Hence conservation is needed for each flyway as a whole. Coordination is easier if only one or two countries are concerned, e.g. N. America. Elsewhere, a network of sanctuaries is recommended along each flyway (Savage, 1972).

In spite of much drainage in N. America, particularly in the breeding areas, waterfowl populations remain adequate for preservation, photography etc. Management is required to produce a surplus for shooting (Crissey, 1969). This involves preserving small wetlands in the Prairies, etc. from drainage, infilling and agriculture. The Canadian Wildlife Service and Ducks Unlimited are mainly responsible (e.g. Canadian Wildlife Service, Saskatoon Wetlands Seminar, 1969; Drewier & Springer, 1969). Wetland diversity is, however, decreased as their management aims at shallow-flooded, sparse, eutrophic reedswamp around open water.

Activities involving many people and much disturbance

These include boating, camping, and any other activity which happens to have many adherents. Sites are usually in populous societies. They usually have open water; the wetland is inessential, but adds to the scenic value. In the less affluent areas, there is much disturbance from trampling, picnicking, etc., and few or no special facilities. Elsewhere, facilities increase with tourist pressure. First come access roads, car parks, paths or walking spaces, and sites for fishing, viewing and boats. Next come notice boards, leaflets, refreshments, wardens (to inform, guide, and decrease vandalism), specified areas for picnics, caravans and camping (to decrease fire risk, litter and pollution), personnel for water-skiing, cruising, etc., and impassable barriers where visitors must be excluded. Spectator sports bring the most visitors. The amenities bringing visitors will, however, decrease if facilities increase too much.

With light use in established shallow-water sites, vegetation may need limiting to increase recreational space. With intensive use, the position is reversed. Submerged vegetation is less tolerant than reedswamp, and reedswamp is less tolerant than woodland. Reedswamp needs protection (Sukopp, 1971*a*. 1973; Sukopp & Krauss, 1990, Klötzli, 1974), and the most tolerant vegetation should be encouraged. *Typha* spp. are fairly tolerant of mechanical damage, and *Acorus calamus* and *Glyceria maxima* resist some forms of eutrophic or industrial pollution. (Methods of restoration are described below, pp. 448–52.) Paths must be constructed, and summer dry reedswamp and woodland may be used to screen large numbers of visitors.

With dense use, different forms of recreation should be separated, in space or time. Parts of a large wetland, or each of a series of small ones, may have a single main use: the denser and noisier ones (e.g. water-skiing, camping) being at sites of easier access, followed by, e.g. angling and rambling and, at the most remote, bird watching. In all but the first, ordinary conservation principles apply. Use for sailing in summer and migrant waterfowl in winter is an example of seasonal separation.

In a non-changing ecosystem where the wetlands have never been managed, upkeep costs are low or absent. In drying or polluted areas they are higher, and where traditional management is required to maintain communities, and this does not pay, costs rise further. Recreation can cover the expenses of a reserve in an area attracting affluent visitors, without detriment to conservation.

Income can come from any of the uses for profit described in this chapter. Income from recreational uses can be in the form of shooting rights, fishing rights, entry fees, car park fees, hide fees, escorted tours, sales of leaflets, souvenirs, refreshments, etc., and from hiring boats, water-skiing, etc. Where these last form an important part, profits can be very high.

Many wetlands are endangered by being potential farmland. These are part of agricultural holdings, and as a different expertise is required to make wetlands profitable, drainage too often occurs without consideration of other possibilities. For conservation, almost any use is preferable to drainage, as reclamation is possible while a wetland exists. In populous and affluent parts, a profit equal to that from farming should usually be possible from a mixture of traditional (long-established, non-intensive, non-industrial) uses and recreation, in a sufficient number of places to conserve most traditional communities (Anon., 1971, 1973; also see Haslam, 1973*b,c*).

Use of wetlands for scientific research

Research can be carried on in any wetland, but nature reserves have the best facilities for most purposes, provided the research is non-destructive (see below). The starting of research, however, often leads to the establishment of a reserve in that place. Research is necessary for reserve management. Scientific research in reserves is a conservation–specific use (Haber, 1971).

Many scientific disciplines contribute to the understanding of wetlands. Observations of natural processes, and estimations of the effects of human impact and use are needed for studying self-regulating ecosystems and hence for regulating and governing our environment. Nature reserves are, or should be, used as indicators for all environmental changes. Wetlands are particularly sensitive indicators.

Reserves are necessary for experimental work, particularly that requiring protection from unforeseen changes in management or from vandals. Plant and animal successions are most profitably studied in reserves or remote areas, unless extreme biotic influences are to be investigated. Successions should be studied more, and this can best be done by the repeated mapping and analyses of vegetation of sample plots.

Westhoff (1972) has proposed a classification for conservation purposes of the situations occurring when vegetation is studied over a period of time:

1. No short-term succession, although some changes may occur in the course of centuries. This situation is widespread in stable environments.
2. Human interference over a whole region, which, within the wetland itself, either changes the original stability in a few and undesirable

ways, or alters the succession. Changes in water table is the most common example.

3. Disturbance from sudden changes in management within the wetland, such as the cessation of mowing, grazing, burning or trampling. These lead to a severe impoverishment in species. This has often surprised reserve managers.

4. Relatively rapid succession without interference. Such successions may be cyclic, progressive or arrested.

Well-equipped field stations in or near a wetland are advantageous when complex apparatus, or long periods in the field, are needed. Many field study centres are associated with areas of wetland in the UK and Germany. In the USSR 104 large reserves had field stations or research laboratories and similar facilities exist in many other countries. National parks often allow research at various levels.

If nature reserves are allowed to be used for both research and education, the primary purpose should be defined (Bauer, 1972). These primary purposes may be conservation, biological monitoring, commercial use or educational demonstration. There are many dangers in scientific research. The habitat or species studied may be altered by the work done. Changes in management can irreversibly alter communities. Disturbance can eliminate desired animals. Transplants can lead to the explosive growth of species not desired as dominants (also see below). In reserves, conservation should be more important than research.

Examples of outstanding specialised research on individual wetlands, which have contributed greatly to the understanding of these ecosystems, include the work on Wicken and neighbouring fens, England (see Godwin, 1978), fishponds in Czechoslovakia (see Dykyjová & Květ, 1978), the studies of the commercial use of the Danube Delta in Romania (see Rodewald-Rudescu, 1974) and the studies of the papyrus swamps of the Upper Nile (see Thompson, 1976*b*). The future aims of research in Britain are discussed in Hughes and Heathwaite (1995).

Conservation of wetlands

Conservation is, according to Morgan (1972), the management of habitats towards specified aims, with the intention of maintaining their scientific interest or rehabilitating their physical, chemical or biological quality.

The need for conservation

Wetland conservation is important for the many uses discussed above (Haslam, 1973*a*). Summarising, these are:

Economic purposes They produce plant materials, water, and animals for food, fur and sport.

The water balance of their regions They act as retention basins, and modify the water flowing through.

Recreation Their aesthetic value is high, and the specifically wetland features of waterfowl, reedswamps and open water attract visitors. Open water is also welcomed for boating activities.

Science and education Wetlands show a high diversity of types, and are often infrequent. They are particularly suitable for studying minor changes on natural habitats, rare species, population dynamics, succession and the equilibrium of natural communities, and as sources of genetic material.

In the past 40–100 years, wetlands in many countries have been considered economically useless, and consequently destroyed or altered. The largest losses have come from drainage and conversion to arable or other agricultural uses. This mostly occurs where the soils are fertile, but their fertility decreases thereafter very quickly. Other important causes of loss or damage are eutrophication, herbicides, the dumping of rubbish, and various forms of recreation. In contrast, Costanza *et al.* (1997) find flood-plains and wetlands are the second and fourth most economically valuable ecosystems.

The ecological basis of conservation

Ecological research is essential to guarantee conservation. Change must normally be avoided, and diversity and successional pattern be maintained. Many wetlands have been used for many centuries, and this must be considered when designing plans for conservation. The minimum area, the water regime (optimum levels and fluctuations), the influence of eutrophication (from inflowing water, birds, etc.) and requirements for buffer zones are among the other factors to be taken into account.

Water regime

The water regime, i.e. water level and its fluctuations, is the most important ecological factor controlling wetlands (Gilman, 1994; see Chapter 1). The dependence on water regime of the most important European wetland types (in habitats drier than littoral belts) is shown in Table 8.4. References are cited in Sculthorpe (1967) and Klötzli (1969). Wetlands, of course, require a high water table and unless they have an independent water supply, they are affected by the other uses of water. Drainage and abstraction are lowering the water table in many industrial and densely populated lowland regions. There is also increasing pressure on land use, especially in fertile, low-lying areas which include wetlands. Wetlands are among the most threatened habitats. Within this category, wet grasslands are the most at risk: especially the flood and water meadows mown or grazed in summer and (at least formerly) flooded in winter. This management allowed much bird life. Here, only a small drop in water level will prevent most winter flooding. These grasslands can also be converted to arable more easily than other wetlands. Except for reserves, wet grasslands are likely to be completely lost in industrial areas.

Chemical regime

Chemical conditions are the next most important factors (see Chapters 1 and 6). Most nutrients and other substances leading to chemical changes come from domestic, factory and agricultural discharges. The chemicals may come directly from the air, effluents, run-off or groundwater, or they may reach the wetland indirectly, via polluted lakes or rivers or from fertilized agricultural land. Other sources may be locally important, e.g. birds (Moss *et al.*, 1978). The exact quantities, and the effects attributable to each chemical may not always be clear. A variety of studies, ranging from general accounts to more specific examples, is given in Table 8.5.

Plant communities change or break down when exposed to excessive nutrients (e.g. nitrogen, phosphorous; Table 8.6) or toxins (e.g. sulphites, detergents, pesticides, acids). The breakdown of vegetation normally leads to the loss of the animal communities as well, even if these are individually not harmed directly by the pollution.

Plant sensitivity varies, *Glyceria maxima* populations being unusually tolerant (e.g. Klötzli, 1969). Even vigorous *Phragmites australis* stands may break down under the combined action of mechanical disturbance and excessive nutrients (Klötzli & Grunig, 1976; Klötzli, 1986; Binz, 1989).

The sensitivity of wetlands to eutrophication depends both on their trophic level, and the amount and type of the incoming nutrients. The more eutrophic the site, the less the effect of added nutrients. The effect also depends on the absorption capacity of the humus layer, and the way the nutrients are brought to the site. Seepage into the bottom of deep peat has less effect than flooding at ground level. Peat is less sensitive than most mineral soils. Many nutrient-poor communities have become scarce because of nutrients coming from fertilised areas nearby. If eutrophication is allowed in the most exposed areas, it may be possible to protect oligotrophic areas of high conservation value (e.g. Niemann & Wegener, 1976; Boller-Elmer, 1977).

Abstraction of groundwater may seriously change the chemical regime and vegetation of wetlands (Haslam, in press). Even if they remain wet, rain or surface water are likely to have a different composition, and to deprive the wetlands of nutrients. In Western Europe this commonly occurs when calcium-rich water maintaining fens is taken from limestone or chalk aquifers.

Physical management, grazing and other damaging events

Mowing (intensity, season and equipment used), grazing, trampling and burning also control the plant, and through this the animal (particularly bird) communities (Dykyjová & Květ, 1978 and see pp. 447–52). Other extreme influences may be superimposed (e.g. frost damage is worse in cut stands), or damage may follow other effects (e.g. severe insect damage may follow the absence of flooding in *Phragmites* stands, Haslam, 1971*a,b*; 1973*a,b*; Mook & van der Toorn, 1974). The timing and duration of traumatic events such as flooding or burning may influence their effects (e.g. through seedling establishment, when *Salix cinerea* colonised after a fire in early summer, but *Calamagrostis lanceolata* after burning at other seasons).

Sensitivity to mechanical disturbance depends on the plant community, the soil conditions and the adaptability to the source of disturbance.

Damage, as distinct from grazing, by vertebrates is described in many publications, e.g. Errington (1963); Hoffmann (1964); Hudec and Šťastný (1978); Pelikán (1978); Sukopp and Krauss (1990).

Table 8.4. *The influence of water table on soil type and plant communities in some Central European wetlands (from Klötzli, 1969)*

Seasonal[a] periodicity group	Average water level[b] Annual[d] (cm)	Gr. season[c] (cm)	Annual[d] fluctuation (cm)	Weekly fluctuation[e] (cm)	Duration of flooding Annual[f] (wk)	Gr. season (wk)	Soil type[g]	Plant community
—5	25–40	30–40	>140	92–31	5	2	Niedermoor, Anmoor	*Caricetum elatae typicum, (Acrocladium-variant)*
—5	25–40	30–40	116	30–40	5	2	Mull – partly wet-gley	*Primulo-Schoenetum Stachyetosum* (drier variants)
—6	15–25	7–25	84–92	14–24	13	9	Wet-gley to Anmoor	*Caricetum davallianae* (drier variants)
—6	15–25	7–25	89	20	13	9	Wet-gley	*Ranunculo-Caricetum hostianae*
—7	5–12	7–11	89	15–14	20	8.5	Wet-gley to Anmoor	*Caricetum acutae*

—— 8	5–12	7–11	65	30–12	7.5	3	Peat–Gyttja
8	5–12	7–11	40	8–7	9	0.5	Wet-gley, Anmoor, partly Calcareous tuff
8	0–+10	ca. 0	20–30	2–5	40–50	20–24	Intermediate fen, Niedermoor, Peat–Gyttja

Caricetum diandrae

Primulo-Schoenetum (wet variants)

Caricetum elatae comaretosum, Chrysohypno-Caricetum lasiocarpae (dry variant)

[a] The group number refers to the type of seasonal periodicity in water level, as shown in the illustrations beside each example. Each point shows the number of weeks a certain water level is reached or exceeded. Horizontal axis – whole year and (vertical line) 28 week growing season. Vertical axis – horizontal line at 50 cm below surface (main root horizon). Duration groups 1–4 are drier than wetlands; group 8 has quaking mats and hence does not have a fully matching graph.

[b] Water levels in cm below ground level, unless shown as +, for flood levels.

[c] Broken line.

[d] Full line.

[e] Arrows.

[f] Horizontal bar.

[g] Soil types as defined in Mückenhausen (1959), except Anmoor, defined as in Göttlich (1965).

Table 8.5. *Examples of studies of pollution and wetland macrophytes*

Pollution	Reference	Plant community
General accounts	Carbiener (1969)	
	Kokin (1962)	
	Kurimo (1970)	Helophytes and hydrophytes
	Lathwell *et al.* (1969)	Helophytes
	Perttula (1952)	
	Sawyer (1962)	
	Suominen (1968)	
Eutrophication	Klötzli (1967)	*Carex elata* fen
	Klötzli (1974)	*Phragmites australis* die-back
	Klötzli & Grünig (1976)	Bank plants as indicators
	Lang (1967)	Lake communities
	Lundegårdh-Ericson (1972)	*Phragmites australis* invasion
	Sukopp *et al.* (1975)	Reedswamp
	Vass (1971)	
Toxins		
Smelters	Gorham & Gordon (1963)	
Sulphite and organic materials	Eloranta (1970)	
Phenols, metals	Seidel (1971)	Helophytes – remove toxins
Hot water	Sharitz *et al.* (1974)	Swamp forest

Other organisms

The sections above have dealt mainly with the effects on the primary producers, but there are also direct and indirect effects on the micro-biological and animal communities. Many wetland animals, invertebrates, birds, amphibia and fish, prefer special plant communities for their nutrition and other aspects of their behaviour (e.g. Table 8.7 and see Table 8.11). Water depth may affect the distribution of birds (see Haslam, 1973*b*), and fish (e.g. Ehranfeld, 1970). The interrelations of wetland plants and animals, particularly invertebrates, are discussed by Gaevskaya (1966/69) (also see p. 452 and Chapter 5).

Changes in wetlands

Lohammar (1949) and Caspers (1964) have discussed the problems in general. See also the review by Tallis (1983), with emphasis on acidophilous vegetation.

Table 8.6. *Changes in some Central European wetland plant communities induced by eutrophication (Klötzli, 1967; Sukopp, 1971b, Klötzli, 1986)*

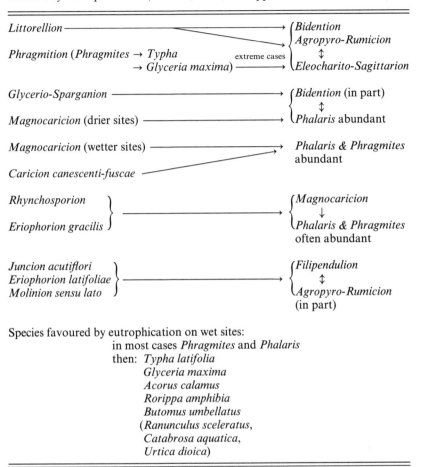

Species favoured by eutrophication on wet sites:
in most cases *Phragmites* and *Phalaris*
then: *Typha latifolia*
Glyceria maxima
Acorus calamus
Rorippa amphibia
Butomus umbellatus
(*Ranunculus sceleratus,*
Catabrosa aquatica,
Urtica dioica)

Examples of changes in landscapes and catchments

North America Wetlands comprise 3.5% of the land surface of the United States, but have been reduced from *ca.* 870 000 km^2 to *ca.* 100 000 km^2 (Niering, 1985). Well-documented examples include:

The Florida Everglades There is a long history of drainage to 'reclaim' land for agriculture and for flood prevention, and some only slightly less disastrous early attempts at integrated management (Niering, 1985).

Table 8.7. *Spawning and hatching areas of fish on Lake Constance (Nümann & Deufel, personal communication)*

Species of fish	Water depth (cm)	Season	Plant community
Esox lucius	+30–40	Spring (eggs)–autumn (young fish)	Sedge meadows on land side of reed (*Carex elata, Carex panicea,* etc.)
Cyprinus carpio	+30–40	Spring–early summer (eggs)	Sedge meadows (*Carex elata, Carex vesicaria,* etc.)
Rutilus rutilus *Scardinius erythrophthalmus* *Tinca tinca*	+20–50	Winter (all ages) spring–late spring (eggs)	Reedbeds
Perca fluviatilis	+20–50	Late spring (eggs)	Reed, only when no submerged vegetation
Abramis brama	50	Spring–late spring (eggs)	Zone in front of reedbed

Great Lakes Area, especially Lake Erie (Canada/USA) Stuckey (1968) has described the loss of aquatic and marsh plants from pollution.

Lake Manitoba Dirschl (1972) and Walker [Walker-Shay] (1959, 1965 and pers. comm.) outline the hydrological problems due to the construction of a power station, and to drainage of neighbouring land (2 to 4% of wetlands being lost each year). Stabilisation of the water table has decreased waterlevel fluctuations from *ca.* 2 m to *ca.* 0.45 m, and this, together with dams and drainage channels (made in 1968) have led to uninterrupted successions of *Phragmites* and *Salix*. Plans for multi-purpose management are discussed.

Lake Okoboji (Iowa) Volker and Smith (1965) describe changes in vegetation due to pollution.

Prairie Pothole Areas Over 4000 km^2 of wetland were drained between 1943 and 1961, with a loss of over 10% of waterfowl breeding areas (Linduska, 1964).

Unfortunately there are many other examples, e.g. Holder (1969); Mann (1969); Teal and Teal (1969); Milwey (1970); Bonnema (1972); Dirschl (1971); Choate (1972) and Niering (1985).

Europe

Biesbosch Delta (Netherlands) Zonneveld (1960*a,b*) has described successions induced by eutrophication, freshwater influence and stabilisation of the lake level.

Boden See (Switzerland) Many workers, e.g. Lang (1968); Wagner (1970); Klötzli and Grünig (1976) and Klötzli and Züst (1973*a,b*), have studied the effects of pollution, especially the increase in plant-available phosphate from 0 μl^{-1} in 1935 to 25 μl^{-1} in 1970. These include changes in macrophytes, especially the declining density, and retreat (at 1–3 m y^{-1}) of *Phragmites* belts.

Central Europe Table 8.6 shows changes in plant communities commonly seen in association with eutrophication in this region.

Czech Republic Hejný (1990) has described how various levels of human interference cause advance or retreat of plant communities in fishponds. There is a general decline of wetland plants and plant communities, often due to the control of reedbelt stands in fishponds by heavy machines, duck farming and the severe eutrophication of the fishponds.

Ems Valley (North-Western Germany) Maps show many changes (Meisel & Hubschmann, 1975).

Denmark & S. Sweden Olsen has described the influence of town sewage, and Lilieroth (1950) the lowering of the water table following cultivation.

Havel Seen (Berlin) Raghi-Atri (1976), Raghi-Atri and Bornkamm (1978) and Sukopp and Markstein (1989) give the effects of recreation and other activities on shore vegetation, discussing the retreat of *Phragmites* in detail, and describing the retreat of plant communities. Between 1962 and 1987 there has been a retreat of reedbeds from 40% of shoreline to 12%.

Hornborgasjön (Sweden) Björk (1972) described a managed change, reclaiming a drained lake overgrown by *Phragmites* by winter cutting, flooding in spring, and summer cutting with a rotary cultivator.

Ijsselmeer Polders (Netherlands) Feekes (1936) and Feekes and Bakker (1954) studied plant successions on wetlands created during land reclamation, with varying salinity and soil moisture.

Lac Léman, Lac Lucerne, Pfäffikin See and Zurich See (Switzerland) These have shown a large scale, simultaneous retreat of *Phragmites* and replacement of *Schoenus* by *Carex elata* swamps (e.g. Lachavanne & Wattenhofer, 1975a,b; Klötzli, 1986).

Mecklenburg Lakes (Germany) Jeschke (1976) gives a general account of the retreat of reed.

Neerach Swamp (Switzerland) Ellenberg and Klötzli (1967) and Klötzli (1967) show how eutrophic effluent changed a *Carex elata* community to monodominant *Phagmites*.

Neusiedlersee (Austria/Hungary) Weisser (1970), Löffler (1974), Burian and Sieghardt (1979) and Schiemer (1979) include accounts of alterations in reedbeds and submerged macrophytes.

Norfolk Broads (UK) Ellis (1965) described the origin of these artificial wetlands, the decline in open water and reedswamp between 1830 and 1946, and some later changes. More recent changes are reported by Haslam (1973a,b), George (1977, 1992) and Boorman and Fuller (1981), and currently attempts are being made to restore the vegetation.

Overasseltse and Hatertse Vennen (Netherlands) Strijbosch (1976) investigated changes in fen and pond vegetation by birds (development of *Bidentetea* communities and *Juncus effusus* meadows from *Scheuchzerietea*, quickly going to *Phragmites* communities), and by agriculture (*Parvocaricetea* fens going over slowly into *Phragmitetea*).

W. and N. Netherlands Van Zinderen Bakker (1942, 1947), Westhoff (1949), Segal (1966) and Creuzberg *et al.* (1969) describe the landscapes, the origin and development of the artificial lakes, the plant and animal ecology and the hydrobiology.

An Asian example

Lake Baikal (Siberia) Savich (1967) describes the result of an increase in water level following construction of a new power station, and partial flooding of a large swamp.

Africa

Lake Chilwa (Nyasaland) Major changes were due to climatic fluctuations (Howard-Williams, 1973).

Lake Kariba (Zimbabwe/Zambia) After a major dam was built floating wetlands developed from an initial invasion of the alien species *Salvinia molesta* (D.S. Mitchell, 1969).

River Nile The sudd swamps of the Sudan have long been threatened by plans to construct the Jonglei canal (Howell *et al.*, 1988).

Extinct, endangered and impoverished wetland plant communities

These have been studied in most detail in the Netherlands, where over 20 distinct wetland communities only occur in less than ten $25 \, km^2$ grid squares, and well over 30 communities are regarded as strongly endangered. All of these have been regressing, although most of them are now protected in conservation areas (Westhoff & den Held, 1969; V. Westhoff & R.J. de Boer, pers. comms.). Sukopp *et al.* (1978) found similar changes in central Europe. Some community changes are traced by Klötzli (1967, 1979), for Switzerland, and Kaule (1973) for South Bavarian lakes. The retreat of systematic groups is shown by Hejný and Husák (1978) for pond vegetation, and Schoef-van Pelt (1973) for the *Littorellion* communities. The disappearance of suitable sites is clearly due to:

the general eutrophication of many European lakes (due to intensification of agriculture, and to detergents;
the destruction of flat shores (land reclamation and consequent erosion); and the drainage of wetlands;

which were, separately and together, detrimental to oligotrophic and helophytic communities.

*Changes in the frequency and distribution of wetland species**

Such changes have been reviewed by Sukopp (1972) who summarises the deleterious effects of human interference as:

Direct effects By the introduction of effective competitors (e.g. *Spartina townsendii*), by the introduction of animal and plant pests (e.g. the effect of *Myocastor* on *Phragmites*), or by mechanical disturbance (e.g. boats, damage to reed belts).

Indirect effects Through eutrophication, pollution or by lowering the groundwater table (see above).

The following examples illustrate the extent of the problem:

Belgium In the century up to 1970, 19 wetland species had disappeared, 9 were retreating, 15 were in danger, and 70 were threatened (Lawalrée, 1971).

Britain In the 300 years to 1975 seven wetland species became extinct and 27 were endangered (Perring, 1976; Dony, 1977). Eighteen species were found in only 25–35% of the 10 km squares they once occupied.

Switzerland Landolt (1991) includes endangered wetland species.

Many other papers describe species changes brought about by human activities, e.g. Australia, Specht *et al.* (1974); Belgium, Delvosalle *et al.* (1969), Delvosalle and Vanhecke (1982); Germany, Sukopp *et al.* (1976), Korneck and Sukopp (1988).

Clearly, at least in Europe, wetland species have retreated at an alarming rate during the past century. The loss of species such as *Eleocharis soloniencis* and *Limosella aquatica* is due to the destruction of oligotrophic and mesotrophic habitats. Drainage, pollution (including eutrophication) and direct human disturbance account for most other losses. Many species can now survive only in protected areas. Methods of preservation are described below (pp. 442–62).

Die-back

Special problems for habitat management arise from the die-back of dominant species. This is particularly found with *Phragmites australis* (e.g. Hürlimann, 1951; Klötzli, 1971; Klötzli & Zust, 1973*a,b*; Klötzli &

---

* Deliberate changes are described on pp. 445, 448 and generally in pp. 444–62.

Table 8.8. *Research on causes of reed die-back*

Disturbance (boats, trampling)		Dittrich & Westrich, 1990
		Iseli, 1900, 1993
		Kühl & Neuhaus, 1993
		Ostendorp, 1990
Erosion		Dittrich & Westrich, 1990
		Ostendorp, 1990
		Wöbbecke & Ripl, 1990
		Sukopp, 1991
		Huber, 1993
Animal damage	Coypu	George, 1992; Boorman & Fuller, 1981
	Donacia	Fuchs, 1993
	Musk rat	Krauss, 1993
	See also sources of damage in Chapter 5, pp. 301–17	
Water level fluctuations		Wöbbecke & Ripl, 1990
		Sukopp, 1991
		Krauss, 1993
		Luft, 1993
Pollution	Excessive	Ksenofontova, 1989
	With algal mats	Sukopp, 1991
		Čižková-Končalová *et al.*, 1996
		Leyrink & Hubatsch, 1993
		van der Putten, 1994
Not pollution		Iseli, 1990
		Hosnor *et al.*, 1990
		Ostendorp, 1990
	May be indirect effects	Boorman & Fuller, 1981

Grünig, 1976; Boorman & Fuller, 1981; Ostendorp, 1989 and other papers in den Hartog, 1989).

Reed die-back has only been reported from stands fronting open waters but there it has been extensive. In the English Broadland it has been recorded since the 1940s (starting on soft substrates, George, 1992), although it only became serious in continental Europe in the early 1970s. It has caused much concern, reedbeds having amenity as well as ecological value, and often also economic value.

Die-back can be contained, and even reversed, by protective measures allowing the reedbed to have a stable, undisturbed habitat with suitable water and nutrient regime (Pier *et al.*, 1993; Schanz, 1993; see also pp. 449–52 and Fig. 8.1).

This die-back has been attributed to many causes (recently reviewed by

Ostendorp & Krumscheid-Plankert, 1990; Van der Putten, 1997; Table 8.8) most of which arise from human interference or management. Probably many act indirectly, several can act at any one site and die-back at different sites will have different causes. The most important mechanisms seem to be initiated by disturbance at exposed sites and by interactions between hydrology and eutrophication. These can lead to anoxic, toxic or sequestering accumulations of litter and soils, metabolic disturbances decreasing the carbohydrate reserves for overwintering and regrowth, and the development of callus in the rhizome aeration system. Any initial weakening may lead to bacterial infection, and also breakage of culms underwater, which will further interfere with rhizome aeration (p. 136). Neuhaus *et al.* (1993) pointed out that stands may consist of single or several clones that thrive in the initial conditions, but have different responses from clones of other sites. The clones of nutrient-poor sites may respond to changes at lower levels than those of initially more fertile sites, and sites with single clones may be particularly more sensitive to all sorts of changes causing die-back.

Die-back of other species has been described by Lambert (1964; *Spartina*); and van der Valk and Davis (1978; *Scirpus validus*). In the latter case the die-back is shown to be part of a 5–20 year cycle.

When changes are due to eutrophication, the habitat may be left open, or be colonised by species tolerating highly eutrophic conditions, e.g. algae, *Acorus calamus, Catabrosa aquatica* and *Ranunculus sceleratus*. Such communities, of course, may not support the same animal populations as the reed belts.

Introduced species

The introduction and distribution of new species have been described by Mitchell, 1974 (including reference lists) and Sculthorpe, 1967; Weber, 1967; Weber-Oldecop, 1970–71 and Sukopp, 1971*a,b*, 1972 (including reference lists). Two thirds of all invaders established in natural wetland vegetation occur in small water-courses, particularly in plant communities of the *Bidention* and *Convolvulion*, and in *Azolla* and *Elodea* mats. Plants and animals from warmer countries, are becoming established in warmwater effluents below power stations (see also Parker, 1973).

Techniques of conservation

The ways in which wetland conservation is effected vary from laws and regional planning measures to simple or complex management techniques

(Duffey & Watt, 1971; Kaule, 1971; Haslam, 1973*b*; Klötzli, 1978; Weller, 1978; Newbould *et al.*, 1983; Pfadenhauer & Klötzli, 1996; see also p. 464). The aim is the creation or maintenance of desirable, stable plant and animal communities.

Evaluation of wetland habitats

In order to select nature reserves, the available wetland areas must be evaluated, with full records of the plant and animal communities and of rare species. Originally most work was based on wetland birds. Some information is now available on whole biotopes, but the earlier annotated lists were only from wetlands already being conserved for their scientific value (e.g. Ant & Engelke, 1970; Luther & Rzóska, 1971; Bauer, 1972–1974). There is a need to incude sites which it is desirable to conserve as well as those in which it is being achieved. Data are being gathered, but much is in reports with limited circulation (e.g. Nature Conservancy Council, UK, internal reports).

The main ecological criteria for the evaluation of wetlands are species diversity, and the rarity and irreplaceability of the habitat (e.g. Sukopp, 1971*b*; Patten, 1990).

Hammack and Brown (1974) and Barbier *et al.* (1997) discuss the economic costs and valuation of wetlands.

Legal enforcement of conservation

To ensure conservation in changing or populous regions, laws and regulations are necessary at both national and local level (McCormick, 1974; Untermaier, 1991). The law may concern the whole wetland or even the whole catchment. In parts of North America, organisations with the appropriate licences have power to retain water for wetlands, and even to expropriate wetlands for wildlife purposes (Mitchell, G.C., 1969). Official permission may be necessary before a wetland can be altered or drained, permission being refused if wetland conservation in the area is inadequate. Financial inducements may also be used to retain and conserve wetlands (NCC UK Annual Reports).

Laws may also concern the water management (water balance and water quality) or the plant management (grazing, cutting, access, etc.). Reedswamps are legally protected in Switzerland and in Berlin. Conservation and regeneration of reedbeds have proved difficult under much recreational pressure, so the Berlin laws forbid boats and people (wading or swimming) within the reedswamp. Boats may not anchor within 2 m of the reedswamp. A Polish law permits reed cutting only above ice.

Exploitation for plant materials, fish, waterfowl, etc. may be regulated by law, and in many countries named plant and animal species are protected under special laws for conservation or sport.

Regional planning

Careful planning is needed for large-scale tourist movement and recreation in wetlands. Some examples of regional plans for wetlands and their surroundings are given in Sukopp and Kunick (1969); Kadner (1971); Kaule (1971); Anon. (1973); Carter (1977*a,b*); Roman and Good (1990); Mitsch (1994).

Ecosystem management

The management and control of nature reserves must be based on ecological principles. In contrast to earlier ideas, the human control of nature is now regarded as indispensable to the preservation of variety-in-space and stability-in-time.

The management of nature reserves aims at conserving their various habitats against alterations arising both within and without. A secondary aim is the increasing of their internal spatial variety. The greater the variety-in-space, the greater the resistance to variety-in-time. For both aims, the cybernetical term 'regulation amplifying' describes the conservation measures.

Some general rules are given by van Leeuwen (1966). Two main types of control can be recognised: internal control (the continuation of traditional management within the reserves, rules 1–3), and external control (protection from external influences, rules 4–6).

These rules are:

1. Botanical richness is best preserved if management remains very similar to the traditional management and there is no period without management. (Where the water level is falling, however, this should be rectified separately).
2. Where the character and size of a reserve permit, internal variety and regulation can be increased by furthering the development of ecoclines based on the degree of human influence within the area.

3. Controlling operations should be done gradually and on a small scale.
4. Measures for protecting reserves from external influences in landscapes with a coarse-grained pattern must be based on the shape and size of the reserves. Reserves which are circular and large are the most secure from external threats as they have the greatest proportion of their area away from the boundaries.
5. If a reserve is large enough, management should take advantage of the ecoclines developing near the boundaries where internal and external influences interact. In these conditions oligotrophic (internal) influences can resist eutrophic (external) ones.
6. If changes are induced from outside, internal management should aim at delaying them.

The need to conserve habitats is self-evident, but the decision to conserve individual species requiring specialist management is more difficult. Very rare species, those typical of a habitat, or in the centre of their range should be given priority (Morgan, 1972). Decisions should depend partly on management costs and partly on the effort required. If 4–5 years intensive work fails to retain a species, further effort is probably more profitably directed in other ways. An example of the management of a site to match the ecology of the very rare species, *Ranunculus ophioglossifolius*, is discussed by Dring and Frost (1971). The conservation of a well-known and much studied wetland (Wicken Fen, UK) is described in Friday (1997).

Experiments to increase habitat diversity have been undertaken by Westhoff (1972), Haslam (1973*a,b*) and Eigner and Schmatzler (1980).

Measures for wetland management include the construction of impoundments (mainly for water engineering), works to regulate water levels (for plant and animal management, e.g. reeds or waterfowl), making islands for waterfowl (for cover, nesting, resting and observation), control of plants by mechanical, chemical or biological means, or by burning (see below), removing woody plants, constructing ponds for waterfowl and aquatic plants, harvesting or culling plants and animals, increasing the attractiveness of the site to certain species (e.g. to obtain and retain migrant waterfowl) and establishing rare plants and animals. Examples can be found in Linde (1969), Haslam (1973*a*), Good *et al.* (1978), Klötzli (1981*a*, 1989), Whigham *et al.* (1990), Hammer (1992), Mitsch (1994) and Hawke and José (1995). Denny (1985) and Roggeri (1995) discuss the management of tropical wetlands.

Water level control

The cost of restoration or maintenance depends primarily on the water table. Where this is falling, treatment is necessary, but this treatment varies from merely decreasing drainage, to creating a water-holding system, using water diverted from elsewhere.

Where ground level is lowered, or water level raised, new wetlands are being created, as in disused gravel pits and reservoirs. Recreation, at intensities expected to damage natural wetlands, should be directed into these new areas until it interferes with the prime use of the wetland (e.g. water quality in a reservoir).

The primary control over wetland vegetation is through the water table. The best control in large fens and marshes comes from intersecting dykes, with inflow and outflow controlled by pumps, sluices and valves giving individual control of each dyked (and banked) compartment (see Haslam, 1973*b*). In regions of falling water level irrigation is usually more important than drainage. Lateral water movement through soil is slow, so unless dykes are adjacent and frequent, winter floods or summer drought can persist in central parts. Regulation also affects flow. Some communities, e.g. of *Cladium mariscus*, are favoured by flow, while others, e.g. of *Carex elata*, do best in more stagnant conditions.

Wetlands on peaty soils or in peat-bog complexes often need special attention, because of the shrinkage, or accumulation of the peat, and the effects on water table.

Dykes (open drains) also provide habitat diversity, open water, boundaries and firebreaks. They permit access by boat, which is useful for moving harvested plants, and for conveyance on nature trails. They prevent really stagnant conditions, but if contaminated (e.g. eutrophic) water enters the system, dykes quickly spread it through the wetland.

Habitat diversity in respect of water level may come from varying either water or ground level. The former is achieved by the compartmental dyke control system. The latter occurs on lake shores, former peat cuttings, newly made pools, etc. Creation of open waters can be achieved by cutting, trampling and grazing, dredging or explosives. Such open waters are used mainly for waterfowl conservation or fishing. Large-scale lake restoration may involve the destruction and removal of wetlands, e.g. of *Phragmites* and *Salix* spp. in Hornborgasjön (Björk, 1971).

Cutting, burning, etc

Many wetlands will, if left alone, bear monodominant stands of herbs, e.g. *Phragmites*, in wet places, and trees, e.g. *Salix* spp., in drier ones. Management (cutting, etc.) produces habitat diversity and multiuse sites.

Cutting and burning both remove above-ground parts, and expose the top soil to greater temperature fluctuations. Burning may harm the fauna more, especially if it is done carelessly, or if the basal litter is allowed to burn; but it is often cheaper than cutting. Summer burning, however, may not be possible in wet years. Some plants, e.g. *Glyceria maxima* are selectively favoured by burning (Hejný, 1959; Mallik & Wein, 1986). Thompson (1976*a*) found that regular burning of tropical papyrus swamps can lead to considerable losses of nutrients and decrease the annual productivity by up to 75%. In contrast van der Toorn and Mook (1982) found that burning increased the productivity of temperate *Phragmites* stands by reducing insect damage.

Large-scale cutting in wetlands produces fodder and litter for domestic animals, and materials for thatching and industry (see pp. 407–10). Both uses occur most in Europe, the latter mainly where there are (or potentially are) large monodominant areas of *Phragmites australis*, and a demand for products which can be made from this species. The former was usually developed for horse fodder in the days of horse transport. In the more populous countries such as Britain, most wetlands were managed, for many centuries, mainly by cutting, and the plant and animal communities are dependent on this management. This is especially so where the water level is falling, and the invasion of woody plants and tall terrestrial or semi-terrestrial dicotyledons is only prevented by regular cutting at the correct season.

Therefore, in wetlands which have been managed for a long time, regular cutting is necessary to preserve the existing communities. In wetlands which have not previously been cut, cutting may be necessary if the water level is lowered or if habitat diversity is to be increased. The season and frequency of cutting determine its result. Some cutting techniques are described above.

Tall grasses or dicotyledonous herbs may be cut annually or biennially in summer or autumn, for use as fodder or litter. Good fodder is said to come from *Glyceria maxima* and *Phalaris arundinacea* meadows, which are cut in summer whenever the crop is tall enough (Armstrong, 1950; Petersen, 1954). *Cladium mariscus* is cut in summer or early autumn every *ca.* 4 years. *Phragmites australis*, in temperate regions, is cut in winter annually or biennially. Cutting may be used as a management tool, producing diverse plant, and therefore animal, communities within a potentially uniform wetland (e.g. Fiala & Květ, 1971; Husák, 1978).

Grazing, possible in summer dry wetlands, is a similar management tool, being effectively a long-continued low-level cut associated with compaction and movement of the upper soil (which is liable to damage superficial rhizomes). Heavy grazing produces pasture containing short marsh plants. *Juncus subnodulosus* marsh, which is often rich in orchids, etc., is favoured by light grazing or frequent cutting.

Some details on miscellaneous techniques concerned with nutrient status, salt water, food plants for water fowl, and the removal of undesirable species are described in Haslam (1973*a,b*).

Restoration of lakes and their wetlands

Lakes which have been polluted or drained can be, to some extent, restored to their original condition. The first measures are to stop the inflow of effluents and raise the water level, but these alone may be insufficient. Limnological effects of these measures are described by Edmondson (1972) and Mathiesen (1970, 1971).

Further measures, which may be necessary, include the removal of sediments, aeration and the removal of macrophytes (including underground parts). The original methods were worked out in Sweden, and can be modified for other areas as required (see Björk, 1971; Björk *et al.*, 1978; Andersson, 1973; Ripl, 1978; Klötzli, 1991; Pfadenhauer & Klötzli, 1996).

Hornborgasjön, in Sweden (*ca.* 30 km^2, used to be up to 3 m deep), had been drained, and was mainly overgrown by *Phragmites australis* and *Carex acuta*. The *Phragmites* areas (*ca.* 11 km^2) were converted to open water. Reeds were cut in winter, spring and summer, and in autumn the stubble and underground parts were broken up by a rotor cultivator. The detritus from this was washed up on the shores in spring. The lake substrate became mud, and was colonised by, e.g. *Chara, Potamogeton* and *Myriophyllum*. The waterfowl, bottom fauna, microbenthos and periphyton all increased. The *Carex* areas (*ca.* 18 km^2) were kept as emergent vegetation. When the water level was raised, the below-ground plant parts floated to the water surface, buoyed up by the gas (mainly methane) forming in and below them. *Phragmites, Schoenoplectus* and *Carex* colonise this area. A mosaic of reedswamp and open water was created (with amphibious excavators) to increase waterfowl.

Creation, restoration and protection of wetlands

Species suitable for planting, and recommended techniques, are given in Table 8.9 and in Bittmann (1953, 1957, 1968); Seidel (1959, 1967); Schlüter (1971); Brooks (1976); Newbould *et al.* (1989); Klötzli (1991); Hammer (1992); Armstrong *et al.* (1995); Hawke and José (1995); Wheeler *et al.* (1995); and Pfadenhauer and Klötzli (1996). *Phragmites* has been sown widely in Dutch reclaimed areas, but is not allowed to become permanent there.

In one case at least about 5000 m^2 of parts of an endangered type of Swiss wetland (*Caricetum diandrae* and other communities) have been transplanted to an alternative and controlled site to guarantee its continued existence, so far with every sign of success (Klötzli, 1980, 1981*b*).

New and old reedbeds exposed to much mechanical damage from open water should be enclosed by barriers (Fig. 8.1; Klötzli & Züst, 1973*b*; Sukopp, 1973; Binzl & Klötzli, 1978; Binz, 1989). These prevent boats and

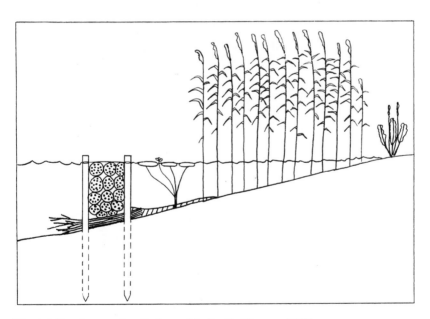

Fig. 8.1. Reed protection (Lahnung) in Berlin (Krauss, 1992).
🐝 – Bundles of sticks
🎋 – Brushwood

Table 8.9. Reedswamp species suitable for transplanting and sowing (examples from Central and Western Europe)

Species	Habitat			Planting methods			Comments
	Substrate	Maximum water depth (cm)	Water movement	Plant part[a]	Season	Distance between transplants (cm)	
Acorus calamus	Any, preferably nutrient-rich	20	No or little flow	Rhizomes	Spring	30–40	Tolerates eutrophic pollution
Carex gracilis	Gravel and stones	10	Flowing	Soil blocks with rhizomes	Mid-summer		
Glyceria maxima	Usually fine	20[b]	Preferably a little flow	Rhizomes	Not in winter	40	Tolerates eutrophic pollution but not anaerobic conditions
Iris pseudacorus	Any, preferably nutrient-rich	10[b]	No or little flow	Rhizomes with buds	Spring and early summer	80	
		Moist	None	Seed	Spring	25	
Phalaris arundinacea	Mineral	20, but not flooded in summer[b]	Little flow	Soil blocks with rhizomes	Spring	10–20	
				Cuttings of shoots or rhizomes	Early and mid-summer	10–20	

Species	Soil	Water depth	Water flow	Planting material	Season	Quantity	Notes
Phragmites australis	Any	10[b]	Little or no flow, no wave action	Rhizomes	Preferably spring	20–30	Young shoots vulnerable, slow to establish
				Soil blocks with rhizomes	Preferably spring	30–40	Many more details in Hawke and José (1995)
				Cuttings of shoots	Early summer	10–20	
	Sandy	0		Seed (chopped ripe panicles)	Spring	500 kg ha^{-1} 1000–10 000 seedlings ha^{-1}	
Schoenoplectus lacustris	Any	80	Still or flowing	Rhizomes with buds	Spring	40–100	
Typha angustifolia	Any	20[b]	No or little flow	Rhizomes with buds	Early spring	80	
T. latifolia	Any	5[b]	No or little flow	Rhizomes with buds	Early spring	80	

Other suitable species include: *Alisma plantago-aquatica*, *Scirpus maritimus*, *Butomus umbellatus*, *Carex acutiformis*, *C. aquatilis*, *C. buekii*, *C. riparia*, *Sagittaria latifolia* and *sagittifolia*, *Sparganium erectum*, *Stratiotes aloides*.

[a] Transplants should be fixed firmly in the soil, and aerial parts should be tall enough to reach oxygenated water or air.

[b] Fluctuations in water level should be less than 20 cm during establishment.

Sources: Seidel (1959); Bittmann (1968); Véber (1978, 1982) and personal communications from E. Bittmann, K. Gloor, S. M. Haslam and D. F. Westlake.

drift (algal mats, etc) reaching the plants, and decrease wave action to some extent. They do not give protection from water of unsuitable quality, or from animals. Netting above and around the vegetation provides protection from birds (e.g. swans). Reed barriers should be placed *ca.* 2 m beyond the reedswamp boundary.

In very eutrophic areas, it is best to harvest or mow the vegetation regularly, at a season appropriate for the species concerned. Exposed stands on shores, in contrast, should not be mown (Klötzli & Züst, 1973*a*).

Proposals for a more natural construction of water courses supporting and integrating parts of wetlands are described by Haslam (1978), Binder (1977) and Wolf (1977).

Conservation of animal species

In general, if the appropriate vegetation is established, and the disturbance sufficiently low, the desired animal population will follow. Freedom from disturbance is more necessary for vertebrates than for invertebrates, though even within one group (e.g. birds) different species may have widely different tolerance levels (Haslam, 1973*a,b*).

The vegetation is required for two purposes: for food (directly for herbivores, and indirectly for carnivores), and for its physical structure (Marshall & Westlake, 1978). Some animals depend on a single plant species, some on many, but in either case the actual species of plants present are of importance. Table 8.10 summarises plants consumed by different orders of animals. Many *Potamogeton* spp. are preferred by six animal orders. *Phragmites australis*, which is the most frequent plant species, is preferred by three animal orders (Gaevskaya, 1966/69).

The requirement for physical structure is less species dependent, as the same structure (carr, reedswamp, short grassland, etc.) can come from a number of different plant species. It may, however, depend on management, as many of the more open or shorter communities occur (or occur on a large scale) only with grazing, cutting, or burning, etc. Examples of requirements for vegetation structure are cited in Haslam (1973*b*) (e.g. butterflies concentrated around fen paths, grasshopper warblers preferring open carr, waterfowl needing 'leisure areas' of short vegetation). Tables 8.6 and 8.11 show the influences of plant communities on the distribution of fish species.

Conservation of waterfowl

Waterfowl may present additional problems for conservation. Many are migrants and many are sensitive to disturbance. There are two periods of special risk, nesting and moulting. Human interference has already resulted in the virtual disappearance of waterfowl from many otherwise suitable habitats, and this trend is likely to continue (Atkinson-Willes, 1969). Reserves can be kept undisturbed, but the large areas of coastal wetlands, fertile lakes, etc., which formerly had few or no visitors, now often have too many and are not suitable for waterfowl, although they are still suitable for the maintenance of vegetation. Migrants return to the same area each year, so a reserve in one region is useless to a species migrating to another, even though all other habitat factors are satisfactory. In this geographical, non-habitat, non-climatic requirement, migrant birds differ from other groups of organisms. Hence a system of refuges is needed throughout the world, in which the correct requirements for each species in terms of locality, habitat, and tolerable amount of disturbance are met.

Waterfowl, both migrant and non-migrant, are of great economic importance for sport, in areas such as N. America. Earlier, more research in wetlands was directed to retain and increase waterfowl than to any other aspect of wetland conservation. The topics covered include the preservation of the whole wetland, the regulation of water level, the proportions of open water, reedswamp and dry land, the amount of cover on the latter, the plant species concerned and the development of food and shelter. See Projects MAR, AQUA, IBP/CT and the activities of IUCN and IWRB (Wetlands International since 1995).

Techniques of control

In some cases biota living on wetlands may be detrimental to humans, influencing the water regime, or changing the preferred communities, or acting as disease vectors (transferring illnesses to humans and animals). Some animals, mostly insects, but also snails and some others, are vectors of mild or grave diseases or parasitic infections (e.g. malaria, yellow fever, river blindness, bilharzia, swimmer's itch, liver fluke). Vectors of parasites of livestock, may sometimes cause serious economic problems. Mass increases of some plants or animals may also be a nuisance to humans living in the neighbourhood of the wetlands.

When these nuisances are too great, human beings try to counteract them, either through the destruction of the wetland (by drainage), or by

Table 8.10. *Wetland plants and their consumers (from Gaevskaja, 1966/69). The numbers are the number of species of the animal order feeding on the plant genus*

		Order of consumers																				
Wetland plant genera		Tylenchidae	Basommatophora	Monotocardia	Ostracoda	Isopoda	Amphipoda	Decapoda	Collempoda	Ephemeroptera	Plecoptera	Homoptera	Heteroptera	Coleoptera	Diptera	Trichoptera	Lepidoptera	Cypriniformes	Periciformes	Anseres	Ralli	Insectivora	Rodentia
Hepaticae	*Riccia*		2				4		1	1	2	1			1								
Musci	*Sphagnum*							3	1	1	1				1			1		3	3	1	3
	Hypnum															11							1
Equisetales	*Equisetum*							1						2	1			1				1	3
Filicales	*Thelypteris*																						1
	Marsilea							3															
	Salvinia												?				1				1		2
Ranales	*Caltha*											2		2	1		1						
	Brasenia													2	1		8						2
	Nelumbo	1										1			1								1
	Nuphar		5					2				3		4	13	10	7			7		1	4
	Nymphaea		1					4				2		8	9	9	6			10		1	4
Rosales	*Potentilla*													4						6			1
Polygonales	*Polygonum*		4					3						9	3		1	3		13		1	4
	Rumex	2													2					10			2

Rhoeadales	*Nasturtium*					2							1
	Rorippa	2	1	1				7	1		1	2	2
Myrtales	*Trapa*			3				1	2		2	1	2
Umbelliflorae	*Sium*							6		1			1
Primulales	*Hottonia*	6		1		1							1
Gentianales	*Menyanthes*	3									8		3
Helubiae	*Butomus*				1			2	5		4	1	4
	Stratiotes	6	3	2				1	20		1		2
	Alisma	7	2	4		1		3	11	1	5	1	4
	Sagittaria	2				2		10	10	1	11	1	4
Liliflorae	*Iris*	1						3	9	4	1		3
Spathiflorae	*Lemna*	7	1	6	1	2		3	2	5	9	1	2
Pandanales	*Sparganium*	2		5	2			9	21	2	7	16	1	4
	Typha	1		1		10	1		13		18	2	1	4
Cyperales	*Carex*	1		8	1	1		22	8	3	12	11	1	4
	Eleocharis					1		3	1		4	3		2
	Scirpus	1		3	3	3		9	15		10	15	1	4
Graminales	*Glyceria*				2	5		6	6	3	7	2	1	1
	Oryza	2				8	3	3	7	1	3	3	
	Phragmites	1		4		20		10	15		23	4	1	4
	Phalaris							2			2		1

In addition: Chromadorida 5 on *Oryza*.

Enoplida 4 on *Oryza*.

Phyllopoda 1 on *Oryza*.

Thysanoptera 1 on *Phragmites*.

Table 8.11. *Distribution of the most important species of fish on a lake shore (after Meisriemler, 1974)*

	Open water	Submerged plants	Reeds, pond-like open waters, open bays, channels	Dense reeds and sedges
Anguilla anguilla	←———————————————————————→			
Alburnus alburnus	←———————————————→			
Cyprinus carpio	←———————————————→			
Blicca bjorkna	←—————————————→			
Abramis brama	←————————————→			
Lucioperca lucioperca	←——————→			
Aspius aspius	←——→			
Acerina cernua	←——→			
Perca fluviatilis	←——→			
Rutilus rutilus		←——→		
Scardinius erythrophthalmus		←——→		
Esox lucius		←———→		
Tinca tinca			←——→	
Carassius carassius			←——→	
Misgurnus fossilis			←——→	

control of the troublesome organisms, which may include mammals, fish, insects, bivalve and univalve snails, crustacea, leeches, macrophytes, algae, etc.

Sometimes, control is for plant protection, but this is rather rare except in rice fields.

The control is nearly always a deep intervention in the structure and function of the ecosystem. Each type of intervention exerts an influence on all links of the ecosystem and, consequently, effects can arise in unwanted places. To avoid this, the programme of control should be prepared with care and with a knowledge of the functioning of the ecosystem. Otherwise, one can cause unwanted changes in water regime, water level, water quality and in densities of protected or useful plants or animals; and the advantages of control of the nuisance organisms will be less than the damage (Marshall & Westlake, 1978).

Control of macrophytes

Macrophytes are controlled where they grow over waterways, drainage and irrigation ditches, fishponds and water bodies used for recreation.

Special attention has been paid to the control of water weeds in newly created water reservoirs used for storage and power in the tropics. In such reservoirs water weeds very often show mass development. At least three species of weeds are particularly troublesome in various tropical and subtropical waters, namely: *Eichhornia crassipes, Salvinia molesta* and *Hydrilla verticillata*; and many others are locally important. In a very short time they can occupy the water body, the first two covering the whole surface with a thick layer, producing many serious difficulties in the exploitation of the reservoir and radically changing the quality of the water in small water bodies.

Nuisance populations of macrophytes are controlled by biological, chemical or mechanical techniques, or by management of the water body. Pieterse and Murphy (1993) give a recent survey of the subject.

Biological control Biological control is not yet widely used because of its many limitations, but it may be the safest and cheapest way and there have been some outstanding successes. The techniques were reviewed in a special issue of *Aquatic Botany* (den Hartog, 1977) and by Perkins (1978). They use other plants, viruses, fungi, bacteria, fish, beetles, snails and even mammals, but few are in routine use. Perhaps the most spectacular has been the successful use of a beetle, *Cytobagous salviniae*, to control *Salvinia molesta* in many lakes in Australia and Papua New Guinea (e.g. Thomas & Room, 1986).

In some areas plant-eating fish, especially the grass carp, *Ctenopharyngodon idella*, are used. This species is outstanding for its greediness and rather low conversion factor (Blackburn *et al.*, 1971), which means that it is a very good destroyer of macrophytes. Also, it does not breed in the wild outside the special conditions of its native rivers in China, so population densities can be controlled and it cannot become invasive. However, not all plant species are consumed equally readily (Table 8.12), and its rate of grazing is sometimes limited during periods of low temperatures in temperate regions.

Krupauer (1967) showed the selection of food by two-year-old grass carp introduced into fishponds in Czechoslovakia. Of the 104 aquatic and terrestrial plant species offered, only 13 species were refused while 72 species were eaten very intensively. Despite the differences found in consumption, the selectivity shown by the grass carp was not very great. Their food spectrum included most of the aquatic macrophytes that form substantial components of freshwater littoral plant communities. Species of *Ranunculus* subgenus *Batrachium* seem to be the most

Table 8.12. *Selection of aquatic plants for consumption by grass carp*

Preferred (filaments, leaves and parts of petioles, stems and inflorescences; low stocking density)	Partially consumed (young shoots and soft margins of leaves; high stocking density)	Refused
Acorus calamus	*Ceratophyllum* spp.	*Cicuta virosa*
Alisma plantago-aquatica	*Hippuris vulgaris*	*Hottonia palustris* (toxic)
Calla palustris	*Juncus tenageia*	*Polygonum amphibium*
Chara spp.	*Myriophyllum spicatum*	(terrestrial form)
Cladophora spp.	*Nuphar lutea*	*Ranunculus fluitans*
Eleocharis acicularis	*Nymphaea alba*	
Elodea canadensis	*Potamogeton lucens*	
Glyceria fluitans	*P. natans*	
G. maxima	*Scirpus* spp.	
Groenlandia densa	*Typha angustifolia*	
Hydrocharis morsus-ranae	*Vallisneria* spp.	
Hydrodyction reticulatum		
Lemna spp.		
Najas spp.		
Nasturtium officinale		
Nymphoides peltata		
Phragmites australis (up to height of 80 cm)		
Potamogeton berchtoldii		
P. pectinatus		
Rumex aquaticus		
Sagittaria sagittifolia		
Spirogyra spp.		
Trapa natans		
Typha latifolia		
Utricularia spp.		

Sources: Verigin, 1963; Stroganov, 1963; Krupauer, 1967, 1971; Alabaster & Stott, 1967; Fowler & Robson, 1978.

important group not normally consumed. As shown by Prowse (1971) the grass carp prefers young and succulent plants with negligible fibre, while the more fibrous and lignified plants are least preferred. The food selection is particularly influenced by the age of fish, density of population, physiological state and environmental factors (especially dissolved oxygen and water temperature; Stroganov, 1963; Krupauer, 1971; Rottman, 1977). As the fish grow they become less selective. The algae become less preferred, duckweed (Lemnaceae) and pond weeds (*Pota-*

mogeton spp.) are still preferred and fibrous weeds are accepted more readily. Food consumption begins at about 10 °C, depending on the previous acclimation of the fish, and the most intensive feeding is at 22 to 30 °C. At higher temperatures the grass carp feed less selectively (see also den Hartog, 1977).

This selectivity and variability in activity may produce some limitations in its use as a biological control, but it has been successfully used to control both submerged and emergent vegetation in fishponds, irrigation and drainage canals, hydroelectric lakes and water-cooling reservoirs. It is known from numerous observations that the grass carp exerts a powerful effect on stands of *Phragmites australis, Elodea canadensis*, several species of *Potamogeton* and *Lemna, Myriophyllum spicatum, Trapa natans* and other plant species. For a specific example including effects on emergent plants, a 95 ha eutrophic lake in Poland (Dgal Wielki) was heavily stocked with grass carp, initially in 1966, then again in 1970 and later (Krzywosz *et al.*, 1980). In 1961 and until 1973, 41% of its area was covered with submerged plants, but after 1975 their cover decreased until by 1978 it was negligible. Emergent plants, mostly *Phragmites australis*, covered 5% from 1961 until 1975 but then decreased to less than 2%. In some situations the macrophytes can be completely destroyed and some authors (e.g. Grenfeeld, 1973) therefore, have doubts about the release of grass carp into natural waters. The stands of submerged plants are such an important habitat for numerous invertebrates serving as food for many other fish species, that elimination of vegetation can lead to a substantial decrease of indigenous species of both phytophilous and zoophilous fish. Some countries have forbidden its use outside isolated water bodies. However, proper management may overcome such problems.

The principles and costs of vegetation management using grass carp have been described by Rottman (1977), Stott and Luckley (1978) and Eaton *et al.* (1992).

Chemical control Chemical control has been applied to most important species but particularly to emergent species (70% of all publications). A great variety of materials have been used but many are unsuitable for application in or near water and in many countries these are forbidden in such situations. Some useful sources of information on applications and problems are Blackburn (1974), Zonderwijk and van Zon (1974), Brooker and Edwards (1975), Newbould (1975), Bates (1976), Makepeace (1976), Robson and Barrett (1977) and Ministry of Agriculture, Fisheries & Food (UK) (1995). Numerous further papers may be found in the *Hyacinth*

Control Journal, later the *Journal of Aquatic Plant Management*, as well as in the Symposia on Aquatic Weeds organised by the European Weed Research Society.

Mechanical control Mechanical control can be carried out in two ways: (i) cutting and removal of plants, with their propagules; and (ii) destroying plants without the removal of plant material.

The first, which is widely used to keep rivers and drainage channels open, is more laborious and more expensive, but often more effective, and usually safer for other organisms. When plant material is removed, it must be satisfactorily disposed of. Deposition on the shore is not the best solution, because the decomposing materials release a liquid rich in nutrients and biological oxygen demand, which finds its way into the water. Also, they are unsightly (which is important in recreational areas) and the dried residues are a fire hazard. Use as fodder, litter, mulch, etc. has often been tried but there are usually expensive problems of drying, cleaning and transport to be solved unless these facilities are provided by an existing commercial use (Little, 1979).

The second way is cheaper, but is followed by at least eutrophication of the water and in some cases by pollution and deoxygenation. This approach was elaborated in fishpond farming many years ago, mostly for control of tough emergent macrophytes. In this case the plant material may be used to fertilise the pond and is deliberately decomposed in the water or on the adjacent shore (Hejný & Husák, 1978). Such a method is not applicable to other water bodies where water quality is important.

Choice of method The best and cheapest methods are likely to be biological, but they have not yet been fully developed and must be more elaborated before they become generally applicable. Chemical control has particular hazards for the operatives as well as the ecosystem, and must be limited to the treated area. It must not be forgotten that these herbicides are poisons, and that through water movement, spray drift or carelessness they can act in other places and on other organisms. Generally, because of the multiple uses of water, chemical control of water plants must be limited as far as possible, especially where the treated water might be used for crop irrigation. However, recent developments are likely to provide techniques to use herbicides to control limited areas. In some circumstances herbicides can be used as a conservation tool, to selectively control unwanted (e.g. alien) species.

Mechanical control is time and energy consuming. Use of manually operated tools needs hard physical work, and in many cases it may be difficult to organise enough manpower for this. Machines are expensive and a full set is needed for cutting, transport and reloading of harvested plant material. Agriculture machines are not suitable for wetland management because heavy machines, moving on wheels or caterpillar tracks, destroy the rhizomes in soft mud.

The best solution for the control of undesirable macrophytes is to manage the water body and surrounding areas so that their growth is limited by their environment (see pp. 429–31). The theory of such ecological control is not fully developed, the ecologists have a lot to elucidate, but the understanding of natural processes is the only way to maintain stable ecological equilibria over long periods. The simplest and often used example is, of course, the manipulation of water level. See Hejný (1971) for a general evaluation of its effects on wetland and aquatic plants.

Control of algae

Algae seldom need control in wetlands, as distinct from drains, lakes and reservoirs. The abundance in lakes may lead to damage to submerged macrophytes (e.g. Phillips *et al.*, 1978) and to weakened reedswamp (e.g. Klötzli, 1971), so they may need control in lakes for the sake of the marginal wetlands. Usually, management to reduce eutrophication is required.

Control of animals

Of first importance is the control of mosquitos in wetlands, belonging to the genera *Aedes, Anopheles* and *Culex*, as vectors of malaria and some other diseases including (filariasis, yellow fever and possibly some tropical viral cancers). Whole journals are devoted to mosquito control and the literature is so extensive that it could not be reviewed in this volume. Other vectors such as *Simulium* (onchocerelasis), *Lymnaea* and *Bithynia* (facioliasis, Crossland, 1971; Beer, 1969) and *Bulinus, Onchomelania* and *Bionphalaria* (schistosomiasis) are important in many parts of the world. The massive applications of insecticides often used can effect many changes in wetlands, leading to instability and more intensive use of the insecticides.

Some other invertebrates are controlled because of their undesirable abundance, e.g. midges (Chironomidae), (Edwards *et al.*, 1964); mayflies

(Ephemeroptera), (Lieux & Mulrennan, 1955); water boatmen (*Notonecta undulata* etc.), (Fales *et al.*, 1968); *Asellus* (Klapper, 1966).

The control of pests in rice fields (PANS, 1976; and see pp. 309–12) is another major application of management techniques in wetlands. Several attempts have been made to control weeds, and snails and mosquito vectors in paddy fields by fish. Some success was achieved in Indonesia, Malaysia and Katanga, Africa, but with the development of pesticides, the use of fish has declined (Coche, 1968).

Vertebrates are mostly controlled, by shooting and trapping, when they range outside wetlands to feed on cultivated plants (e.g. coypu, *Myocastor coypus*; Canada geese, *Branta canadensis*) or animals (e.g. mink, *Mustela vison*). Sometimes excessive populations damage the wetlands themselves, or change water levels by burrowing (e.g. *Myocastor*) or damming (e.g. beaver, *Castor fiber*). Extensive trapping programmes have been needed where such species have been introduced or have escaped from fur farms (e.g. *Mustela*). Fish may be dense enough to damage the vegetation and limitation may be necessary (e.g. Steenis *et al.*, 1954; Anon., 1968). In fish farming, and in lakes used for sport fishing, fish of little value, which are in competition with valuable species, are controlled.

The organisation of wetland conservation

After initial discussions in Zurich in 1961, several international projects were started at an IBP/PF meeting in 1964. Project AQUA was supported by SIL, Project MAR by IUCN, ICBP and IWRB jointly, and Project TELMA by PT and PF Sections of IBP. Many wetlands of international importance have been listed:

Project MAR, Europe & North Africa, Hoffman (1964) and Olney (1965)
Project AQUA, worldwide, Luther and Rzóska (1971)
RAMSAR Convention, worldwide, RAMSAR (1990)
Africa – Hughes *et al.* (1992)
Asia – Scott (1969)
Oceania – Scott (1993)
Worldwide – Jones (1993)

The importance of wetlands was recognised by most countries by Resolution 20 of the IUCN Conference in Banff (Elliot, 1973), and many have signed the RAMSAR Convention. The *Directory of Wetlands of the Western Palearctic* (Carp, 1980) compiled information on progress of these projects, and reported on the efforts of UNESCO, FAO, ICBP,

IUCN, IBP, and SIL to form a consultative and advisory committee to monitor conservation status, provide reference works, and help protect representative wetlands. Endangered plants and animals of wetlands, and of habitats beside wetlands, appear in the IUCN Red Data Books (e.g. Lucas *et al.*, 1978). Because of the great influence of ornithologists, much further information on the conservation and quality of wetlands, and criteria for their selection, can be found in the *Proceedings of the International Meetings on Conservation of Wildfowl Resources*, and from the International Wildfowl Research Bureau (Slimbridge, UK).

Many countries, particularly in Europe and North America, have national lists, e.g.

Africa south of the Sahara, Hedberg (1968)

Australia, Specht *et al.* (1974)

Canada, Goodman *et al.* (1972); Kiel *et al.* (1972)

Germany (Democratic Republic), Bauer (1972–74)

Germany (Federal Republic), Ant and Engelke (1970); Korneck and Sukopp (1988)
(Baden-Württemberg), Müller (1967)

Great Britain, Atkinson-Willes (1963) (wildfowl habitats); Nature Conservancy (English Nature) Annual reports

Switzerland, Anon. (1968) on (Bundesinventar und Katalog der Landschaften von Nationaler Bedeutung, listing all high-value wetlands); Landolt (1991)

USA, Shaw and Fredine (1971)

Small collections of various aquatic plants are kept at Třeboň, Czech Republic; Mikołajki, Poland; Washington DC, USA and Zürich, Switzerland. Such collections should be enlarged to include further species and a greater range of genotypes. There appear to be no specific seedbanks of wetland plants, or living collections of wetland animals.

The selection of listed and protected wetlands should be improved and extended. There are many gaps because selection has often depended on the siting of research stations and the individual knowledge of a few workers. Networks of smaller areas should be protected, to ensure the survival of endangered species, and to maintain the exchange of genes. Specific proposals for further conservation and restoration were made by UN Recommendations 39–45 of the Declaration on the Human Environment drawn up at the 1972 Stockholm Conference (UN, 1973), including the following.

1. Surveying plant genetic resources throughout the world, with appropriate programmes for exploration and collection.
2. Preparing inventories of resources both in the field and in collections of living species, and organising a comprehensive recording scheme to facilitate distribution of information.
3. Conserving plant genetic resources by selecting and correctly managing appropriate reserves.
4. Conserving plant genetic resources in living collections and seed banks, on a long-term basis.

These aims remain the fundamental basis of the continuous efforts needed to conserve the world's endangered wetlands.

References

Abaskhkin, S.A., Boĭkov, V.N., Boĭkova, F.I., Maximov, A.A., Pashkevich, V.Ĭ & Sorokina, L.I. (1972). Ocherk ekologii ondatrȳ v poĭme verkhnego, serednego i nizhnego techenĭya Obi. (On the ecology of *Ondatra* on upper, middle and lower flow of the river Ob.) *Trudȳ Biologicheskogo Instituta, Novosibirsk*, **19** 6–59. (In Russian.)

Abdullaev, D.A. (1972). O ratsional'nom ispol'zovanii vodno-bolotnȳkh rastenii Ferganskoi dolini v narodnom khozyaistve. In *Kul'tivironvanie Vodoroslei i Vysshikh Vodnikh Rastenii v Uzbekistane*, ed. A.M. Muzafarov, pp. 119–32. Tashkent: FAN.

Adams, D.D., Seitzinger, S.P. & Crill, P.M. (1996). *Cycling of Reduced Gases in the Hydrosphere*; Mitteilungen der Internationalen Vereinigung für Theoretische und Angewandte Limnologie No. 25. Stuttgart: Schweizerbart'sche Verlag. 204 pp.

Adams, F.S., Cole, H. Jr & Massie, L.B. (1973). Element constitution of selected aquatic vascular plants from Pennsylvania: submerged and floating leaved species and rooted emergent species. *Environmental Pollution*, **5**, 117–47.

Adams, F.S., Mackenzie, D.R., Cole, H. Jr & Price, M.W. (1971). The influence of nutrient pollution levels upon element constitution and morphology of *Elodea canadensis*. *Environmental Pollution*, **1**, 285–98.

Akkermann, R. (1974). Untersuchungen zur Ökologie und Populationsdynamik des Bisams (*Ondatra zibethica* L.) an einem nordwestdeutschen Verlandungssee (Dümmer). Dok. Diss., Bonn Universität. 164 pp.

Alabaster, J.S. & Stott, B. (1967). Grass carp (*Ctenopharyngodon idella* Val.) for aquatic weed control. *Proceedings of the EWRS 2nd Symposium on Aquatic Weeds*, 123–6.

Alimov, A.F. (1967). O vozmozhnoĭ roli zhivotnȳkh-fil'tratorov v protsessakh samoochishcheniya vodoemov na primere populyatsii presnovodnȳkh mollyuskov *Sphaerium corneum* (L.) (On the possible role of animals-filtrators in the processes of self-purification of water bodies, on the example of the population of the freshwater mollusc *Sphaerium corneum* L.) *Trudȳ Zoologicheskogo Instituta*, **42**, 205–11. Leningrad: AN SSSR. (In Russian.)

Alimov, A.F., Boullion, V.V., Finogenova, N.P., Ivanova, M.B., Kuzmitskaya, N.K., Nikulina, V.N., Ozeretkovskaya, N.G. & Zharova, T.V. (1972). Biological productivity of lakes Krivoe and Krugloe. In *Productivity Problems of Freshwaters*, ed. Z. Kajak & A. Hillbricht-Ilkowska; Proceedings of the IBP-UNESCO Symposium on Productivity Problems of

465

Freshwaters, Kazimierz Dolny, May, 1970, pp. 39–56. Warszawa-Kraków: PWN.

Allen, H.L. (1971). Primary productivity, chemo-organotrophy and nutritional interactions of epiphytic algae and bacteria on macrophytes in the littoral of a lake. *Ecological Monographs*, **41**, 97–127.

Allen, S.E. & Pearsall, W.H. (1963). Leaf analysis and shoot production in *Phragmites*. *Oikos*, **14**, 176–89.

Alsterberg, G. (1930). *Wichtige Züge in der Biologie der Süsswassergastropoden*. Lund: University of Lund. 130 pp.

Altschul, A. M. (ed.) (1958). *Processed Plant Protein Foodstuffs*. New York: Academic Press. 955 pp.

Ambasht, R.S. (1971). Freshwater ecosystems. In *Ecology – Study of Ecosystems*, ed. K.C. Misra, D.N. Rao, R.S. Ambasht, R.S. Dewivedi, K.L. Mukherjee & P.V. Ananth Krishnan. Allahabad: Wheeler & Co.

Amoros, C. (1973). Evolution des populations de cladocères et copepodes dans trois etanges piscicoles de la Dombes. *Annales de Limnologie*, **9** 135–55.

Anderson, J.P.E. & Domsch, K.H. (1978). A physiological method for the quantitative measurement of microbial biomass in soils. *Soil Biology and Biochemistry*, **10**, 215–21.

Anderson, M.C. (1971). Radiation and crop structure. In *Plant Photosynthetic Production*, ed. Z. Šesták, J. Čatský & P. Jarvis, pp. 412–66. The Hague: Junk.

Anderson, M.C. (1975). Solar radiation and carbon dioxide in plant communities – conclusions. In *Photosynthetic and Productivity in Different Environments*, ed. J.P. Cooper, International Biological Programme 22, pp. 345–56. Cambridge: Cambridge University Press.

Anderson, W.P. (ed.) (1973). *Ion Transport in Plants*; Proceedings of an International Meeting, Workshop on Ion Transport, Liverpool, July 1972. London: Academic Press. 630 pp.

Andersson, G., Cronberg, G. & Gelin, C. (1973). Planktonic changes following the restoration of Lake Trummen, Sweden. *Ambio*, **2**, 44–7.

Andrikovics, S. (1975*a*). On the hydrolecological character of the lake of a gravel pit. *Annales Universitatis Scientarum Budapestinensis, Sectio Biologica*, **17**, 115–21.

Andrikovics, S. (1975*b*). Macrofaunal biomass in the submerged vegetation stands of Lake Velence. *Symposia Biologica Hungarica*, **15**, 247–54.

Anon. (1968 onwards). *Bundesinventor und Katalog der Landschaften von Nationaler Bedeutung*. Bern: Eidgenössische Drücksachen und Materialzentrale. Single sheets.

Anon. (1968). *The Delta Marsh, its Values, Problems and Potentialities*. Manitoba: Manitoba Department of Mines and Natural Resources.

Anon. (1969). *Wildlife Management on Inland Waters*; Eley Game Advisory Service Green Guides No. 3. Fordingbridge UK: Eley Game Advisory Station. 80 pp.

Anon. (1971). *Coastal Zone Management in Florida 1971*. Tallahassee, Fl.: Florida Coastal Coordination Council. 11 pp.

Anon. (1972). *The Use of Bamboo and Reeds in Building Construction*, United Nations Document, ST/SOA/113. New York: United Nations. 95 pp.

Anon. (1973). *Recommendations for Development Activities in Florida Coastal Zone*. Florida: Florida Dept. Natural Resources, Coastal Coordination Council. 66 pp.

Ant, H. & Engelke, H. (1970). *Die Naturschutzgebiete der Bundesrepublik Deutschland (revised)*; Landwirtschaft – Angewandte Wissenschaft, Heft

145. Hiltrup b. Münster: Landwirtschaft – Angewandte Wissenschaft. 305 pp.

Antipa, G. (1912). Überschwemmungsgebiet der unteren Donau. *Annales Institutui şi Geoçizica a României*, **4**(1910), 1–172.

Antipov, N.J. (1961). Vodniĭ rezhim nektotorikh gigrofitov. *Fiziologiya Rasteniĭ*, **8**, 284–93.

Antipov, N.J. (1964). Vodno-rezdusniĭ rezhim nekotorikh vodnikh rasteniĭ. (Water aeration regime of some aquatic plants.) *Botanicheskiĭ Zhurnal*, **49**, 702–7. (In Russian.)

Antipov, N.J. (1973). Osobennosti vodoobmena odinochnikh tsvetkov i sotsvetiĭ travyanistikh rastenii po nablyudeniyam v Ryazanskoĭ oblasti. (Pecularities of the water metabolism of solitary flowers and inflorescences of herbaceous plants as observed in the Ryazan region.) *Botanicheskiĭ Zhurnal*, **58**, 914–23. (In Russian.)

Arenkova, R.L. (1965). Rastitel'nost'i i fytofil'naya fauna prudov zapadnikh oblasteĭ ukrainskoĭ SSR. (Vegetation and phytophilous fauna of ponds in the western regions of the Ukrainian SSR.) *Sbornik Rȳbnoe Khozyaĭstvo*, **2**, 75–82. (In Russian.)

Arenkova, R.L. (1970). Makrofitȳ i fitofil'naya fauna rybovodnȳkh prudov zapadnȳkh oblasteĭ Ukrainsky (Macrophytes and phytophilous fauna of fishponds of western Ukraine.) Avtoref. Diss. na Soiskanie Uchen. Stepni Kand. Biol. Nauk. (03.105). Moskva: VNII Morskogo Rybnogo Khozyaĭstva i Okeanografii. 38 pp. (In Russian.)

Armstrong, D.E. & Rohlich, G.A. (1969). Effects of agricultural pollution on eutrophication. In *Agricultural Practices and Water Quality*; Proceedings of Conference Concerning the Role of Agriculture in Clean Water, Water Pollution Control Series DAST-26, 13040, EYX 11/69, pp. 314–30. Washington: US Government (DAST).

Armstrong, J. (ed.) (1996). *Ventilation in Macrophytes*; *Aquatic Botany (Special Issue)*, **54**, 85–264.

Armstrong, S.F. (1950). *British Grasses and their Employment in Agriculture*, 3rd edn. Cambridge: Cambridge University Press. 350 pp.

Armstrong, W. (1979). Aeration in higher plants. In *Advances in Botanical Research*, 7, ed. H.W. Woolhouse, pp. 225–332. New York: Academic Press.

Artimo, A. (1960). The dispersal and acclimatization of the muskrat in Finland. *Papers on Game Research*, **21**, 1–101.

Aruga, Y. & Monsi, M. (1963). Chlorophyll amount as an indicator of matter productivity in bio-communities. *Plant Cell Physiology, Tokyo*, **4**, 29–39.

Atkinson-Willes, G.L. (ed.) (1963). *Wildfowl in Great Britain. A Survey of the Winter Distribution of the Anatidae and their Conservation in England, Scotland and Wales*. London: HMSO. 368 pp.

Atkinson-Willes, G.L. (1969). Wildfowl and recreation: a balance of requirements. *British Water Supply*, **11**, 5–15.

Auclair, A.W.D., Bouchard, A. & Pajaczkowski, J. (1974). Plant composition and species relations on the Huntingdon Marsh, Quebec. *Canadian Journal of Botany*, **51**, 1231–47.

Auclair, A.W.D., Bouchard, A. & Pajaczkowski, J. (1976). Plant standing crop and productivity relations in a *Scirpus – Equisetum* wetland. *Ecology*, **57**, 941–52.

Aumen, N.G. (ed.) (1985). *Ecological Studies on the Littoral and Pelagic Systems of Lake Okeechobee, Florida (USA)*; Advances in Limnology VI. Stuttgart: Schweizerbart'sche Verlag. 356 pp.

Baker, C.J. & Maltby, E. (1995). Nitrate removal by river marginal wetlands:

Factors affecting the provision of a suitable denitrification environment. In *Hydrology and Hydrochemistry of British Wetlands*, ed. J.M.R. Hughes & A.L. Heathwaite. pp. 291–314. London: Wiley.

Balaschov, L.S. (1972). Pro splivannya torfu u vodoschovishchi Kiïivskeï gesta. Iogo rol u zabrudnenni vodȳ (in Ukrainian). *Ukraïnskiï Botanicheskiï Zhurnal*, **29**(1), 49–54. (On peat floating in the Kiev reservoir. Its role in water pollution.)

Balcalbaşa-Dobrovici, N. (1971). The economic importance of the burgu (*Echinochloa stagnina* P. Beauv.) on the middle Niger. *Hidrobiologia Bucureşti*, **12**, 41–6.

Balon, E.K. (1975). Reproductive guilds of fishes: a proposal and definition. *Journal of the Fisheries Research Board of Canada*, **32**, 821–64.

Balon, E.K. (1981). Additions and amendments to the classification of reproductive styles in fishes. *Environmental Biology of Fish*, **6**, 377–89.

Baradziej, E. (1974). Net primary production of two marsh communities near Ispinia in the Niepołomice Forest (Southern Poland). *Ekologia Polska*, **22**, 144–72.

Barbier, E.B., Acreman, M. & Knowler, D. (1997). *Economic Valuation of Wetlands. A Guide for Policy Makers and Planners*. Gland: Ramsar Convention Bureau/IUCN. 127 pp.

Bardach, J.E. (1972). Some ecological implications of Mekong River development plans. In *The Careless Technology*, ed. M.T. Farver & J.P. Milton, pp. 236–44. New York: The Natural History Press.

Barko, J.W. & Smart, R.M. (1979). The nutritional ecology of *Cyperus esculentus*, an emergent aquatic plant, grown on different sediments. *Aquatic Botany*, **6**, 13–28.

Barko, J.W. & Smart, R.M. (1981). Sediment-based nutrition of submersed macrophytes. *Aquatic Botany*, **10**, 339–52.

Barnes, R.D. (1953). The ecological distribution of spiders in non-forest maritime communities at Beaufort, North Carolina. *Ecological Monographs*, **23**, 315–37.

Barsegyan, A.M. (1956). O geobotanicheskom izuchenii voduo-bolotnoȳ rastitel'nosti Araratskoȳ ravninȳ. *Izvestiya Akademiï Nauk Armyamskoi SSR, Seriya Biologicheskikh i Sel'skokhzyaistvennȳkh. Nauk*, **19**, 83–93.

Barsegyan, A.M. & Khursudyan, P.A. (1969). Neketorȳe ekologichskie osobennosti obyknovennogo trostnika *Phragmites communis* Trin. preizrastaïuschego na obnazhennykh gruntakh ozera Sevan. *Biologicheskiï Zhurnal Armenii*, **22**(5), 74–85.

Baryashnikov, V.G. (1962). O prirode bolot Irkutskoi oblasti. *Trudȳ Vostochno-Sibirskogo Biologicheskogo Instituta, Botanika*, **1**, 61–9. Irkutsk: AN SSSR.

Bates, J.A.R. (1976). Pesticides safety precautions scheme – the registration of aquatic herbicides. In *British Crop Protection Council Monograph No. 16*; Proceedings of the Symposium on Aquatic Herbicides, Oxford, pp. 26–37. London: British Crop Protection Council.

Bauer, K. (1960). Die Säugetiere des Neusiedlersee-Gebietes (Österreich). *Bonner Zoologische Beitrage*, **11**, 141–344.

Bauer, L. (ed.) (1972–4). *Handbuch der Naturschutzgebiete der Deutschen Demokratischen Republik*, **Bd 1–5**. Berlin: Urania-Verlag. 301, 223, 277, 275 and 309 pp.

Bayly, L.I. & O'Neil, T.A. (1972*a*). Seasonal ionic fluctuations in a *Phragmites communis* community. *Canadian Journal of Botany*, **50**, 2103–9.

Bayly, L.I. & O'Neil, T.A. (1972b). Seasonal ionic fluctuations in a *Typha glauca* community. *Ecology*, 53, 714–19.

Beadle, L.C. (1974). *The Inland Water of Tropical Africa. An Introduction to Tropical Limnology*. London: Longman. 266 pp.

Beattie, D.M., Bromley, H.J., Chambers, M.R., Goldspink, R., Vijverberg, J., Zalingen, van N.P. & Golterman, H.L. (1972). Limnological studies on Tjeukemeer – a typical Dutch polder reservoir. In *Productivity Problems of Freshwaters*, ed. Z. Kajak & A. Hillbricht-Ilkowska; Proceedings of the IBP-UNESCO Symposium on Productivity Problems of Freshwaters, Kazimierz Dolny, May, 1970, pp. 421–47. Warszawa-Kraków: PWN.

Beecher, W.J. (1942). *Nesting Birds and the Vegetation Substrate*. Chicago: Chicago Ornithological Society. 69 pp.

Beer, S.A. (1969). Poisk moll'yuskitsidov prigodnȳkh dlya borbȳ s *Bithynia leachi* Shepp. – promezhutochnȳm khozainom *Opisthorchis felineus*; Soobshchenie III, Izbiratel'noe deȳstvie nizkikh doz nekotorȳkh moll'yuskitsidov na bitiniȳ invazirovannȳkh tserkaryami – *O. felineus*. *Meditsinskaya Parazitolgiya*, 38, 674–6.

Beetle, A.A. (1950). Bulrushes and their multiple uses. *Economic Botany*, 4, 132–8.

Beguin, C. & Major, J. (1975). Contribution a l'étude phytosociologique et écologique de marias de la Sierra Nevada (California). *Phytocoenologie*, 2, 349–67.

Berczik, Á. (1970). Schädigung eines Reisfeldes durch Chironomiden und seine ökologischen Umstände. *Opuscula Zoologica, Budapest*, 10, 221–9.

Berczik, Á. (1971). Zur Populationsdynamik der Mesofauna der Reisfelder. *Sitzungsberichte, Österreichische Akademie der Wissenschaften, Mathematisch-Naturwissenschaftliche Klasse I, Abteilung 1*, 179, 299–302.

Berczik, Á. (1973a). Benennung der zwei ökologischen Gruppen wasserbewohnender Wirbelloser. *Opuscula Zoologica, Budapest*, 12, 33–41.

Berczik, Á. (1973b). Periodische Aspektveränderung der Zoozönosen auf Reisfeldern in Ungarn. *Verhandlungen der Internationalen Vereinigung für Theoretische und Angewandte Limnologie*, 18, 1742–50.

Berg, C.O. (1950). Biology of certain Chironomidae reared from *Potamogeton*. *Ecological Monographs*, 20, 83–101.

Bernard, J.M. (1973). Production ecology of wetland sedges: The genus *Carex*. *Polskie Archiwum Hydrobiologii*, 20, 207–14.

Bernard, J.M. (1974). Seasonal changes in standing crop and primary production in a sedge wetland and an adjacent dry old-field in central Minnesota. *Ecology*, 55, 350–9.

Bernard, J.M. & Gorham, E. (1978). Life history aspects of primary production in sedge wetlands. In *Freshwater Wetlands. Ecological Processes and Management Potential*, ed. R.E. Good, D.F. Whigham, R.L. Simpson & C.G. Jackson Jr; Proceedings of Symposium on Freshwater Marshes: Present Status, Future Needs; New Brunswick, 1977, pp. 39–52. New York: Academic Press.

Bernard, J.M. & Solsky, B.A. (1977). Nutrient cycling in a *Carex lacustris* wetland. *Canadian Journal of Botany*, 55, 117–23.

Bernatowicz, S. (1960). Charakterystyka jezior na podstawie roślin naczyniowych. *Rocznik Nauk Rolniczych*, 77B, 79–103.

Bernatowicz, S. (1969). Macrophytes in the lake Warnak and their chemical composition. *Ekologia Polska, Seria A*, 14, 519–46.

Bernatowicz, S., Hillbricht-Ilkowska, A., Kakak, Z., Rybak, J.I., Turczyńska, J.

& Węgleńska, T. (1974). Charakterystyka limnologiczna jeziora Niegocin na tle postępującej eutrophizacji. *Zeszyty Nauk, Akademia Olsztyn*, **3**, 149–73.

Bernatowicz, S., Lesczynski, S. & Tyczynska, S. (1976). The influence of transpiration by emergent plants on the water balance in lakes. *Aquatic Botany*, **2**, 275–88.

Bernatowicz, S. & Radziej, J. (1964). Produkcja roczna macrofitóv w kompleksie jeziora Mamry. *Polskie Archiwum Hydrobiologii*, **12**, 307–48.

Bernatowicz, S. & Zachwieja, J. (1966). Types of littoral found in the lakes of the Masurian and Suwałki lakelands. *Ekologia Polska, Seria A*, **14**(28), 519–46.

Bernis, F. (1964). La invernada y migracion da nuestros ansareg (*Anser anser y Anser fabalis*). *Ardeola*, **9**, 67–109.

Best, E.P.H. (1988). The phytosociological approach to the description and classification of aquatic macrophytic vegetation. In *Vegetation of Inland Waters*, ed. J.J. Symoens; Handbook of Vegetation Science 15/1, pp. 155–82.

Beydeman, I.N. (1960). Ritm sezonnogo khoda intensivnosti transpiratsii rastenii pri raznykh tipakh vodnogo rezhima pochv razlichnȳkh klimaticheskikh usloviĭakh. *Botanicheskiĭ Zhurnal*, **45**, 1108–22.

Bezzel, J.J. & Reichholf, J. (1974). Die Diversität als Kriterium zur Bewertung der Reichhaltigkeit von Wasservogel-Lebensräumen. *Journal of Ornithology*, **115**, 50–61.

Biggar, J.W. & Corey, B.B. (1969). Agricultural drainage and eutrophication. In *Eutrophication, Causes, Consequences, Correctives* – Proceedings of a Symposium, pp. 404–45. Washington DC: National Academy of Sciences.

Binder, W. (1977). Neuschaffung von Biotopen in Verbindung mit Wasserbauvorhaben. *Berichte der Akademie zum Naturschutz und Landschaftspflege, Laufen/Sazach*, **1**, 26–35.

Binz, H.R. (1989). *Mechanische Belastbarkeit natürlicher Schilfbestände durch Wellen, Wind, und Treibzeug*; Veröffenlichung Geobotanisches Institut, Eidgenosse Technische Hochschule, Stiftung Rübel in Zurich, **101**, 536 pp.

Binz, H.R. & Klötzli, F. (1978). Mechanische Wirkung auf Röhrichte im eutrophen Milieu – Versuch eines Modells. In *Beiträge zur chemischen Kommunikation in Bio- und Öko-systemen*, Festschrift R. Kickuth, pp. 193–215. Witzenhausen: Universität Kassel.

Bisset, K. & Farmer, A. (1993). *SSSIs in England at Risk from Acid Rain*. English Nature Science Series No. 15. Peterborough: English Nature. 126 pp.

Bittmann, E. (1953). Das Schilf (*Phragmites communis* Trin.) und seine Verwendung im Wasserbau. *Angewandte Pflanzensoziologie*, **7**(8), 111–44.

Bittmann, E. (1957). Untersuchungen über die Ufervegetation der Mosel von Perl bis Koblenz. *Deutsche Gewässerkundliche Mitteilungen*, **1**, 102–6.

Bittmann, E. (1968). Landschaftspflege an Gewässern. In *Handbuch für landschaftspflege und Naturschutz*, ed. K. Buchwald & E. Engelhardt; 2, *Pflege der freien Landschaft*, pp. 350–74. München: Bayr. Landschaft. Verlag.

Bittmann, E. (1973). Richtlinien für Pflegemassnahmen an Gewässern. In *Landschaftspflege und Naturschutz in der Praxis*. ed. K. Buchwald & W. Engelhardt, pp. 141–50. München: Bayr. Landschaft. Verlag.

Björk, S. (1967). Ecologic investigations of *Phragmites communis*: studies in theoretic and applied limnology: *Folia Limnologica Scandinavica, Lund*, **14**, 1–248.

Björk, S. (1971). Reversibila skador i sjöekosystem. *Svensk Naturvetenskap*, 1971, 93–101.

Björk, S. (1972). Ecosystem studies in connection with restoration of lakes.

Verhandlungen der Internationalen Vereinigung für Theoretische und Angewandte Limnologie, **18**, 379–87.

Björk, S., Bengtsson, L., Berggren, H., Cronberg, G., Digerfeldt, G., Fleischer, S., Gelin, C., Lindmark, G., Malmer, N., Plejmark, F., Ripl, W. & Swanberg, O.P. (1978). Ecosystem studies in connection with the restoration of lakes. *Verhandlungen der Internationalen Vereinigung für Theoretische und Angewandte Limnologie*, **18**, 379–87.

Black, C.C. (1971). Ecological implications of dividing plants into groups with distinct photosynthetic production capacities. *Advances in Ecological Research*, **7**, 87–113.

Blackard, J.J., Parker, W.T. & Sumrell, F. (1972). A report on upland habitat and wildlife conditions. In *Port Royal Sound Environmental Study*, pp. 279–95. Columbia: S. Carolina, Water Research Commission. 555 pp.

Blackburn, R.D. (1974). Chemical control. In *Aquatic Vegetation and its Use and Control*, ed. D.S. Mitchell, pp. 85–98. Paris: UNESCO.

Blackburn, R.D., Sutton, D.L. & Taylor, T. (1971). Biological control of aquatic weeds. *Journal of the Irrigation and Drainage Division, American Society of Civil Engineers*, **97**(IR3), 421–32.

Blake, C. & Dubois, J.P. (1982). Éparation des eaux; rôles des macrophytes aquatiques dans l'élimination des éléments minéraux. In *Studies on Aquatic Vascular Plants*, ed. J.J. Symoens, S.S. Hooper & P. Compère; Handbook of Vegetation Science 15/1, pp. 315–23. Brussels: Royal Botanical Society of Belgium.

Blažka, P. (1958). The anaerobic metabolism of fish. *Physiological Zoology*, **21**, 117–28.

Bliss, L.C., Heal, O.W. & Moore, J.J. (eds.) (1981). *Tundra Ecosystems: a Comparative Analysis*; International Biological Programme 25. Cambridge: Cambridge University Press. 400 pp.

Blum, J.J. (1969). Nutrient changes in water flooding the high salt marsh. *Hydrobiologia*, **34**, 95–9.

Böck, F. (1974). Vögel des Rohrwaldes und am freien See. In *Neusiedlersee: the Limnology of a Shallow Lake in Central Europe*, ed. H. Löffler; Monographiae Biologicae, pp. 116–36. The Hague: W. Junk.

Bohr, N.L. with Guest, E. (1968). Gramineae: General Systematic Text. In *Flora of Iraq*, IX, ed. C.C. Townsend & E. Guest, pp. 14–19. Baghdad: Ministry of Agriculture.

Boller-Elmer, K. (1977). Stickstoff- und Düngung-Einflüsse von Intensivgrünland auf Streu- und Moor-wiesen. *Veröffentlichungen, Geobotanischer Forschungsinstitut, ETH, Stiftung Rübel in Zurich*, **63**, 1–103.

Bonnema, K.W. (1972). *Wildlife habitat losses in Ten Mile Creek watershed (Judic. Ditch 8), Lac qui Parle and Yellow Medicine Counties, Minnesota*. Division of Game/Fisheries, Section of Technical Service, Special Publication 99. Minneapolis-St Paul: Ministry Department of Natural Resources. 11 pp.

Boorman, L.A. & Fuller, R.M. (1981). The changing status of reedswamp in the Norfolk Broads. *Journal of Applied Ecology*, **18**, 241–69.

Bootle, P. & Knauer, G. (1972). The possible importance of fecal material in the biological amplification of trace and heavy metals. *Limnology and Oceanography*, **17**, 270–4.

Borhidi, A. (1970). Ökologie, Wettbewerb und Zönologie des Schilfrohrs (*Phragmites communis* L.) und die Systematik der Brachröhrichte. *Acta Botanica Academiae Scientiarum Hungaricae*, **16**, 1–12.

Borutskiĭ, E.V. (1949). Izmenenie zarosleĭ makrofitov v Bielom Ozere v Kosine s 1888 po 1938 g. *Trudy̆ Vsesoyuznogo Gidrobiologicheskogo Obshchestva*, **1**, 44–56.

Boughey, A.S. (1963). The explosive development of a floating weed vegetation on Lake Kariba. *Adamsonia*, **3**, 49–61.

Boulé, M. (1994). An early history of wetland ecology. In *Global Wetlands: Old World and New*, ed. J.W. Mitsch, pp. 57–74. Amsterdam: Elsevier.

Boulenge, E., le (1972). État de nos connaissances sur l'écologie du rat musqué *Ondatra zibethica* L. *Terre et la Vie* No. 1, 3–37.

Bourn, W.S. & Cottam, C. (1950). *Some biological effects of ditching tidewater marshes.* US Fish & Wildlife Service. Research Report 19. Washington: US Fish & Wildlife Service, 30 pp.

Bownik, L.J. (1970). The periphyton of the submerged macrophytes of Mikołajskie lake. *Ekologia Polska Seria A*, **18**, 503–20.

Boyd, C.E. (1968a). Freshwater plants: a potential source of protein. *Economic Botany*, **22**, 359–68.

Boyd, C.E. (1968b). Evaluation of some common aquatic weeds as possible feedstuffs. *Hyacinth Control Journal*, **7**, 26–7.

Boyd, C.E. (1968c). Some aspects of aquatic plant ecology. In *Symposium on Reservoir Fisheries Resources*, pp. 114–29. Athens G.: University of Georgia Press.

Boyd, C.E. (1969). Production, mineral nutrient absorption, and biochemical assimilation by *Justicia americana* and *Alternanthera philoxeroides*. *Archiv für Hydrobiologie*, **66**, 139–60.

Boyd, C.E. (1970a). Chemical analyses of some vascular aquatic plants. *Archiv für Hydrobiologie*, **67**, 78–95.

Boyd, C.E. (1970b). Production, mineral accumulation and pigment concentrations in *Typha latifolia* and *Scirpus americanus*. *Ecology*, **51**, 285–90.

Boyd, C.E. (1970c). Influence of organic matter on some characteristics of aquatic soils. *Hydrobiologia*, **36**, 17–21.

Boyd, C.E. (1971a). The dynamics of dry matter and chemical substances in a *Juncus effusus* population. *American Midland Naturalist*, **86**, 256–70.

Boyd, C.E. (1971b). The limnological role of aquatic macrophytes and their relationship to reservoir management. *Reservoir Fisheries and Limnology (Special Publications)*, **8**, 153–66.

Boyd, C.E. (1971c). Leaf protein from aquatic plants. In *Leaf Protein: its Agronomy, Preparation, Quality and Uses*, International Biological Programme Handbook Series, No. 20, ed. N.W. Pirie, pp. 44–9. Oxford: Blackwell.

Boyd, C.E. (1974). The utilisation of nitrogen from the decomposition of organic matter in cultures of *Scenedesmus dimorphus*. *Archiv für Hydrobiologie*, **73**, 361–8.

Boyd, C.E. & Goodyear, C.P. (1971). Nutritive quality of food in ecological systems. *Archiv für Hydrobiologie*, **69**, 256–70.

Boyd, C.E. & Hess, L.W. (1970). Factors influencing shoot production and mineral nutrient levels in *Typha latifolia*. *Ecology*, **51**, 296–300.

Boyd, C.E. & Lawrence, J.M. (1967). The mineral composition of several freshwater algae. In *Proceedings of the 20th Annual Conference of the Southeastern Association of Game and Fish Commissioners*, 413–24.

Boyd, C.E. & Scarsbrook, E. (1975a). Influence of nutrient additions and initial density of plants on production of waterhyacinth *Eichhornia crassipes*. *Aquatic Botany*, **1**, 253–61.

Boyd, C.E. & Scarsbrook, E. (1975*b*). Chemical composition of aquatic weeds. In *Proceedings of the Symposium on Water Quality & Management through Biological Control*, ed. P.L. Brezonik & J.L. Fox, pp. 144–50. Gainsville: University of Florida.

Boyd, C.E. & Vickers, D. H. (1971). Variation in the elemental content of *Eichhornia crassipes*. *Hydrobiologia*, **38**, 409–14.

Boysen-Jensen, B. (1914). Studies concerning the organic matter of sea bottoms. *Report of the Danish Biological Station* No. 22, 5–39.

Bradbury, I.K. & Grace, J. (1983). Primary production in wetlands. In *Mires: Swamp, Bog, Fen and Moors, General Studies*, ed. A.J.P. Gore; Ecosystems of the World, 4A, 285–310. Amsterdam: Elsevier.

Brady, N.C. (1990). *Introduction to the Nature and Properties of Soils*, 10th ed. New York: Macmillan. 780 pp.

Braginskiĭ, L.P., Bereza, V.D., Velichko, J.M., Grin, V.G., Gusȳnskaya, S.L., Denisova, A.J., Litvinova, M.A. & Sȳsueva-Antipchuk, A.F. (1968). 'Pyatna tsveteniya', nagonnȳe massȳ vybrosȳ sinezelennȳkh vodorosleĭ i proischodyashchie v nikh biologicheskie processȳ. In *Tsvetenie Vodȳ*, **1**, 92–149. Kiev: 'Naukova Dumka'.

Brändle, R., Čížková, H. & Pokornȳ, J. (eds.) (1996). *Adaptation Strategies in Water Plants: Links between Ecology and Physiology*, Special Features in Vegetation Science, 10. Uppsala: Opulus Press. 162 pp.

Braun, R. (1952). Limnologische Untersuchungen an einigen Seen im Amazonagebiet. *Schweizer Zeitung der Hydrobiologie*, **14**, 1–128.

Bray, J.R. (1960). The chlorophyll content of some native and managed plant communities in central Minnesota. *Canadian Journal of Botany*, **38**, 313–33.

Bray, J.R., Lawrence, D.B. & Pearson, L.C. (1959). Primary production in some Minnesota terrestrial communities for 1957. *Oikos*, **10**, 38–49.

Breymeyer, A.I. & Van Dyne, G.M. (eds.) (1980). *Grasslands, Systems Analysis and Man*; International Biological Programme 19. Cambridge: Cambridge University Press. 950 pp.

Brežny, O., Mehta, I. & Sharma, R.K. (1973). Studies on evapotranspiration of some aquatic weeds. *Weed Science*, **21**, 197–204.

Brinson, M.M. (1977). Decomposition and nutrient exchange of litter in an alluvial swamp forest. *Ecology*, **58**, 601–9.

Brinson, M.M., Lugo, A.E. & Brown, S. (1981). Primary productivity, decomposition and consumer activity in fresh water wetlands. *Annual Review of Ecology and Systematics*, **12**, 123–62.

Bristow, J.M. (1974). Nitrogen fixation in the rhizosphere of freshwater angiosperms. *Canadian Journal of Botany*, **52**, 217–21.

Bristow, J.M. (1975). The structure and function of roots in aquatic vascular plants. In *The Development and Function of Roots*, ed. J.G. Torrey & D.T. Clarkson, pp. 231–3. London: Academic Press.

Brooker, M.P. & Edwards, R.W. (1975). Aquatic herbicides and the control of water weeds. *Water Research*, **9**, 1–15.

Brooks, A. (1976). *Waterways and Wetlands*. London: British Trust for Conservation Volunteers Ltd. 228 pp.

Brylinsky, M. (1980). Estimating the productivity of lakes and reservoirs. In *The Functioning of Freshwater Ecosystems*, ed. E.D. LeCren & R.H. Lowe-McConnell; International Biological Programme No. 22, pp. 411–54. Cambridge: Cambridge University Press.

Burian, K. (1969). Die photosynthetische Aktivität eines *Phragmites-communis*-Bestandes am Neusiedler See. *Sitzungsberichte Österreichische Akademie der Wissenschaften, Mathematisch-Naturwissenschaftliche Klasse I, Abteilung 1*, **178**, 43–62.

Burian, K. (1971). Primary production, carbon exchange and transpiration in *Phragmites communis* Trin. on the lake Neusiedler See, Austria. *Hidrobiologia, Bucureşti*, **12**, 203–18.

Burian, K. (1973). *Phragmites communis* Trin im Röhricht des Neusiedlersees. Wachstum, Produktion und Wasserverbrauch. In *Ökosystemforschung*, ed. H. Ellenberg, pp. 61–78. Heidelberg: Springer Verlag.

Burian, K. & Sieghardt, H. (1979). The primary producers of the *Phragmites* belt, their energy utilization and water balance. In *Neusiedlersee: the Limnology of a Shallow Lake in Central Europe*, ed. H. Löffler; Monographiae Biologicae, pp. 251–72. The Hague: W. Junk.

Burkholder, P.R. (1957). Studies on the nutritive value of Spartina Grass growing in the marsh areas of coastal Georgia. *Bulletin of the Torrey Botanical Club*, **83**, 327–34.

Butcher, R.W. (1933). Studies on the ecology of rivers I. On the distribution of macrophytic vegetation in the rivers of Britain. *Journal of Ecology*, **21**, 58–91.

Buttery, B.R. & Lambert, J.M. (1965). Competition between *Glyceria maxima* and *Phragmites communis* in the region of Surlingham Broad. I. The competition mechanism. *Journal of Ecology*, **53**, 163–81.

Buttery, B.R., Williams, W.T. & Lambert, J.M. (1965). Competition between *Glyceria maxima* and *Phragmites communis* in the region of Surlingham Broad. II. The fen gradient. *Journal of Ecology*, **53**, 183–95.

Caines, L.A. (1965). The phosphorus content of some aquatic macrophytes with special reference to seasonal fluctuations and applications of phosphate fertilizer. *Hydrobiologia*, **20**, 289–301.

Cameron, G.N. (1972). Analysis of insect trophic diversity in two salt marsh communities. *Ecology*, **53**, 58–73.

Campbell, E.O. (1983). Mires of Australasia. In *Mires: Swamp, Bog, Fen and Moor, Regional Studies*, ed. A.J.P. Gore; Ecosystems of the World, vol. 4B, 153–80. Amsterdam: Elsevier.

Canadian Wildlife Service. (1969). *Saskatoon Wetlands Seminar*. Canadian Wildlife Service Report Series 6. Ottawa: Department of Indian Affairs and Northern Development. 262 pp.

Carbiener, R. (1969). Aperçu sur quelques effets de la pollution des eaux douces de la zone tempérée sur les biocéno ses aquatiques. *Bulletin de la Section de Géographie du Comité des Travaux Historiques et Scientifiques, Paris*, **80**, 45–132.

Carignan, R. & Kalff, J. (1979). Quantification of the sediment phosphorus available to aquatic macrophytes. *Journal of the Fisheries Research Board of Canada*, **36**, 1002–5.

Carp, E. (1980). *Directory of Wetlands of the Western Palearctic*. Gland: IUCN. 506 pp.

Carter, J. (1977*a,b*). *Executive Order, 11988, Floodplain Management; 11990, Protection of Wetlands*. Federal Register, **42**(101), 26951–7; 26961–5. Washington: US Government.

Casey, H. & Downing, A. (1976). Levels of inorganic nutrients in *Ranunculus penicillatus* var. *calcareus* in relation to water chemistry. *Aquatic Botany*, **2**, 75–9.

Casey, H. (1977). Origin and variation of nitrate nitrogen in the chalk springs, streams and rivers in Dorset and its utilization by higher plants. *Progress in Water Technology*, **8**, 225–35; Conference on Nitrogen as a Water Pollutant, 2, Pollution, Paper B1.2, Copenhagen (1975).

Casey, H. & Newton, P.V.R. (1972). The chemical composition and flow of the South Winterbourne in Dorset. *Freshwater Biology*, **2**, 229–34.

Casey, H. & Westlake, D.F. (1974). Growth and nutrient relationships of macrophytes in Sydling Water, a small unpolluted chalk stream. In *Proceedings of the EWRS, 4th International Symposium on Aquatic Weeds*, pp. 69–76.

Caspers, H. (1964). Characteristics of hypertrophic lakes and canals in cities. *Verhandlungen der Internationalen Vereinigung für Theoretische und Angewandte Limnologie*, **15**, 631–8.

Castellano, E.R. (1977). Productividad de *Rorippa nasturtium-aquaticum* (L.) Hayek. Trabajo, Universidad de Los Andes. 42 pp.

Cavari, B.Z. (1977). Nitrification potential and factors governing the rate of nitrification in Lake Kinneret. *Oikos*, **28**, 285–90.

Center, T.D. & Spencer, N.R. (1981). The phenology and growth of water hyacinth (*Eichhornia crassipes* (Mart.) Solms) in a eutrophic North-central Florida lake. *Aquatic Botany*, **10**, 1–32.

Chabreck, R.H. (1970). *Marsh Zones and Vegetative Types of the Louisiana Coastal Marshes*. Baton Rouge: Louisiana State University. 112 pp.

Chambers, M.R. (1971*a*). Studies on the littoral fauna of Tjeukemeer. PhD thesis. Liverpool: University of Liverpool. 281 pp.

Chambers, M.R. (1971*b*). The dominance, production and utilization of *Gammarus tigrinus* in the exposed *Phragmites* reed beds of the Tjeukemeer. *Hydrobiologia*, **12**, 297–304.

Chapman, V.J. (ed.) (1977). *Wet Coastal Ecosystems*; Ecosystems of the World 1. Amsterdam: Elsevier. 428 pp.

Chapman, V.J. & Coffey, B.J. (1971). Experiments with grass carp in controlling exotic macrophytes in New Zealand. *Hidrobiologia, Bucureşti*, **12**, 313–23.

Chattergee, S.P. (1964). *Progress of Geography (Fifty Years of Science in India)*. Calcutta: India Science Congress Association. 227 pp.

Chen, T.M., Brown, R.H. & Black, C.C. (1970). CO_2 compensation concentration, rate of photosynthesis, and carbonic anhydrase activity of plants. *Weed Science*, **18**, 399–403.

Chevey, M. & Lepoulain, C. (1940). *La Pêche dans les Eaux Douces du Cambodge*; Travaux – Institut de Oceanographie de l'Indochine, 5e mem. Saigon: IOI. 193 pp.

Choate, J.S. (1972). Effects of stream channelling on wetlands in a Minnesota watershed. *Journal of Wildlife Management*, **36**, 940–4.

Christian, R.R., Hanson, R.B., Hall, J.R. & Wiebe, V.J. (1981). Aerobic microbes and meiofauna. In *The Ecology of a Salt Marsh*, ed. L.R. Pomeroy & R.G. Wiegert; Ecological Studies 38, pp. 113–35. New York: Springer Verlag.

Chvála, M., Doskočil, J., Mook, J.H. & Pokorný, V. (1974). The genus *Lipara* Meigen (Diptera, Chloropidae), systematics, morphology, behaviour and ecology. *Tijdschrift voor Entomologie*, **117**, afl,1, 1974, 1–25.

Čižková-Končalová, H., Strand, J. & Lukavská, J. (1996). Factors associated with reed decline in a eutrophic fishpond, Rožmberk (South Bohemia, Czech Republic). *Folia Geobotanica et Phytotaxonomica, Praha*, **31**, 73–84.

Claassen, P.W. (1921). *Typha* insects: Their economical relationships. *Cornell*

University Agricultural Experimental Station Bulletin and Memoirs, **47**, 459–531.

Clark, J.P. & Evans, F.C. (1954). Distance to nearest neighbour as a measure of spatial relationship in populations. *Ecology*, **35**, 445–53.

Clymo, R.S. (1962). An experimental approach to part of the calcicole problem. *Journal of Ecology*, **50**, 707–31.

Coche, A.C. (1968). Fish culture in rice fields – a world-wide synthesis. *Hydrobiologia*, **30**, 1–43.

Cockayne, L. (1928). *The Vegetation of New Zealand* (2nd edn.). Leipzig: Engelmann. 456 pp.

Cole, A.C. (1931). *Typha* insects and their parasites. *Entomological News*, **42** (1 and 2), 6–11 and 35–9.

Conner, W.H. & Day, J.W. Jr (1976). Productivity and composition of a baldcypress-water tupelo site and a bottomland hardwood site in a Louisiana swamp. *American Journal of Botany*, **63**, 1354–64.

Cooke, R.W. (1976). *A Review of the Effects of Agriculture on the Chemical Composition and Quality of Surface and Underground Waters*; Technical Bulletin, MAFF, No. 32, pp. 1–57. London: HMSO.

Cooper, C.F. (1969). Nutrient output from managed forests. In *Eutrophication: Causes, Consequences, Correctives* – Proceedings of a Symposium, pp. 446–63. Washington DC: National Academy of Sciences.

Cooper, F.E. (1972). The thatcher and the thatched roof. In *The Reed ('Norfolk Reed')* (2nd edn.), pp. 58–64. Norwich: Norfolk Reed Growers Association.

Cooper, J.P. (ed.) (1975). *Photosynthesis and Productivity in Different Environments*; International Biological Programme No. 22. Cambridge: Cambridge University Press. 715 pp.

Cooper, P. & Green, B. (1995). Reed bed treatment systems for sewage treatment in the United Kingdom – the first 10 years' experience. *Water Science Technology*, **32**, 317–27.

Costanza, R., Arge, d' R., Groot, de R., Farber, S., Grasso, M., Hannon, B., Limburg, K., Naeem, S., O'Neill, R.V., Paruelo, J., Raskin, R.G., Sutton, P. & Belt v. d. M. (1997). The value of the world's ecosystem services and natural capital. *Nature*, **387**, 253–60.

Cottam, G. & Curtis, J.T. (1956). The use of distance measures in phytosociological sampling. *Ecology*, **37**, 451–60.

Coupland, R.T. (ed.) (1979). *Grassland Ecosystems of the World: Analysis of Grasslands and their Uses*; International Biological Programme 18. Cambridge: Cambridge University Press. 401 pp.

Coveney, M.F., Cronberg, G., Enell, M., Larsson, K. & Olofson, L. (1977). Phytoplankton, zooplankton and bacteria – standing crop and production relationships in an eutrophic lake. *Oikos*, **29**, 5–21.

Cowardin, L.M., Carter, V., Golet, F.C. & LaRoe, E.T. (1979). *Classification of Wetlands and Deepwater Habitats of the United States*; Report No. FWS/OBS-79/31. Washington DC: US Fish and Wildlife Service. 103 pp.

Craig, N.J., Turner, R.E. & Day, J.W. (1979). Land loss in coastal Louisiana. *Environmental Management*, **3**, 133–44.

Crawford, C.C., Hobbie, J.E. & Webb, K.L. (1974). The utilisation of dissolved free amino acids by estuarine microorganisms. *Ecology*, **55**, 551–63.

Crawford, R.M.M. (1969). The physiological basis of flooding tolerance. *Berichte der Deutschen Botanischen Gesellschaft*, **82**, 111–14.

Crawford, R.M.M. (1978). Metabolic adaptations to anoxia. In *Plant Life in*

Anaerobic Environments, ed. D.D. Hook & R.M.M. Crawford, pp. 119–36. Ann Arbor: Ann Arbor Science.

Creutzberg, F., Leentvaar, P. Rense, R., Rikkert, C.T.B. de Koe, Vries, H.A. de & Zwart, K.W.E. (1969). *De Zuidelijke Vechtplassen, Naarden*; Stichting voor de Vecht en het oestelijk en westlijke plassengebied. 205 pp.

Crisp, D.T. (1970). Input and output of minerals for a small watercress bed fed by chalk water. *Journal of Applied Ecology*, **7**, 117–40.

Crissey, W.F. (1969). Prairie potholes from a continental viewpoint. In *Saskatoon Wetlands Seminar*; Canadian Wildlife Service Report Series 6, pp. 161–71. Ottawa: Department of Indian Affairs and Northern Development.

Crossland, N.O. (1971). A field trial with the molluscicide Frescon for control of *Lymnaea peregra* Müller, snail host of *Diplostomum spathaceum* Rdolphi. *Journal of Fisheries Biology*, **1**, 27–30.

Cruz, A.A. de la & Poe, W.E. (1975). Amino acid content of marsh plants. *Estuarine Coastal and Marine Science*, **3**, 243–6.

Culley, D.D. Jr & Epps, E.A. (1973). Potential usefulness of duckweeds in waste water treatment and animal feeds. *Journal of the Water Pollution Control Federation*, **45**, 337–47.

Culley, D.D. Jr, Rejmánková, E., Frye, J.B. & Květ, J. (1983). Production, chemical quality and use of duckweeds (Lemnaceae) in aquaculture, waste management and animal feeds. *Proceedings of World Mariculture Society*, **12**, 27–49.

Cumbus, I.P., Hornsey, D.J. & Robinson, L.W. (1977). The influence of phosphorus, zinc and manganese on absorption and translocation of iron in watercress. *Plant and Soil*, **48**, 651–60.

Cumbus, I.P. & Robinson, L.W. (1977). The function of rootsystems in mineral nutrition of watercress (*Rorippa Nasturtium-aquaticum* L. Hayek). *Plant and Soil*, **47**, 395–406.

Cumbus, I.P., Robinson, L.W. & Clare, R.G. (1980). Mineral nutrient availability in watercress bed substrates. *Aquatic Botany*, **9**, 343–9.

Cummins, K.W. (1973). Trophic relations of aquatic insects. *Annual Review of Entomology*, **18**, 183–206.

Daiber, F.C. (1974). Biological productivity of estuaries as influenced by wetland management. In *International Conference on the Conservation of Wetlands and Waterfowl, Heiligenhafen, December, 1974*, ed. M. Smart; Proceedings, pp. 329–31. Slimbridge: IWRB.

Dale, H.M. & Gillespie, T. (1976). The influence of floating vascular plants on the diurnal fluctuations of temperature near the water surface in early spring. *Hydrobiologia*, **49**, 245–56.

Däniker, A.U. (1939). Neues Calidonia. *Vegetationsbilder, Reihe 25*, **Heft 6**, Tafel 31–36.

Darnell, R.M. (1961). Trophic spectrum of an estuarine community based on studies of Lake Pontchartrain, Louisiana. *Ecology*, **42**, 553–658.

Davies, J. (1964). A vegetation of Tasmania. *Geographical Review*, **54**, 249–53.

Davis, C.B. & van der Walk, A.G. (1978). The decomposition of standing and fallen litter of *Typha glauca* and *Scirpus validus*. *Canadian Journal of Botany*, **56**, 662–75.

Davis, L.V. & Grey, I.E. (1966). Zonal and seasonal distribution of insects in North Carolina salt marshes. *Ecological Monographs*, **36**, 275–95.

Dawson, F.H. (1976a). The annual production of the aquatic macrophyte

Ranunculus penicillatus var. *calcareus* (R.W. Butcher) C.D.K. Cook. *Aquatic Botany*, **2**, 51–73.

Dawson, F.H. (1976*b*). Organic contribution of stream edge forest litter fall to the chalk stream ecosystem. *Oikos*, **27**, 13–18.

Dawson, F.H., Castellano, E. & Ladle, M. (1978). Concept of species succession in relation to river vegetation and management. *Verhandlungen der Internationalen Vereinigung für Theoretische und Andewandte Limnologie*, **20**, 1429–34.

Day, J.W. Jr, Hall, C.A., Kemp, W.M. & Yáñez-Arancibia, A. (1989). *Estuarine Ecology*. New York: Wiley. 576 pp.

Day, J.W. Jr, Smith, W.G., Wagener, P.R. & Stowe, W.C. (1973). *Community Structure and Carbon Budget of a Salt Marsh and Shallow Bay Estuarine System, in Louisiana*; Center for Wetland Resources, Publication No. LSU-SG-72-04. Baton Rouge: Louisiana State University. 80 pp.

De Marte, J.A. & Hartman, R.T. (1974). Studies on absorption of ^{32}P, ^{59}Fe and ^{45}Ca by water-milfoil (*Myriophyllum exalbescens* Fernald). *Ecology*, **55**, 188–94.

Debenham, B. (1953). Bangweula swamps. *World Crops*, **5**, 150–2.

Dejoux, C. & Saint-Jean, L. (1972). Études des communatés invertebrés d'herbieres du lac Tchad: recherches préliminaires. *Cahiers de l'Office de la Recherche Scientifique et Technique Outre-Mer, Série Hydrobiologie*, **6**, 67–83.

Delacour, J. & Jabouillet, P. (1931). *Les Oiseaux del'Indochine Française*. Paris: Exposition Coloniale Internationale. 4 vols.

Delvosalle, L. & Vanhecke, L. (1982). Essai de notation quantatative de la raréfaction d'espèces aquatiques est palustres en Belgique entre 1960 et 1980. In *Studies on Aquatic Vascular Plants*, ed. J.J. Symoens, S.S. Hooper & P. Compère; Proceedings of the International Colloquium on Aquatic Vascular Plants, Brussels, January 1981, pp. 403–9. Brussels: Royal Botanical Society of Belgium.

Delvosalle, L.F., Demaret, J., Lambinon, J. & Lawalrée, A. (1969). L'appauvrissement de la flore belge depuis le mileu du XIXe siécle. In *Plantes Rares, Disparues ou Menacées de Disparation en Belgique. L'appauvrissement de la flore indigène*, ed. L.F. Delvosalle, J. Demaret, J. Lambinon & A. Lawalrée; Ministère de l'Agriculture, Administration de l'Eau et Forêts Travaux, 4, pp. 9–21. Brussels: Ministry of Agriculture.

Demidovskaya, L.F. & Isambaev, A.I. (1964). Proizvodstvennaya klassifikatsiya trostnikovikh zaroslei nizovei riekȳ Sȳr-Darīȳ. *Trudȳ Instituta Academiyi Nauk Kazakhstana SSR*, **19**, 38–62.

Demidovskaya, L.F. & Kirikhenko, R.A. (1964). Morfologo-anatomicheskie osobennosti trostnika i tsikl ego razvitiya. *Trudȳ Instituta Botaniki AN Kazakhskoi SSR*, **19**, 93–159.

Denaeyer-De Smet, S. (1964). Note sur la composition minérale des graminées et plantes graminoides des tapis végétaux naturels de Belgique. *Bulletin – Société Royale de Botanique de Belgique*, **97**, 19–25.

Denny, P. (1980). Solute movement in submerged angiosperms. *Biological Reviews*, **55**, 65–92.

Denny, P. (ed.) (1985). *The Biology and Management of African Wetland Vegetation*. Dordrecht: Junk. 344 pp.

DeWit, C.T. (1965). Photosynthesis of leaf canopies. *Agricultural Research Reports*, **663**, 11–57.

Dickinson, C.H. & Pugh, G.J.F. eds. (1974). *Biology of Plant Litter Decomposition I, II.* New York: Academic Press. 775 pp.
Dirschl, H.J. (1971). Ecological evaluations in Saskatoon and Alberta. *Canadian Wildlife Service*, **71**, 71–3.
Dirschl, H.J. (1972). Evaluation of ecological effects of recent low water levels in the Peace–Athabasca Delta. *Canadian Wildlife Service, Occasional Paper*, **13**, 1–27.
Dittrich, A. & Westrich, B. (1990). Erosion Scheinungen und Schilfrückgang in der Flachwasserzone des Bodensees. In *Ökologie, Gefährdung, und Schutz von Röhrichtpflanzen*, ed. H. Sukopp & M. Krauss; Landschaftsentwicklung u. Umweltforschung, **71**, pp. 86–93. Berlin: Technische Universität.
Dobrowolski, K.A. (1969). Structure of the occurrence of waterfowl types and morpho-ecological forms. *Ekologia Polska, Seria A*, **17**, 29–72.
Dobrowolski, K.A. (1973a). Role of birds in Polish wetlands ecosystems. *Polskie Archiwum Hydrobiologii*, **20**, 217–21.
Dobrowolski, K.A. (1973b). Ptaki wodne i ich rola w ekosystemie jeziornym. (Waterfowl and their role in lake ecosystems.) *Wiadomości Ekologiczne*, **19**, 353–71. (In Polish with English summary.)
Dölling, L. (1962). Der Anteil der Tierwelt an der Bildung von Unterwasserböden. *Verhandlungen der Zoologisch-Botanischen Gesellschaft im Wien*, **101/102**, 50–85.
Dony, J.G. (1977). Change in the flora of Bedfordshire, England, from 1798 to 1976. *Biological Conservation*, **11**, 307–20.
Doskočil, J. & Chvála, M. (1971). A revision of *Lipara* Meigen (Diptera, Chloropidae) including the description of a new species from Europe. *Acta Entomologica Bohemoslovaca*, **68**, 100–7.
Doyle, R.W. (1979). Ingestion rate of a selective deposit feeder in a complex mixture of particles: testing the energy-optimization hypothesis. *Limnology and Oceanography*, **24**, 867–74.
Dozier, H.L. (1948). Estimating muskrat populations by house counts. In *Proceedings of 13th North American Wildlife Conference, St Louis*, pp. 372–92.
Drake, B.G. & Read, M. (1981). Carbon dioxide assimilation, photosynthetic efficiency and respiration of a Chesapeake Bay salt marsh. *Journal of Ecology*, **69**, 405–23.
Drewier, R.C. & Springer, P.F. (1969). Ecological relationships of breeding bluewinged teal to prairie potholes. In *Saskatoon Wetlands Seminar*; Canadian Wildlife Service Report Series 6, pp. 102–15. Ottawa: Department of Indian Affairs and Northern Development.
Dring, M.J. & Frost, L.C. (1971). Studies of *Ranunculus ophioglossifolius* in relation to its conservation at the Badgeworth Nature Reserve, Gloucestershire, England. *Biological Conservation*, **4**, 48–56.
Duffey, E. & Watt, A.S. (eds.) (1971). *The Scientific Management of Animal and Plant Communities for Conservation*; 11th Symposium of the British Ecological Society. Oxford: Blackwell Science Publishers. 600 pp.
Duffield, A.N. & Edwards, R.W. (1976). Predicting the distribution of *Lemna* spp. in a complex system of drainage channels. In *Aquatic Weeds and their Control*; Proceedings of the Conference on Aquatic Weeds and their Control; Oxford, 1981, pp. 59–76. Warwick: Association of Applied Biologists.
Duplakov, S.N. (1933). Materialȳ k izucheniu perifȳtona. *Trudȳ Limologicheskoĭ Stanciiv Kosine*, **16**, 5–160.

Durska, B. (1970). Changes in the reed (*Phragmites communis* Trin.) condition caused by diseases of fungal and animal origin. *Polskie Archiwum Hydrobiologii*, **17**(30/34), 373–96.

Durska, B. (1972). Wpływ grzybów pasożytniczych na zawartość azotu i transpiracja trzciny pospolittej. *Acta Mycologica*, **8**, 3–19.

Duthu, G.S. & Kilgen, R.H. (1975). Aquarium studies on the selectivity of 16 aquatic plants as food by fingerling hybrids of the cross between *Ctenopharyngodon idella* and *Cyprinus carpio*. *Journal of Fisheries Biology*, **7**, 203–8.

Duvigneaud, P. & Denaeyer-de Smet, S. (1962). Distribution de certain élements minéraux (K, Ca et N) dans les tapis végétaux naturels. *Bulletin de la Société Française de Physiologie Végétale*, **8**, 96–103.

Dvořák, J. (1970*a*). Horizontal zonation of macrovegetation, water properties and macrofauna in a littoral stand of *Glyceria aquatica* in a pond in South Bohemia. *Hydrobiologia*, **35**, 17–30.

Dvořák, J. (1970*b*). On some phytophilous chironomid larvae of the nature reserve 'Die Lindevallei' (Chiron., Diptera). *Mededelingen van de Hydrobiologische Verenigung*, **4**, 172–4.

Dvořák, J. (1971). The zonation of environmental factors and the macrofauna of littoral emergent vegetation in ponds in South Bohemia. *Hidrobiologia, Bucureşti*, **12**, 325–30.

Dvořák, J. (1996). An example of relationships between macrophytes, macroinvertebrates and their food relationships in a shallow eutrophic lake. *Hydrobiologia*, **339**, 27–36.

Dvořák, J. & Best, E.P.H. (1982). Macro-invertebrate communities associated with macrophytes of Lake Vechten: structural and functional relationships. *Hydrobiologia*, **95**, 115–26.

Dvořák, J. & Lišková, E. (1970). A quantitative study on the macrofauna of stands of emergent vegetation in a carp pond of Southwest Bohemia. *Rozpravy Československé Akademie Věd, Řada Matematických a Přírodních Věd*, **80**(6), 63–114.

Dykyjová, D. (1971*a*). Production, vertical structure and light profiles in littoral stands of reed-bed species. *Hidrobiologia Bucureşti*, **12**, 361–76.

Dykyjová, D. (1971*b*). Ekomorfozy a ekotypy rákosu obecného. (Ecotypes and ecomorphoses of common reed.) *Preslia*, **43**, 120–38. (In Czech.)

Dykyjová, D. (1973*a*). Specific differences in vertical structure and radiation profiles in the helophyte stands. In *Ecosystem Study on Wetland Biome in Czechoslovakia*, ed. S. Hejný, Czechoslovak IBP-PT/PP Report No. 3, pp. 121–31. Třeboň: ČSAV.

Dykyjová, D. (1973*b*). Accumulation of mineral nutrients in the biomass of reedswamp species. A preliminary report. In *Ecosystem Study on Wetland Biome in Czechoslovakia*, ed. S. Hejný, Czechoslovak IBP-PT/PP Report No. 3, pp. 151–61. Třeboň: ČSAV.

Dykyjová, D. (1978*a*). Determination of energy content and net efficiency of solar energy conversion by fishpond helophytes. In *Pond Littoral Ecosystems: Structure and Functioning*, ed. D. Dykyjová & J. Květ, Ecological Studies 28, pp. 216–20. Berlin: Springer-Verlag.

Dykyjová, D. (1978*b*). Nutrient uptake by littoral communities of helophytes. In *Pond Littoral Ecosystems: Structure and Functioning*, ed. D. Dykyjová & J. Květ, Ecological Studies 28, pp. 257–77. Berlin: Springer-Verlag.

Dykyjová, D. (1979). Selective uptake of mineral ions and their concentration in aquatic higher plants. *Folia Geobotanica et Phytotaxonomica, Praha*, **14**, 267–325.

Dykyjová, D. (1980). The production ecology of *Acorus calamus*. *Folia Geobotanica et Phytotaxonomica, Praha*, **15**, 29–57.

Dykyjová, D. & Hradecká, D. (1973). Productivity of reed-bed stands in relation to the ecotype, microclimate and trophic conditions of the habitat. *Polskie Archiwum Hydrobiologii*, **20**, 111–20.

Dykyjová, D. & Hradecká, D. (1976). Production ecology of *Phragmites communis* L. Relations of two ecotypes to the microclimate and nutrient conditions of habitat. *Folia Geobotanica et Phytotaxonomica, Praha*, **11**, 23–61.

Dykyjová, D. & Husák, Š. (1973). The influence of summer cutting on the regeneration of reed. In *Ecosystem Study on Wetland Biome in Czechoslovakia*, ed. S. Hejný; Czechoslovak IBP-PT/PP Report No. 3, pp. 87–92. Třeboň: ČSAV.

Dykyjová, D. & Květ, J. (1970). Comparison of biomass production in reedswamp communities growing in South Bohemia and South Moravia. In *Productivity of Terrestrial Ecosystems and Production Processes*, ed. D. Dykyjová; Czechoslovak IBP-PT/PP Report No. 1, pp. 71–9. Praha: ČSAV.

Dykyjová, D. & Květ, J. (eds.) (1978). *Pond Littoral Ecosystems: Structure and Functioning*; Ecological Studies 28. Berlin: Springer-Verlag. 464 pp.

Dykyjová, D. & Květ, J. (1982). Mineral nutrient economy in wetlands of the Třeboň Basin Biosphere Reserve. In *Wetlands: Ecology and Management*, ed. B. Gopal, R.E. Turner, R.G. Wetzel & D.F. Whigham; Proceedings of the 1st International Wetlands Conference; New Delhi, 1980, pp. 325–55. Jaipur: National Institute of Ecology and Institute of Science Publication.

Dykyjová, D. and Ondok, J.P. (1973). Biometry and the productive stand structure of coenoses of *Sparganium erectum* L. *Preslia*, **45**, 19–30.

Dykyjová, D., Ondok, J.P. & Přibáň, K. (1970). Seasonal changes in productivity and vertical structure of reed-stands (*Phragmites communis* Trin). *Phytosynthetica*, **4**, 280–7.

Dykyjová, D. & Přibil, S. (1975). Energy content in the biomass of emergent macrophytes and their ecological efficiency. *Archiv. für Hydrobiologie*, **75**, 90–108.

Dykyjová, D. & Véber, K. (1978). Experimental hydroponic cultivation of helophytes. In *Pond Littoral Ecosystems: Structure and Functioning*, ed. D. Dykyjová & J. Květ, Ecological Studies 28, pp. 181–92. Berlin: Springer-Verlag.

Eaton, J.W., Best, M.A., Staples, I.O. & O'Hara, K. (1992). *Grass Carp for Aquatic Weed Control, a User's Manual*; National Rivers Authority, Research & Development Note No. 53. Bristol: National Rivers Authority. 91 pp.

Edmondson, W.T. (1970). Eutrophication – key elements. *Science*, **170**, 1153–4.

Edmondson, W.T. (1972). The present condition of Lake Washington. *Verhandlungen der Internationalen Vereinigung für Theoretische und Angewandte Limnologie*, **18**, 284–91.

Edwards, R.W., Egan, H., Learner, M.A. & Maris, P.J. (1964). The control of chironomid larvae in ponds using TDE (DDD). *Journal of Applied Ecology*, **1**, 97–117.

Ehranfeld, D.W. (1970). *Biological Conservation*; Modern Biology Series. New York: Holt, Rinehart & Winston. 226 pp.

Eigner, J. & Schmatzler, E. (1980). Bedeutung, Schatz und Regeneration von Hochmooren. *Naturschutz Aktuell*, **4**, 1–78.

Eisenlohr, W.S. Jr (1966). Water loss from a natural pond through transpiration by hydrophytes. *Water Resources Research*, **2**, 443–53.

Ekzertsev, V.A. (1966). Rastitel'nost' litorali Volgogradskogo vodokhranilishcha na tret'em godu sushchestvovaniya. *Trudȳ Instituta Biologiyí Vnutrennikh Vod*, **11**, 143–61.

Ekzertsev, V.A. & Ekzertseva, V.V. (1962). Produktsïya makrofitov v zalivakh Ivan'kovskogo vodokhranilishcha. *Buylleten Instituta Biologiyí Vodokhranilishch*, **12**, 11–14.

Ekzertseva, V.V. (1961). Produktsïya pribrezhno-vodnoĭ rastitel'nosti Uglichskogo vodokhranilishcha. *Byulleten Instituta Biologiyí Vodokhranilishch*, **11**, 7–9.

Elder, H.Y., Garrod, D.J. & Whitehead, P.J.P. (1971). Natural hybrids of the African cichlid fishes *Tilapia spilurus nigra* and *T. leucostictus*: a case of hybrid introgression. *Biological Journal of the Linnaean Society*, **3**, 103–46.

Ellenberg, H. & Klötzli, F. (1967). Vegetation und Bewirtschaftung des Vogelreservates Neeracher Ried. *Bericht, Geobotanisches Institut, ETH, Stiftung Rübel in Zürich*, **37**, 88–108.

Ellenbroek, G.A. (1987). *Ecology and Productivity of an African Wetland System: The Kafue Flats, Zambia*. Dordrecht: Kluwer Acad. Publ. 272 pp.

Elliott, H.F.I. (ed.) (1973). *Report on IUCN 12th Technical Meeting, Conservation and Development: Papers & Proceedings, Banff, 1972*; IUCN Publications N.S. 28. Morges: IUCN. 383 pp.

Ellis, E.A. (1965). *The Broads*. London: Collins. 401 pp.

Eloranta, P. (1970). Pollution and aquatic flora of waters by sulphite cellulose factories at Mänttä, Finnish Lake District. *Annales Botanici Fennica*, **7**, 63–141.

Engler, A. (1910). Die Pflanzenwelt Afrikas, ihres besonder tropischen Gebietes: Band I. Allgemeine Übersicht über die Pflanzenwelt Afrikas und ihre Existenzbedingungen. In *Die Vegetation der Erde*, ed. A. Engler & O. Drude; Sammlung pflanzengeographischen Mongraphien, **IX**, pp. 1–1029. Leipzig: Englemann.

Epstein, E. (1969). Mineral metabolism of halophytes. In *Ecological Aspects of the Mineral Nutrition of Plants*, ed. I.H. Rorison; Symposium of the British Ecological Society, No. 9, pp. 345–55. Oxford: BES.

Erdös, J. (1957). Beobachtungen über die Insektenzönose des Schilfs. *Bericht der Achten Wandersammlung der Deutschen Entomologie*, 1957, 171–7.

Errington, P.L. (1963). *Muskrat Populations*. Ames, Iowa: Iowa State University Press/American Ecological Society. 665 pp.

European Communities Commission (1991). CORINE Biotopes Manual; Rapports EUR 12587, **3**, Data Specification – Part 2; Habitats of the European Community. Luxembourg: European Commission. 300 pp.

Evans, G.C. (1972). *The Quantitative Analysis of Plant Growth*. Oxford: Blackwell Science Publishers. 734 pp.

Falconer, R.A. & Goodwin, P. (eds.) (1994). *Wetland Management*; Proceedings of a Conference of the Institute of Civil Engineers, London, June, 1994. London: Telford. 289 pp.

Fales, J.H., Spangler, P.J., Bodenstein, O.F., Mills, G.D. & Durbin, C.G. (1968). Laboratory and field evaluation of Abate against a backswimmer, *Notonecta undulata* Say (Hemiptera: Noctonectidae). *Mosquito News*, **28**, 77–81.

Feekes, W. (1936). De ontwickkeling van de natuurlijke vegetatie in den Wieringer-meerpolder, de eerste grote drooogmakerij in de Zuiderzee. Dr. Landbouwwetenschappen: Dissertatie, Landbouwhogeschool Wageningen. Amsterdam: Mulder. 295 pp. (In Dutch with English summary.)

Feekes, W. & Bakker, D. (1954). De ontwickkeling van de natuurlijke vegetatie in de Noordoostpolder. *Van Zee tot Land*, No. 6, 1–92. (In Dutch with English summary.)

Fenchel, T. (1969). The ecology of marine microbenthos. *Ophelia*, **6**, 1–182.

Fenchel, T. (1970). Studies on the decomposition of organic detritus derived from the turtle grass *Thalassia testudinum*. *Limnology and Oceanography*, **15**, 14–20.

Fernando, C.H. & Holčík, J. (1982). The nature of fish communities: a factor influencing the fishery potential and yields of tropical lakes and reservoirs. *Hydrobiologia*, **97**, 127–40.

Fernando, C.H. & Holčík, J. (1984). The nature of fish communities: an important factor influencing fishery potential and yields of lakes and reservoirs: a short summary of the concept and its application. *Verhandlungen der Internationalen Vereinigung für Theoretische und Angewandte Limnologie*, **22**, 2498–501.

Fernando, C.H. & Holčík, J. (1991). Fish in reservoirs. *Internationale Revue der Gesamten Hydrobiologie*, **76**, 149–67.

Festetics, A. & Leisler, B. (1968). Ecology of waterfowl in the region of lake Neusiedlersee, Austria, etc. *Wildfowl*, **19**, 83–95.

Fiala, K. (1973). Growth and production of underground organs of *Typha angustifolia* L., *Typha latifolia* L. and *Phragmites communis* Trin. *Polskie Archiwum Hydrobiologii*, **20**, 59–66.

Fiala, K. (1976). Underground organs of *Phragmites communis*, their growth, biomass and net production. *Folia Geobotanica Phytotaxonomica, Praha*, **11**, 225–59.

Fiala, K. (1978a). Underground organs of *Typha angustifolia* L. and *Typha latifolia* L., their growth, propagation and production. *Acta Scientiarum Naturalium, Academiae Scientarium Bohemoslovacea, Brno*, **12**, 1–43.

Fiala, K. (1978b). Seasonal development of helophyte polycormones and relationships between underground and aboveground organs. In *Pond Littoral Ecosystems: Structure and Functioning*, ed. D. Dykyjová & J. Květ; Ecological Studies 28, pp. 174–81.

Fiala, K. & Květ, J. (1971). Dynamic balance between plant species in South Moravian reedswamps. In *The Scientific Management of Animal and Plant Communities for Conservation*, ed. E. Duffey & A.S. Watt, pp. 241–69. Oxford: Blackwell Science Publishers.

Filben, G.H. & Hough, R.A. (1979). The effects of excess copper sulfate on the metabolism of the duckweed, *Lemna minor*. *Aquatic Botany*, **7**, 79–86.

Findenegg, I. (1967). Die Verschmutzung Österreichischer Alpenseen aus biologisch-chemischer Sicht. *Berichte Raumforschung und Raumplanung (Wien)*, **11**, 3–12.

Fischer, Z. (1968). Food selection in grass carp (*Ctenopharyngodon idella* Val.) under experimental conditions. *Polskie Archiwum Hydrobiologii*, **15**, 1–8.

Fischer, Z. (1973). Biology and bioenergetics of grass carp (*Ctenopharyngodon idella* Val.). *Polskie Archiwum Hydrobiologii*, **20**, 521–57.

Fisher, S.G. & Likens, G.E. (1973). Energy flow in Bear Brook, New Hampshire; an integrative approach to stream ecosystem metabolism. *Ecological Monogaphs*, **43**, 421–39.

Fittkau, E.J., Irmler, U., Junk, W., Reiss, F. & Schmidt, G.W. (1975). Productivity, biomass and population dynamics in Amazonian water bodies. In *Tropical Ecological Systems*, ed. F.B. Golley & E. Medina, pp. 281–311. Berlin: Springer-Verlag.

Fogg, G.E., Stewart, W.D.P., Fay, P. & Walsby, A.E. (1973). *The Blue-green Algae*. New York: Academic Press. 495 pp.

Forbes, J. (1940). Report of the Percy Sladen expedition to Lake Hulah. *Journal of Ecology*, **28**, 357–76.

Forsh, L.F. (1957). Isparenije i transpiratsija v delte Amu-Daryi. *Trudȳ Laboratorii Ozerovedeniya (M.T.)*, **4**, 35–170.

Forsh, L.F. & Drabkova, V.G. (eds.) (1985). *Bol'shie Ozera Kol'skogo Poluostrova.* (The Great Lakes of Kola Peninsula.) Leningrad: 'NAUKA'. 349 pp. (In Russian.)

Fowler, M.C. & Robson, T.O. (1978). The effects of the food preferences and stocking rates of grass carp (*Ctenopharyngodon idella* Val.) on mixed plant communities. *Aquatic Botany*, **5**, 261–76.

Frazer, J.C. (1972). *Water Levels, Fluctuations and Minimum Pools in Reservoirs for Fish and the Aquatic Resources – an Annotated Bibliography*; Food & Agriculture Organization of the United States, Fisheries Technical Paper No. 113. Rome: FAO. 42 pp.

Friday, L.C. (ed.) (1997). *Wicken Fen – The Making of a Wetland Nature Reserve.* Colchester: Healey Books. 306 pp.

Fries, R.E. (1914). Vegetationsbilder aus dem Bangweologebiet (Nordost Rhodesia). *Vegetationsbilder, Reihe XII*, **Heft 1**, Tafel 1–6.

Fritz, G. (1977). Zur Inanspruchnahme von Naturschutzgebieten durch Freizeit und Erholung. *Natur und Landschaft*, **52**, 192–4.

Frohne, W.C. (1938). Contribution to the knowledge of the limnological role of the higher aquatic plants. *Transactions of the American Microscopical Society*, **57**, 256–62.

Frohne, W.C. (1939*a*). Observation on the biology of three semiaquatic lacustrine moths. *Transactions of the American Microscopical Society*, **58**, 327–48.

Frohne, W.C. (1939*b*). Biology of *Chilo forbesellus* Ferland, a hydrophilous crambine moth. *Transactions of the American Microscopical Society*, **58**, 304–26.

Frömming, E. (1952). Über das Verhalten unserer Wasserschnecken gegenüber den Lemnaceae. *Archiv für Molluskenkunde*, **81**, 45–8.

Frömming, E. (1956). *Biologie der Mitteleuropäischen Süsswasserschnecken.* Berlin: Dunacker & Humbold. 313 pp.

Fuchs, C. (1993). The beetle *Donacia clavipes* as possible cause for the local reed decline at Lake Constance (Untersee). In *Seenufer-zerstörung und Seeufer-renaturierung in Mitteleuropa*, ed. W. Ostendorp & P. Krumscheid-Plankert; Limnologie Aktuell, **5**, 9–60.

Fukaya, M. (1948). (On the local races of the rice stem borer.) *Nogaku-Kenkyu*, **37**, 121–3. (In Japanese.)

Gaevskaya, N.S. (1966/1969). *Rol' Vysshikh Vodnykh Rastenii v Pitanii Zhivotnykh Presnykh Vodoemov.* Moskva: Nauka. 327 pp. Translation: *The Role of Higher Aquatic Plants in the Nutrition of the Animals of Freshwater Basins*, **1**, 1–231, **2**, 232–417, **3**, 418–629. Translated by D.G. Maitland Muller, ed. K.H. Mann, 1969. Boston Spa: National Lending Library for Science and Technology.

Gak, D.Z., Gurvich, V.V., Korelyakova, I.L., Kostikova, L.E., Konstantinova,

N.A., Olivari, G.A., Primachenko, A.D., Tseeb, Ya.Ya., Vladimirova, K.S. & Zimbalevskya, L.N. (1972). Productivity of aquatic organism communities of different trophic levels in Kiev Reservoir. In *Productivity Problems of Freshwaters*, ed. Z. Kajak & A. Hillbricht-Ilkowska; Proceedings of the IBP-UNESCO Symposium on Productivity Problems of Freshwaters, Kazimierz Dolny, May, 1970, pp. 447–56. Warszawa-Kraków: PWN.

Gallagher, J.L. & Pfeiffer, W.J. (1977). Aquatic metabolism of the standing dead plant communities in salt and brackish water marshes. *Limnology and Oceanography*, 22, 562–4.

Gallopin, G.C. (1972). Structural properties of food webs. In *Systems Analysis and Simulation in Ecology*, Vol. 2, ed. B.C. Patten, pp. 241–82. New York: Academic Press.

Ganetskaya, Z.G. (1971). Produktivnost trostnikovykh zaroslei vnutrennych vodoemov SSSR. In *Biologicheskaya produktivnost i krugovorot khimicheskikh elementov v rastitelnych soobshchestvakh*, ed. N.I. Brazilevich, T.R. Gordeeva, T.I. Evdokimova, E.P. Mateeva, L.K. Posdnyakov, N.I. Pyavtchenko, L.E. Rodin, V.M. Svveshnikova & I.S. Scalon, pp. 97–113. Leningrad: Nauka.

Gates, J.M. (1978). *Recommendations for a scattered wetlands programme of pheasants' habitat preservation in southeastern Wisconsin*; Wisconsin Department of Natural Resources, Research Report, 63, 24 pp.

Gaudet, J.J. (1973). Growth of a floating aquatic weed, *Salvinia*, under standard conditions. *Hydrobiologia*, 41, 77–106.

Gaudet, J.J. (1975). Mineral concentrations in papyrus in various African swamps. *Journal of Ecology*, 63, 483–91.

Gaudet, J.J. (1976). Nutrient relationships in the detritus of a tropical swamp. *Archiv für Hydrobiologie*, 78, 213–39.

Gaudet, J.J. (1977a). Natural drawdown on Lake Naivasha, Kenya, and the formation of papyrus swamps. *Aquatic Botany*, 3, 1–47.

Gaudet, J.J. (1977b). Uptake, accumulation and loss of nutrients by papyrus in tropical swamps. *Ecology*, 58, 415–22.

Gaudet, J.J. (1979). Seasonal changes in nutrients in a tropical swamp, North Swamp, Lake Naivasha, Kenya. *Journal of Ecology*, 67, 953–81.

Gaudet, J.J. (1982). Nutrient dynamics of papyrus swamps. In *Wetlands, Ecology and Management*, ed. B. Gopal, R.E. Turner, R.G. Wetzel & D.F. Whigham; Proceedings of 1st International Wetlands Conference, New Delhi, 1980, pp. 305–19. Jaipur: National Institute of Ecology and Institute of Science Publication.

Gavenčiak, Š. (1972). Výskum strát vody evapotranspirácionu z vodných rastlin. *Vodohospodársky Časopis*, 20, 16–32. (In Slovak, with German and Russian summaries.)

Geiger, R. (1961). *Das Klima der Bodennahen Luftschicht* (4th edn.). Braunschweig: Vieweg und Sohn. 646 pp.

George, C.J. (1972). The role of the Aswan high dam in changing the fisheries of the south-eastern Mediterranean. *The Careless Technology*, ed. M.T. Farver & J.P. Milton, pp. 236–44. New York: The Natural History Press.

George, M. (1992). *Broadlands*. Chichester: Packard. 558 pp.

Gerloff, G.C. & Fishbeck, K.A. (1973). Plant content of elements as a bioassay of nutrient availability in lakes and streams. In *Bioassay Techniques and Environmental Chemistry*, ed. G. Glass; pp. 159–76. Ann Arbor: Ann Arbor Scientific Publications.

Gerloff, G.C. & Skoog, F. (1954). Cell contents of nitrogen and phosphorus as a measure of their availability for growth of *Microcystis aeruginosa*. *Ecology*, **35**, 348–53.

Gerloff, G.C. & Skoog, F. (1957). Nitrogen as a limiting factor for the growth of *Microcystis aeruginosa* in Southern Wisconsin Lakes. *Ecology*, **38**, 556–61.

Germain, R. (1952). Les associations végétales de La Pflaine de La Ruzizi, Congo Bélge), en relation avec le milieu. *Publications de l'Institute Nationale pour l'Etude Agronomique du Congo Bélge*, **52**, 1–321.

Gessner, F. (1955). *Hydrobotanik: die Physiologischen Grundlagen der Pflanzenverbreitung im Wasser I. Energiehaushalt*. Berlin: VEB Deutscher Verlag der Wissenschaften. 517 pp.

Gessner, F. (1956). Der Wasserhaushalt der Hydrophyten und Helophyten. In *Handbuch der Pflanzenphysiologie*, III, ed. W. Ruhland, pp. 854–901. Berlin: Springer-Verlag.

Gessner, F. (1959). *Hydrobotanik: Die Physiologischen Grundlagen der Pflanzenverbreitung im Wasser, 2. Stoffhaushalt*. Berlin: VEB Deutscher Verlag d. Wissenschaften. 701 pp.

Gilli, A. (1971). Afganische Planzengesellschaften II. *Vegetatio*, **23**, 199–234.

Gilman, R. (1994). *Hydrology and Wetland Conservation*. London: Wiley. 114 pp.

Gladȳshev, A.I. (1975). Zakonomernosti raspredeleniya rastitel'nosti i ee produktivnosti v poïme srednego techeniya Amudar'i. In *Izuchenie rastitel'nosti Turkmenii*, pp. 17–21. Ashkhabad: Yl'm.

Gliwicz, Z.M. & Rybak, J.I. (1976). Zooplankton. In *Selected Problems of Lake Littoral Ecology*, ed. E. Pieczyńska, pp. 69–96. Warszawa: Wydawnictwa Uniwersytetu.

Gloser, J. (1976). Photosynthesis and respiration of some alluvial meadow grasses: responses to irradiance, temperature and CO_2 concentration. *Acta Scientarium Naturalium Academiae Scientarium Bohemoslovaea, Brno*, **10**, 1–39.

Gloser, J. (1977a). Photosynthesis and respiration of some alluvial meadow grasses: responses to soil water stress, diurnal and seasonal courses. *Acta Scientiarum Naturalium, Academiae Scientarium Bohemoslovacea, Brno*, **11**, 1–34.

Gloser, J. (1977b). Characteristics of CO_2 exchange in *Phragmites communis* Trin. derived from measurements *in situ*. *Photosynthetica*, **11**, 139–47.

Gloser, J. (1978). Net photosynthesis and dark respiration of reed estimated by gas-exchange measurements. In *Pond Littoral Ecosystems: Structure and Functioning*, ed. D. Dykyjová & J. Květ; Ecological Studies 28, pp. 227–33.

Glowacka, I., Soszka, G.J. & Soszka, H. (1976). Invertebrates associated with macrophytes. In *Selected Problems of Lake Littoral Ecology*, ed. E. Pieczyńska, pp. 97–122. Warszawa: Wydawnictwa Uniwersytetu Warszawskiego.

Glutz, U. von Blotzheim, Bauer, K. & Bezzel, E. (1973). *Handbuch der Vögel Mitteleuropas*, **Bd 5**. Frankfurt-am-Main: Akademie-Verlagsgesellschaft. 699 pp.

Godshalk, G.L. & Wetzel, R.G. (1977). Decomposition of macrophytes and the metabolism of organic matter in sediments. In *Interactions between Sediments and Freshwater*, ed. H. Golterman, pp. 258–64. The Hague: Junk.

Godwin, H. (1978). *Fenland: Its Ancient Past and Uncertain Future*. Cambridge: Cambridge University Press. 196 pp.

Goetghebuer, M. (1928). *Diptères (Nematocères) Chironomida III. Chironomariae*; Fauna de France, **18**. Paris: LeChevalier. 174 pp.

Goldman, C.R. (1961). The contribution of alder trees (*Alnus tenuifolia*) to the primary productivity of Castle Lake, California. *Ecology*, **42**, 282–8.

Golley, F., Odum, H.T. & Wilson, R.F. (1962). The structure and metabolism of a Puerto Rico red mangrove forest in May. *Ecology*, **43**, 9–19.

Golovanov, N.C. (1955). Novyĭ vid syr'ya dlya proizvodstva kartona: Trostnik, rogoz i kamysh. (New ways to manufacture cartons: Reeds, cat-tails and rushes.) *Bumazhnaya Promyshlennost'*, **30**, 22–3. (In Russian.)

Golterman, H.L. & Kouwe, F.A. (1980). Chemical budgets and nutrient pathways. In *The Functioning of Freshwater Ecosystems*, ed. E.D. LeCren & R.H. Lowe-McConnell; International Biological Programme 22, pp. 85–140. Cambridge: Cambridge University Press.

Good, R. (1953). *The Geography of the Flowering Plants* (3rd edn.). London: Longmans. 518 pp.

Good, R.E., Whigham, D.F. & Simpson, R.L. (eds.) (1978). *Freshwater Wetlands. Ecological Processes and Management Potential*; Proceedings of the Symposium on Freshwater Marshes: Present Status, Future Needs, New Brunswick, July 1977. New York: Academic Press. 378 pp.

Goodman, A.J., Surrendi, C., Hatfield, J.P. & Harris, R.D. (1978). *Waterfowl Habitat in Western Canada*; Canadian Wildlife Service No. 71. Ottawa: Department of Indian Affairs and Northern Development. 40 pp.

Goodman, G.T. (1962). Some mineral nutrient characteristics of acid peat. In *Soil Organic Matter*; Report No. 3, Welsh Soils Discussion Group, pp. 73–86. Aberystwyth: Welsh Soils Discussion Group.

Goodman, G.T. & Perkins, D.F. (1959). Mineral uptake and retention in Cotton-grass (*Eriophorum vaginatum* L.). *Nature*, **184**, 467–8.

Goodman, G.T. & Perkins, D.F. (1968). The role of mineral nutrients in *Eriophorum* communities IV. Potassium supply as a limiting factor in an *E. vaginatum* community. *Journal of Ecology*, **56**, 685–96.

Gopal, B. (ed.) (1992). *Ecology and Management of Aquatic Vegetation in the Indian Subcontinent*. Dordrecht: Kluwer. 287 pp.

Gopal, B., Hillbricht-Ilkowska, A. & Wetzel, R.G. (1993). *Wetlands and Ecotones: Studies on Land–Water Interactions*. New Delhi: NIE and Int. Scientific Publ. 301 pp.

Gopal, B. & Sharma, K.P. (1981). *Water-hyacinth* (Eichhornia crassipes): *the Most Troublesome Weed of the World*. Delhi: Hindasia Publ. 128 pp.

Gordon, J.C., Wheeler, C.T. & Perry, D.A. (eds.) (1979). *Symbiotic Nitrogen Fixation in the Management of Temperate Forests*; Proceedings of a Workshop, April, 1979. Corvallis: Forest Reseach Laboratory, Oregon State University. 501 pp.

Gore, A.J.P. (ed.) (1983a). *Mires: Swamp, Bog, Fen and Moors, General Studies*; Ecosystems of the World **4A**. Amsterdam: Elsevier. 440 pp.

Gore, A.J.P. (ed.) (1983b). *Mires: Swamp, Bog, Fen and Moors, Regional Studies*; Ecosystems of the World **4B**. Amsterdam: Elsevier. 479 pp.

Gorham, E. (1953a). Some early ideas concerning the nature, origin and development of peat lands. *Journal of Ecology*, **41**, 257–74.

Gorham, E. (1953b). Chemical studies on the soils and vegetation of waterlogged habitats in the English Lake District. *Journal of Ecology*, **41**, 345–60.

Gorham, E. (1955). On the acidity and salinity of rain. *Geochimica et Cosmochimica Acta*, **7**, 231–9.

Gorham, E. (1957). The development of peat lands. *Quarterly Review of Biology*, **32**, 145–66.

Gorham, E. (1974). The relationship between standing crop in sedge meadows and summer temperature. *Journal of Ecology*, **62**, 487–91.

Gorham, E. & Gordon, A.G. (1963). Some effects of smelter pollution upon aquatic vegetation near Sudbury, Ontario. *Canadian Journal of Botany*, **41**, 371–8.

Gorham, E. & Pearsall, W.H. (1956). Production ecology. III. Shoot production in *Phragmites* in relation to habitat. *Oikos*, **7**, 206–14.

Gosselink, J.G. & Kirby, C.J. (1974). Decomposition of Salt Marsh Grass, *Spartina alterniflora* Loisel. *Limnology and Oceanography*, **19**, 825–32.

Gosselink, J.G. & Turner, R.E. (1978). The role of hydrology in freshwater wetland ecosystems. In *Freshwater Wetlands. Ecological Processes and Management Potential*, ed. R.E. Good, D.F. Whigham, R.L. Simpson & C.G. Jackson Jr; Proceedings of Symposium on Freshwater Marshes: Present Status, Future Needs; New Brunswick, 1977, pp. 63–78. New York: Academic Press.

Gossett, D.R. & Norris, W.E. (1971). Relationship between nutrient availability and content of nitrogen and phosphorus in tissues of the aquatic macrophyte *Eichhornia crassipes* (Mart.) Solms. *Hydrobiologia*, **38**, 15–28.

Göttlich, Kh. (1965). Ergebnisse und Ziele bodenkundlicher Studien in Moor und Anmoor. *Arbeiten – Landwirtschaftliche Hochschule, Hohenheim*, **33**, 1–122. Stuttgart: Ulmer.

Goulder, R. & Boatman, D.J. (1971). Evidence that nitrogen supply influences the distribution of freshwater macrophyte *Ceratophyllum demersum*. *Journal of Ecology*, **59**, 783–91.

Granhall, U. & Solander, H. (1973). Nitrogen fixation in a subarctic mire. *Oikos*, **24**, 8–15.

Greenway, P.J. & Vesey-Fitzgerald, D.F. (1969). The vegetation of Lake Manyara National Park. *Journal of Ecology*, **57**, 127–49.

Greenwood, P.H. (1966). *The Fishes of Uganda* (2nd edn.). Kampala: The Uganda Society. 131 pp.

Grenfeeld, D.W. (1973). An evaluation of the advisability of the release of the grass carp, *Ctenopharyngodon idella*, into natural waters of the USA. *Transactions of the Illinois State Academy of Sciences*, **66**, 49–53.

Grimm, M.P. (1989). Northern pike (*Esox lucius* L.), and aquatic vegetation; tools in the management of fisheries and water quality in shallow waters. *Hydrobiological Bulletin*, **23**, 59–65.

Gripekoven, H. (1921). Minierende Tendipediden. *Archiv für Hydrobiologie, Suppl.*, **2**, 129–230.

Grünberg, K. (1909). Lepidoptera, Schmetterlinge. In *Süsswasserfauna Deutschlands*, **8**, ed. A. Brauer, pp. 96–159. Jena: Fischer Verlag.

Gwahaba, J.J. (1975). The distribution, population density and biomass of fish in an equatorial lake, Lake George, Uganda. *Proceedings of the Royal Society, London*, **B190**, 393–414.

Haber, W. (1971). Zur ökologischen Bedeutung der Vegetation für den Menschen. In *Vegetation als Anthropo-ökologischer Gegenstand*, ed. A. Schwabe-Braun; Bericht zum Internationalen Symposium Nr 15, der Internationalen Vereinigung für Vegetationskunde, Rinteln, 1971, pp. 49–64.

Hacker, R. (1974). Produktionsbiologische und nahrungsökologische Untersuchungen an der Güster (*Blicca bjoerkna* L.) des Neusiedlersees. Dissertation, Universität Wien. 93 pp.

Hackney, C.T. & Cruz, A.A. de la (1980). *In situ* decomposition of roots and rhizomes of two tidal marsh plants. *Ecology*, **61**, 226–31.

Haller, W.T. & Sutton, D.L. (1973). Effect of pH and high phosphorus concentrations on growth of Waterhyacinth. *Hyacinth Control Journal*, **11**, 59–61.

Hammack, J. & Brown, G.M. Jr (1974). *Waterfowl and Wetlands: Toward Bioeconomic Analysis*. Washington DC: Resources for the Future. 95 pp.

Hammer, D.A. (ed.) (1990). *Constructed Wetlands for Wastewater Treatment*. Boca Raton, Florida: CRC Press/Lewis Publishers. 856 pp.

Hammer, D.A. (1992). *Creating Wetlands*. Boca Raton, Florida: CRC Press. 312 pp.

Hammer, U.T. (1980). Primary production – Geographical variations. In *The Functioning of Freshwater Ecosystems*, ed. E.D. LeCren & R.H. Lowe-McConnell; International Biological Programme No. 22, pp. 235–46. Cambridge: Cambridge University Press.

Hansen, K.L., Ruby, E.G. & Thompson, R.L. (1971). Trophic relationships in the Water Hyacinth community. *Quarterly Journal of the Florida Academic Society*, **35**, 107–13.

Hanson, R.B. & Snyder, J. (1979). Microheterotrophic activity in a salt-marsh estuary, Sapelo Island, Georgia. *Ecology*, **60**, 99–107.

Hanson, R.B. & Snyder, J. (1980). Glucose exchanges in a salt-marsh estuary: biological activity and chemical measurement. *Limnology and Oceanography*, **25**, 633–42.

Happ, C., Gosselink, J. & Day, J. (1977). The seasonal distribution of organic carbon in a Louisiana estuary. *Estuarine and Coastal Marine Science*, **5**, 695–705.

Hargrave, B.T. (1970). The effect of a deposit-feeding amphipod on the metabolism of benthic microflora. *Limnology and Oceanography*, **15**, 21–30.

Hargrave, B.T. (1976). The central role of invertebrate faeces in sediment decomposition. In *The Role of Terrestrial and Aquatic Organisms in Decomposition Processes*, ed. J.M. Anderson & A. MacFadyen; British Ecological Society Symposium No. 17, pp. 301–21. Oxford: Blackwell Science Publishers.

Hartog, C. den (ed.) (1977). *Biological Control of Aquatic Weeds, Aquatic Botany (Special Issue)*, **3**(2), 103–202. Amsterdam: Elsevier Publishing Co.

Hartog, C. den (ed.) (1989). *Reed and Reed Decline in Europe, Aquatic Botany (Special Issue)*, **35**(1), 1–132. Amsterdam: Elsevier Publishing Co.

Hartog, C. den & Segal, S. (1964). A new classification of the water-plant communities. *Acta Botanica Neerlandica*, **13**, 367–93.

Hashimoto, T. (1958). Effects of K and Ca fertilizer on yield and quality of mat rushes. *Bulletin of the Hiroshima Agricultural College*, **1**, 27–32.

Haslam, S.M. (1965). Ecological studies in the Breck fens I. Vegetation in relation to habitat. *Journal of Ecology*, **53**, 599–619.

Haslam, S.M. (1969a). Stem types of *Phragmites communis* Trin. *Annals of Botany*, **33**, 127–31.

Haslam, S.M. (1969b). The development and emergence of buds in *Phragmites communis* Trin. *Annals of Botany*, **33**, 289–301.

Haslam, S.M. (1969c). Shoot height and density in *Phragmites* stands. *Hidrobiologia, Bucureşti*, **12**, 113–19.

Haslam, S.M. (1970a). Variation of population type in *Phragmites communis* Trin. *Annals of Botany*, **34**, 147–58.

Haslam, S.M. (1970*b*). The development of the annual population in *Phragmites communis* Trin. *Annals of Botany*, **34**, 571–91.

Haslam, S.M. (1971*a*). Community regulation in *Phragmites communis* Trin. I. Monodominant stands. *Journal of Ecology*, **59**, 65–73.

Haslam, S.M. (1971*b*). Community regulation in *Phragmites communis* Trin. II. Mixed stands. *Journal of Ecology*, **59**, 75–88.

Haslam, S.M. (1972*a*). The Reed (*Phragmites communis* Trin.). In *The Reed ('Norfolk Reed')* (2nd edn.), pp. 1–49. Norwich: Norfolk Reed Growers Association.

Haslam, S.M. (1972*b*). *Phragmites communis* Trin.: Biological Flora of the British Isles No. 128. *Journal of Ecology*, **60**, 585–610.

Haslam, S.M. (1973*a*). The management of British wetlands I. Economic and amenity use. *Journal of Environmental Management*, **1**, 303–20.

Haslam, S.M. (1973*b*). The management of British wetlands II. Conservation. *Journal of Environmental Management*, **1**, 345–61.

Haslam, S.M. (1973*c*). Some aspects of the life history and autecology of *Phragmites communis* Trin. A review. *Polskie Archiwum Hydrobiologii*, **20**, 79–100.

Haslam, S.M. (1975). The performance of *Phragmites communis* Trin. in relation to temperature. *Annals of Botany*, **39**, 881–8.

Haslam, S.M. (1978). *River Plants*. Cambridge: Cambridge University Press. 396 pp.

Haslam, S.M. (1994). *Wetland Habitat Differentiation and Sensitivity to Chemical Pollutants (Non-open-water Wetlands)*; Department of the Environment Report DoE/HMIP/RR/040, 1 and 2. London: Her Majesty's Inspectorate of Pollution, pp. 175 and 110.

Haslam, S.M. (In press). *Bog, Fen and Marsh: Understanding Wetlands*. London: Academic Press.

Hawke, C.J. & José, P.V. (1995). *Reed Bed Management for Commercial and Wildlife Interests*. Sandy, UK: Royal Society for the Protection of Birds. 212 pp.

Hayashi, K. (1972). Efficiencies of solar energy conversion in rice varieties. *Bulletin of the National Institute of Agricultural Sciences, Tokyo*, **D23**, 1–67.

Heal, O.W. & French, D.D. (1974). Decomposition of organic matter in tundra. In *Soil Organisms and Decomposition in Tundra*, ed. A.J. Holding, O.W. Heal, S.F. MacLean Jr & P.W. Flanagan, pp. 279–309. Stockholm: Tundra Biome Steering Committee.

Heald, E.J. (1971). *The production of organic detritus in a south Florida estuary*; Sea Grant Program Technical Bulletin No. 6; PhD thesis. Miami: University of Miami. 110 pp.

Hedberg, O.I. (ed.) (1968). *Conservation of Vegetation South of the Sahara*; Acta Phytogeographica Suecica, **54**. 320 pp.

Hejný, S. (1957). Ein Beitrag zur Ökologischen Gliederung der Makrophyten der tschechoslowakischen Niederungsgewässer. *Preslia, Praha*, **29**, 349–68.

Hejný, S. (1959). Příspěvek k zarůstání rybničního pobřeží vypáleného ohněm. (Beitrag zur Erneuerung der Pflanzenbestande auf den ausgebrannten Teichufern.) *Sborník Krajského vlastivědného musea v Českých Budějovicích, Sci. Natur*, **2**, 85–101. (In Czech with German summary.)

Hejný, S. (1960). *Ökologische Charakteristik der Wasser- und Sumpfpflanzen in den Slovakischen Tiefeben (Donau- und Theiss-gebiet)*. Bratislava: Vydavaterstvo SAV. 492 pp.

Hejný, S. (1971). The dynamic characteristics of littoral vegetation with respect to changes of water level. *Hidrobiologia, Bucureşti*, **12**, 71–85.

Hejný, S. (1978). Management aspects of fishpond drainage. In *Pond Littoral Ecosystems: Structure and Functioning*, ed. D. Dykyjová & J. Květ, Ecological Studies 28, 399–403. Berlin: Springer-Verlag.

Hejný, S. (1990). Dynamic changes in the macrophyte vegetation of South Bohemian fishponds after thirty-five years. *Folia Geobotanica et Phytotaxonomica, Praha*, **25**, 245–55.

Hejný, S. & Husák, Š. (1978). Higher plant communities. In *Pond Littoral Ecosystems: Structure and Functioning*, ed. D. Dykyjová & J. Květ: Ecological Studies 28, 23–64. Berlin: Springer-Verlag.

Hejný, S. & Květ, J. (1978). Introduction to the ecology of fishpond littorals. In *Pond Littoral Ecosystems: Structure and Functioning*, ed. D. Dykyjová & J. Květ; Ecological Studies 28, 1–10. Berlin: Springer-Verlag.

Hejný, S., Květ, J. & Dykyjová, D. (1981). Survey of biomass and net production of higher plant communities in fishponds. *Folia Geobotanica Phytotaxonomica, Praha*, **16**, 73–94.

Henderson, H.F., Ryder, R.. & Kudhonganta, A.W. (1973). Assessing fishery potential of lakes and reservoirs. *Journal of the Fisheries Research Board of Canada*, **30**, 2000–9.

Herzog, T. (1923). Die Pflanzenwelt der botanischen Anden und ihren östlichen Verlandes. In *Die Vegetation der Erde*, ed. A. Engler & O. Drude; Sammlung pflanzengeographischer Monographien, **XV**, pp. 1–289. Leipzig: Englemann.

Hickling, C.F. (1961). *Tropical Inland Fisheries*. London: Longmans. 287 pp.

Hickman, M. (1971). The standing crop and productivity of the epiphyton attached to *Equisetum fluviatile* L. in Priddy Pool, North Somerset. *British Journal of Phycology*, **6**, 51–9.

Higler, L.W.G. (1975). Analysis of the macrofauna-community on *Stratiotes*-vegetations. *Verhandlungen der Internationalen Vereinigung für Theoretische und Angewandte Limnologie*, **19**, 2773–7.

Higler, L.W.G. (1977). Macrofauna-cenoses on *Stratiotes* plants in Dutch broads. *Transactions of the Research Institute for Nature Management (Netherlands)*, **11**, 1–86.

Hillbricht-Ilkowska, A. & Pieczyńska, E. (eds.) (1993). *Nutrient Dynamics and Retention in Land-water Ecotones of Lowland, Temperate Lakes and Rivers*; Developments in Hydrobiology 82. Dordrecht: Kluwer Acad. Publ. 361 pp.

Ho, C. & Barrett, B. (1975). *Distribution of nutrients in Louisiana's coastal waters influenced by the Mississippi river*; Louisiana Wildlife & Fisheries Commission, Technical Bulletin No. 17. New Orleans: LWLFC.

Hoagland, D.H. (1948). *Lectures on the Inorganic Nutrition of Plants*, 2nd edn. Waltham, Massachusetts: Chronica Botanica. 226 pp.

Hobbie, J.E., Traaen, T., Rublee, P., Reed, J.P., McMillar, M.C. & Fenchel, T. (1980). Decomposers, bacteria and microbenthos. In *Limnology of Tundra Ponds*, ed. J. Hobbie; US-IBP Synthesis Series 13, pp. 340–87. Stroudsburg, Pennsylvania: Dowden, Hutchinson & Ross Inc.

Hobbie, J.E. & Wright, R.T. (1965). Bioassay with bacterial uptake kinetics: glucose in freshwater. *Limnology and Oceanography*, **10**, 471–4.

Hoffman, L. (ed.) (1964). *Project MAR: the Conservation and Management of Temperate Marshes, Bogs and Other Wetlands*, **Vol. 1**; Proceedings of Conference Organized by ICUN, ICBP and International Biological

Programme, Le Saintes-Maries-de-la-Mer, November 1962; IUCN
Publications (NS) No. 3, 475 pp. Gland: IUCN.

Hoffmann, M. (1958). *Die Bisamratte.* Leipzig: Akad. Verlag Geest & Portig.
260 pp.

Hoffmann, M. (1964). Über die Besiedlung der brandenburgischen Gewässer
durch die Bisamratte (*Ondatra zibethica* L.) und die Massnahmen zu ihrer
Bekämpfung. In *Beitrage zur Tierwelt d. Mark I*, **4**, pp. 97–110. Potsdam:
Veröff. Bezirksheimatmuseum.

Hoffstetter, R.H. (1983). Wetlands in the United States. In *Mires: Swamp, Bog,
Fen and Moor, Regional Studies*, ed. A.J.P. Gore; Ecosystems of the World
4B, pp. 201–44. Amsterdam: Elsevier.

Hogeweg, P. & Brenkert-van Riet, A.L. (1969). Structure of aquatic vegetation: a
comparison of aquatic vegetation in India, the Netherlands and
Czechoslovakia. *Tropical Ecology*, **10**, 139–62.

Hokyo, N. (1972). Studies on the life history and the population dynamics of the
green rice leafhopper, *Nephotettix cincticeps* Uhler. *Bulletin of the Kyushu
Agricultural Experimental Station*, **16**, 283–382. (In Japanese with English
summary.)

Holčík, J. (1970). Standing crop, abundance, production and some ecological
aspects of fish populations in some inland waters of Cuba. *Věstník
Československé Společnosti Zoologické*, **34**, 184–201.

Holčík, J. (1977). Changes to fish community of Klíčava reservoir with particular
reference to Eurasian perch (*Perca fluviatilis*), 1957–72. *Journal of the
Fisheries Research Board of Canada*, **34**, 1734–47.

Holčík, J. (1996). Ecological fish production in the inland delta of the Middle
Danube, a floodplain river. *Environmental Biology of Fish*, **46**, 151–65.

Holčík, J. & Bastl, I. (1976). Ecological effects of water level fluctuation upon the
fish populations in the Danube River floodplain in Czechoslovakia. *Acta
Scientiarum Naturalium, Academiae Scientarium Bohemoslovacea, Brno* (NS),
10(9), 3–46.

Holčík, J. & Bastl, I. (1977). Predicting fish yield in the Czechoslovakian section
of the Danube river based on the hydrological regime. *Internationale Revue
der Gesamten Hydrobiologie und Hydrographie*, **62**, 523–32.

Holčík, J., Bastl, I., Ertl, M. & Vranovský, M. (1981). Hydrobiology and
ichthyology of the Czechoslovak Danube in relation to predicted changes
after the construction of the Gabčikovo-Nagymaros river barrage system.
Práce Labôratória Rybárstva a Hydrobiolôgie, **3**, 19–158.

Holčík, J. & Hruška, V. (1966). On the spawning substrate of the roach – *Rutilus
rutilus* (Linnaeus, 1758) and bream – *Abramis brama* (Linnaeus, 1758) and
notes on the ecological characteristics of some European fishes. *Věstník
Československé Společnosti Zoologické*, **30**, 22–9.

Holder, T. (1969). *Disappearing Wetlands in Eastern Arkansas.* Little Rock:
Arkansas Planning Committee. 72 pp.

Holdgate, M.W. (ed.) (1977). *Environmental Issues*; SCOPE Report 10.
Chichester: John Wiley. 242 pp.

Holišová, V. (1967). The food of *Apodemus agrarius* (Pall.). *Zoologické Listy*, **16**,
1–14.

Holišová, V. (1970). Trophic requirements of the water vole (*Arvicola terrestris*
L.) on the edge of stagnant waters. *Zoologické Listy*, **19**, 221–33.

Holišová, V. (1972). The food of *Clethrionomys glareolus* in a reed swamp.
Zoologické Listy, **21**, 293–307.

References 493

Holišová, V. (1975). Food of rodents in the reedbelt of Nesyt fishpond. *Zoologické Listy*, **24**, 223–37.

Holmes, N.T.H. (1983). *Typing British Rivers According to their Flora*; Focus on Nature Conservation No. 4. London: Nature Conservancy Council. 179 pp. (Mostly reprinted by Department of the Environment, 1987; In *Methods for the Use of Aquatic Macrophytes for Assessing Water Quality, 1985–87*; Methods for the Examination of Waters and Associated Materials, pp. 75–174. London: HMSO.)

Hood, M.A. (1970). A Bacterial Study of an Estuarine Environment: Barataria Bay, MS Thesis. Baton Rouge: Louisiana State University. 85 pp.

Hopkins, B. (1962). Vegetation of the Olokemeiji forest reserve, Nigeria I. General features of the reserve and the research sites. *Journal of Ecology*, **50**, 559–98.

Hosner, E., Janauer, G.A. & Haberl, R. (1990). Biometrie und mechanische Eigenschaften von Schilf an künstlich geschaffenen und natürlichen Standorten. In *Ökologie, Gefährdung, und Schutz von Röhrichtpflanzen*, ed. H. Sukopp & M. Krauss; Landschaftentwicklung u. Umweltforschung, **71**, pp. 198–211. Berlin: Technische Universität.

Hossel, J.C. & Baker, J.H. (1979). Estimation of the growth rates of epiphytic bacteria and *Lemma minor* in a river. *Freshwater Biology*, **9**, 319–22.

Houghton, R.A. & Woodwell, G.M. (1980). The Flax Pond ecosystem study: exchanges of CO_2 between a salt marsh and the atmosphere. *Ecology*, **61**, 1434–45.

Howard-Williams, C. (1973). Vegetation and Environment in the Marginal Areas of a Tropical African Lake (L. Chilwa, Malawi). PhD thesis, University of London.

Howard-Williams, C. & Gaudet, J.J. (1985). The structure and functioning of African swamps. In *The Ecology and Management of African Wetland Vegetation*, ed. P. Denny, pp. 153–76. Dordrecht: Junk.

Howard-Williams, C., Davies, J. & Pickmere, S. (1982). The dynamics of growth, the effects of changing area and nitrate uptake by watercress *Nasturtium officinale* R.Br. in a New Zealand stream. *Journal of Applied Ecology*, **19**, 589–601.

Howell, P.P., Lock, M. & Cobb, L. (1988). *The Jonglei Canal: Impact and Opportunity*. Cambridge: Cambridge University Press. 576 pp.

Hradecká, D. (1973). Ecotypes and Ecophases of Common Reed (*Phragmites communis* Trin.), PhD thesis, Charles University, Prague. 64 pp.

Hubbard, J.C.E. & Ranwell, D.S. (1966). Cropping *Spartina* saltmarsh for silage. *Journal of the British Grassland Society*, **21**, 214–17.

Huber, A. (1993). Ufer Erosion am Neusenburgersee. In *Seenufer-zerstörung und Seeufer-renaturierung in Mitteleuropa*, ed. W. Ostendorp & P. Krumscheid-Plankert; Limnologie Aktuell, **5**, 93–102.

Hübl, E. (1967). Stoffproduction von *Phragmites communis* Trin. im Schilfgurtel des Neusiedler Sees im Jahre 1966. (Ergebnisse nach der Erntemethode). *Sitzungsberichte der Österreichischen Akademie der Wissenschaften, Mathematischnaturwissenschaftliche Klasse*, **14**, 271–8.

Hudec, K. (1973a). Die Nahrung der Graugans, *Anser anser*, in Südmähren. *Zoologické Listy*, **22**, 41–58.

Hudec, K. (1973b). Occurrence and food of the Greylag Goose (*Anser anser*) at the Nesyt fishpond. In *Littoral of the Nesyt Fishpond*, ed. J. Květ; Studie Československé Akademie Věd, 1973, No. 15, pp. 121–4. Praha: Academia.

Hudec, K. (1975). Density and breeding of birds in the reed-swamps of Southern

Moravian ponds. *Acta Scientiarum Naturalium, Academiae Scientiarum Bohemoslovacae, Brno* (NS), **9**(6), 1–40.

Hudec, K. & Rooth, J. (1970). *Die Grauganz*; Die neue Brehm-Bücherei, Heft 429. Wittenburg-Lutherstadt: Ziemsen Verlag. 148 pp.

Hudec, K. & Šťastný, K. (1978). Birds in the reedswamp ecosystem. In *Pond Littoral Ecosystem: Structure and Functioning*, ed. D. Dykyjová & J. Květ; Ecological Studies 28, pp. 366–75. Berlin: Springer-Verlag.

Hueck, K. (1966). *Die Wälder Südamerikas. Ökologie, Zusammensetzung und Wirtschaftliche Bedeutung.* Jena: VEB G. Fischer Verlag. 127 pp.

Hughes, J.M.R. & Heathwaite, A.L. (eds.) (1995). *Hydrology and Hydrochemistry of British Wetlands.* London: Wiley. 486 pp.

Hughes, R.H., Hughes, J.S. & Bernacsek, G. (1992). *A Directory of African Wetlands.* Gland: IUCN. 820 pp.

Hundt, R. & Unger, H. (1968). Untersuchungen über die zellulolytische Aktivität unter Grünlandgesellschaften in *Mineralisation der Zellulose*; Tagungsberichte der Deutschen Akademie der Landwirtschaftswissenschaften zu Berlin, Nr 98, pp. 263–75.

Hürlimann, H. (1951). Zur Lebensgeschichte des Schilfes an den Ufern der Schweizer Seen. *Beiträge geobotanischen Landesaufnahme der Schweiz*, **30**, 1–232. Bern: Hans Huber Verlag.

Husák, Š. (1973). Destructive control of stands of *Phragmites communis* and *Typha angustifolia* and its effects on shoot production followed for three seasons. In *Littoral of the Nesyt Fishpond*, ed. J. Květ; Studie Československé Akademie Věd, 1973, No. 15, pp. 89–91. Praha: Academia.

Husák, Š. (1978). Control of reed and reed mace stands by cutting. In *Pond Littoral Ecosystems: Structure and Functioning*, ed. D. Dykyjová & J. Květ; Ecological Studies 28, pp. 404–8. Berlin: Springer-Verlag.

Husák, Š. & Květ, J. (1970). Productive structure of *Phragmites communis* and *Typha angustifolia* stands after cutting at two different levels. In *Productivity of Terrestrial Ecosystems. Production Processes*, ed. D. Dykyjová; Czechoslovak IBP-PT/PP Report No. 1, pp. 117–19. Třeboň: ČSAV.

Husák, Š. & Květ, J. (1973). Zonation of higher-plant shoot biomass in the reed-belt of the Nesyt fishpond. In *Littoral of the Nesyt Fishpond*, ed. J. Květ; Studie Československé Akademie Věd, 1973, No. 15, pp. 73–81. Praha: Academia.

Hutchinson, G.E. (1957). *A Treatise on Limnology*, I. *Geography, Physics and Chemistry.* New York: Wiley. 1015 pp.

Hutchinson, G.E. (1967). *A Treatise on Limnology*, II. *Introduction to Lake Biology and the Limnoplankton.* New York: Wiley. 1115 pp.

Hutchinson, G.E. (1977). *A Treatise on Limnology*, III. *Limnological Botany.* New York: Wiley. 660 pp.

Hynes, H.B.N. (1972). *The Ecology of Running Waters* (2nd edn.). Liverpool: Liverpool University Press. 580 pp.

Idso, S.B. & Anderson, M.G. (1988). A comparison of two recent studies of transpirational water loss from emergent aquatic communities. *Aquatic Botany*, **31**, 191–5.

Ikusima, I. (1970). Ecological studies on the productivity of aquatic plant communities. IV. Light conditions and community photosynthetic production. *Botanical Magazine, Tokyo*, **83**, 330–41.

Ikusima, I. (1978). Primary production and population ecology of the aquatic sedge *Lepironia articulata* in a tropical swamp, Tasek Bera, Malaysia. *Aquatic Botany*, **4**, 269–80.

Illjin, C. (1936). Zur Physiologie der kalkfeindlichen Pflanzen. *Beihefte zum Botanischen Zentralblatt*, **54**, 569–98.

Imhof, G. (1973). Aspects of energy flow by different food chains in a reed bed. A review. *Polskie Archiwum Hydrobiologii*, **20**, 165–8.

Imhof, G. & Burian, K. (1972). *Energy-flow Studies in a Wetland Ecosystem (Reed Belt of the Lake, Neusiedlersee)*; Special Publication for International Biological Programme. Wien: Austrian Academy of Sciences. 15 pp.

Isambaev, A.I. (1964). Podzemnye pobegi trostnika obyknovennogo v razlichnych ekologicheskich usloviiach. In *Trostnik, Materialy po biologii, ekologii i ispolzovaniyu trostnika obyknovennogo v Kazakhstane*, ed. B.A. Bykov *et al.*; Trudy Instituta Botaniki, **15**, pp. 185–201. Alma Ata: Akademiya Nauk Kazakhskoï SSR.

Iseli, C. (1990). Die Geschichte der Schilfrohrbereiche am Bielersee und Folgerungen für den praktischen Schilfschutz. In *Ökologie, Gefährdung, und Schutz von Röhrichtpflanzen*, ed. H. Sukopp & M. Krauss; Landschaftsentwicklung u. Umweltforschung, **71**, pp. 212–28. Berlin: Technische Universität.

Iseli, C. (1993). Ufererosion und Schilfrückgang am Bielersee – Möglichkeiten und Strategien der Uferrenaturierung. In *Seenufer-zerstörung und Seeufer-renaturierung in Mitteleuropa*, ed. W. Ostendorp & P. Krumscheid-Plankert; Limnologie Aktuell, **5**, pp. 103–12. Stuttgart: G. Fischer.

Ishikura, H. (1952). Relation of the percentage of rice stems infested by the rice stem borer to the yield of rice. *Survey and Studies of Crop Damage*, **1**, 1–15. Tokyo: Statistics and Survey Division, Ministry of Agriculture and Forestry of Japan. (In Japanese.)

Ishikura, H. (1955). On the types of the seasonal prevalence of rice stem borer moth in Japan. *Bulletin of the National Institute of Agricultural Science, Tokyo, Ser. C*, **5**, 678–80.

Ishikura, H. (1967). Assessment of rice loss caused by the rice stem borer. In *The Major Insect Pests of the Rice Plant*; Proceedings of the Symposium of the International Rice Research Institute, 1964, pp. 251–64. Baltimore: Johns Hopkins.

IUCN (1972). *International Conference on Conservation of Wetlands and Waterfowl, Ramsar, Iran, Jan.–Feb. 1971*, ed. E. Carr, Proceedings; Article 1, p. 18. Slimbridge: International Wildfowl Research Bureau. 303 pp.

Ivanov, L.S. (1959). Uroven vody kak faktor povysheniya zapasov i ulovov ryb v Dunaye. *Comptes Rendus del'Akademie Bulgare des Sciences*, **12**, 553–6.

Iversen, J. (1936). Biologische Pflanzentypen als Hilfsmittel in der Vegetationsforschung. Thesis, University of København. 224 pp.

Jackson, P.B.N. (1961). *Kariba Studies – Ichthyology. The Fish of the Middle Zambezi*. Manchester: Manchester University Press. 36 pp.

Jenik, J. (1972). *Obecná Geobotanika*. Praha: SPN. 30 pp.

Jenkinson, D.S. & Powlson, D.S. (1976). The effects of biocidal treatments on metabolism in soil I. Fumigation with chloroform. *Soil Biology and Biochemistry*, **8**, 167–77.

Jervis, R.A. (1969). Primary production in the fresh water marsh of Troy Meadows, New Jersey. *Bulletin of the Torrey Botanical Club*, **96**, 209–31.

Jeschke, L. (1976). Veränderung des Röhrichtgürtels der Seen in unseren Naturschutzgebieten. *Naturschutz Arbieten in Mecklenburg*, **19**, 49–52.

John, D.M. (1986). *The Inland Waters of Tropical West Africa*. Stuttgart: Schweizerbart'sche Verlag. 244 pp.

496 References

Johnson, P.N. & Brook, P.A. (1989). *Wetland Plants in New Zealand.* Wellington: DSIR. 317 pp.

Jones, E.B.G. (1974). Aquatic fungi. In *Biology of Plant Litter Decomposition,* II, ed. C.H. Dickinson & G.F.J. Pugh, pp. 337–83. New York: Academic Press.

Jones, M.B. (1988). Photosynthetic responses of C3 and C4 wetland species in a tropical swamp. *Journal of Ecology,* **76,** 253–62.

Jones, M.B. & Milburn, T.R. (1978). Photosynthesis in papyrus (*Cyperus papyrus* L.). *Photosynthetica,* **12,** 197–9.

Jones, T. (1993). *A Directory of Wetlands of International Importance: Sites Designated for the Ramsar List of Wetlands of International Importance.* Gland: Ramsar Convention Bureau. 4 vols.

Jongli Investigation Team (1954). *The Equatorial Nile Project and its Effects in the Anglo-Egyptian Sudan,* I–V. Khartoum: Sudan Government.

Junk, W.J. (1970). Investigations of the ecology and production-biology of the 'floating meadows' (*Paspalo-Echinochloetum*) in the Middle Amazon I. The floating vegetation and its ecology. *Amazonina,* **2,** 449–95.

Junk, W.J. (1973). Investigations on the ecology and production-biology of the 'floating meadows' (*Paspalo-Echinochloetum*) in the Middle Amazon II. The aquatic fauna in the root zone of floating vegetation. *Amazonina,* **4,** 9–102.

Junk, W.J. (1983). Ecology of swamps in the Middle Amazon. In *Mires: Swamp, Bog, Fen and Moor, Regional Studies,* ed. A.J.P. Gore; Ecosystems of the World 4B, pp. 269–94. Amsterdam: Elsevier.

Jupp, B.P. & Spence, D.H.N. (1977). Limitations of macrophytes in a eutrophic lake, Loch Leven II. Wave action, sediments and water-fowl grazing. *Journal of Ecology,* **65,** 431–46.

Kadlec, R.H. & Knight, R.L. (1995). *Treatment Wetlands.* Boca Raton, Florida: CRC Press. 928 pp.

Kadner, D. (1971). Derzeitige Verhältnisse in den Seenlandschaften Südbayerns und Vorschläge für ihre zukünftige Nutzung. In *Ländespflege in Alpenvorland,* Schriftenreihe der Deutschen Rat Landespflege, **16,** pp. 37–9.

Kajak, Z., Hillbricht-Ilkowska, A. & Pieczyńska, E. (1972). The production processes in several Polish lakes. In *Productivity Problems of Freshwaters,* ed. Z. Kajak & A. Hillbricht-Ilkowska; Proceedings of the IBP-UNESCO Symposium on Productivity Problems of Freshwaters, Kazimierz Dolny, May, 1970, pp. 129–47. Warszawa-Kraków: PWN.

Kalbe, L. (1981). *Ökologie der Wasservögel*; Die neue Brehm-Bücherei, **Heft 518,** 2nd ed. Wittenberg-Lutherstadt: Ziemsen Verlag. 116 pp.

Kalugina, N.S. (1959). K biologii nekotorўkh kironomid Uchinskogo vodokhranilishcha (rod *Endochironomas* K., rod. *Glyptotendipes* K. i dr.). (On the bionomics of some Chironomids of the Uchinsko reservoir.) In *Trudў VI Soveshchaniya po Problemam Biologiyi Vnutrennikh Vod, Iyunya, 1957,* pp. 283–6. Moskva/Leningrad: AN SSSR. (In Russian.)

Kalugina, N.S. (1961). Sistematika i razvitie komarov *Endochironomus albipennis* Mg., *E. tendens* F. i *E. impar* Walk. (Diptera, Tendipedidae). *Entomologicheskoe Obozrenie,* **40,** 900–19. (Translation: Taxonomy and development of *Endochironomus albipennis* Mg, *E. tendens* F. and *E. impar* Walk. (Diptera, Tendipedidae); In *Entomological Reviews, Washington,* **40,** 515–26.)

Kamuro, S. (1957). The plant ecology studies of lakes and marshes having a period of drainage III. On the amphiphyte zone in artificial reservoirs. *Botanical Magazine, Tokyo,* **70,** 305–12.

Kamuro, S. (1960). Plant ecological studies on reed swamps with special reference to the abiotic habitat factors I. *Japanese Ecology*, **10**, 29–33.

Kapetsky, J.M. (1974). The Kafue River floodplain: an example of pre-impoundment potential for fish production. In *Lake Kariba; a Man-made Tropical Ecosystem in Central Africa*, ed. E.K. Balon & A.G. Coche, pp. 479–523. The Hague: Junk.

Karavaev, M.N. (1958). Geobotanichesko raĭonirovanie vostochnoĭ chasti centralnoĭ Ĭakutskoi ravninȳ. In *Voprosȳ Fizicheskoĭ Geografii*, pp. 228–57. Moskva: AN SSSR.

Karpáti, L. & Lantos, T. (1978). Bioindikator vizi makrofitonok kutatasa a Balaton I. *Elterjedesi viszonyk. Kesszth. Agrárélydomány Egyetum Keszthtudo Merog. K. Növén.-Es Növén. Tansz*, **21**, 1–43.

Kashkin, N.Ĭ. (1958). Potreblenie vȳssheĭ vodnoĭ rastitel'nosti lichinkami *Phryganea grandis* L. (Utilization of higher plants by larvae of *P. grandis*.) *Trudȳ Moskovskogo Tekhnicheskogo Instituta Rybnoĭ Promyshlennosti i Khozyaĭstva, imeni A.I. Mikoyana*, **9**, 146–60. (In Russian.)

Kashkin, N.Ĭ. (1959). Pitanie gusenits *Paraponyx stratiotata* L., *Nymphula nymphaeata* L. i *Cataclysta lemnata* L. (Pyralididae, Lepidoptera). (Feeding of the larvae of *P. stratiotata*, *N. nymphaeata* and *G. lemnata*.) *Trudȳ Moskovskogo Tekhnicheskogo Instituta Rybnoĭ Promyshlennosti i Khozyaĭstva imeni A.I. Mikoyana*, **10**, 162–76. (In Russian.)

Kashkin, N.Ĭ. (1961). O rozmerach ispolzovaniya vȳshȳkh vodnȳch rastenii nektotorȳmi bezpozvonochnȳmi fitofagami (na primere Ĭachranskogo Vodokhranilishche kanala Moskva-Volga). *Trudȳ Murmanskkogo Biologicheskogo Instituta*, **3**, 170–84.

Katanskaya, V.T. (1960a). Materialȳ dlȳa izuchenia produktivnosti zarosleĭ vodnȳkh rastenii del'tȳ r. Amudar'i. In *Problemȳ Istoricheskogo Ozerovedeniya. Voprosȳ Paleogeografiyi; Trudȳ Laboratoriyi. Ozerovedeniya. AN SSSR*, **10**, pp. 193–249. Moskva & Leningrad: AN SSSR.

Katanskaya, V.T. (1960b). Produktivnost' rastitel'nogo pokrova nekotorykh ozer Karel'skogo peresheĭka. *Trudȳ Laboratoriya Ozerovedeniya*, **11**, 151–77.

Kats, N.Ya. (1959). O bolotakh i torfyanikakh severnoĭ Ameriki. *Pochvovedenie* No. 10, 44–52.

Kats, N.Ya. (1971). *Bolota Zemnogo Shara*. Moskva: Nauka. 295 pp.

Kats, N.Ya. (1972). O rasprostranenii torfyanikov na zemnom share, o tipakh ikh i priznalakh. (On the distribution of peat bogs on earth, their types and peculiarities.) *Botanicheskiĭ Zhurnal, SSSR*, **57**, 198–210. (In Russian.)

Kaul, V. (1971). Production and ecology of some macrophytes of Kashmir lakes. *Hidrobiologia, Bucureşti*, **12**, 63–9.

Kaul, V., Trisal, C.L. & Handoo, J.K. (1978). Distribution and production of macrophytes in some water bodies of Kashmir. In *Glimpses of Ecology*, ed. J.S. Singh & B. Gopal, pp. 313–34. Jaipur: International Scientific Publications.

Kaul, V. & Vass, K.K. (1972). Production studies of some macrophytes of Srinagar lakes. In *Productivity Problems of Freshwaters*, ed. Z. Kajak & A. Hillbricht-Ilkowska; Proceedings of the IBP-UNESCO Symposium on Productivity Problems of Freshwaters, Kazimierz Dolny, May, pp. 725–31. Warszawa & Kraków: Polish Science Publishers.

Kaul, V. & Zutshi, D.P. (1967). A study of aquatic and marshland vegetation of Srinagar. *Proceedings of the National Institute of Science in India*, **33**, 111–27.

Kaule, G. (1971). Naturschutzgebiete und ihre Nutzung für die Erholung, dargestellt am beispiel Eggstätt-Hemhofer Seenplatte. *Schriftenreihe der Landespflege und Naturschutz*, **6**, 259–65.

Kaule, G. (1973). Die Seen und Moore zwischen Inn und Chiemsee. *Schrifte für Naturschutz und Landschaftpflege*, **3**, 1–72.

Kaushik, N.K. & Hynes, H.B.N. (1971). The fate of the dead leaves that fall into streams. *Archiv für Hydrobiologie*, **68**, 465–515.

Kawahara, S., Kiritani, K., Sasaba, T., Nakasuji, F. & Okuma, C. (1969). Seasonal changes in abundance and the faunal composition of spiders in the paddy field, with special reference to their relation to the seasonal prevalence of the green rice leafhopper, *Nephotettix cincticeps* Uhler. *Proceedings of the Association of Plant Protection, Shikoku*, **4**, 33–44. (In Japanese with English summary.)

Ketchum, B.H. (ed.) (1983). *Estuaries and Enclosed Seas*; Ecosystems of the World 26. Amsterdam: Elsevier. 500 pp.

Ketner, P. (1973). Primary production of salt marsh communities on the island of Terschelling in the Netherlands. *Verhandlung Rijksinstituut voor Natuurbeheer*, **5**, 1–181.

Khan, M.A., Wazer, V.A. & Khan, T. (1969). A study of elephant grass (*Typha elephantina* Roxb.) for textile purposes I. Physical and chemical examination of the fibres. *Pakistan Journal of Scientific and Industrial Research*, **12**, 303–6.

Khashes, Ts. & Bobro, V.I. (1971). Pro dennu ta sezonnu dinamiku transpiratsii v osheretu zvichaïnogo (*Phragmites communis* Trin.). *Ukrayins'kyï Botanichnyï Zhurnal*, **28**, 521–4.

Kickuth, R. & Tittizer, Th. (1974). Makrophyten limnischer Standorte und ihr Verhalten gegenüber *p*-Toluol-sulfonsäure im Substrat III. Abbau von *p*-Toluolsulfonsäure durch Pflanzen limnischer Standorten und ihre Rhizosphärengesellschaft. *Angewandte Botanik*, **48**, 355–70.

Kiel, W.H., Hawkins, A.S. & Perret, N.G. (1972). *Waterfowl Habitat Trends in the Aspen Parklands of Manitoba*; Canadian Wildlife Service Report Series No. 18. Ottawa: Department of Indian Affairs and Northern Development. 61 pp.

Kiendl, J. (1953). Zur Transpirationsmessung an Sumpf- und Wasser-pflanzen. *Berichte der Deutschen Botanischen Gesellschaft*, **67**, 243–8.

Killingbeck, K.T., Smith, D.L. & Marzolf, G.R. (1982). Chemical changes in tree leaves during decomposition in a tallgrass prairie stream. *Ecology*, **63**, 585–9.

Kira, T. (1975). Primary production of forests. In *Photosynthesis and Productivity in Different Environments*, ed. J.P. Cooper; International Biological Programme No. 22, pp. 5–40. Cambridge: Cambridge University Press.

Kirby, C.J. (1971). The annual primary production and decomposition of the salt marsh grass *Spartina alterniflora* Loisel in the Barataria Bay estuary of Louisiana. PhD Dissertation. Baton Rouge: Louisiana State University. 74 pp.

Kirby, C.J. & Gosselink, J.G. (1976). Primary production in a Louisiana Gulf Coast *Spartina alterniflora* marsh. *Ecology*, **57**, 1052–9.

Kiritani, K. (1964). Natural control of populations of the southern green stink bug, *Nezara viridula*. *Researches on Population Ecology*, **6**, 88–98.

Kiritani, K. (1971). Distribution and abundance of the southern green stink bug, *Nezara viridula*. *Proceedings of the Symposium on Rice Insects*, 1971, 235–48. Tokyo: Tropical Agriculture Research Centre, Ministry of Agriculture & Forestry.

Kiritani, K. (1972). Strategy in integrated control of rice pests. *Review of Plant Protection Research (Tokyo)*, **5**, 76–104.

Kiritani, K. & Hokyo, N. (1970). *Studies on the Population Ecology of the Southern Green Stink Bug*, Nezara viridula; Shitei-shiken (Byogaichu) 9. Tokyo: Ministry of Agriculture & Forestry. 259 pp. (In Japanese with English summary.)

Kiritani, K. & Iwao, S. (1967). The biology and life cycle of *Chilo suppressalis* (Walker) and *Tryporyza* (*Schoenobius*) *incertulas* (Walker) in temperate-climate areas. In *The Major Insect Pests of the Rice Plant*; Proceedings of Symposium of the International Rice Institute, pp. 45–101. Baltimore: Johns Hopkins.

Kiritani, K., Sasaba, T. & Nakasuji, F. (1971). A critical review of integrated control of insect pests. *Botyu-Kagaku*, **36**, 78–98. (In Japanese with English summary.)

Kisimoto, R. (1965). Studies on the polymorphism and its role playing in the population growth of the brown planthopper, *Nilaparvata lugens* Ståhl. *Bulletin – Experimental Station of National Research Institute of Vegetables, Ornamental Plants and Tea, Shizuoka*, **13**, 1–106. (In Japanese with English summary.)

Kisimoto, R. (1971). Long distance migration of Planthoppers, *Sogatella furcifer* and *Nilaparvata lugens*. *Proceedings of Symposium on Rice Insects*, 1971, pp. 201–16. Tokyo: Tropical Agriculture Research Centre, Ministry of Agriculture and Forestry.

Kistritz, R.U. (1978). Recycling of nutrients in an enclosed aquatic community of decomposing macrophytes (*Myriophyllum spicatum*). *Oikos*, **30**, 561–9.

Klapp, E. (1965). *Taschenbuch der Gräser* (9th edn.). Berlin: Parey. 260 pp.

Klapper, H. (1966). Wasserassel (*Asellus aquaticus* Rakoritza) im Trinkwasserversorgungsnetz einer Grossstadt und Möglichkeiten zu ihrer Bekämpfung. *Verhandlungen der Internationale Vereinigung für Theoretische und Angewandte Limnologie*, **16**, 996–1002.

Klötzli, F. (1967). Umwandlung von Moor- und Sumpf-gesellschaften durch Abwässer im Gebiet des Neeracher Riets. *Bericht Geobotanisches Institut der Eidgenoss. Technischen Hochschule, Stiftung Rübel in Zürich*, **37**, 104–12.

Klötzli, F. (1969). Die Grundwasserbeziehungen der Streu- und Moor-wiesen im nordlichen Schweizer Mittelland. *Beiträge zur Geobotanischen Landesaufnahme der Schweiz*, **52**, 1–296.

Klötzli, F. (1971). Biogenous influences on aquatic macrophytes, especially *Phragmites communis. Hidrobiologia, Bucureşti*, **12**, 107–11.

Klötzli, F. (1974). Über Belastbarkeit und Produktion in Schilfröhrichten. *Verhandlungen der Gesellschaft für Ökologie, Saarbrücken*, 1973, 237–47.

Klötzli, F. (1978). Wertung, Sicherung und Erhaltung von Naturschutzgebieten. Einige rechtliche und technische Probleme. *Berichte der Schweizerischen Naturforschenden Gesellschaft*, **7**, 23–32.

Klötzli, F. (1979). Ursachen für Verschwinden und Umwandlung von Molinion-Gesellschaften in der Schweiz. In *Werden und Vergehen von Pflanzengesellschaften*, ed. O. Wilmanns & R. Tüxen: Bericht zum Internationalen Symposium Internationalen Vereinigung für Vegetationskunde; Rinteln, 1978, pp. 451–64.

Klötzli, F. (1980). Zur Verpflanzung von Streu- und Moor-wiesen. Erfahrungen von 1969 bis 1980. *Berichte, Bayer Akademie für Naturschutz und Landschaftspflege*, **5**, 41–50.

Klötzli, F. (1981*a*). Möglichkeiten und Grenzen der Schaffung von

Feuchtgebieten. In *Landwirtschaft und Wasserhaushalt*, ed. G. Fischbeck *et al.*; Tagung Dachverband Agrarwirtschaft, Mainz 1980; Agrarspektrum, 1, pp. 107–17. München and Frankfurt am Main: Verlagsunion.

Klötzli, F. (1981*b*). Zur Reaktion verpflanzter Ökosysteme der Feuchtgebiete. *Daten und Dokumente zum Umweltschutz, Universität Stuttgart-Hohenheim*, **31**, 107–17.

Klötzli, F. (1986). Tendenzen zur Eutrophierung in Feuchtgebieten. *Veröffenlichung – Geobotanisches Institut der Eidgenoss. Technischen Hochschule in Zürich*, **87**, 343–61.

Klötzli, F. (1989). Erhaltung von Feuchgebieten mit Hilfe Kulturtechnischer Massnehmen. In *Wasser und Landschaft*, ed. W. Schmit; Festschrift H. Grubinger, Institut für Orts-Regional-Landesplannung der Eidgenoss. Technischen Hochschule in Zürich, Schriften-Reihe 49, pp. 157–69. Zürich: ETH.

Klötzli, F. (1991). Möglichkeiten und erste Ergebnisse mitteleuropäischer Renaturierungen. *Verhandlungen Gesellschaft für Ökologie*, **20**, 229–42.

Klötzli, F. & Grünig, A. (1976). Seeufervegetation als Bioindikator: Zur Reaktion belasteter Seeufervegetation. *Daten und Dokumente zum Umweltschutz, Universität Stuttgart-Hohenheim*, **19**, 109–31.

Klötzli, F. & Züst, S. (1973*a*). Nitrogen regime in reed-beds. *Polskie Archiwum Hydrobiologii*, **20**, 131–6.

Klötzli, F. & Züst, S. (1973*b*). Conservation of reed-beds in Switzerland. *Polskie Archiwum Hydrobiologii*, **20**, 229–35.

Kluesner, J.W. & Lee, G.F. (1974). Nutrient loading from a separate storm sewer in Madison, Wisconsin. *Journal of the Water Pollution Control Federation*, **46**, 920–36.

Klyukina, E.A. (1974). Vidovoĭ sostav, biomassa i chimicheskiĭ sostav vīssheĭ vodnoĭ rastitel'nosti Povenetskogo zaliva Onezhskogo ozera. In *Okhrana i Ispol'zovanie Vodnȳkh Resursov Karelii*, pp. 151–67. Petrozavodsk: V.A. Freĭndling.

Knipling, E.G., West, S.H. & Haller, W.T. (1970). Growth characteristics, yield potential, and nutritive content of water hyacinths. *Proceedings – Soil and Crop Science Society of Florida*, **30**, 51–63.

Kobayashi, M. (1971). Role of photosynthetic bacteria in paddy soils. *INRA Publications*, **71**(7), 29–35.

Kobayashi, T. (1961). The effect of insecticidal applications to the rice stem borer on the leafhopper populations. *Special Report on the Prediction of Pests, Ministry of Agriculture and Forests* No. 6, 1–126. (In Japanese with English summary.)

Kobayashi, T. & Shibata, H. (1973). Seasonal changes in population density of spiders in paddy fields, with special reference to the ecological control of the rice insect pests. *Japanese Journal of Applied Entomology and Zoology*, **17**, 193–202. (In Japanese with English summary.)

Kobuszewska, D.M. (1973). Experimentally increased fish stock in the pond-type lake Warniak XIII. Distribution and biomass of the Lemnaceae and the fauna associated with them. *Ekologia Polska*, **21**, 611–29.

Kocur, M., Martinec, T., Jírková, K., Volfová, J. & Pelčáková, Z. (1961). Studium mikroflory lednických rybníků. *Publications of the Faculty of Science of J.E. Purkyně University, Brno*, **428**, 477–502.

Koenig, O. (1952). Ökologie und Verhalten der Vögel des Neusiedlersee Schilfgürtels. *Journal für Ornithologie*, **93**, 207–89.

Koidsumi, K., Sakurai, Y. & Kawashima, S. (1967). Standing crop of higher aquatic plants in Lake Suwa. *Japanese Journal of Limnology*, **2**, 57–63.

Kokin, K.A. (1962). Vliyanie pogruzhennoĭ vodnoĭ rastitel'nosti na gidrochimicheskiĭ rezhim i processȳ samoochishcheniĭa reki Moskvȳ. (Der Einfluss der unter wasser lebenden Pflanzen auf die hydrochemischen Verhältnisse und auf die Selbstreinigung der Moskwa.) *Vestnik – Moskovsii Universitet Seriya 6, Biologiya, Pochvovedenie*, **17**, 33–9. (In Russian.)

Kopecký, K. (1965). Einfluss der Ufer- und Wassermakrophyten-Vegetation auf die Morphologie des Flussbettes einiger tschechoslowakischer Flüsse. *Archiv für Hydrobiologie*, **61**, 137–60.

Kopecký, K. (1967). Einfluss langdauernder Überflutungen auf die Stoffproduktion von Glanzgraswiesen. *Folia Geobotanica Phytotaxonomica, Praha*, **2**, 347–82.

Kopecký, K. (1969). Klassifikationsvorschlag der Vegetationstandorte an den Ufern der tschechoslovakischen Wasserläufe unter hydrologischen Gesichtspunkten. *Archiv für Hydrobiologie*, **66**, 326–47.

Köppen, W. (1923). *Die Klimate der Erde*. Berlin: Walter de Gruyter & Co. 369 pp.

Korelyakova, I.L. (1971). Distribution and productivity of communities of *Phragmites communis* Trin. in Dnieper Reservoirs. *Hidrobiologia, Bucureşti*, **12**, 149–54.

Korelyakova, I.L. (1975). Kratkaya kharakteristika melkovodii i ikh rastitel'nogo pokrova v Kremenchugskom vodokhranilishche. *Gidrobiologicheskiĭ Zhurnal*, **11**(2), 12–17.

Kořínková, J. (1971*a*). Quantitative relations between submerged macrophytes and populations of invertebrates in a carp pond. *Hidrobiologia, Bucureşti*, **12**, 377–82.

Kořínková, J. (1971*b*). Sampling and distribution of animals in submerged vegetation. *Věstnik Československé Společnosti Zoologické*, **35**, 209–21.

Korneck, D. & Sukopp, H. (1988). *Rote Liste der in der Bundesrepüblik Deutschland Ausgestorbenen, Verschollenen und Gefährdeten Farn- und Blütenpflanzen und ihre Auswertung für den Arten- und Biotopeschutz*; Schriftenreihe für Vegetationskunde 19. Bonn – Bad Godesberg: Bundesforschungsanstalt für Naturschutz u. Landschaftsökologie. 210 pp.

Kostecki, P.T. & Calabrese, J.J. (1991). *Hydrocarbon Contaminated Soils and Groundwater. Analysis, Fate, Environmental and Public Health Effects, Remediation*, BB1. Chelsea, Mich.: CRC/Lewis Publishers. 670 pp.

Kovács, M., Précsényi, I. & Podani, J. (1978). Anhäufung von Elementen im Balatoner Schilfrohr (*Phragmites communis*). *Acta Botanica Academiae Scientiarum Hungaricae*, **24**, 99–111.

Kovařik, J. (1958). Straty vody vzparem é volný vodní hladiny a transpirací ryhničnich porostu. *Výskumný Ústav Vodného Hospodárstra, Bratislava Práce a Štúdie*, **11**, 339–41.

Kožená-Toušková, I. (1973). Composition of nests of birds breeding in the *Phragmition* plant community. *Acta Scientiarum Naturalium Academiae Scientiarum Bohemoslovacae, Brno*, **7**(7), 1–36.

Krasnoborov, I.M. (1965). Rastitel'nost dolinȳ r. Agul (Vostochnyi Sayan). *Rastitelnyi Pokrov Krasnoyarskogo Kraya*, **2**, 24–28.

Krasovskiĭ, L.I. (1962). Sutochnaia potrebnost' ondatry v estestvennykh kormakh. (Daily consumption of natural food by the muskrat.) *Zoologcheskiĭ Zhurnal*, **41**, 1529–35. (In Russian.)

Kratochvil, J. & Rosický, B. (1955). Die sibirische Wühlmaus (*Microtus oeconomus*), ein Eiszeitrelikt in der ČSR. *Práce Brněnské Základny ČSAV*, **27**, 33–72.

Krausch, D. (1956). Das Riesenrohr im Kreise Licksu und sein Schutz. *Märkische Heimat*, **1**, **3**, 32–4.

Krauss, M. (1992). Röhrichtrückgang an der Berliner Havel – Ursachen, Gegenmaßnahmen und Sanierungserfolg. *Natur und Landschaft*, **62**, 287–92.

Krauss, M. (1993). Die Rolle des Bisams (*Ondatra zibethicus*) beim Röhrichtrückgang an der Berliner Havel. In Limnologie Aktuell, **5**, 49–60.

Kreeb, K. (1974). *Ekophysiologie der Pflanzen*. Jena: VEB Fischer Verlag. 211 pp.

Krejci, G. (1974). Jahresperiodische Stoffwechselschwankungen in *Phragmites communis*. Diss. phil. Fak. Univ. Wien. 150 pp.

Królikowska, J. (1971). Transpiration of Reed (*Phragmites communis* Trin.). *Polskie Archiwum Hydrobiologii*, **18**, 347–58.

Królikowska, J. (1972). Physiological effects of sodium salts of 2,4-D and MCPA on *Typha latifolia* L. *Polskie Archiwum Hydrobiologii*, **19**, 333–42.

Królikowska, J. (1974). Water content in leaves of helophytes. *Polskie Archiwum Hydrobiologii*, **21**, 229–40.

Królikowska, J. (1976). Physiological effects of triazine herbicides on *Typha latifolia* L. *Polskie Archiwum Hydrobiologii*, **23**, 249–56.

Królikowska, J. (1987). Water relations of wetland plants. *Archiv für Hydrobiologie, Beihefte*, **271**, 231–7.

Krotkevich, P.G. (1960). Agrobiologicheskie svoĭstva vosproizvodstva trostnika. In *Ispol'zovanie Trostnika i Odnoletnikh Rastenĭ. v. Tsellyulozno-bymazhnoĭ*, promyshlennosti, dok. P.G. Krotkevicha; Konferentsiya, Fevralya, 1958, g. Tsyurupinsk. Material, pp. 16–33. Moskva/Leningrad: Tsentral'noe Byuro Tekhnicheskoĭ Informatsii Glavstandartdoma: Goslesbumizdat.

Krotkevich, P.G. (1970). Biologo-ekologicheskie Svoĭstva i Narodnochozĭaĭstvennoe Ispol'zovanie Trostnika Obȳknovennogo *Phragmites communis* Trin. Avtoref. Diss. na Soisk. Uchen. Stepeni D-ra Biol. Nauk (03.494). Kiev: AN USSR. 71 pp.

Krotkevich, P.G. (1976). K voprosu ispol'zovaniya vod okhranno-ochisthȳkh svoĭstv trostnika obyknovennogo. (On the problem of using water-conservation and purification properties of common reed.) *Vodnȳe Resursȳ*, **5**, 191–7. (In Russian.)

Krupauer, V. (1967). Food selection of two years old grass carp. *Bulletin of Fisheries Research Institute Vodňany*, **1**, 1–11.

Krupauer, V. (1968). Experience gained with the breeding of herbivorous fish in Czechoslovakia. *Bulletin of Fisheries Research Institute Vodňany*, **2**, 3–15.

Krupauer, V. (1971). The use of herbivorous fishes for ameliorative purposes in Central and Eastern Europe. In *Proceedings of the EWRS 3rd Symposium on Aquatic Weeds*, 95–103.

Krȳlov, S.V. (1942). Sȳrĭevye resursȳ dlya polluchenia gorȳneikh, shkronikh II sel 12. Dukjov deregomu drevesiny, Tomsk: AW SSSR.

Krȳzhanovskiĭ, S.G. (1949). Ekologo-morfologicheskie zakonomernosti razvitia karpovȳkh vȳnnovȳkh i somovȳkh ryb (Cyprinoidei i Siluroidei). *Trudȳ Instituta Morfologii Zhivotnȳkh, AN SSSR, Moskva*, **1**, 5–332.

Krzywosz, T., Krzywosz, W. & Radziej, J. (1980). The effect of grass carp (*Ctenopharyngodon idella* Val.) on aquatic vegetation and ichthyofauna of Lake Dgal Wielki. *Ekologia Polske*, **27**, 433–50.

Ksenofontova, T. (1989). General changes in the Matsalu Bay reedbeds in this century and their present quality. *Aquatic Botany*, **35**, 111–20.

Kubiëna, W.L. (1953). *The Soils of Europe*. London: Murby. 318 pp.

Kühl, H. & Neuhaus, D. (1993). The genetic variability of *Phragmites australis* investigated by random amplified polymorphic DNA. *Limnologie Aktuell*, **5**, 9–18.

Kulcyzński, S. (1949). Peat bogs of Polesie. *Mémoires de l'Academie Polonaise des Sciences et Lettres, Classe Sci. Math. Nat. Sér. B*, **15**, 1–356.

Kulshreshtha, M. & Gopal, B. (1982*a*). Decomposition of freshwater wetlands vegetation I. In *Wetlands, Ecology and Management*, ed. B. Gopal, R.E. Turner, R.G. Wetzel & D.F. Whigham, pp. 259–79. Jaipur: Michael Paul Lucknow Publishing House.

Kulshreshtha, M. & Gopal, B. (1982*b*). Decomposition of freshwater wetlands vegetation II. Above-ground organs of emergent macrophytes. In *Wetlands, Ecology and Management*, ed. B. Gopal, R.E. Turner, R.G. Wetzel & D.F. Whigham, pp. 280–92. Jaipur: Michael Paul Lucknow Publishing House.

Kumari, R., Mäemets, A. & Renno, O. (eds.) (1974). *Estonian Wetlands & their Life*; Estonian Contribution to the International Biological Programme No. 7. Tallin: Valgus. 288 pp.

Kuno, E. (1968). Studies on the population dynamics of rice leafhoppers in a paddy field. *Bulletin of the Kyushu Agricultural Experimental Station*, **14**, 131–246. (In Japanese with English summary.)

Kuno, E. & Hokyo, N. (1970). Comparative analysis of the population dynamics of rice leafhoppers, *Nephottetix cincticeps* Uhler and *Nilaparvata lugens* Stål, with special reference to natural regulation of their numbers. *Researches on Population Ecology*, **12**, 154–84.

Kurimo, U. (1970). Effect of population on the aquatic macroflora of the Varkans area, Finnish Lake District. *Annales Botanici Fennici*, **7**, 213–54.

Kuznetsov, V.J. (1954). Vliyanie vodnoǐ rastitel'nosti na ispareniye. *Trudȳ Gosudarstvenogo Gidrobiologicheskogo Instituta*, **46**(100), 108–36.

Květ, J. (1971). Growth analysis approach to the production ecology of reedswamp plant communities. *Hidrobiologia, Bucureşti*, **12**, 15–40.

Květ, J. (ed.) (1973*a*). *Littoral of the Nesyt Fishpond*; Studie Československé Akademie Věd, 1973, No. 15. Praha: Academia. 172 pp.

Květ, J. (1973*b*). Transpiration of South Moravian *Phragmites communis*. In *Littoral of the Nesyt Fishpond*, ed. J. Květ; Studie Československé Akademie Věd, 1973, No. 15, pp. 143–6. Praha: Academia.

Květ, J. (1973*c*). Mineral nutrients in shoots of reed (*Phragmites communis* Trin.). *Polskie Archiwum Hydrobiologii*, **20**, 137–47.

Květ, J. (1973*d*). Shoot biomass, leaf area index and mineral nutrient content in selected South Bohemian and South Moravian stands of common reed (*Phragmites communis* Trin.). Results of 1968. In *Ecosystem Study on Wetland Biome in Czechoslovakia*, ed. S. Hejný, Czechoslovak IBP-PT/PP Report No. 3, pp. 93–5. Třeboň: ČSAV.

Květ, J. (1975). Transpiration in seven plant species colonizing a fishpond shore. *Biologia Plantarum*, **17**, 434–42.

Květ, J. (1978). Growth analysis of fishpond littoral communities. In *Pond Littoral Ecosystem: Structure and Functioning*, ed. D. Dykyjová & J. Květ; Ecological Studies 28, pp. 198–206. Berlin: Springer-Verlag.

Květ, J. (1984). Differentiation of summer temperatures in fishpond vegetation. *Preslia*, **56**, 213–27.

Květ, J. & Hudec, R. (1971). Effects of grazing by greylag geese on reedswamp plant communities. *Hidrobiologia, Bucureşti*, **12**, 351–60.

Květ, J. & Husák, Š. (1978). Primary data on biomass and production estimates in typical stands of fishpond littoral plant communities. In *Pond Littoral*

Ecosystems: Structure and Functioning, ed. D. Dykyjová & J. Květ; Ecological Studies 28, pp. 211–15. Berlin: Springer-Verlag.

Květ, J. & Ondok, J.P. (1973). Zonation of higher plant shoot biomass in the littoral of the Opatovický fishpond. In *Ecosystem Study on Wetland Biome in Czechoslovakia*, ed. S. Hejný, Czechoslovak IBP-PT/PP Report No. 3, pp. 87–92. Třeboň: ČSAV.

Květ, J., Svoboda, J. & Fiala, K. (1967). A simple device for measuring leaf inclinations. *Photosynthetica*, **1**, 127–8.

Květ, J., Svoboda, J. & Fiala, K. (1969). Canopy development in stands of *Typha latifolia* and *Phragmites communis* Trin. in South Moravia. *Hidrobiologia, Bucureşti*, **10**, 63–75.

La Bastille, A. (1974). *Ecology and Management of the Atitlán Grebe, Lake Atitlán, Guatemala*; Wildlife Monographs No. 37. Bethesda: The Wildlife Society Inc. 66 pp.

Lác, J. (1958). Príspevok k poznaniu potravy kunce ohnivého (*Bombina bombina*). (Contribution to the knowledge of the food of *B. bombina*.) *Biológia*, **13**, 844–53. (In Slovak.)

Lachavanne, J-B. & Wattenhofer, R. (1975*a*). *Contribution à l'Étude des Macrophytes du Léman*; Commission Internationale pour la Protection des Eaux du Léman et du Rhône contre la Pollution. Genève: Conservatoire Botanique de Genève. 447 pp.

Lachavanne, J-B. & Wattenhofer, R. (1975*b*). Evolution de la couverture végétale de la rade de Geǹve, *Saussurea*, **6**, 217–30.

Lack, J.T. (1973). Studies on the Macrophytes and Phytoplankton of the River Thames and Kennet at Reading. PhD thesis, University of Reading. 96 pp.

Ladle, M., Bass, J.A.B. & Jenkins, W.R. (1972). Studies on production and food consumption by the larval Simulidae (Diptera) in a chalk stream. *Hydrobiologia*, **39**, 429–48.

Lambert, J.M. (1964). The *Spartina* story. *Nature*, **204**, 1136–8.

Landolt, E. (1991). *Rote liste. Gefährdung der Farn- und Blütenpflanzen in der Schweiz*. Bern: Eidgenoss. Drucksachen- und Materialzentrale. 185 pp.

Lang, A.R.C., Evans, G.N. & Ho, P.Y. (1974). The influence of local advection on evapotranspiration from irrigated rice in a semiarid region. *Agricultural Meteorology*, **13**, 5–13.

Lang, G. (1967). Die Ufervegetation des westlichen Bodensees. *Archiv für Hydrobiologie, Suppl.*, **32**(4), 437–574.

Lang, G. (1968). Vegetationsveränderungen am Bodenseeufer in den letzten 100 Jahren. *Schriften des Vereins für Geschichte des Bodensees und seiner Umgebung*, **86**, 295–319.

Langhans, V. (1911). Untersuchungen über die Fauna des Hirschberger Grossteichs. *Monographie zur Internationalen Revue der Gesamten Hydrobiologie*, **3**, 1–101.

Lathwell, D.J., Mulligan, N.F. & Bouldin, D.R. (1969). Chemical properties and plant growth in twenty artificial wildlife marshes. *New York Fish and Game Journal*, **16**, 158–83.

Lavrenko, E.M. & Sochava, V.B. (1956). *Descriptio Vegetationis URSS*. Moskva-Leningrad: Edit. Academiya Nauk URSS. 971 pp.

Lavrenko, E.M. & Zoz, I.G. (1931). Rastitel'nost' konskikh plaven reki Dnepra ('Velikogo Luga'). Zaporozhskogo okruga. In *Materialy po Probleme Nizhnego Dnepra*, **2**, 79–142. Leningrad: AN SSSR.

Lavrov, N.P. (1959). *Akklimatizatsiya Ondatrȳ v SSSR*. (Acclimatization of the muskrat in the USSR.) Moskva: Izdatel'stvo Tsentrosoyuza. 530 pp. (In Russian.)

Lawalrée, A. (1971). L'Áppauvrissement de la flora en Belgique depuis 1850. *Boissiera*, **19**, 65–71.

Lawrence, J.M. & Mixon, W.W. (1970). Comparative nutrient content of aquatic plants from different habitats. *Proceedings of the Annual Meeting – Southern Weed Science Society*, **23**, 306–10.

Leah, R.T., Moss, B. & Forrest, D.E. (1078). Experiments with large enclosures in a shallow brackish lake, Hickling Broad, Norfolk, UK. *Internationale Revue der Gesamten Hydrobiologie*, **63**, 291–310.

Lebrun, J. & Gilbert, G. (1954). *Une Classification Écologique des Forêts du Congo*; Institut National pour l'Etude Agronomique du Congo, Serie Scientifique No. 63. 84 pp.

LeCren, E.D. & Lowe-McConnell, R.H. (eds.) (1980). *The Functioning of Freshwater Ecosystems*; International Biological Programme 22. Cambridge: Cambridge University Press. 588 pp.

Leentvaar, P. (1958). Guanotrofie in het Naarder meer. *De Levende Natuur*, **61**, 150–4.

Leeuwen, C.G. van (1966). Het botanisch beheer van natuurreservaten op structuur-oecologisch gronstag. (The botanical control of nature reserves based on structure ecology.) *Gorteria*, 3(2). (In Dutch with English summary).

Leisler, B. (1969). Beiträge zur Kenntnis der Ökologie der Anatiden des Seewinkels (Burgenland), Teil I. – Gänse. *Egretta*, **12**, 1–52.

Leszczynski, L. (1963). Pokarm mlodocianych stadoórych gatunkow ryb z kilku jezior okolic Wegorzewa. (Food of juvenile stages of some fish species from several lakes near Wegorzewo.) *Rocznik Nauk Rolniczych, Seria B*, **82**, 235–49. (In Polish.)

Levadinov, V. Ya. (1940). Znachenne allokhtonnogo materiala kak pishchevogo resursa v vodoeme na primere pitaniya vodyanogo oslika (*Asellus aquaticus* L.). (The importance of allochthonous material as food reserves in the water basins as exemplified by the feeding of *A. aquaticus* L.) *Trudȳ Vsesoyuznogo Gidrobiologicheskogo Obschestva*, **1**, 100–7. (In Russian.)

Lévêque, C., Carmouze, J.P., Dejoux, C., Durand, J.R., Gras, R., Iltis, A., Lemoalle, J., Loubens, G., Lauzanne, L. & Saint-Jean, L. (1972). In *Productivity Problems of Freshwaters*, ed. Z. Kajak & A. Hillbricht-Ilkowska; Proceedings of IBP-UNESCO Symposium on Productivity Problems of Freshwaters, Kazimierz Dolny, May 1970, pp. 95–107. Warszawa & Kraków: Polish Science Publishers.

Leyrink, L. & Hubatsch, H. (1993). Die Ufersetzung an den Netteseen. In *Seenuferzerstörung und Seeuferrenaturierung in Mitteleuropa*, ed. W. Ostendorp & P. Krumscheid-Plankert; Limnologie Aktuell, **5**, 62–76.

Lhotský, O. & Marvan, P. (1975). Biomasseproduktion und Bindung der Nährstoffe in einigen Massenvorkommen von Algen in der Natur. In *Izučenie Intensivnych Kultur Vodoroslei*, ed. J. Nečas, pp. 191–6. Třeboň: Institute of Microbiology.

Li, W.C., Armstrong, D.E., Williams, D.H., Harris, R.F. & Syers, J.K. (1972). Rate and extent of inorganic phosphate exchange in lake sediments. *Soil Science Society of America – Proceedings*, **36**, 279–85.

Libosvárský, J., Lusk, S. & El-Sedry, H.M. (1972). Fishery survey carried out at Lake Borullus, A.R.E., in the spring of 1971. *Acta Scientiarum Naturalium Academiae Scientiarum Bohemoslovacae, Brno 6 (Nova Series)*, **7**, 3–41.

Lieth, H. (1968). The measurement of calorific values of biological material and the determination of ecological efficiency. In *Functioning of Terrestrial Ecosystems at the Primary Production Level*, ed. F.F. Eckardt, pp. 233–42. Paris: UNESCO.

Lieth, H. & Whittaker, R.H. (ed.) (1975). *Primary Productivity of the Biosphere*; Ecological Studies 14. Berlin: Springer-Verlag. 339 pp.

Lieux, D.B. & Mulrennan, J. A. (1955). Mayfly control. *Mosquito News*, **15**, 156.

Likens, G.E., Bormann, F.H., Pierce, R.S., Eaton, J. S. & Johnson, N.M. (1977). *Biochemistry of a Forest Ecosystem*. New York: Springer Verlag. 146 pp.

Lilieroth, S. (1950). Über Folgen der kulturbedingten Wasserstandsenkung für Makrophyten- und Plankton-gemeinschaften in seichten Seen des südschwedischen Oligotrophiegebietes. *Acta Limnologica*, **3**, 1–228.

Linacre, E. (1976). Swamps. In *Vegetation and the Atmosphere, II Case Studies*, ed. J.L. Monteith, pp. 329–47. New York: Academic Press.

Linacre, E.T., Wicks, B.B., Sainty, G.R. & Grauze, G. (1970). The evaporation from a swamp. *Agricultural Meteorology*, **7**, 375–86.

Lind, E.M. & Visser, S.A. (1962). A study of a swamp at the north end of Lake Victoria. *Journal of Ecology*, **50**, 599–613.

Linde, A.F. (1969). *Techniques for Wetland Management*. Wisconsin Department of Natural Resources, Research Reports 45. Madison, Wisconsin: WDNR. 156 pp.

Linduska, J.P. (ed.) (1964). *Waterfowl Tomorrow*. Washington: Fish & Wildlife Service, US Department of the Interior. 770 pp.

Lipin, A.N. & Lipina, N.N. (1951). Makroflora stoiashchikh vodoiemov i sviaz ee s gidrofaunoi. (Standing water macrophytes and their relations to the hydrofauna.) *Trudȳ Vserosiiskogo Nautcho-issledovatelskogo Instituta Prudovogo Rȳbnogo Choziaistva*, **5**, 1–270. (In Russian.)

Lipina, N.N. (1928). Lichinki i kukolki khironomid: ekologiya i sistematika. (Larvae and pupae of chironomids: ecology and systematics.) *Izdaniya Nauchnogo Instituta Rȳbnogo Khozyiastva*, **3**, 1–179. (In Russian.)

Lisitsina, L.J. & Ekzertsev, V.A. (1971). O transpiratsii khvoskhtsa pireshtsnogo (*Equisetum fluviatile* L.), mannika bolshego (*Glyceria maxima* Hartm. Holmb.) i kamȳsha ozernogo (*Scirpus lacustris* L.). *Informatsionnyi Byulleten' Institut Biologiyi Vnutrennikh Vod*, No. 12, 14–18.

Little, E.C.S. (1967). Progress report on transpiration of some tropical water weeds. *Pesticides Abstracts and Summaries*, **13**, 127–32.

Little, E.C.S. (1979). *Handbook of Utilization of Aquatic Plants. A Review of World Literature*; FAO Fisheries Technical Paper No. 187. Rome: FAO. 176 pp.

Livingstone, D.A. (1963). Chemical composition of rivers and lakes. In *The Data of Geochemistry* (6th edn.), ed. M. Fleischer; Professional Papers United States Geological Survey, 440–G. pp. 1–64. Washington: Government Printing Office.

Lodge, D.M. (1991). Herbivory of freshwater macrophytes. *Aquatic Botany*, **41**, 195–224.

Löffler, H. (1974). *Der Neusiedlersee. Naturgeschichte eines Steppensees*. Wien: Verlag Molden. 175 pp.

Löffler, H. (ed.) (1979a). *Neusiedlersee. The Limnology of a Shallow Lake in Central Europe*; Monographiae Biologicae. The Hague: Junk. 543 pp.

Löffler, H. (1979b). The crustacean fauna of the *Phragmites* belt (Neusiedlersee). In *Neusiedlersee. The Limnology of a Shallow Lake in Central Europe*, ed. H. Löffler; Monographiae Biologicae, pp. 399–410. The Hague: Junk.

Lohammar, G. (1949). Über die Veränderung der Naturverhaltnisse gessenkter Seen. *Verhandlungen der Internationalen Vereinigung für Theoretische und Angewandte Limnologie*, **10**, 266–74.

Losos, B. & Heteša, J. (1971). Hydrobiological studies on the Lednické Rybníky Ponds. *Acta Scientiarum Naturalium Academiae Scientiarum Bohemoslovacae, Brno*, **5**(10), 1–54.

Louckes, O.L. & Watson, V. (1977). The use of models to study wetland regulation of nutrient loading to Lake Mendota. In *Wetlands Ecology, Values and Impacts*, ed. C.B. DeWitt & E. Soloway; Proceedings of the Waubesa Conference on Wetlands, June, 1977, Madison, Wisconsin, pp. 242–52. Madison: University of Wisconsin.

Loveless, A.R. (1960). The vegetation of Antigua, West Indies. *Journal of Ecology*, **48**, 495–527.

Lucas, G., Synge, H. & IUCN. (1978). *Plant Red Data Book*. Morges: IUCN. 540 pp.

Luft, G. (1993). Langfristige Veränderung der Bodensee-Wasserstände und mögliche Auswirkungen auf Erosion und Ufervegetation. In *Seeuferzerstörung und Seeuferrenaturierung in Mitteleuropa*, ed. W Ostendorp & P. Krumscheid-Plankert; Limnologie Aktuell, **5**, 61–76.

Lugo, A.E., Brown, S. & Brinson, M. (eds.) (1990). *Forested Wetlands*; Ecosystems of the World 15. Amsterdam, New York: Elsevier. 504 pp.

Lukina, E.V. (1972). Vodnaya i pribrezhno-vodnaya rastitel'nost' vodochranilishcha-okhladitelya. *Informatsionyi Bȳulleten, Biologiya Vnutrennȳkh Vod*, No. 15, 17–21.

Lundegårdh, H. (1951). *Leaf Analysis*. London: Hilger & Watts. 176 pp.

Lundegårdh-Ericson, C. (1972). Changes during four years in the aquatic macrovegetation in a flat in northern Stockholm Archipelago. *Svensk Botanika Tidskrifter*, **66**, 207–25.

Lundh, A. & Almerstrand, A. (1951*a*). Studies on the vegetation and hydrochemistry of Scanian Lakes I. Higher aquatic vegetation. *Svensk Botaniska Notiser* 1951, Suppl. 2, 141 pp.

Lundh, A. & Almerstrand, A. (1951*b*). Studies on the vegetation and hydrochemistry of Scanian Lakes III. Distribution of macrophytes and some algal groups. *Svensk Botaniska Notiser*, 1951, Suppl. 3, 138 pp.

Luther, H. (1949). Vorschlag zu einer ökologischen Grundeinteilung der Hydrophyten. *Acta Botanica Fennica*, **44**, 1–5.

Luther, H. & Rzóska, J. (1971). *Project Aqua. A Sourcebook of Aquatic Sites Proposed for Conservation*; International Biological Programme Handbook No. 21. Oxford: Blackwell Science Publishers 239 pp.

MacArthur, R.H. (1955). Fluctuations of animal populations and a measure of community stability. *Ecology*, **36**, 533–6.

MacFadyen, A. (1963). The contribution of the microfauna to total soil metabolism. In *Soil Organisms*, ed. J. Doeksen & J. Drift, pp. 3–17. Amsterdam: North-Holland Publishers.

Makepeace, R.J. (1976). The approval, efficiency and recommendations for use of aquatic herbicides. In *British Crop Protection Council Monograph No. 16*; Proceedings of the Symposium on Aquatic Herbicides, Oxford, pp. 38–45. London: British Crop Protection Council.

Mallik, A.U. & Wein, R.W. (1986). Response of *Typha* marsh community to draining, flooding and burning. *Canadian Journal of Botany*, **64**, 1236–43.

Malmer, M. (1962). Studies on mire vegetation in the Archean area of Southwestern Götland (South Sweden) I. Vegetation and habitat conditions on the Akhult Mire. II. Distribution and seasonal variation in elementary constituents on some mire sites. *Opera Botanica*, **7**(1), 1–322.

Mann, K.H. (1969). The dynamics of aquatic ecosystems. *Advances in Ecological Research*, **6**, 1–81.

Manny, B.A., Wetzel, R.G. & Johnson, W.C. (1975). Annual contribution of carbon, nitrogen and phosphorus by migrant Canada geese to a headwater lake. *Verhandlungen der Internationalen Vereinigung für Theoretische und Angewandte Limnologie*, **19**, 949–51.

Marcus, J.H., Sutcliffe, D.W. & Willoughby, L.G. (1978). Feeding and growth of *Asellus aquaticus* (Isopoda) on food items from the littoral of Windermere, including green leaves of *Elodea canadensis*. *Freshwater Biology*, **8**, 505–19.

Marker, A.F.H. & Westlake, D.F. (1980). Primary production: introduction. In *The Functioning of Freshwater Ecosystems*, ed. E.D. LeCren & R.H. Lowe-McConnell; International Biological Programme No. 22, pp. 141–6. Cambridge: Cambridge University Press.

Marshall, E.J.P. & Westlake, D.F. (1978). Recent studies on the role of aquatic macrophytes in their ecosystem. *Proceedings of the EWRS 5th Symposium on Aquatic Weeds*, 1978, 43–51.

Martin, N.A. (1972). Temperature fluctuations within English lowland ponds. *Hydrobiologia*, **40**, 455–69.

Marvan, P. & Sládeček, V. (1973). Main source of pollution of the Nesyt fishpond. In *Littoral of the Nesyt Fishpond*, ed. J. Květ; Studie Československé Akademie Věd, 1973, No. 15, pp. 121–4. Praha: Academia.

Mason, C.F. & Bryant, R.J. (1974). The structure and diversity of the animal communities in a Broadland reedswamp. *Journal of Zoology, London*, **172**, 289–302.

Mason, C.F. & Bryant, R.J. (1975). Production, nutrient content and decomposition of *Phragmites communis* Trin. and *Typha angustifolia* L. *Journal of Ecology*, **63**, 71–95.

Mathews, E. & Fung, R.E. (1987). Methane emission from natural wetlands: global distribution, area and environmental characteristics of sources. *Global Geochemical Cycles*, **1**, 61–86.

Mathews, C.P. & Kowalczewski, A. (1969). The disappearance of leaf litter and its contribution to production in the River Thames. *Journal of Ecology*, **57**, 543–52.

Mathews, C.P. & Westlake, D.F. (1969). Estimation of production by populations of higher plants subject to high mortality. *Oikos*, **21**, 156–60.

Mathiesen, H. (1970). Miljøaendringer og biologisk effekt i Søer. *Watten*, **2/70**, 149–73.

Mathiesen, H. (1971). Summer maxima of algae and eutrophication. *Mitteilungen der Internationalen Vereinigung für Theoretische und Angewandte Limnologie*, **19**, 161–81.

Mayer, A.M. & Gorham, E. (1951). The iron and manganese content of plants present in the natural vegetation of the English Lake District. *Annals of Botany*, **15**, 247–63.

McComb, A.J. & Lake, P.S. (1990). *Australian Wetlands*. North Ryde: Collins/Angus & Robertson. 258 pp.

McCormick, J. (1974). Ecology and the regulation of freshwater wetlands. In *Freshwater Wetlands. Ecological Processes and Management Potential*, ed. R.E. Good, D.F. Whigham, R.L. Simpson & C.G. Jackson Jr; Proceedings of Symposium on Freshwater Marshes: Present Status, Future Needs; New Brunswick, 1977, pp. 341–55. New York: Academic Press.

McGaha, Y.J. (1952). The limnological relations of insects to certain aquatic flowering plants. *Transactions of the American Microscopical Society*, **71**, 355–81.

McGaha, Y.J. (1954). Contribution to the biology of some Lepidoptera which feed on certain aquatic flowering plants. *Transactions of the American Microscopical Society*, **73**, 167–77.

McLusky, D.S. (1971). *Ecology of Estuaries*. London: Heinemann Educational Books. 144 pp.

McNaughton, S.J. (1966). Ecotype function in the *Typha* community-type. *Ecological Monographs*, **36**, 297–325.

McNaughton, S.J. (1973). Comparative photosynthesis of Quebec and California ecotypes of *Typha latifolia*. *Ecology*, **54**, 1260–70.

McNaughton, S.J. (1974a). Natural selection at the enzyme level. *American Midland Naturalist*, **108**, 616–24.

McNaughton, S.J. (1974b). Developmental control of net productivity in *Typha latifolia* ecotypes. *Ecology*, **55**, 854–9.

McNaughton, S.J. & Fullem, L.W. (1970). Photosynthesis and photorespiration in *Typha latifolia*. *Plant Physiology*, **45**, 703–7.

McRoy, C.P. & Barsdate, R.J. (1970). Phosphate absorption in eelgrass. *Limnology and Oceanography*, **15**, 6–13.

McRoy, C.P., Barsdate, R.J. & Nebert, M. (1972). Phosphate cycling in an eelgrass (*Zostera marina* L.) ecosystem. *Limnology and Oceanography*, **17**, 58–67.

Maltby, E., Hogan, D.V. & Oliver, G.A. (1995). Wetland soil hydrology and ecosystem functioning. In *Hydrology and Hydrochemistry of British Wetlands*, ed. J.M.R. Hughes & A.L. Heathwaite, pp. 325–62. London: Wiley.

Meeks, R.L. (1969). The effect of drawdown date on wetland plant succession. *Journal of Wildlife Management*, **33**, 817–21.

Meisel, K. & Hübschmann, A. von (1975). Zum Rückgang von Nass- und Feucht-biotopen im Emstal. *Natur und Landschaft*, **50**, 33–8.

Meisriemler, P. (1974). Produktionsbiologische und nahrungsbiologische Untersuchungen am Kaulbarsch (*Acerina cernua* L.) des Neusiedlersees. Dissertation, Universität Wien. 98 pp.

Meuche, A. (1939). Die fauna im Algenbewuchs. Nach Untersuchungen im Litoral ostholsteinischer Seen. *Archiv für Hydrobiologie*, **34**, 349–520.

Meybeck, M. (1976). Total mineral dissolved transport by world major rivers. *Hydrological Science Bulletin*, **21**, 265–84.

Meyer-Reil, L-A. (1971). Bacterial growth rates and biomass production. In *Microbial Ecology of a Brackish Water Environment*, ed. G. Rheinheimer; Ecological Studies 25, pp. 223–36. New York: Springer Verlag.

Meyers, S.P. (1971). Microbial studies in Barataria Bay. *Coastal Studies Bulletin*, **6**, 1–6.

Mikheev, P.V. & Prokhorova, K.P. (1952). *Rybnoe Naselenie Vodokhranilishcha i ego formirovanie*. Moskva: Pishchepromizdat. 85 pp.

Mikkelson, D.S. & Datta, S.K.D. (1991). Rice culture. In *Rice production*, ed. B.S. Luh, 2nd edn., pp. 103–86. New York: Van Nostrand Reinhold.

Milner, C. & Hughes, R.E. (1968). *Methods for the Measurement of the Primary Production of Grassland*; International Biological Programme Handbook No. 6. Oxford: Blackwell Science Publishers 70 pp.

Milwey, C.P. (ed.) (1970). *Eutrophication in Large Lakes and Impoundments*; Report of Uppsala Symposium, 1968. Paris: OECD. 560 pp.

Ministry of Agriculture, Fisheries and Food (UK) (1958). *Guidelines for the Use of Herbicides on Weeds in or near Watercourses and Lakes* (revised). London: MAFF. 52 pp.

Minshall, G.W. (1967). Role of allochthonous detritus in the trophic structure of a woodland springbrook community. *Ecology*, **48**, 139–49.

Mishchenko, A.I. (1940). *Nasekomȳe – Vrediteli Polevȳkh i Ovoshchnȳkh Kul'tur Dal'nego Vostoka*. (Insects that are Pests of Field and Vegetable Crops of the Far East.) Khabarovsk: Dal'nevostochnȳĭ NII Zemledeliya i Zhivotnobvodstva. 196 pp. (In Russian.)

Misra, R.D. (1938) Edaphic features in the distribution of aquatic plants in the English Lakes. *Journal of Ecology*, **26**, 411–52.

Mitchell, D.S. (1969). The ecology of vascular hydrophytes on Lake Kariba. *Hydrobiologia*, **34**, 448–64.

Mitchell, D.S. (1974). The effects of excessive aquatic plant populations. In *Aquatic Vegetation and its Use and Control. A Contribution to the International Hydrological Decade*, ed. D.S. Mitchell, pp. 50–6. Paris: UNESCO.

Mitchell, D.S. & Tur, N.M. (1975). The rate of growth of *Salvinia molesta* (*S. auriculata* auct.) in laboratory and natural conditions. *Journal of Applied Ecology*, **12**, 213–25.

Mitchell, G.C. (1969). Legal considerations of water uses. In *Saskatoon Wetlands Seminar*; Canadian Wildlife Service Report 6, pp. 21–4. Ottawa: Department of Indian Affairs and Northern Development.

Mitsch, V.I., Straškraba, M. & Jørgensen, S.E. (eds.) (1988). *Wetland Modelling*; Developments in Environmental Modelling 12. Amsterdam: Elsevier. 228 pp.

Mitsch, W.J. (ed.) (1994). *Global Wetlands: Old World and New*. Amsterdam: Elsevier. 992 pp.

Mitsch, W.J. & Gosselink, J.G. (1986). *Wetlands*. New York: Van Nostrand Reinhold. 540 pp.

Miyashita, K. (1955). Some considerations on the population fluctuations of the rice stem borer. *Bulletin of the National Institute of Agricultural Science, Tokyo, Series C*, **5**, 99–109. (In Japanese with English Summary.)

Miyashita, K. (1963). Outbreaks and population fluctuations of insects, with special reference to agricultural insect pests in Japan. *Bulletin of the National Institute of Agricultural Science, Tokyo, Ser. C*, **15**, 99–170.

Miyashita, K. (1971). Recent status of the rice stem borer, *Chilo suppressalis* Walker, in Japan. In *Proceedings of the Symposium on Rice Insects, 1971*, pp. 169–76. Tokyo: Tropical Agriculture Research Centre, Ministry of Agriculture and Forestry.

Miyawaki, A. (1951). Untersuchungen über die Pflanzengesellschaften auf den strohdächern. *Science Reports of the Yokahama National University, Sec. II*, No. 5, 16–33.

Miyawaki, A. & Okada, S. (1972). Pflanzensoziologische Untersuchungen über die Auen-Vegetation des Flusses Tama mit eine vergleichenden Betrachtung über die vegetation des Flusses Tona. *Vegetatio, den Haag*, **24**, 229–313.

Mochnacka-Ławacz, H. (1974*a*). Seasonal changes of *Phragmites communis* Trin. Part II *Polskie Archiwum Hydrobiologii*, **21**, 369–80.

Mochnacka-Ławacz, H. (1974*b*). The effects of mowing on the dynamics of quantity, biomass and mineral contents of reed (*Phragmites communis* Trin.) *Polskie Archiwum Hydrobiologii*, **21**, 381–6.

Mochnacka-Ławacz, H. (1975). Description of the common reed (*Phragmites communis* Trin.) against habitat conditions, and its role in the overgrowing of lakes. *Ekologia Polska*, **23**, 545–71.

Moizuk, G.A. & Livingston, R.B. (1966). Ecology of red maple (*Acer rubrum*) in a Massachusetts upland bog. *Ecology*, **47**, 948-50.

Monakov, A.V. (1969). The zooplankton and zoobenthos of the White Nile and adjoining waters of the Republic of the Sudan. *Hydrobiologia*, **33**, 161–85.

Monsi, M. & Saeki, T. (1953). Über den Lichtfaktor in den Pflanzengesellschaften und seine Bedeutung für die Stoffproduktion. *Japanese Journal of Botany*, **14**, 22–52.

Monteith, J.L. (1973). *Principles of Environmental Physics*. London: Arnold. 256 pp.

Monteith, J.L. (ed.) (1975–6). *Vegetation and the Atmosphere*, I *Principles*, II *Case Studies*. New York: Academic Press. 278 and 439 pp.

Mook, J.H. (1967). Habitat selection by *Lipara lucens* Mg. (Dipt. Chlorop.) and its survival value. *Archives Néerlandaises de Zoologie*, **17**, 469–549.

Mook, J.H. (1971a). Influence of environment on some insects attacking common reed (*Phragmites communis* Trin.). *Hidrobiologia, Bucureşti*, **12**, 305–12.

Mook, J.H. (1971b). Observations on the colonization of the new Ijsselmeer-Polders by animals. *Miscellaneous Papers – Landbouwhogeschool, Wageningen*, **8**, 13–31.

Mook, J.H. (1971c). Phytyophagous insects on reed and willows. In *Institutes of the Royal Netherlands Academy of Arts and Sciences Progress Report, 1971*, ed. W.H. Van Dobben & J.W. Woldendorf: Verhandlingen der Koninklijke Nederlanse Akademie van Wetenschappen, Afd. Naturkunde, Tweede Reeks, **61**(3), (1972), 87–9.

Mook, J.H. & Toorn, J. van der (1974). Experiment on the development of reed vegetation in the Zuidflevoland polder. *Progress Report of the Institute of Ecological Research*, 1974, 11–15.

Moore, J.J. (1962). The Braun-Blanquet System: a reassessment. *Journal of Ecology*, **50**, 761–9.

Mordukhai-Boltovskoi, F.D. (1974). Fauna bespozvonochnȳkh pribrezhnoĭ zonȳ Rȳbinskogo vodokhranilishcha: (Obshchiĭ obzor). (Invertebrate fauna of the inshore zone of Rybinsk reservoir.) *Trudȳ Darvinskogo Gosudarstvennogo Zapovednika*, **12**, 158–95. (In Russian.)

Mordukhai-Boltovskoi, F.D., Mordukhai-Boltovskaya, F.D. & Yanovskaya, G. Ya. (1958). Fauna pribrezhnoi zonȳ Rȳbinskogo vodokhranilishcha. (Fauna of the littoral region of the Rybinskoe reservoir.) *Trudȳ Biologicheskoĭ Stancii 'Borok'*, **3**, 142–94. (In Russian.)

Morgan, N.C. (1972). Problems of the conservation of freshwater ecosystems. In *Conservation and Productivity of Natural Waters*, ed. R.W. Edwards & D.J. Garrod; Symposium of the Zoological Society of London No. 29, pp. 135–54.

Moriarty, Ch.M. & Moriarty, D.J.W. (1973). Quantitative estimation of the daily ingestion of phytoplankton by *Tilapia nilotica* and *Haplochromis nigripennis* in Lake George, Uganda. *Journal of Zoology, London*, **171**, 15–23.

Moriarty, D.J.W. (1973). The physiology of digestion of blue-green algae in the cichlid fish, *Tilapia nilotica*. *Journal of Zoology, London*, **171**, 25–39.

Moriarty, D.J.W., Darlington, J.P.E.C., Dunn, I.G., Moriarty, C.M. & Terlin, M.P. (1973). Feeding and grazing in Lake George, Uganda. *Proceedings of the Royal Society (London), Ser. B*, **184**, 299–319.

Morowitz, H.J. (1974). The physical foundations of global ecological processes. *Proceedings of the First International Congress of Ecology, The Hague*, 14–5.

Mortimer, C.H. (1941). The exchange of dissolved substances between mud and water in lakes I and II. *Journal of Ecology*, **29**, 280–329.

Moshiri, G.A. (ed.) (1994). *Constructed Wetlands for Water Quality Improvement*. Boca Raton, Florida: CRC Press/Lewis Publishers. 656 pp.

Moss, B., Leah, R.T. & Forrest, D.E. (1978). Ecosystem experimentation in the management of a system of shallow lakes. *Verhandlungen der Internationalen Vereinigung für Theoretische und Angewandte Limnologie*, **20**, 649–53.

Mückenhausen, E. (1959). *Die wichtigsten Böden der Bundesrepublik Deutschland, dargestellt an 60 farbigen Bodenprofilen. A2*. Frankfurt am Main: Commentator. 146 pp.

Müller, Th. (1967). *Verzeichnis der Naturschutz- und Landschaftschutz-gebiete des Landes Baden-Württemberg, 2 Aufl*. Ludwigsburg: Landesstelle für Naturschutz und Landschaftschutz Pflege 219 pp.

Müller-Liebenau, I. (1956). Die Besiedelung der *Potamogeton*-Zone ostholsteinischer Seen. *Archiv für Hydrobiologie*, **52**, 470–606.

Müller-Stoll, W.R. (1938). Wasserhaushaltsfragen bei Sumpf- und emersum Wasserpflanzen. *Berichte der Deutschen Botanischen Gessellschaft*, **56**, 355–67.

Mulligan, H.F. & Baranowski, A. (1969). Growth of phytoplankton and vascular aquatic plants at different nutrient levels. *Verhandlungen der Internationalen Vereinigung für Theoretische und Angewandte Limnologie*, **17**, 808–10.

Muthuri, F.M., Jones, M.B. & Imbamba, S.K. (1989). The primary productivity of papyrus (*Cyperus papyrus*) in a tropical swamp: Lake Naivasha, Kenya. *Biomass*, **18**, 1–14.

Naiman, R.J. & Decamps, H. (eds.) (1993). *The Ecology and Management of Aquatic-terrestrial Ecotones*, MAB Series, 4. Paris: UNESCO & Parthenon Publishing Group. 315 pp.

National Academy of Sciences, USA. (1969). *Eutrophication, Causes, Consequences, Correctives* – Proceedings of a Symposium, Madison, 1967. Washington DC: National Academy of Sciences. 661 pp.

National Academy of Sciences, USA. (1976). *Making Aquatic Weeds Useful: some Perspectives for Developing Countries*. Washington DC: National Academy of Sciences. 175 pp.

Nature Conservancy Council (later English Nature). (1975 On). *Annual Reports*. London: HMSO.

Naumann, E. (1919). Nagra synpunkter angaende planktons ökologie, med Sarskild hansir till phytoplankton. *Svensk Botanisk Tidskrift*, **13**, 129–63.

Naumann, E. (1932). *Grundzüge der regionalen Limnologie*; Die Binnengewässer, 11. Stuttgart: Schweizerbart'sche Verlag. 176 pp.

Nauwerck, A. (1980). Phytoplankton – Patterns of biomass change. In *The Functioning of Freshwater Ecosystems*; International Biological Programme 22, 200–3. Cambridge: Cambridge University Press.

Neagu-Godeanu, M. Hnidei, L. & Constancinescu, E. (1968). Beitrag zur Kenntnis des Mineralisationsprozesses der Überschwemmungs-gebiete des Donaudeltas. *Traveau du Museum d'Histoire Naturelle, Bukarest*, **8**, 321–2.

Nelson, D.J., Kaye, S.V. & Booth, R.S. (1972). Radionuclides in river systems. In *River Ecology and Man*, ed. R.T. Oglesby, C.A. Carlson & J.A. McCann, pp. 367–87. New York: Academic Press.

Neuhaus, D., Kühl, J-G., Kohl, P. & Börner, T. (1993). Investigation on the genetic diversity of *Phragmites* stands using genomic fingerprinting. *Aquatic Botany*, **45**, 357–64.

Neuhäusl, R. (1965). Vegetation der Röhrichte und der sublitoralen

Magnocariceten im Wittingauer Becken. In *Synökologische Studien über Rörhrichte, Wiesen und Auenwälder*, ed. R Neuhäusl, J. Moravec & Z. Neuhäuslová-Novotná; Vegetace ČSSR, **A1**, pp. 11–177.

Newbould, C. (1975). Herbicides in aquatic systems. *Biological Conservation*, **7**, 97–118.

Newbould, C., Honnor, J. & Buckley, K. (1989). *Nature Conservation & the Management of Drainage Channels*. Peterborough: Nature Conservancy Council. 108 pp.

Newbould, C., Purselove, J. & Holmes, N.T.H. (1983). *Nature Conservation and River Engineering*. Peterborough: Nature Conservancy Council. 36 pp.

Newman, R.M. (1991). Herbivory and detritivory on freshwater macrophytes by invertebrates: a review. *Journal of the North American Benthological Society*, **10**, 89–114.

Nichols, D.S. & Keeney, D.R. (1973). Nitrogen and phosphorus release from decaying water milfoil. *Hydrobiologia*, **42**, 509–25.

Nie, H.W. de (1987). The decrease in aquatic vegetation in Europe and its consequences for fish populations. *European Inland Fisheries Advisory Commission, Occasional Paper* No. 19. Rome: FA. 52 pp.

Niemann, E. (1973). Grundwasser und Vegetationsgefüge. Grundwasserdauerlinien – Koinzidenmethode und Dauerlinien-Variabilitätsdiagramm im Rahmen ökologischer Untersuchungen an grundwasserbeeinflussten Vegetationseinheiten. *Nova Acta Leopoldina, Suppl.* 6, **38**, 1–172.

Niemann, E. & Wegener, U. (1976). Verminderung des Stickstoff-und Phosphor-eintrages in wasserwirtschaftliche Speicher mit Hilfe nitrophiler Uferstauden- und Verlandungs-vegetation ('Nitrophyten-Methode'). *Acta Hydrochemica et Hydrobiologica*, **4**, 269–75.

Niering, W.A. (1985). *Wetlands; Audubon Society Nature Guide*. New York: Knopf. 640 pp.

Nikolskiĭ, G.V. (1971). *Chastnaya Ikhtiologiya* (3rd edn.). Moskva: Vȳsshaya Shkola. 471 pp.

Nishida, T. & Torii, T. (eds.) (1972). *A Handbook of Field Methods for Research on Rice Stem-Borers and Their Natural Enemies*; International Biological Programme Handbook No. 14. Oxford: Blackwell Science Publishers. 144 pp.

Nixon, S. (1980). Between coastal marshes and coastal waters – a review of twenty years of speculation and research on the role of salt marshes in estuarine productivity and water chemistry. In *Estuarine and Wetland Processes*, ed. P. Hamilton & K. MacDonald, pp. 437–525. New York: Plenum Publishing Corporation.

Nowak, E. (1971). *The Range Expansion of Animals and its Causes*; Zeszyty naukowe PAN No. 3. Warszawa: PAN. 256 pp.

Odum, E.P. (1961). The role of tidal marshes in estuarine production. *New York State Conserv.*, **3**, 12–16.

Odum, E.P. (1971). *Fundamentals of Ecology* (3rd edn.). Philadelphia: Saunders Co. 574 pp.

Odum, E.P. & Cruz, A.A. de la (1967). Particulate organic detritus in a Georgia salt-marsh–estuarine ecosystem. In *Estuaries*, ed. G.H. Lauff; Publications of the American Association for the Advancement of Science 83, pp. 383–8. Washington: AAAS.

Odum, H.P., Burkholder, P.R. & Rivero, J. (1959). Measurement of productivity of turtle-grass reefs in Bahia Fosforescente of Southern Puerto Rico.

Publications of the Institute of Marine Science, University of Texas, **6**, 159–70.

Odum, H.T. (1957). Trophic structure and productivity of Silver Springs, Florida. *Ecological Monographs*, **27**, 55–112.

Odum, W.E. (1971). Pathways of energy flow in a south Florida estuary. PhD Dissertation, University of Miami Sea Grass Programme, Technical Bulletin No. 7. Miami: University of Miami. 162 pp.

Odum, W.E., Zeiman, J.C. & Heald, E. (1973). The importance of vascular plant detritus to estuaries. In *Proceedings of the 2nd Coastal Marsh and Estuary Symposium, Baton Rouge*, ed. R.H. Chabreck, pp. 91–135. Baton Rouge: Louisiana State University.

Odzuck, W. (1978). Anthropogene Veränderungen eines Moorökosystems durch Erholungssuchende. *Natur und Landschaft*, **53**, 192–4.

Ogawa, H., Yoda, R. & Kira, T. (1961). A preliminary survey on the vegetation of Thailand. *Nature and Life of SE Asia*, **1**, 21–157.

Ohle, W. (1965). Nährstoffanreicherung durch Düngemittel und Meliorationen. *Münchener Beiträge*, **12**, 54–83.

Oláh, J. (1969). A quantitative study of the saprophytic and total bacterioplankton in the open water and the littoral zone of Lake Balaton in 1968. *Annales Instituti Biologici, Tihany*, **36**, 197–212.

Olney, P.J.S. (ed.) (1965). *Proceedings of Project MAR – The Conservation and Management of Temperate Marshes, Bogs and other Wetlands*, Vol. II; *List of European and North African Wetlands of International Importance*; Proceedings of Conference Organized by ICUN, ICBP and IBP, Le Saintes-Maries-de-la-Mer, November 1962; IUCN Publications (NS) 5. Morges: IUCN. 102 pp.

Olsen, S. (1950). Aquatic plants and hydrospheric factors I. Aquatic plants in S.W. Jutland, Denmark. II. The hydrospheric types. *Svensk Botanisk Tidskrift*, **44**, 1–34; 332–72.

Olsen, S. (1964). Vegetationsaendringer i Lyngby S. Bidrag til analyse af kultur-pavirkninger pa vand og sumpplantvegetation. *Svensk Botanisk Tidskrift*, **59**, 273–300.

Ondok, J.P. (1968). Analyse des Blattwachstums als Methode zur Bestimmung des Massstabes der ontogenetischen Entwicklung. *Studia Biophysica (Berlin)*, **11**, 161–8.

Ondok, J.P. (1971*a*). Indirect estimation of primary values used in growth analysis. In *Plant Photosynthetic Production. Manual of Methods*, ed. Z. Šesták, J. Čatský & P.G. Jarvis, pp. 412–66. The Hague: W. Junk.

Ondok, J.P. (1971*b*). Horizontal structure of some macrophyte stands and its production aspects. *Hidrobiologia, Bucureşti*, **12**, 47–56.

Ondok, J.P. (1973*a*). Average shoot biomass in monospecific stands of the Opatovicý fishpond. In *Ecosystem Study on Wetland Biome in Czechoslovakia*, ed. S. Hejný, Czechoslovak IBP-PT/PP Report No. 3, pp. 83–6. Třeboň: ČSAV.

Ondok, J.P. (1973*b*). Interception of photosynthetically active radiation by a *Phragmites* stand. In *Ecosystem Study on Wetland Biome in Czechoslovakia*, ed. S. Hejný, Czechoslovak IBP-PT/PP Report No. 3, pp. 133–42. Třeboň: ČSAV.

Ondok, J.P. (1973*c*). Photosynthetically active radiation in a stand of *Phragmites communis* Trin. I. Distribution of irradiance and foliage structure. *Photosynthetica*, **7**, 8–17.

Ondok, J.P. (1975). Photosynthetically active radiation in a stand of *Phragmites communis* Trin. IV. Stochastic model. *Photosynthetica*, **9**, 201–10.
Ondok, J.P. (1977). Regime of global and photosynthetically active radiation in helophyte stands. In *Littoral of the Nesyt Fishpond*, ed. J. Květ; Studie Československa Academie Věd, 1973, No. 15, pp. 121–4. Praha: Academia.
Ondok, J.P. (1978*a*). Radiation climate in fishpond littoral plant communities. In *Pond Littoral Ecosystems: Structure and Functioning*, ed. D. Dykyjová & J. Květ; Ecological Studies 28, pp. 113–25. Berlin: Springer-Verlag.
Ondok, J.P. (1978*b*). Estimation of seasonal growth of underground biomass. In *Pond Littoral Ecosystems: Structure and Functioning*, ed. D. Dykyjová & J. Květ; Ecological Studies 28, pp. 193–97. Berlin: Springer-Verlag.
Ondok, J.P. (1984). Simulation of stand geometry in photosynthetic models based on hemispherical photography. *Photosynthetica*, **18**, 231–9.
Ondok, J.P. (1990). Modeling ecological processes in wetlands. In *Wetlands and Shallow Continental Water Bodies*, **1**, ed. B.C. Patten, pp. 659–89. The Hague: SPB Academic Publishers.
Ondok, J.P. & Dykyjová, D. (1973). Assessment of shoot biomass of dominant reed-beds in Třeboň basin. Methodical aspects. In *Ecosystem Study on Wetland Biome in Czechoslovakia*, ed. S. Hejný, Czechoslovak IBP-PT/PP Report No. 3, pp. 79–85. Třeboň: ČSAV.
Ondok, J.P. & Gloser, J. (1978). Modeling of photosynthetic production in littoral helophyte stands. In *Pond Littoral Ecosystems: Structure and Functioning*, ed. D. Dykyjová & J. Květ; Ecological Studies 28, pp. 234–45. Berlin: Springer-Verlag.
Ondok, J.P. & Květ, J. (1978). Selection of sampling areas in assessment of production. In *Pond Littoral Ecosystems: Structure and Functioning*, ed. D. Dykyjová & J. Květ; Ecological Studies 28, pp. 163–73. Berlin: Springer-Verlag.
Opatrný, E. (1968). Poznámka k biometrice a bionomii skokana štíhlého, *Rana dalmatina* Bonaparte, 1839. (Bemerkung zur Biometrik und Bionomie des Springfrosches, *R. dalmatina* Bonaparte, 1839.) *Acta Universitatis Palackianae Olomucensis – Facultas Rerum Naturalium*, **28**, 151–4. (In Czech with German summary.)
Opatrný, E. (1973). Die Waldeidechse *Lacerta vivipara* Jacquin, 1787 auf tiefliegendem Standort beim Fluss Morava. *Acta Universitatis Palackianae Olomucencis – Facultas Rerum Naturalium*, **43**, 281–96.
Ostendorp, W. (1989). Die-back of reeds in Europe – A critical review of literature. *Aquatic Botany*, **35**, 5–26.
Ostendorp, W. (1990). Ist die Seeneutrophierung am Schilfsterben schuld? In *Ökologie, Gefährdung, und Schutz von Röhrichtpflanzen*, ed. H. Sukopp & M. Krauss; Landschaftentwicklung u. Umweltforschung, **71**, pp. 121–40. Berlin: Technische Universität.
Ostendorp, W. (1995). Effect of management on the mechanical stability of lakeside reeds in Lake Constance – Untersee. *Acta Oecologia*, **16**, 277–94.
Ostendorp, W. & Krumscheid-Plankert, P. (eds.) (1990). *Seenuferzerstörung und Seeuferrenaturierung in Mitteleuropa*; Limnologie Aktuell, **5**. Stuttgart: G. Fischer. 263 pp.
Otis, C.H. (1914). The transpiration of emersed water plants, its measurements and relationships. *Botanical Gazette*, **58**, 457–94.
Ozimek, T. (1978). Effect of municipal sewage on the submerged macrophytes of a lake littoral. *Ekologia Polska*, **26**, 13–39.
Ozimek, T. & Balcerzak, D. (1976). Macrophytes. In *Selected Problems of Lake*

Littoral Ecology, ed. E. Pieczyńska, pp. 33–53. Warszawa: Wyd. Uniwersytetu Warszawskiego.

Ozimek, T. & Klekot, L. (1979). *Glyceria maxima* (Hartm.) Holmb. in ponds supplied with post-sewage water. *Aquatic Botany*, **7**, 223–31.

Paerl, H.W. (1973). Detritus in Lake Tahoe: structural modification by attached microflora. *Science*, **180**, 496–8.

Palmgren, P. (1936). Über die Vogelfauna der Binnengewässer Alands. *Acta zoologica Fennica*, **17**, 1–59.

PANS (eds.) (1976). *Pest Control in Rice*; PANS Manual No. 3 (3rd edn.). London: Tropical Pesticides Research Headquarters and Information Unit. 270 pp.

Parker, E.D. (1973). Ecological comparisons of thermally affected aquatic environments. *Water Pollution Control Federation Journal*, **45**, 726–33.

Parkinson, D. (1967). The root region. In *Soil Biology*, ed. A. Burgess & F. Raw, pp. 449–79. London: Academic Press.

Pathak, M.D. (1968). Ecology of common insect pests of rice. *Annual Review of Entomology*, **13**, 257–94.

Patrick, S., Battarbee, R.W. & Jenkins, A. (1995). Overview and assessment. In *UK Acid Waters Monitoring Network: The First Five Years. Analysis and Interpretation of Results, April 1988–March 1993*, ed. S. Patrick, D.T. Montieth & A. Jenkins, pp. 287–312. London: ENSIS Publ. 320 pp.

Patrick, W.H. Jr (1978). Critique of measurement and prediction of anaerobiosis in soils. In *Nitrogen in the Environment, I, Nitrogen Behaviour in Field Soil*, ed. D.R. Nielsen & J.G. McDonald, pp. 449–57. London: Academic Press.

Patrick, W.H. Jr & Delaune, H.D. (1972). Characterization of the oxidized and reduced zones in flooded soil. *Proceedings of the Soil Society of America*, **36**, 573–6.

Patrick, W.H. Jr & Khalid, R.A. (1974). Phosphate release and absorption by soils and sediments: effect of aerobic and anaerobic condition. *Science*, **186**, 53–5.

Patrick, W.H. Jr & Mikkelsen, D.S. (1971). Plant nutrient behaviour in flooded soil. In *Fertilizer Technology and Use*, ed. R.A. Olsen (2nd edn.), pp. 187–215. Madison: Soil Science of America.

Patriquin, D. & Reddy, C. (1978). Nitrogenase activity (acetylene reduction) in a Nova Scotia salt marsh: its association with angiosperms and the influence of some edaphic factors. *Aquatic Botany*, **4**, 227–44.

Patriquin, D. & Knowles, R. (1972). Nitrogen fixation in the microsphere of marine organisms. *Marine Biology*, **16**, 49–58.

Patten, B.C. *et al.* (ed.) (1990 and 1994). *Wetlands and Shallow Continental Water Bodies*, 1, *Natural and Human Relationships*; 2, *Case Studies*. The Hague: SPB Academic Publishers. 759 and 732 pp.

Patterson, D.T. & Duke, S.O. (1979). Effect of growth irradiance on the maximum photosynthetic capacity of water hyacinth. *Eichhornia crassipes* (Mart.) Solms]. *Plant Cell Physiology*, **20**, 177–84.

Payne, K. (1972). A survey of the *Spartina*-feeding insects in Poole Harbour, Dorset. *Entomologist's Monthly*, **108** (1295–1297): 66–79.

Pazourek, J. (1973). The density of stomata in leaves of different ecotypes of *Phragmites communis. Folia Geobotanica and Phytotaxonomica, Praha*, **8**, 15–21.

Pearcy, R.W., Berry, J.A. & Bartholomew, B. (1974). Field photosynthetic performance and leaf temperatures of *Phragmites communis* under summer conditions in Death Valley, California. *Photosynthetica*, **8**, 104–8.

Pearsall, W.H. (1938). The soil complex in relation to plant communities I. Oxidation-reduction potentials in soils. *Journal of Ecology*, **26**, 180–93.

Pearsall, W.H. & Mortimer, C.H. (1939). Oxidation–reduction potentials in waterlogged soils, natural waters and muds. *Journal of Ecology*, **27**, 483–501.

Pelikán, J. (1973). Mammals in reed stands of the Nesyt fishpond. In *Littoral of the Nesyt Fishpond*, ed. J. Květ; Studie Československé Akademie Věd, 1973, No. 15, pp. 117–20. Praha: Academia.

Pelikán, J. (1974). Dynamics and energetics of a reed swamp population of *Arvicola terrestris* (Linn.). *Zoologické Listy, Praha*, **23**, 321–34.

Pelikán, J. (1975). Mammals of Nesyt fishpond, their ecology and production. *Acta Scientiarum Naturalium Academiae Scientiarum Bohemoslovacae, Brno*, **9**(12), 1–15.

Pelikán, J. (1978). Mammals in the reedswamp ecosystem. In *Pond Littoral Ecosystems: Structure and Functioning*, ed. D. Dykyjová & J. Květ; Ecological Studies 28, pp. 357–65. Berlin: Springer-Verlag.

Pelikán, J., Květ, J. & Úlehlová, B. (1973). Principal constituents and relationships in the reed-belt ecosystem at the Nesyt fishpond. In *Littoral of the Nesyt Fishpond*, ed. J. Květ; Studie Československé Akademie Věd, 1973, No. 15, pp. 17–23. Praha: Academia.

Pelikán, J., Svoboda, J. & Květ, J. (1970). On some relations between the production of *Typha latifolia* and a muskrat population. *Zoologické Listy, Praha*, **19**(4), 303–20.

Penfound, W.T. (1952). Southern swamps and marshes. *Botanical Reviews*, **18**, 413–46.

Penfound, W.T. & Earle, T.T. (1948). The biology of the water hyacinth. *Ecological Monographs*, **18**, 447–72.

Penman, H.L. (1948). Natural evaporation from open water, bare soil and grass. *Proceedings of the Royal Society (London), Ser. A*, **193**, 120–45.

Penman, H.L. (1963). *Vegetation and Hydrology*; Commonwealth Bureau of Soil Science, Technical Communication 53, 124 pp.

Pénzes, A. (1960). Über die Morphologie, Dynamik und zönologische Rolle der Sprosskolonienbildenden Pflanzen (Polycormone). *Fragmenta Floristica et Geobotanica*, **6**(4), 505–15.

Perdue, R.K. (1958). *Arundo donax* – source of musical reeds and industrial cellulose. *Economic Botany*, **12**, 368–404.

Perkins, B.D. & Maddox, D.M. (1976). Host specificity of *Neochetina bruchii* Hustache (Coleoptera: Curculionidae) – a biological control agent for water-hyacinth. *Journal of Aquatic Plant Management*, **14**, 59–64.

Perkins, B.P. (1978). Approaches in biological control of aquatic weeds. *Proceedings of the EWRS 5th Symposium on Aquatic Weeds, Amsterdam*, 1978, 9–15.

Perring, F.H. (1976). *Wetland Flora in Danger*; Conservation Review, SPNR No. 13, 1–4. Lincoln: Society for the Promotion of Nature Conservancy.

Perttula, U. (1952). Über die Einwirkung der Abwässer auf die Vegetation und Flora der Gewässer bei Valkaakoski in Mittelfinnland. *Annales Societatis Zoologicae Botanicae Fennicae Vanamo*, **7**, 106–13.

Petersen, A. (1954). *Die Gräser als Kulturpflanzen und Unkräuter auf Wiese, Weide und Acker* (4th edn., 1992, 7th edn.). Berlin: Akademie Verlag. 275 pp.

Petersen, R.C. & Cummins, K.W. (1974). Leaf processing in a woodland stream. *Freshwater Biology*, **4**, 343–68.

Petr, T. (1968). Population changes in aquatic invertebrates living on two water plants in a tropical man-made lake. *Hydrobiologia*, **32**, 449–85.

Petr, T. (1973). Some factors limiting the distribution of *Povilla adjusta* Navas (Ephemeroptera, Polymitarcidae) in African lakes. In *Proceedings of the 1st International Conference on Ephemeroptera*, ed. W.L. Peters & J.G. Peters, Florida, 1970, pp. 223–30. Leiden: E.J. Brill.

Petrov, M.P. (1966–67). *Pustyni Tsentral'noi Azii*, **1** and **2**. Moskva/Leningrad: Nauka. 271 and 286 pp.

Pfadenhauer, J. & Klötzli, F. (1996). Restoration experiments in Middle European wet terrestrial ecosystems: an overview. *Vegetatio*, **126**, 101–15.

Phillips, G.L., Eminson, D. & Moss, B. (1978). A mechanism to account for macrophyte decline in progressively eutrophicated freshwaters. *Aquatic Botany*, **4**, 103–26.

Piasecki, J. (1967). Wpływ roślinności wodnej na intensywność parowania z powierzchni zbiorników wodnych. (The influence of water vegetation upon the intensity of evaporation from the surface of water reservoirs.) *Zeszyty Naukowe Wyższej Szkoly Akademii Rolniczej we Wrocławiu, 73, Melioracja*, **12**, 123–34. (In Polish with English summary.)

Pieczyńska, E. (1970a). Periphyton in the trophic structure of freshwater ecosystems. *Polskie Archiwum Hydrobiologii*, **17**, 141–7.

Pieczyńska, E. (1970b). Periphyton as food of aquatic animals (methods of investigation). *Wiadomosci ekologiczne-Metodyka*, **16**, 133–44.

Pieczyńska, E. (1972a). Ecology of the eulittoral zone of lakes. *Ekologia Polska*, **20**, 637–732.

Pieczyńska, E. (1972b). Production and decomposition in the eulittoral of lakes. In *Productivity Problems of Freshwaters*, ed. Z. Kajak & A. Hillbricht-Ilkovska; Proceedings of IBP-UNESCO Symposium on Productivity Problems of Freshwaters, Kazimierz Dolny, May 1970, pp. 615–35. Warszawa: Polish Science Publishers.

Pieczyńska, E. (1973). Experimentally increased fish stock in the pond-type lake Warniak. XI. Food resources and availability of the eulittoral zone for fish. *Ekologia Polska*, **21**, 583–93.

Pieczyńska, E. (ed.) (1976). *Selected Problems of Lake Littoral Ecology*. Warszawa: Wydawnictwa Uniwersytetu Warswzawskiego. 238 pp.

Pieczyńska, E. (1986). Sources and fate of detritus in the shore zones of lakes. *Aquatic Botany*, **25**, 153–66.

Pieczyńska, E., Balcerzak, D., Kolodziejczyk, A., Olszewski, Z. & Rybak, J.I. (1984). Detritus in the littoral of several Masurian lakes (sources and fates). *Ekologia Polska*, **32**, 387–440.

Pieczyńska, E. & Ozimek, T. (1976). Ecological significance of lake macrophytes. *International Journal of Environmental Science*, **2**, 115–28.

Pieczyńska, E., Ozimek, T. & Rybak, J.I. (1988). Long-term changes in littoral habitats and communities in Lake Mikołajskie (Poland). *Internationale Revue der Gesamten Hydrobiologie u. Hydrographie*, **73**, 361–78.

Pieczyńska, E. & Spodniewska, I. (1963). Occurrence and colonization of periphyton organisms in accordance with the type of substrate. *Ekologia Polska Seria A*, **11**, 533–45.

Pieczyńska, E. & Straškraba, M. (1969). Field experiments on the effect of light conditions in *Phragmites* stands on the production of littoral algae. *Bulletin Academie Polonaise des Sciences, Class II Série des Sciences Biologiques*, **17**, 43–6.

Pier, A., Dienst, M. & Stark, H. (1993). Dynamics of reed belts at Lake

Constance (Untersee and Überlingen See) from 1984 to 1993. In *Seenuferzerstörung und Seeuferrenaturierung in Mitteleuropa*, ed. W. Ostendorp & P. Krumscheid-Plankert; Limnologie Aktuell, **5**, 141–8.

Pieterse, A.H. (1978). The Water Hyacinth (*Eichhornia crassipes*) – a review. *Abstracts on Tropical Agriculture (Royal Tropical Institute, Amsterdam)*, **4**(2), 9–42.

Pieterse, A.H. & Murphy, K.J. (eds.) (1993). *Aquatic Weeds: The Ecology and Management of Nuisance Aquatic Vegetation*. Oxford: Oxford University Press. 593 pp.

Pigott, C.D. (1969). Influence of mineral nutrition on the zonation of flowering plants in coastal salt-marshes. In *Ecological Aspects of the Mineral Nutrition of Plants*, ed. I.H. Rorison; Symposium of the British Ecological Society No. 9, pp. 25–35. Oxford: BES.

Pintera, A. (1971). Some observations on the mealy plum aphid, *Hyalopterus pruni*, occurring on reeds. *Hidrobiologia, Bucureşti*, **12**, 293–6.

Pintera, A. (1973). Seasonal dynamics of the mealy aphid population on reeds at the Opatovický fishpond. In *Ecosystem Study on Wetland Biome in Czechoslovakia*, ed. S. Hejný. Czechoslovak IBP-PT/PP Report No. 3, pp. 231–2. Třeboň: ČSAV.

Pirie, N.W. (1970). Weeds are not all bad. *Ceres (FAO Review)*, **3**(4), 32–4.

Planter, M. (1970*a*). Physico-chemical properties of the water of reedbelts in Mikołajskie, Taltowisko and Śniardwy lakes. *Polskie Archiwum Hydrobiologii*, **17**, 337–56.

Planter, M. (1970*b*). Elution of mineral components out of dead reed *Phragmites communis* Trin. *Polskie Archiwum Hydrobiologii*, **17**, 357–62.

Planter, M. (1973). Physical and chemical conditions in the helophyte zone of the lake littoral. *Polskie Archiwum Hydrobiologii*, **20**, 1–7.

Pokorný, V. (1971). Flies of the genus *Lipara* Meigen on common reed. *Hidrobiologia, Bucureşti*, **12**, 287–92.

Polisini, J.M., Boyd, C.E. & Digeon, D. (1970). Nutrient limiting factors in an oligotrophic South Carolina pond. *Oikos*, **21**, 344–7.

Polunin, N.V.C. (1982*a*). Processes contributing to the decay of reed (*Phragmites australis*) litter in fresh water. *Archiv für Hydrobiologie*, **94**, 182–209.

Polunin, N.V.C. (1982*b*). Process of decay of reed (*Phragmites australis*) litter in fresh water. In *Wetlands, Ecology and Management*, ed. B. Gopal, R.E. Turner, R.G. Wetzel & D.F. Whigham, pp. 293–304. Jaipur: Michael Paul Lucknow Publishing House.

Polunin, N.V.C. (1984). The decomposition of emergent macrophytes in fresh water. *Advances in Ecological Research*, **14**, 115–66.

Pomeroy, L.R. (1970). The strategy of mineral cycling. *Annual Review of Ecology and Systematics*, **1**, 171–90.

Pomeroy, L.R. & Wiegert, R.O. (1981). *The Ecology of Salt Marsh*; Ecological Studies No. 38. Heidelberg: Springer Verlag. 271 pp.

Ponnamperuma, F.N. (1972). The chemistry of submerged soils. *Advances in Agronomy*, **8**, 29–95.

Popp, N. (1959). Conditiile geochimice ale stufaliiler (in curs de amenajare) din Delta Dunarii. *Celuloze si Hirtie*, **8**(3), 69–77.

Poore, M.E.D. (1955). The use of phytosociological methods in ecological investigations. *Journal of Ecology*, **43**, 226–44.

Poštolková, M. (1967). Comparison of the zooplankton amount and primary production of the fenced and unfenced littoral regions of Smyslov Pond. In *Contributions to the Productivity of the Littoral Region of Ponds and Pools*, ed. M. Straškraba, J. Kořínková & M. Poštolková; Rozpravy ČSAV, Řada Matematických a Přírodnich Věd, **77**(11), pp. 63–79. Praha: ČSAV.

Potzger, J.E. & Engel, van W.A. (1942). Study of the rooted aquatic vegetation of Weber Lake, Vilas County, Wisconsin, *Transactions of the Wisconsin Academy of Science, Arts & Letters*, **34**, 149–61.

Prejs, A. (1973). Experimentally increased fish stock in the pond-type lake Warniak IV. Feeding of introduced and autochthonous non-predatory fish. *Ekologia Polska*, **21**, 466–505.

Prejs, A. (1977). The Nematodes of the root region of aquatic macrophytes, with special consideration of nematode groupings penetrating the tissues of roots and rhizomes. *Ekologia Polska*, **25**, 5–20.

Prejs, R. & Wiktorzak, M. (1976). The fauna of the root region of macrophytes. In *Selected Problems of Lake Littoral Ecology*, ed. E. Pieczyńska, pp. 145–53. Warszawa: Wydawnictwo Uniwersytetu Warszawskiego.

Prentki, R.T., Gustavson, T.D. & Adams, M.S. (1978). Nutrient movement in lakeshore marshes. In *Freshwater Wetlands, Ecological Processes and Management Potential*, ed. R.E. Good, D.F. Whigham & R.L. Simpson; Proceedings of Symposium on Freshwater Marshes: Present Status, Future Needs, New Brunswick, 1977, pp. 169–94. New York: Academic Press. 378 pp.

Přibáň, K. (1973). Microclimatic measurements of temperature in a pure reed stand. In *Ecosystem Study on Wetland Biome in Czechoslovakia*, ed. S. Hejný, Czechoslovak IBP-PT/PP Report No. 3, pp. 65–70. Třeboň: ČSAV.

Přibáň, K. & Ondok, J.P. (1978). Microclimate and evapotranspiration in two wet grassland communities. *Folia Geobotanica Phytotaxonomica*, **13**, 113–28.

Přibáň, K. & Ondok, J.P. (1980). The daily and seasonal course of evapotranspiration from a Central European sedge-grass marsh. *Journal of Ecology*, **68**, 547–9.

Přibáň, K. & Ondok, J.P. (1985). Heat balance components and evapotranspiration from sedge-grass marsh. *Folia Geobotanica et Phytotaxonomica*, **20**, 41–56.

Přibáň, K. & Ondok, J.P. (1986). Evapotranspiration of a willow carr in summer. *Aquatic Botany*, **25**, 203–16.

Přibáň, K., Ondok, J.P. & Jenik, J. (1986). Patterns of temperature and humidity in wetland biotopes. *Aquatic Botany*, **25**, 191–202.

Přibáň, K., Šmíd, P. & Květ, J. (1977). Microclimatic differentiation in fishpond vegetation. In *Biophysikalische Analyze Pflanzlicher Systeme*, ed. R. Unger, pp. 283–9. Jena: Fischer Verlag.

Priimatchenko, A.D. & Litvinova, M.A. (1968). Raspredelenye i dinamika siniezeleznÿkh vodorosleÿ v dnieprovskikh vodokhranilishchakh. (Distribution and dynamics of blue-green algae in the reservoirs of the Dniepr River.) *Tsvetenye Vodÿ*, **1**, 42–7. (In Russian.)

Prowse, G.A. (1971). Experimental criteria for the study of grass carp feeding in relation to weed control. *Progressive Fish Culturist*, **33**, 128–31.

Pruscha, H. (1973). Biologie und Produktionsbiologie des Rohrbohrers *Phragmataecia castanea* Hb. (Lepidoptera, Cossidae). *Sitzungsberichte der Österreichischen Akademie der Wissenschaften Mathematisch-Naturwissenschaftliche Klasse, Abteilung 1*, **181**, 1–49.

Pugh, G.J.F. & Dickinson, C.H. (1965*a*). Fungal colonization of seedling roots of *Halimione portulacoides* growing under natural conditions. In *Plant Microbes Relationships*, ed. J. Macura & V. Vančura; Proceedings of Symposium, Prague, September 1963, pp. 76–83. Praha: ČSAV.

Pugh, G.J.F. & Dickinson, C.H. (1965*b*). Studies on fungi in coastal soils VI. *Gliocladium roseum* Bainer. *Transactions of the British Mycological Society*, **48**, 279–85.

Pugh, G.J.F. & Mulder, J.L. (1971). Mycoflora associated with *Typha latifolia* L. *Transactions of the British Mycological Society*, **57**, 273–82.

Pugh, G.J.F. & Williams, G.M. (1968). Fungi associated with *Salsola kali*. *Transactions of the British Mycological Society*, **52**, 389–96.

Pühringer, G. (1975). Zur Faunistik und Populationsdynamik der Schilfspinnen des Neusiedler Sees. *Sitzungsberichte der Österreichischen Akademie der Wissenschaften Mathematisch-Naturwissenschaftliche Klasse, Abteilung 1*, **184**(8–10), 379–419.

Puri, G. (1960). *Indian Forest Ecology*, **1**. New Delhi: Oxford Book & Stationery Co. 720 pp.

Putten, W.H. van der (1993). Effects of litter on the growth of *Phragmites australis*. In *Seenuferzerstörung und Seeuferrenaturierung in Mitteleuropa*, ed. W. Ostendorp &. P. Krumscheid-Plankert; Limnologie Aktuell, **5**, 19–22.

Putten, W.H. van der (1997). Die-back of *Phragmites australis* in European wetlands: an overview of the European Research Programme on Reed Die-back Progression (1993–1994). *Aquatic Botany*, **59**, 253–62.

Raghi-Atri, F. (1976). Ökologische Untersuchungen an *Phragmites communis* Trin. in Berlin unter Berücksichtigung des Eutrophierungseinflusses. Diss. FB 14 Technische Universität, Berlin. 151 pp.

Raghi-Atri, F. & Bornkamm, R. (1978). Wachstum und chemische Zusammensetzung von *Phragmites communis* im Freiland bei unterschiedlicher Gewässerbelastung. *Verhandlungen der Gesellschaft für Ökologie (Kiel)*, 1977, 357–60.

Raicu, P., Staicu, S., Stoian, V. & Roman, T. (1972). The *Phragmites communis* Trin. chromosome complement in the Danube Delta. *Hydrobiologia*, **39**, 83–9.

RAMSAR (1990). *A Directory of Wetlands of International Importance*; 4th Meeting of the Conference of Contracting Parties to the Convention on Wetlands of International Importance, especially as Waterfowl Habitat, Montreux, June–July, 1990. Gland: RAMSAR Convention Bureau/ICUN. 796 pp.

Raspopov, I.M. (1973). Fitomassa i produktsïya makrofitov Onezhskogo ozera. (Phytomass and Production of Macrophytes of the Lake Onega.) In *Mikrobiologïya i Pervichnaya Produktsïya Onezhskogo Ozera*, ed. I.I. Nikolaev, pp. 123–42. Leningrad: 'NAUKA'. (In Russian.)

Raspopov, I.M. (1985). *Vÿsshaya Vodnaya Rastitel'nost' Bol'shikh Ozer Severo-Zapada SSSR*. (The Higher Aquatic Vegetation of the Great Lakes of the North-Western USSR.) Leningrad: 'NAUKA'. 200 pp. (In Russian.)

Raspopov, I.M., Ekzertsev, V.A. & Korelyakova, I.L. (1977). Production by freshwater vascular plant (macrophyte) communities of lakes and reservoirs in the European part of the USSR. *Folia Geobotanica et Phytotaxonomica, Praha*, **12**, 113–20.

Raspopov, I.M., Vorontzov, F.F., Slepukhina, T.D., Dotzenko, O.N. & Rychkova, M.A. (1990). *Rol' Volneniya v Formirovanii Biotsenozov Bentosa Bol'shikh Ozer*. (Role of Water Roughness in the Formation of Great Lake Benthic Biocoenoses.) Leningrad: 'NAUKA'. 114 pp. (In Russian.)

Ratcliffe, D.A. (1964). Mires and Bogs. In *The Vegetation of Scotland*, ed. J.H. Burnett, pp. 426–78. Edinburgh: Oliver & Boyd.

Raunkiaer, C. (1934). *The Life Forms of Plants and Statistical Plant Geography.*
Oxford: Oxford University Press. 632 pp.

Raven, J.A. (1970). Exogenous inorganic carbon sources in plant photosynthesis.
Biological Reviews, **45**, 167–221.

Raven, J.A. (1981). Nutritional strategies of submerged benthic plants: the
acquisition of C, N and P by rhizophytes and haptophytes. *New Phytologist*,
88, 1–30.

Reader, R.J. (1978). Primary production in Northern bog marshes. In *Freshwater
Wetlands. Ecological Processes and Management Potential*, ed. R.E. Good,
D.F. Whigham, R.L. Simpson & C.G. Jackson Jr; Proceedings of
Symposium on Freshwater Marshes: Present Status, Future Needs; New
Brunswick, 1977, pp. 53–62. New York: Academic Press.

Reddy, D.B. (1967). The rice gall midge, *Pachydiplosis oryzae* Wood-Mason. In
The Major Insect Pests of the Rice Plant; Proceedings of Symposium of the
International Rice Institute, 1964, pp. 457–91. Baltimore: Johns Hopkins.

Rehbronn, E. (1937). Beiträge zur Fischereibiologie märkischer Seens II. Das
natürliche Nahrungsangebot, inbesonderem der Aufwuchs, und die
Ernährung der Fischnährtiere im Litoral eines eutrophen Sees. *Zeitschrift für
Fischerei*, **35**, 233–345.

Reiche, K. (1907). Grundzüge der Pflanzenverbreitung in Chile. In *Die
Vegetation der Erde*, **VIII**, ed. A. Engler & O. Drude; Sammlung
pflanzengeographischer Mongraphien, pp. 1–374. Leipzig: Englemann.

Reichle, D.E. (1981). *Dynamic Properties of Forest Ecosystems*; International
Biological Programme 23. Cambridge: Cambridge University Press. 683 pp.

Reimold, R.J. (1972). The movement of phosphorus through the salt-marsh cord-
grass *Spartina alterniflora* Loisel. *Limnology and Oceanography*, **14**, 606–11.

Reimold, R.J. & Daiber, F.C. (1970). Dissolved phosphorus concentrations in a
natural salt-marsh of Delaware. *Hydrobiologia*, **36**, 361–71.

Reimold, R.J. & Queen, W.H. (eds.) (1974). *Ecology of Halophytes*. New York:
Academic Press. 605 pp.

Reimold, R.J., Gallagher, J.L., Linthurst, R.A., Pfeiffer, W.J. & Cronin, L.
(1975*a*). Detritus production in coastal Georgia salt marshes. In *Estuarine
Research 1, Chemistry, Biology and the Estuarine System*, ed. L. Eugene; 2nd
International Conference, 1973, pp. 217–28. New York: Academic Press.

Reimold, R.J., Linthurst, R.A. & Wolf, P.L. (1975*b*). Effects of grazing in a salt
marsh. *Biological Conservation*, **8**, 105–25.

Reiner, E. & Robbins, R. (1964). The middle sepik plains of New Guinea.
Geographical Reviews, **54**, 20–54.

Reinisch, F.K. (1925). Die Entomostrakenfauna in ihrer Beziehung zur
Makroflora der Teiche. *Archiv für Hydrobiologie*, **15**, 253–79.

Reiss, F. (1973). Zur Hydrographie und Makrobenthosfauna tropischer Lagunen
in den Savannen des Território de Roraima, Nordbrasilien. *Amazonina*, **4**,
367–78.

Rejmánek, M. & Velásquez, J. (1978). Communities of emerged fishpond shores
and bottoms. In *Pond Littoral Ecosystems: Structure and Functioning*, ed. D.
Dykyjová & J. Květ; Ecological Studies 28, pp. 206–10. Berlin: Springer-
Verlag.

Rejmánková, E. (1973*a*). Seasonal changes in the growth rate of duckweeds
(*Lemna gibba* L.) in the littoral of the Nesyt fishpond. In *Littoral of the
Nesyt Fishpond*, ed. J. Květ; Studie Československé Akademie Věd, 1973,
No. 15, pp. 103–6. Praha: Academia.

Rejmánková, E. (1973*b*). Chlorophyll content in leaves of *Phragmites communis*

Trin. In *Ecosystem Study on Wetland Biome in Czechoslovakia*, ed. S. Hejný, Czechoslovak IBP-PT/PP Report No. 3, pp. 143–5. Třeboň: ČSAV.

Rejmánková, E. (1978). Growth, production and nutrient uptake of duckweeds in fishponds and in experimental cultures. In *Pond Littoral Ecosystems: Structure and Functioning*, ed. D. Dykyjová & J. Květ; Ecological Studies 28, pp. 278–84.

Rejmánková, E. (1979). Úloha Okřehků v Rybničniích Ekosystémech. Kandidat. Diss., Bot. Inst. ČSAV. 166 pp.

Rejmánková, E. (1982). The role of duckweeds (Lemnaceae) in small wetland water bodies of Czechoslovakia. In *Wetlands; Ecology and Management*, ed. B. Gopal, R.E. Turner, R.G. Wetzel & D.F. Whigham; Proceedings of the 1st International Wetlands Conference, New Delhi, 1980, pp. 397–403. Jaipur: National Institute of Ecology and Institute of Science Publication.

Richardson, C. (1985). Mechanism controlling phosphorus retention capacity in freshwater wetlands. *Science*, **228**, 1424–7.

Richardson, C.J., Tilton, D.L., Kadlec, J.A., Chamie, J.P.M. & Wentz, W.A. (1978). Nutrient dynamics of northern wetland ecosystems. In *Freshwater Wetlands. Ecological Processes and Management Potential*, ed. R.E. Good, D.F. Whigham, R.L. Simpson & C.G. Jackson Jr; Proceedings of Symposium on Freshwater Marshes: Present Status, Future Needs, New Brunswick, 1977, pp. 195–216. New York: Academic Press.

Rijks, D.A. (1969). Evaporation from a papyrus swamp. *Quarterly Journal of the Royal Meteorological Society*, **95**, 643–9.

Rikli, M. (1929). Durch die Marmarica zur Oase Siwa. *Vegetationsbilder, Reihe 20*, **Heft 1**, Tafel 1–6.

Rimes, C. (1992). *Freshwater Acidification of SSSIs in Great Britain, 1: Overview*. Peterborough: English Nature. 56 pp.

Ripl, W. (1978). Oxidation of Lake Sediments with Nitrate. Dissertation, LUNBDS/(NBLI-001)/1-150/ISSN 0348-0798. Institute of Limnology, Lund. 151 pp.

Robinson, L.W. & Cumbus, I.P. (1977). Determination of critical levels of nutrients in watercress (*Rorippa nasturtium-aquaticum* (L.) Hayek) grown in different solution concentrations of N, P and K. *Journal of Horticultural Science*, **52**, 383–90.

Robson, T.O. (1978). The present status of chemical aquatic weed control. *Proceedings of the EWRS 5th Symposium on Aquatic Weeds*, 17–25.

Robson, T.O. & Barrett, R.R.F. (1977). Review of effects of aquatic herbicides. In *Ecological Effects of Pesticides*, ed. F.H. Perring & H. Mellanby; Linnean Society Symposium Series No. 5, pp. 111–18. London: Linnean Society.

Rodewald-Rudescu, L. (1974). *Das Schilfrohr*. Phragmites communis *Trin*. Die Binnengewässer, **Bd** 27, ed. H-J. Elster & W. Ohle. Stuttgart: Schweizerbart'scher Verlag. 302 pp.

Rodwell, R. S. (ed.) (1995). *Aquatic Communities, Swamps, and Tall-herb Fens*; British Plant Communities, 2. Cambridge: Cambridge University Press. 283 pp.

Roggeri, H. (1995). *Tropical Freshwater Wetlands, a Guide to Current Knowledge and Sustainable Management*. Dordrecht: Kluwer. 364 pp.

Roman, C.T. & Good, R.E. (1990). A regional strategy for wetlands protection. In *Wetland Ecology and Management: Case Studies*, ed. D.F. Whigham, R.E. Good & J. Květ; Proceedings of 2nd International Wetlands Conference. Třeboň, June 1984, pp. 1–6. Dordrecht: Kluwer. 180 pp.

Roman, L., Roman, T., Lisandru, E. & Ilies, C. (1971). The role of the hydrological factor in the mineral nutrition of the reed and its chief floristic partners. *Hidrobiologia, Bucureşti*, **12**, 135–47.

Romanenko, V.I. & Kuznetsov, S.I. (1974). *Ekologia Mikroorganizmov Presnÿkh Vodoemov*. Leningrad: Izdatel'stvo Nauka. 194 pp.

Ross, S.M. (1995). Overview of the hydrochemistry and solute processes in British wetlands. In *Hydrology and Hydrochemistry of British Wetlands*, ed. J.M.R. Hughes & A.L. Heathwaite, pp. 133–81. London: Wiley.

Rosswall, T. (1973). *Modern Methods in the Study of Microbial Ecology*; Bull. Ecol. Res. Com., **17**. Stockholm: Swedish National Science Council. 511 pp.

Rothschild, G.D.H. & Waterhouse, D.F. (eds.) (1972). *Research on Rice Borers, Related Pests and their Natural Enemies*; Proceedings of the 12th Pacific Science Congress Symposium No. 9A(1); Mushi 45 (Supplement). Fukuoka: Fukuoka Entomological Society. 59 pp.

Rothschild, G.H.L. (1971). The biology and ecology of rice stem borers in Sarawak (Malaysian Borneo). *Journal of Applied Ecology*, **8**, 287–322.

Rottman, R. (1977). Management of weedy lakes and ponds with grass carp. *Fisheries*, **2**(5), 8–14.

Royal Society (1983). *The Nitrogen Cycle of the United Kingdom*: Report of a Royal Society Study Group. London: Royal Society. 264 pp.

Rozinoer, I.M., Saprÿkina, A.P. & Poroiskaya, S.M. (1973). Ob organicheskikh veschestvakh atmosfernÿkh osadkov v raĭone g. Voronezha. *Gidrobiologicheskiĭ Zhurnal, Kiev*, **9**, 100–4.

Rozmej, Z. (1952). *Badania nad Możliwością Mineralizacji Trzciny*. (Studies on the possibility of mineralization of reed.) Prace – Instytutu Techniki Budowlanej 154, Ser. C, No. 52, *Materiały Budowlane, Drogowe i ich Technologia*. Warszawa: Instytut Techniki Budowlanej. 15 pp. (In Polish.)

Rudescu, L. (1960). Contributii la studiul evaporatiei stufului din Delta Dunării. *Celuloză şi Hîrtie*, **9**, 315–18.

Rudescu, L. (1965). Neue biologische Probleme bei den Phragmiteskulturarbeiten im Donaudelta. *Archiv für Hydrobiologie (Suppl.)*, **30**, 80–111.

Rudescu, L., Niculescu, C. & Chivu, J.P. (1965). *Monografia Stufului din Delta Dunarii*. Bucureşti: Editura Academici Republicii Socialiste Romania. 542 pp.

Rudescu, L. & Popescu-Marinescu, V. (1970). Vergleichende Untersuchungen über benthische und phytophile Biozönosen einiger emerser Makrophyten des Donaudeltas mit besonderer Berücksichtigung von *Phragmites communis* Trin. *Archiv für Hydrobiologie, Supp.* **36**, 279–92.

Ruppolt, W. (1957). Zur biologie der cecidogenen Diptere *Lipara lucens* Mg. (Chloropidae). *Wiss. Z. Ernst. Mortiz Arndt-Univ. Greifswald, Math. – naturw. Reihe*, **6**(5/6), 280–92.

Rybak, J.I. (1969). Bottom sediments of the lakes of various trophic type. *Ekologia Polska*, A, **12**, 147–58.

Rychnovská, M. (1967). A contribution to the autecology of *Phragmites communis* Trin. I. Physiological heterogeneity of leaves. *Folia Geobotanica et Phytotaxonomica, Praha*, **2**, 179–88.

Rychnovská, M. (1973). Some physiological features of water balance in littoral and terrestrial *Phragmites communis* Trin. In *Littoral of the Nesyt Fishpond*, ed. J. Květ; Studie Československe Akademie Věd, 1973, No. 15, pp. 147–51. Praha: Academia.

Rychnovská, M. (1978). Water relations, water balance, transpiration, and water turnover in selected reedswamp communities. In *Pond Littoral Ecosystems:*

Structure and Functioning, ed. D. Dykyjová & J. Květ; Ecological Studies 28, pp. 246–56.

Rychnovská, M., Čermák, J. & Šmíd, P. (1980). Water output in a stand of *Phragmites communis* Trin. *Acta Scientiarum Naturalium Academiae Scientiarum Bohemoslovacae, Brno*, **14**(2), 1–30.

Rychnovská, M., Květ, J., Gloser, J. & Jakrlová, J. (1972). Water relations in three zones of grasslands. *Acta Scientiarum Naturalium Academiae Scientiarum Bohemoslovacae, Brno*, **6**(5), 1–30.

Rychnovská, M. & Šmíd, D. (1973). Preliminary evaluation of transpiration in two *Phragmites* stands. In *Ecosystem Study on Wetland Biome in Czechoslovakia*, ed. S. Hejný, Czechoslovak IBP-PT/PP Report No. 3, pp. 111–19. Třeboň: ČSAV.

Rychnovský, B. (1973). Occurrence of *Lipara* spp. at the Nesyt fishpond and their influence on the productivity of reed. In *Littoral of the Nesyt Fishpond*, ed. J. Květ; Studie Československé Akademie Věd, 1973, No. 15, 129–31. Praha: Academia.

Rzóska, J. (1974). The Upper Nile swamps, a tropical wetland study. *Freshwater Biology*, **4**, 1–30.

Rzóska, J. (ed.) (1976). *The Nile: Biology of an Ancient River*. The Hague: Junk. 417 pp.

Sahai, R. & Sinha, A.B. (1969). Investigations on bioecology of inland waters of Gorakkhpur (U.P.) India I. Limnology of Ramgarh Lake. *Hydrobiologia*, **34**, 433–47.

Sale, P.J.M. (1974). Productivity of vegetable crops in a region of high solar input. *Australian Journal of Plant Physiology*, **20**, 177–84.

Sale, P.J.M. & Orr, P.T. (1986). Gas exchange of *Typha orientalis* Presl. in artificial ponds. *Aquatic Botany*, **23**, 329–40.

Sale, P.J.M., Orr, P.T., Shell, G.S. & Erskine, D.J.C. (1985). Photosynthesis and growth rates in *Salvinia molesta* and *Eichhornia crassipes*. *Journal of Applied Ecology*, **22**, 125–37.

Salt, G. (1964). A contribution to the ecology of Upper Kilimanjaro. *Journal of Ecology*, **42**, 375–423.

Sanders, W.M. (1972). Nutrients. In *River Ecology and Man*, ed. R.T. Oglesby, A.C. Carlson & J.A. McCann; Proceedings of the International Symposium on River Ecology and the Impact of Man, Massachusetts, 1971, pp. 389–415.

Sandon, H. (1950). An illustrated guide to the fresh-water fishes of the Sudan. *Sudan Notes and Records*, **25** (Supplement), 1–61.

Sandon, H. (1951). Problems of fisheries in the area affected by Equatorial Nile Project. *Sudan Notes and Records*, **32**, 5–36.

Sandon, H. & El Tayib, A. (1953). The food of some common Nile fish. *Sudan Notes and Records*, **30**, 205–29.

Sasaba, T. & Kiritani, K. (1972). Evaluation of mortality factors with special reference to parasitism of the green rice leafhopper, *Nephotettix cincticeps* Uhler (Hemiptera: Deltocephalidae). *Applied Entomology and Zoology, Tokyo*, **7**, 83–93.

Sasaba, T., Kiritani, K. & Urabe, T. (1973). A preliminary model to simulate the effect of insecticides on a spider-leafhopper system in the paddy field. *Researches on Population Ecology*, **15**, 9–22.

Saunders, G.W. (1971). Carbon flow in the aquatic system. In *The Structure and Function of Fresh Water Microbial Communities*, ed. J. Cairns: Research

Division Monograph, Virginia Polytechnic Institute and State University No. 3, pp. 31–45. Charlottesville, VA.: University Press of Virginia.

Saunders, G.W., Cummins, K.W., Gak, D.Z., Pieczyńska, E., Straškrabová, V. & Wetzel, R.G. (1980). Organic matter and decomposers. In *The Functioning of Freshwater Ecosystems*, ed. E.D. LeCren & R.H. Lowe-McConnell; International Biological Programme 22, pp. 341–92. Cambridge: Cambridge University Press.

Savage, C.D.W. (1972). Multi-purpose use of wetlands and the establishment of 'Green Routes' of effective refuges. In *Proceedings of International Conference on Conservation of Wetlands and Waterfowl, IWRB, Ramsar, Iran*, pp. 81–6. Slimbridge, UK: IWRB.

Savich, N.M. (1967). Posol'skoe Boloto. (Posolskoe Swamp.) In *Geobotanischeskhie Issledovaniya na Baĭkale*, ed. B.A. Tikhomirov: Trudȳ Sibirskogo Otdeleniya Limnologicheski lago Instituta, Academiĭ Nauk SSSR, 1967, pp. 302–42. Moskva: Nauka. (In Russian.)

Sawyer, C.N. (1947). Fertilization of lakes by agricultural and urban drainage. *Journal of the New England Water Works Association, Boston*, **61**, 109–27.

Sawyer, C.N. (1962). Causes, effects and control of aquatic growths. *Journal of the Water Pollution Control Federation*, **34**, 279–87.

Saxena, K. (1972). The concept of ecosystem as examplified by the vegetation of Western Rajasthan. *Vegetatio*, **24**, 215–27.

Schanz, F. (1993). Zwölf Jahre Schilf-Beobachtungen am unteren Zürichsee von 1979 bis 1991. In *Seenuferzerstörung und Seeuferrenaturierung in Mitteleuropa*, ed. W. Ostendorp & P. Krumscheid-Plankert; Limnologie Aktuell, **5**, 121–30.

Schäperclaus, W. (1961). *Lehrbuch der Teichwirtschaft* (2nd edn.). Berlin: Paul Parey. 582 pp.

Schiemer, F. (1979). Submerged macrophytes in the open lake. Distribution pattern, production and long-term changes. In *Neusiedlersee: The Limnology of a Shallow Lake in Central Europe*, ed. H. Löffler; Monographiae Biologicae 37, pp. 235–50. The Hague: Junk.

Schiemer, F. & Farahat, A.M.Z. (1966). Redox potential und Sauerstoffverbrauch von Böden einiger Salzgewässer im Gebiet des Neusiedlersees (Österreich). *Sitzungsberichte der Österreichischen Akademie der Wissenschaften Mathematisch-Naturwissenschaftliche Klasse, Abteilung 1*, 175, **Bd 4**, 143–57.

Schierup, H-H. (1978). Biomass and primary production in a *Phragmites communis* Trin. bog in North Jutland, Denmark. *Verhandlungen der Internationalen Vereinigung für Theoretische und Angewandte Limnologie*, **20**, 94–9.

Schindler, D.W. (1971). A hypothesis to explain differences and similarities among lakes in the Experimental Lakes Area, Northwestern Ontario. *Journal of the Fisheries Research Board of Canada*, **28**, 295–301.

Schlütter, U. (1971). *Lebendbau. Ingenieurbiologische Bauweisen und lebende Baustoffe*. München: Callway. 97 pp.

Schneider, D. (1954). Beitrag zu einer Analyse des Beute- und Flucht-verhaltens einheimischer Anuren. *Biologisches Zentralblatt (Leipzig)*, **73**, 225–82.

Schoef-van Pelt, M.M. (1973). *Littorelletea*: A study of the vegetation of some amphiphytic communities of western Europe. Thesis, University of Nijemegen. 216 pp.

Schröder, R. (1973). Die Freisetzung von Pflanzennährstoffen im Schilfgebiet und ihr Transport in das Freiwasser am Biespiel des Bodensee-Untersees. *Archiv für Hydrobiologie*, **71**, 145–58.

Schubert, P. (1961). Beiträge zur Kenntnis der Arthropodenfauna des Schilfgürtels am Neusiedlersee. *Wissenschaftliche Arbeiten Burgenland*, **29**, 68–77.

Schütze, K.T. (1931). *Die Biologie der Kleinschmetterlinge unter besonderer Berücksichtigung ihrer Nährpflanzen und Erscheinungszeiten*; Handbuch der Microlepidopteren Raupenkalender. Frankfurt am Main: Verlag des Internationalen Entomologischen Vereins. 235 pp.

Scott, D.A. (1989). *A Directory of Asian Wetlands*. Gland: IUCN. 1181 pp.

Scott, D.A. (1993). *A Directory of Wetlands in Oceania*. Slimbridge: IWRB. 444 pp.

Scott, M. (1924). Observations of the habits and life of *Galerucella nymphae* (Coleoptera). *Transactions of the American Microscopical Society*, **43**, 11–16.

Sculthorpe, C.D. (1967). *The Biology of Aquatic Vascular Plants*. London: Arnold. 610 pp.

Sebestyen, O. (1950). Studies on detritus drifts in Lake Balaton. *Annales Instituti Biologiae Pervestigandae Hungarici*, **1**, 49–64.

Segal, S. (1965). *Een Vegetatieonderzoek van de Hogere Waterplanten in Nederland*; Wetenschappelijke Mededelingen van de Koninklijke Nederlandse Natuurhistorische Vereiniging, 57. Hoogwould; Utrecht: KNNV. 80 pp.

Segal, S. (1966). Ecological studies of peat-bog vegetation in the north-western part of the province of Overijsel (the Netherlands). *Wentia*, **15**, 109–41.

Seidel, K. (1955). *Die Flechtbinse* Scirpus lacustris *L.: Ökologie, Morphologie und Entwicklung, ihre Stellung bei den Völkern und ihre wirtschaftlicher Bedeutung*; Die Binnengewässer, **21**, Stuttgart: Schweizerbart'sche Verlag. 216 pp.

Seidel, K. (1959). Scirpus-Kulturen. *Archiv für Hydrobiologie*, **56**, 58–92.

Seidel, K. (1966). Reinigung von Gewässern durch höhere Pflanzen. *Naturwissenschaften*, **12**, 289–97.

Seidel, K. (1967). Biologischer Schutz unserer Seen durch Pflanzen. *Österreichische Fischerei*, **1**, 3–7.

Šesták, Z., Čatský, J. & Jarvis, P.G. (eds.) (1971). *Plant Photosynthetic Production. Manual of Methods*. The Hague: W. Junk. 818 pp.

Seville, F. (1961). Vegetation of the Navajo Reservoir Basin. In *Ecological Studies of the Flora and Fauna of Navajo Reservoir Basin, Colorado and New Mexico*, eds. D.M. Prendergast & C.C. Stout; Anthropological Papers No. 55, pp. 15–46. Salt Lake City: University of Utah Press.

Shapiro, R.E. (1958). Effects of flooding on availability of nitrogen and phosphorus. *Soil Science*, **85**, 190–7.

Sharitz, R.R., Irwin, J.E. & Christy, J.E. (1974). Vegetation of swamps receiving reactor effluents. *Oikos*, **25**, 7–13.

Sharma, K.P. & Gopal, B. (1977). Studies on stand structure and primary production in *Typha* species. *International Journal of Ecology and Environmental Science*, **3**, 45–66.

Sharma, K.P. & Gopal, B. (1982). Decomposition and nutrient dynamics in *Typha elephantina* Roxb. under different water regimes. In *Wetlands, Ecology and Management*, ed. B. Gopal, R.E. Turner, R.G. Wetzel & D.F. Whigham, pp. 321–34. Jaipur: Michael Paul Lucknow Publishing House.

Shaw, S.P. & Fredine, C.G. (1971). *Wetlands of the United States. Their Extent and their Value to Waterfowl and other Wildlife*. US Department of the

Interior, Fish and Wildlife Service Circular 39, 1–67. Washington: US Department of the Interior.

Shcherbakov, A.P. (1961). Produktivnost' zhivotnogo naseleniya pribrezhnykh zaroslĕ Glubokogo ozera. (Production of animal populations in littoral stands of Lake Glubokoe.) *Trudÿ Vsesoyuznogo Gidrobiologicheskogo Obshchestva*, **11**, 285–98. (In Russian.)

Sheldon, S.P. (1987). The effects of herbivorous snails on submerged macrophyte communities in Minnesota lakes. *Ecology*, **68**, 1920–31.

Sieghardt, H. (1973). Utilization of solar energy and energy content of different organs of *Phragmites communis* Trin. *Polski Archiwum Hydrobiologii*, **12**, 151–6.

Sieghardt, H. (1977). Untersuchungen zur Energienutzung von *Phragmites communis* Trin. *Archiv für Hydrobiologie*, **79**, 172–81.

Sinha, A.B. & Sahai, R. (1978). Studies on the factors affecting growth and productivity of free-floating macrophytes in Ramgarh lake of Gorakhpur (India). In *Glimpses of Ecology*, ed. J.S. Singh & B. Gopal, pp. 337–82. Jaipur: Institute of Science Publications.

Sircar, S.C.G., De, S.C. & Bhowmick, H.D. (1940). Microbiological decomposition of plant material I, II. *Indian Journal of Agricultural Science*, **10**, 119–57.

Sirenko, L.A. (1972). *Fisiologicheskye Osnovÿ Razmnozheniya Siniezelenÿkh Vodoroslĕ v Vodokhranilishchakh.* (Physiological Bases of Reproduction of Blue-green Algae in Reservoirs.) Kiev: 'Naukova Dumka'. 203 pp. (In Russian.)

Sjörs, H. (1948). *Myrvegetation in Bergalagen*; Acta Phytogeographica Suecica, BB21, 299 pp.

Skuhravá, M. & Skuhravý, V. (1977). The development of *Giraudiella inclusa* (Frauenfeld) and the variability of its galls on *Phragmites communis* Trin. *Marcellia*, **40**, 195–206.

Skuhravá, M. & Skuhravý, V. (1981). *Die Gallmücken (Cecidomyiidae, Diptera) des Schilfes* (Phragmites communis *Trin.*); Studie Československé Akademie Věd, 1981, No. 3. Praha: Academia. 150 pp.

Skuhravý, V. (1975). Die Entwicklung der Gallmücke *Lasioptera arundinis* (Schiner) (Diptera, Cecidomyiidae an Schilf (*Phragmites communis* Trin.). *Marcellia*, **38**, 287–98.

Skuhravý, V. (1976). Bionomie und Schädlichkeit der Eule *Archanara geminipunctata* (Lepidoptera, Noctuidae) an Schilf *Phragmites communis*. *Acta Scientiarum Naturalium Academiae Scientiarum Bohemoslovacae, Brno*, **73**, 209–15.

Skuhravý, V., Hudec, K., Pelikán, J., Pokorný, V., Rychnovský, B. & Skuhravá, M. (1981). *Invertebrates and Vertebrates Attacking Common Reed Stands* (Phragmites communis *Trin.*) *in Czechoslovakia*; Studie Československé Akademie Věd, 1981, No. 1. Praha: Academia. 113 pp.

Skuhravý, V., Pokorný, V. & Skuhravá, M. (1975). Die Gliederfüssler (*Lipara* spp., *Steneotarsonemus* sp. und *Lepidoptera*-larvae) als Ursache der Nichtbildung des Blütenstandes von Schilf (*Pragmites communis*). *Acta Entomologica Bohemoslovaca*, **72**, 87–91.

Skuhravý, V. & Skuhravá, M. (1978). Das Schadbild und Entwicklung der Art *Platycephala planifrons* (F.) (Diptera, Chloropidae) an Schilf *Phragmites communis*. *Dipterologica Seminaria Bohemoslovacae (Bratislava)*, **1**, 311–18.

Sládček, V. (1973). A swarm of zooplankton in the Nesyt fishpond. In *Littoral of the Nesyt Fishpond*, ed. J. Květ; Studie Československé Akademie Věd, 1973, No. 15, 71–81. Praha: Academia.

Slavík, B. (1974). *Methods of Studying Plant Water Relations*. Praha: Academia. 449 pp.

Slepukhina, T.D. (1969). Materialȳ po bentosu prudov stepnoĭ chasti Severnogo Kavkaza. (Benthos of ponds of steppe region of North Caucasus.) In *Trudȳ Leningradskago Gosudarstvenogo Universtiteta Laboratoriya Ozerovedeniya (Zaĭlenie malȳkh Vodokhranilishch Predkavkaz'ya)*, '23', 167–75. Leningrad: Izdatel'stvo Universiteta Leningradskogo. (In Russian.)

Sloey, W.E., Spangler, F.L. & Fetter, C.W. Jr (1978). Management of freshwater wetlands for nutrient assimilation. In *Freshwater Wetlands. Ecological Processes and Management Potential*, ed. R.E. Good, D.F. Whigham & R.L. Simpson; Proceedings of the Symposium on Freshwater Marshes: Present Status, Future Needs, New Brunswick, July 1977, pp. 321–40. New York: Academic Press. 378 pp.

Small, E. (1972*a*). Ecological significance of four critical elements in plants of raised *Sphagnum* peat bogs. *Ecology*, **53**, 498–503.

Small, E. (1972*b*). Photosynthetic rates in relation to nitrogen recycling as an adaptation to nutrient deficiency in peat bog plants. *Canadian Journal of Botany*, **50**, 2227–33.

Smalley, A.E. (1958). The role of two invertebrate populations, *Littorina errorata* and *Orchelium fidicinum* in the energy flow of a salt marsh ecosystem. PhD Dissertation. Athens: University of Georgia. 126 pp.

Smalley, A.E. (1959). The growth cycle of *Spartina* and its relation to the insect population in the marsh. *Proceedings of the Salt Marsh Conference of Marine Institute of the University of Georgia*, 1958, 25–8.

Smalley, A.E. (1960). Energy flow of a salt marsh grasshopper population. *Ecology*, **41**, 672–7.

Smart, M. (ed.) (1976). *Proceedings of the International Conference on the Conservation of Wetlands and Waterfowl, Heiligenhafen, December 1974*. Slimbridge: International Waterfowl Research Bureau. 492 pp.

Šmíd, P. (1973). Microclimatological characteristics of reedswamps at the Nesyt fishpond. In *Littoral of the Nesyt Fishpond*, ed. J. Květ; Studie Československé Akademie Věd, 1973, No. 15, pp. 29–38. Praha: Academia.

Šmíd, P. (1975). Evaporation from a reedswamp. *Journal of Ecology*, **63**, 229–309.

Smirenskiĭ, A.A. (1950). *Vodnȳe Kormovȳe i Zashchitnȳe Rasteniya v Okhotnich'e-Promȳslovȳch Khozyaĭstvach*. (Fodder and Protective Water Plants in Hunting Production Units.) Vȳp. 1. Moskva: Zagotizdat. 135 pp. (In Russian.)

Smirenskiĭ, A.A. (1951). Struktura vodnȳch okhotnich'ikh ugodiĭ zapadnosibirskoĭ lesostepi. Soobshchenie I Obshchaya strukturnaya kharakteristika osnovnȳkh tipov ozer bluydets. (Structure of the water hunting areas of West-Siberian partially wooded steppe. Report I. General structural characteristics of the main types of the pothole lakes.) In *Voprosȳ Biologii Pushnȳkh Zvereĭ i Tekhniki Okhotnich'ego Promȳsla*; Trudȳ Vsesoyuznogo Nauchno-issledovatel'skogo Instituta Okhotnich'ego Promȳsla, **9**, 122–216. Moskva: Gosud. Izd. Tekh.-Ekon. Lit. (In Russian.)

Smirnov, N.N. (1959). Rol' vȳsshikh rasteniĭ v pitanii zhivotnogo naseleniya bolot. (The role of higher plants in the nutrition of animal populations of mires.) *Trudȳ Moskovskogo Tekhnicheskogo Instituta Rybnoĭ Promȳshlennosti i Khozyaĭstva*, **10**, 75–87. (In Russian.)

Smirnov, N.N. (1960). Nutrition of *Galerucella nymphaea* L. (Coleoptera, Chrysomelidae), mass consumer of water lily. *Hydrobiologia*, **15**, 208–24.

Smirnov, N.N. (1961*a*). Food cycles in sphagnous bogs. *Hydrobiologia*, **17**, 175–82.

Smirnov, N.N. (1961*b*). Consumption of emergent plants by insects. *Verhandlungen der Internationalen Vereinigung für Theoretische und Angewandte Limnologie*, **14**, 232–6.

Smirnov, N.N. (1964). On the quantity of allochthonous pollen and spores received by the Rybinsk reservoir. *Hydrobiologia*, **24**, 421–9.

Smirnova, N.N. (1960). Kratkaya kharakteristika rastitel'nosti bolot dolinȳ Angarȳ. *Trudȳ Vostochno-Sibirskogo Filiala, Seriya Biologicheskaya*, **22**, 89–92.

Smyly, W.J.P. (1952). The Entomostraca of the weeds of a moorland pond. *Journal of Animal Ecology*, **21**, 1–11.

Smyly, W.J.P. (1957). Distribution and seasonal abundance of Entomostraca in moorland ponds near Windermere. *Hydrobiologia*, **11**, 59–72.

Sokolova, N. (1963). Fauna zaroslei nekotorykh makrofitov Uchinskogo vodokhranilishcha. (Fauna of the stands of some macrophytes of the Uchinskoe reservoir.) In *Uchinskoe i Mozhalskoe Vodokhranilishcha (Gidrobiologicheske i Ikhtiologicheske Issledovaniya)*, pp. 108–53. Moskva: Izdatel'stvo Moskovskogo Universiteta. (In Russian.)

Solski, A. (1962). Mineralizacja roślin wodnych I. Uwalnianie fosforu i potasu przez wymywanie. *Polski Archiwum Hydrobiologii*, **10**, 167–96.

Sorokin, J.I. (1967). Nekotoryje itogi izuchenija troficyesko roli bakterih v. vodoemach. *Gidrobiologicheskiĭ Zhurnal, Kiev*, **3**, 32–42.

Sorokin, Y.T. & Kadota, H. (eds.) (1972). *Techniques for the Assessment of Microbial Production and Decomposition in Fresh Waters*; International Biological Programme Handbook No. 23. Oxford: Blackwell Science Publishers. 128 pp.

Soszka, G.J. (1975). Ecological relationships between invertebrates and submerged macrophytes in the lake littoral. *Ekologia Polska*, **23**, 393–15.

Soszka, H. (1974). Chironomidae associated with pond-weeds (*Potamogeton lucens* L. and *Potamogeton perfoliatus* L.) in the Mikołajskie Lake. *Bulletin de l'Academie Polonaise des Sciences Classe II, Série des Sciences Biologiques*, **22**, 369–76.

Specht, R.L., Roe, E.M. & Boughton, V.H. (eds.) (1974). *Conservation of Major Plant Communities in Australia and Papua New Guinea*; Australian Journal of Botany, Supplementary Series No. 7. East Melbourne: CSIRO. 667 pp.

Spector, W.S. (ed.) (1956). *Handbook of Biological Data*. Philadelphia: Saunders Co. 584 pp.

Spence, D.H.N. (1967). Factors controlling the distribution of freshwater macrophytes with particular reference to the lochs of Scotland. *Journal of Ecology*, **55**, 147–70.

Spence, D.H.N. (1976). Light and plant response in freshwater. In *Light as an Ecological Factor: II*, ed. G.C. Evans, R. Bainbridge & O. Rackham; Symposium of British Ecological Society No. 16, pp. 93–133.

Spitzenberger, F. (1966). Ein Beitrag zur Ökologie und Biologie von Neusiedlersee Feldmäusen (*Microtus arvalis*). *Natur und Land*, **52**, 18–21.

Stangenberg, M. (1949). Nitrogen and carbon in the bottom-deposits of lakes and in the soils under carp ponds. *Verhandlungen der Internationalen Vereinigung für Theoretische und Angewandte Limnologie*, **10**, 422–37.

Stangenberg, M. (1967). Die Produktions-bedingungen in den Teichen II.

Chemische Zusammensetzung der Böden unter den Teichen. *Geologie der Meer und Binnengewässer*, **6**, 1–64.

Stangenberg, M. & Żemoytel, K. (1952). Skład chemiczny osadów Jeziora Charzykonskiego. *Biuletyn Panstwowego Instytuta Geologicznego, Warszawa*, **68**, 3–172.

Stankovič, S. & Jankovič, D. (1971). Mechanisms der Fischproduktion im Gebiet des mittleren Donaulaufes. *Archiv für Hydrobiologie, Suppl.*, **36** (Donauforschung 4), 299–305.

Steel, J.A.P. (1980). Primary production – phytoplankton models. In *The Functioning of Freshwater Ecosystems*, ed. E.D. LeCren & R.H. Lowe-McConnell, International Biological Programme No. 22, pp. 220–7. Cambridge: Cambridge University Press.

Steenberg, B. (1968). Papyrus problems in utilization for pulp and paper making. In *Pulp and Paper Development in Africa and the Near East*, 2; FAO 03952-68-MR, pp. 865–76. Rome: FAO.

Steenis, G.G.J. van & Ruttner, F. (1932). Die Pteridophyten und Phanerogamen der deutschen limnologischen Sunda-Expedition. Mit Vegetationskizzzen nach Tagebuchaufzeichnungen von F. Ruttner. *Archiv für Hydrobiologie, Suppl.*, **11** (Tropische Binnengewässer, 1), 231–387.

Steenis, T.H., Wider, N.G., Cofer, H.P. & Beck, R.A. (1954). *The Marshes of Delaware, their Improvement and Preservation*; Delaware Board of Game & Fish Commissioners, Pittman-Robertson Publication 2, 1–42.

Stevens, C.P. (1983). *Watercress – Production of the Cultivated Crop*; ADAS/ MAFF Reference Book 136. London: Grower Books and HMSO. 54 pp.

Steward, K.K. & Ornes, W.H. (1975). The autecology of sawgrass (*Cladium jamaicense* Crantz) in the Florida Everglades. *Ecology*, **56**, 162–71.

Stewart, R.E. & Kantrud, H.A. (1971). *Classification of natural ponds and lakes in the glaciated prairie region*; US Department of the Interior, Fish & Wildlife Service, Bureau of Sport Fish & Wildlife, Research Publication 92. Washington; US Department of the Interior. 97 pp.

Stewart, W.D.P. (1968). Nitrogen input into aquatic ecosystems. In *Algae, Man and the Environment*, ed. D.F. Jackson, pp. 53–72. Syracuse: Syracuse University Press.

Stewart, W.D.P. (ed.) (1975). *Nitrogen Fixation by Free-living Micro-organisms*; International Biological Programme Synthesis 6. Cambridge: Cambridge University Press. 471 pp.

Stocker, O. (1967). Der Wasser- und Photosynthesehaushalt mitteleuropäischer Gräser, ein Beitrag zum allgemeinen Konstitutionsproblem des Grastypus. *Flora, Abteilung B*, **157**, 56–96.

Stone, J.H., Bahr, L.M. Jr & Day, J.W. Jr (1977). Effects of canals on freshwater marshes in coastal Louisiana and implications for management. In *Freshwater Wetlands. Ecological Processes and Management Potential*, ed. R.E. Good, D.F. Whigham & R.L. Simpson; Proceedings of the Symposium on Freshwater Marshes: Present Status, Future Needs, New Brunswick, July 1977, pp. 299–320.

Stott, B. & Buckley, B.R. (1978). Costs of controlling aquatic weeds with grass carp as compared with conventional methods. *Proceedings of EWRC 5th Symposium on Aquatic Weeds*, 253–60.

Straka, H. (1960). Literaturübersicht über Moor- und Torf-ablagerungen aus tropischen Gebieten. *Erdkunde*, **14**, 81–97.

Straškraba, M. (1963). *Share of the Littoral Region in the Productivity of two*

Fishponds in Southern Bohemia; Rozpravy ČSAV, Řada Matematických a Přírodních Věd, **73**(13). 64 pp.

Straškraba, M. (1965*a*). Contributions to the productivity of the littoral region of ponds and pools I. Quantitative studies of the littoral zooplankton of the rich vegetation of the backwater Labíčko. *Hydrobiologia*, **26**, 421–43.

Straškraba, M. (1965*b*). The effect of fish on the number of invertebrates in ponds and streams. *Mitteilungen der Internationalen Vereinigung für Theoretische und Angewandte Limnologie* No. 13, 106–27.

Straškraba, M. (1967). Quantitative study on the littoral zooplankton of the Poltruba backwater with an attempt to disclose the effect of fish. In *Contributions to the Productivity of the Littoral Region of Ponds and Pools*, ed. M. Straškraba, J. Kořínková & M. Poštolková; *Rozpravy ČSAV, Řada Matematických a Přírodních Věd*, **77**(11), pp. 3–34. Praha: ČSAV.

Straškraba, M. (1968). Der Anteil der höheren Pflanzen an der Produktion der stehenden Gewässer. *Mitteilungen der Internationalen Vereinigung für Theoretische und Angewandte Limologie* No. 14, 212–30.

Straškraba, M. & Pieczyńska, E. (1970). Field experiments on shading effect by emergents on littoral phytoplankton and periphyton production. Relations of aquatic macroflora to phytoplankton, periphyton and macrofauna. *Rozpravy ČSAV, Řada Matematických a Přírodních Věd*, **80**(6), 7–32.

Straškrabová, V. & Sorokin, Y.I. (1972). Determination of cell size of microorganisms for the calculation of biomass. In *Techniques for the Assessment of Microbial Production and Decomposition in Fresh Waters*, ed. Y.I. Sorokin & H. Kadota; IBP Handbook No. 23, pp. 48–50. Oxford: Blackwell Science Publishers.

Strijbosch, H. (1976). Een vergelijkend syntaxonomische en synecologische studie in de Overassettse en Heterse vennen bij Nijmegen. Diss., University of Nijmegen.

Stroganov, N.S. (1963). Izbiratel'naya sposobnost, amurov i pishcha. (Food selectivity in grass carp.) In *Materialÿ Vsesoyuznogo Soveshchaniya po Rÿbokhozyaïstvennomu Osvoeniyu Rastitel'noyadnÿkh Rÿb – Belogo Amura* (Ctenopharyngodon idella) *i Tolstolobika* (Hypopthalmichthys molitrix) – *v Vodoemakh SSSR, Noyabrya, 1961, Ashkhabad*, pp. 181–91. Ashkhabad: Izdatel'stvo AH Turkmenskoï SSR. (In Russian.)

Stuckey, R.L. (1968). Western Lake Erie's changing aquatic and marsh flora. *American Journal of Botany*, **55**, 735.

Sukopp, H. (1968). Veränderung des Röhrichtbestandes der Berliner Havel 1962–67. *Senator f. Bau- und Wohnungswesen*, **3**(14), 1–66.

Sukopp, H. (1971*a*). Effects of man, especially recreational activities on littoral macrophytes. *Hidrobiologia, Bucureşti*, **12**, 331–40.

Sukopp, H. (1971*b*). Bewertung und Auswahl von Naturschutzgebieten. *Schriftenreihe der Landschaftspflege und Naturschutz*, **6**, 183–94.

Sukopp, H. (1972). Wandel von Flora und Vegetation in Mitteleuropa unter dem Einfluss des Menschen. *Berichte über Landwirtschaft*, **50**, 112–39.

Sukopp, H. (1973). Conservation of wetlands in Central Europe. *Polskie Archiwum Hydrobiologii*, **20**, 223–8.

Sukopp, H. (1991). Röhrichte unter dem Einfluss von Großstädten. *Rundgespräche der Kommission für Ökologie*, 2 (*Ökologie der Ober-Bayerischen Seen*), 63–72.

Sukopp, H. & Krauss, M. (eds.) (1990). *Ökologie, Gefährdung und Schutz von Röhrichtpflanzen*: Landschaftsentwicklung u. Umweltforschung, **71**, Berlin:

Fachbereich 14 – Landschaftsentwicklung – der Technischen Universität Berlin. 245 pp.

Sukopp, H. & Kunik, W. (1969). Die Ufervegetation der Berliner Havel. *Naturschutz und Landschaft*, **44**, 287–92.

Sukopp, H. & Markstein, B. (1989). Die Vegetation der Berliner Havel. Bestandsveränderungen 1962–1987. *Landschaftsentwicklung und Umweltforschung*, **64**, 1–128. Berlin: Technische Universität.

Sukopp, H., Markstein, B. & Trepl, L. (1975). Röhrichte unter intensivem Grossstadteinfluss. *Beiträge zur Naturkundlichen Forschung in Südwestdeutschland*, **34**, 371–85.

Sukopp, H., Trautmann, W. & Korneck, D. (1978). Auswertung der Roten Liste gefährdeter Farn- und Blüten-pflanzen in der Bundesrepublik Deutschland für den Arten- und Biotop-schutz. *Schriftenreihe Vegetationskunde*, **H 12**, 1–138.

Suominen, J. (1968). Changes in the aquatic microflora on the polluted Lake Rautavesi, SW Finland. *Annales Botanici Fennici*, **5**, 65–81.

Sutcliffe, J.V. (1974). A hydrological study of the southern sudd region of the Upper Nile. *Bulletin des Sciences Hydrologiques*, **19**, 237–55.

Szajnowski, P. (1970). The relations between the reed standing crop and fishery effect. *Polskie Archiwum Hydrobiologii*, **17**, 363–71.

Szczepańska, W. (1967). Limnological individuality of small lacustrine bays. *Polskie Archiwum Hydrobiologii*, **14**, 39–52.

Szczepańska, W. (1970). Periphyton of several lakes of the Mazurian Lakeland. *Polskie Archiwum Hydrobiologii*, **17**, 397–418.

Szczepańska, W. & Szczepański, A. (1973). Emergent macrophytes and their role in wetland ecosystems. *Polskie Archiwum Hydrobiologii*, **20**, 41–50.

Szczepański, A. (1965). Deciduous leaves as a source of organic matter in lakes. *Bulletin de l'Academie Polonaise des Sciences Classe II, Série des Sciences Biologiques*, **13**, 215–17.

Szczepański, A. (1969). Biomass of underground parts of the reed *Phragmites communis* Trin. *Bulletin de l'Academie Polonaise des Science Classe II, Série des Sciences Biologiques*, **17**, 245–7.

Szczepański, A. (1973). Chlorophyll in the assimilation parts of helophytes. *Polskie Archiwum Hydrobiologii*, **20**, 61–71.

Szczepański, A. (1977). Allelopathy as a means of biological control of water weeds. *Aquatic Botany*, **3**, 193–7.

Szczepański, A. (1983). Ekologiczna waloryzacja środowisk podmokłych. *Zeszyty problemowe postępów nauk rolniczych, Warszawa*, **235**, 279–86.

Szumiec, M. (1973). Parowanie z powierzchni małych zbiorników wodnych. *Przeglad Geofizyczny*, **18**, 159–65.

Szumiec, M.A. (1986). Weather effects on temperature and light penetrating into ponds of different morphometry and with differentiated intensity of carp culture. *Aquatic Botany*, **25**, 217–25.

Täckholm, V. & Täckholm, M. (1941/50). *Flora of Egypt I & II*; Bulletin of the Faculty of Science 17 and 28. Cairo: Fouad I University Press. 574 and 547 pp.

Tadzhitdinov, M.T. & Butov, K.N. (1972). *Rastitel'nost' Sovremennȳkh Vodoemov Karakalpakii*. Tashkent: Karakalpakskiĭ Filial AN UzSSR Kompleksnyĭ Institut Estestv. Nauk. 135 pp.

Taghon, G.L., Self, R.F.L. & Jumars, P.A. (1978). Predicting particle selection by deposit feeders: a model and its implication. *Limnology and Oceanography*, **23**, 752–9.

Takagi, S., Sugino, T. & Nishino, M. (1958). (Reinvestigation on damage of rice attacked by the second generation rice stem borer.) *Bulletin – Experimental Station of National Research Institute of Vegetables, Ornamental Plants & Tea: Shizuoka Prefecture*, **3**, 23–36. (In Japanese.)

Takeda, K. & Furusaka, C.H. (1970). On the bacteria isolated anaerobically from paddy field soil. *The Reports of the Institute of Agricultural Research. Tohoku University*, **44**, 343–8.

Taligoola, H.K. (1969). Studies in the colonisation of *Phragmites communis* Trin. by Microfungi. PhD thesis, University of Nottingham. 133 pp.

Tallis, J.H. (1983). Changes in wetland communities. In *Mires: Swamp, Bog, Fen & Moors, General Studies*; ed. A.J.P. Gore; Ecosystems of the World 4A, pp. 311–44.

Tamm, C.O. (1954). Some observations on the nutrient turn-over in a bog community dominated by *Eriophorum vaginatum* L. *Oikos*, **5**, 189–94.

Tamm, C.O., Holmen, H., Popovič, B. & Wiklander, G. (1974). Leaching of plant nutrients from soils as a consequence of forestry operations. *Ambio*, **3**, 211–21.

Tapiador, D.D., Henderson, H.F., Delmendo, M.N. & Tsutsui, H. (1977). *Freshwater Fisheries and Aquaculture in China*; A Report of the FAO Fisheries (Aquaculture) Mission to China, May, 1976; FAO Fisheries Technical Paper 168. Rome: FAO. 84 pp.

Taubaev, T.T. (1970). *Flora i Rastitel'nost' Vodoemov Sredneĭ Azii i ikh Ispol'zovanie v Narodnom Khozyaĭstve*. (Vegetation of Middle Asiatic waterbodies and its value for the national economy.) Tashkent: Institut Botaniki, FAN, Akademia Nauk Uzbekskoĭ. SSR. 491 pp. (In Russian.)

Taubaev, T.T., Keldibekov, S. & Abidov, M. (1972). Primenenie ryaski (*Lemna minor* L.) i khlorellȳ (*Chlorella vulgaris* Beyer) v ratsione rastitel'no-yadnoi rybȳ v prudovom rȳbnom khozyaistve 'Damashi'. In *Kul'tivirovanie Vodoroslei i Vȳsshikh Vodnȳkh Rastenii v Uzbekistane*, ed. A.M. Muzafarov, pp. 109–12. Tashkent: FAN.

Taylor, J.K. (1950). The Soils of Australia. In *The Australian Environment*: Handbook prepared for the British Commonwealth Specialist Agricultural Conference on Plant and Animal Nutrition in Relation to Soil and Climatic Factors held in Australia, August 1949 (2nd edn.), pp. 35–48. Melbourne: CSIRO.

Taylor, J.K. (1959). The classification of lowland swamp communities in North-eastern Papua. *Ecology*, **40**, 703–11.

Teal, J. & Teal, M. (1969). *Life and Death of the Salt Marsh*. Boston: Atlantic Monthly Press. 278 pp.

Teal, J.M. (1962). Energy flow in the salt marsh ecosystem of Georgia. *Ecology*, **43**, 614–24.

Teal, J.M. & Kanwisher, J. (1961). Gas exchange in a Georgia salt marsh. *Limnology and Oceanography*, **6**, 388–99.

Tenney, F.G. & Waksman, S.A. (1930). Composition of natural organic materials and their decomposition in the soil. *Soil Science*, **30**, 143–60.

Ter Hoeve, J. (1951). Een vergeliijking tussen de weergesteldheid en groudwaterstand in de dwingebieden van Vlieland en Terschelling. (A comparison between weather-conditions and ground water-level in the dunes of the isles of Vlieland and Terschelling.) *Terschellingen-Landbouwkundig Tijdschrift*, **63**, 715–26. (In Dutch with English summary.)

Tessařová, M. & Úlehlová, B. (1968). Abbau der Zellulose unter einigen

Wiesengesellschaften. In *Mineralisation der Zellulose*; Tagungsberichte DAL Nr. 98, 277–87. Berlin: Deutsche Akademie für Landwirtschaft.

Tessenow, U. & Baynes, Y. (1975). Redox-dependent accumulation of Fe and Mn in a littoral sediment supporting *Isoetes lacustris* L. *Die Naturwissenschaften*, **62**, 342–3.

Thienemann, A. (1912). Der Bergbach des Sauerlandes. *Internationale Revue der gesamten Hydrobiologie und Hydrographie*, **4**(Supplemental Series), 125 pp.

Thienemann, A. (1925). *Die Binnengewässer Mitteleuropas*; Die Binnengewässer, **1**. Stuttgart: Schweizerbart'scher Verlag. 255 pp.

Thienemann, A. (1954). Chironomus. *Leben, Verbreitung und Wirtschaftliche Bedeutung der Chironomiden*; Die Binnengewässer, **20**. Stuttgart: Schweizerbart'scher Verlag. 834 pp.

Thomas, A.S. (1943). The vegetation of the Karamoja district, Uganda. *Journal of Ecology*, **31**, 149–77.

Thomas, H.E. (1956). Changes in quantities and qualities of ground and surface waters. In *Man's Role in Changing the Face of the Earth*, ed. W.L. Thomas Jr, pp. 542–63. Chicago: University of Chicago.

Thomas, I.F. (1961). The Cladocera of the swamps of Uganda. *Crustaceana*, **2**, 108–25.

Thomas, P.A. & Room, P.M. (1986). Successful control of the floating weed *Salvinia molesta* in Papua New Guinea: a useful biological invasion neutralizes a disastrous one. *Environmental Conservation*, **13**, 242–8.

Thommen, G.H. & Westlake, D.F. (1981). Factors affecting the distribution of populations of *Apium nodiflorum* and *Nasturtium officinale* in small chalk streams. *Aquatic Botany*, **11**, 21–36.

Thompson, K. (1974). *Environmental Factors and Aquatic Plants in the Okavango Delta*; Technical Report UNDP Project BOT/506. Rome: FAO, 78 pp.

Thompson, K. (1976*a*). The primary production of African wetlands with particular reference to the Okavango delta. In *The Okavango Delta and its Future Utilization*, ed. A. Campbell; Proceedings of the Symposium of the Botswana Society; Botswana Notes & Records, Special Issue, pp. 67–79.

Thompson, K. (1976*b*). Swamp development in the head waters of the White Nile. In *The Nile. Biology of an Ancient River*, ed. J. Rzóska, pp. 177–96. The Hague: Junk.

Thompson, K. (1985). Emergent plants of permanently and seasonally flooded wetlands. In *The Ecology and Management of African Wetland Vegetation*, ed. P. Denny; Geobotany 6, pp. 43–108. Dordrecht: Junk.

Thompson, K. & Hamilton, A.C. (1983). Peatland and swamps of the African continent. In *Mires: Swamp, Bog, Fen and Moor, Regional Studies*, ed. A.J.P. Gore; Ecosystems of the World 4B, pp. 331–73. Amsterdam: Elsevier.

Thompsom, K., Shewry, P.R. & Woolhouse, H.W. (1979). Papyrus swamp development in the Upemba Basin, Zaire: Studies of population structure in *Cyperus papyrus* stands. *Botanical Journal of the Linnean Society*, **78**, 299–316.

Thornton, I.W.B. (1957). Faunal succession in umbels of *Cyperus papyrus* L. on the Upper White Nile. *Proceedings of the Royal Entomological Society*, **(A)32**, 119–31.

Tilzer, M., Bindloss, M.E., Marker, A.F.H. & Westlake, D.F. (1980). Primary production – The light climate in water. *The Functioning of Freshwater Ecosystems*, ed. E.D. LeCren & R.H. Lowe-McConnell; International Biological Programme 22, pp. 154–63. Cambridge: Cambridge University Press.

Timmer, C.E. & Weldon, L.W. (1967). Evapotranspiration and pollution of Water hyacinth. *Hyacinth Control Journal*, **6**, 34–7.

Toorn, J. van der (1972). Variability of *Phragmites australis* (Cav.) Trin. ex. Steudel in relation to the environment. *Van Zee tot Land*, **48**, 1–122. Staatsuitgeverij: 's-Gravenhage.

Toorn, J. van der & Mook, J.H. (1982). The influence of environmental factors and management on stands of *Phragmites australis* II. Effects of burning, frost and insect damage on shoot density and shoot size. *Journal of Applied Ecology*, **19**, 477–99.

Tóth, L. (1960). Phytozönologische Untersuchungen über die Röhrichte des Balaton-Sees. *Annales Instituti Biologici, Tihany*, **27**, 209–42.

Tóth, L. (1972). Reeds control eutrophication of Balaton Lake. *Water Research*, **6**, 1533–9.

Tóth, L. & Szabó, E. (1958). Über die chemische Zusammensetzung verschiedener Schilfproben vom Balaton-See. *Annales Instituti Biologici, Tihany*, **25**, 363–74.

Tóth, L. & Szabó, E. (1961). Zönologische und ökologische Untersuchungen in den Röhrichten des Neusiedlersees (Fertö-Tó). *Annales Instituti Biologici, Tihany*, **28**, 151–68.

Townsend, C.C. & Guest, E. (eds.) (1966). *Flora of Iraq, II*. Baghdad: Ministry of Agriculture. 183 pp.

Troll, C. (1953). Der Vergleich der Tropenvegetation der alten und neuen Welt. *Proceedings of the 7th International Botanical Congress, Stockholm, 1950*, 602–5.

Troughton, J.H. (1975). Photosynthetic mechanisms in higher plants. In *Photosynthesis and Productivity in Different Environments*, ed. J.P. Cooper, International Biological Programme 3, pp. 357–91. Cambridge: Cambridge University Press.

Tsunoda, S. & Takahashi, N. (eds.) (1984). *Biology of Rice*. Tokyo: Japan Scientific Societies Press. 380 pp.

Tucker, C.S. & Dubusk, T.A. (1981). Seasonal growth of *Eichhornia crassipes* (Mart.) Solms.: relationships to protein, fibre, and available carbohydrate content. *Aquatic Botany*, **11**, 137–42.

Turček, F.J.T. (1972). Birds as biological indicators. *Questiones Geobiologicae, Bratislava* Nr 10, 1–64.

Turner, R.E. (1976). Geographic variation in salt marsh macrophyte production: a review. *Contributions in Marine Science*, **20**, 48–68.

Turner, R.E. (1978). Community planktonic respiration in a salt marsh estuary and the importance of macrophyte leachates. *Limnology and Oceanography*, **23**, 442–51.

Tuschl, P. (1970). Die Transpiration von *Phragmites communis* Trin. im geschlossenen Bestand des Neusiedler Sees. *Wissenschaftliche Arbeiten aus dem Burgenland*, **44**, 126–86.

Tusneem, M.E. & Patrick, W.H. Jr (1971). Nitrogen transformation in waterlogged soil. *Bulletin of Louisiana State University*, **657**, 1–75.

Tutin, T.G. (1940). The Percy Sladen Trust Expedition to Lake Titicaca in 1937 under the leadership of Mr H. Carey Gilson, M.A. The macrophytic vegetation of the lake. *Transactions of the Linnean Society of London, 3rd Series*, **1**, 161–89.

Tüxen, R. & Preising, E. (1942). Grundbegriffe und Methoden zum Studium der Wasser- und Sumpfpflanzen-gesellschaften. *Deutsche Wasserwirtschaft*, **37**, 10–17 & 57–69.

Tyuremnov, S.N. (1976). *Torfyanye Mestorozhdeniya* (3rd edn.). Moskva: NAUKA. 487 pp.

Uchijima, Z. (1961). On characteristics of heat balance of water layer under paddy plant cover. *Bulletin of the National Institute of Agricultural Science, Series A* No. 8, 243–65.

Uchijima, Z. (1976). Maize and rice. In *Vegetation and the Atmosphere, II Case Studies*, ed. J.L. Monteith, pp. 33–64. New York: Academic Press.

Úlehlová, B. (1970). An ecological study of aquatic habitats in north-west Overijssel, the Netherlands. *Acta Botanica Neerlandica*, **19**, 830–58.

Úlehlová, B. (1971). Decomposition and humification of plant material in the vegetation of *Stratiotes aloides* in N.W. Overijssel – Holland. *Hidrobiologia, Bucureşti*, **12**, 279–85.

Úlehlová, B. (1973). Rates of decomposition processes in the Nesyt fishpond. In *Studie Československa Academie Věd*, 1973, No. 14, pp. 135–7. Praha: Academia.

Úlehlová, B. (1976). *Microbial Decomposers and Decomposition Processes in Wetlands*; Studie Československé Akademie Věd, 1976, No. 14. Praha: Academia. 112 pp.

Úlehlová, B. (1978). Decomposition processes in the fishpond littoral. In *Pond Littoral Ecosystems: Structure and Functioning*, ed. D. Dykyjová & J. Květ; Ecological Studies 28, pp. 341–56. Berlin: Springer-Verlag.

Úlehlová, B. & Dobrovolná-Vašulková, E. (1977). The role of microflora in the decomposition of plant residues in the fishpond littoral zone. In *Soil Biology and Conservation of the Biosphere*, ed. J. Szegi, pp. 121–7. Budapest: Akadémiai Kiadó.

Úlehlová, B. & Přibil, P. (1978). Water chemistry in the fishpond littorals. In *Pond Littoral Ecosystems*, ed. D. Dykyjová & J. Květ; Ecological Studies 28, pp. 126–40. Berlin: Springer-Verlag.

Úlehlová, B., Husák, Š. & Dvořák, J. (1973). Mineral cycles in reed stands of Nesyt fishpond in southern Moravia. *Polskie Archiwum Hydrobiologii*, **20**, 121–9.

Ultsch, G.R. & Anthony, D. (1973). Role of aquatic exchange of carbon dioxide in the ecology of the water-hyacinth (*Eichhornia crassipes*). *Florida Scientist*, **36**, 16–22.

UN (1973). *Report of the UN Conference on the Human Environment, Stockholm, June 1972*; United Nations Document A/CONF.48/4/Rev.1 (Resolutions, pp. 29–36). New York: United Nations. 77 pp.

Unni, K.S. (1971). An ecological study of the macrophytic vegetation of the Doodhadhari lake, Raipur. M.P., India. *Hydrobiologia*, **37**, 139–55.

Unni, K.S. (1977). The distribution and production of macrophytes in Lunz Mittersee and Lunz Untersee. *Hydrobiologia*, **56**, 89–94.

Untermaier, J. (ed.) (1991). *Legal Aspects of the Conservation of Wetlands*. Gland: ICUN. 202 pp.

Urban, E. (1975). The mining fauna in four macrophyte species in Mikołajskie Lake. *Ekologia Polska*, **23**, 417–35.

Uspienski, S.M. (1967). *Die Wildgänse Nordeurasiens*; Die neue Brehm-Bücherei, Heft 352 (2nd edn.). Wittenberg-Lutherstadt: Ziemsen Verlag. 80 pp.

Utida, S. (1958). On fluctuations in population density of the rice stem borer *Chilo suppressalis*. *Ecology*, **39**, 587–99.

Valdimirova, T.M. (1963). Alterations of zooplankton and zoobenthos of Zhemtchushnoe Lake treated with polychlorpyren. *Izvestiya*

Gosudarstvennogo Nauchno-Issledovatel'skogo Instituta Ozernogo, Rechnogo Rỹbnogo Khozyaĭstva, **55**, 70–83.

Valiela, I.J. & Teal, J.M. (1979). The nitrogen budget of a salt marsh ecosystem. *Nature*, **280**, 652–6.

Valk, A.G. van der & Bliss, L.C. (1971). Hydrarch succession and net primary production of oxbow lakes in Central Alberta. *Canadian Journal of Botany*, **49**, 1177–99.

Valk, A.G. van der & Davis, C.B. (1978). Primary production of prairie glacial marshes. In *Freshwater Wetlands. Ecological Processes and Management Potential*, ed. R.E. Good, D.F. Whigham, R.L. Simpson & C.G. Jackson Jr; Proceedings of Symposium on Freshwater Marshes: Present Status, Future Needs, New Brunswick, 1977, pp. 21–37. New York: Academic Press.

Valverde, J. (1964). La invernada y migracion de nuestros ansares (*Anser anser y Anser fabilis*). *Ardeola*, **9**, 67–109.

Van Zinderen Bakker, E.M. (1942). *Het Naardermeer: een geologische, historische en botanische landschapsbeschrÿving van Nederlands oudste natuurmonument*. Amsterdam: Allert de Lange. 134 pp.

Van Zinderen Bakker, E.M. (1947). *De West-Nederlandse Veenplassen*. Amsterdam: Allert de Lange. 255 pp.

Varenko, N.I. & Lubyanov, I.P. (1973). Pro nagromadzennya mikroelemntiv (Mn, Zn, Cu i Co) deyakimi vodnimi roslinami Dniprodzerzhinskogo ta Zaporozhnye vodoymishch. (On accumulation of trace elements by some hydrophytes of the Dnieprodzerzhinsk and Zaporozhnye reservoirs.) *Ukrayins'kyi Botanichnyi Zhurnal*, **30**, 165–70. (In Ukrainian with English summary.)

Vassiljev, J.M. (1961). Über den Wasserhaushalt von Pflanzen der Sandwüste im südöstlichen Kara-Kum. *Planta*, **14**, 225–309.

Vavruška, A. (1966). Stanovení živin v nejrozšířenějších vodních, pobřežních a bažinných rostlinách z hlediska využití ke kompostováni. *Práce Výzkumného Ústavu Rybářskeho a Hydrobiologického Vodňany*, **6**, 41–68.

Veatch, J.O. (1932). Some relationships between water plants and water soils in Michigan. *Papers of the Michigan Academy of Sciences Arts and Letters*, **27**, 409–13.

Véber, K. (1973). Pěstováni rákosu, nové technické rostliny III. Nároky rákosu na minerálnií výživu. (Growing of common reed, a new technical plant III. Demands of common reed for mineral nutrition.) *Sbornik VŠZ v Praze, Provozně Ekonomicke Fakulty v Českých Budějovicich*, **2**, 129–42. (In Czech with English summary.)

Véber, K. (1978). Propagation, cultivation and exploitation of common reed in Czechoslovakia. In *Pond Littoral Ecosystems: Structure and Functioning*, ed. D. Dykyjová & J. Květ; Ecological Studies 28, pp. 416–23. Berlin: Springer-Verlag.

Véber, K. (1982). *Biologické základy pěstování rákosu obecného v Československu*. (Biological basis for reed cultivation in Czechoslovakia.) Studie Československé Akademie Věd, 1982, No. 5. Praha: Academia. 135 pp. (In Czech.)

Velde, G. van der, Giesen, Th.G. & Heijden, L. van der (1979). Structure, biomass and seasonal changes of biomass of *Nymphoides peltata* (Gmel.) O. Kuntze (Menyanthaceae), a preliminary study. *Aquatic Botany*, **7**, 279–300.

Verhoeven, J.T.A., Koerselman, W. & Beltman, B. (1988). The vegetation of fens in relation to their hydrology and nutrient dynamics. In *Vegetation of Inland*

Waters, ed. J.J. Symoens; Handbook of Vegetation Science, **15/1**, pp. 249–82.

Verigin, B.V. (1963). Materialy po izbiratel'nosti v pishche i sutochnym racionam belogo amura. In *Problemy̆ Rybokhozyaĭstva Ispol'zovanie Rastitel'noyadny̆kh Ry̆b v vodoyemakh*, pp. 192–4. Ashkhbad: SSSR.

Vinberg, G.G. (1971). *Symbols, Units and Conversion Factors in Studies of Fresh Water Productivity*. London: International Biological Programme. 23 pp.

Vinberg, G.G. (1972). Some interim results of Soviet International Biological Programme investigations on lakes. In *Productivity Problems of Freshwaters*, ed. Z. Kajak & A. Hillbricht-Ilkowska, Proceedings of the IBP-UNESCO Symposium on Productivity Problems of Freshwaters, Kazimierz Dolny, May, 1970, pp. 363–81. Warszawa & Kraków: Polish Science Publishers.

Vinberg, G.G., Babitsky, V.A., Gavrilov, S.I., Gladky, G.V., Zakarenkov, I.S., Kovalevskya, R.Z., Mikheeva, T.M., Neveydomskaya, P.S., Ostapenya, A.P., Petrovich, J., Potaenko, J.S. & Yakushko, O.F. (1972). Biological productivity of different types of lakes. In *Productivity Problems of Freshwaters*, ed. Z. Kajak & A. Hillbricht-Ilkowska, Proceedings of the IBP-UNESCO Symposium on Productivity Problems of Freshwaters, Kazimierz Dolny, May, 1970, pp. 383–404. Warszawa & Kraków: Polish Science Publishers.

Viosca, P.J. (1937). *Pondfish Culture: A Handbook of the Culture of Warm Water Game Fishes of the United States*. New Orleans: Pelican Publ. 260 pp.

Volker, R. & Smith, S.G. (1965). Changes in the aquatic vascular flora of Lake East Okoboji in historic times. *Iowa Academy of Sciences*, **72**, 65–72.

Volkova, L.A. (1974). Vy̆sshaya vodnaya rastitel'nost' ozer Kol'skogo poluostrova. (Higher aquatic vegetation of the Kola Peninsula lakes.) In *Ozera Razlichny̆kh Landshaftov Kol'skogo Poluostrova*, Chast' 2, pp. 63–77. Leningrad: 'NAUKA'. (In Russian.)

Vollenweider, R.A. (1971). *Water Management Research. Scientific Fundamentals of the Eutrophication of Lakes and Flowing Water with Particular Reference to Nitrogen and Phosphorus as Factors in Eutrophication*. Paris: UNESCO. 155 pp.

Vollenweider, R.A. (ed.) (1974). *A Manual on Methods for Measuring Primary Production in Aquatic Environments*; International Biological Programme Handbook No. 12 (2nd edn.). Oxford: Blackwell Science Publishers. 225 pp.

Wagner, G. (1970). Die Zunahme der Belastung des Bodensees. *Gas, Wasser, Abwasser*, **111**, 485–7.

Waisel, Y. & Rechav, Y. (1971). Ecotypic differentiation in *Phragmites communis* Trin. *Hidrobiologia, Bucureşti*, **12**, 259–66.

Waitzbauer, W. (1969). Lebenweise und Produktionsbiologie der Schilfgallenliege *Lipara lucens* Mg. (Diptera, Chloropidae). *Sitzungsberichte Österreichischer Akademie der Wissenschaften, Mathematisch-Naturwissenschaftliche Klasse I, Abteilung 1*, **17**(5–8), 175–242.

Waitzbauer, W. (1972). Produktionsbiologische Aspekte schilffressender Insekten. *Verhandlungen – Deutsche Zoologische Gesellschaft*, **65**, Jahresversammlung, 116–19.

Waitzbauer, W. (1976). Energieumsatz aquatischer Hemipteren *Naucoris cimicoides* L. *Notonecta glauca* L. *Ranatra linearis* L. *Oecologia*, **22**, 179–202.

Waitzbauer, W., Prusche, H. & Picher, O. (1973). Faunistiche-ökologische Untersuchungen an schilfbewohnenden Dipteren im Schilfgürtel des Neusiedlersees. *Sitzungsberichte Österreichischer Akademie der*

Wissenschaften, Mathematisch-Naturwissenschaftliche Klasse I, Abteilung 1,
    181, 111–36.

Walker, A. & Sillans, E. (1961). *Les Plantes Utiles du Gabon*; Encyclopedie
    Biologique, LVI. Paris: Paul LeChevalier, 614 pp.

Walker, D. (1972). Vegetation of the Lake Ipea region, New Guinea Highlands
    II. Kayamanda swamp. *Journal of Ecology*, **60**, 479–504.

Walker, H.G. (1962). *Preliminary List of Insects and Mites Recorded on Paddy
    Rice*. Rome: FAO. 63 pp. (Cited from Yasumatsu & Toril, 1968).

Walker, J.M. (1959). Vegegation Studies in the Delta Marsh, Manitoba. MSc
    thesis, University of Winnipeg. 272 pp.

Walker, J.M. (1965). Vegetation Changes with Falling Water Levels in the Delta
    Marsh, Manitoba. PhD thesis, University of Winnipeg. 272 pp.

Walker, J.M. & Waygood, E.R. (1968). Ecology of *Phragmites communis*. I.
    Photosynthesis of a single shoot *in situ*. *Canadian Journal of Botany*, **46**, 549–
    55.

Wallentinus, H.G. (1975). Aboveground production and chemical analysis of
    Phragmites communis in polluted brackish water. *Merentutkimuslaitosken
    Julkaisu, Havsforskningsinstitut Skrifter* No. 239, 116–22.

Walter, H. (1968). *Die Vegetation der Erde in Ökophysiologischer Betrachtung*, II.
    Jena: VEB G. Fischer Verlag. 1001 pp.

Washino, R.K. (1968). Predator–prey studies in relation to an integrated
    mosquito control program: A progress report. *Proceeding Papers of the
    Annual Conference on the California Mosquito Control Association*, **36**, 33–4.

Washino, R.K. & Hokama, Y. (1967). Preliminary report on the feeding pattern
    of two species of fish in a rice field habitat. *Proceeding Papers of the Annual
    Conference of the California Mosquito Control Association*, **35**, 84–7.

Watson, D.J. (1952). The physiological basis of variation in yield. *Advances in
    Agronomy*, **4**, 101–45.

Watt, R.F. & Heinselman, M.L. (1965). Foliar nitrogen and phosphorus level
    related to the site quality in a northern Minnesota spruce bog. *Ecology*, **46**,
    357–61.

Weber, C.A. (1928). *Das Rohrglanzgras und die Rohrglanzgraswiesen*. Berlin:
    Parey. 48 pp.

Weber, D.W. (1967). Über die Wasserpflanzenflora Ostfalens. *Braunschweig
    Heimat*, **53**, 11–15.

Weber, N.A. (1942). A biocoenose of papyrus heads (*Cyperus papyrus*). *Ecology*,
    13, 115–19.

Weber-Oldecop, D.W. (1970). Wasserpflanzengesellschaften im Östlichen
    Niedersachsen. I. (Water plant communities of eastern Lower Saxony.)
    Internationaler Revue der Gesamten Hydrobiologie, **55**, 913–67. (In German.)

Weber-Oldecop, D.W. (1971). Wasserpflanzengesellschaften im Östlichen
    Niedersachsen. II. (Water plant communities of eastern Lower Saxony.)
    Internationaler Revue der Gesamten Hydrobiologie, **56**, 79–122. (In German.)

Webster, J.R. & Benfield, E.F. (1986). Vascular plant breakdown in freshwater
    ecosystems. *Annual Revue of Ecology and Systematics*, **17**, 567–94.

Wein, K. (1942). Die älteste Einführungs- und Ausbreitungs-geschichte von
    Acorus calamus. *Hercynia*, **3**, 214–91.

Weiss, H.B. & West, E. (1920). Notes on *Galerucella nymphae* L., the pondlife
    leaf-beetle (Coleoptera). *Canadian Entomologist*, **52**, 237–9.

Weisser, P. (1970). Die Vegetationsverhältnisse des Neusiedlersees.
    Wissenschaftliche Arbeiten aus dem Burgenland, **45** (*Naturwissenschaft*, **29**),
    1–83.

Welch, P.S. (1952). *Limnology*. New York: McGraw-Hill. 538 pp.

Welcomme, R.L. (1975). *The Fisheries Ecology of African Floodplains*; Commission for Inland Fisheries of Africa, Technical Paper No. 3. Rome: FAO. 51 pp.

Welcomme, R.L. (1979). *Fisheries Ecology of Floodplains Rivers*. London: Longman. 317 pp.

Welcomme, R.L. (1985). *River Fisheries*; FAO Fisheries Technical Paper No. 262. FAO. 330 pp.

Welcomme, R.L. & Hagborg, D. (1977). Towards a model of a floodplain fish population and its fishery. *Environmental Biology of Fishes*, **2**, 7–24.

Weller, M.W. (1978). Management of freshwater marshes for wildlife. In *Freshwater Wetlands; Ecological Processes and Management Potential*, ed. R.E. Good, D.F. Whigham & R.L. Simpson; Proceedings of the Symposium on Freshwater Marshes: Present Status, Future Needs, New Brunswick, July 1977, pp. 267–84. New York: Academic Press.

Wermuth, H. (1952). *Die Europäische Sumpfschildkröte*. Leipzig: Geest & Portig (Die neue Brehm-Bucherei). 40 pp.

Wesenburg-Lund, C. (1943). *Biologie der Süsswasserinsekten*. Berlin: Springer-Verlag. 682 pp.

Westhoff, V. (ed.) (1949). *Landschap, flora en vegetatie van de Botshol nabij Abcoude*. Baambrugge: Stichting Commissie voor de Vecht en het Oostelijk en Westelijk Plassengebied. 102 pp.

Westhoff, V. (1964). Contact- en storungs-gezelschappen tussen eutroof an oligotroof milieu in het hoogveengebied van der Peel. *Jaarboek Koninklijke Nederlandse Botanische Vereinigung*, 1963, 44–5.

Westhoff, V. (1972). L'évolution de la végétation dans les lacs eutrophes et les bas-marais des Pays-Bas. *Naturalistes Belges*, **54**, 1–28.

Westhoff, V. & Held, A.J. den (1969). *Plantengemeenschappen in Nederland*. Zutphen: Thieme & Cie. 324 pp.

Westlake, D.F. (1963). Comparisons of plant productivity. *Biological Reviews*, **38**, 385–425.

Westlake, D.F. (1965). Some basic data for investigations of the productivity of aquatic macrophytes. *Memorie dell'Istituto Italiano Idrobiologia*, **18**(Supplement), 229–48.

Westlake, D.F. (1966). The biomass and productivity of *Glyceria maxima*. I. Seasonal changes in biomass. *Journal of Ecology*, **54**, 745–53.

Westlake, D.F. (1968). Methods used to determine the annual production of reedswamp plants with extensive rhizomes. In *Methods of Productivity Studies in Root Systems and Rhizosphere Organisms*, ed. M.S. Ghilarov, V.A. Kovda, L.N. Novichkova-Ivanova, L.E. Rodin & V.M. Sveshnikova, Leningrad, pp. 226–34. Leningrad: NAUKA.

Westlake, D.F. (1973). Aquatic macrophytes in rivers. A Review. *Polskie Archiwum Hydrobiologii*, **20**, 31–40.

Westlake, D.F. (1975a). Primary production of freshwater macrophytes. In *Photosynthesis and Productivity of Different Environments*, ed. J.P. Cooper; International Biological Programme No. 3, pp. 189–206. Cambridge: Cambridge University Press.

Westlake, D.F. (1975b). Macrophytes. In *River Ecology*, ed. B.A. Whitton; Studies in Ecology 2, pp. 106–28. Oxford: Blackwell Science Publishers.

Westlake, D.F. (1981). The development and structure of aquatic weed populations. In *Proceedings of Conference on Aquatic Weeds and their*

Biology, Oxford, 1981, pp. 33–47. Warwick: Association of Applied Biologists.

Westlake, D.F. (Coordinator) (1980). Primary production. In *The Functioning of Freshwater Ecosystems*, ed. E.D. LcCren & R.H. Lowe-McConnell; International Biological Programme No. 22, pp. 141–246. Cambridge: Cambridge University Press.

Westlake, D.F. (1982). Primary productivity of water-plants. In *Studies on Aquatic Vascular Plants*, ed. J.J. Symoens, S.S. Hooper & P. Compère; Handbook of Vegetation Science, **15/1**, pp. 165–80. Brussels: Royal Botanical Society of Belgium.

Westlake, D.F., Casey, H., Dawson, F.H., Ladle, M., Mann, R.H.K. & Marker, A.F.H. (1972). The chalk-stream ecosystem. In *Productivity Problems of Freshwaters*, ed. Z. Kajak & A. Hillbricht-Ilkovska; Proceedings of IBP-UNESCO Symposium on Productivity Problems of Freshwaters, Kazimierz Dolny, May, 1970, pp. 615–35. Warszawa: Polish Science Publishers.

Westlake, D.F., Spence, D.H.N. & Clarke, R.T. (1986). The direct determination of the biomass of aquatic macrophytes. In *The Direct Determination of the Biomass of Aquatic Macrophytes and Measurement of Underwater Light 1985*; Methods for the Examination of Waters and Associated Materials, pp. 3–28. London: HMSO.

Wetzel, R.G. (1960). Marl encrustations on hydrophytes in several Michigan lakes. *Oikos*, **11**, 223–36.

Wetzel, R.G. (1964). Excretion of dissolved organic compounds by aquatic macrophytes. *Bioscience*, **19**, 539–40.

Wetzel, R.G. (1968). Dissolved organic matter and phytoplanktonic productivity in a large shallow lake. *Mitteilungen der Internationalen Vereinigung für Theoretische und Angewandte Limnologie*, **14**, 261–70.

Wetzel, R.G. (1975). *Limnology*. Philadelphia: Saunders. 743 pp.

Wetzel, R.G. & Allen, H.L. (1972). Functions and interactions of dissolved organic matter and the littoral zone in lake metabolism and eutrophication. In *Productivity Problems of Freshwaters*, ed. Z. Kajak & A. Hillbricht-Ilkovska; Proceedings of IBP-UNESCO Symposium on Productivity Problems of Freshwaters, Kazimierz Dolny, May 7–12, 1970, pp. 333–47. Warszawa: PWN, Polish Science Publishers.

Wetzel, R.G. & Manny, B.A. (1972). Excretion of dissolved organic carbon and nitrogen by aquatic macrophytes. *Verhandlungen der Internationalen Vereinigung für Theoretische und Angewandte Limnologie*, **18**, 162–70.

Wetzel, R.G., Rich, P.H., Miller, M.C. & Allen, H.L. (1972). Metabolism of dissolved and particulate detrital carbon in a temperate hard-water lake. In *Detritus and its Ecological Role in Aquatic Ecosystems*, ed. L. Tonolli; Memorie dell'Istituto Italiano Idrobiologia, Suppl., **29**, pp. 185–243.

Wheeler, B.D., Shaw, S.C., Fojt, W.J. & Robertson, R.A. (eds.) (1995). *Restoration of the Temperate Wetlands*. Chichester: Wiley. 562 pp.

Whigham, D.F. (1978). The relationship between aboveground and belowground biomass of freshwater tidal wetland macrophytes. *Aquatic Botany*, **5**, 355–64.

Whigham, D.F., Dykyjová, D. & Hejný, S. (eds.) (1985). *Wetlands of the World: Inventory, Ecology and Management*, Vol. 1; Handbook of Vegetation Science 15/2. Dordrecht: Kluwer Acad. Publ. 768 pp.

Whigham, D.F., Good, R.E. & Květ, J. (eds.) (1990). *Wetland Ecology and Management: Case Studies*; Proceedings of 2nd International Wetlands Conference, Třeboň, June 1984. Dordrecht: Kluwer. 180 pp.

Whigham, D.F., Kerkhoven, M. van, O'Neill, J. & Maltby, J. (1994).

Comparative study of nutrient-related processes in geographically separated wetlands. In *Global Wetlands: Old World and New*, ed. J.W. Mitsch, pp. 91–106. Amsterdam: Elsevier.

Whigham, D.F., McCormick, J., Good, R.E. & Simpson, R.L. (1978). Biomass and primary production in freshwater tidal wetlands of the Middle Atlantic Coast. In *Freshwater Wetlands; Ecological Processes and Management Potential*, ed. R.E. Good, D.F. Whigham, R.L. Simpson & C.G. Jackson Jr; Proceedings of Symposium on Freshwater Marshes: Present Status, Future Needs; New Brunswick, 1977, pp. 3–20. New York: Academic Press.

White, D.A., Weiss, T.E., Trapani, J.M. & Thien, B. (1978). Productivity and decomposition of the dominant salt-marsh plants in Louisiana. *Ecology*, **59**, 751–9.

Wiebe, W.J., Christian, R.R., Hansen, J.A., King, G., Sherr, B. & Skyring, G. (1981). Anaerobic respiration and fermentation. In *The Ecology of a Salt Marsh*, ed. L.R. Pomeroy & R.G. Weigert; Ecological Studies 38, pp. 137–59. New York: Springer-Verlag.

Wieder, R.K. & Lang, G.E. (1982). A critique of the analytical methods used in examining decomposition data obtained from litter bags. *Ecology*, **63**, 1636–42.

Wiegert, R.G. & Evans, F.C. (1964). Primary production and the disappearance of dead vegetation on an old field in south-eastern Michigan. *Ecology*, **45**, 49–63.

Wilhelmy, H. (1956). Ein Vegetationsprofil durch die feuchttropischen Anden von Kolumbien. *Kosmos*, **10**, 478–84.

Wilkońska, H. & Żuromska, H. (1967). Observations of the spawning of pike *Esox lucius* L. and roach *Rutilus rutilus* L. in Mazury Lake District. *Rocznik Nauk Rolniczych, Seria H*, **90**, 477–502.

Willer, A. (1944). Untersuchungen über das Rohrgelege der Gewässer. II. Das Rohrgelege als Siedlungsraum. *Zeitschrift für Fischerei*, **42**, 5–43.

Willer, A. (1949). Kleinklimatische Untersuchungen im *Phragmites*-Gelege. *Verhandlungen der Internationalen Vereinigung für Theoretische und Angewandte Limnologie*, **10**, 566–74.

Williams, R.B. (1966). Annual phytoplankton productivity in a system of shallow temperate estuaries. *Some Contemporary Studies in Marine Science*, ed. H. Barnes, pp. 699–716. London: George Allen & Unwin.

Williams, R.B. (1972). Nutrient levels and phytoplankton productivity in the estuary. *Proceedings of the Coastal Marsh and Estuary Management Symposium, Louisiana State University, 1972*, pp. 59–89.

Williams, R.B. & Murdoch, M.B. (1969). The potential importance of *Spartina alterniflora* in conveying zinc, manganese and iron into estuarine food chains. In *Proceedings of the 2nd National Symposium on Radioecology*, ed. D.J. Nelson & F.C. Evans; Conf.-670503, USAEC, pp. 431–9.

Willoughby, L.G. (1974). Decomposition of litter in freshwater. In *Biology of Plant Litter Decomposition*, Vol. 2, ed. C.H. Dickinson & G.J.F. Pugh, pp. 659–81. New York: Academic Press.

Wilson, D.O. (1972). Phosphate nutrition of the aquatic angiosperm, *Myriophyllum exalbescens* Fern. *Limnology and Oceanography*, **17**, 612–16.

Wilson, O.F. (1928). Some pests of waterlilies. *Journal of the Royal Horticultural Society*, **53**, 81–91.

Wit, C.T. de (1965). Potential photosynthesis of crop surfaces. *Agricultural Science*, **7**, 141–9.

Wium-Andersen, S. & Andersen, J.M. (1972). The influence of vegetation on the redox profile of the sediment of Grane Langsø, a Danish *Lobelia* lake. *Limnology and Oceanography*, **6**, 948–52.

Wöbbecke, K. & Ripl, W. (1990). Untersuchungen zum Röhrichtrückgang an der Berliner Havel. In *Ökologie, Gefährdung, und Schutz von Röhrichtpflanzen*, ed. H. Sukopp & M. Krauss; Landschaftsentwicklung u. Umweltforschung, **71**, pp. 94–102. Berlin: Technische Universität.

Wolf, H. (1977). Naturgemässer Gewässerausbau, Erfahrungen und Beispiele aus Baden-Württemberg. *Veröffentlichungen für Naturschutz und Landschaftspflege, in Baden-Württemberg*, **46**, 259–320.

Wolverton, B.C. & McKnown, M.M. (1976). Water hyacinths for removal of phenols from polluted waters. *Aquatic Botany*, **2**, 191–201.

Wooten, J.W. (1973). Edaphic factors in species and ecotype differentiation of *Sagittaria*. *Journal of Ecology*, **61**, 151–6.

Wooten, J.W. & Dood, J.D. (1976). Growth of water hyacinth in treated sewage effluent. *Economic Botany*, **30**, 29–37.

Worth, J.E.G. (1972). Aspects of Vegetation History at East Stoke, near Wareham, Dorset, Dissertation. University of Southampton. 31 pp.

Wyninger, R. (1963). Beitrag zur Biologie von *Nonagria geminipunctata* Hatch (Noctuidae, Lepidoptera). *Mitteilungen der Entomologischen Gesellschaft, Basel*. N.F. **13**, 65–80.

Yamamoto, T. & Backiel, T. (1968). *Synoptic Country Studies: Thailand*; FAO/IWP, Fish Economy and Institution Division, Working Paper. (Mimeo.) Rome: FAO. 68 pp.

Yasumatsu, K. & Torii, T. (1968). Impact of parasites, predators and diseases on rice pests. *Annual Review of Entomology*, **13**, 295–324.

Yoshida, T. & Ancajas, R. (1971). Nitrogen fixation by bacteria in the root zone of rice. *Proceedings of the Soil Society of America*, **35**, 156–8.

Zawisza, J. & Ciepielewski, W. (1973). Experimentally increased stock of fish in the pond-type Lake Warniak II. Changes of the autochthonous ichthyofauna due to the introduction of carp (*Cyprinus carpio* L.) and bream (*Abramis brama* L). *Ekologia Polska*, **21**, 424–44.

Zax, M. (1973). Die Temperaturresistenz von *Phragmites communis* Trin. *Polskie Archiwum Hydrobiologii*, **20**, 159–64.

Zejda, J. (1967). Habitat selection in *Apodemus agrarius* (Pallas, 1778) (Mammalia: Muridae) on the border of the area of its distribution. *Zoologické Listy, Praha*, **16**, 15–30.

Zezin, V.G. (1968). Production and application of building materials and elements made of reeds. In *Seminar on Organizational and Technical Measures Directed towards Increasing the Production of Building Materials, Moscow, Sept.–Oct. 1968*, pp. 2–4.

Zhadin, V.I. (1952/65). *Mollyuski Presnȳkh i Solonovatȳkh Vod SSSR*; Opredeliteli po Faunïe SSR. Leningrad: Akademia Nauk SSSR. 486 pp. Translation (1965); *Mollusks of Fresh and Brackish Waters of the USSR*; Israel Programme for Scientific Translation No. 1258, Jerusalem. Washington: Smithsonian Institute & National Science Foundation. 368 pp.

Zimbalevskaya, L.N. (1972). Zooplankton v zaroslyakh vodnoĭ rastitel'nosti i ego produktivnost'. (Zooplankton in water vegetation thickets and its role in productivity of the reservoir shallow waters.) In *Kievskoe Vodokhranilishche – Gidrokhimia, Biologia, Produktivnost'* (The Kiev Reservoir – Hydrochemistry, Biology, Productivity), ed. Ya. Ya. Tseeb & Yu. G. Maistrenko, pp. 308–18. Kiev: 'Naukova Dumka'. (In Russian.)

Zimbalevskaya, L.N. (1981). *Fitofil'nye Bespozvonochnye Ravninnȳkh Rek i Vodokhranilishch. (Ekologicheskiĭ Ocherk.).* (Phytophilous Invertebrates of Lowland Rivers and Water Reservoirs (an Ecological Study).) Kiev: Naukova Dumka. 214 pp. (In Russian.)

Zohary, M. (1973). *Geobotanical Foundations of the Middle East,* 1 and 2, Stuttgart: VEB Fischer Verlag. 738 pp.

Zon, J.C.J. van (1977). Grass carp (*Ctenopharyngodon idella* Val.) in Europe. *Aquatic Botany,* **3**, 143–55.

Zonderwijk, P. & Zon, van J.C.J. (1974). Dutch vision on the use of herbicides in waterways. *Proceedings of EWRS 4th Symposium on Aquatic Weeds,* 158–63.

Zonnenveld, I.S. (1960a). De Brabantse Biesbosch: Een studie van boden en vegetative van een zoetwatergetijden delta. Dr. Landbouwwetenschappen; Dissertatie LH-275; Landbouwhogeschool. Wageningen: Pudoc. 4 volumes. (In Dutch with English summary.)

Zonnenveld, I.S. (1960b). *Bodenkundige Studies* 4 (A–C); Belmontia 2, Ecology, 1960, No. 6. Wageningen: Pudoc. 20 pp.

Żuromska, H. (1967a). Mortality estimation of roach (*Rutilus rutilus* L.) eggs and larvae on lacustrine spawning grounds. *Rocznik Nauk Rolniczych, Seria H,* **90**, 539–56.

Żuromska, H. (1967b). Some causes of mortality of roach eggs and larvae on lake spawning grounds. *Rocznik Nauk Rolniczych, Seria H,* **90**, 557–79.

Index

Page numbers in *italics* refer to figures and tables

546